WONDER WOMAN
THE FOUR HORSEWOMEN

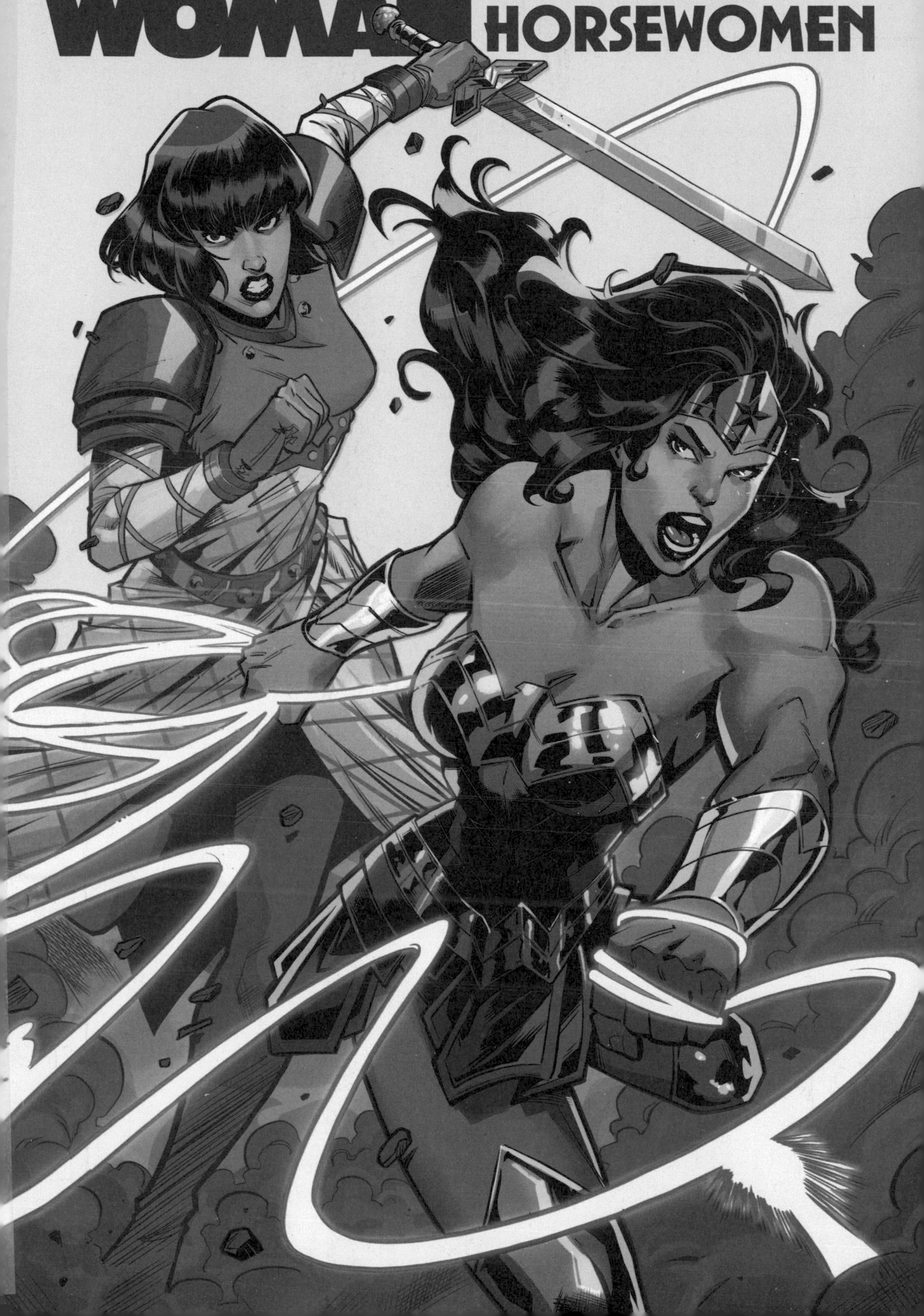

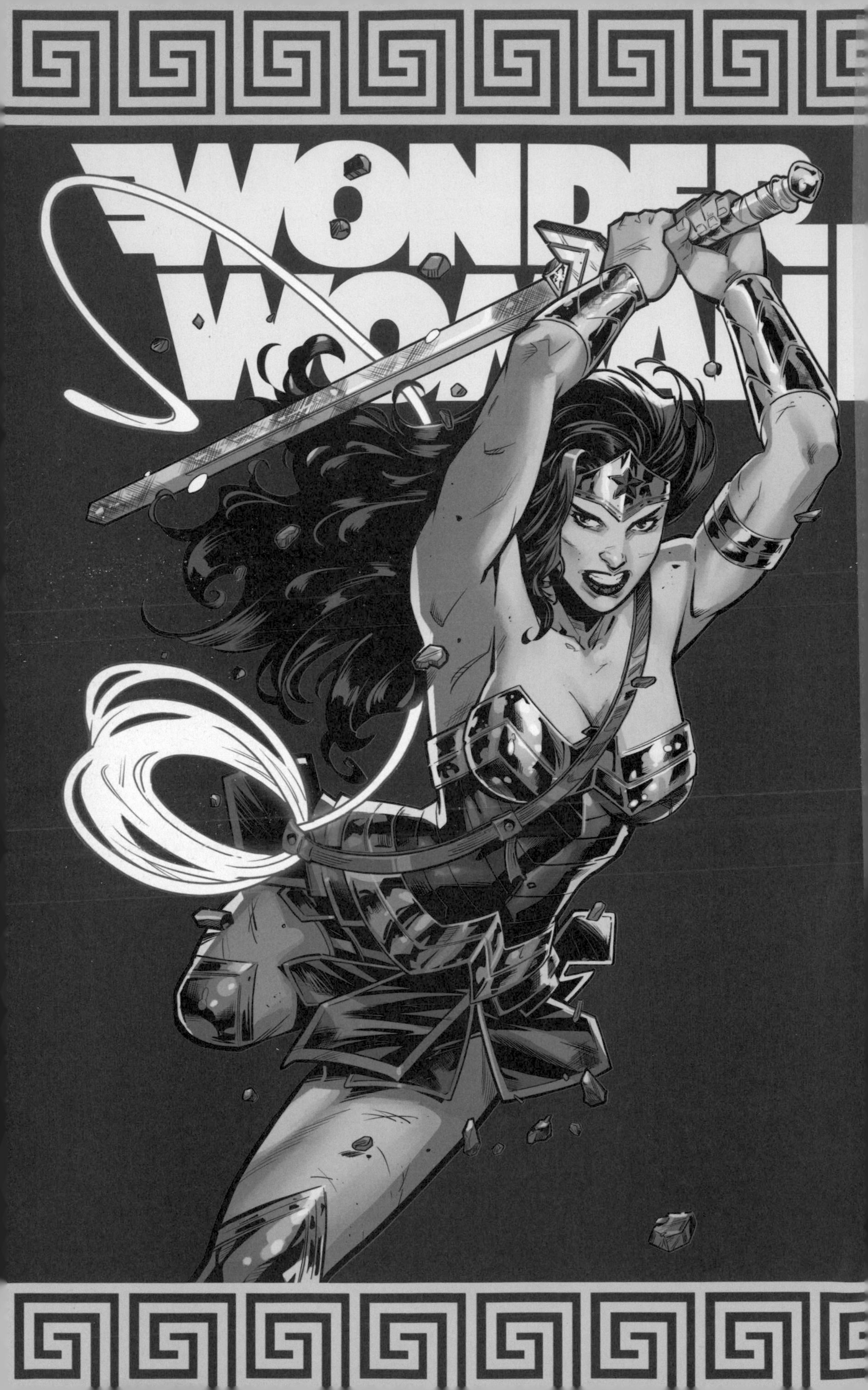
WONDER

THE FOUR HORSEWOMEN

STEVE ORLANDO
WRITER

JESÚS MERINO · V. KEN MARION · KIERAN McKEOWN · JAN DUURSEMA
MAX RAYNOR · GLEB MELNIKOV · EMANUELA LUPACCHINO
JACK HERBERT · JHEREMY RAAPACK · MIGUEL MENDONÇA
PENCILLERS

VICENTE CIFUENTES · SANDU FLOREA · SCOTT HANNA
JAN DUURSEMA · MAX RAYNOR · GLEB MELNIKOV · RAY McCARTHY
JACK HERBERT · NORM RAPMUND · MIGUEL MENDONÇA
INKERS

ROMULO FAJARDO JR. · HI-FI · GABE ELTAEB
COLORISTS

PAT BROSSEAU
LETTERER

ROBSON ROCHA · DANNY MIKI · BRAD ANDERSON
COLLECTION COVER ARTISTS

WONDER WOMAN CREATED BY WILLIAM MOULTON MARSTON

PAUL KAMINSKI, BRIAN CUNNINGHAM & ALEX ANTONE
Editors – Original Series

BRITTANY HOLZHERR
Associate Editor – Original Series & Editor – Collected Edition

STEVE COOK
Design Director – Books

MEGEN BELLERSEN
Publication Design

SUZANNAH ROWNTREE
Publication Production

MARIE JAVINS
Editor-in-Chief, DC Comics

DANIEL CHERRY III
Senior VP – General Manager

JIM LEE
Publisher & Chief Creative Officer

DON FALLETTI
VP – Manufacturing Operations & Workflow Management

LAWRENCE GANEM
VP – Talent Services

ALISON GILL
Senior VP – Manufacturing & Operations

NICK J. NAPOLITANO
VP – Manufacturing Administration & Design

NANCY SPEARS
VP – Revenue

MICHELE R. WELLS
VP & Executive Editor, Young Reader

WONDER WOMAN VOL. 4: THE FOUR HORSEWOMEN

DC Comics, 2900 West Alameda Ave., Burbank, CA 91505
Printed by LSC Communications, Owensville, MO, USA. 3/12/21. First Printing.
ISBN: 978-1-77950-910-9

Library of Congress Cataloging-in-Publication Data is available.

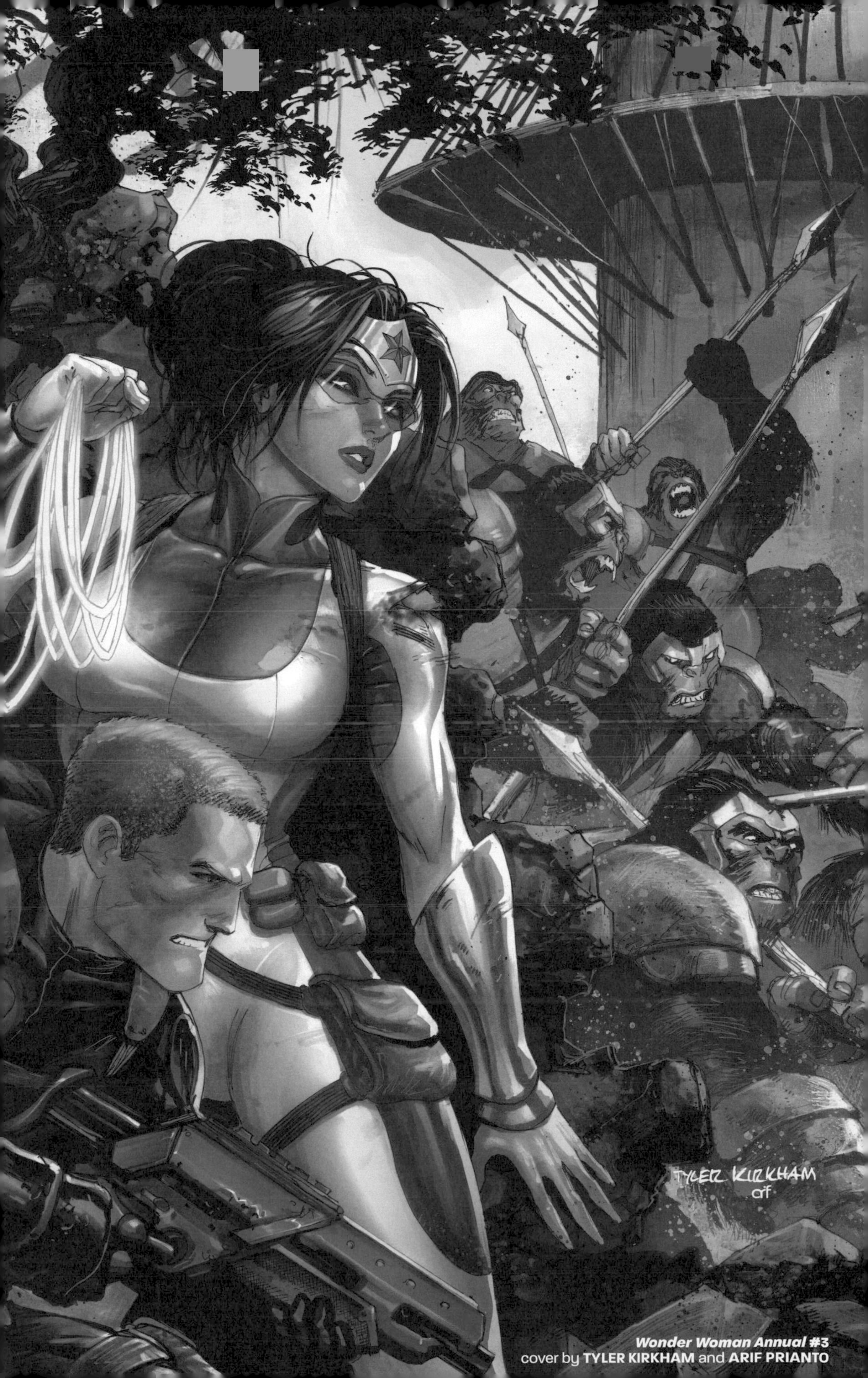
TYLER KIRKHAM

Wonder Woman Annual #3
cover by **TYLER KIRKHAM** and **ARIF PRIANTO**

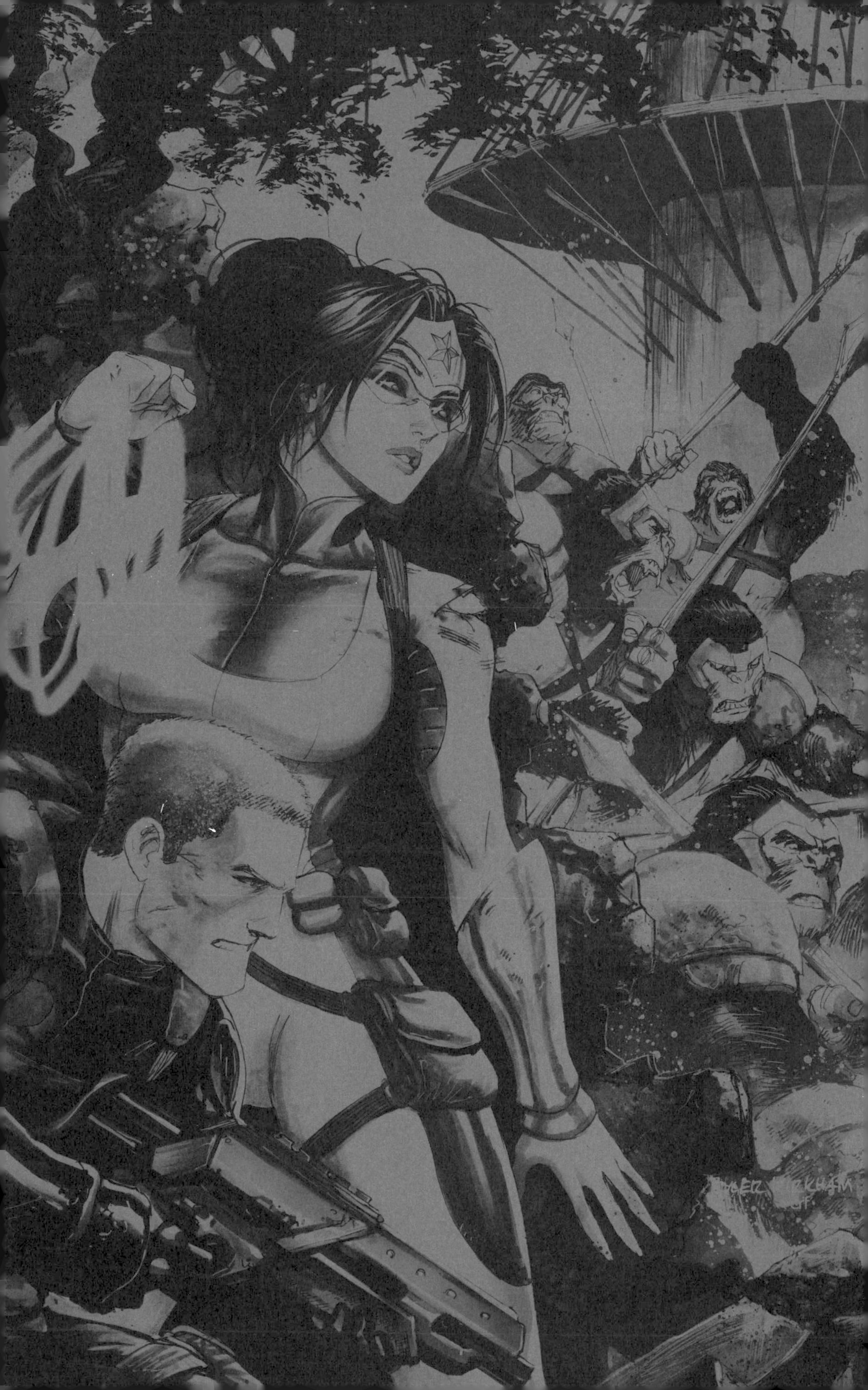

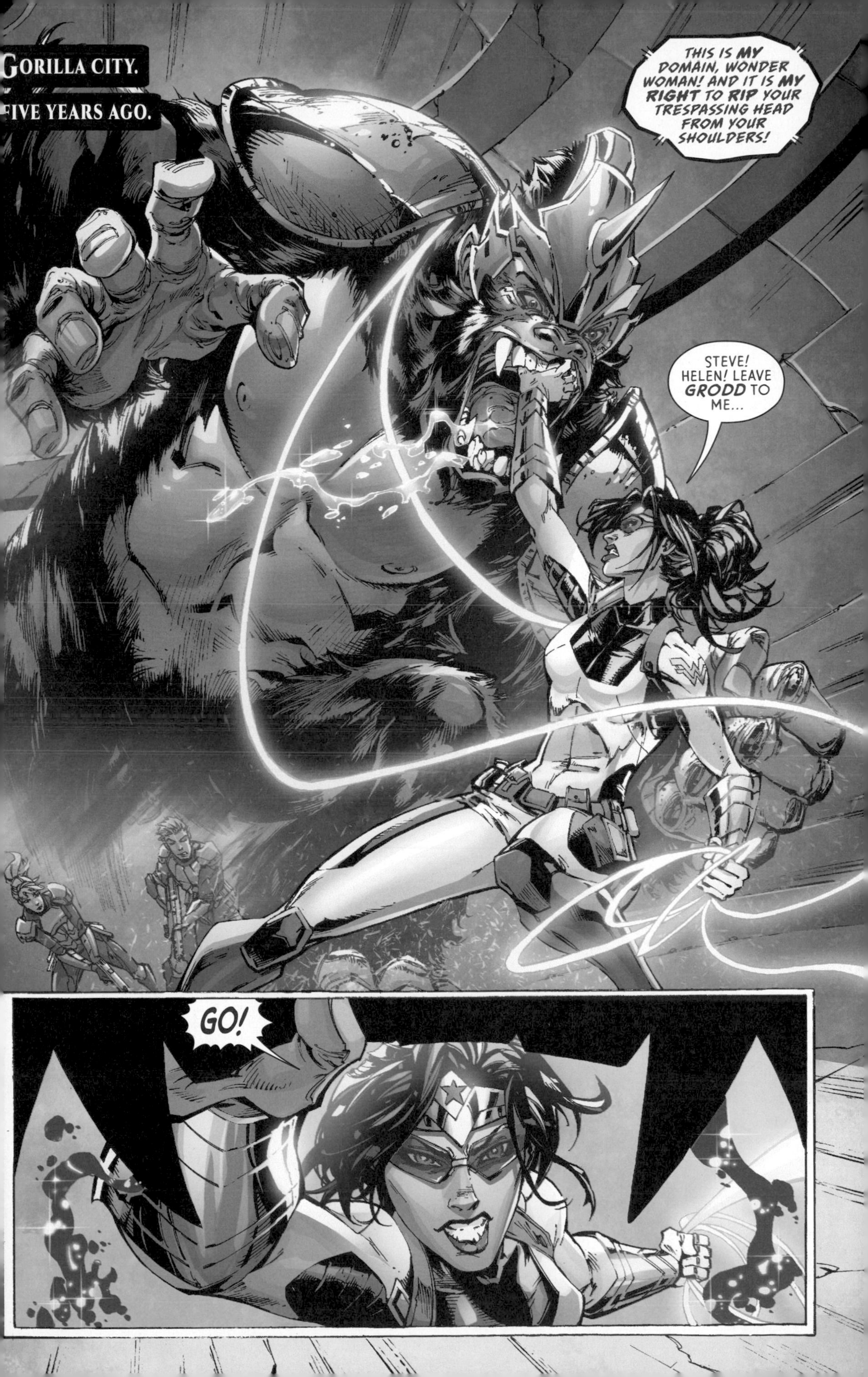
GORILLA CITY.
FIVE YEARS AGO.
THIS IS MY DOMAIN, WONDER WOMAN! AND IT IS MY RIGHT TO RIP YOUR TRESPASSING HEAD FROM YOUR SHOULDERS!
STEVE! HELEN! LEAVE GRODD TO ME...
GO!

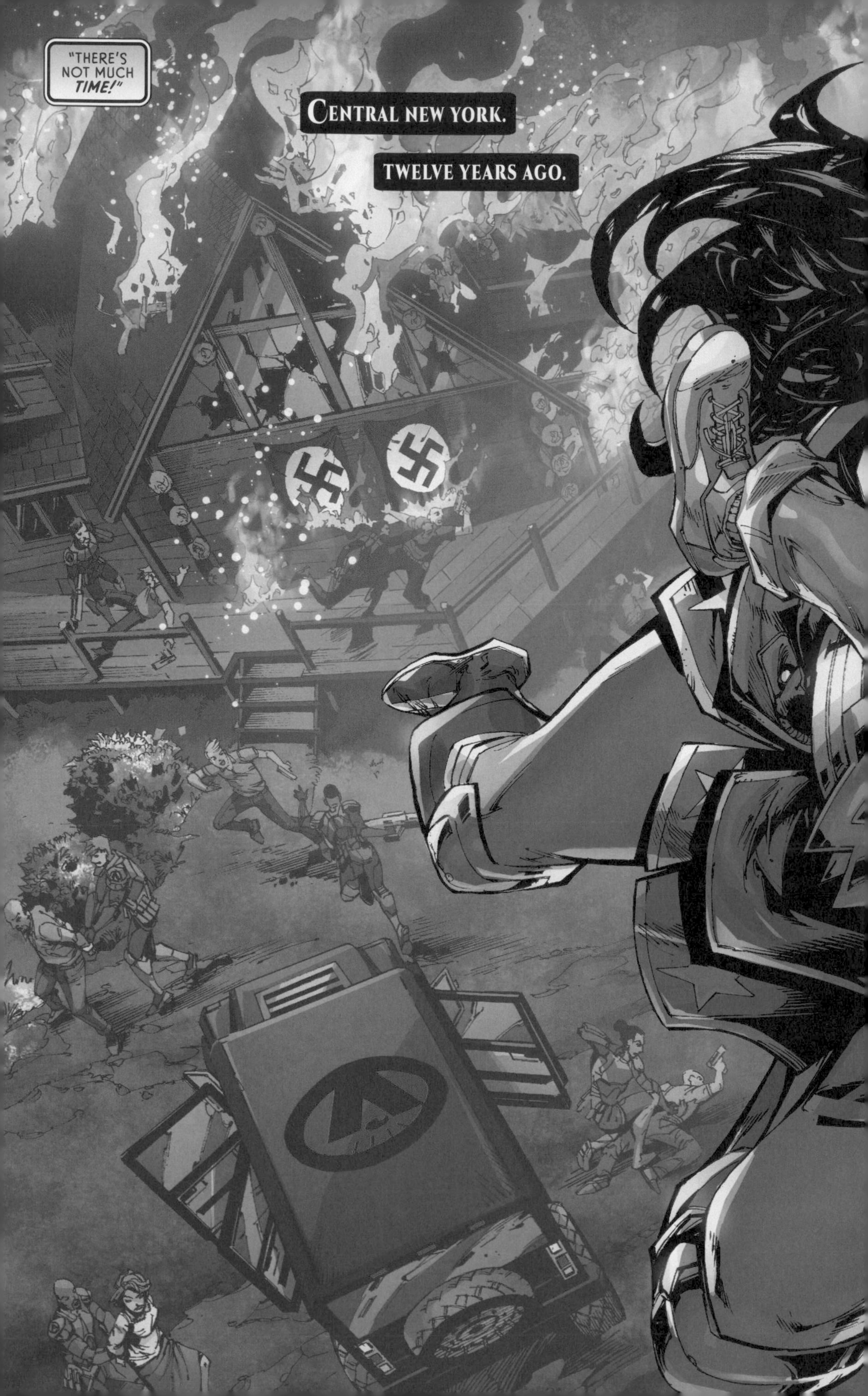
"THERE'S NOT MUCH TIME!"
CENTRAL NEW YORK.
TWELVE YEARS AGO.

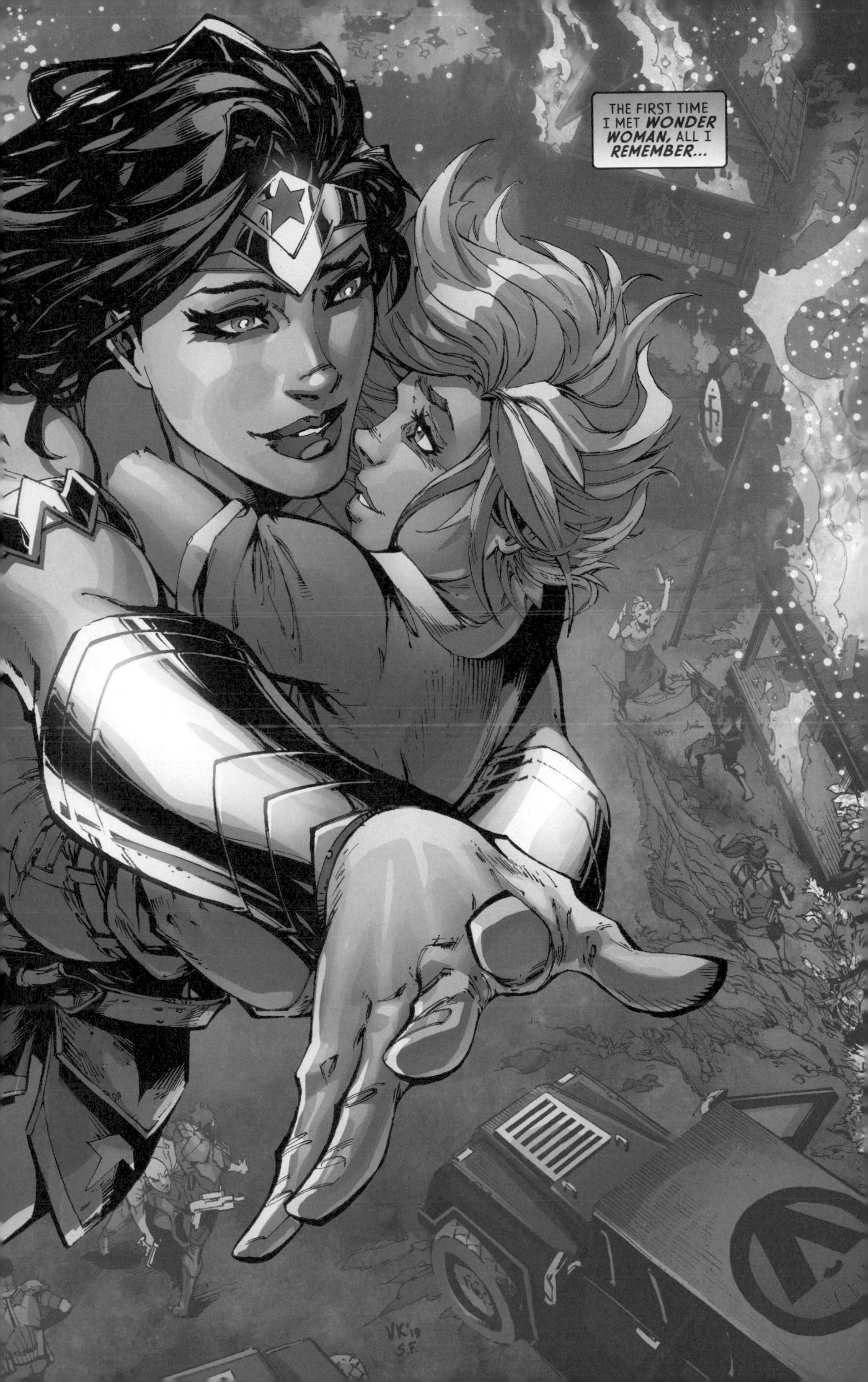
THE FIRST TIME I MET *WONDER WOMAN,* ALL I *REMEMBER...*
VK'19 S.F.

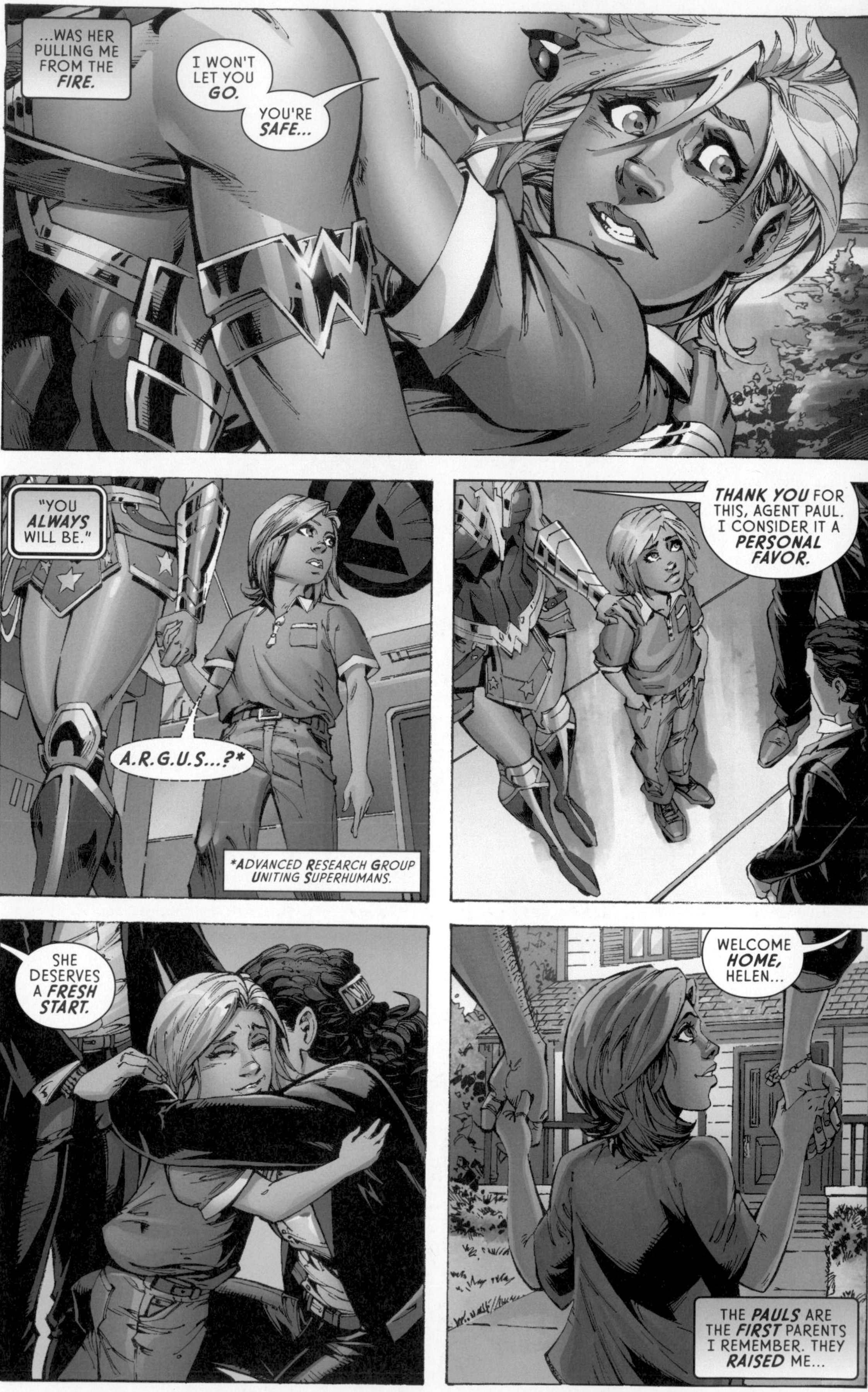
...WAS HER PULLING ME FROM THE FIRE.
I WON'T LET YOU GO.
YOU'RE SAFE...
"YOU ALWAYS WILL BE."
A.R.G.U.S...?*
*ADVANCED RESEARCH GROUP UNITING SUPERHUMANS.
THANK YOU FOR THIS, AGENT PAUL. I CONSIDER IT A PERSONAL FAVOR.
SHE DESERVES A FRESH START.
WELCOME HOME, HELEN...
THE PAULS ARE THE FIRST PARENTS I REMEMBER. THEY RAISED ME...

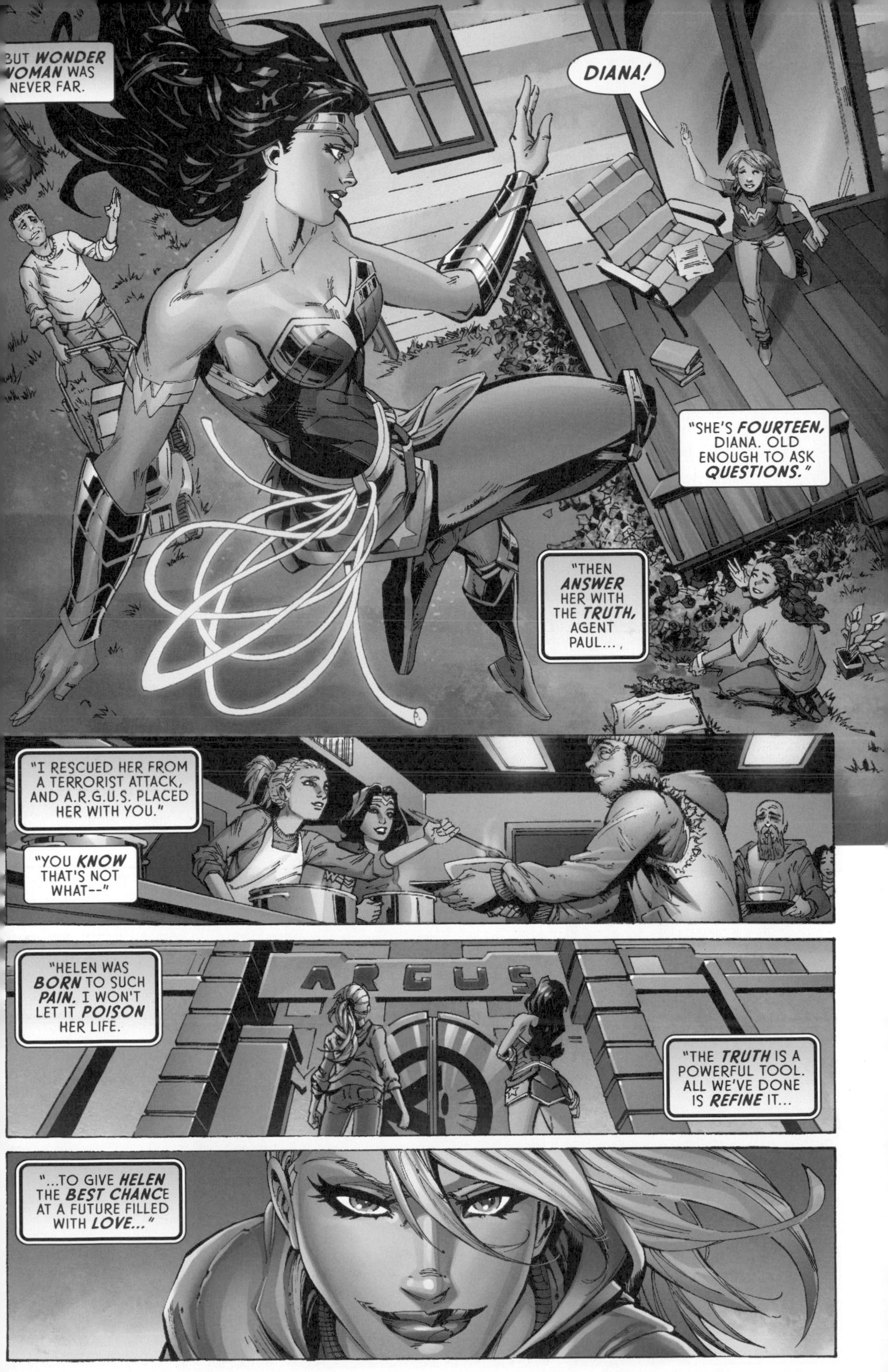
BUT WONDER WOMAN WAS NEVER FAR.
DIANA!
"SHE'S FOURTEEN, DIANA. OLD ENOUGH TO ASK QUESTIONS."
"THEN ANSWER HER WITH THE TRUTH, AGENT PAUL...,
"I RESCUED HER FROM A TERRORIST ATTACK, AND A.R.G.U.S. PLACED HER WITH YOU."
"YOU KNOW THAT'S NOT WHAT--"
"HELEN WAS BORN TO SUCH PAIN. I WON'T LET IT POISON HER LIFE.
ARGUS
"THE TRUTH IS A POWERFUL TOOL. ALL WE'VE DONE IS REFINE IT...
"...TO GIVE HELEN THE BEST CHANCE AT A FUTURE FILLED WITH LOVE..."

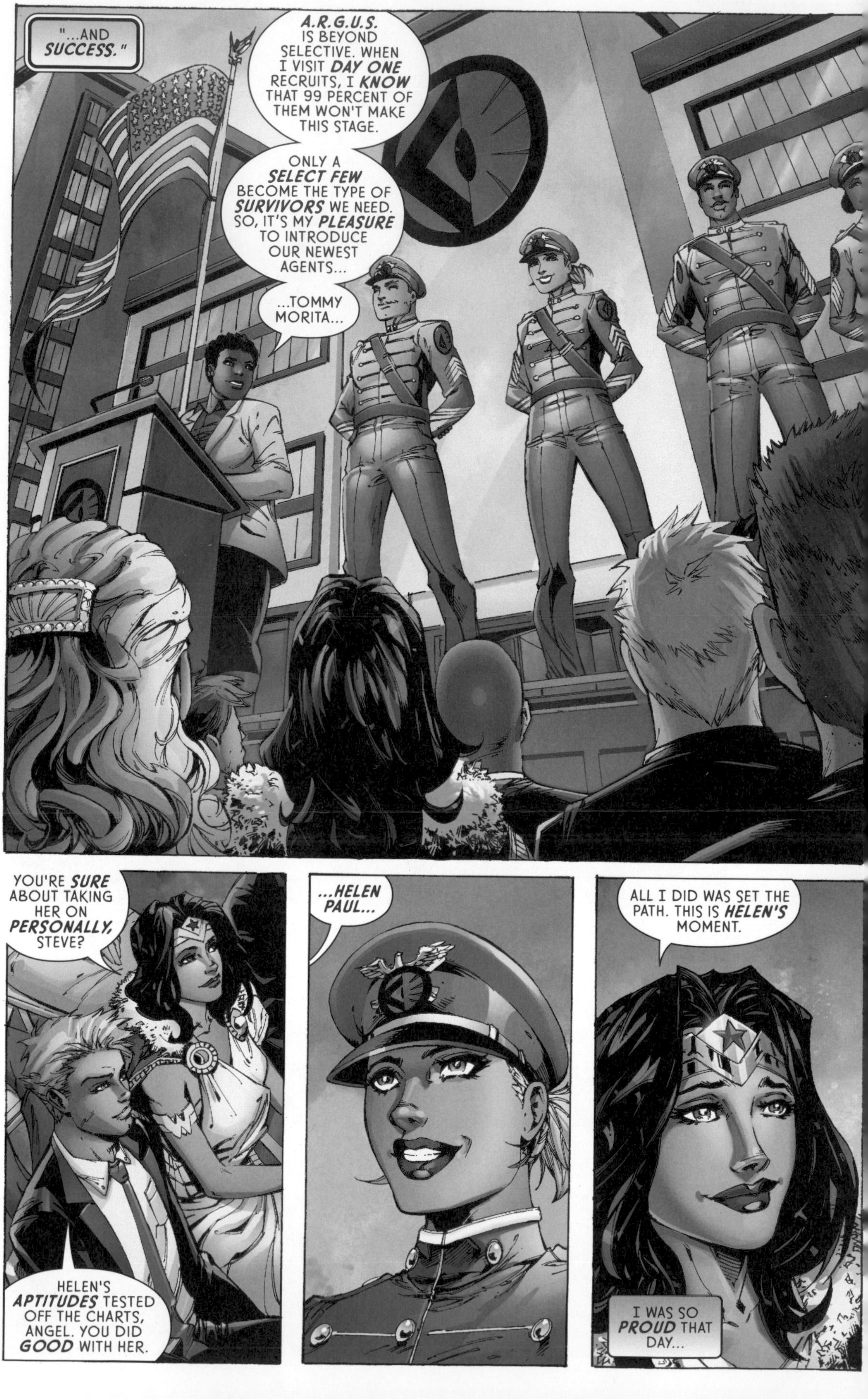
"...AND SUCCESS."
A.R.G.U.S. IS BEYOND SELECTIVE. WHEN I VISIT DAY ONE RECRUITS, I KNOW THAT 99 PERCENT OF THEM WON'T MAKE THIS STAGE.
ONLY A SELECT FEW BECOME THE TYPE OF SURVIVORS WE NEED. SO, IT'S MY PLEASURE TO INTRODUCE OUR NEWEST AGENTS...
...TOMMY MORITA...
YOU'RE SURE ABOUT TAKING HER ON PERSONALLY, STEVE?
HELEN'S APTITUDES TESTED OFF THE CHARTS, ANGEL. YOU DID GOOD WITH HER.
...HELEN PAUL...
ALL I DID WAS SET THE PATH. THIS IS HELEN'S MOMENT.
I WAS SO PROUD THAT DAY...

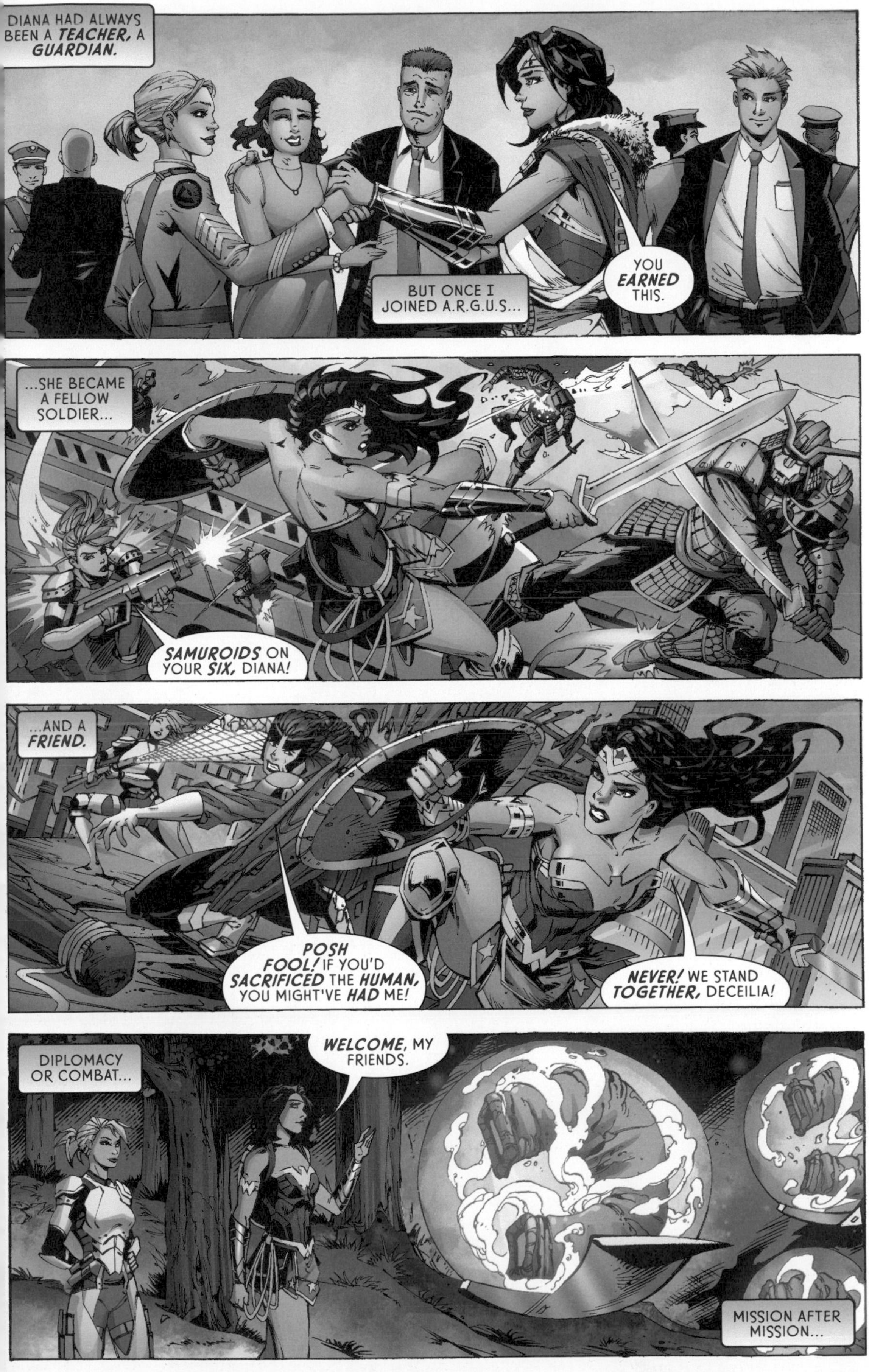
DIANA HAD ALWAYS BEEN A TEACHER, A GUARDIAN.
BUT ONCE I JOINED A.R.G.U.S...
YOU EARNED THIS.
...SHE BECAME A FELLOW SOLDIER...
SAMUROIDS ON YOUR SIX, DIANA!
...AND A FRIEND.
POSH FOOL! IF YOU'D SACRIFICED THE HUMAN, YOU MIGHT'VE HAD ME!
NEVER! WE STAND TOGETHER, DECEILIA!
DIPLOMACY OR COMBAT...
WELCOME, MY FRIENDS.
MISSION AFTER MISSION...

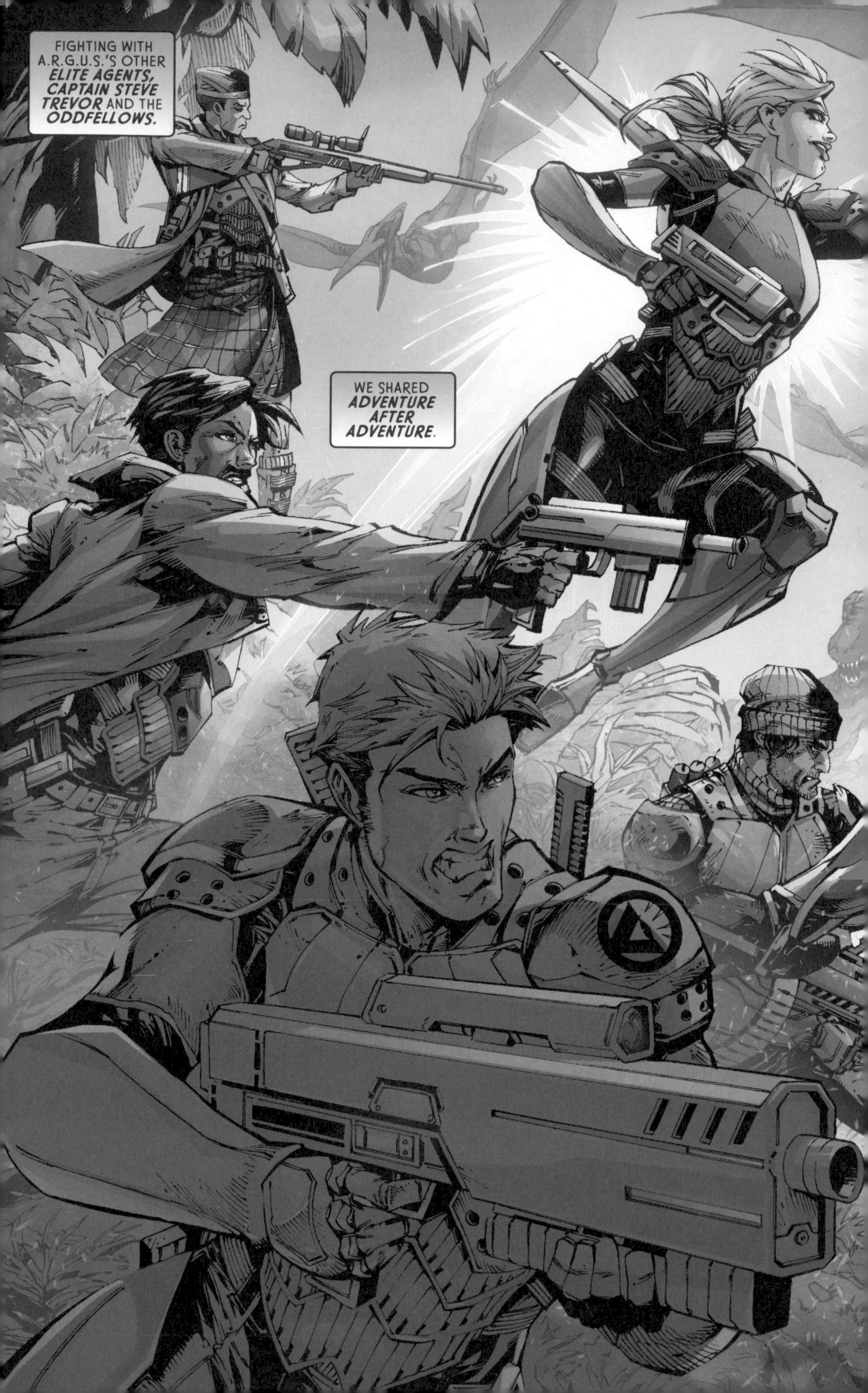
FIGHTING WITH A.R.G.U.S.'S OTHER *ELITE AGENTS, CAPTAIN STEVE TREVOR* AND THE *ODDFELLOWS.*
WE SHARED *ADVENTURE AFTER ADVENTURE.*

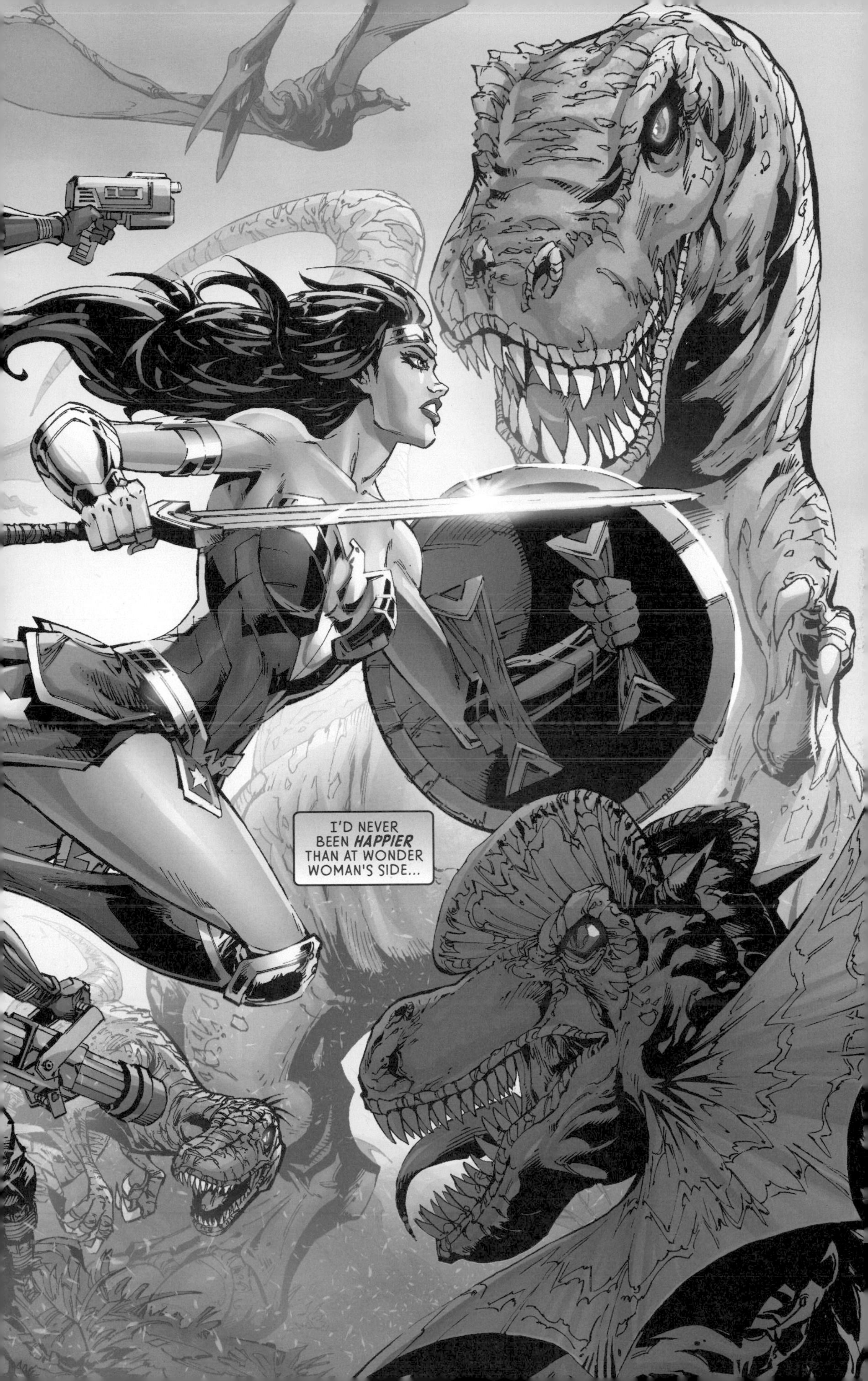
I'D NEVER BEEN HAPPIER THAN AT WONDER WOMAN'S SIDE...

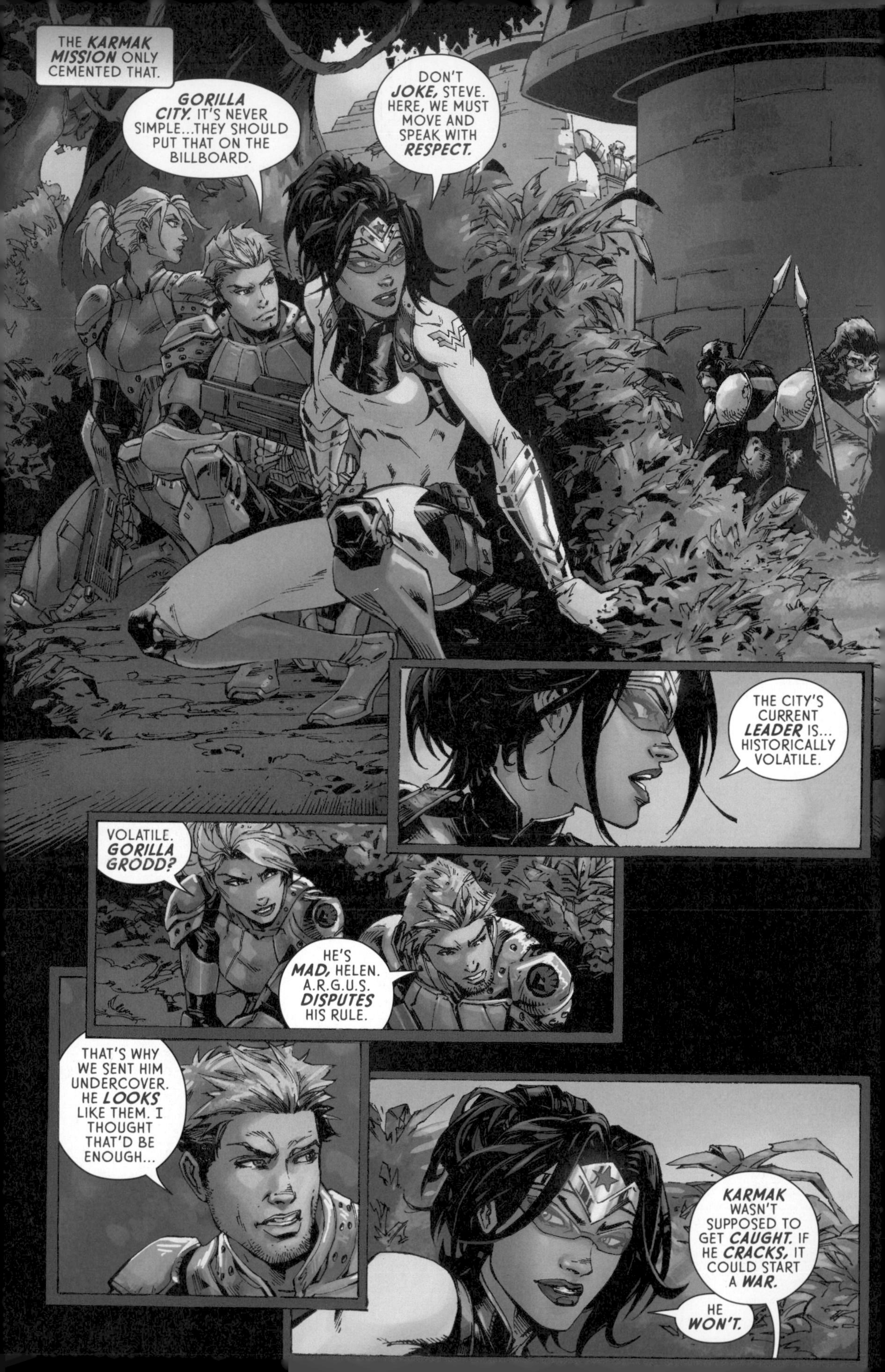
THE KARMAK MISSION ONLY CEMENTED THAT.
GORILLA CITY. IT'S NEVER SIMPLE...THEY SHOULD PUT THAT ON THE BILLBOARD.
DON'T JOKE, STEVE. HERE, WE MUST MOVE AND SPEAK WITH RESPECT.
THE CITY'S CURRENT LEADER IS... HISTORICALLY VOLATILE.
VOLATILE. GORILLA GRODD?
HE'S MAD, HELEN. A.R.G.U.S. DISPUTES HIS RULE.
THAT'S WHY WE SENT HIM UNDERCOVER. HE LOOKS LIKE THEM. I THOUGHT THAT'D BE ENOUGH...
KARMAK WASN'T SUPPOSED TO GET CAUGHT. IF HE CRACKS, IT COULD START A WAR.
HE WON'T.

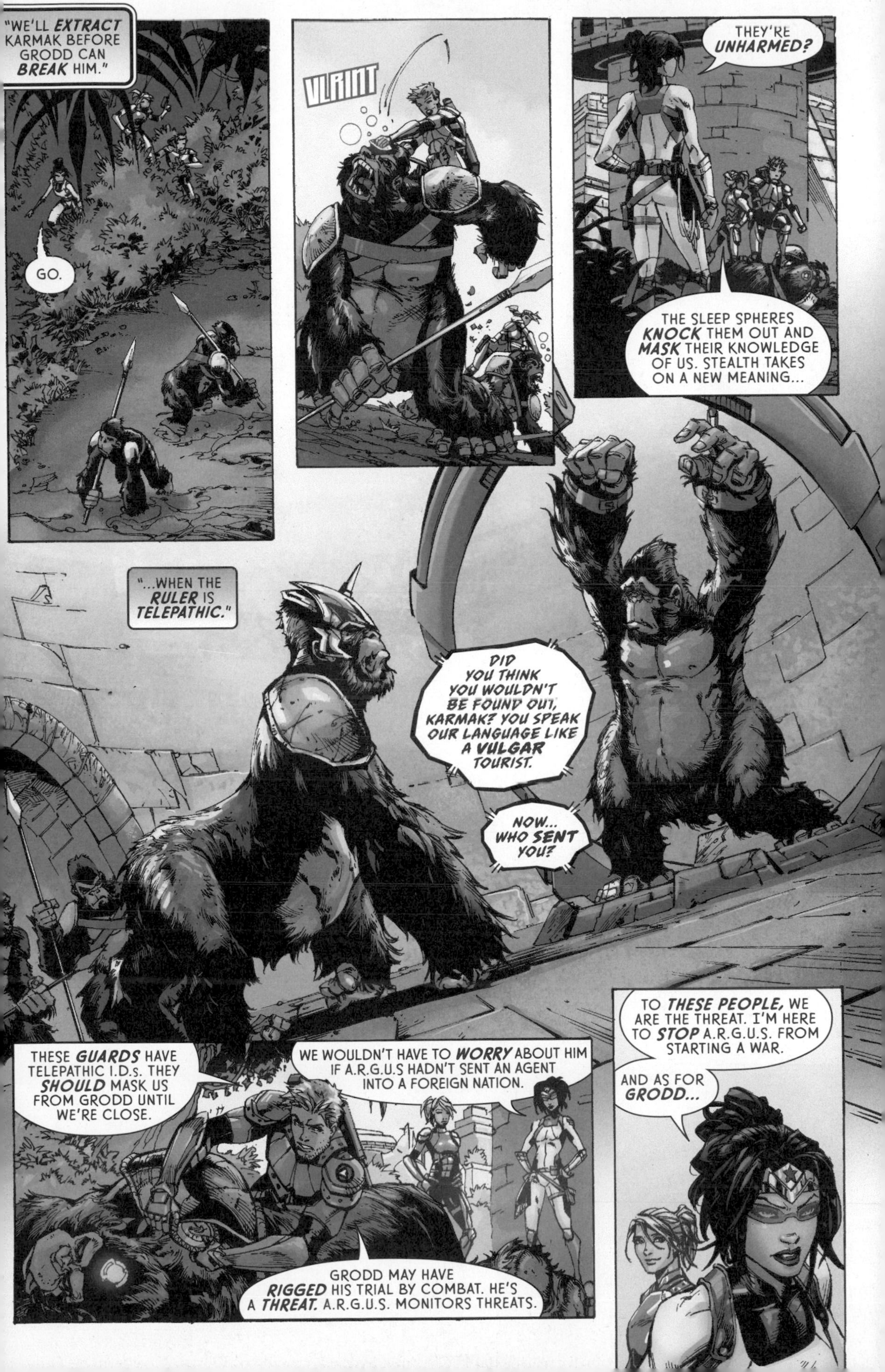
"WE'LL EXTRACT KARMAK BEFORE GRODD CAN BREAK HIM."
GO.
VLRINT
THEY'RE UNHARMED?
THE SLEEP SPHERES KNOCK THEM OUT AND MASK THEIR KNOWLEDGE OF US. STEALTH TAKES ON A NEW MEANING...
"...WHEN THE RULER IS TELEPATHIC."
DID YOU THINK YOU WOULDN'T BE FOUND OUT, KARMAK? YOU SPEAK OUR LANGUAGE LIKE A VULGAR TOURIST.
NOW... WHO SENT YOU?
THESE GUARDS HAVE TELEPATHIC I.D.s. THEY SHOULD MASK US FROM GRODD UNTIL WE'RE CLOSE.
WE WOULDN'T HAVE TO WORRY ABOUT HIM IF A.R.G.U.S HADN'T SENT AN AGENT INTO A FOREIGN NATION.
GRODD MAY HAVE RIGGED HIS TRIAL BY COMBAT. HE'S A THREAT. A.R.G.U.S. MONITORS THREATS.
TO THESE PEOPLE, WE ARE THE THREAT. I'M HERE TO STOP A.R.G.U.S. FROM STARTING A WAR.
AND AS FOR GRODD...

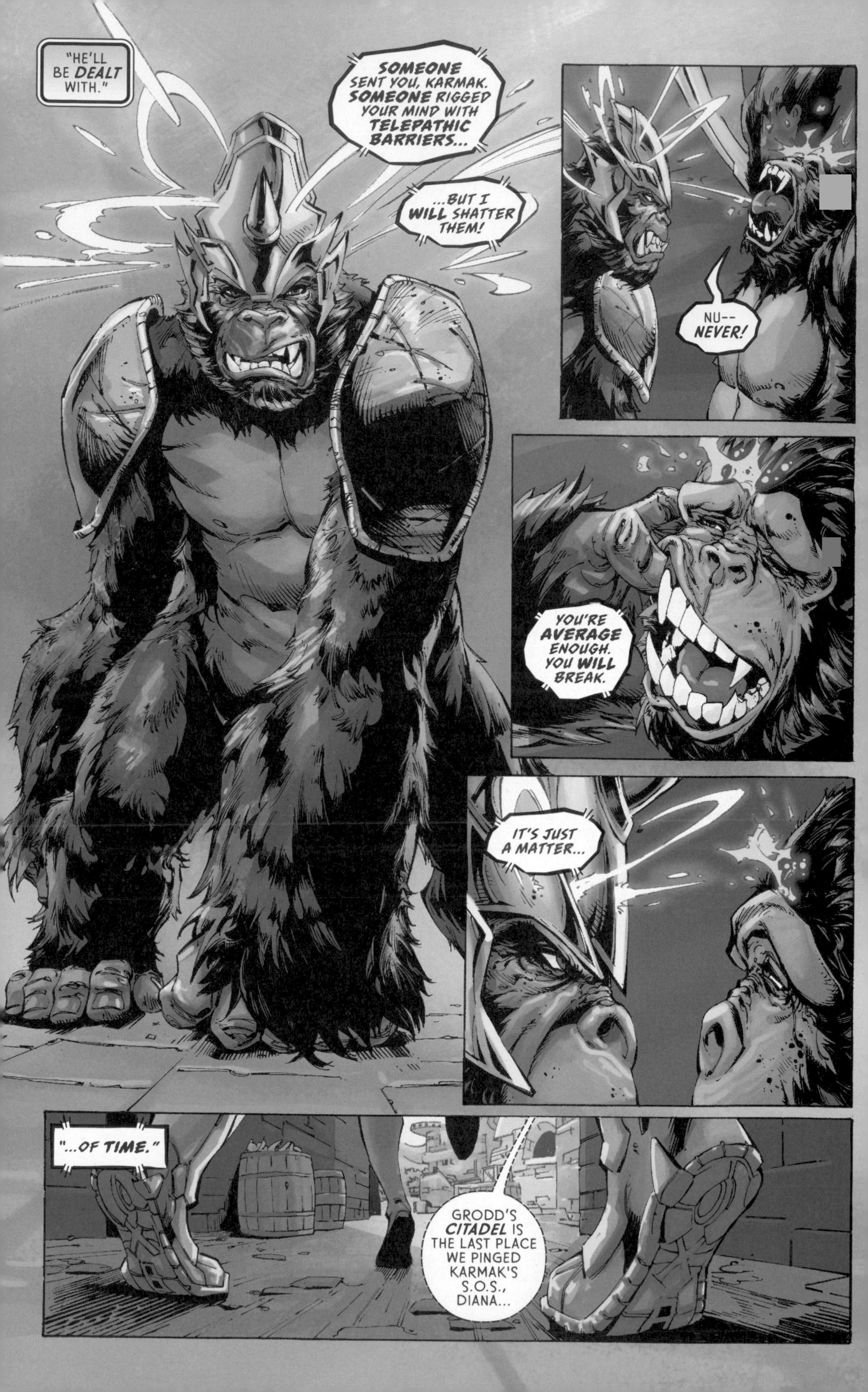
"HE'LL BE DEALT WITH."
SOMEONE SENT YOU, KARMAK. SOMEONE RIGGED YOUR MIND WITH TELEPATHIC BARRIERS...
...BUT I WILL SHATTER THEM!
NU-- NEVER!
YOU'RE AVERAGE ENOUGH. YOU WILL BREAK.
IT'S JUST A MATTER...
"...OF TIME."
GRODD'S CITADEL IS THE LAST PLACE WE PINGED KARMAK'S S.O.S., DIANA...

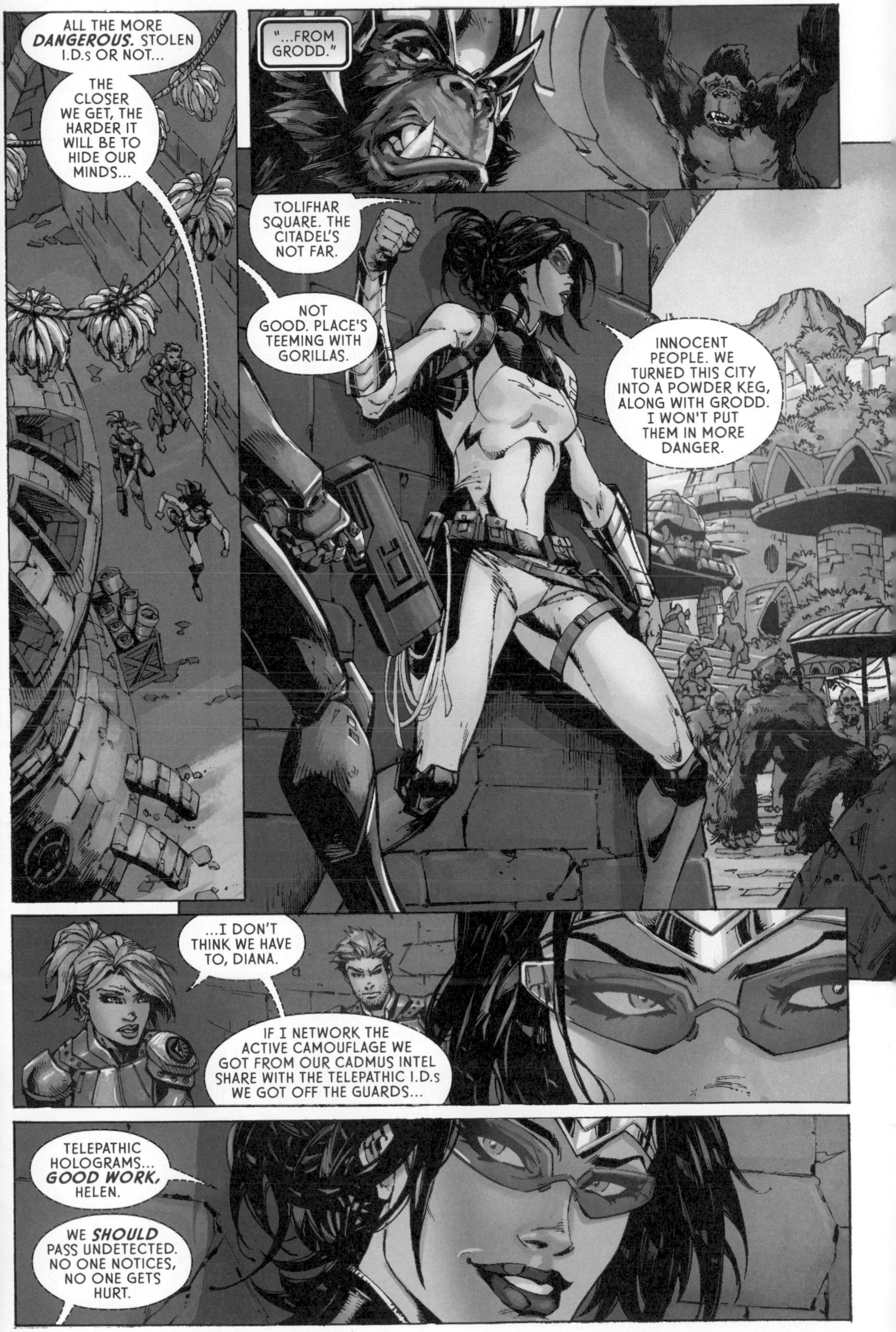
ALL THE MORE DANGEROUS. STOLEN I.D.s OR NOT...
THE CLOSER WE GET, THE HARDER IT WILL BE TO HIDE OUR MINDS...
"...FROM GRODD."
TOLIFHAR SQUARE. THE CITADEL'S NOT FAR.
NOT GOOD. PLACE'S TEEMING WITH GORILLAS.
INNOCENT PEOPLE. WE TURNED THIS CITY INTO A POWDER KEG, ALONG WITH GRODD. I WON'T PUT THEM IN MORE DANGER.
...I DON'T THINK WE HAVE TO, DIANA.
IF I NETWORK THE ACTIVE CAMOUFLAGE WE GOT FROM OUR CADMUS INTEL SHARE WITH THE TELEPATHIC I.D.s WE GOT OFF THE GUARDS...
TELEPATHIC HOLOGRAMS... GOOD WORK, HELEN.
WE SHOULD PASS UNDETECTED. NO ONE NOTICES, NO ONE GETS HURT.

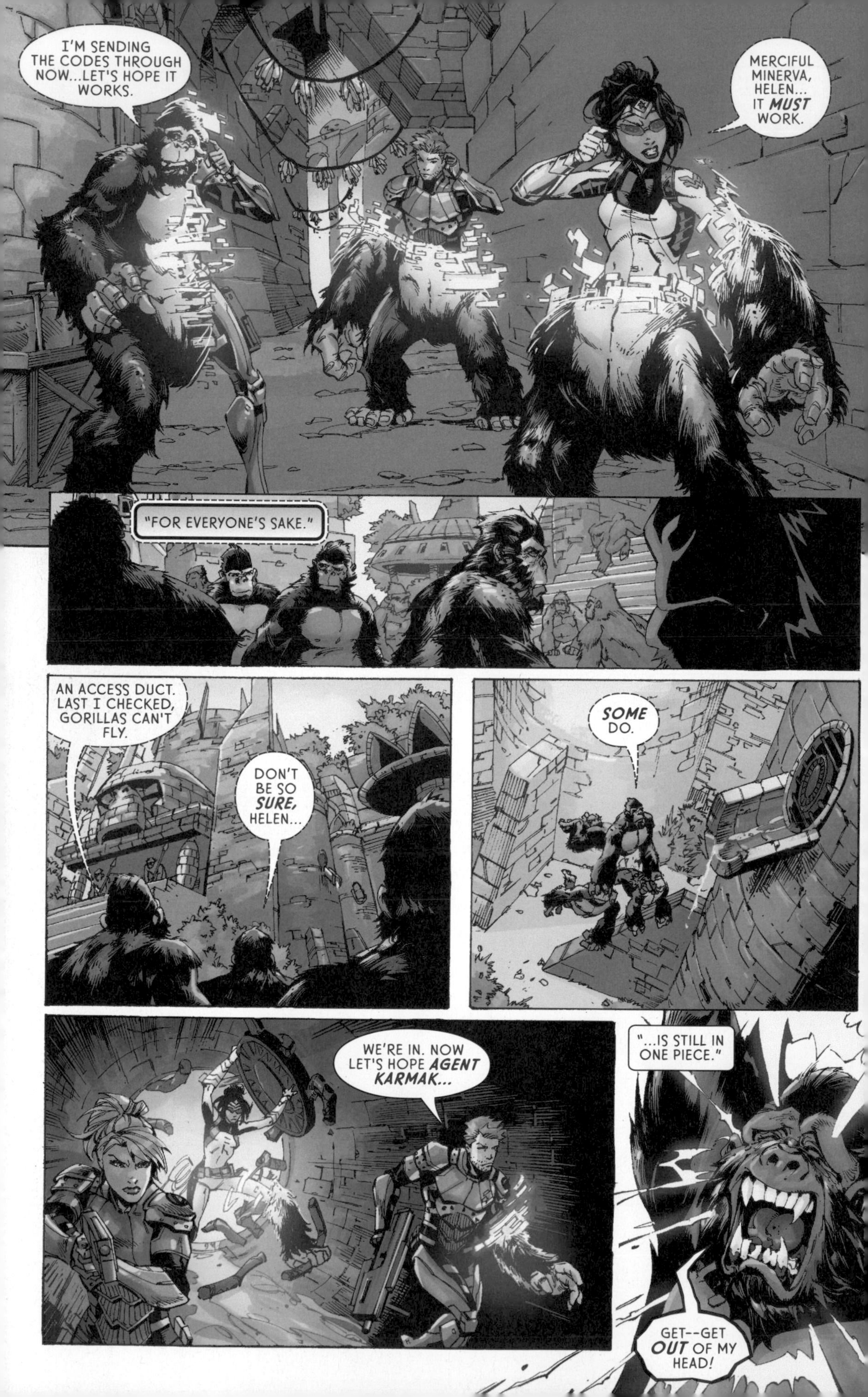
I'M SENDING THE CODES THROUGH NOW...LET'S HOPE IT WORKS.
MERCIFUL MINERVA, HELEN... IT MUST WORK.
"FOR EVERYONE'S SAKE."
AN ACCESS DUCT. LAST I CHECKED, GORILLAS CAN'T FLY.
DON'T BE SO SURE, HELEN...
SOME DO.
WE'RE IN. NOW LET'S HOPE AGENT KARMAK...
"...IS STILL IN ONE PIECE."
GET--GET OUT OF MY HEAD!

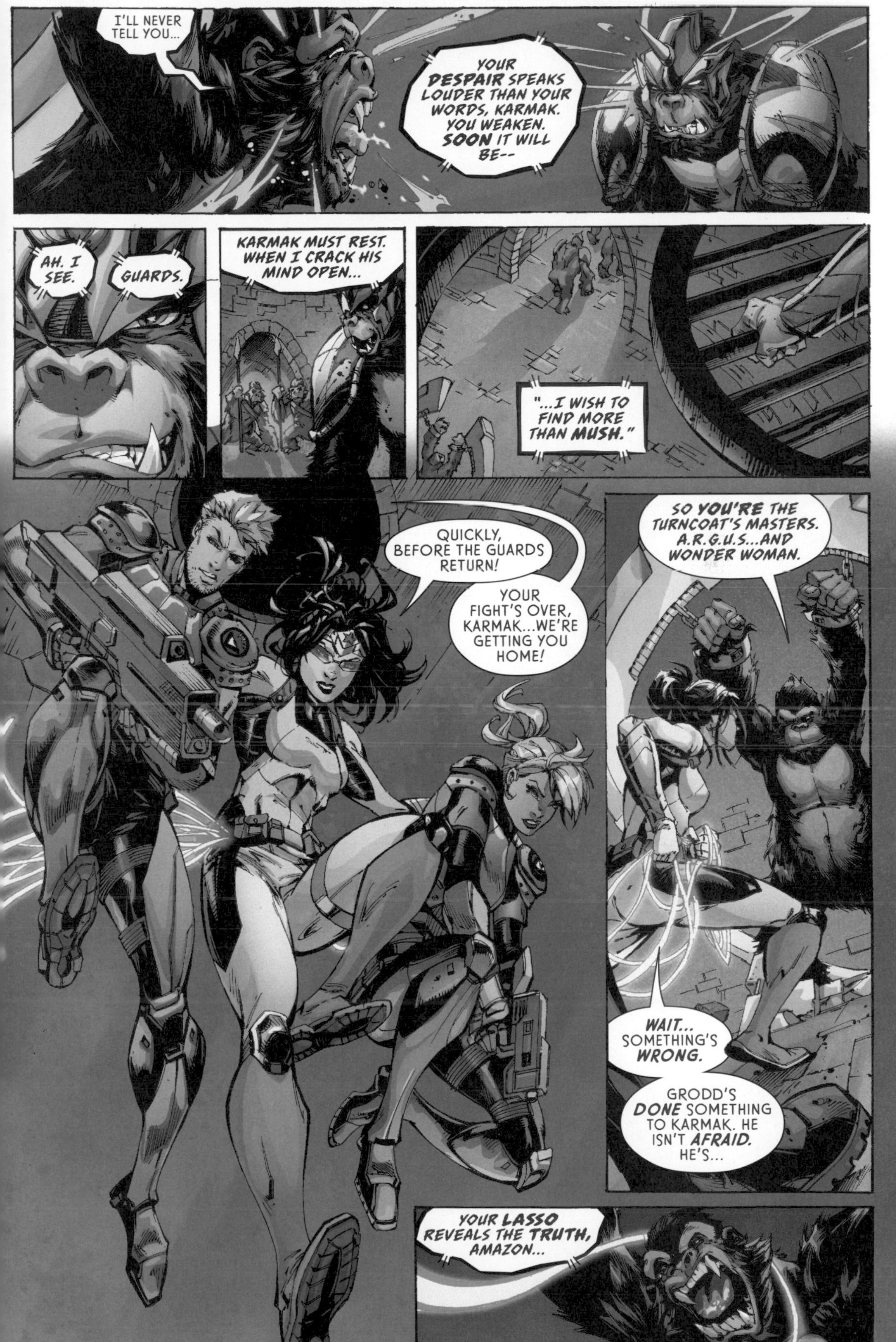

I'LL NEVER TELL YOU...
YOUR DESPAIR SPEAKS LOUDER THAN YOUR WORDS, KARMAK. YOU WEAKEN. SOON IT WILL BE--
AH. I SEE.
GUARDS.
KARMAK MUST REST. WHEN I CRACK HIS MIND OPEN...
"...I WISH TO FIND MORE THAN MUSH."
QUICKLY, BEFORE THE GUARDS RETURN!
YOUR FIGHT'S OVER, KARMAK...WE'RE GETTING YOU HOME!
SO YOU'RE THE TURNCOAT'S MASTERS. A.R.G.U.S....AND WONDER WOMAN.
WAIT... SOMETHING'S WRONG.
GRODD'S DONE SOMETHING TO KARMAK. HE ISN'T AFRAID. HE'S...
YOUR LASSO REVEALS THE TRUTH, AMAZON...

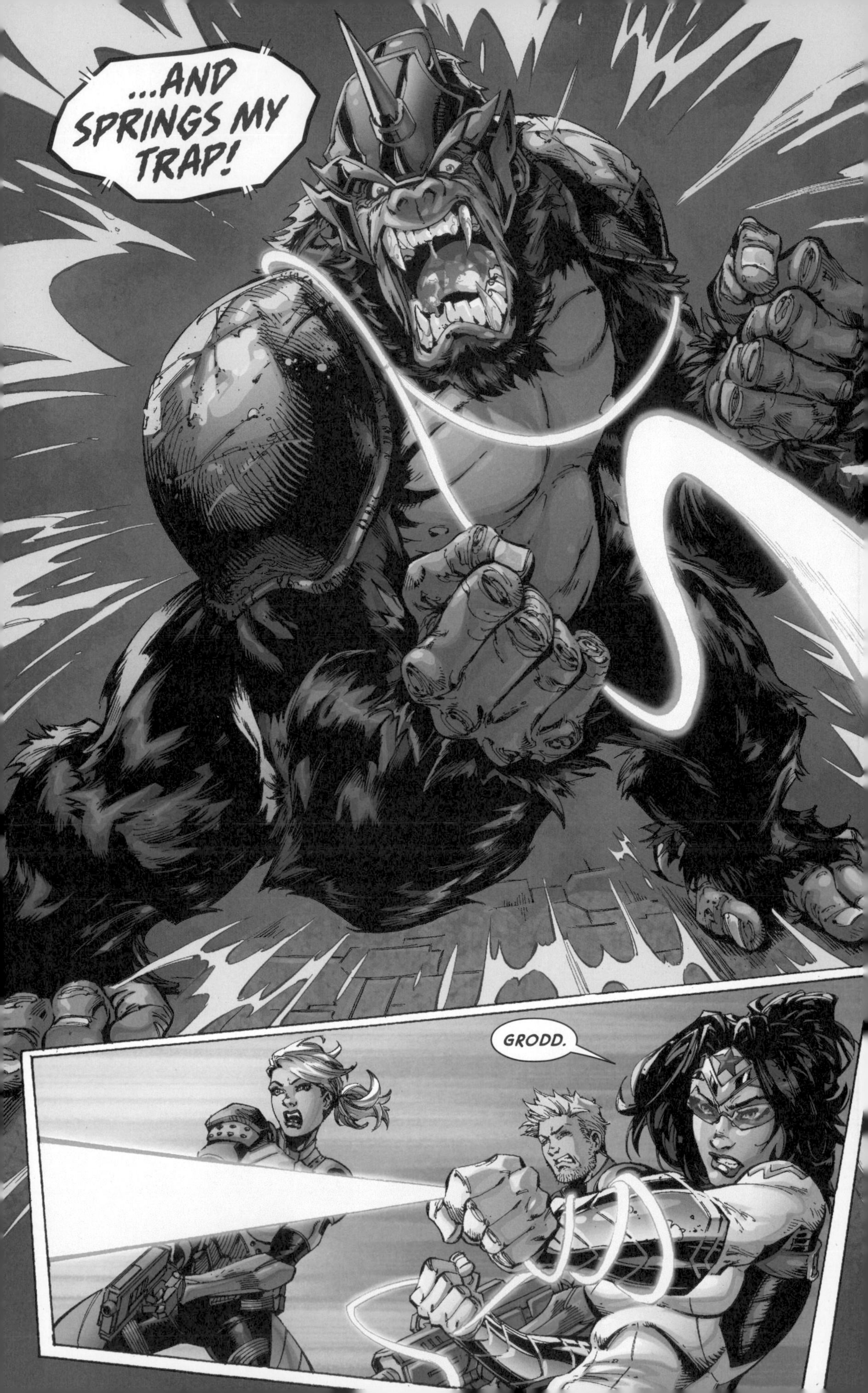
...AND SPRINGS MY TRAP!
GRODD.

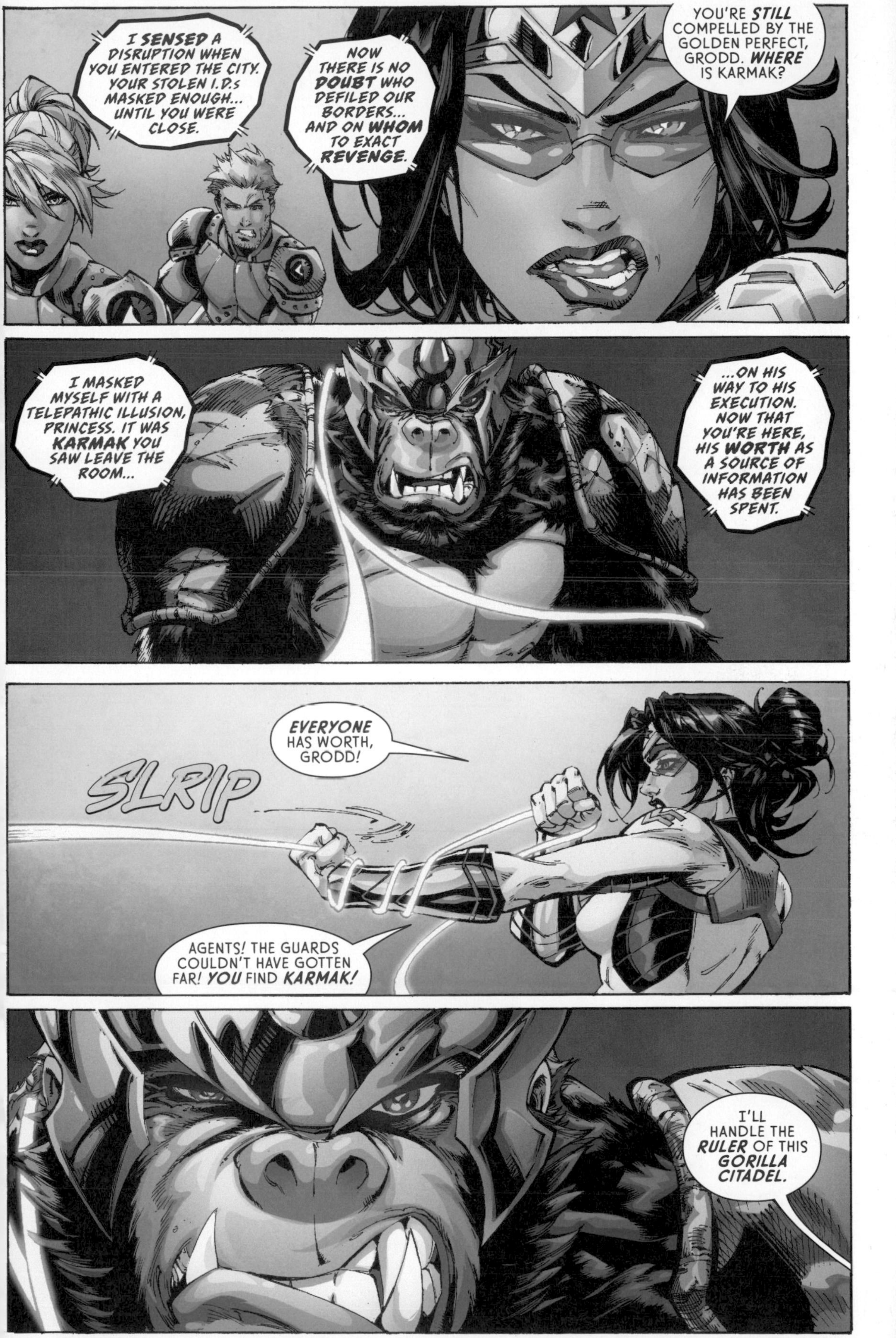
I SENSED A DISRUPTION WHEN YOU ENTERED THE CITY. YOUR STOLEN I.D.s MASKED ENOUGH... UNTIL YOU WERE CLOSE.
NOW THERE IS NO DOUBT WHO DEFILED OUR BORDERS... AND ON WHOM TO EXACT REVENGE.
YOU'RE STILL COMPELLED BY THE GOLDEN PERFECT, GRODD. WHERE IS KARMAK?
I MASKED MYSELF WITH A TELEPATHIC ILLUSION, PRINCESS. IT WAS KARMAK YOU SAW LEAVE THE ROOM...
...ON HIS WAY TO HIS EXECUTION. NOW THAT YOU'RE HERE, HIS WORTH AS A SOURCE OF INFORMATION HAS BEEN SPENT.
EVERYONE HAS WORTH, GRODD!
SLRIP
AGENTS! THE GUARDS COULDN'T HAVE GOTTEN FAR! YOU FIND KARMAK!
I'LL HANDLE THE RULER OF THIS GORILLA CITADEL.

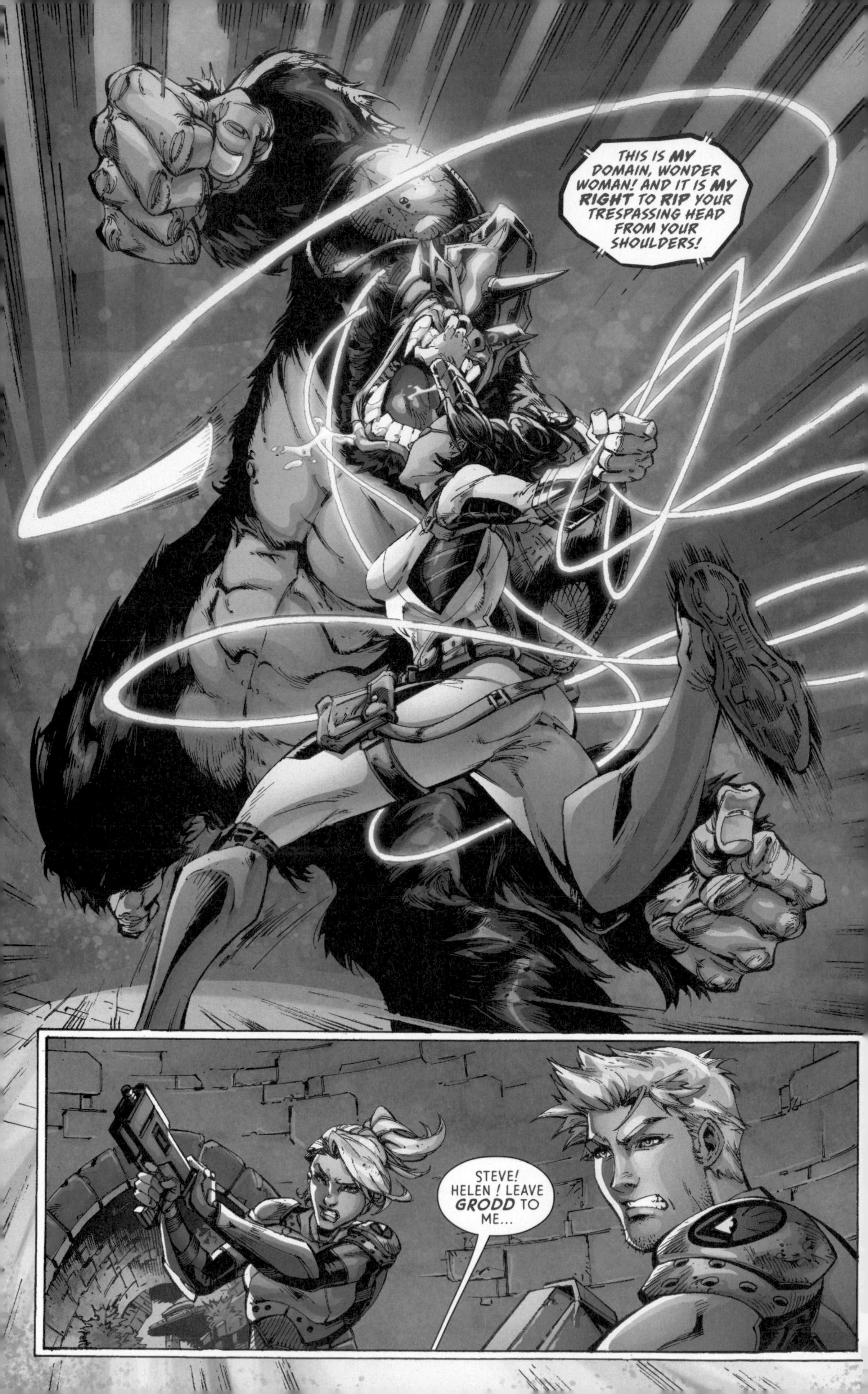
THIS IS MY DOMAIN, WONDER WOMAN! AND IT IS MY RIGHT TO RIP YOUR TRESPASSING HEAD FROM YOUR SHOULDERS!
STEVE! HELEN! LEAVE GRODD TO ME...

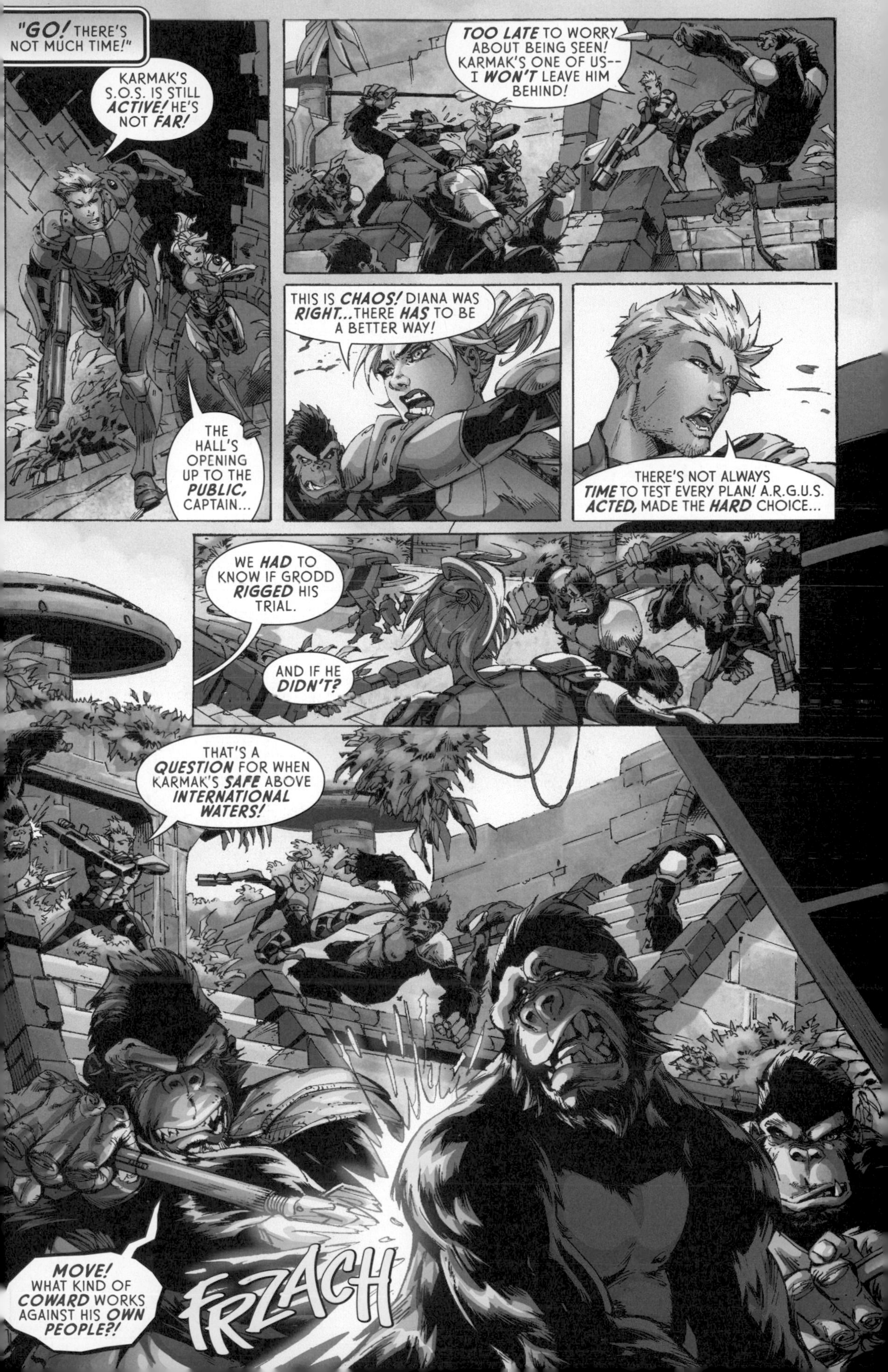
"GO! THERE'S NOT MUCH TIME!"
KARMAK'S S.O.S. IS STILL ACTIVE! HE'S NOT FAR!
THE HALL'S OPENING UP TO THE PUBLIC, CAPTAIN...
TOO LATE TO WORRY ABOUT BEING SEEN! KARMAK'S ONE OF US-- I WON'T LEAVE HIM BEHIND!
THIS IS CHAOS! DIANA WAS RIGHT...THERE HAS TO BE A BETTER WAY!
THERE'S NOT ALWAYS TIME TO TEST EVERY PLAN! A.R.G.U.S. ACTED, MADE THE HARD CHOICE...
WE HAD TO KNOW IF GRODD RIGGED HIS TRIAL.
AND IF HE DIDN'T?
THAT'S A QUESTION FOR WHEN KARMAK'S SAFE ABOVE INTERNATIONAL WATERS!
MOVE! WHAT KIND OF COWARD WORKS AGAINST HIS OWN PEOPLE?!
FRZACH

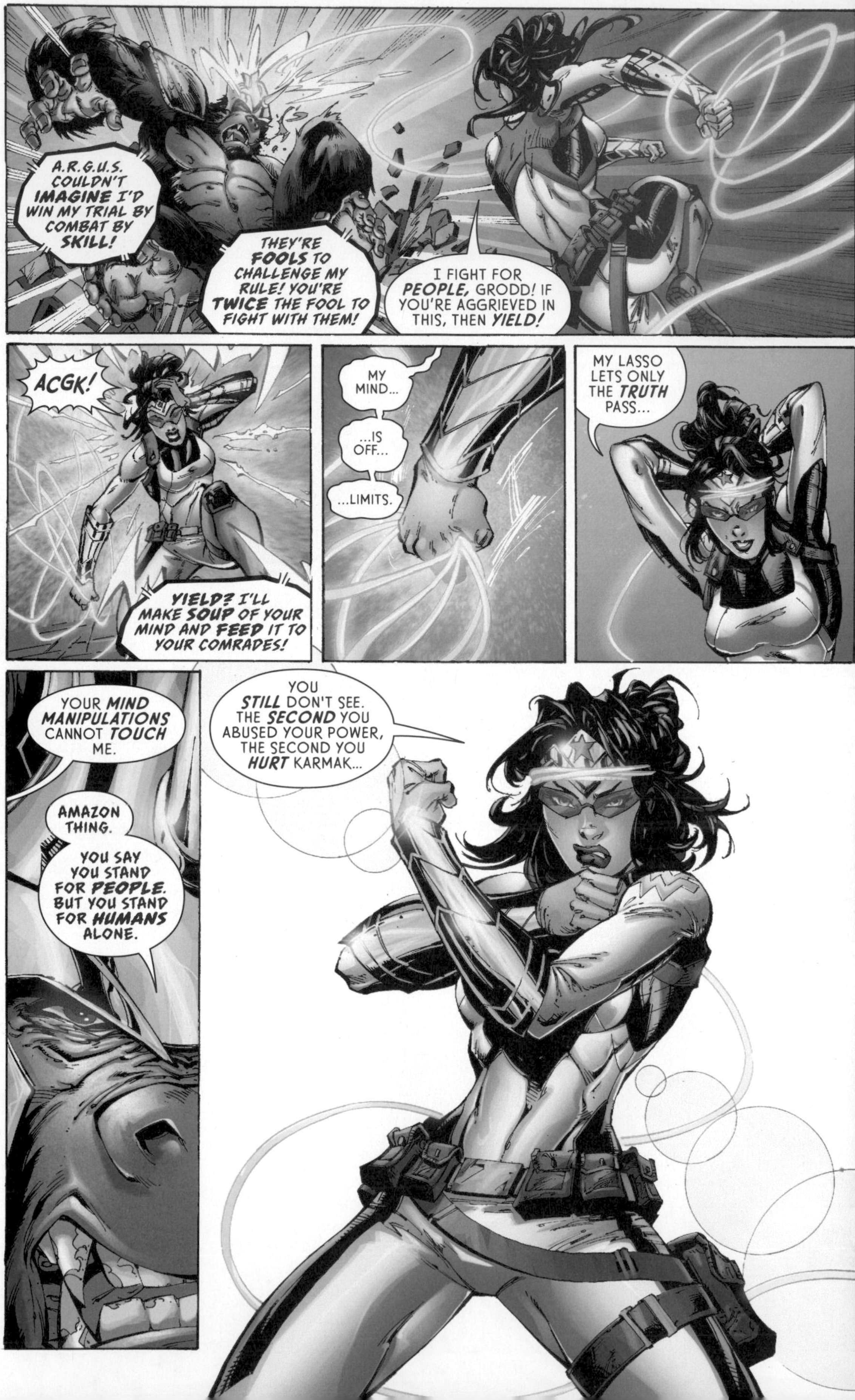
A.R.G.U.S. COULDN'T IMAGINE I'D WIN MY TRIAL BY COMBAT BY SKILL!
THEY'RE FOOLS TO CHALLENGE MY RULE! YOU'RE TWICE THE FOOL TO FIGHT WITH THEM!
I FIGHT FOR PEOPLE, GRODD! IF YOU'RE AGGRIEVED IN THIS, THEN YIELD!
ACGK!
YIELD? I'LL MAKE SOUP OF YOUR MIND AND FEED IT TO YOUR COMRADES!
MY MIND...
...IS OFF...
...LIMITS.
MY LASSO LETS ONLY THE TRUTH PASS...
YOUR MIND MANIPULATIONS CANNOT TOUCH ME.
AMAZON THING.
YOU SAY YOU STAND FOR PEOPLE. BUT YOU STAND FOR HUMANS ALONE.
YOU STILL DON'T SEE. THE SECOND YOU ABUSED YOUR POWER, THE SECOND YOU HURT KARMAK...

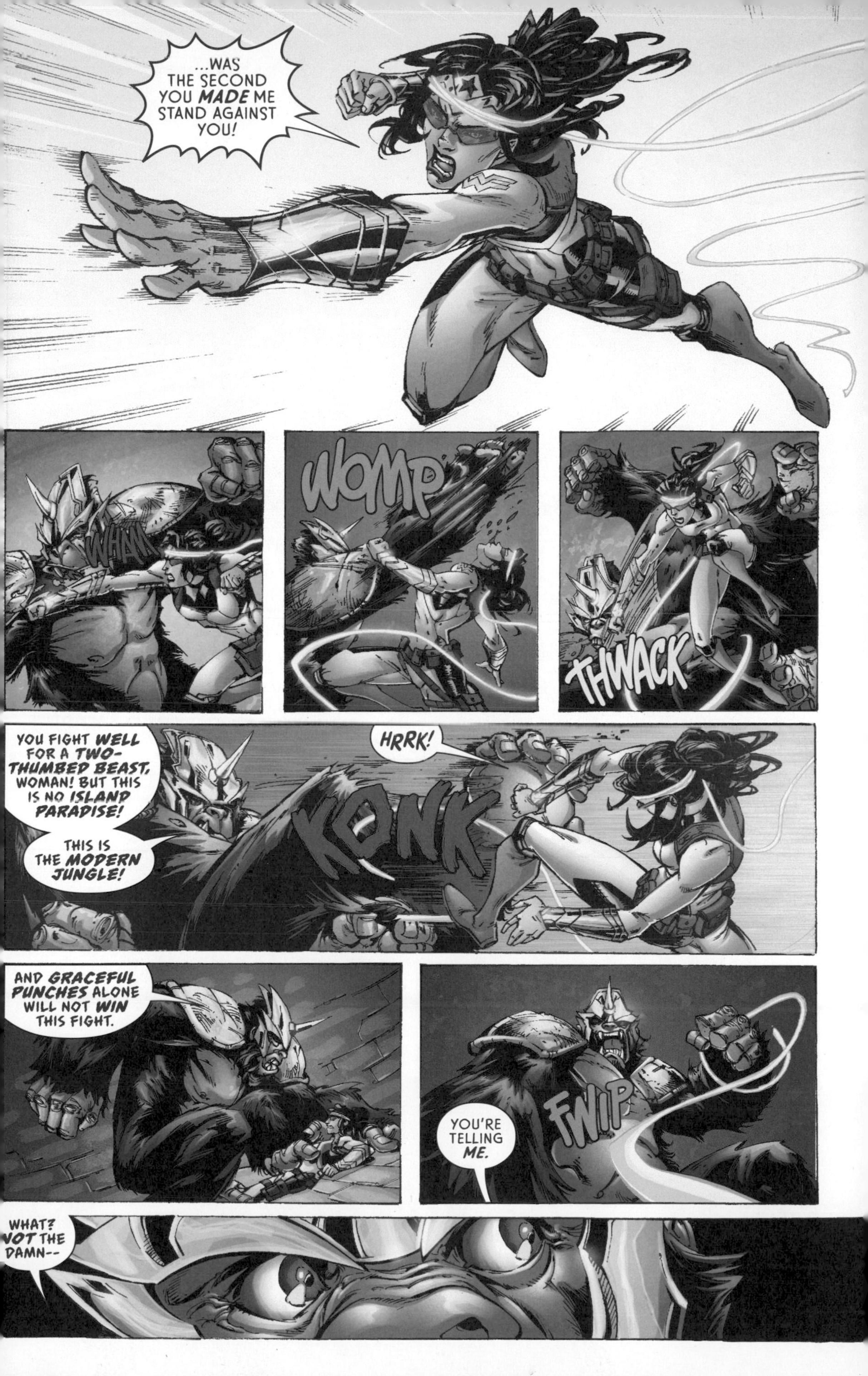

...WAS THE SECOND YOU MADE ME STAND AGAINST YOU!
WHAM
WOMP
THWACK
YOU FIGHT WELL FOR A TWO-THUMBED BEAST, WOMAN! BUT THIS IS NO ISLAND PARADISE!
THIS IS THE MODERN JUNGLE!
HRRK!
KONK
AND GRACEFUL PUNCHES ALONE WILL NOT WIN THIS FIGHT.
FWIP
YOU'RE TELLING ME.
WHAT? NOT THE DAMN--

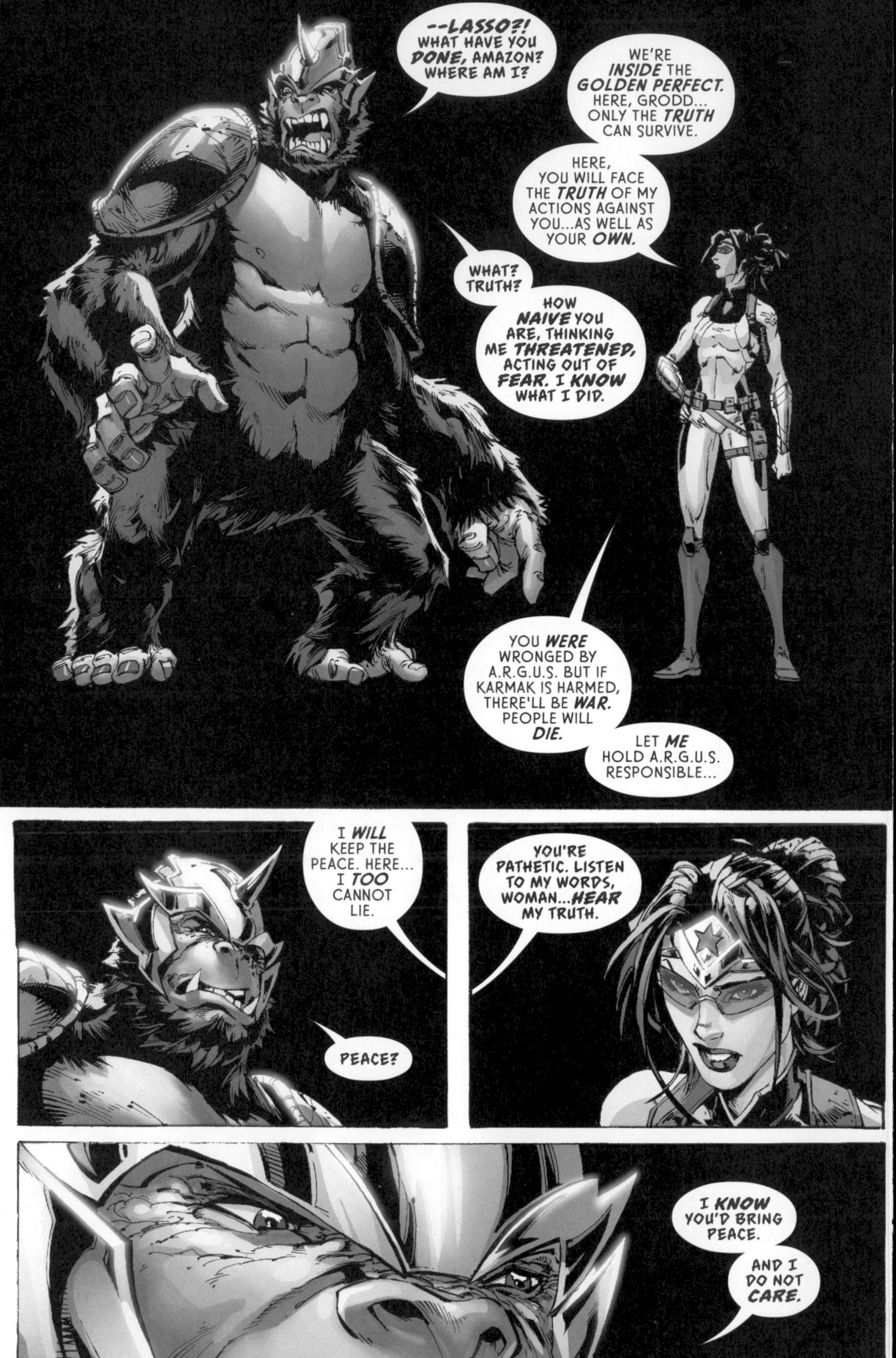
--LASSO?! WHAT HAVE YOU DONE, AMAZON? WHERE AM I?
WE'RE INSIDE THE GOLDEN PERFECT. HERE, GRODD... ONLY THE TRUTH CAN SURVIVE.
HERE, YOU WILL FACE THE TRUTH OF MY ACTIONS AGAINST YOU...AS WELL AS YOUR OWN.
WHAT? TRUTH?
HOW NAIVE YOU ARE, THINKING ME THREATENED, ACTING OUT OF FEAR. I KNOW WHAT I DID.
YOU WERE WRONGED BY A.R.G.U.S. BUT IF KARMAK IS HARMED, THERE'LL BE WAR. PEOPLE WILL DIE.
LET ME HOLD A.R.G.U.S. RESPONSIBLE...
I WILL KEEP THE PEACE. HERE... I TOO CANNOT LIE.
PEACE?
YOU'RE PATHETIC. LISTEN TO MY WORDS, WOMAN...HEAR MY TRUTH.
I KNOW YOU'D BRING PEACE.
AND I DO NOT CARE.

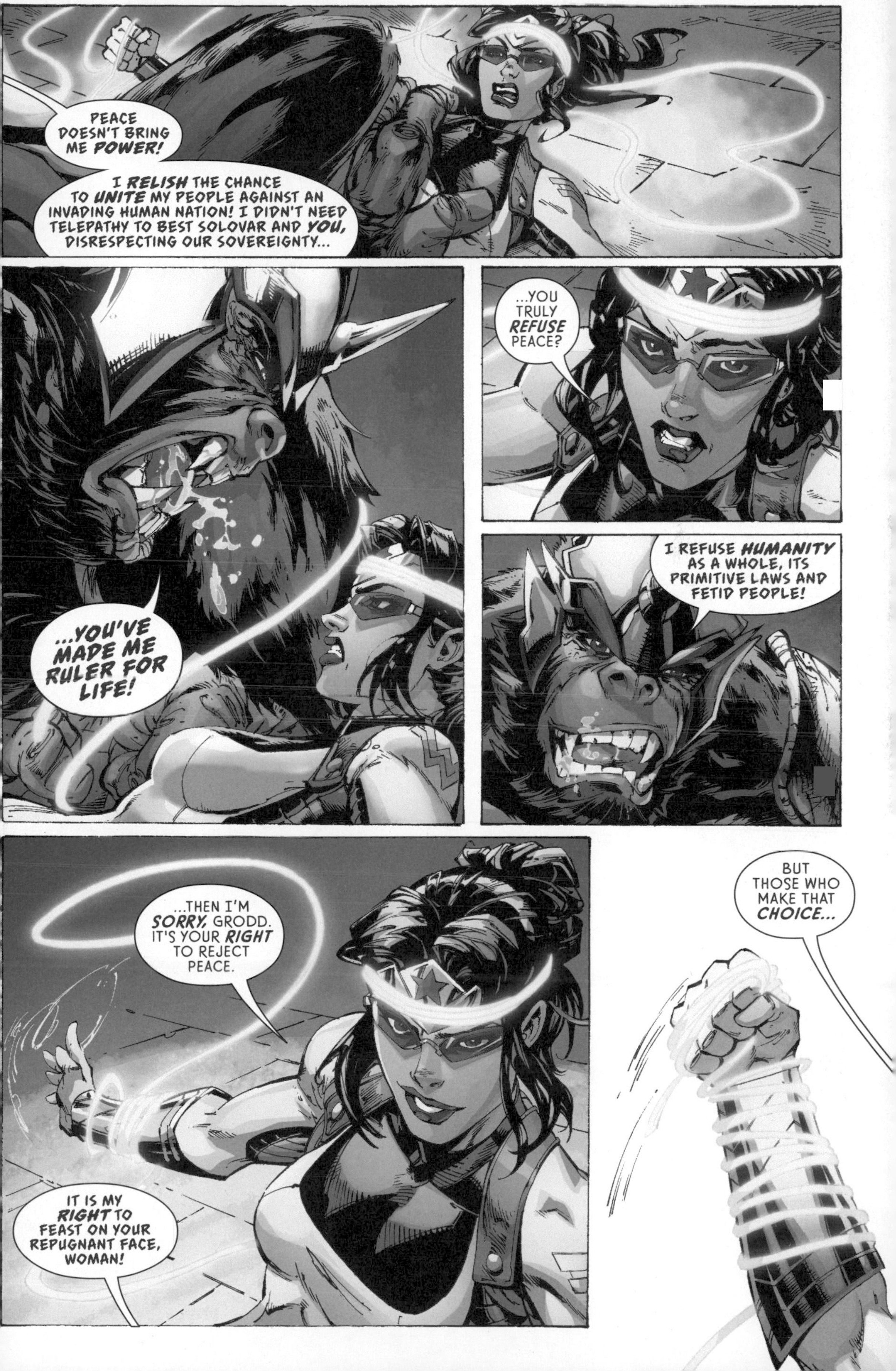
PEACE DOESN'T BRING ME POWER!
I RELISH THE CHANCE TO UNITE MY PEOPLE AGAINST AN INVADING HUMAN NATION! I DIDN'T NEED TELEPATHY TO BEST SOLOVAR AND YOU, DISRESPECTING OUR SOVEREIGNTY...
...YOU'VE MADE ME RULER FOR LIFE!
...YOU TRULY REFUSE PEACE?
I REFUSE HUMANITY AS A WHOLE, ITS PRIMITIVE LAWS AND FETID PEOPLE!
...THEN I'M SORRY, GRODD. IT'S YOUR RIGHT TO REJECT PEACE.
IT IS MY RIGHT TO FEAST ON YOUR REPUGNANT FACE, WOMAN!
BUT THOSE WHO MAKE THAT CHOICE...

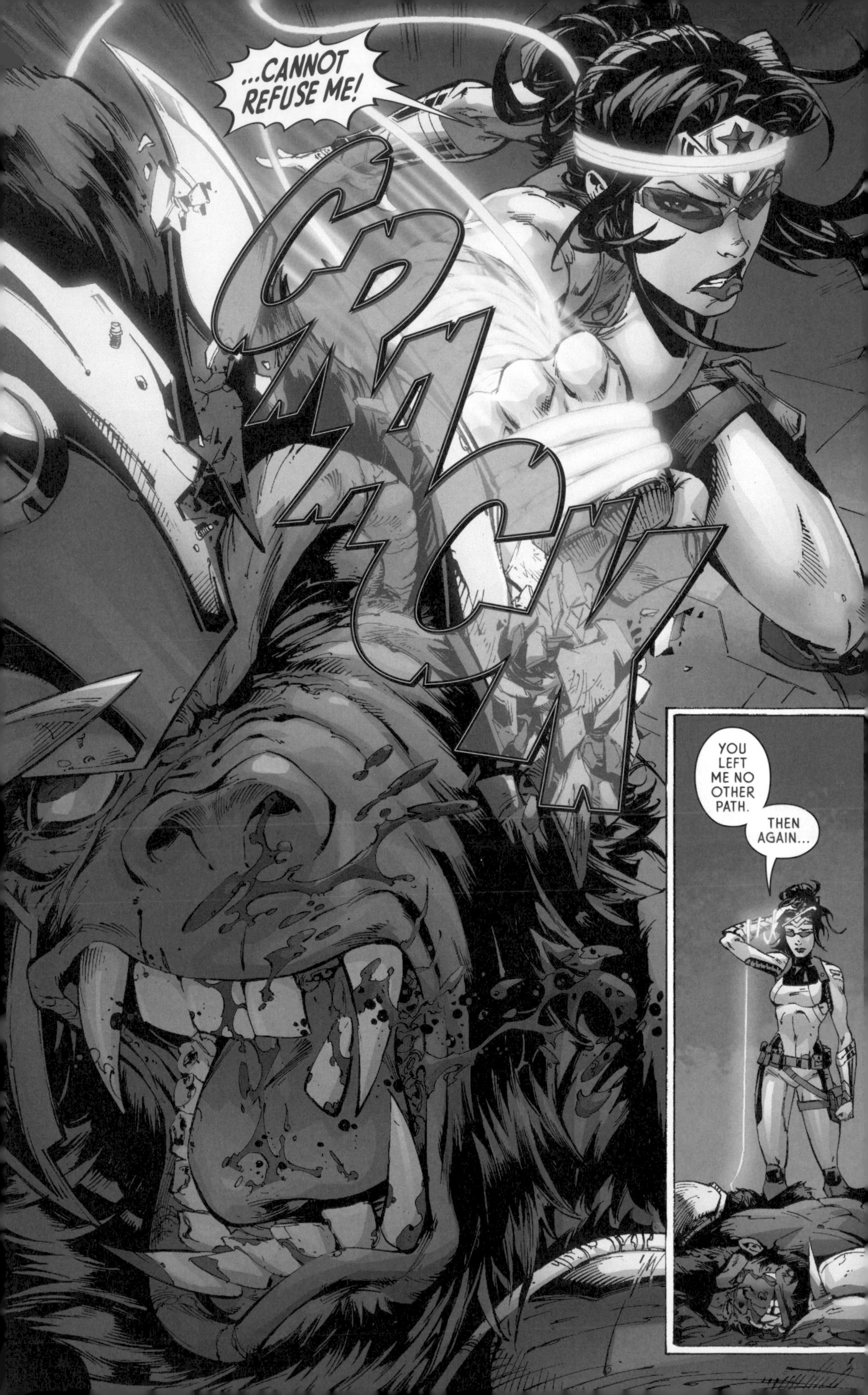

...CANNOT REFUSE ME!
CRACK
YOU LEFT ME NO OTHER PATH.
THEN AGAIN...

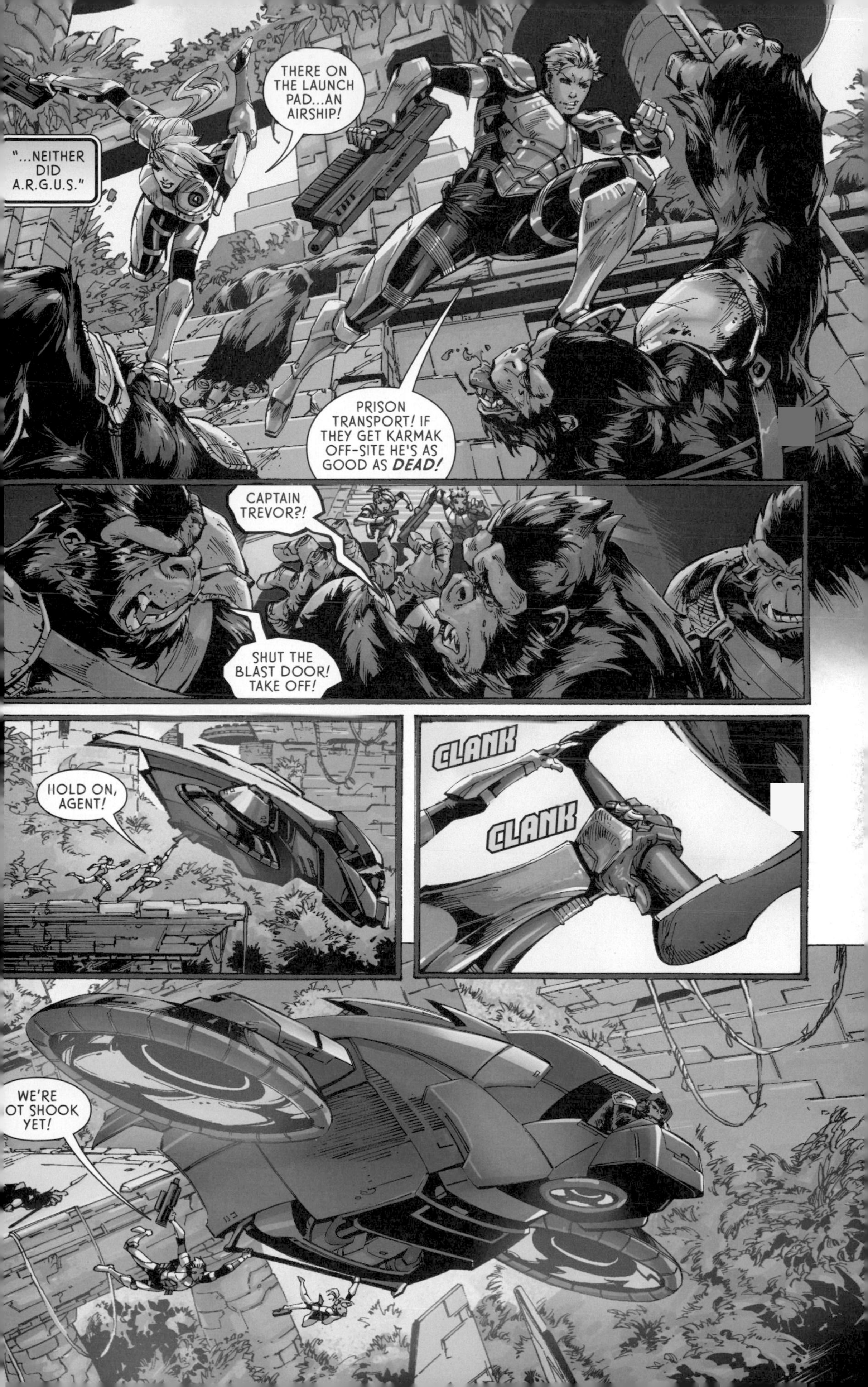
"...NEITHER DID A.R.G.U.S."
THERE ON THE LAUNCH PAD...AN AIRSHIP!
PRISON TRANSPORT! IF THEY GET KARMAK OFF-SITE HE'S AS GOOD AS DEAD!
CAPTAIN TREVOR?!
SHUT THE BLAST DOOR! TAKE OFF!
HOLD ON, AGENT!
CLANK
CLANK
WE'RE OT SHOOK YET!

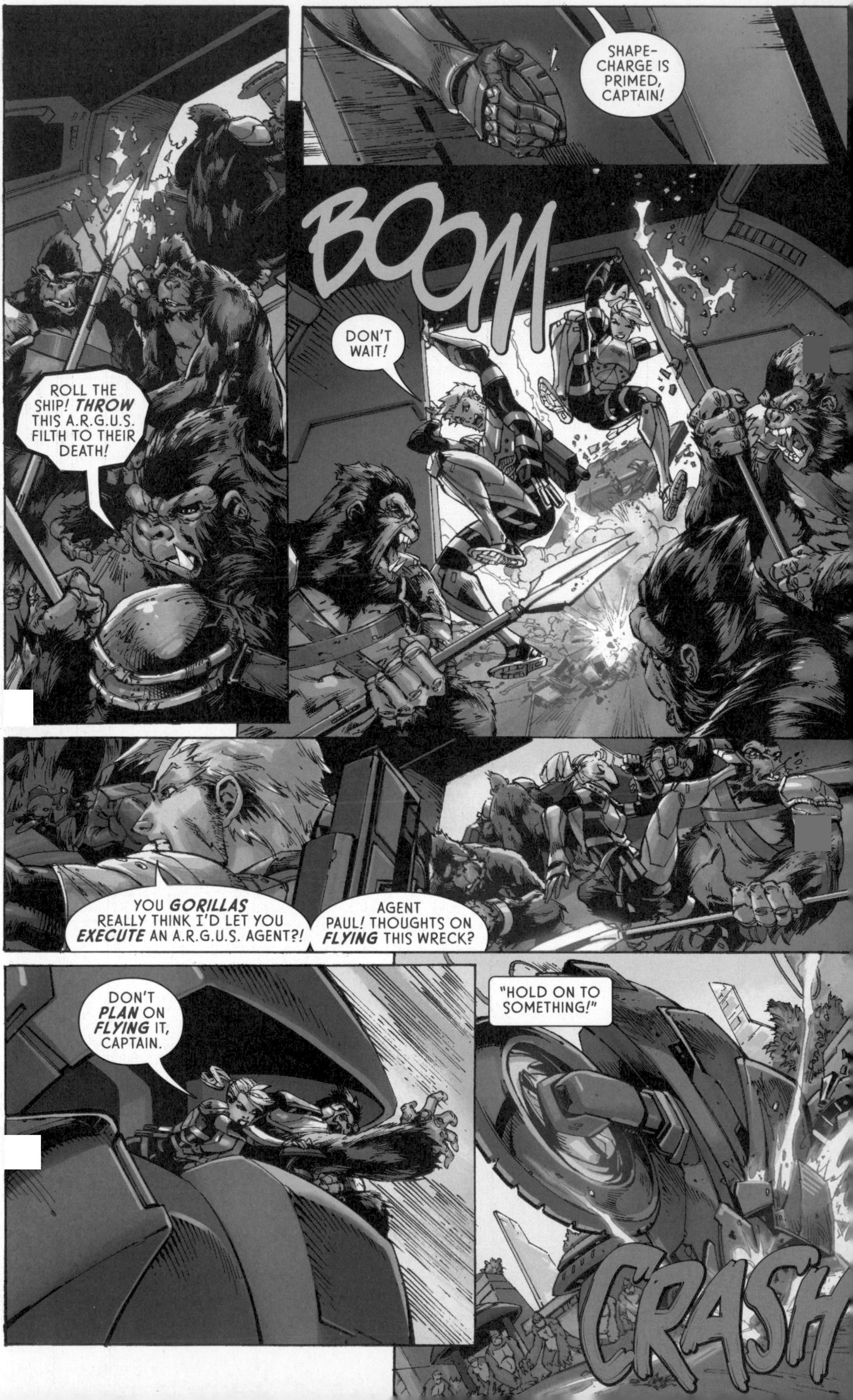
SHAPE-CHARGE IS PRIMED, CAPTAIN!
ROLL THE SHIP! THROW THIS A.R.G.U.S. FILTH TO THEIR DEATH!
BOOM
DON'T WAIT!
YOU GORILLAS REALLY THINK I'D LET YOU EXECUTE AN A.R.G.U.S. AGENT?!
AGENT PAUL! THOUGHTS ON FLYING THIS WRECK?
DON'T PLAN ON FLYING IT, CAPTAIN.
"HOLD ON TO SOMETHING!"
CRASH

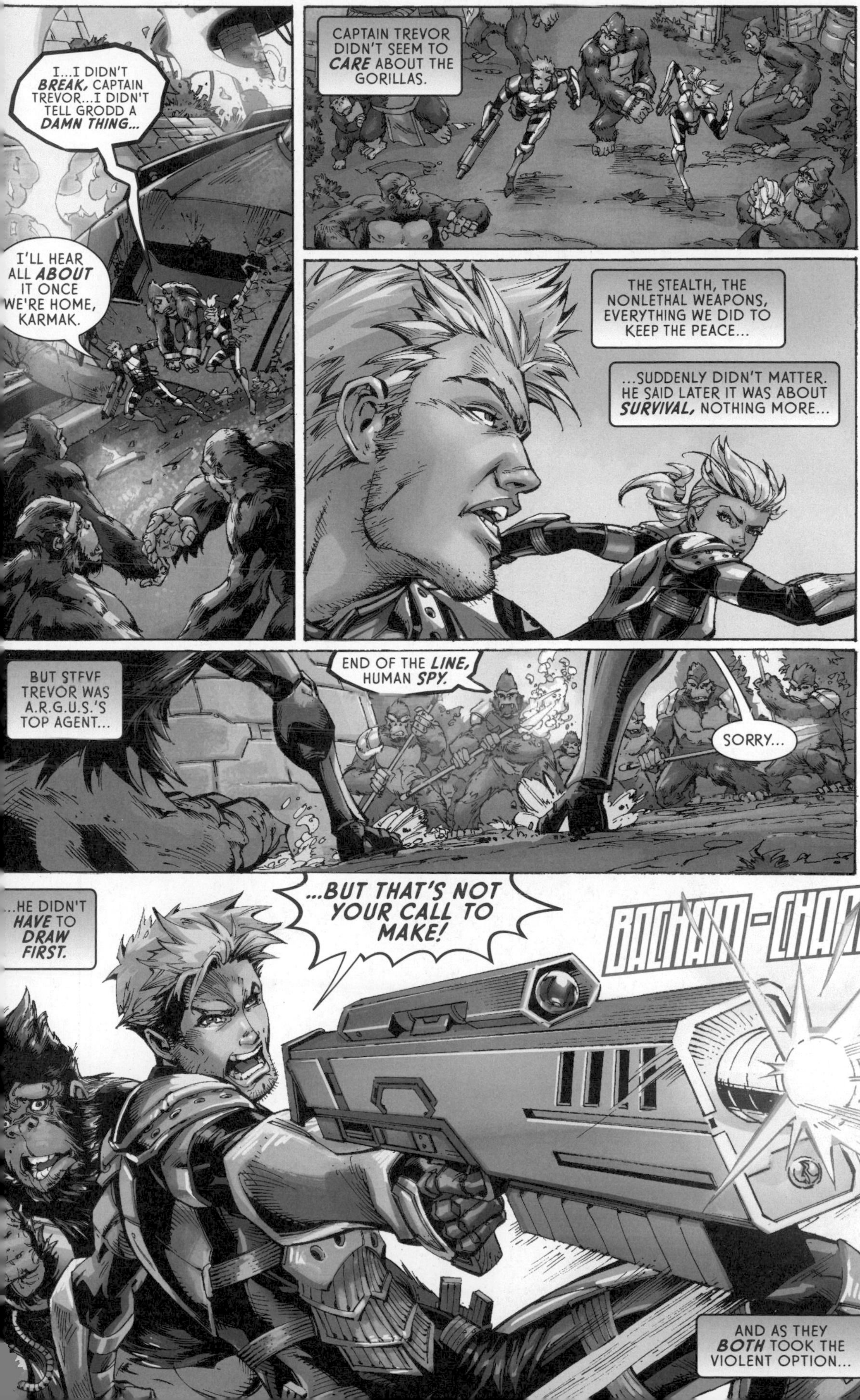
I...I DIDN'T BREAK, CAPTAIN TREVOR...I DIDN'T TELL GRODD A DAMN THING...
I'LL HEAR ALL ABOUT IT ONCE WE'RE HOME, KARMAK.
CAPTAIN TREVOR DIDN'T SEEM TO CARE ABOUT THE GORILLAS.
THE STEALTH, THE NONLETHAL WEAPONS, EVERYTHING WE DID TO KEEP THE PEACE...
...SUDDENLY DIDN'T MATTER. HE SAID LATER IT WAS ABOUT SURVIVAL, NOTHING MORE...
BUT STEVE TREVOR WAS A.R.G.U.S.'S TOP AGENT...
END OF THE LINE, HUMAN SPY.
SORRY...
...HE DIDN'T HAVE TO DRAW FIRST.
...BUT THAT'S NOT YOUR CALL TO MAKE!
BACHAM-CHAM
AND AS THEY BOTH TOOK THE VIOLENT OPTION...

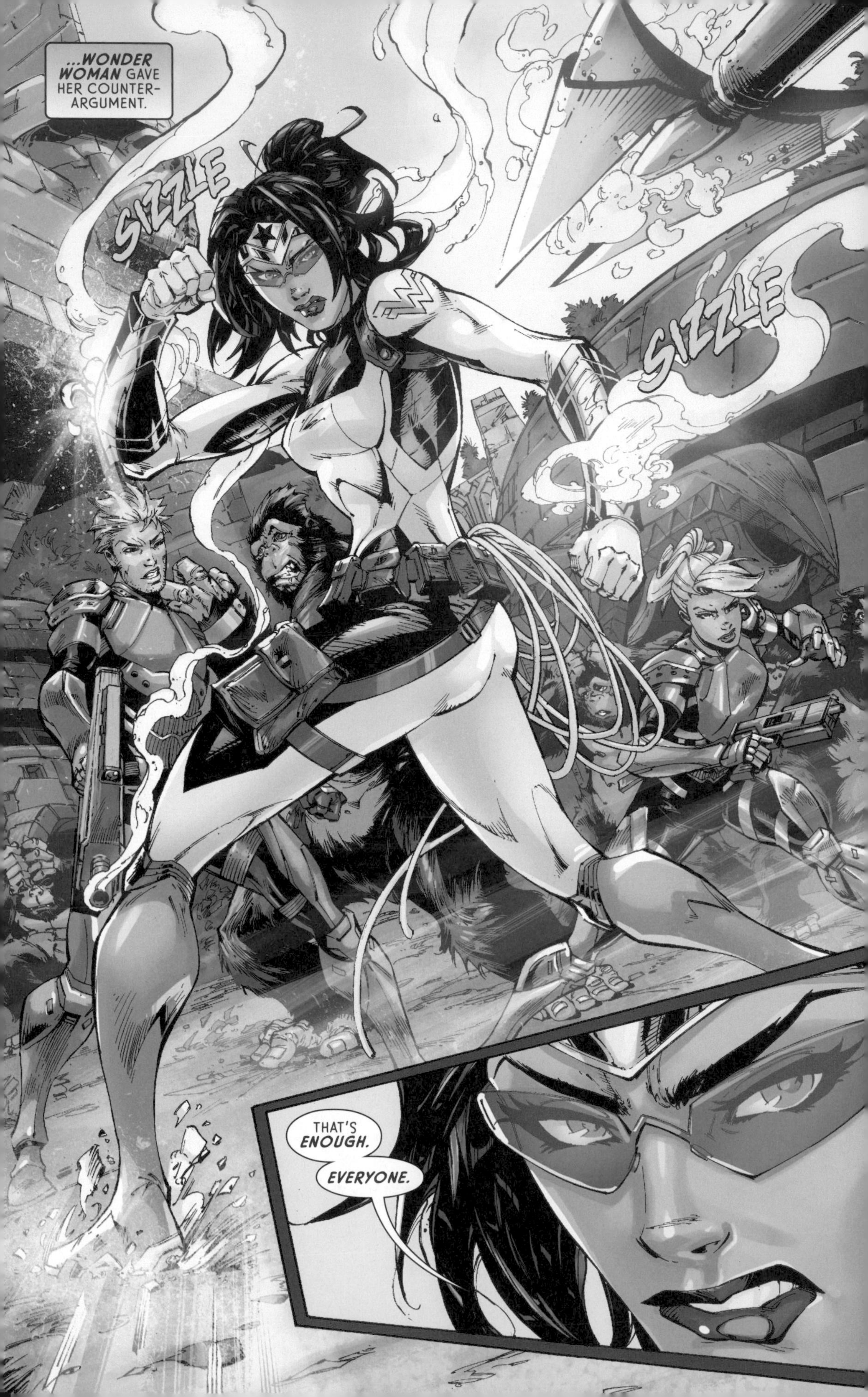
...WONDER WOMAN GAVE HER COUNTER-ARGUMENT.
SIZZLE
SIZZLE
THAT'S ENOUGH.
EVERYONE.

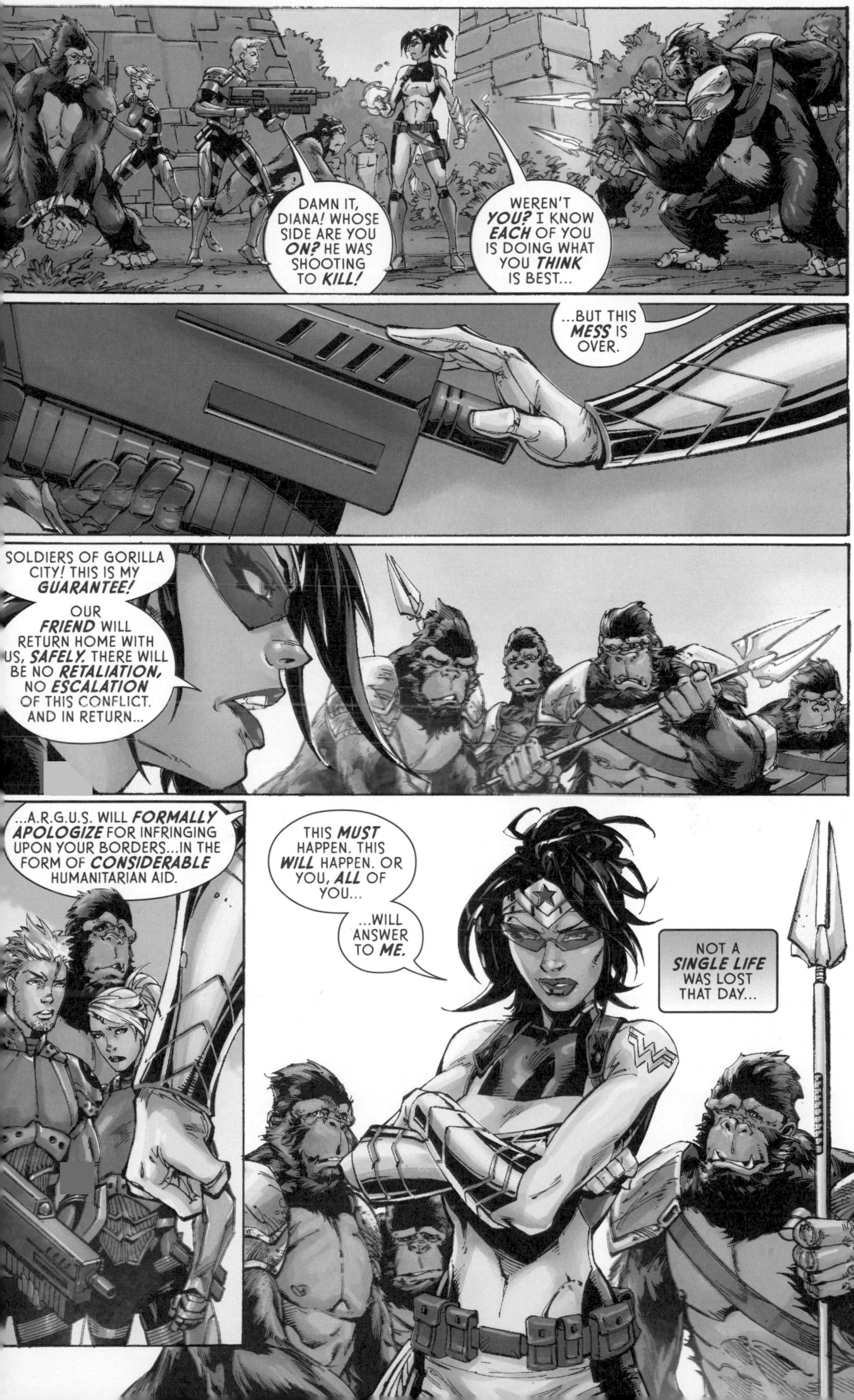
DAMN IT, DIANA! WHOSE SIDE ARE YOU ON? HE WAS SHOOTING TO KILL!
WEREN'T YOU? I KNOW EACH OF YOU IS DOING WHAT YOU THINK IS BEST...
...BUT THIS MESS IS OVER.
SOLDIERS OF GORILLA CITY! THIS IS MY GUARANTEE!
OUR FRIEND WILL RETURN HOME WITH US, SAFELY. THERE WILL BE NO RETALIATION, NO ESCALATION OF THIS CONFLICT. AND IN RETURN...
...A.R.G.U.S. WILL FORMALLY APOLOGIZE FOR INFRINGING UPON YOUR BORDERS...IN THE FORM OF CONSIDERABLE HUMANITARIAN AID.
THIS MUST HAPPEN. THIS WILL HAPPEN. OR YOU, ALL OF YOU...
...WILL ANSWER TO ME.
NOT A SINGLE LIFE WAS LOST THAT DAY...

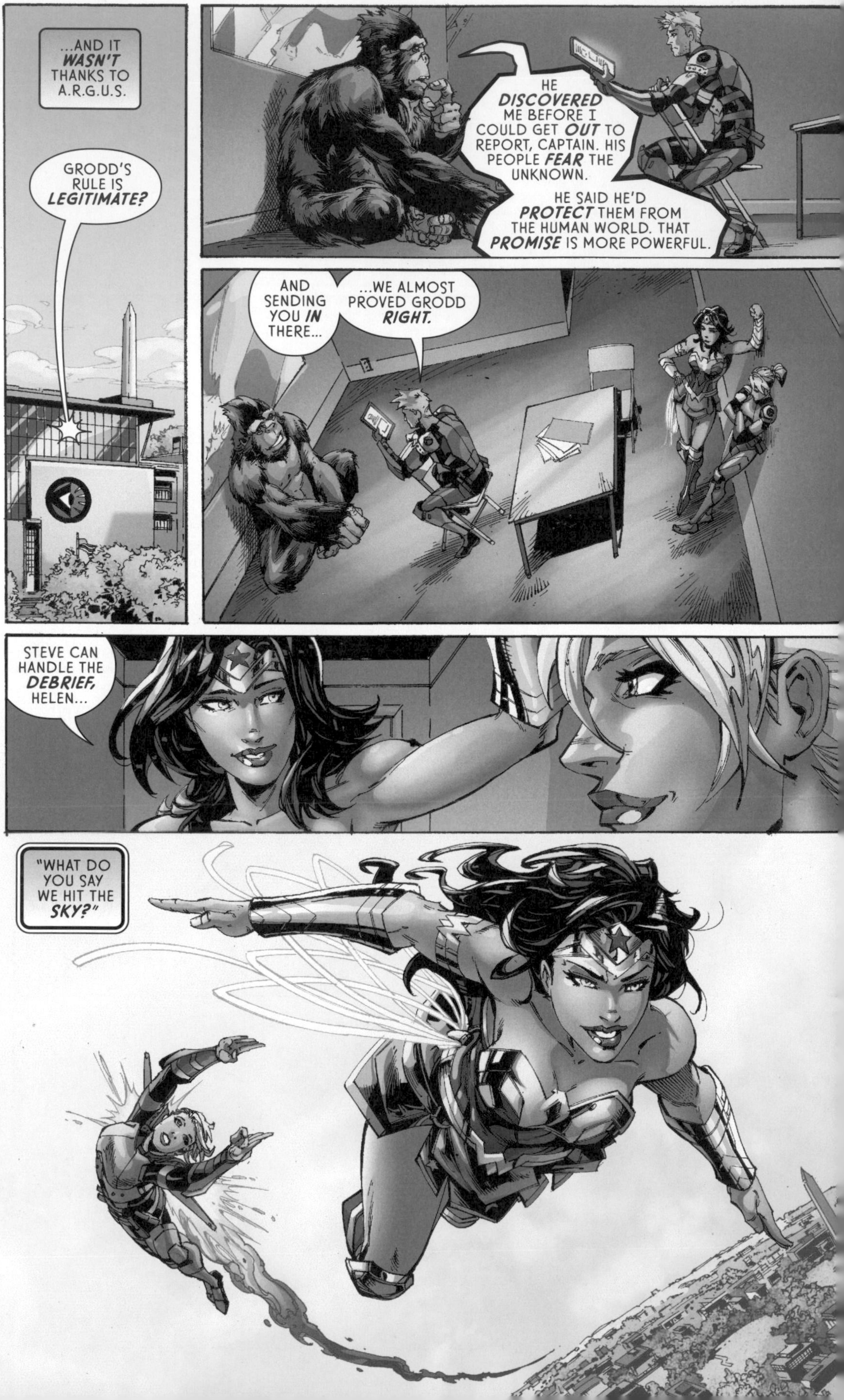

...AND IT WASN'T THANKS TO A.R.G.U.S.
HE DISCOVERED ME BEFORE I COULD GET OUT TO REPORT, CAPTAIN. HIS PEOPLE FEAR THE UNKNOWN.
HE SAID HE'D PROTECT THEM FROM THE HUMAN WORLD. THAT PROMISE IS MORE POWERFUL.
GRODD'S RULE IS LEGITIMATE?
AND SENDING YOU IN THERE...
...WE ALMOST PROVED GRODD RIGHT.
STEVE CAN HANDLE THE DEBRIEF, HELEN...
"WHAT DO YOU SAY WE HIT THE SKY?"

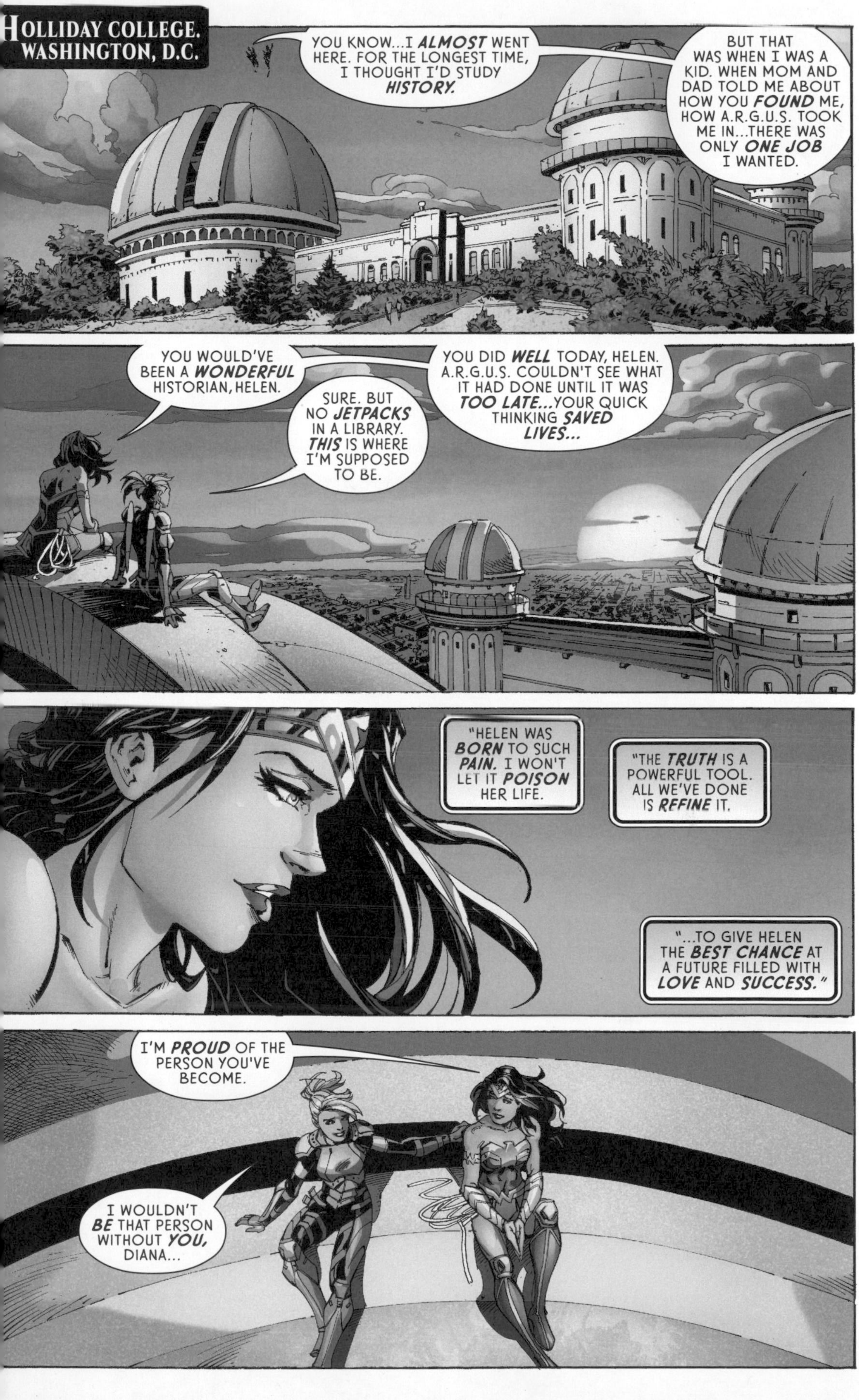
HOLLIDAY COLLEGE. WASHINGTON, D.C.
YOU KNOW...I ALMOST WENT HERE. FOR THE LONGEST TIME, I THOUGHT I'D STUDY HISTORY.
BUT THAT WAS WHEN I WAS A KID. WHEN MOM AND DAD TOLD ME ABOUT HOW YOU FOUND ME, HOW A.R.G.U.S. TOOK ME IN...THERE WAS ONLY ONE JOB I WANTED.
YOU WOULD'VE BEEN A WONDERFUL HISTORIAN, HELEN.
SURE. BUT NO JETPACKS IN A LIBRARY. THIS IS WHERE I'M SUPPOSED TO BE.
YOU DID WELL TODAY, HELEN. A.R.G.U.S. COULDN'T SEE WHAT IT HAD DONE UNTIL IT WAS TOO LATE...YOUR QUICK THINKING SAVED LIVES...
"HELEN WAS BORN TO SUCH PAIN. I WON'T LET IT POISON HER LIFE.
"THE TRUTH IS A POWERFUL TOOL. ALL WE'VE DONE IS REFINE IT.
"...TO GIVE HELEN THE BEST CHANCE AT A FUTURE FILLED WITH LOVE AND SUCCESS."
I'M PROUD OF THE PERSON YOU'VE BECOME.
I WOULDN'T BE THAT PERSON WITHOUT YOU, DIANA...

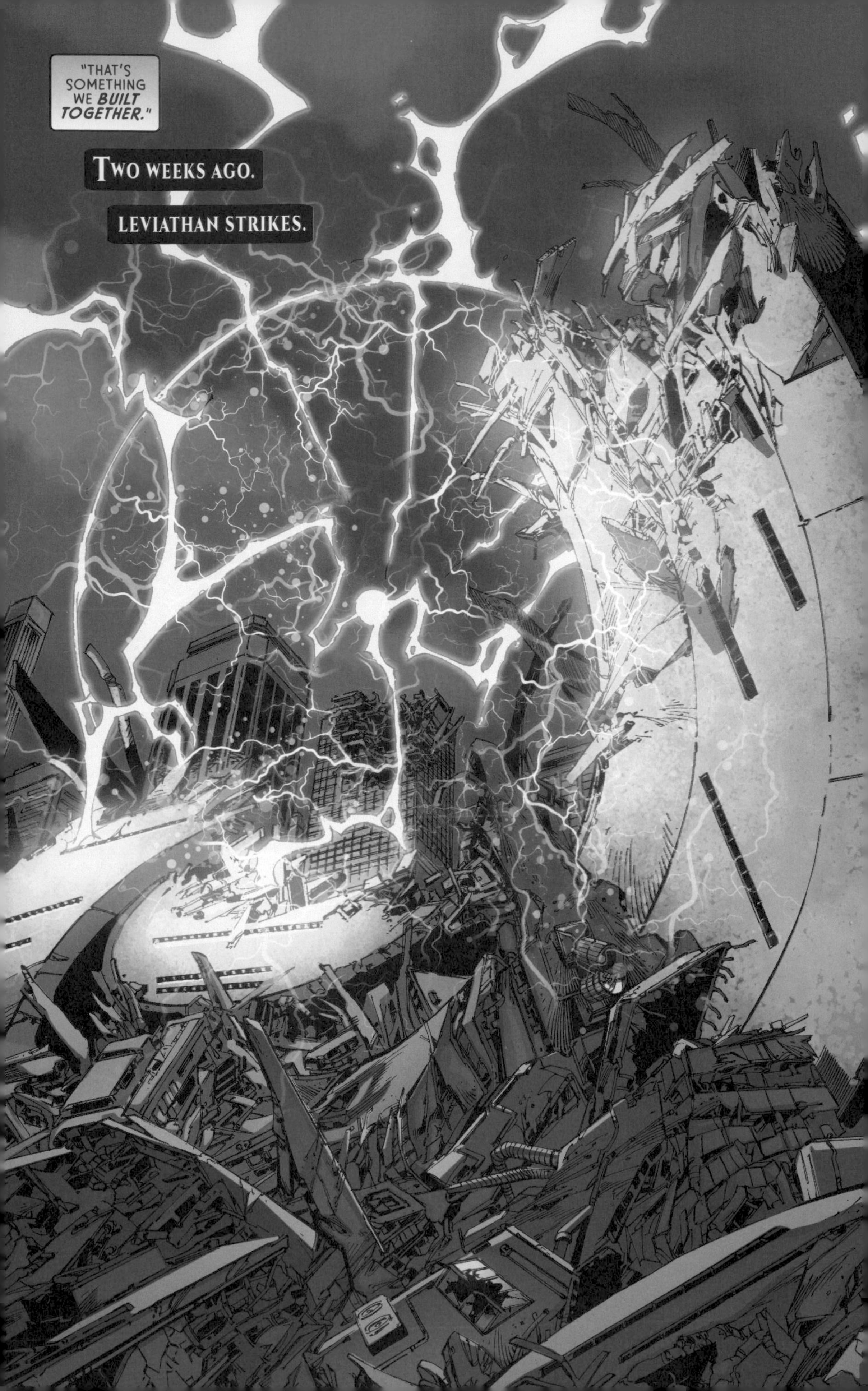
"THAT'S SOMETHING WE *BUILT TOGETHER.*"
TWO WEEKS AGO.
LEVIATHAN STRIKES.

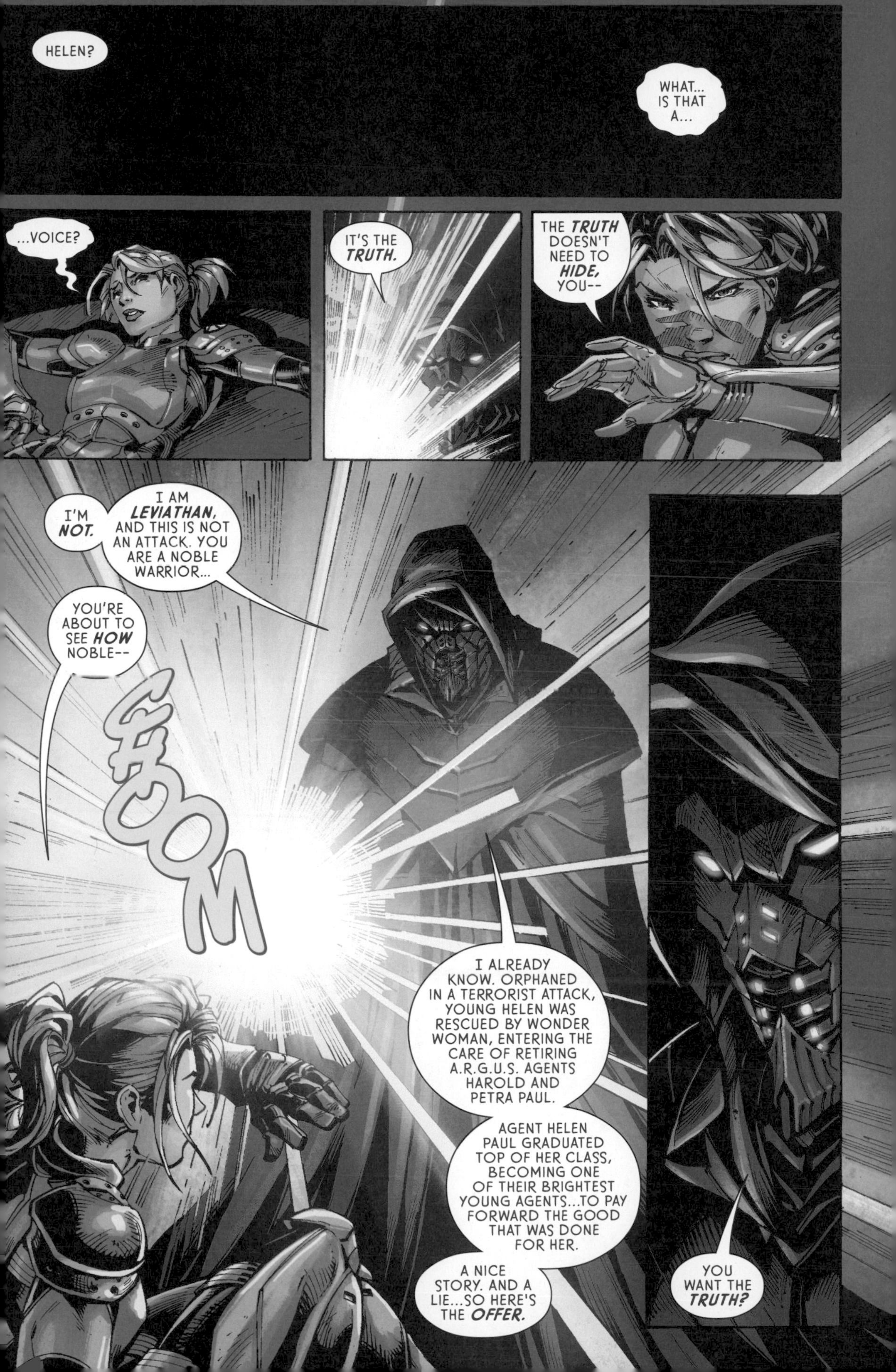
HELEN?
WHAT... IS THAT A...
...VOICE?
IT'S THE TRUTH.
THE TRUTH DOESN'T NEED TO HIDE, YOU--
I'M NOT.
I AM LEVIATHAN, AND THIS IS NOT AN ATTACK. YOU ARE A NOBLE WARRIOR...
YOU'RE ABOUT TO SEE HOW NOBLE--
FOOM
I ALREADY KNOW. ORPHANED IN A TERRORIST ATTACK, YOUNG HELEN WAS RESCUED BY WONDER WOMAN, ENTERING THE CARE OF RETIRING A.R.G.U.S. AGENTS HAROLD AND PETRA PAUL.
AGENT HELEN PAUL GRADUATED TOP OF HER CLASS, BECOMING ONE OF THEIR BRIGHTEST YOUNG AGENTS...TO PAY FORWARD THE GOOD THAT WAS DONE FOR HER.
A NICE STORY. AND A LIE...SO HERE'S THE OFFER.
YOU WANT THE TRUTH?

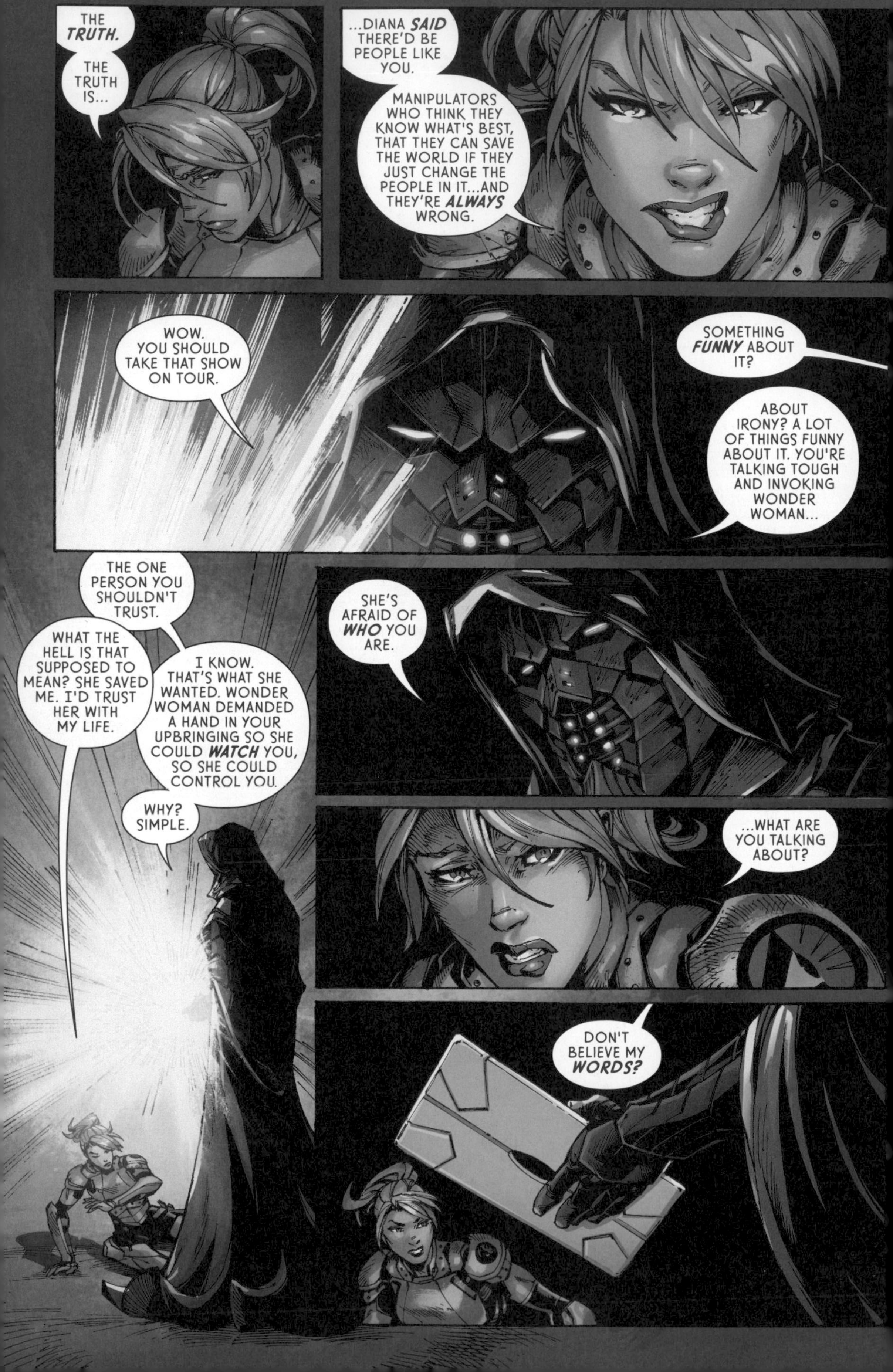
THE TRUTH.
THE TRUTH IS...
...DIANA SAID THERE'D BE PEOPLE LIKE YOU.
MANIPULATORS WHO THINK THEY KNOW WHAT'S BEST, THAT THEY CAN SAVE THE WORLD IF THEY JUST CHANGE THE PEOPLE IN IT...AND THEY'RE ALWAYS WRONG.
WOW. YOU SHOULD TAKE THAT SHOW ON TOUR.
SOMETHING FUNNY ABOUT IT?
ABOUT IRONY? A LOT OF THINGS FUNNY ABOUT IT. YOU'RE TALKING TOUGH AND INVOKING WONDER WOMAN...
THE ONE PERSON YOU SHOULDN'T TRUST.
WHAT THE HELL IS THAT SUPPOSED TO MEAN? SHE SAVED ME. I'D TRUST HER WITH MY LIFE.
I KNOW. THAT'S WHAT SHE WANTED. WONDER WOMAN DEMANDED A HAND IN YOUR UPBRINGING SO SHE COULD WATCH YOU, SO SHE COULD CONTROL YOU.
WHY? SIMPLE.
SHE'S AFRAID OF WHO YOU ARE.
...WHAT ARE YOU TALKING ABOUT?
DON'T BELIEVE MY WORDS?

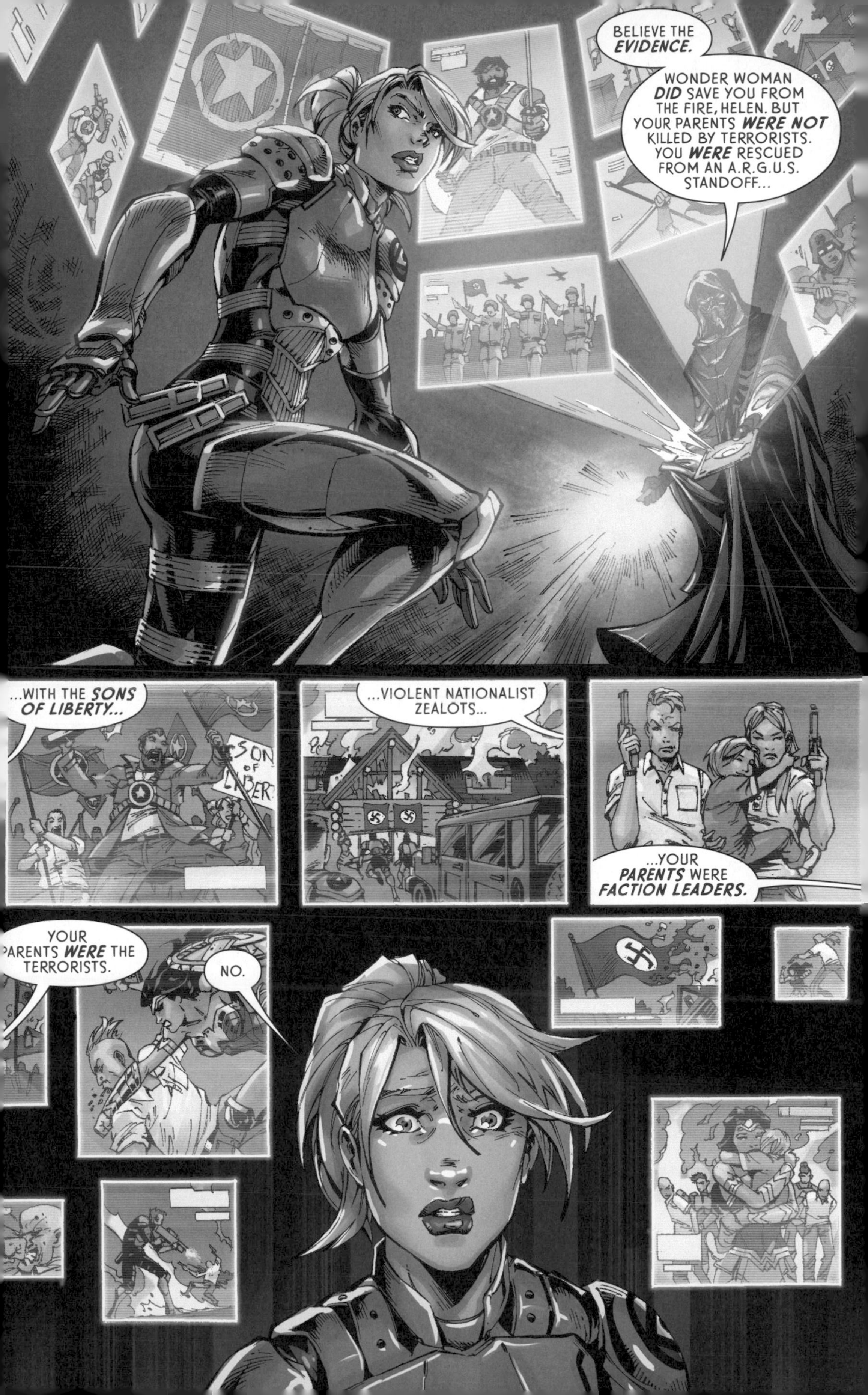
BELIEVE THE *EVIDENCE.*
WONDER WOMAN *DID* SAVE YOU FROM THE FIRE, HELEN. BUT YOUR PARENTS *WERE NOT* KILLED BY TERRORISTS. YOU *WERE* RESCUED FROM AN A.R.G.U.S. STANDOFF...
...WITH THE *SONS OF LIBERTY...*
SONS OF LIBERTY
...VIOLENT NATIONALIST ZEALOTS...
...YOUR *PARENTS* WERE *FACTION LEADERS.*
YOUR PARENTS *WERE* THE TERRORISTS.
NO.

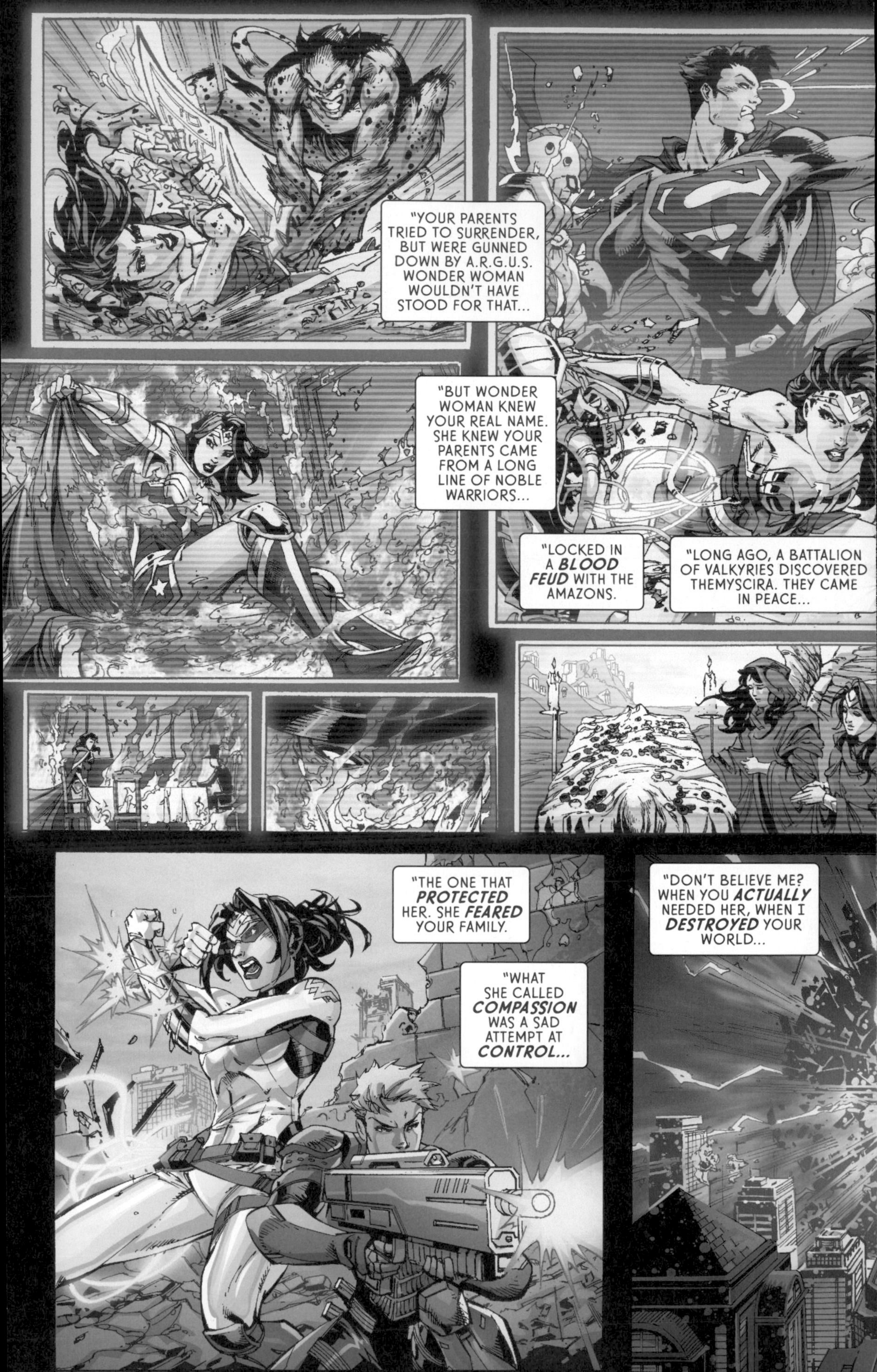
"YOUR PARENTS TRIED TO SURRENDER, BUT WERE GUNNED DOWN BY A.R.G.U.S. WONDER WOMAN WOULDN'T HAVE STOOD FOR THAT...
"BUT WONDER WOMAN KNEW YOUR REAL NAME. SHE KNEW YOUR PARENTS CAME FROM A LONG LINE OF NOBLE WARRIORS...
"LOCKED IN A BLOOD FEUD WITH THE AMAZONS.
"LONG AGO, A BATTALION OF VALKYRIES DISCOVERED THEMYSCIRA. THEY CAME IN PEACE...
"THE ONE THAT PROTECTED HER. SHE FEARED YOUR FAMILY.
"WHAT SHE CALLED COMPASSION WAS A SAD ATTEMPT AT CONTROL...
"DON'T BELIEVE ME? WHEN YOU ACTUALLY NEEDED HER, WHEN I DESTROYED YOUR WORLD...

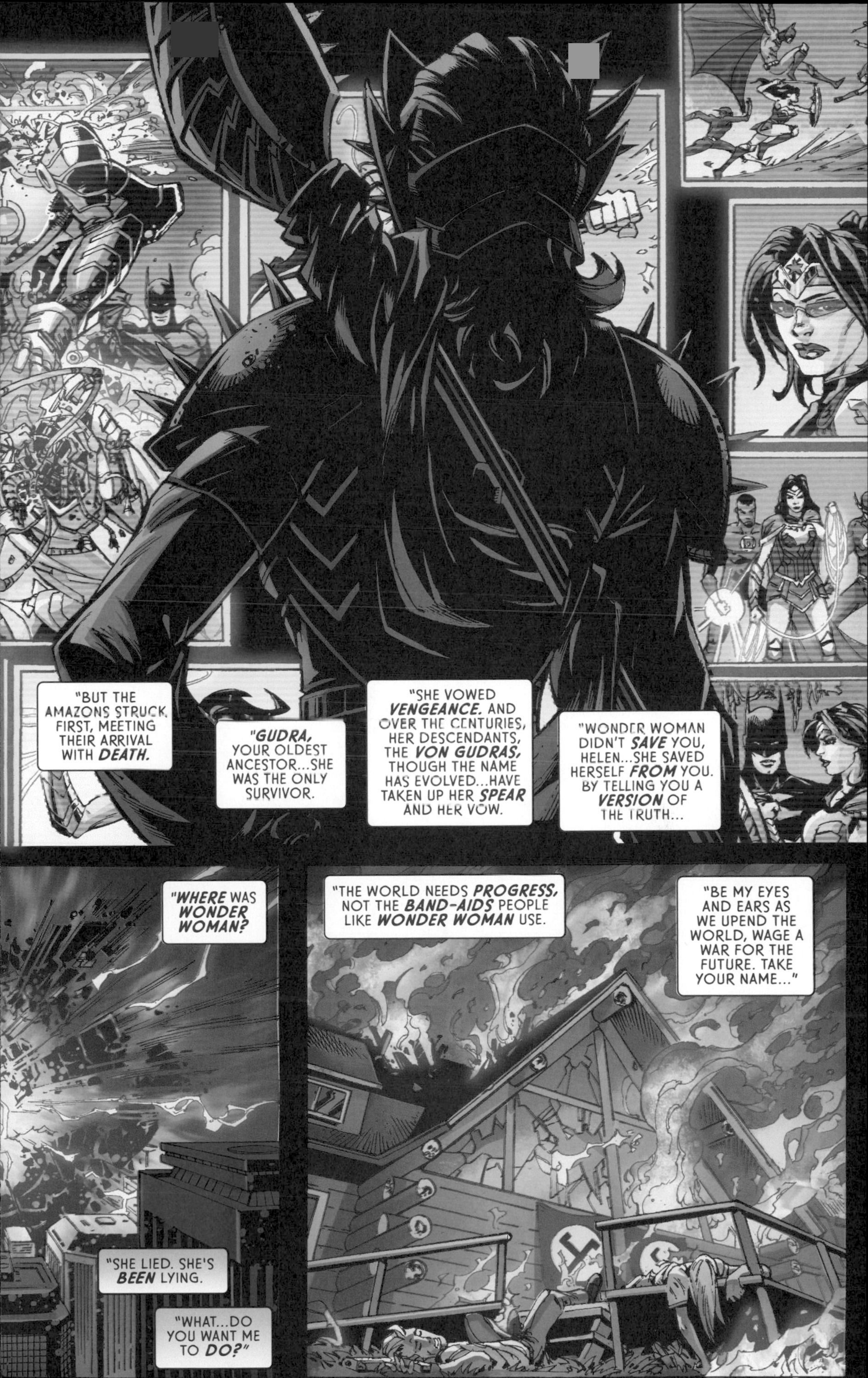
"BUT THE AMAZONS STRUCK FIRST, MEETING THEIR ARRIVAL WITH DEATH.
"GUDRA, YOUR OLDEST ANCESTOR...SHE WAS THE ONLY SURVIVOR.
"SHE VOWED VENGEANCE. AND OVER THE CENTURIES, HER DESCENDANTS, THE VON GUDRAS, THOUGH THE NAME HAS EVOLVED...HAVE TAKEN UP HER SPEAR AND HER VOW.
"WONDER WOMAN DIDN'T SAVE YOU, HELEN...SHE SAVED HERSELF FROM YOU. BY TELLING YOU A VERSION OF THE TRUTH...
"WHERE WAS WONDER WOMAN?
"SHE LIED. SHE'S BEEN LYING.
"WHAT...DO YOU WANT ME TO DO?"
"THE WORLD NEEDS PROGRESS, NOT THE BAND-AIDS PEOPLE LIKE WONDER WOMAN USE.
"BE MY EYES AND EARS AS WE UPEND THE WORLD, WAGE A WAR FOR THE FUTURE. TAKE YOUR NAME..."

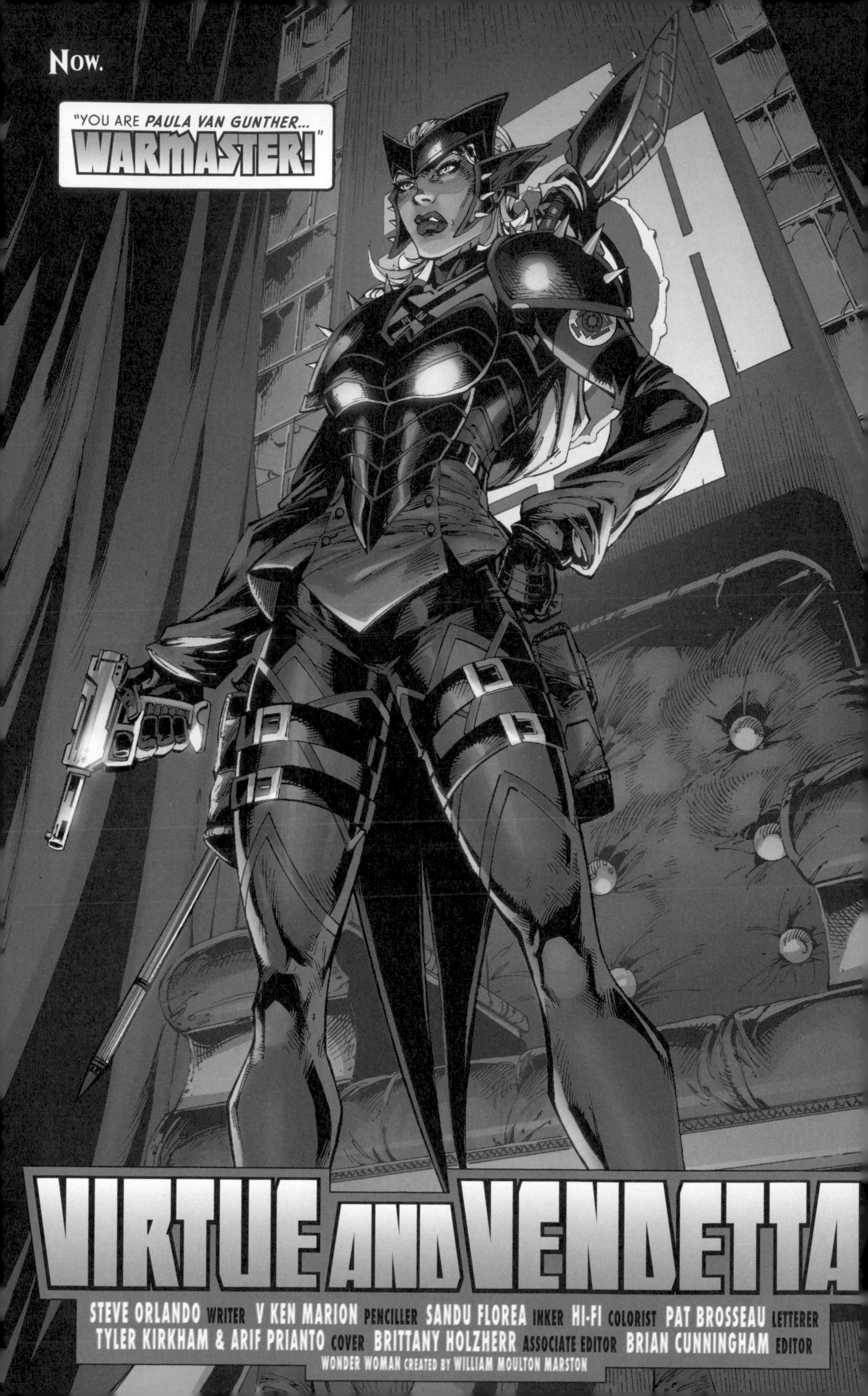
Now.
"YOU ARE PAULA VAN GUNTHER...
WARMASTER!"
VIRTUE AND VENDETTA
STEVE ORLANDO WRITER V KEN MARION PENCILLER SANDU FLOREA INKER HI-FI COLORIST PAT BROSSEAU LETTERER
TYLER KIRKHAM & ARIF PRIANTO COVER BRITTANY HOLZHERR ASSOCIATE EDITOR BRIAN CUNNINGHAM EDITOR
WONDER WOMAN CREATED BY WILLIAM MOULTON MARSTON

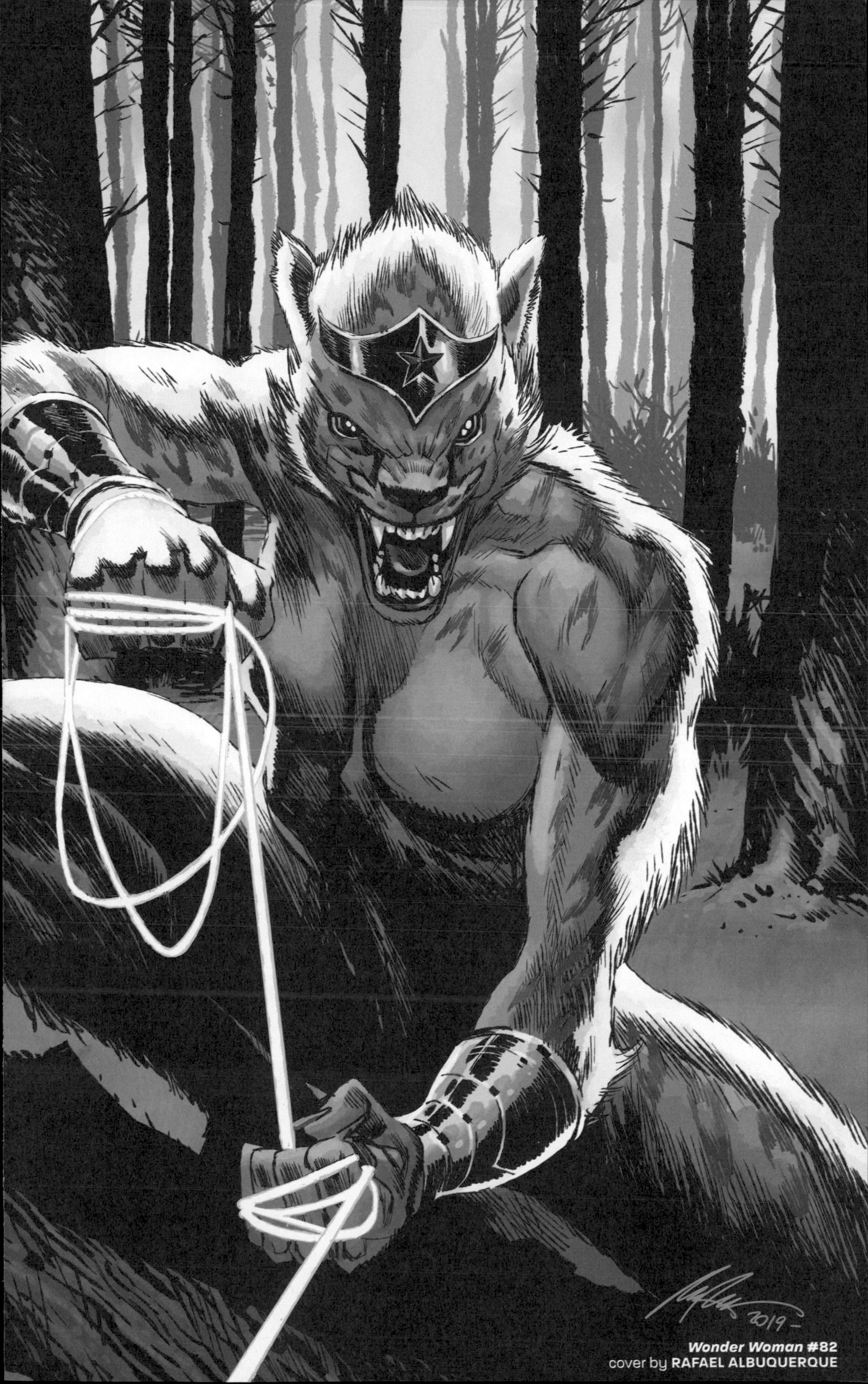

***Wonder Woman* #82**
cover by **RAFAEL ALBUQUERQUE**

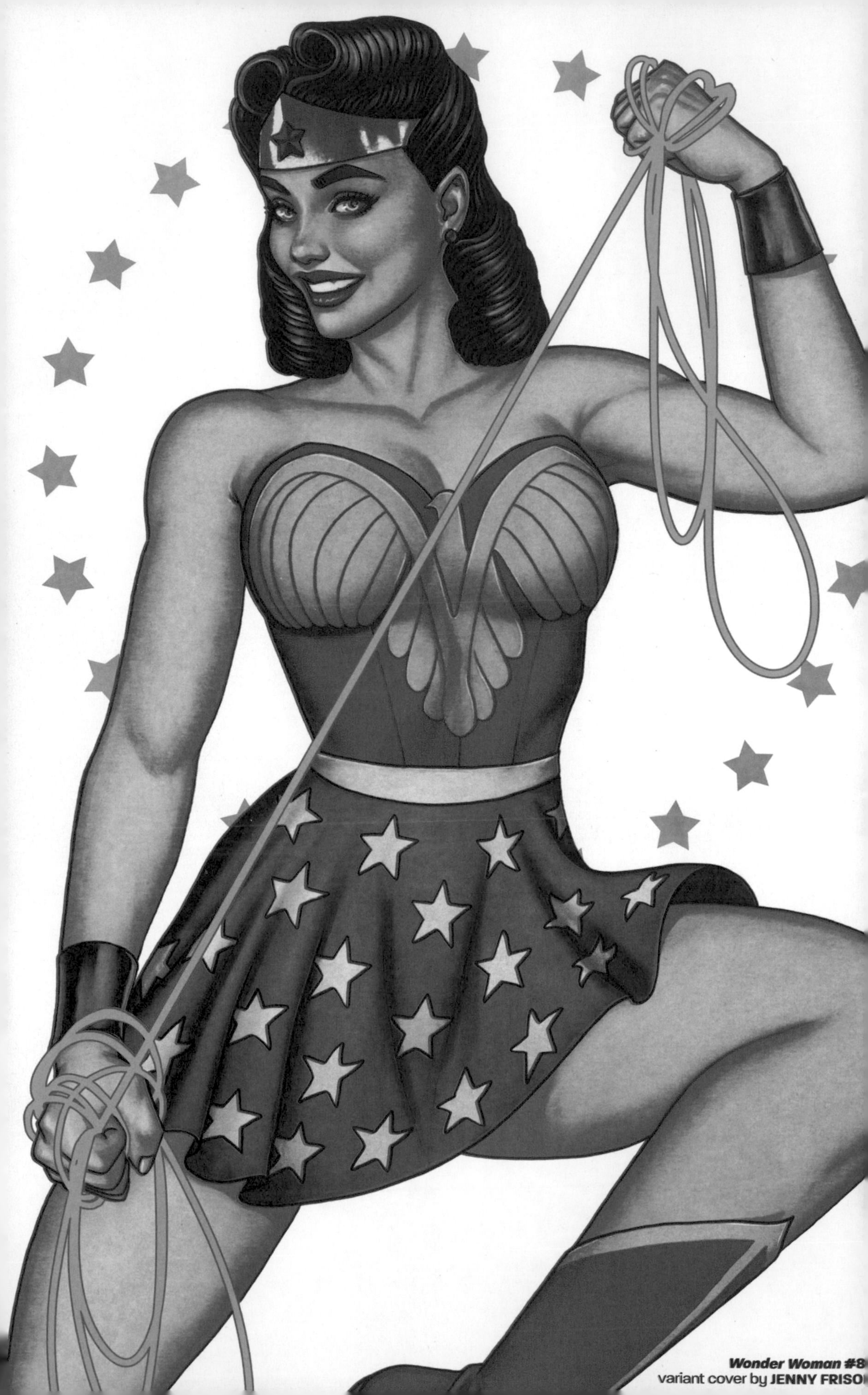

Wonder Woman #8
variant cover by JENNY FRISON

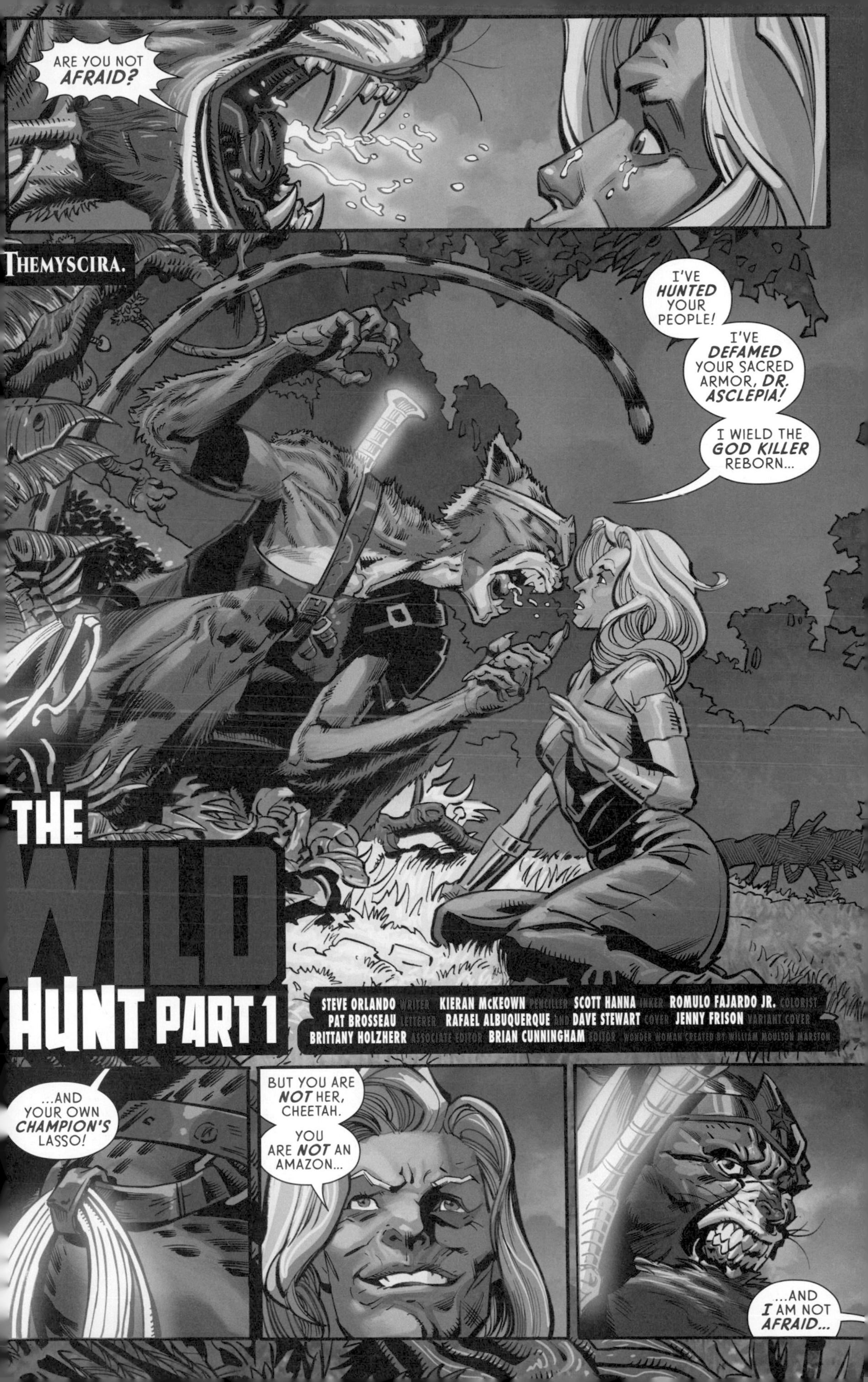
ARE YOU NOT AFRAID?
THEMYSCIRA.
I'VE HUNTED YOUR PEOPLE!
I'VE DEFAMED YOUR SACRED ARMOR, DR. ASCLEPIA!
I WIELD THE GOD KILLER REBORN...
THE WILD HUNT PART 1
STEVE ORLANDO WRITER KIERAN McKEOWN PENCILLER SCOTT HANNA INKER ROMULO FAJARDO JR. COLORIST
PAT BROSSEAU LETTERER RAFAEL ALBUQUERQUE AND DAVE STEWART COVER JENNY FRISON VARIANT COVER
BRITTANY HOLZHERR ASSOCIATE EDITOR BRIAN CUNNINGHAM EDITOR WONDER WOMAN CREATED BY WILLIAM MOULTON MARSTON
...AND YOUR OWN CHAMPION'S LASSO!
BUT YOU ARE NOT HER, CHEETAH.
YOU ARE NOT AN AMAZON...
...AND I AM NOT AFRAID...

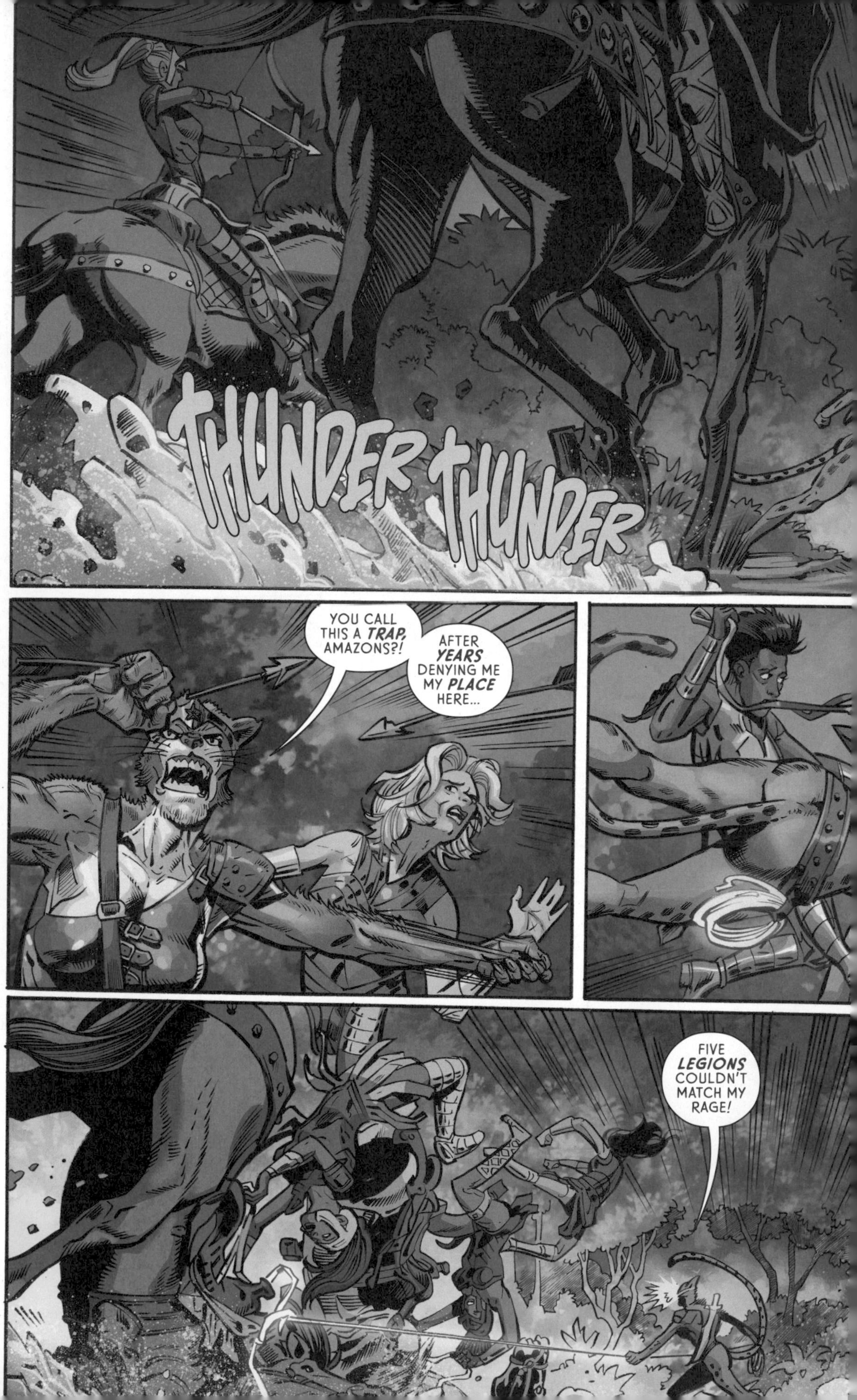
THUNDER THUNDER
YOU CALL THIS A TRAP, AMAZONS?!
AFTER YEARS DENYING ME MY PLACE HERE...
FIVE LEGIONS COULDN'T MATCH MY RAGE!

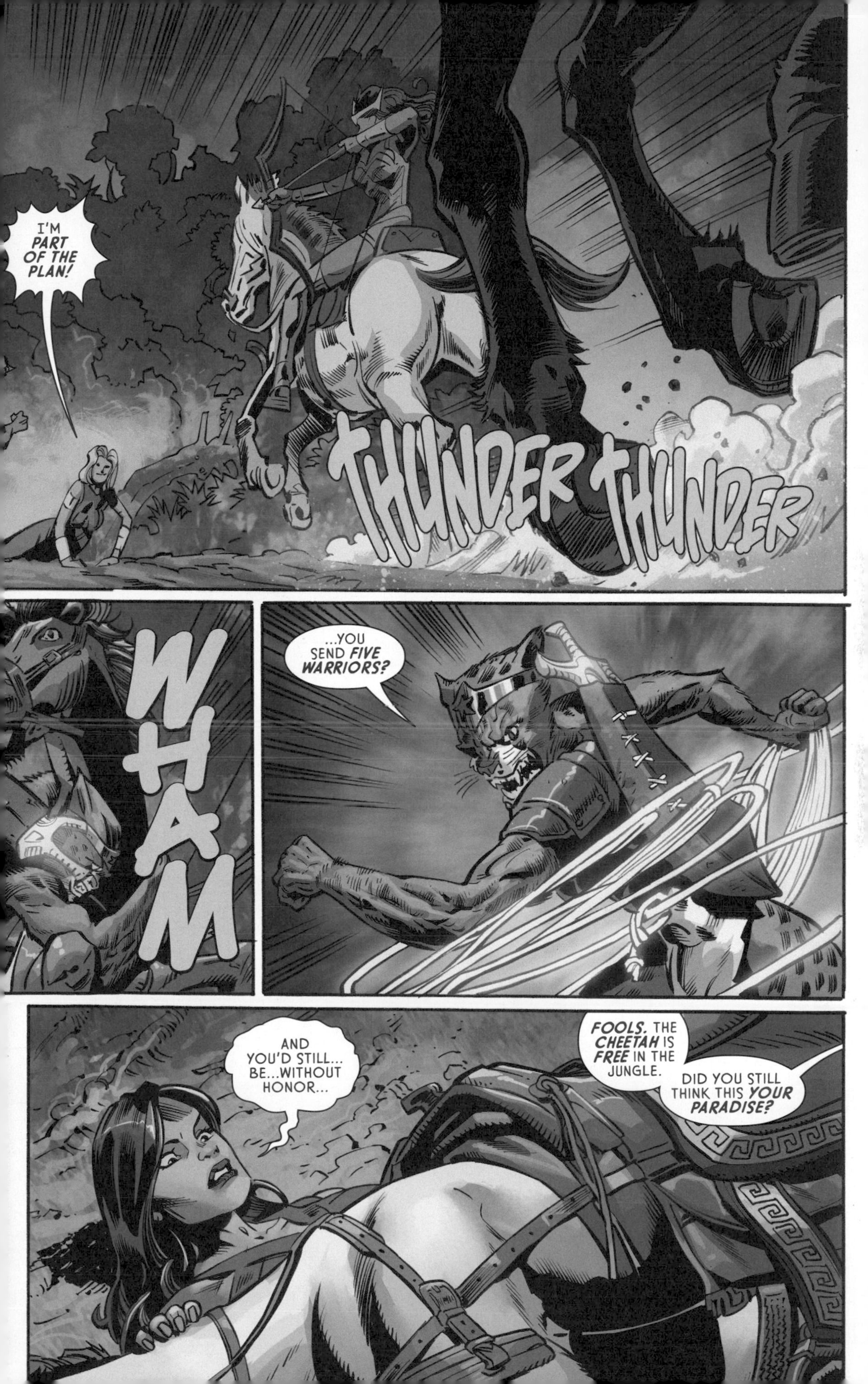
I'M *PART OF THE PLAN!*
THUNDER THUNDER
WHAM
...YOU SEND *FIVE WARRIORS?*
AND YOU'D STILL... BE...WITHOUT HONOR...
FOOLS. THE *CHEETAH* IS *FREE* IN THE JUNGLE.
DID YOU STILL THINK THIS *YOUR PARADISE?*

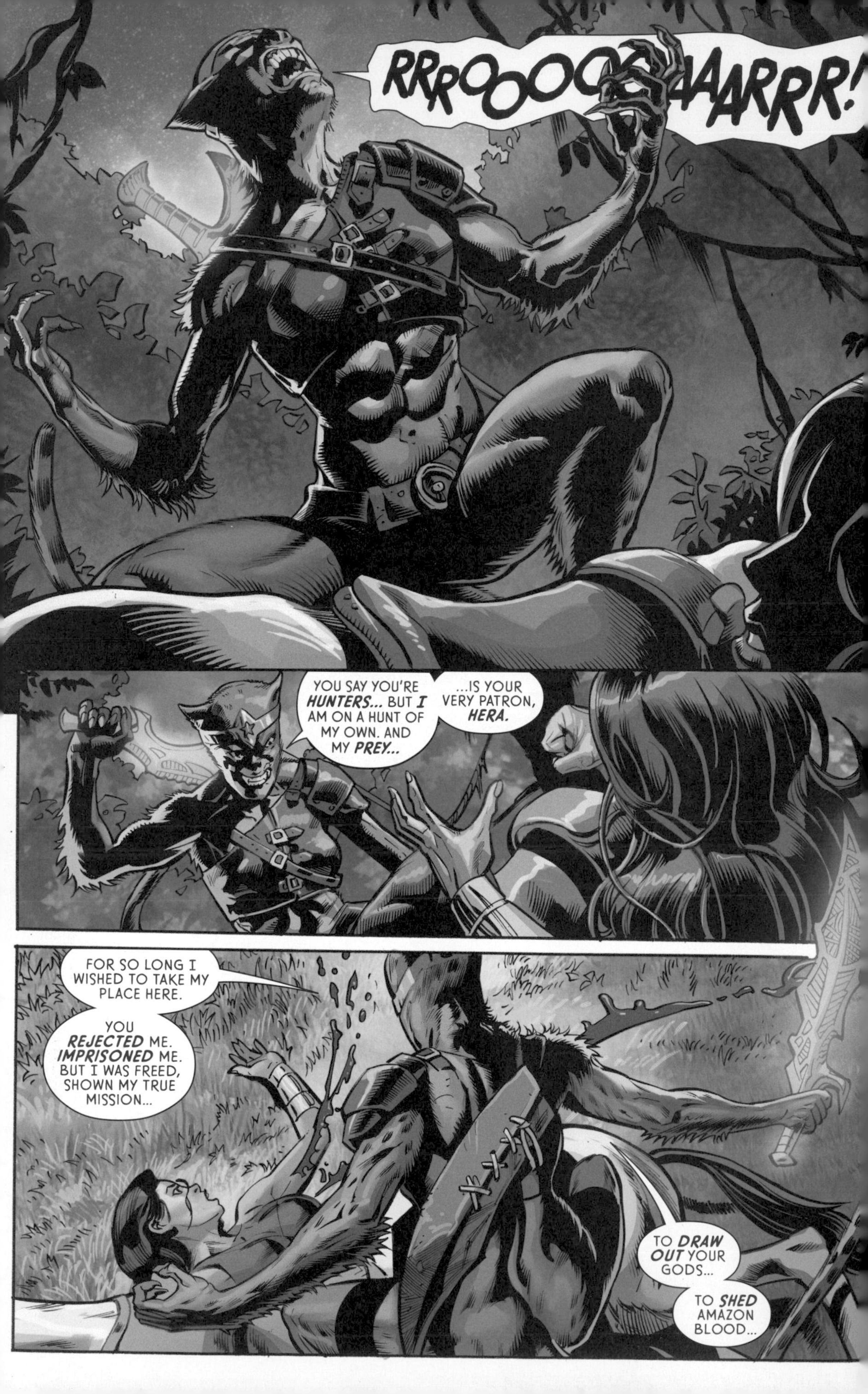
RRROOOOOGHAAARRRR!
YOU SAY YOU'RE **HUNTERS...** BUT ***I*** AM ON A HUNT OF MY OWN. AND MY ***PREY...***
...IS YOUR VERY PATRON, ***HERA.***
FOR SO LONG I WISHED TO TAKE MY PLACE HERE.
YOU ***REJECTED*** ME. ***IMPRISONED*** ME. BUT I WAS FREED, SHOWN MY TRUE MISSION...
TO ***DRAW OUT*** YOUR GODS...
TO ***SHED*** AMAZON BLOOD...

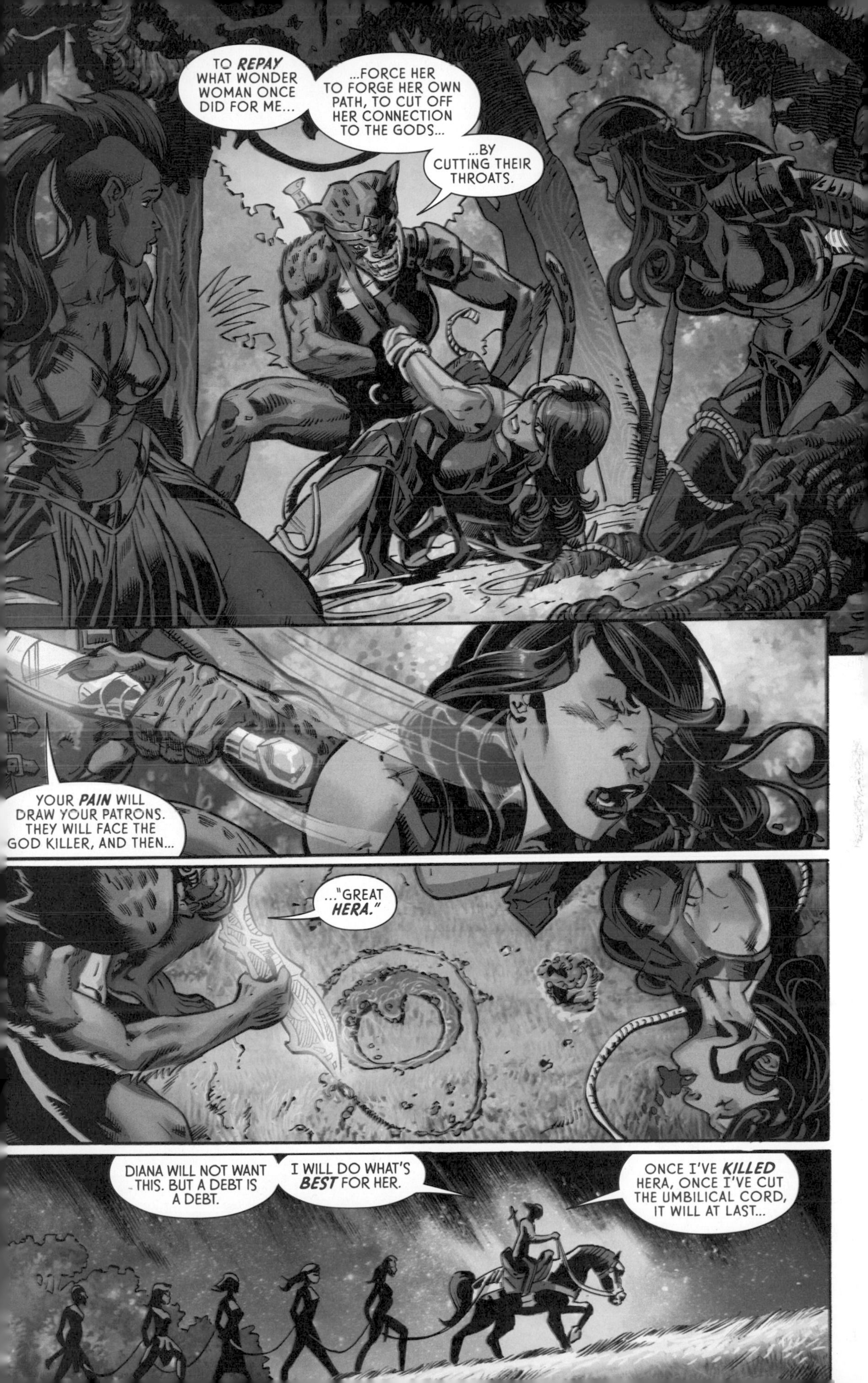
TO *REPAY* WHAT WONDER WOMAN ONCE DID FOR ME...
...FORCE HER TO FORGE HER OWN PATH, TO CUT OFF HER CONNECTION TO THE GODS...
...BY CUTTING THEIR THROATS.
YOUR *PAIN* WILL DRAW YOUR PATRONS. THEY WILL FACE THE GOD KILLER, AND THEN...
..."GREAT *HERA.*"
DIANA WILL NOT WANT THIS. BUT A DEBT IS A DEBT.
I WILL DO WHAT'S *BEST* FOR HER.
ONCE I'VE *KILLED* HERA, ONCE I'VE CUT THE UMBILICAL CORD, IT WILL AT LAST...

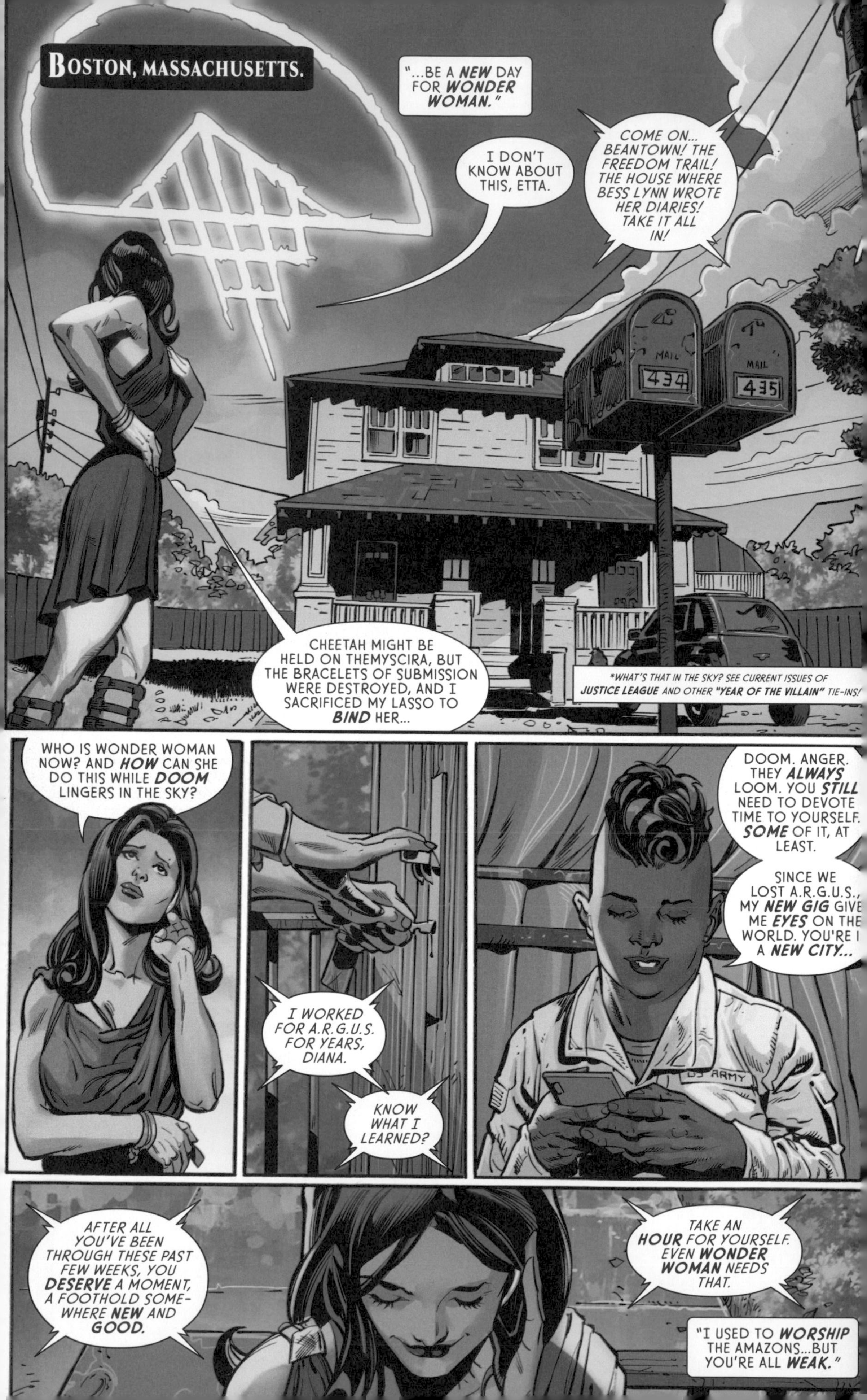
BOSTON, MASSACHUSETTS.
"...BE A NEW DAY FOR WONDER WOMAN."
I DON'T KNOW ABOUT THIS, ETTA.
COME ON... BEANTOWN! THE FREEDOM TRAIL! THE HOUSE WHERE BESS LYNN WROTE HER DIARIES! TAKE IT ALL IN!
MAIL
434
MAIL
435
CHEETAH MIGHT BE HELD ON THEMYSCIRA, BUT THE BRACELETS OF SUBMISSION WERE DESTROYED, AND I SACRIFICED MY LASSO TO BIND HER...
*WHAT'S THAT IN THE SKY? SEE CURRENT ISSUES OF JUSTICE LEAGUE AND OTHER "YEAR OF THE VILLAIN" TIE-INS!
WHO IS WONDER WOMAN NOW? AND HOW CAN SHE DO THIS WHILE DOOM LINGERS IN THE SKY?
I WORKED FOR A.R.G.U.S. FOR YEARS, DIANA.
KNOW WHAT I LEARNED?
DOOM. ANGER. THEY ALWAYS LOOM. YOU STILL NEED TO DEVOTE TIME TO YOURSELF. SOME OF IT, AT LEAST.
SINCE WE LOST A.R.G.U.S., MY NEW GIG GIVE ME EYES ON THE WORLD. YOU'RE I A NEW CITY...
ARMY
AFTER ALL YOU'VE BEEN THROUGH THESE PAST FEW WEEKS, YOU DESERVE A MOMENT, A FOOTHOLD SOME-WHERE NEW AND GOOD.
TAKE AN HOUR FOR YOURSELF. EVEN WONDER WOMAN NEEDS THAT.
"I USED TO WORSHIP THE AMAZONS...BUT YOU'RE ALL WEAK."

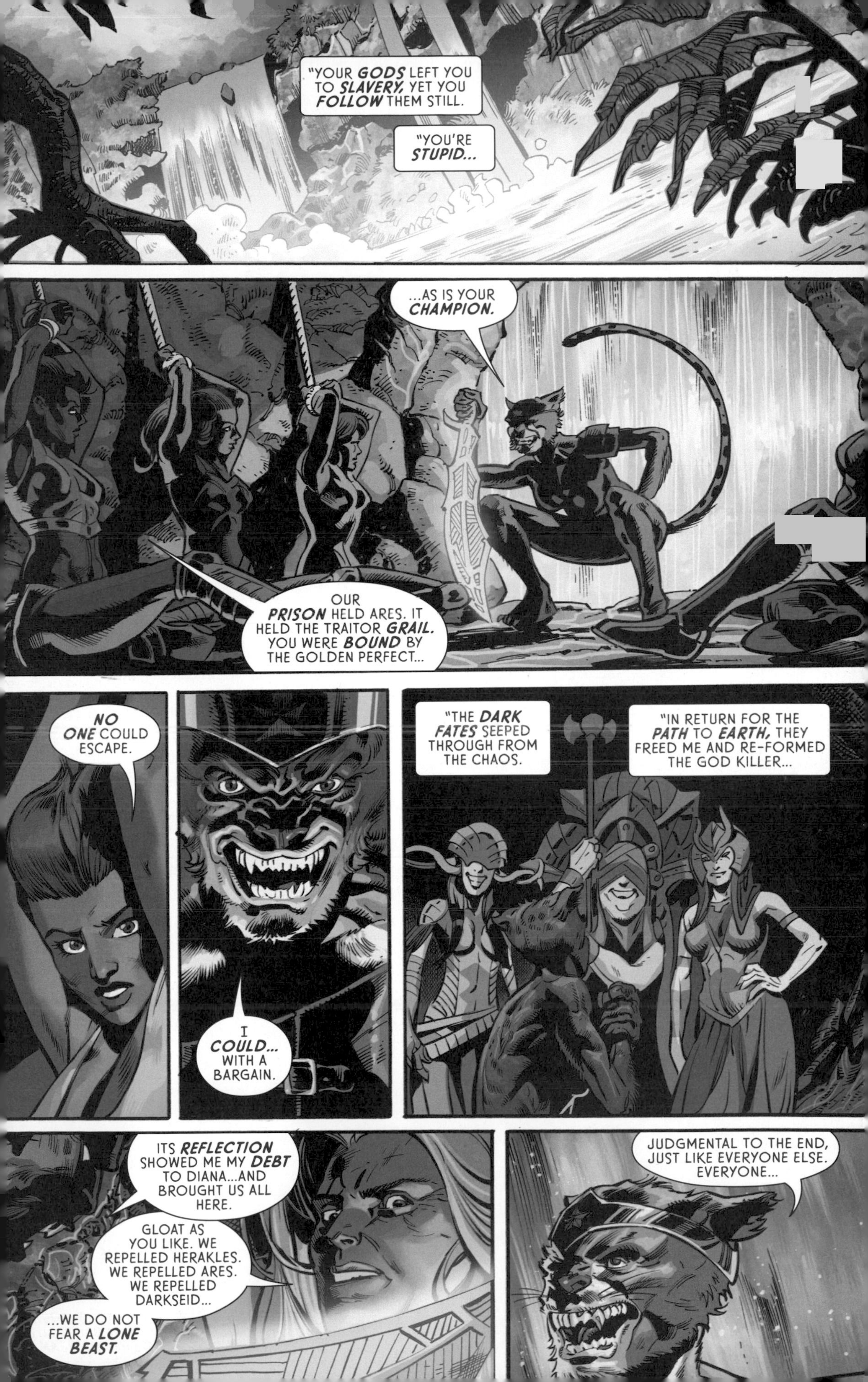
"YOUR GODS LEFT YOU TO SLAVERY, YET YOU FOLLOW THEM STILL.
"YOU'RE STUPID...
...AS IS YOUR CHAMPION.
OUR PRISON HELD ARES. IT HELD THE TRAITOR GRAIL. YOU WERE BOUND BY THE GOLDEN PERFECT...
NO ONE COULD ESCAPE.
I COULD... WITH A BARGAIN.
"THE DARK FATES SEEPED THROUGH FROM THE CHAOS.
"IN RETURN FOR THE PATH TO EARTH, THEY FREED ME AND RE-FORMED THE GOD KILLER...
ITS REFLECTION SHOWED ME MY DEBT TO DIANA...AND BROUGHT US ALL HERE.
GLOAT AS YOU LIKE. WE REPELLED HERAKLES. WE REPELLED ARES. WE REPELLED DARKSEID...
...WE DO NOT FEAR A LONE BEAST.
JUDGMENTAL TO THE END, JUST LIKE EVERYONE ELSE. EVERYONE...

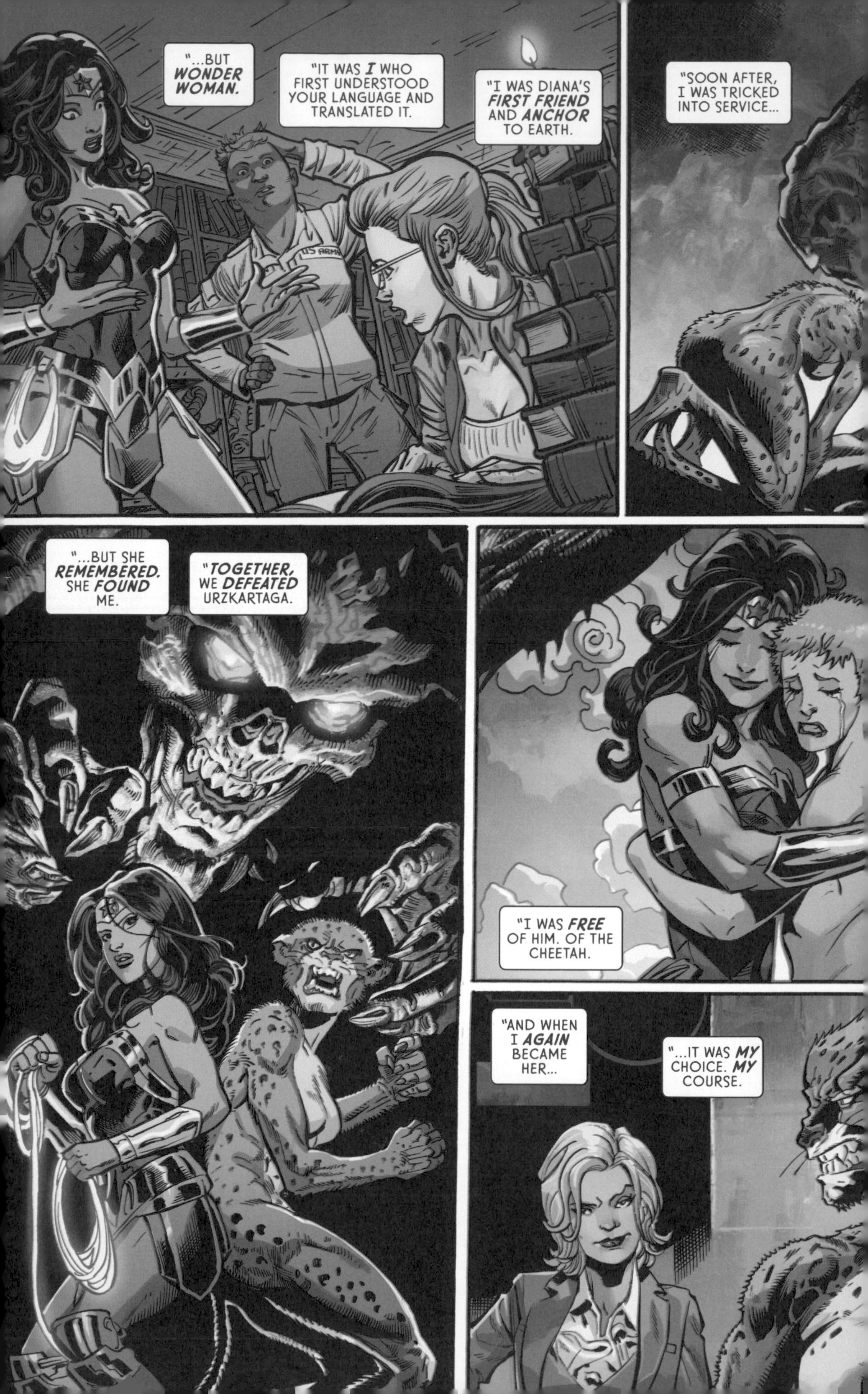
"...BUT WONDER WOMAN.
"IT WAS I WHO FIRST UNDERSTOOD YOUR LANGUAGE AND TRANSLATED IT.
"I WAS DIANA'S FIRST FRIEND AND ANCHOR TO EARTH.
US ARMY
"SOON AFTER, I WAS TRICKED INTO SERVICE...
"...BUT SHE REMEMBERED. SHE FOUND ME.
"TOGETHER, WE DEFEATED URZKARTAGA.
"I WAS FREE OF HIM. OF THE CHEETAH.
"AND WHEN I AGAIN BECAME HER...
"...IT WAS MY CHOICE. MY COURSE.

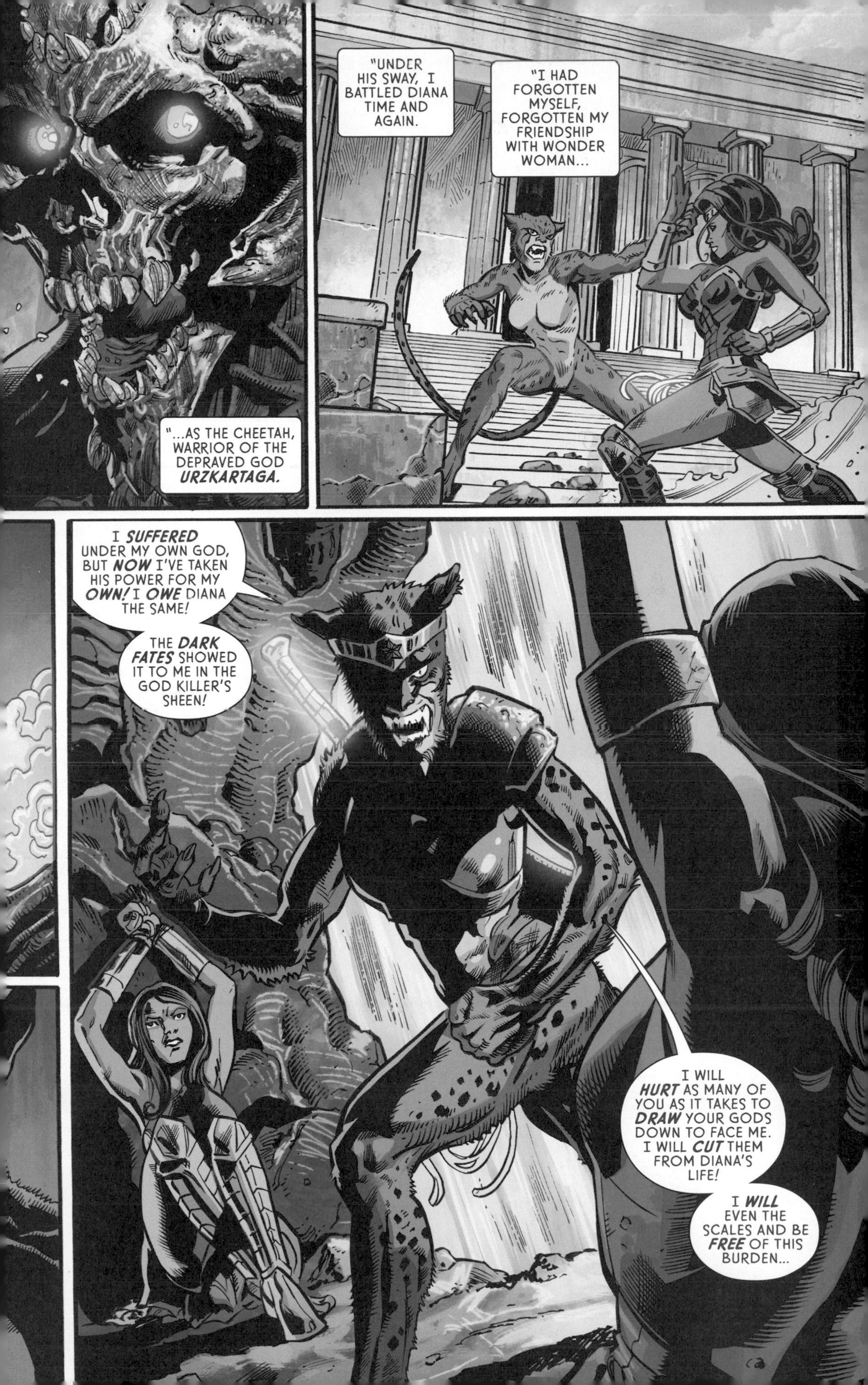
"...AS THE CHEETAH, WARRIOR OF THE DEPRAVED GOD **URZKARTAGA.**
"UNDER HIS SWAY, I BATTLED DIANA TIME AND AGAIN.
"I HAD FORGOTTEN MYSELF, FORGOTTEN MY FRIENDSHIP WITH WONDER WOMAN...
I **SUFFERED** UNDER MY OWN GOD, BUT **NOW** I'VE TAKEN HIS POWER FOR MY **OWN!** I **OWE** DIANA THE SAME!
THE **DARK FATES** SHOWED IT TO ME IN THE GOD KILLER'S SHEEN!
I WILL **HURT** AS MANY OF YOU AS IT TAKES TO **DRAW** YOUR GODS DOWN TO FACE ME. I WILL **CUT** THEM FROM DIANA'S LIFE!
I **WILL** EVEN THE SCALES AND BE **FREE** OF THIS BURDEN...

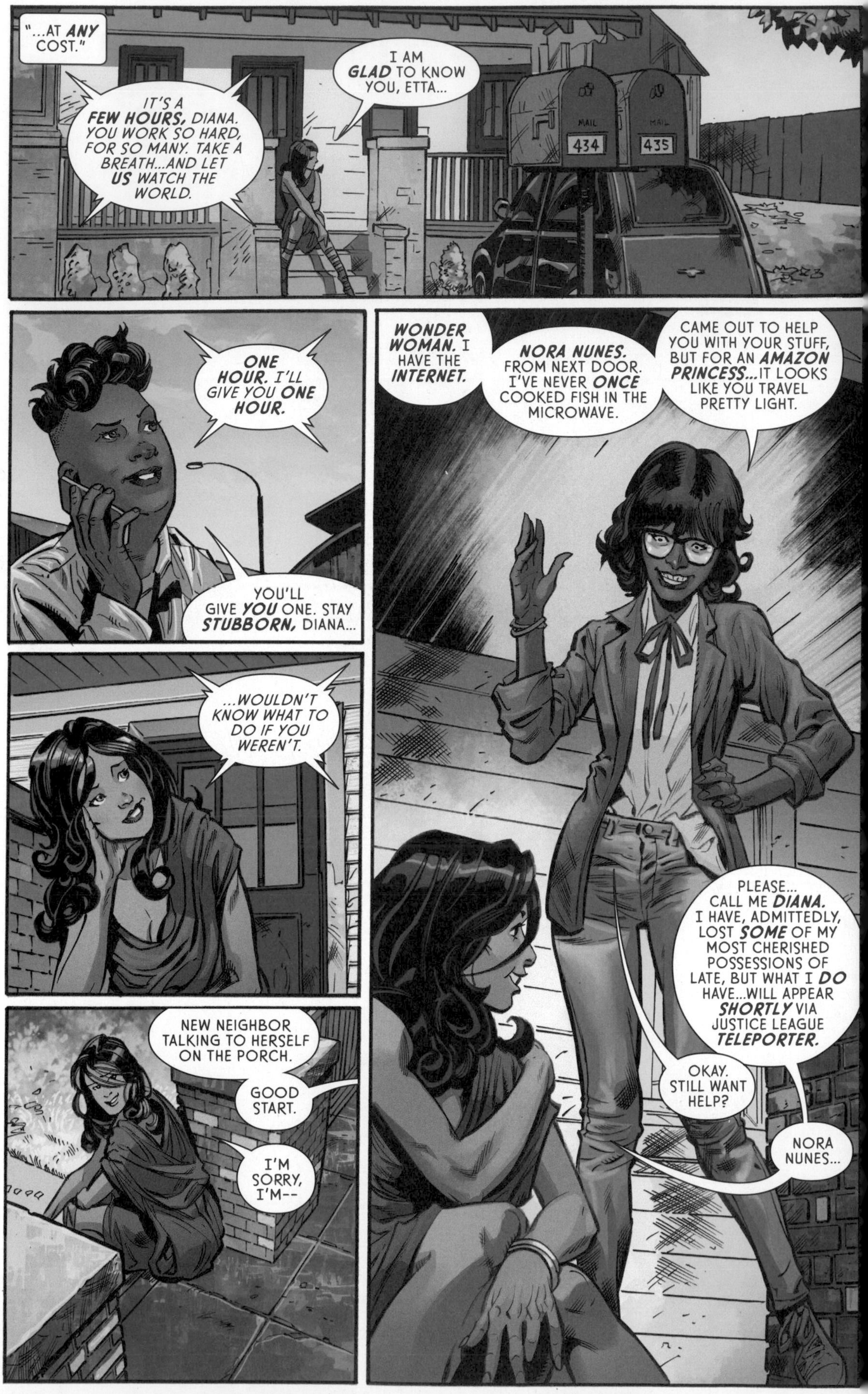

"...AT ANY COST."
IT'S A FEW HOURS, DIANA. YOU WORK SO HARD, FOR SO MANY. TAKE A BREATH...AND LET US WATCH THE WORLD.
I AM GLAD TO KNOW YOU, ETTA...
MAIL
434
MAIL
435
ONE HOUR. I'LL GIVE YOU ONE HOUR.
YOU'LL GIVE YOU ONE. STAY STUBBORN, DIANA...
...WOULDN'T KNOW WHAT TO DO IF YOU WEREN'T.
NEW NEIGHBOR TALKING TO HERSELF ON THE PORCH.
GOOD START.
I'M SORRY, I'M--
WONDER WOMAN. I HAVE THE INTERNET.
NORA NUNES. FROM NEXT DOOR. I'VE NEVER ONCE COOKED FISH IN THE MICROWAVE.
CAME OUT TO HELP YOU WITH YOUR STUFF, BUT FOR AN AMAZON PRINCESS...IT LOOKS LIKE YOU TRAVEL PRETTY LIGHT.
PLEASE... CALL ME DIANA. I HAVE, ADMITTEDLY, LOST SOME OF MY MOST CHERISHED POSSESSIONS OF LATE, BUT WHAT I DO HAVE...WILL APPEAR SHORTLY VIA JUSTICE LEAGUE TELEPORTER.
OKAY. STILL WANT HELP?
NORA NUNES...

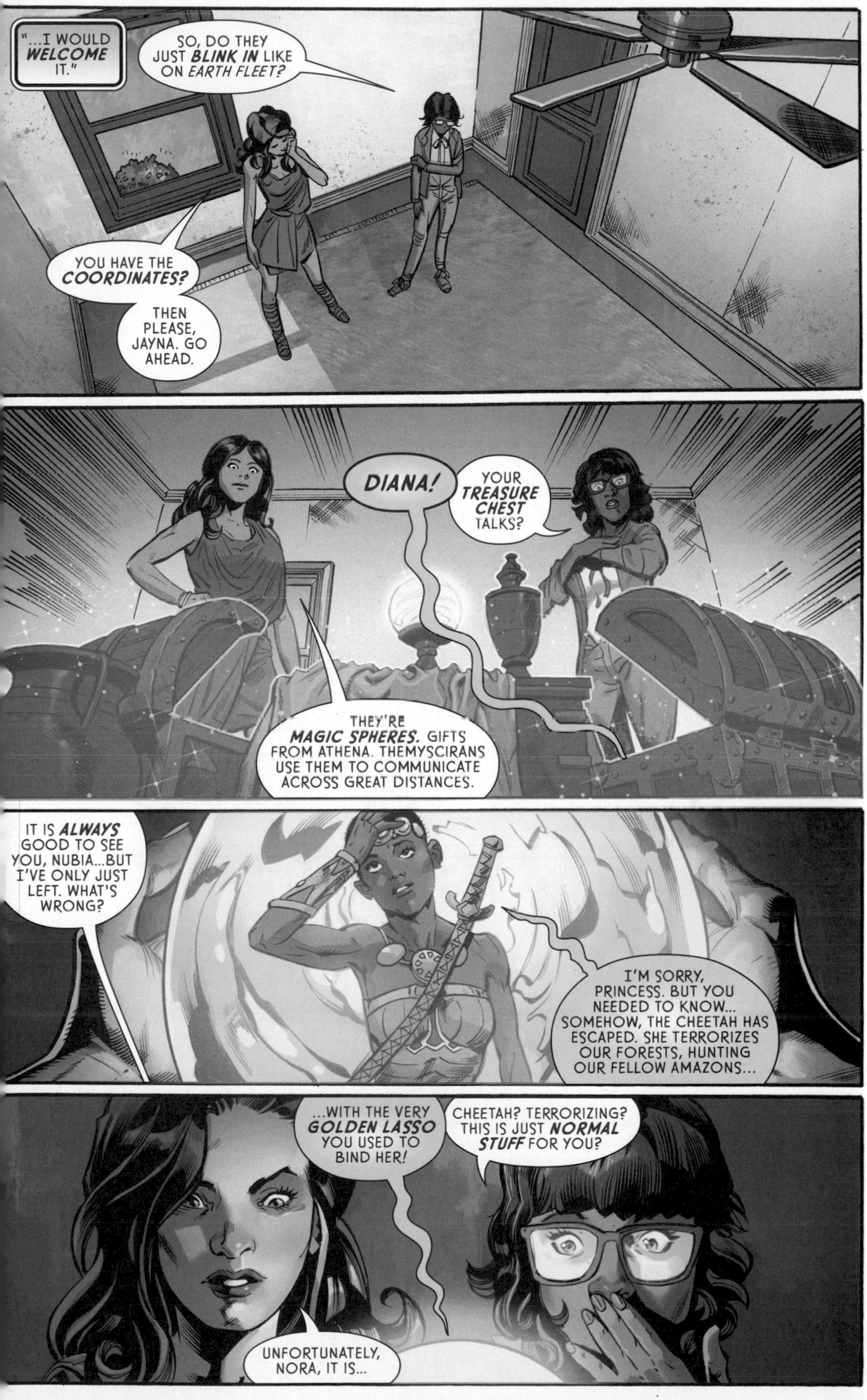
"...I WOULD WELCOME IT."
SO, DO THEY JUST BLINK IN LIKE ON EARTH FLEET?
YOU HAVE THE COORDINATES?
THEN PLEASE, JAYNA. GO AHEAD.
DIANA!
YOUR TREASURE CHEST TALKS?
THEY'RE MAGIC SPHERES. GIFTS FROM ATHENA. THEMYSCIRANS USE THEM TO COMMUNICATE ACROSS GREAT DISTANCES.
IT IS ALWAYS GOOD TO SEE YOU, NUBIA...BUT I'VE ONLY JUST LEFT. WHAT'S WRONG?
I'M SORRY, PRINCESS. BUT YOU NEEDED TO KNOW... SOMEHOW, THE CHEETAH HAS ESCAPED. SHE TERRORIZES OUR FORESTS, HUNTING OUR FELLOW AMAZONS...
...WITH THE VERY GOLDEN LASSO YOU USED TO BIND HER!
CHEETAH? TERRORIZING? THIS IS JUST NORMAL STUFF FOR YOU?
UNFORTUNATELY, NORA, IT IS...

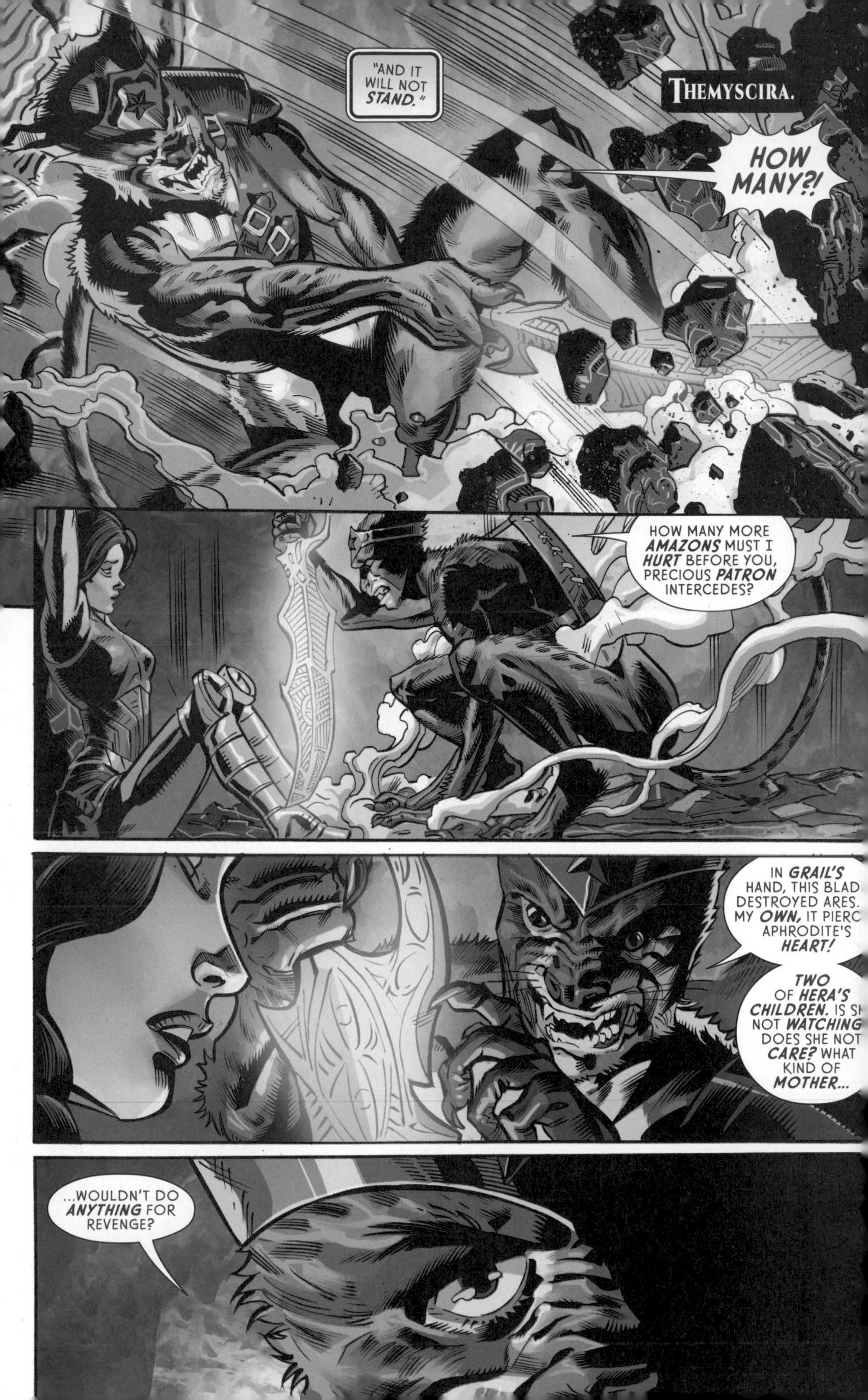
"AND IT WILL NOT STAND."
THEMYSCIRA.
HOW MANY?!
HOW MANY MORE AMAZONS MUST I HURT BEFORE YOU, PRECIOUS PATRON INTERCEDES?
IN GRAIL'S HAND, THIS BLAD DESTROYED ARES. MY OWN, IT PIERC APHRODITE'S HEART!
TWO OF HERA'S CHILDREN. IS S NOT WATCHING DOES SHE NOT CARE? WHAT KIND OF MOTHER...
...WOULDN'T DO ANYTHING FOR REVENGE?

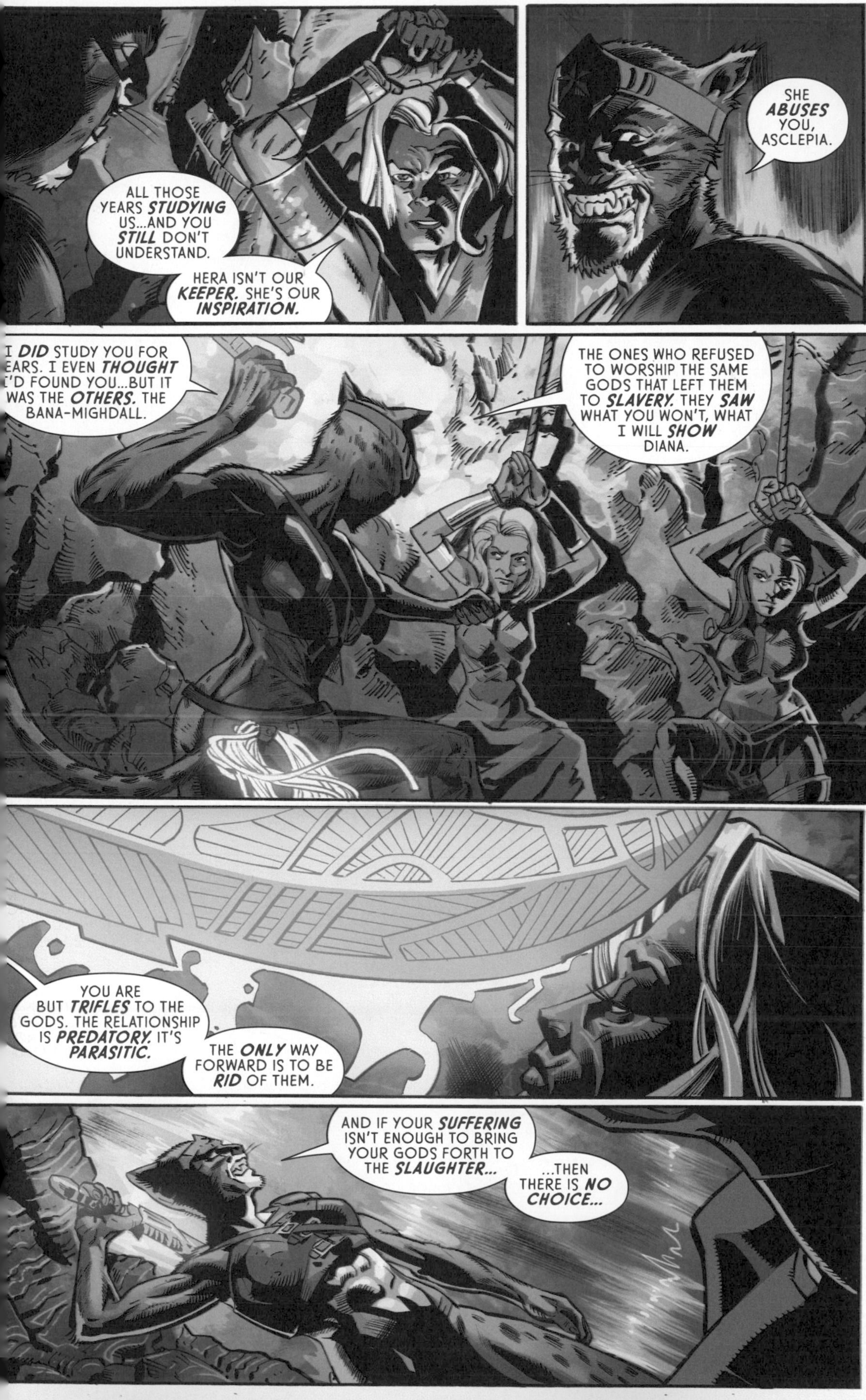
ALL THOSE YEARS STUDYING US...AND YOU STILL DON'T UNDERSTAND.
HERA ISN'T OUR KEEPER. SHE'S OUR INSPIRATION.
SHE ABUSES YOU, ASCLEPIA.
I DID STUDY YOU FOR EARS. I EVEN THOUGHT I'D FOUND YOU...BUT IT WAS THE OTHERS. THE BANA-MIGHDALL.
THE ONES WHO REFUSED TO WORSHIP THE SAME GODS THAT LEFT THEM TO SLAVERY. THEY SAW WHAT YOU WON'T, WHAT I WILL SHOW DIANA.
YOU ARE BUT TRIFLES TO THE GODS. THE RELATIONSHIP IS PREDATORY. IT'S PARASITIC.
THE ONLY WAY FORWARD IS TO BE RID OF THEM.
AND IF YOUR SUFFERING ISN'T ENOUGH TO BRING YOUR GODS FORTH TO THE SLAUGHTER...
...THEN THERE IS NO CHOICE...

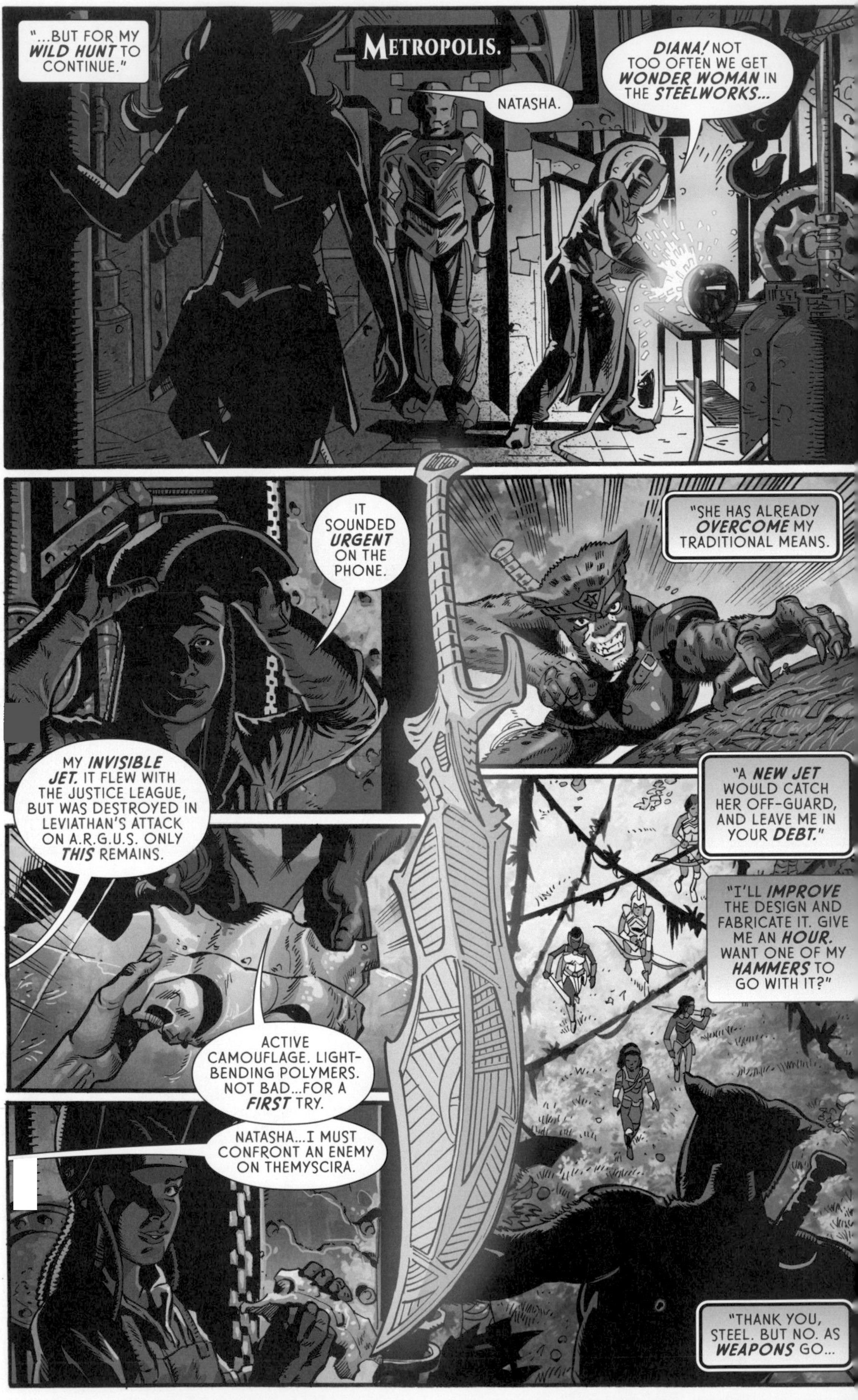
"...BUT FOR MY WILD HUNT TO CONTINUE."
METROPOLIS.
NATASHA.
DIANA! NOT TOO OFTEN WE GET WONDER WOMAN IN THE STEELWORKS...
IT SOUNDED URGENT ON THE PHONE.
"SHE HAS ALREADY OVERCOME MY TRADITIONAL MEANS.
MY INVISIBLE JET. IT FLEW WITH THE JUSTICE LEAGUE, BUT WAS DESTROYED IN LEVIATHAN'S ATTACK ON A.R.G.U.S. ONLY THIS REMAINS.
"A NEW JET WOULD CATCH HER OFF-GUARD, AND LEAVE ME IN YOUR DEBT."
"I'LL IMPROVE THE DESIGN AND FABRICATE IT. GIVE ME AN HOUR. WANT ONE OF MY HAMMERS TO GO WITH IT?"
ACTIVE CAMOUFLAGE. LIGHT-BENDING POLYMERS. NOT BAD...FOR A FIRST TRY.
NATASHA...I MUST CONFRONT AN ENEMY ON THEMYSCIRA.
"THANK YOU, STEEL. BUT NO. AS WEAPONS GO...

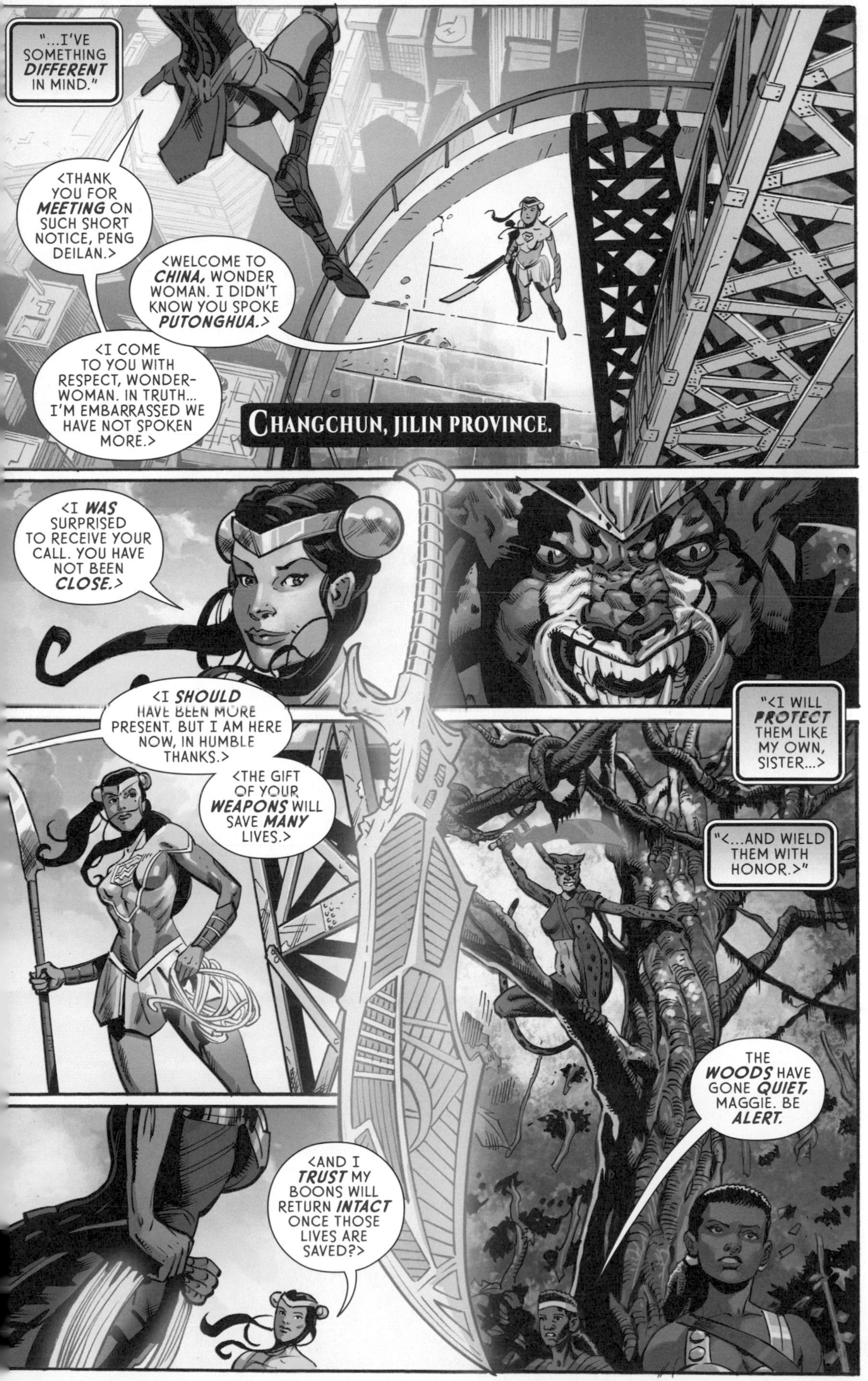

"...I'VE SOMETHING DIFFERENT IN MIND."
<THANK YOU FOR MEETING ON SUCH SHORT NOTICE, PENG DEILAN.>
<WELCOME TO CHINA, WONDER WOMAN. I DIDN'T KNOW YOU SPOKE PUTONGHUA.>
<I COME TO YOU WITH RESPECT, WONDER-WOMAN. IN TRUTH... I'M EMBARRASSED WE HAVE NOT SPOKEN MORE.>
CHANGCHUN, JILIN PROVINCE.
<I WAS SURPRISED TO RECEIVE YOUR CALL. YOU HAVE NOT BEEN CLOSE.>
<I SHOULD HAVE BEEN MORE PRESENT. BUT I AM HERE NOW, IN HUMBLE THANKS.>
<THE GIFT OF YOUR WEAPONS WILL SAVE MANY LIVES.>
"<I WILL PROTECT THEM LIKE MY OWN, SISTER...>
"<...AND WIELD THEM WITH HONOR.>"
<AND I TRUST MY BOONS WILL RETURN INTACT ONCE THOSE LIVES ARE SAVED?>
THE WOODS HAVE GONE QUIET, MAGGIE. BE ALERT.

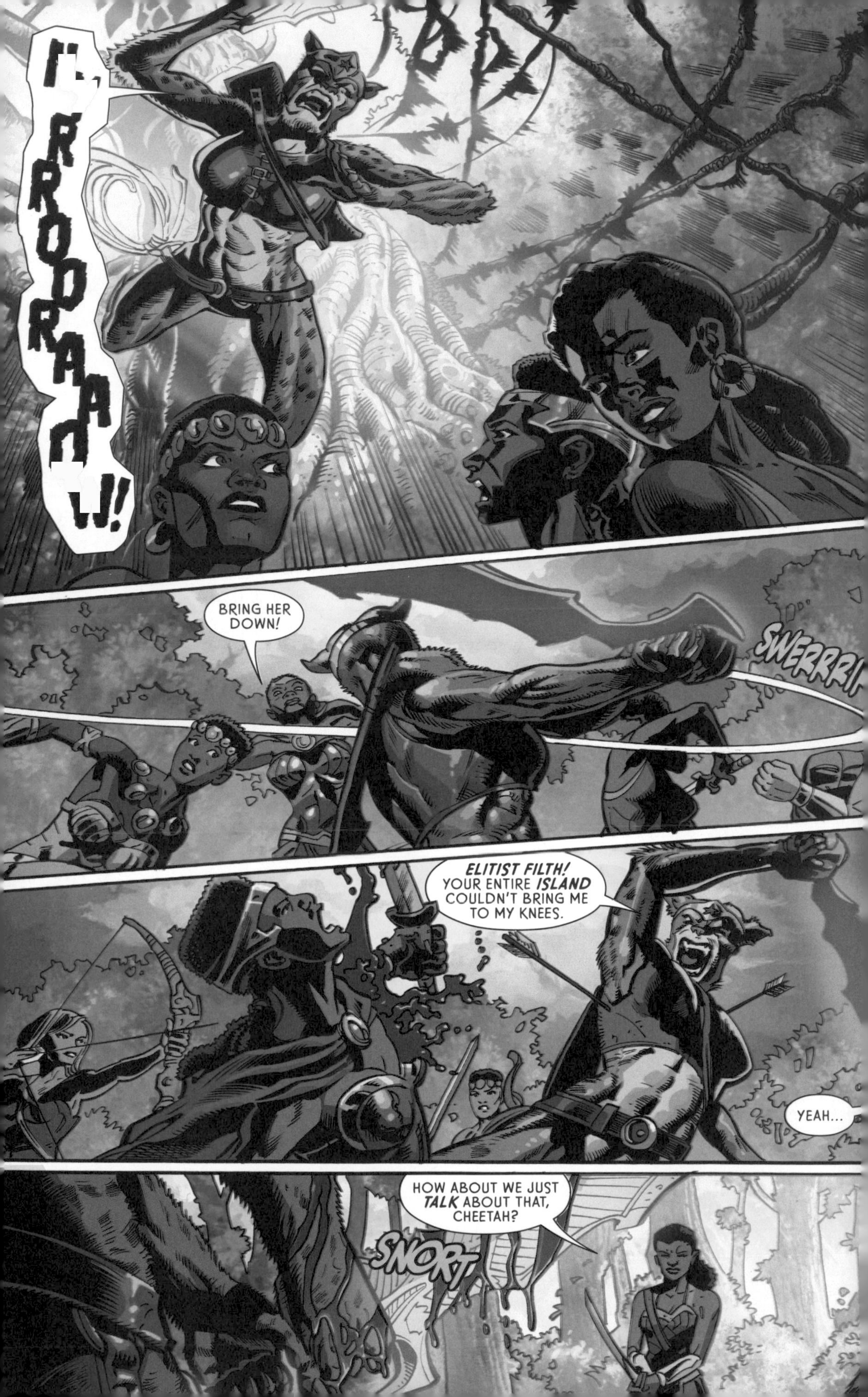
BRING HER DOWN!
SWERRR!
ELITIST FILTH! YOUR ENTIRE *ISLAND* COULDN'T BRING ME TO MY KNEES.
YEAH...
HOW ABOUT WE JUST *TALK* ABOUT THAT, CHEETAH?
SNORT

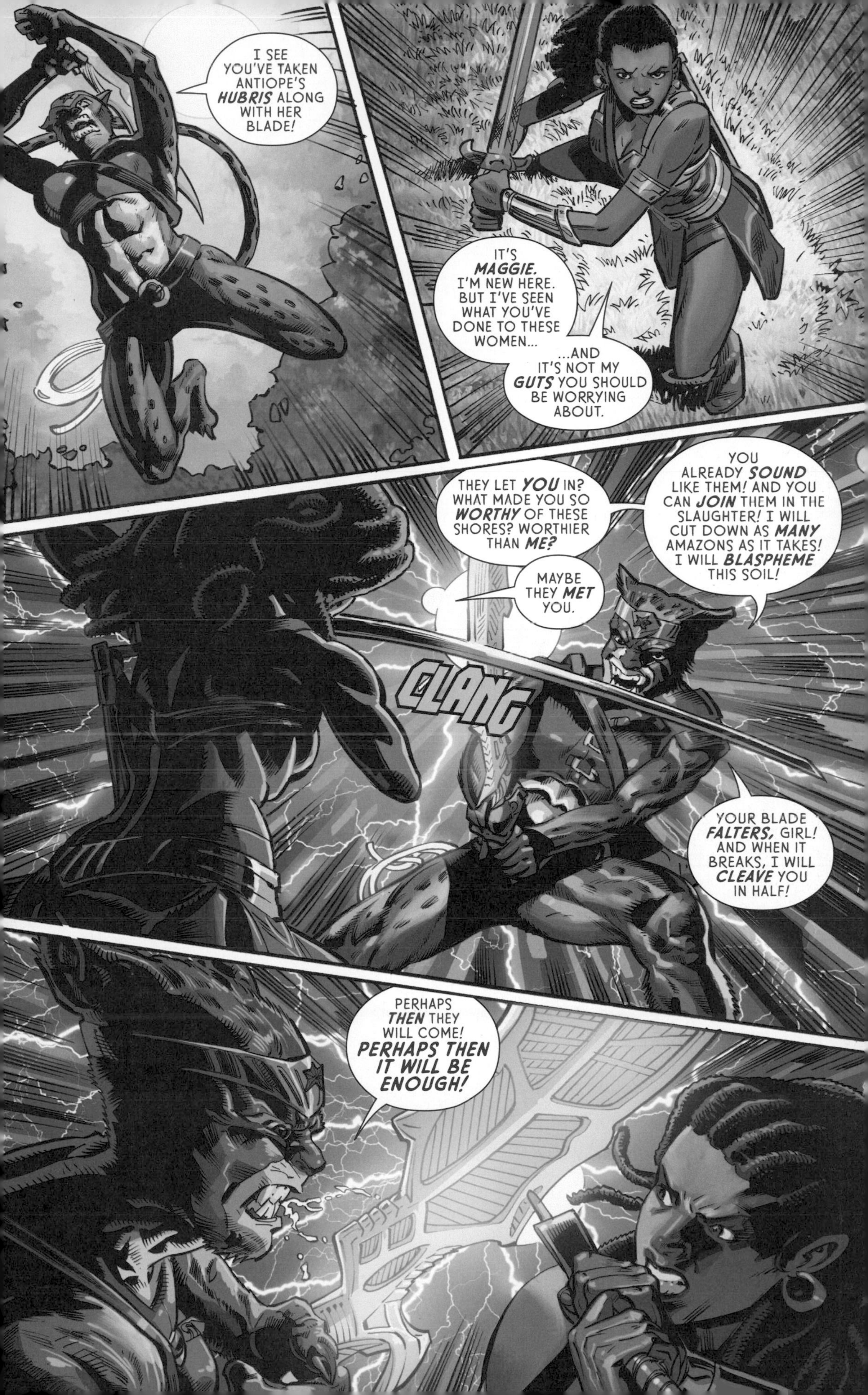
I SEE YOU'VE TAKEN ANTIOPE'S **HUBRIS** ALONG WITH HER BLADE!
IT'S **MAGGIE.** I'M NEW HERE. BUT I'VE SEEN WHAT YOU'VE DONE TO THESE WOMEN...
...AND IT'S NOT MY **GUTS** YOU SHOULD BE WORRYING ABOUT.
THEY LET **YOU** IN? WHAT MADE YOU SO **WORTHY** OF THESE SHORES? WORTHIER THAN **ME?**
MAYBE THEY **MET** YOU.
YOU ALREADY **SOUND** LIKE THEM! AND YOU CAN **JOIN** THEM IN THE SLAUGHTER! I WILL CUT DOWN AS **MANY** AMAZONS AS IT TAKES! I WILL **BLASPHEME** THIS SOIL!
CLANG
YOUR BLADE **FALTERS,** GIRL! AND WHEN IT BREAKS, I WILL **CLEAVE** YOU IN HALF!
PERHAPS **THEN** THEY WILL COME! **PERHAPS THEN IT WILL BE ENOUGH!**

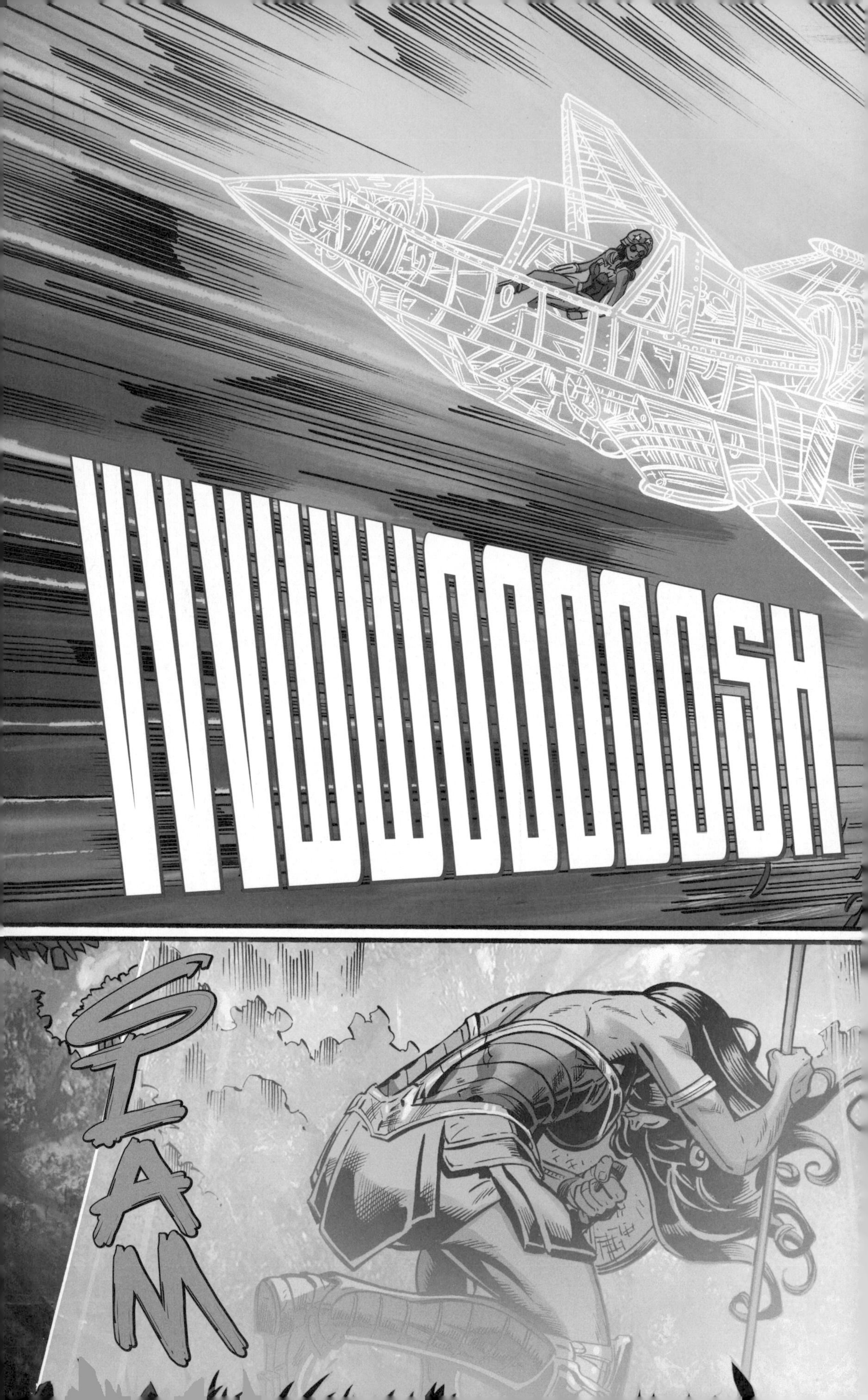
VVWOOOOOSH
SLAM

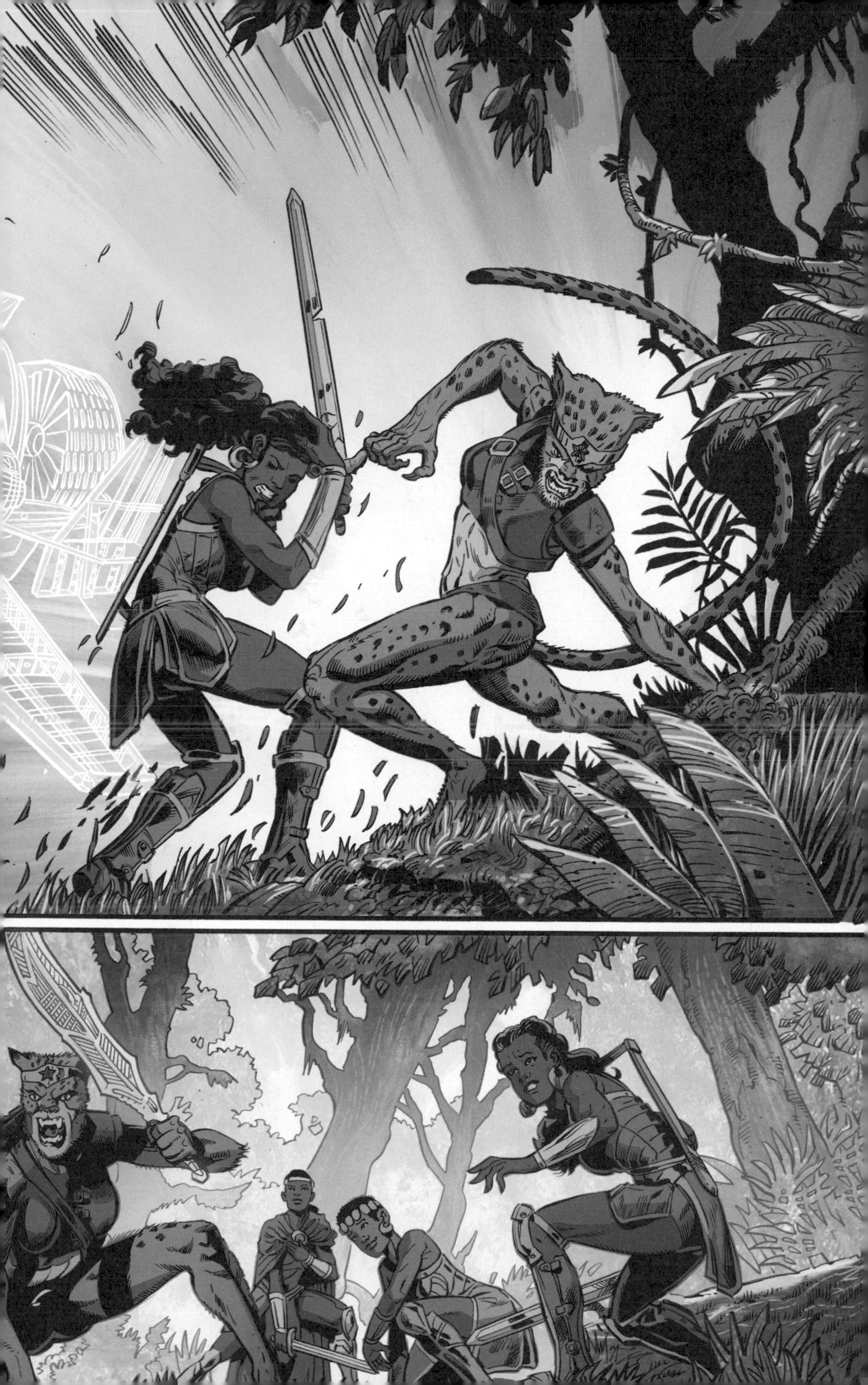

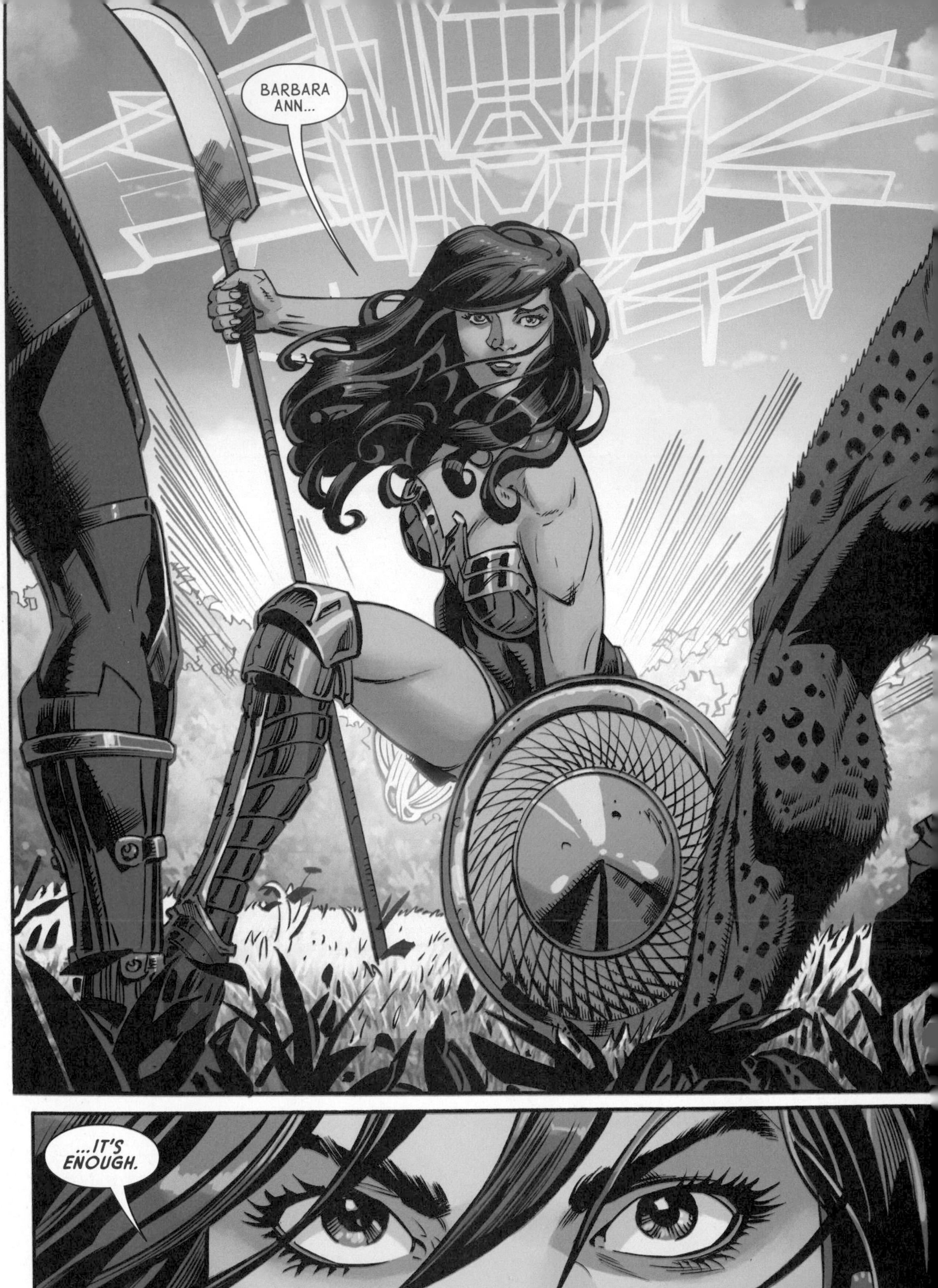
BARBARA ANN...
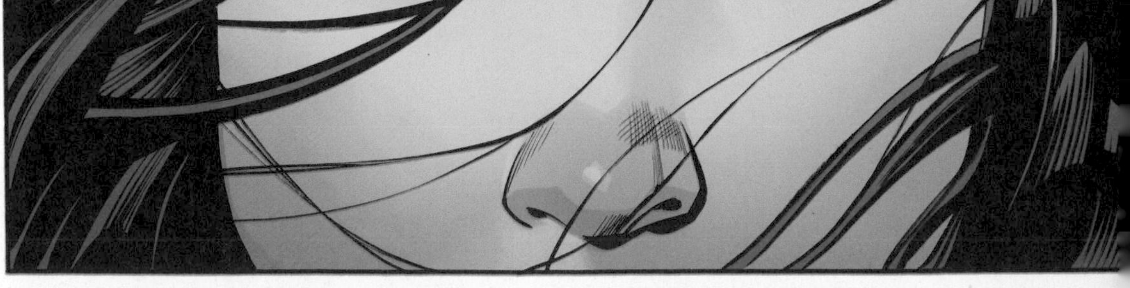
...IT'S ENOUGH.

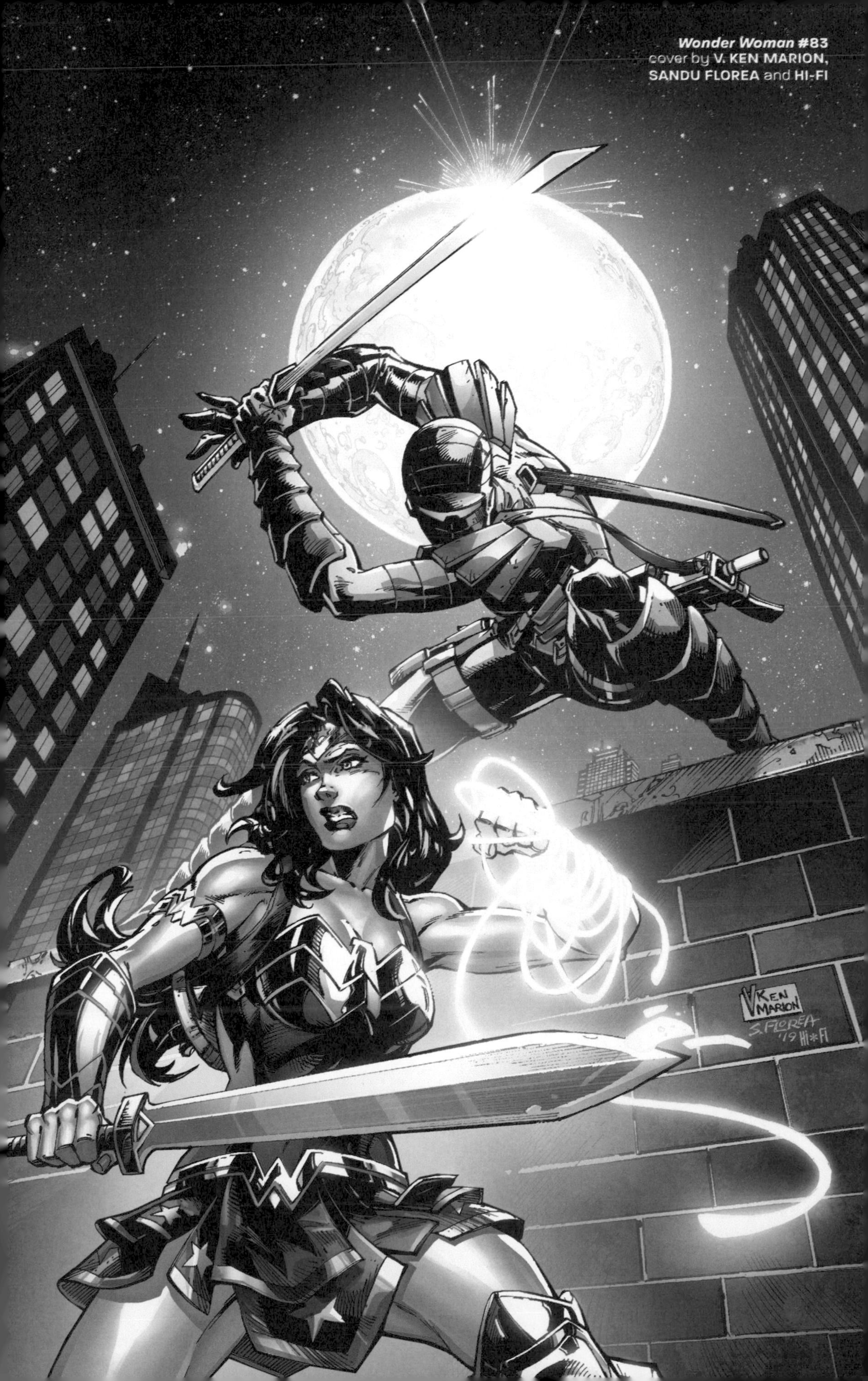
V KEN MARION
S. FLOREA '19 HI*FI

Wonder Woman **#83**
cover by **V. KEN MARION,**
SANDU FLOREA and **HI-FI**

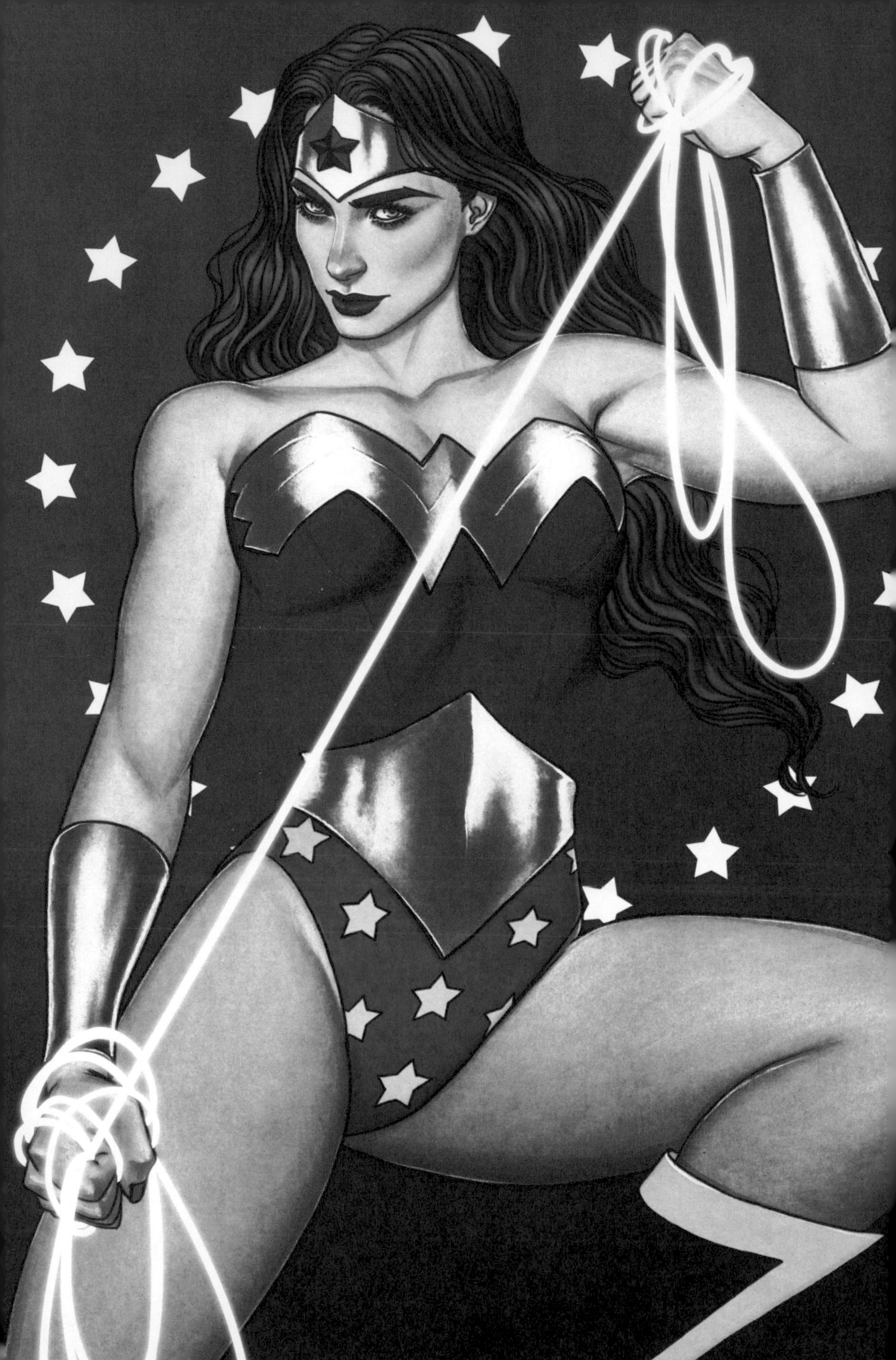

Wonder Woman #
variant cover by **JENNY FRIS**

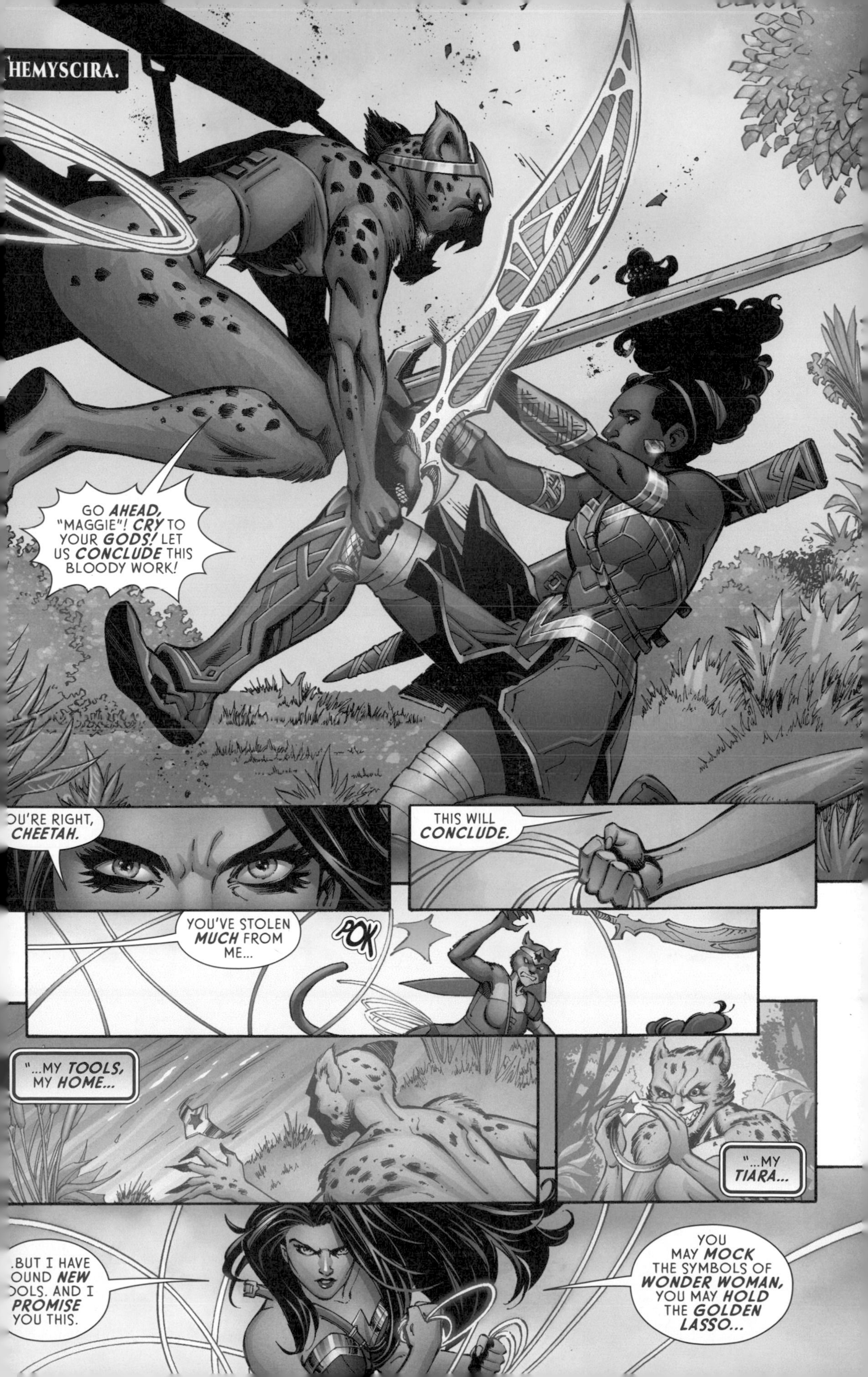
HEMYSCIRA.
GO AHEAD, "MAGGIE"! CRY TO YOUR GODS! LET US CONCLUDE THIS BLOODY WORK!
OU'RE RIGHT, CHEETAH.
THIS WILL CONCLUDE.
YOU'VE STOLEN MUCH FROM ME...
POK
"...MY TOOLS, MY HOME...
"...MY TIARA...
.BUT I HAVE OUND NEW OOLS. AND I PROMISE YOU THIS.
YOU MAY MOCK THE SYMBOLS OF WONDER WOMAN, YOU MAY HOLD THE GOLDEN LASSO...

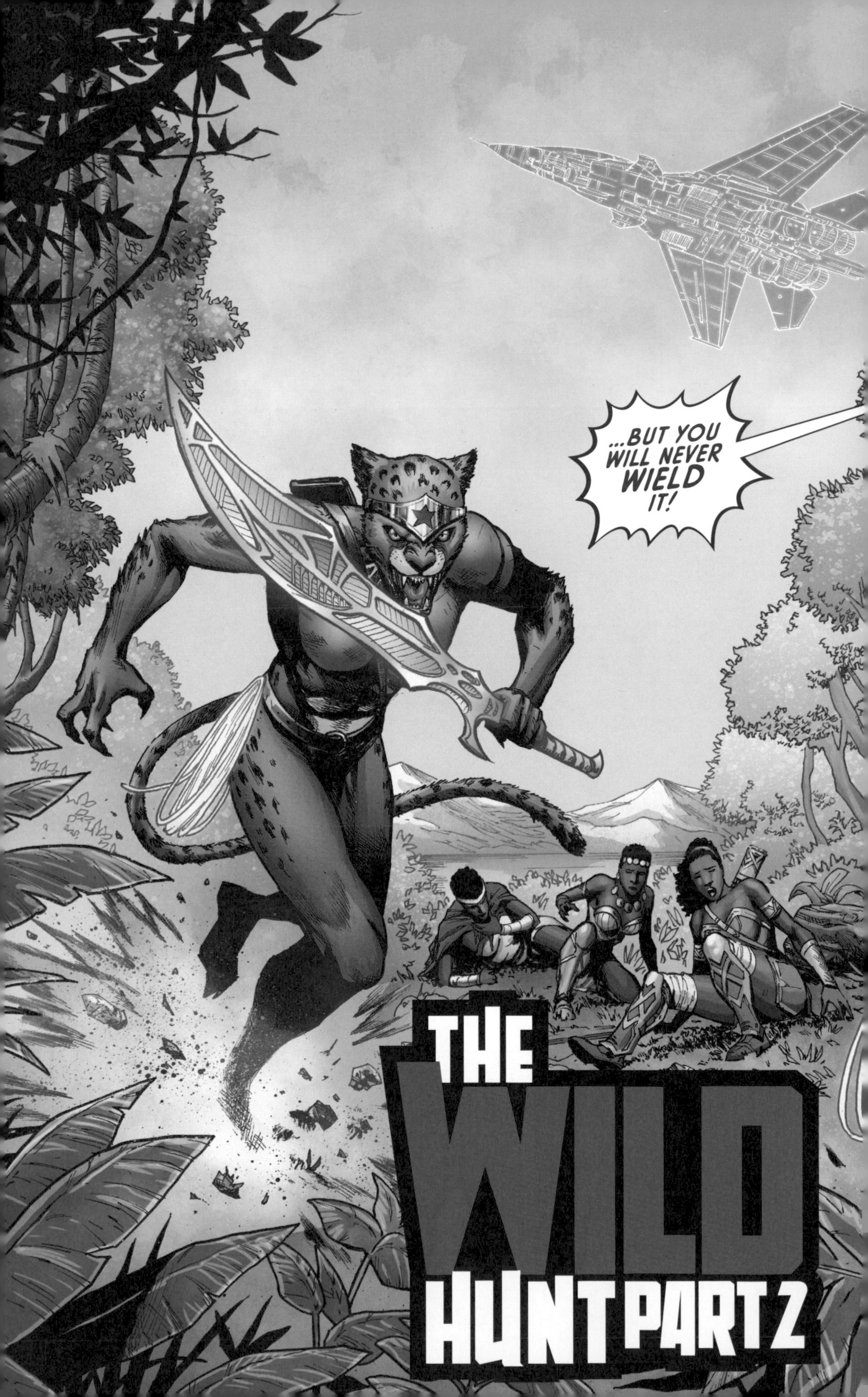
...BUT YOU WILL NEVER WIELD IT!
THE WILD HUNT PART 2

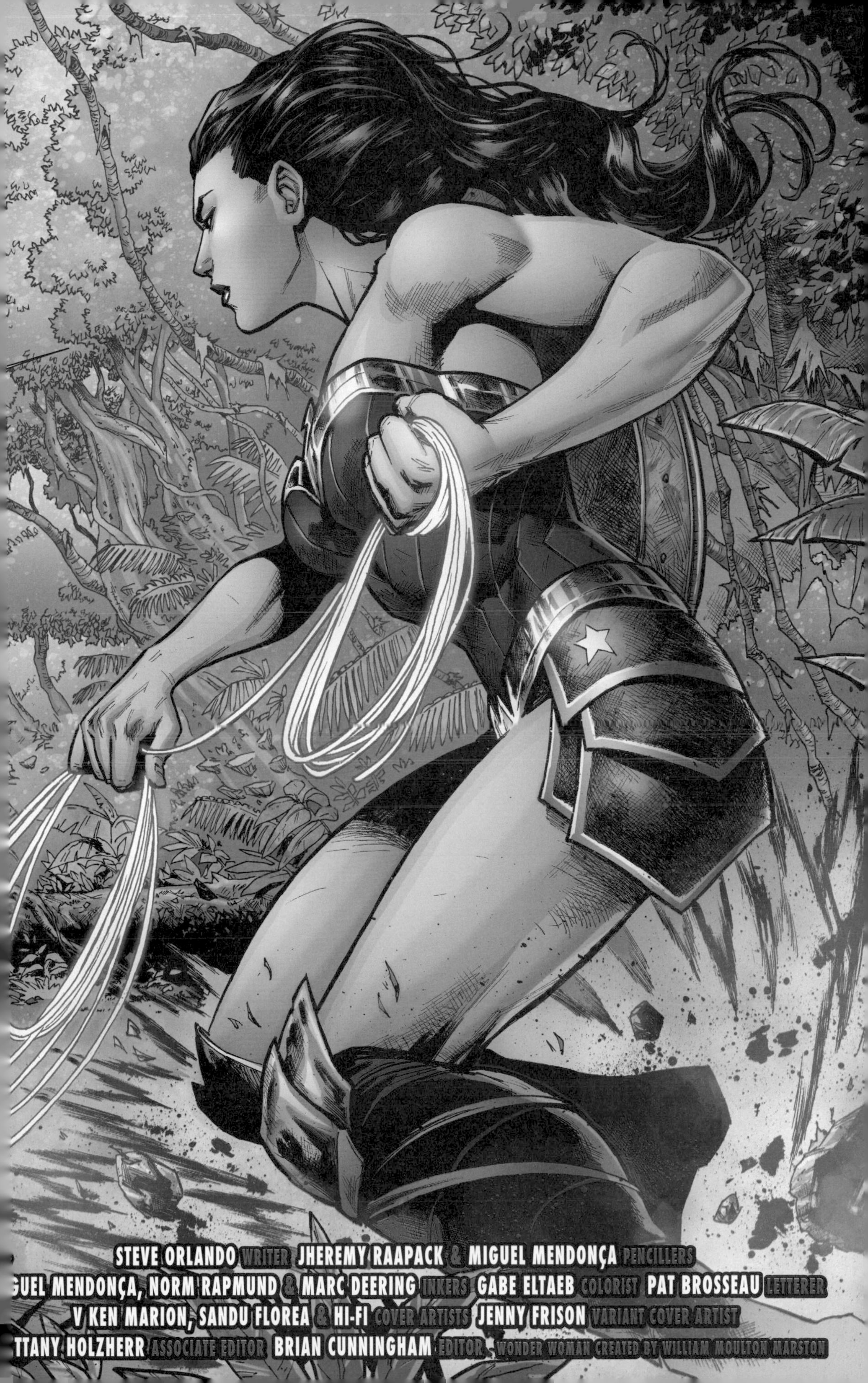
STEVE ORLANDO WRITER JHEREMY RAAPACK & MIGUEL MENDONÇA PENCILLERS
GUEL MENDONÇA, NORM RAPMUND & MARC DEERING INKERS GABE ELTAEB COLORIST PAT BROSSEAU LETTERER
V KEN MARION, SANDU FLOREA & HI-FI COVER ARTISTS JENNY FRISON VARIANT COVER ARTIST
TTANY HOLZHERR ASSOCIATE EDITOR BRIAN CUNNINGHAM EDITOR WONDER WOMAN CREATED BY WILLIAM MOULTON MARSTON

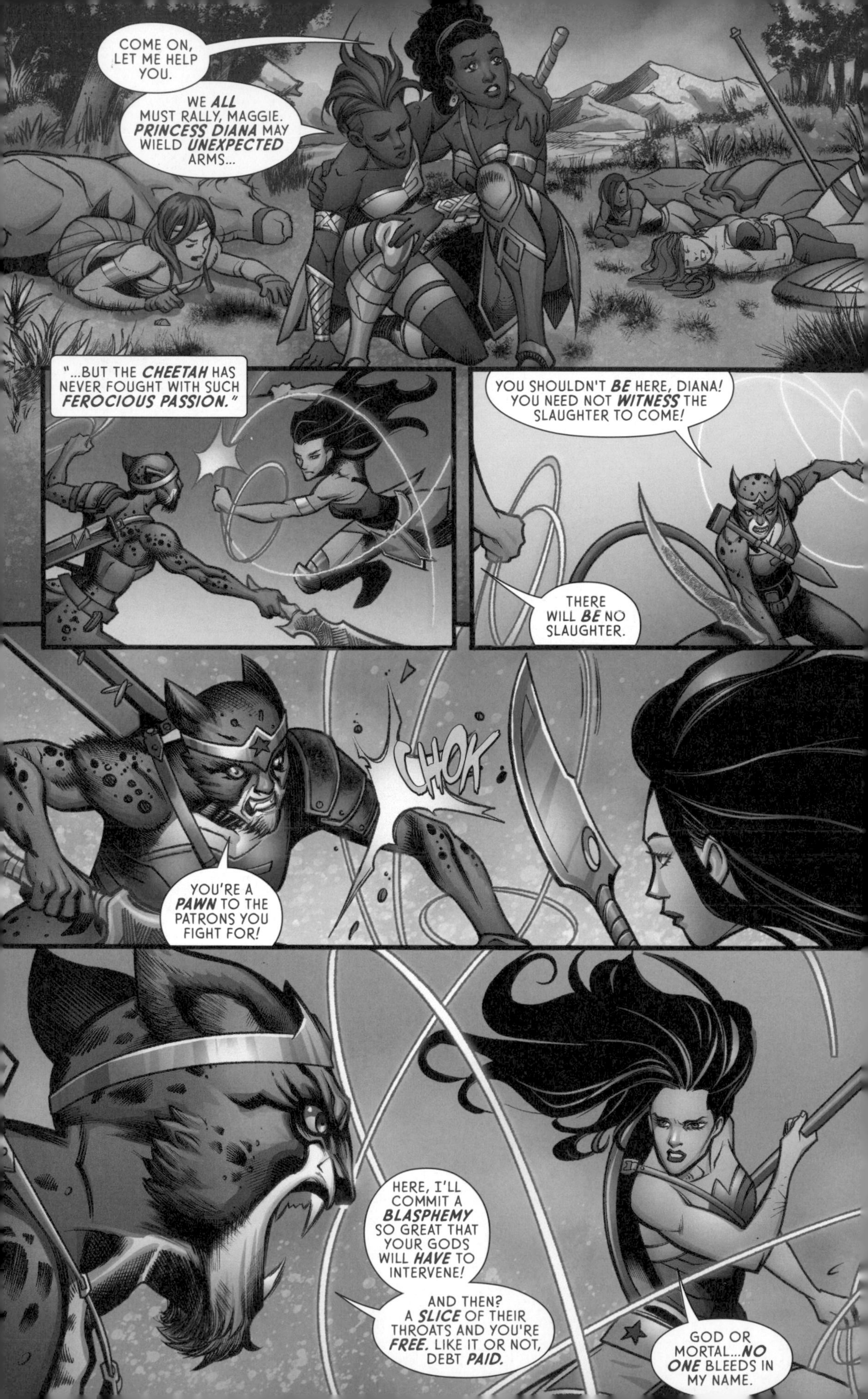

COME ON, LET ME HELP YOU.
WE ALL MUST RALLY, MAGGIE. PRINCESS DIANA MAY WIELD UNEXPECTED ARMS...
"...BUT THE CHEETAH HAS NEVER FOUGHT WITH SUCH FEROCIOUS PASSION."
YOU SHOULDN'T BE HERE, DIANA! YOU NEED NOT WITNESS THE SLAUGHTER TO COME!
THERE WILL BE NO SLAUGHTER.
CHOK
YOU'RE A PAWN TO THE PATRONS YOU FIGHT FOR!
HERE, I'LL COMMIT A BLASPHEMY SO GREAT THAT YOUR GODS WILL HAVE TO INTERVENE!
AND THEN? A SLICE OF THEIR THROATS AND YOU'RE FREE. LIKE IT OR NOT, DEBT PAID.
GOD OR MORTAL...NO ONE BLEEDS IN MY NAME.

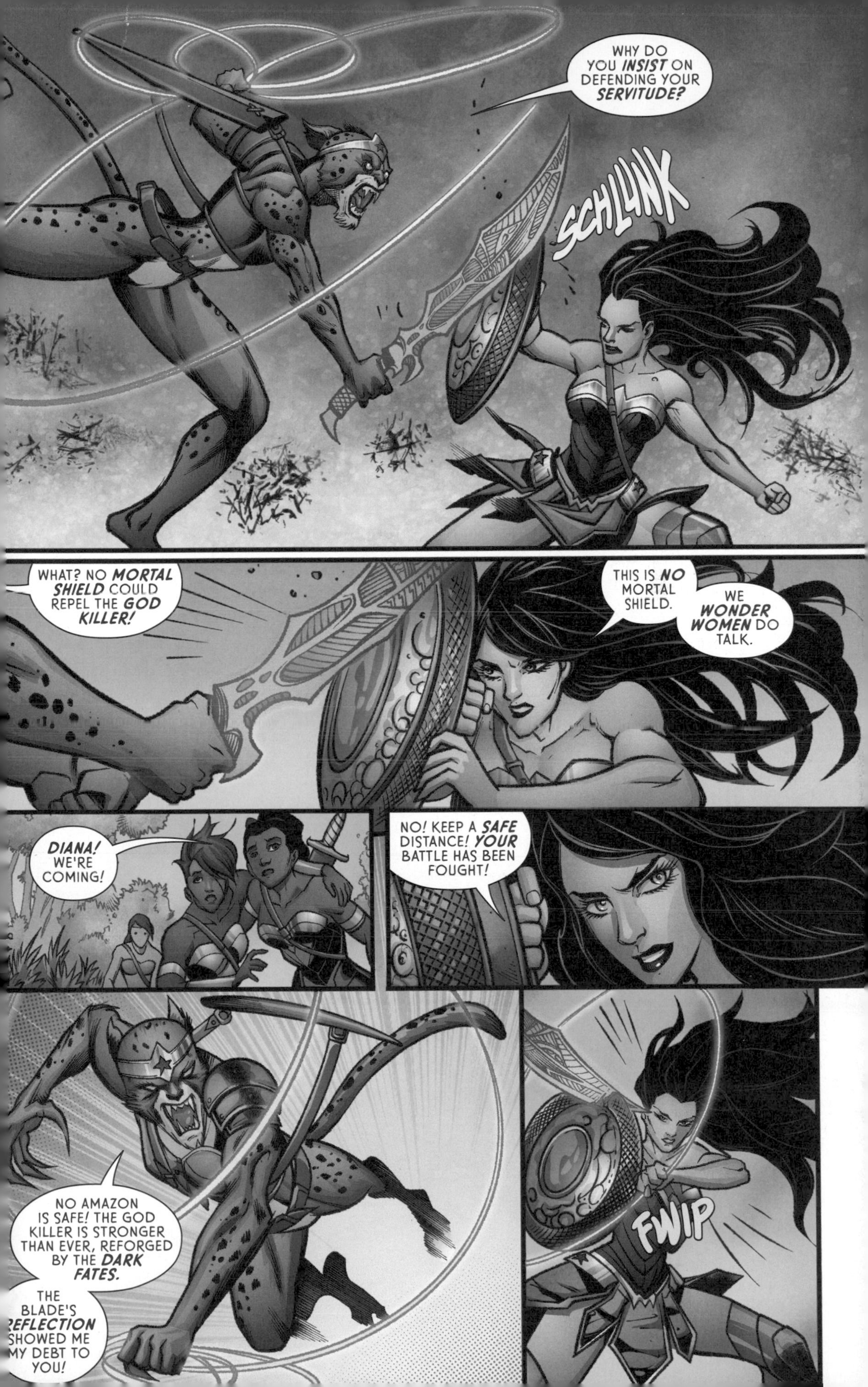

WHY DO YOU INSIST ON DEFENDING YOUR SERVITUDE?
SCHLUNK
WHAT? NO MORTAL SHIELD COULD REPEL THE GOD KILLER!
THIS IS NO MORTAL SHIELD.
WE WONDER WOMEN DO TALK.
DIANA! WE'RE COMING!
NO! KEEP A SAFE DISTANCE! YOUR BATTLE HAS BEEN FOUGHT!
NO AMAZON IS SAFE! THE GOD KILLER IS STRONGER THAN EVER, REFORGED BY THE DARK FATES.
THE BLADE'S REFLECTION SHOWED ME MY DEBT TO YOU!
FWIP

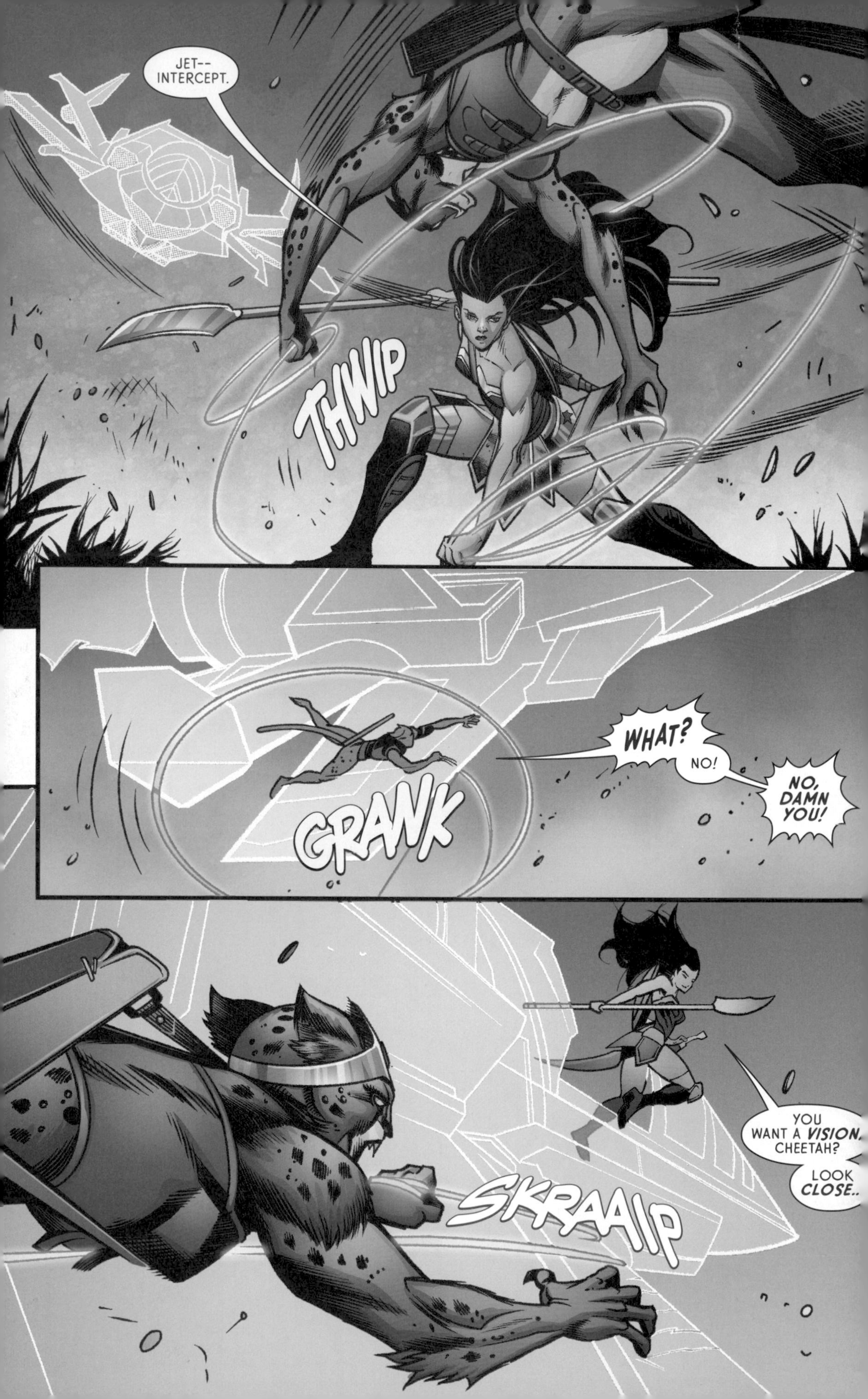
JET--
INTERCEPT.
THWIP
GRANK
WHAT?
NO!
NO, DAMN YOU!
YOU WANT A *VISION*, CHEETAH?
LOOK *CLOSE*..
SKRAAIP

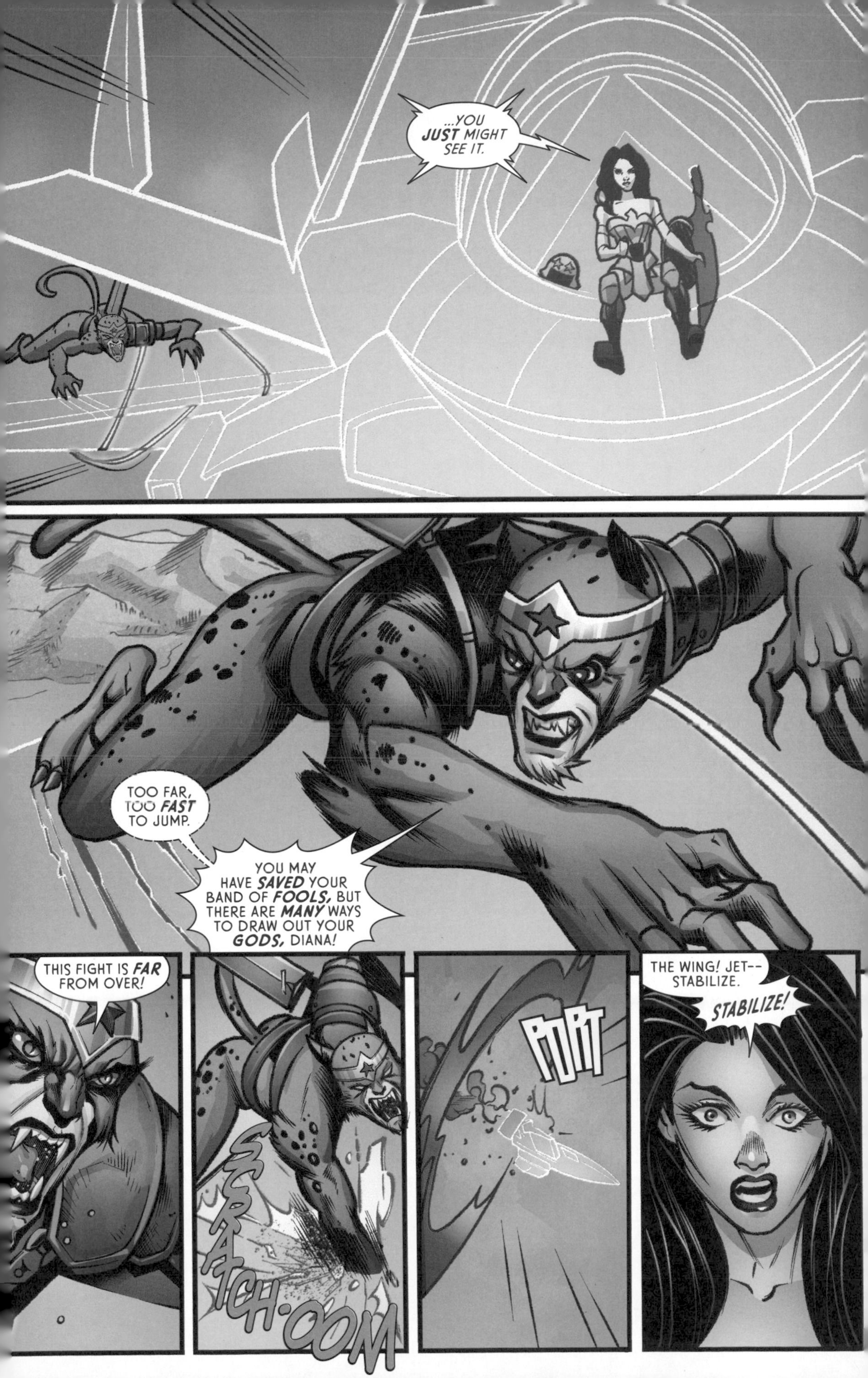
...YOU JUST MIGHT SEE IT.
TOO FAR, TOO FAST TO JUMP.
YOU MAY HAVE SAVED YOUR BAND OF FOOLS, BUT THERE ARE MANY WAYS TO DRAW OUT YOUR GODS, DIANA!
THIS FIGHT IS FAR FROM OVER!
SCRATCH-OOM
PORT
THE WING! JET-- STABILIZE.
STABILIZE!

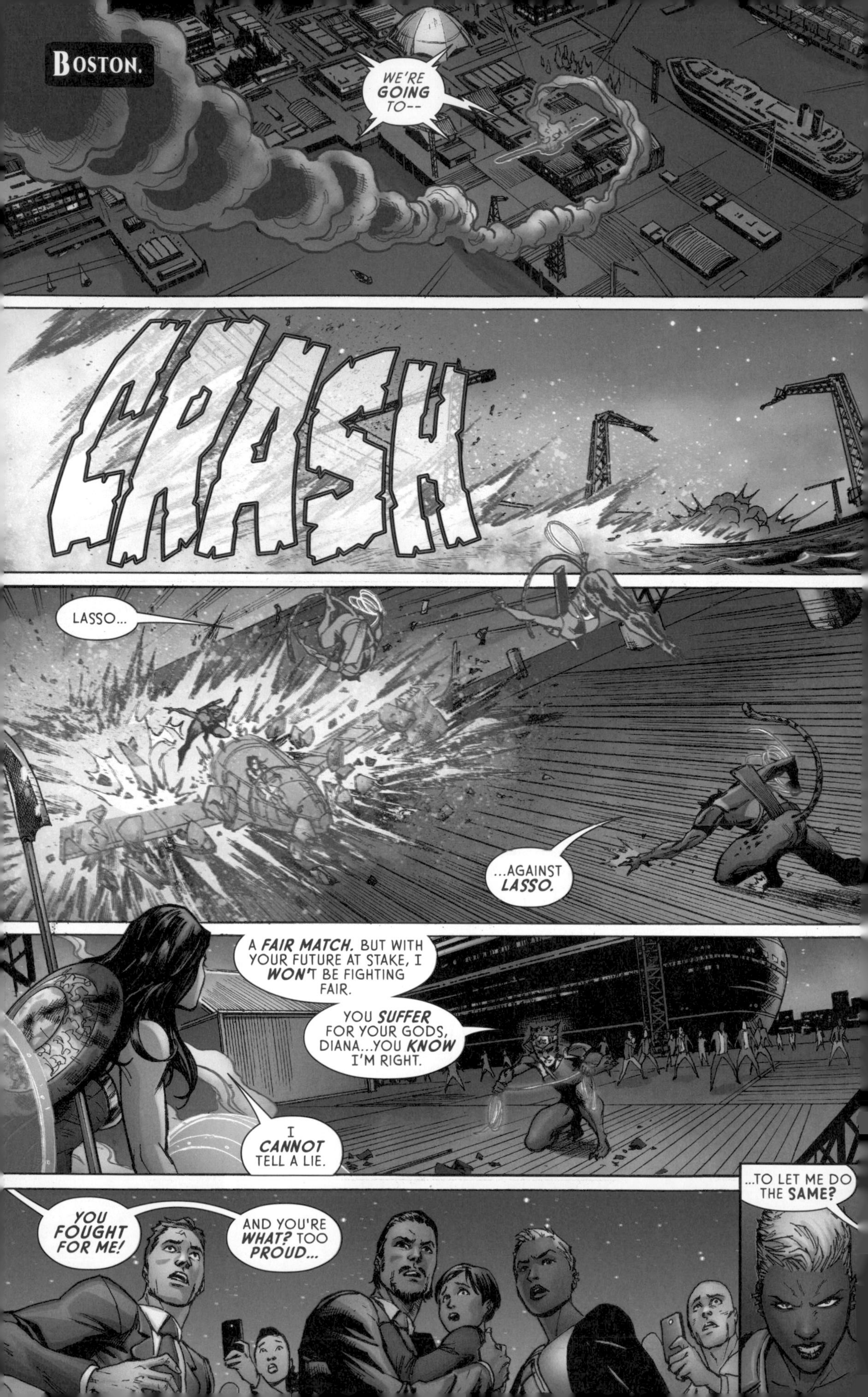
BOSTON.
WE'RE GOING TO--
CRASH
LASSO...
...AGAINST LASSO.
A FAIR MATCH. BUT WITH YOUR FUTURE AT STAKE, I WON'T BE FIGHTING FAIR.
YOU SUFFER FOR YOUR GODS, DIANA...YOU KNOW I'M RIGHT.
I CANNOT TELL A LIE.
YOU FOUGHT FOR ME!
AND YOU'RE WHAT? TOO PROUD...
...TO LET ME DO THE SAME?

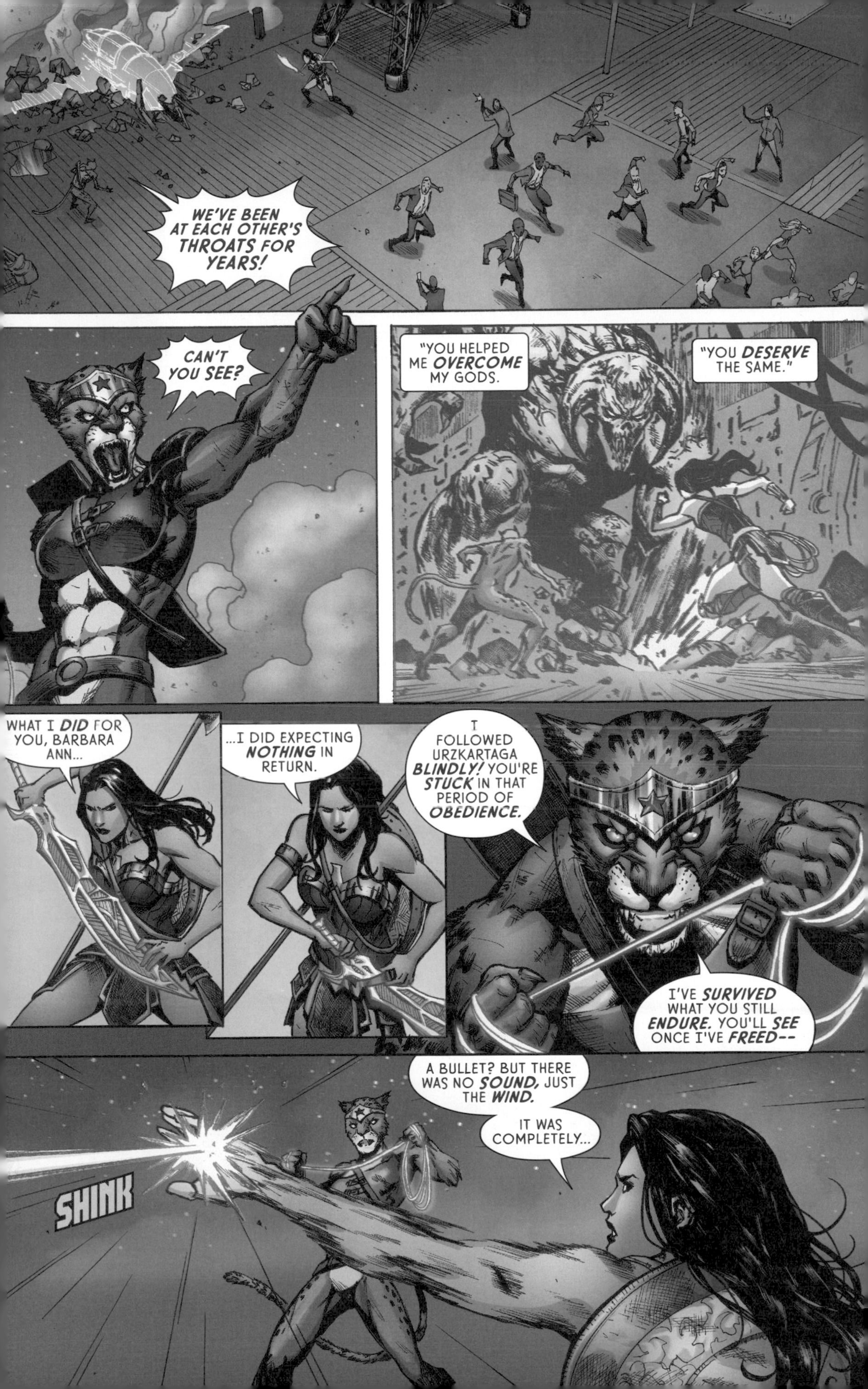
WE'VE BEEN AT EACH OTHER'S THROATS FOR YEARS!
CAN'T YOU SEE?
"YOU HELPED ME OVERCOME MY GODS.
"YOU DESERVE THE SAME."
WHAT I DID FOR YOU, BARBARA ANN...
...I DID EXPECTING NOTHING IN RETURN.
I FOLLOWED URZKARTAGA BLINDLY! YOU'RE STUCK IN THAT PERIOD OF OBEDIENCE.
I'VE SURVIVED WHAT YOU STILL ENDURE. YOU'LL SEE ONCE I'VE FREED--
SHINK
A BULLET? BUT THERE WAS NO SOUND, JUST THE WIND.
IT WAS COMPLETELY...

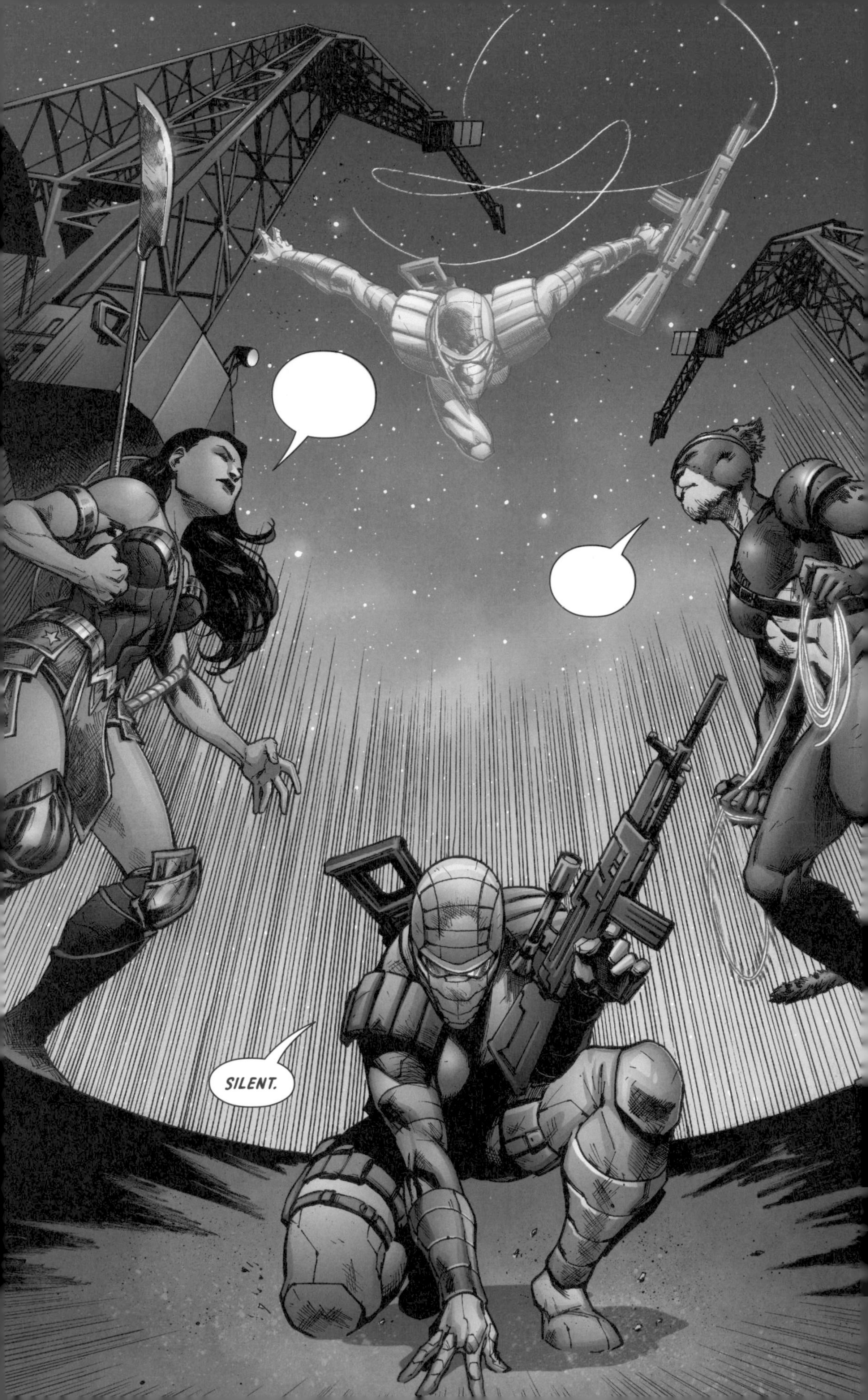
SILENT.

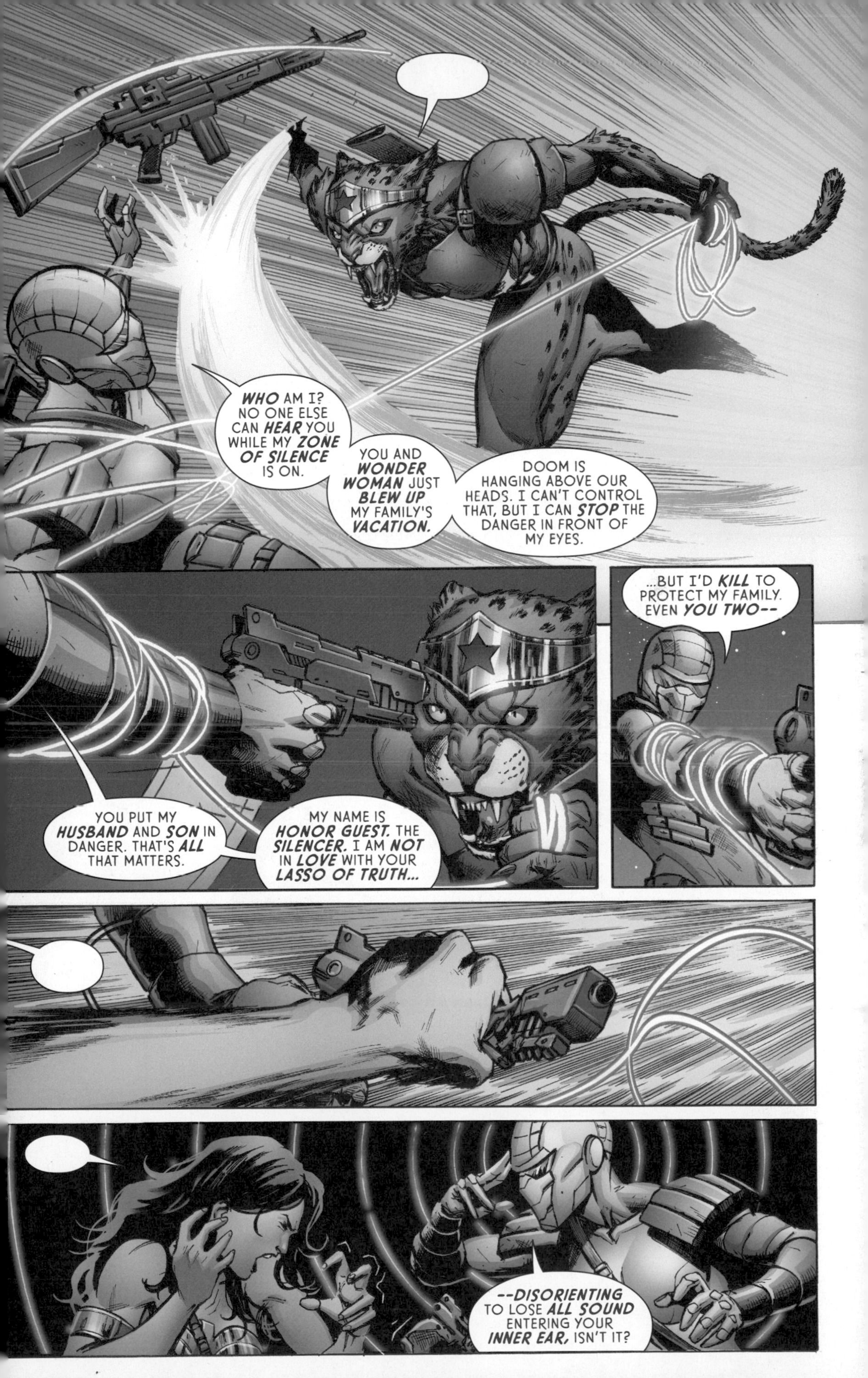
WHO AM I? NO ONE ELSE CAN HEAR YOU WHILE MY ZONE OF SILENCE IS ON.
YOU AND WONDER WOMAN JUST BLEW UP MY FAMILY'S VACATION.
DOOM IS HANGING ABOVE OUR HEADS. I CAN'T CONTROL THAT, BUT I CAN STOP THE DANGER IN FRONT OF MY EYES.
YOU PUT MY HUSBAND AND SON IN DANGER. THAT'S ALL THAT MATTERS.
MY NAME IS HONOR GUEST. THE SILENCER. I AM NOT IN LOVE WITH YOUR LASSO OF TRUTH...
...BUT I'D KILL TO PROTECT MY FAMILY. EVEN YOU TWO--
--DISORIENTING TO LOSE ALL SOUND ENTERING YOUR INNER EAR, ISN'T IT?

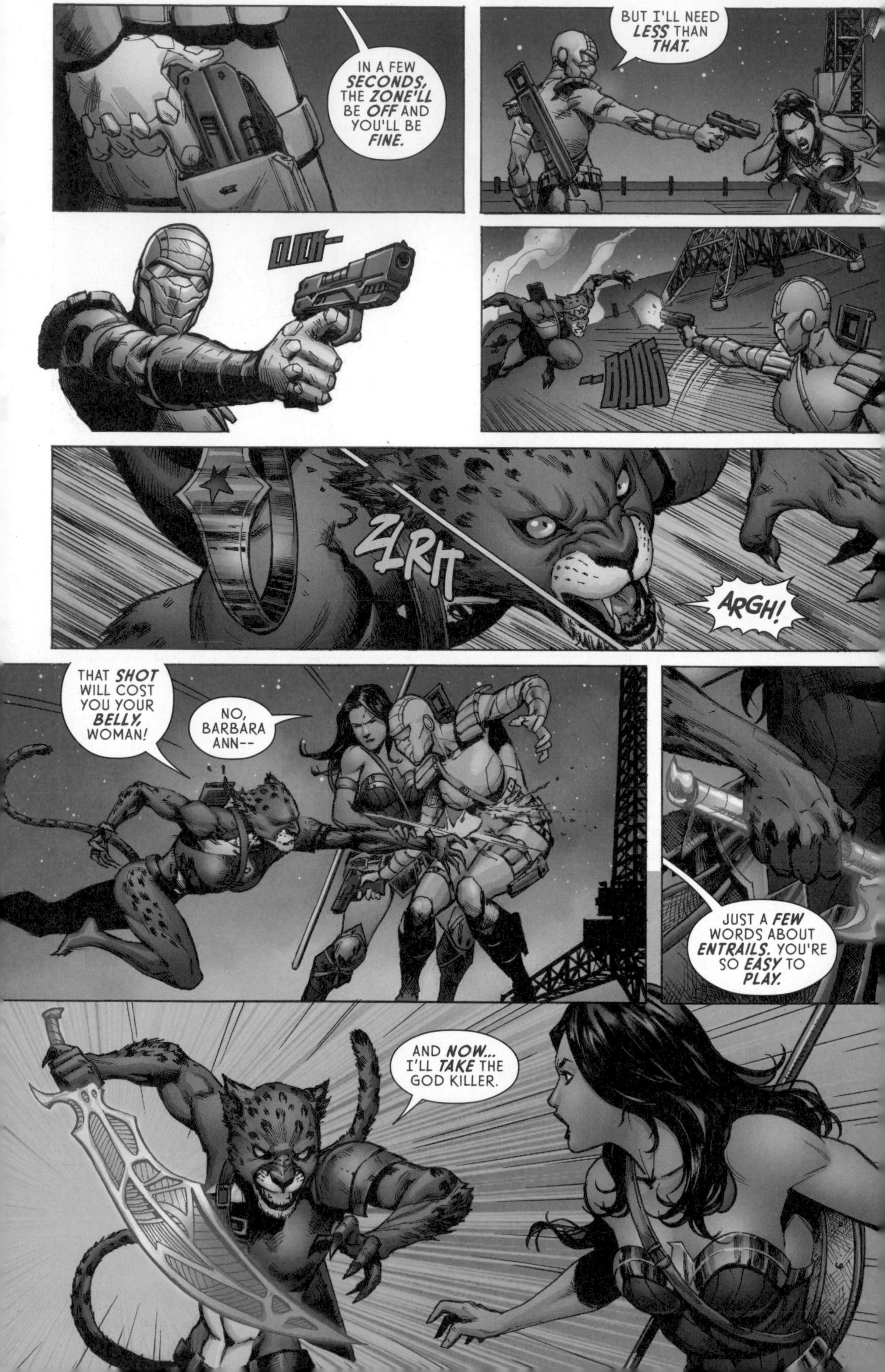
IN A FEW SECONDS, THE ZONE'LL BE OFF AND YOU'LL BE FINE.
BUT I'LL NEED LESS THAN THAT.
CLICK--
--BANG
ZZRIT
ARGH!
THAT SHOT WILL COST YOU YOUR BELLY, WOMAN!
NO, BARBARA ANN--
JUST A FEW WORDS ABOUT ENTRAILS. YOU'RE SO EASY TO PLAY.
AND NOW... I'LL TAKE THE GOD KILLER.

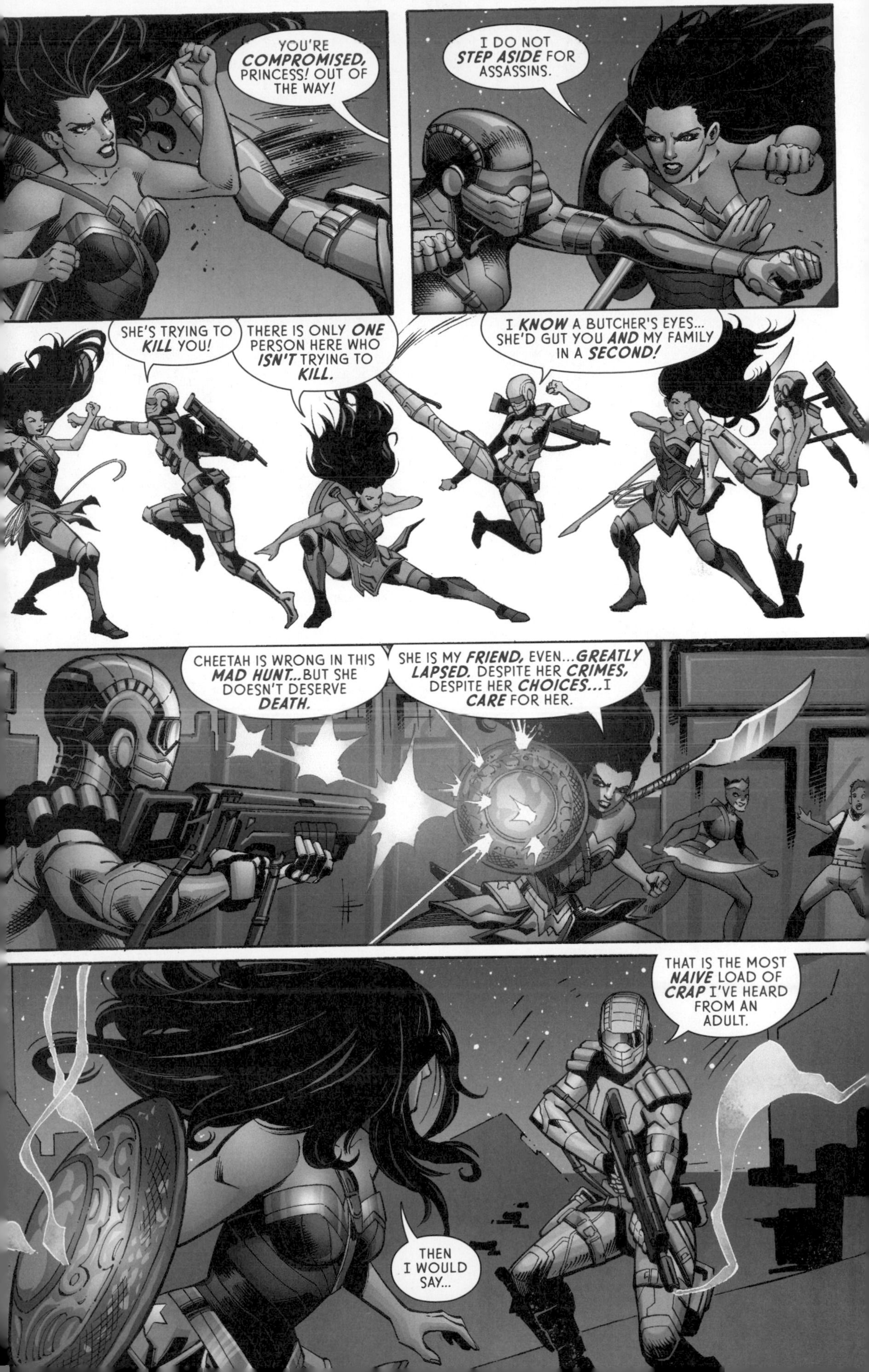
YOU'RE COMPROMISED, PRINCESS! OUT OF THE WAY!
I DO NOT STEP ASIDE FOR ASSASSINS.
SHE'S TRYING TO KILL YOU!
THERE IS ONLY ONE PERSON HERE WHO ISN'T TRYING TO KILL.
I KNOW A BUTCHER'S EYES... SHE'D GUT YOU AND MY FAMILY IN A SECOND!
CHEETAH IS WRONG IN THIS MAD HUNT...BUT SHE DOESN'T DESERVE DEATH.
SHE IS MY FRIEND, EVEN...GREATLY LAPSED. DESPITE HER CRIMES, DESPITE HER CHOICES...I CARE FOR HER.
THAT IS THE MOST NAIVE LOAD OF CRAP I'VE HEARD FROM AN ADULT.
THEN I WOULD SAY...

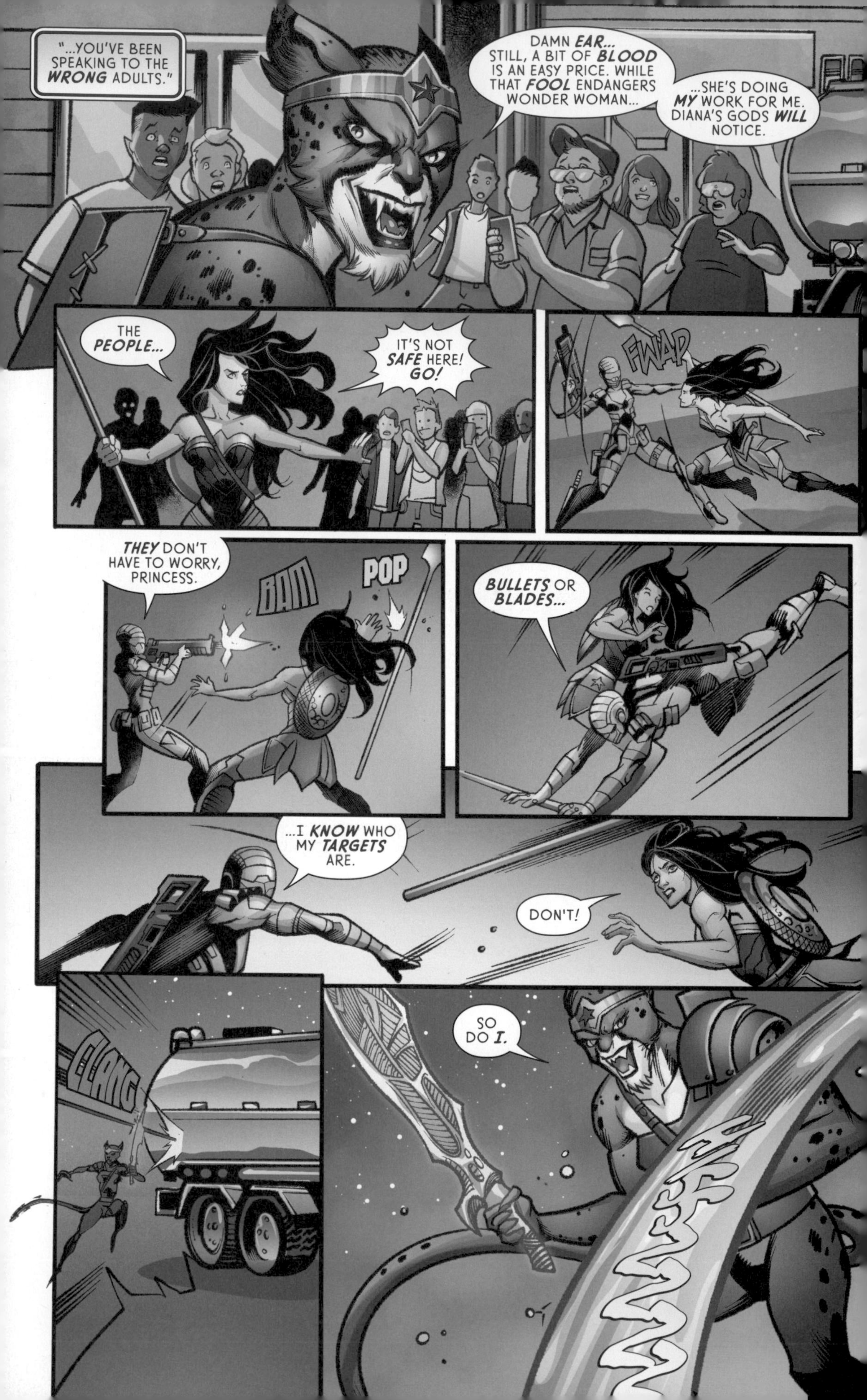
"...YOU'VE BEEN SPEAKING TO THE ***WRONG*** ADULTS."
DAMN ***EAR...*** STILL, A BIT OF ***BLOOD*** IS AN EASY PRICE. WHILE THAT ***FOOL*** ENDANGERS WONDER WOMAN...
...SHE'S DOING ***MY*** WORK FOR ME. DIANA'S GODS ***WILL*** NOTICE.
THE ***PEOPLE...***
IT'S NOT ***SAFE*** HERE! ***GO!***
FWAP
THEY DON'T HAVE TO WORRY, PRINCESS.
BAM
POP
BULLETS OR ***BLADES...***
...I ***KNOW*** WHO MY ***TARGETS*** ARE.
DON'T!
CLANG
SO DO ***I.***

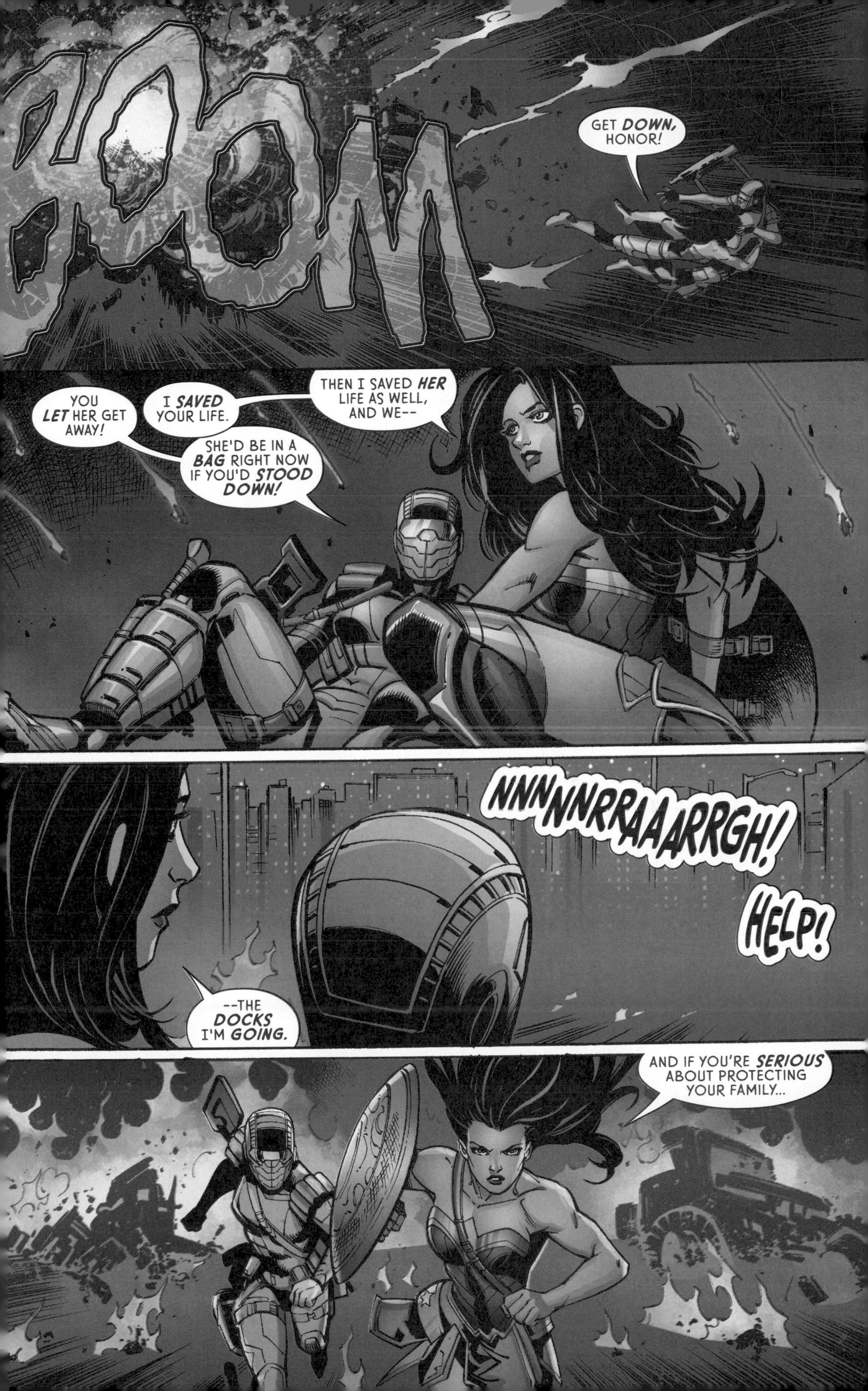
BOOM
GET DOWN, HONOR!
YOU LET HER GET AWAY!
I SAVED YOUR LIFE.
SHE'D BE IN A BAG RIGHT NOW IF YOU'D STOOD DOWN!
THEN I SAVED HER LIFE AS WELL, AND WE--
NNNNNRRAAARRGH!
HELP!
--THE DOCKS I'M GOING.
AND IF YOU'RE SERIOUS ABOUT PROTECTING YOUR FAMILY...

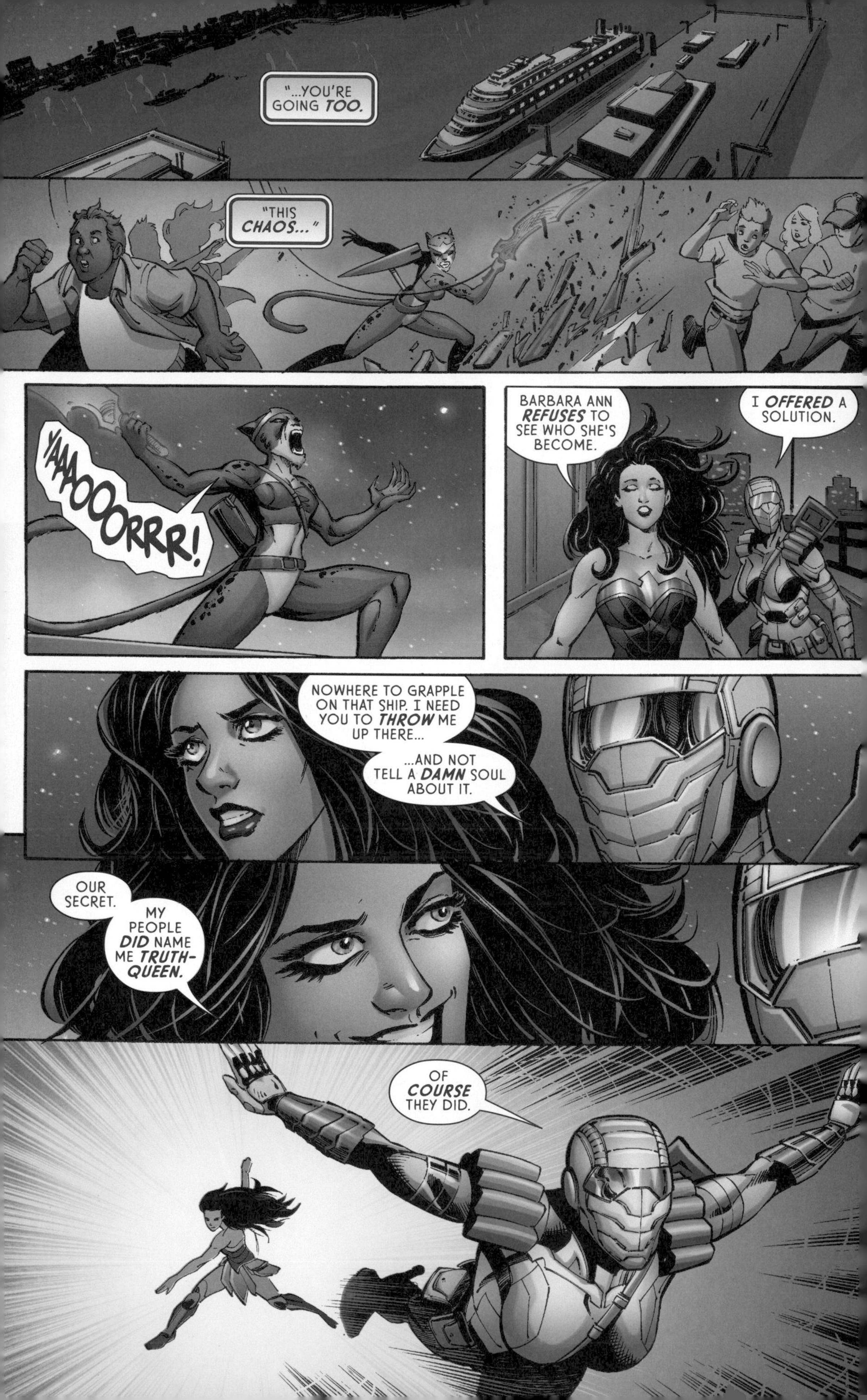
"...YOU'RE GOING TOO.
"THIS CHAOS..."
YAAAOOORRRR!
BARBARA ANN REFUSES TO SEE WHO SHE'S BECOME.
I OFFERED A SOLUTION.
NOWHERE TO GRAPPLE ON THAT SHIP. I NEED YOU TO THROW ME UP THERE...
...AND NOT TELL A DAMN SOUL ABOUT IT.
OUR SECRET.
MY PEOPLE DID NAME ME TRUTH-QUEEN.
OF COURSE THEY DID.

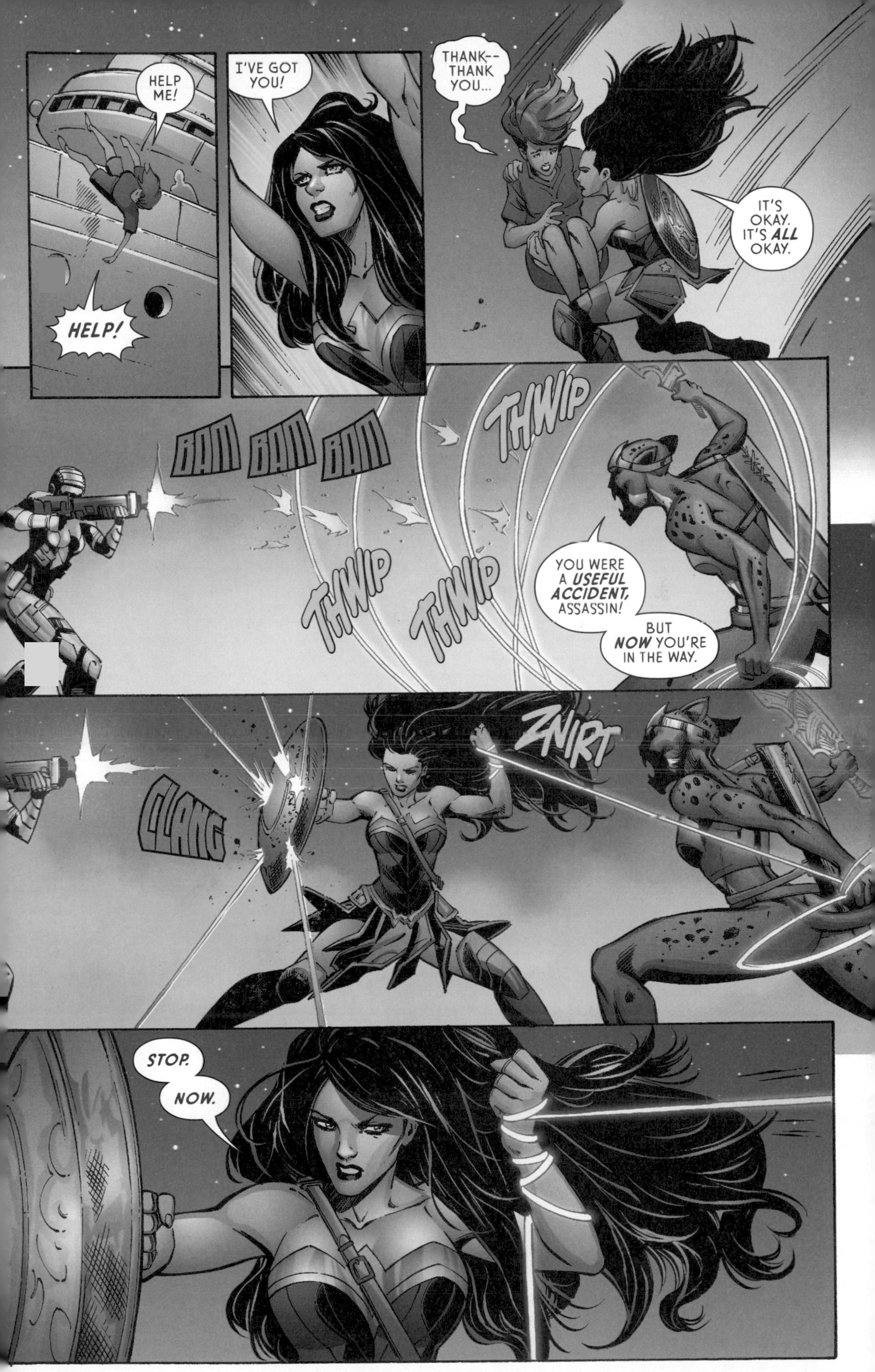
HELP ME!
HELP!
I'VE GOT YOU!
THANK--THANK YOU...
IT'S OKAY. IT'S ALL OKAY.
BAM BAM BAM
THWIP
THWIP
THWIP
YOU WERE A USEFUL ACCIDENT, ASSASSIN!
BUT NOW YOU'RE IN THE WAY.
CLANG
ZNIRT
STOP.
NOW.

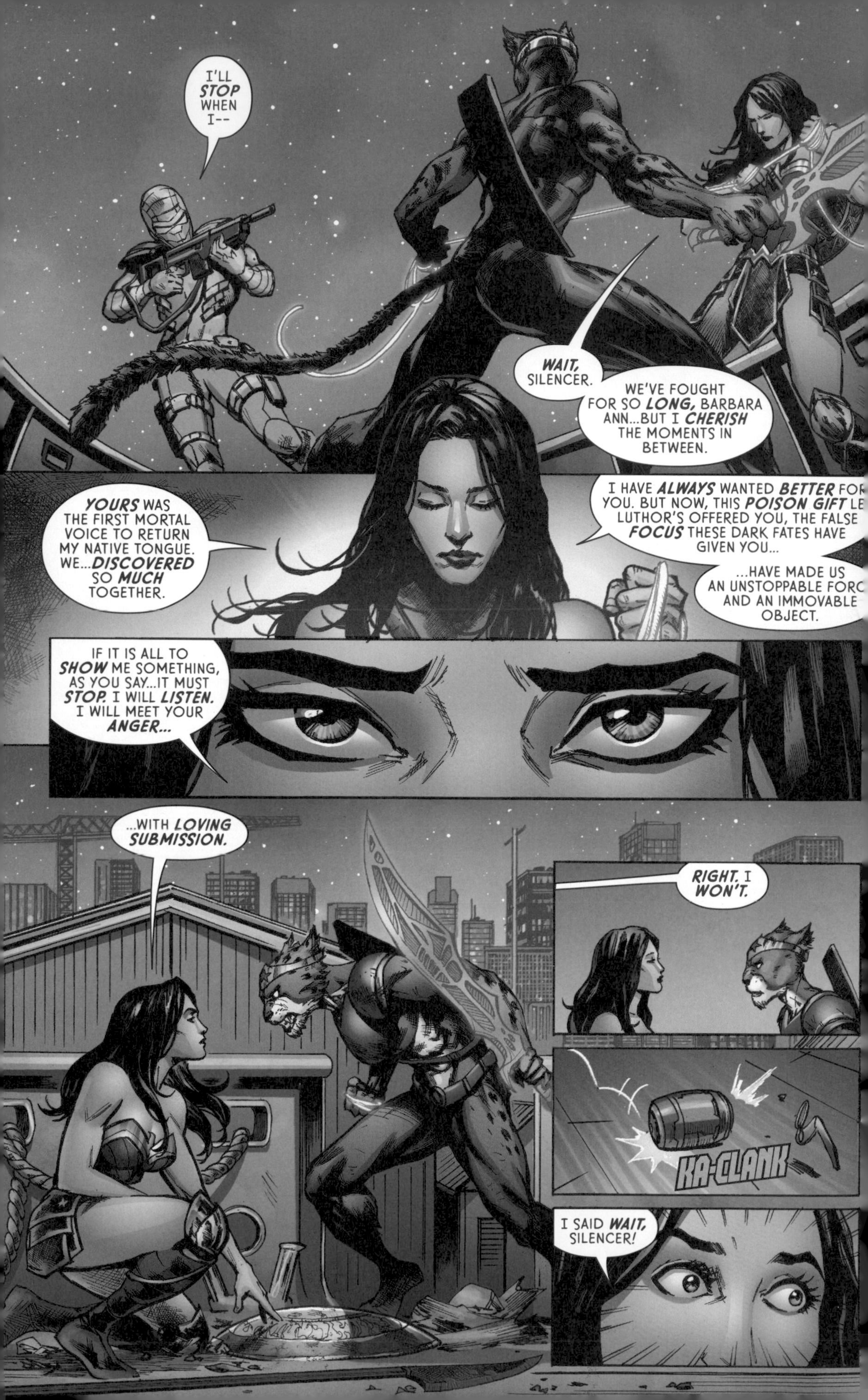
I'LL STOP WHEN I--
WAIT, SILENCER.
WE'VE FOUGHT FOR SO LONG, BARBARA ANN...BUT I CHERISH THE MOMENTS IN BETWEEN.
YOURS WAS THE FIRST MORTAL VOICE TO RETURN MY NATIVE TONGUE. WE...DISCOVERED SO MUCH TOGETHER.
I HAVE ALWAYS WANTED BETTER FOR YOU. BUT NOW, THIS POISON GIFT LE LUTHOR'S OFFERED YOU, THE FALSE FOCUS THESE DARK FATES HAVE GIVEN YOU...
...HAVE MADE US AN UNSTOPPABLE FORC AND AN IMMOVABLE OBJECT.
IF IT IS ALL TO SHOW ME SOMETHING, AS YOU SAY...IT MUST STOP. I WILL LISTEN. I WILL MEET YOUR ANGER...
...WITH LOVING SUBMISSION.
RIGHT. I WON'T.
KA-CLANK
I SAID WAIT, SILENCER!

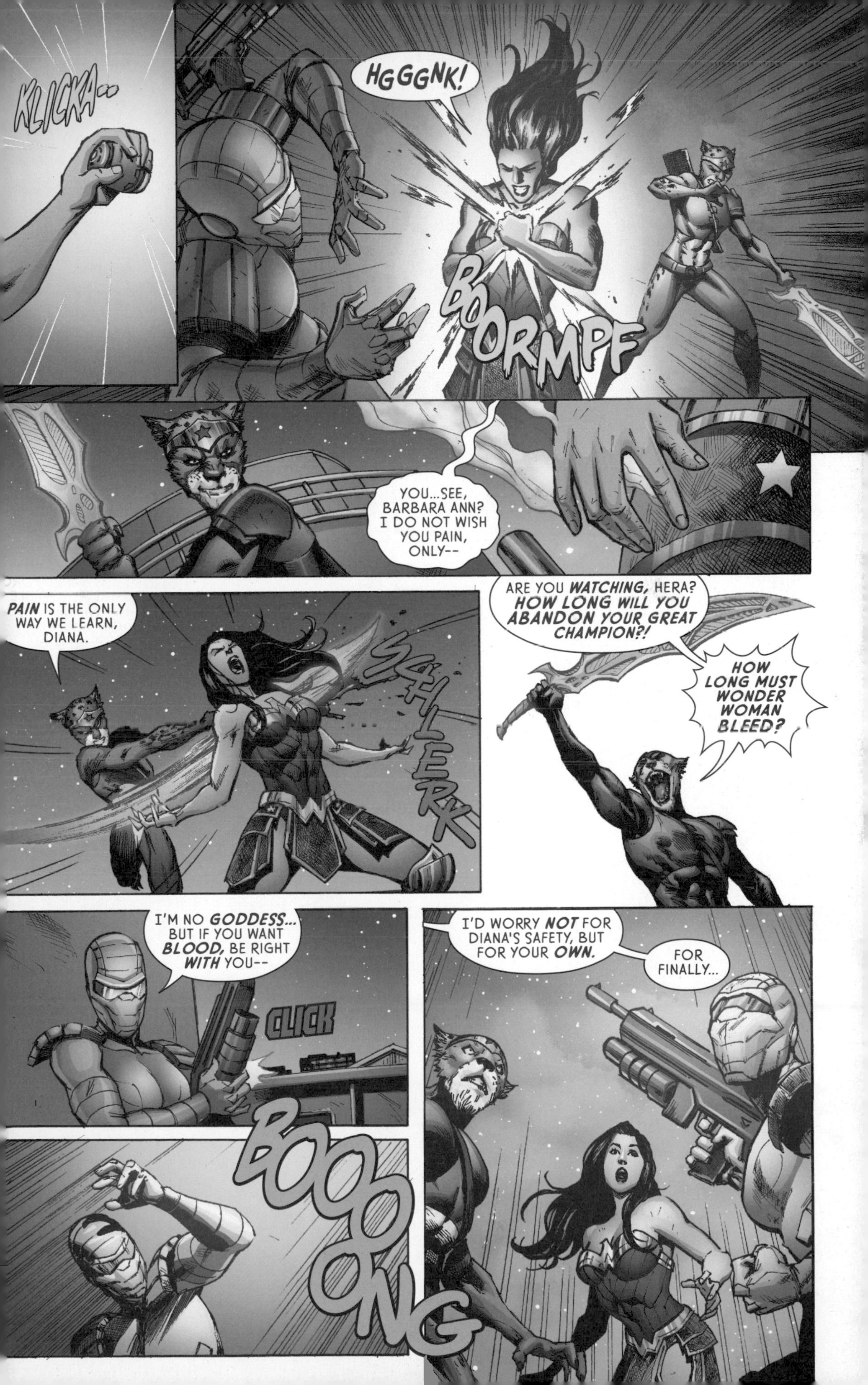
KLICKA--
HGGGNK!
BOORMPF
YOU...SEE, BARBARA ANN? I DO NOT WISH YOU PAIN, ONLY--
PAIN IS THE ONLY WAY WE LEARN, DIANA.
SCHLERK
ARE YOU WATCHING, HERA? HOW LONG WILL YOU ABANDON YOUR GREAT CHAMPION?!
HOW LONG MUST WONDER WOMAN BLEED?
I'M NO GODDESS... BUT IF YOU WANT BLOOD, BE RIGHT WITH YOU--
CLICK
BOOOOONG
I'D WORRY NOT FOR DIANA'S SAFETY, BUT FOR YOUR OWN.
FOR FINALLY...

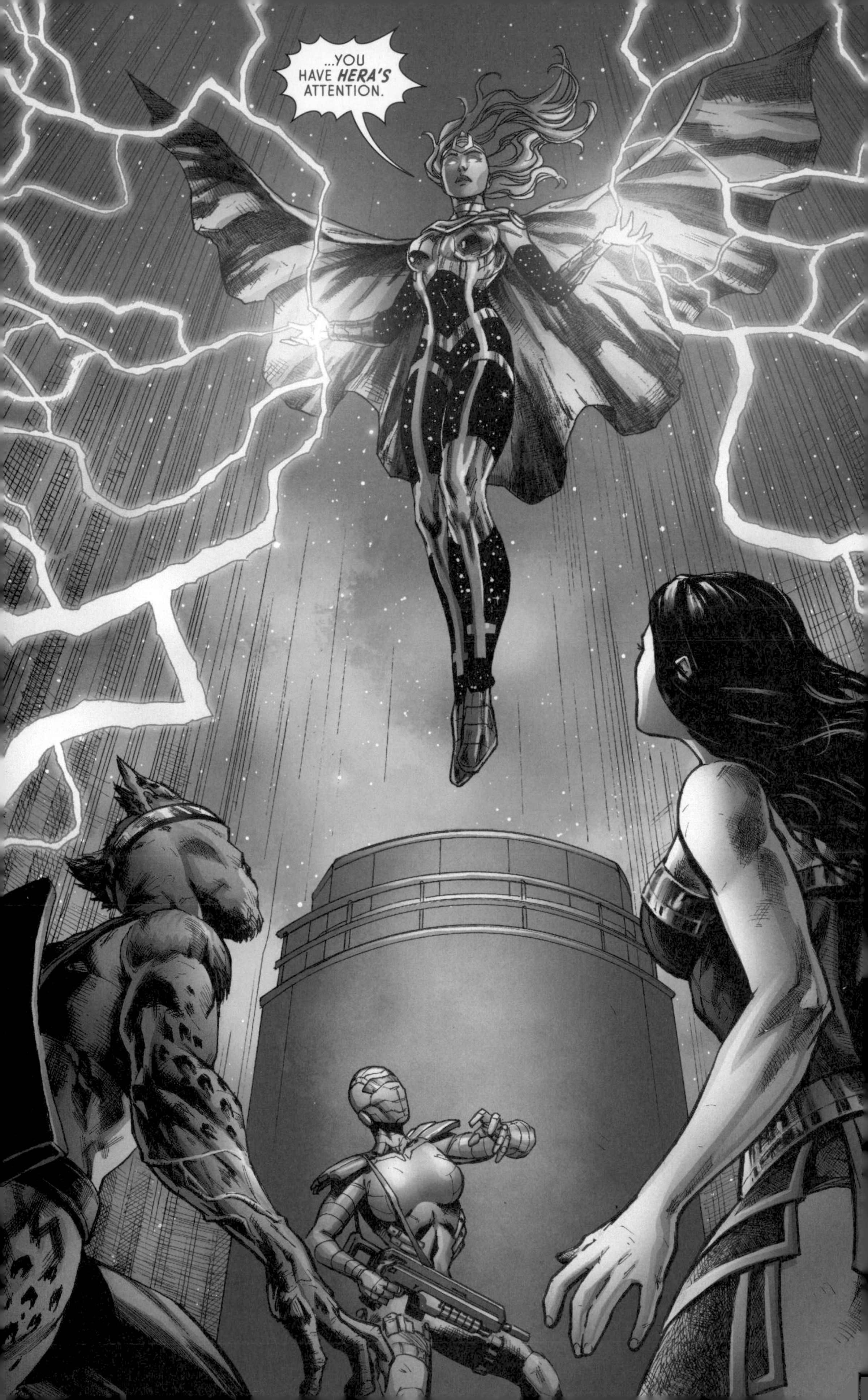
...YOU HAVE HERA'S ATTENTION.

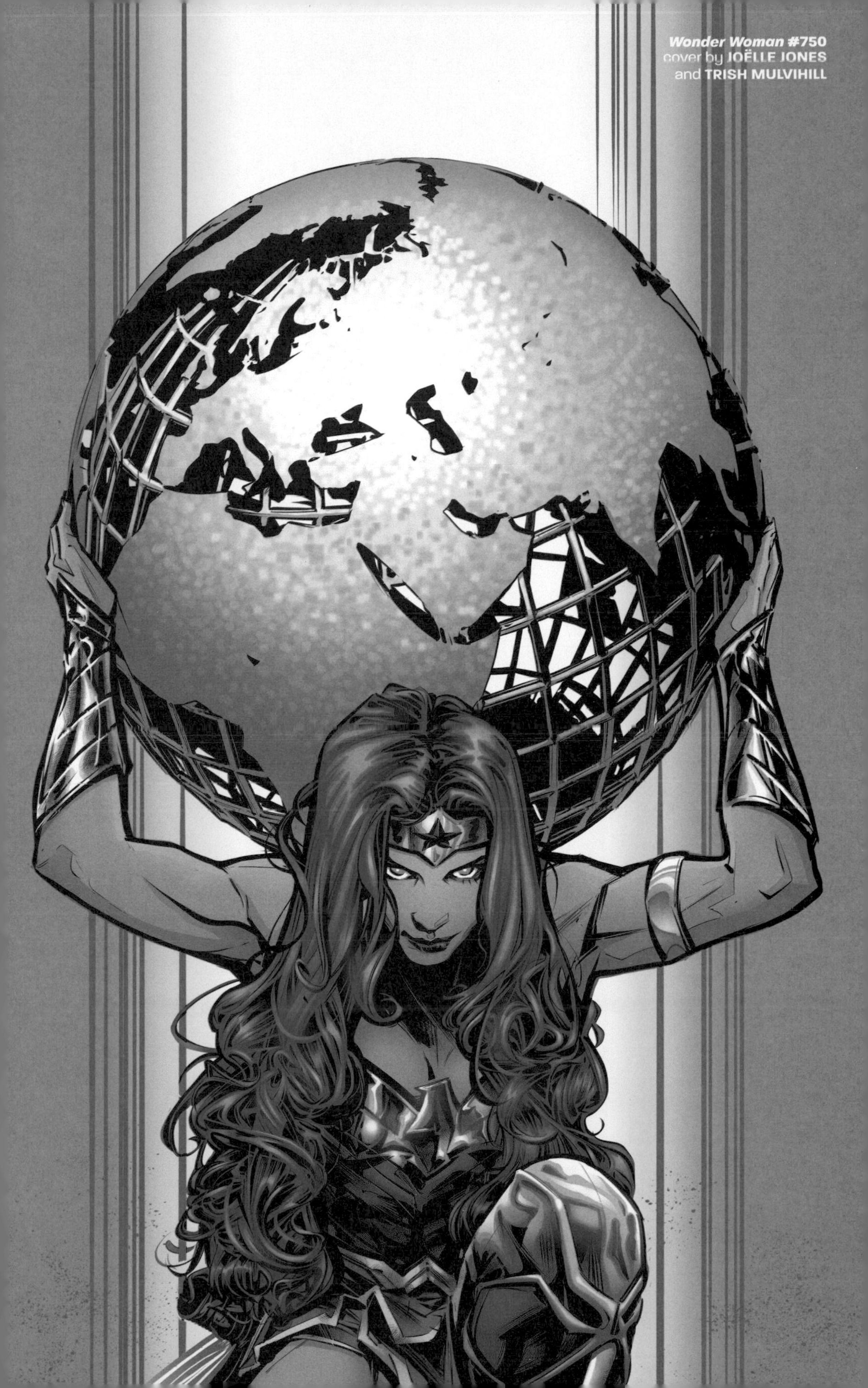

***Wonder Woman* #750**
cover by **JOËLLE JONES**
and **TRISH MULVIHILL**

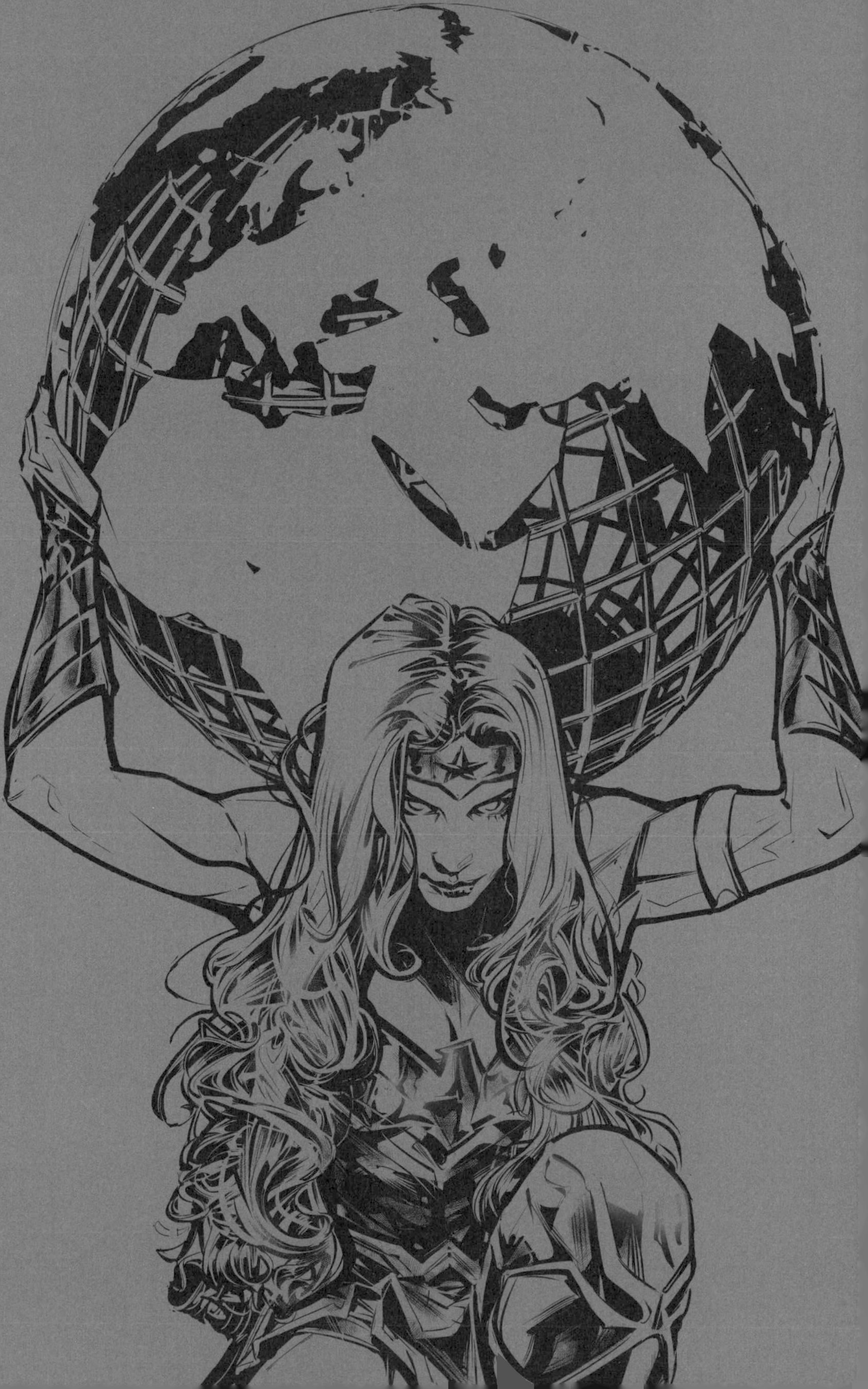

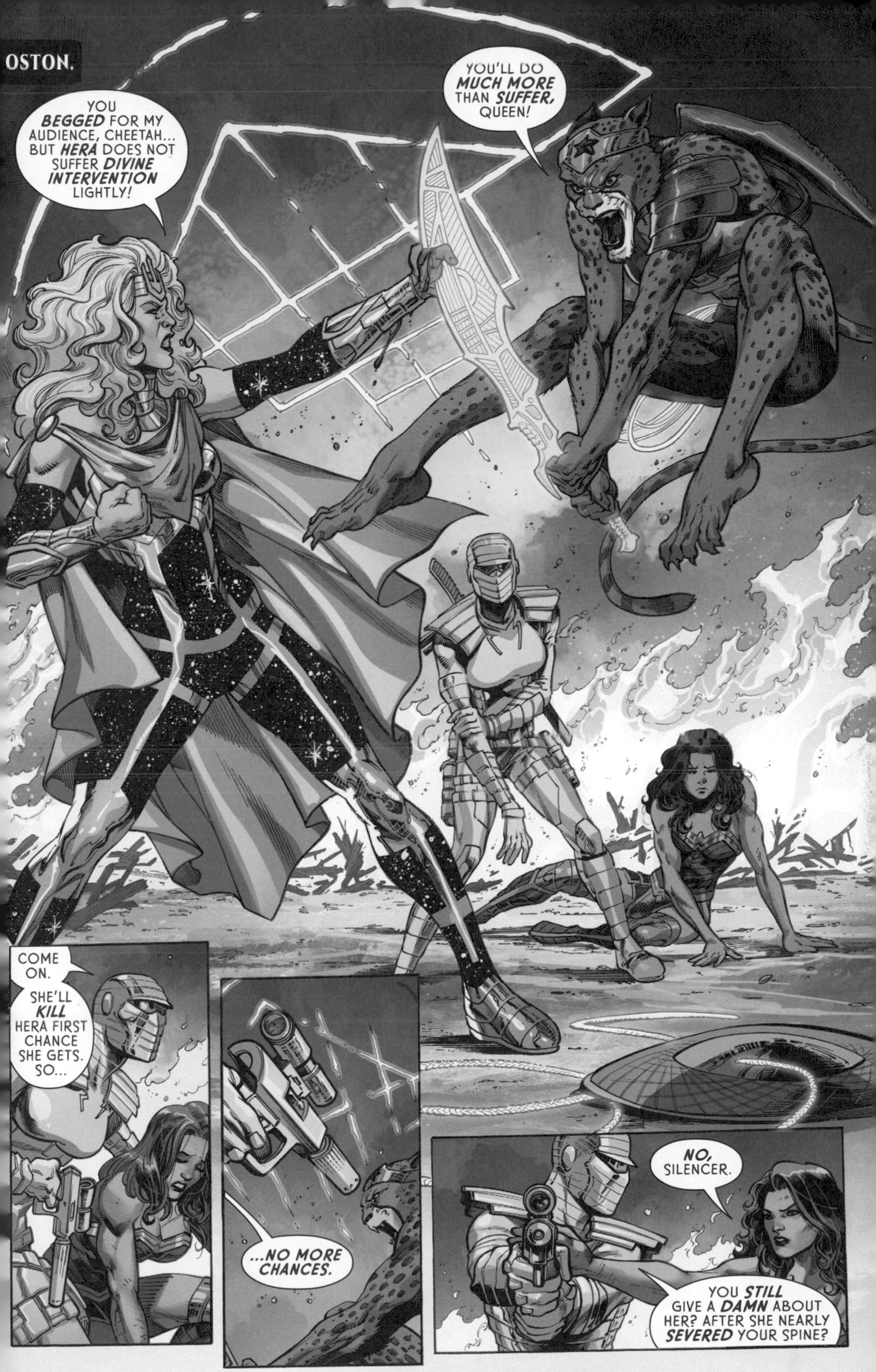
OSTON.
YOU BEGGED FOR MY AUDIENCE, CHEETAH... BUT HERA DOES NOT SUFFER DIVINE INTERVENTION LIGHTLY!
YOU'LL DO MUCH MORE THAN SUFFER, QUEEN!
COME ON.
SHE'LL KILL HERA FIRST CHANCE SHE GETS. SO...
...NO MORE CHANCES.
NO, SILENCER.
YOU STILL GIVE A DAMN ABOUT HER? AFTER SHE NEARLY SEVERED YOUR SPINE?

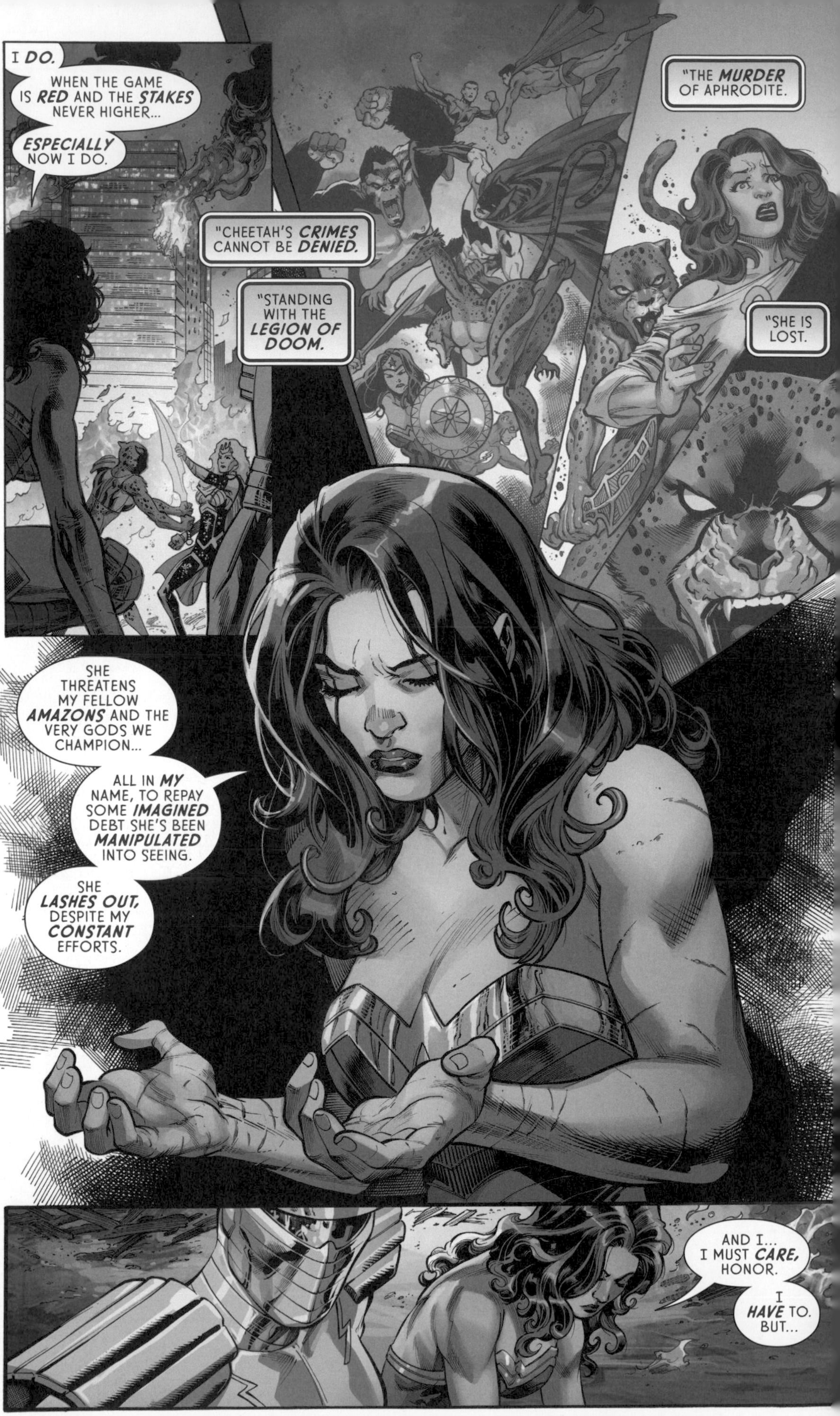
I DO.
WHEN THE GAME IS RED AND THE STAKES NEVER HIGHER...
ESPECIALLY NOW I DO.
"CHEETAH'S CRIMES CANNOT BE DENIED.
"STANDING WITH THE LEGION OF DOOM.
"THE MURDER OF APHRODITE.
"SHE IS LOST.
SHE THREATENS MY FELLOW AMAZONS AND THE VERY GODS WE CHAMPION...
ALL IN MY NAME, TO REPAY SOME IMAGINED DEBT SHE'S BEEN MANIPULATED INTO SEEING.
SHE LASHES OUT, DESPITE MY CONSTANT EFFORTS.
AND I... I MUST CARE, HONOR.
I HAVE TO. BUT...

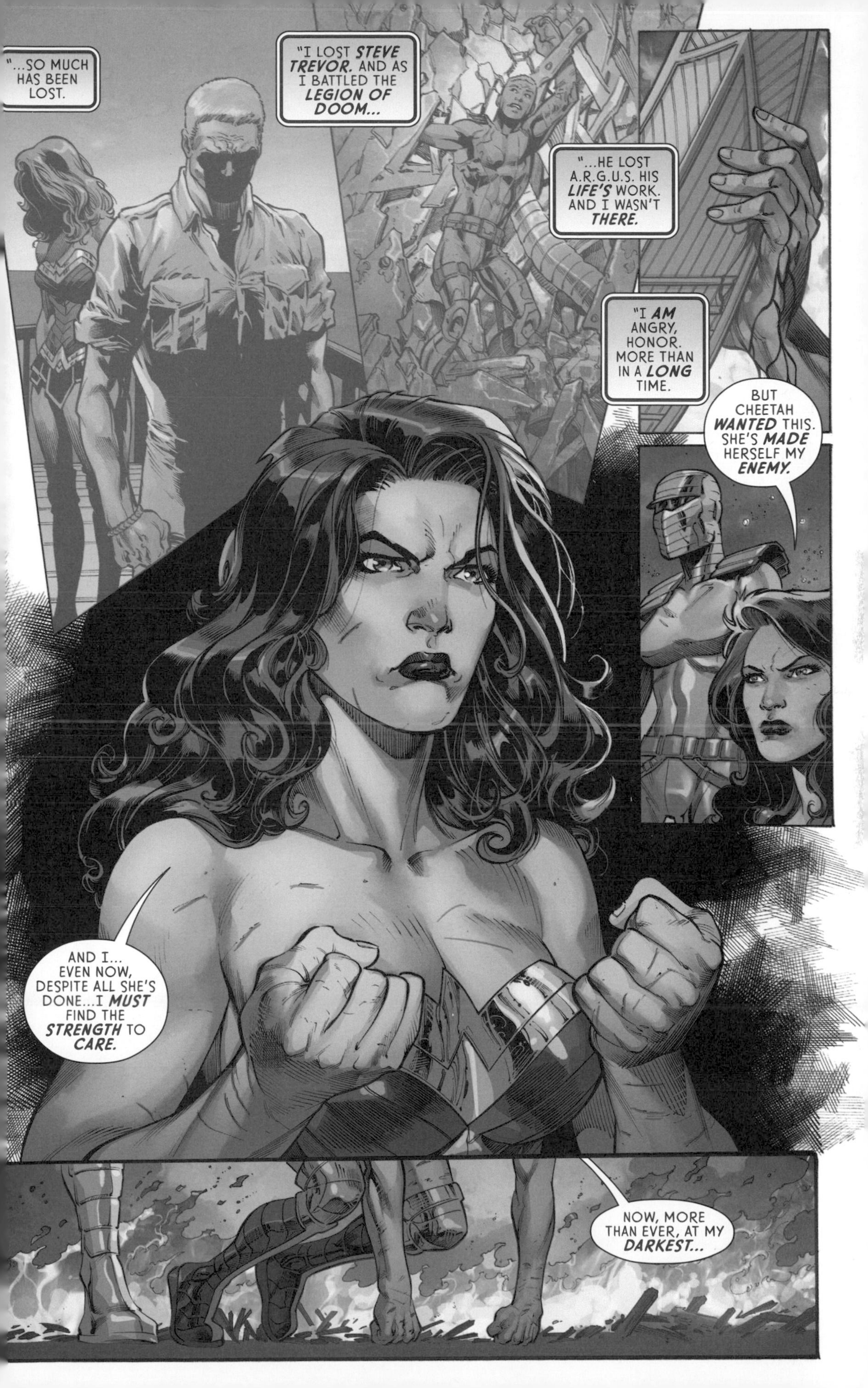
"...SO MUCH HAS BEEN LOST.
"I LOST STEVE TREVOR. AND AS I BATTLED THE LEGION OF DOOM...
"...HE LOST A.R.G.U.S. HIS LIFE'S WORK. AND I WASN'T THERE.
"I AM ANGRY, HONOR. MORE THAN IN A LONG TIME.
BUT CHEETAH WANTED THIS. SHE'S MADE HERSELF MY ENEMY.
AND I... EVEN NOW, DESPITE ALL SHE'S DONE...I MUST FIND THE STRENGTH TO CARE.
NOW, MORE THAN EVER, AT MY DARKEST...

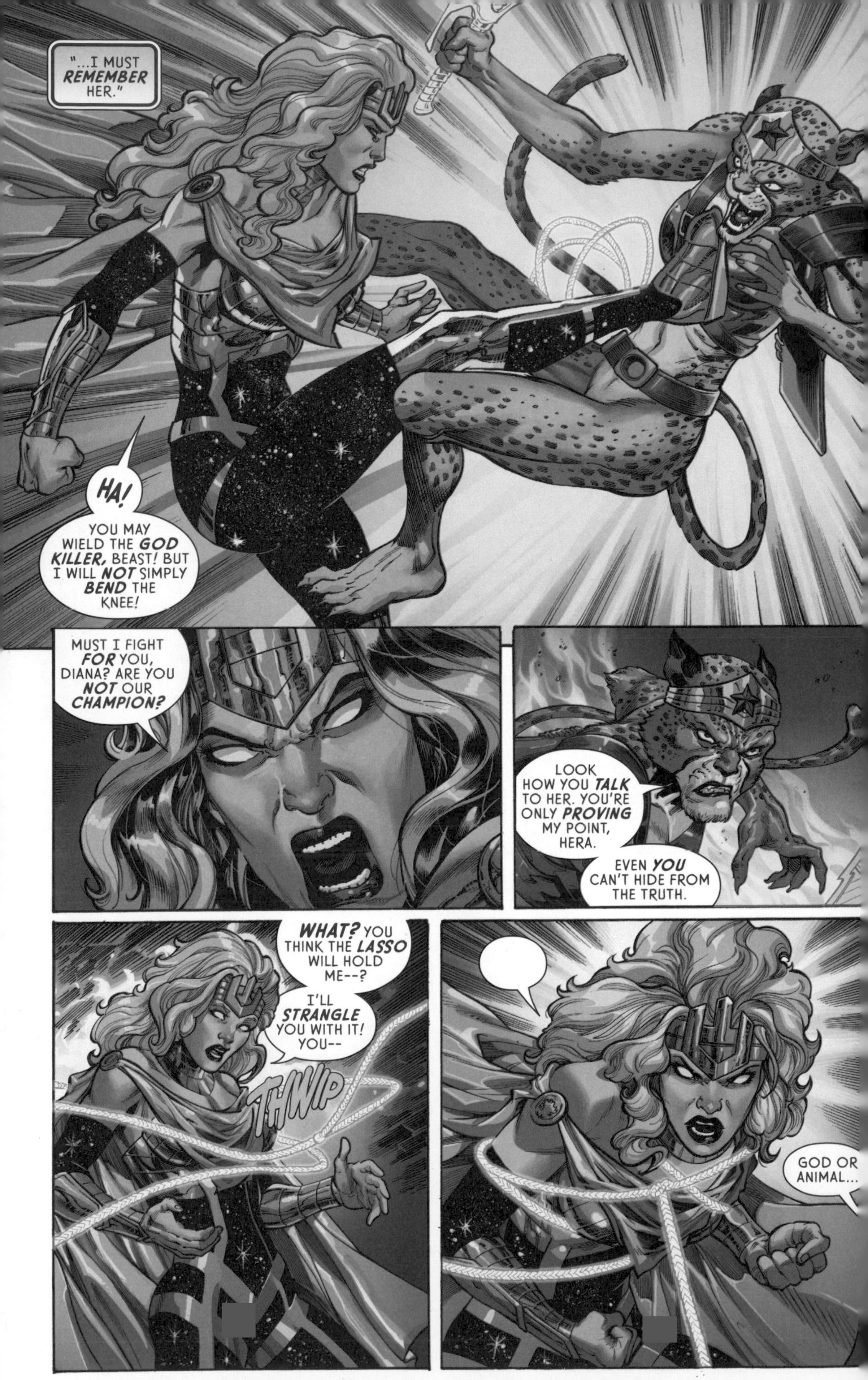
"...I MUST REMEMBER HER."
HA!
YOU MAY WIELD THE GOD KILLER, BEAST! BUT I WILL NOT SIMPLY BEND THE KNEE!
MUST I FIGHT FOR YOU, DIANA? ARE YOU NOT OUR CHAMPION?
LOOK HOW YOU TALK TO HER. YOU'RE ONLY PROVING MY POINT, HERA.
EVEN YOU CAN'T HIDE FROM THE TRUTH.
WHAT? YOU THINK THE LASSO WILL HOLD ME--?
I'LL STRANGLE YOU WITH IT! YOU--
THWIP
GOD OR ANIMAL...

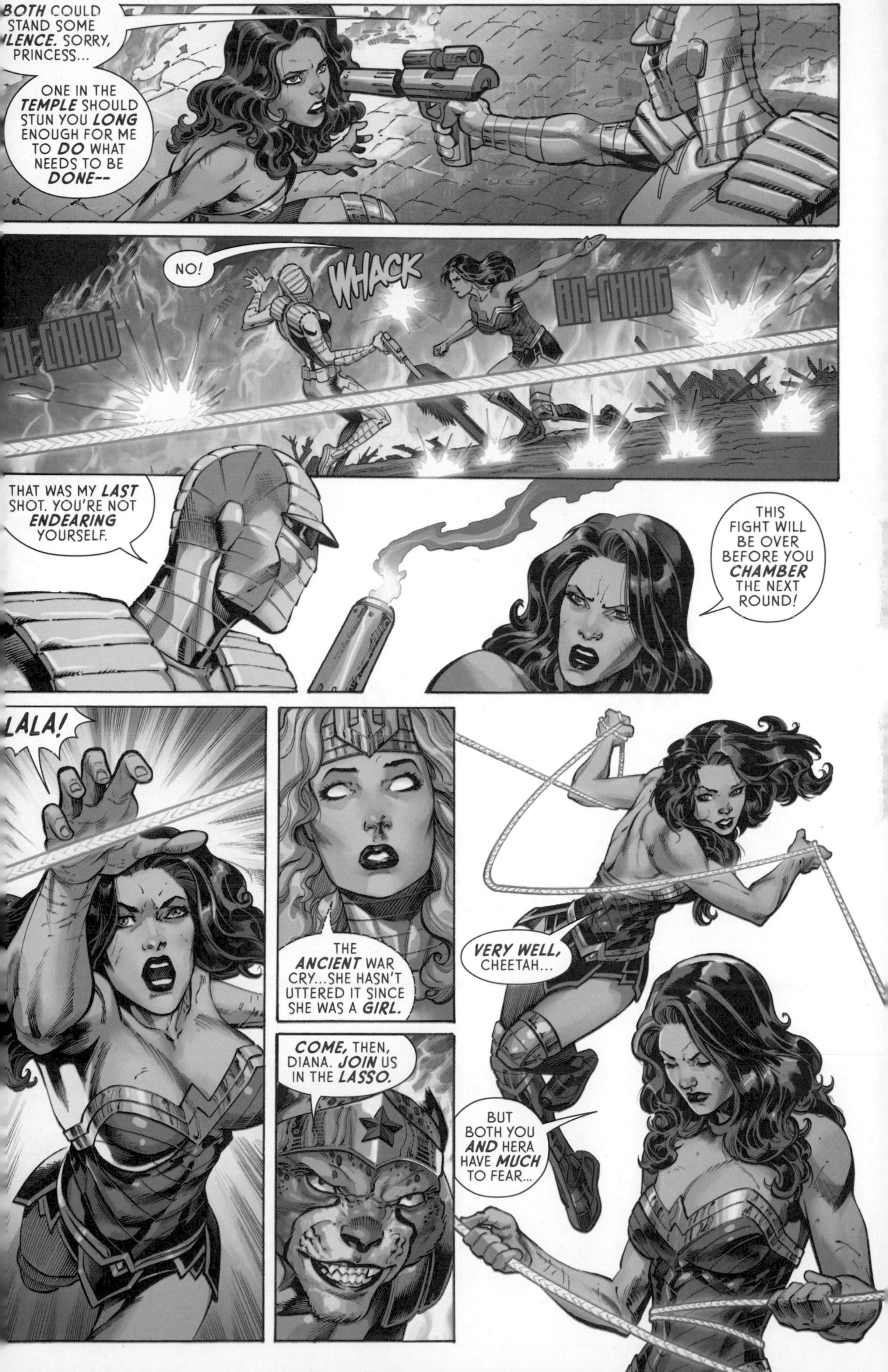

BOTH COULD STAND SOME ILENCE. SORRY, PRINCESS...
ONE IN THE TEMPLE SHOULD STUN YOU LONG ENOUGH FOR ME TO DO WHAT NEEDS TO BE DONE--
NO!
WHACK
BA-CHANG
BA-CHANG
THAT WAS MY LAST SHOT. YOU'RE NOT ENDEARING YOURSELF.
THIS FIGHT WILL BE OVER BEFORE YOU CHAMBER THE NEXT ROUND!
LALA!
THE ANCIENT WAR CRY...SHE HASN'T UTTERED IT SINCE SHE WAS A GIRL.
COME, THEN, DIANA. JOIN US IN THE LASSO.
VERY WELL, CHEETAH...
BUT BOTH YOU AND HERA HAVE MUCH TO FEAR...

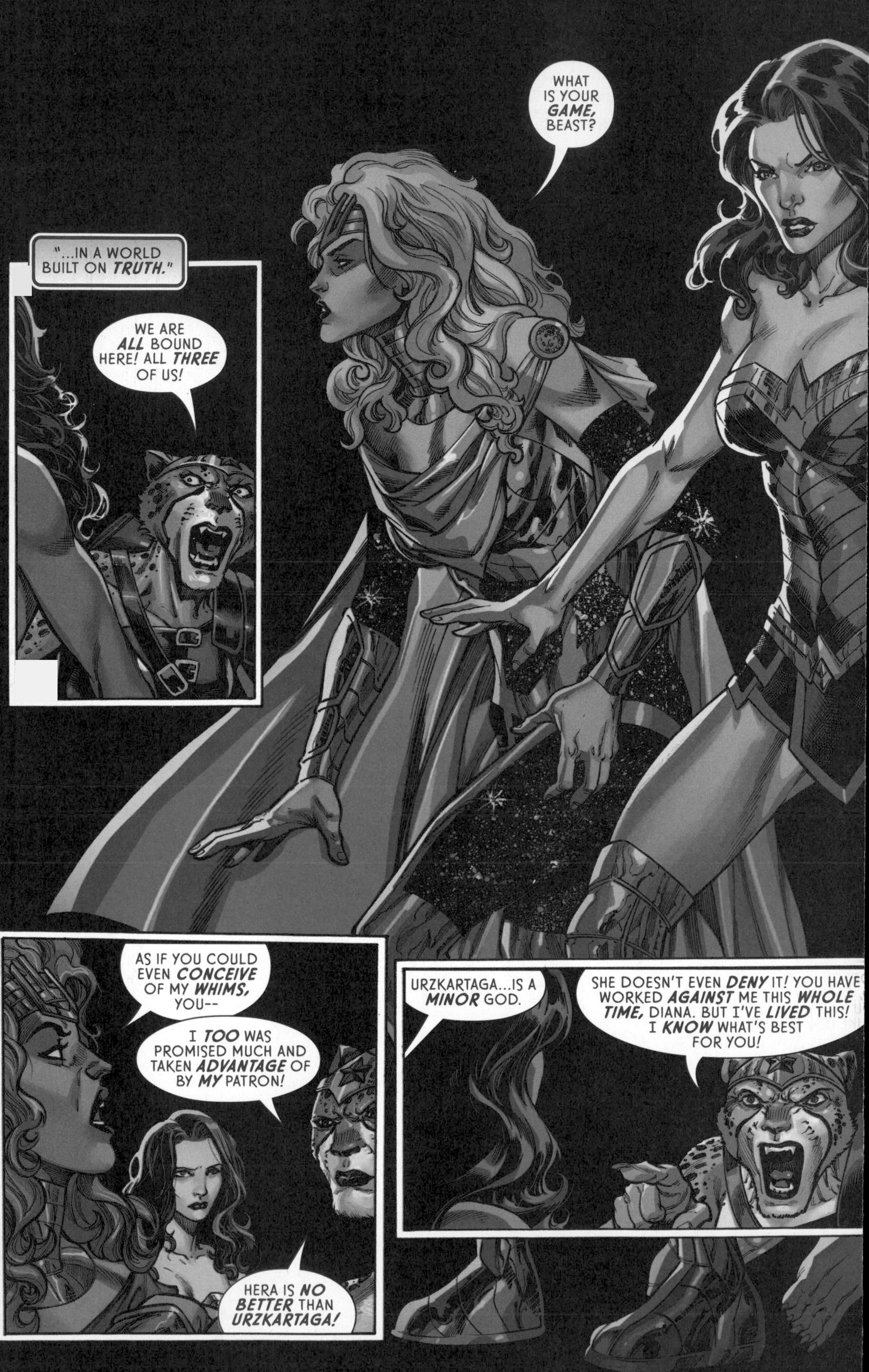
WHAT IS YOUR *GAME,* BEAST?
"...IN A WORLD BUILT ON *TRUTH.*"
WE ARE *ALL* BOUND HERE! ALL *THREE* OF US!
AS IF YOU COULD EVEN *CONCEIVE* OF MY *WHIMS,* YOU--
I *TOO* WAS PROMISED MUCH AND TAKEN *ADVANTAGE* OF BY *MY* PATRON!
HERA IS *NO BETTER* THAN *URZKARTAGA!*
URZKARTAGA...IS A *MINOR* GOD.
SHE DOESN'T EVEN *DENY* IT! YOU HAVE WORKED *AGAINST* ME THIS *WHOLE TIME,* DIANA. BUT I'VE *LIVED* THIS! I *KNOW* WHAT'S BEST FOR YOU!

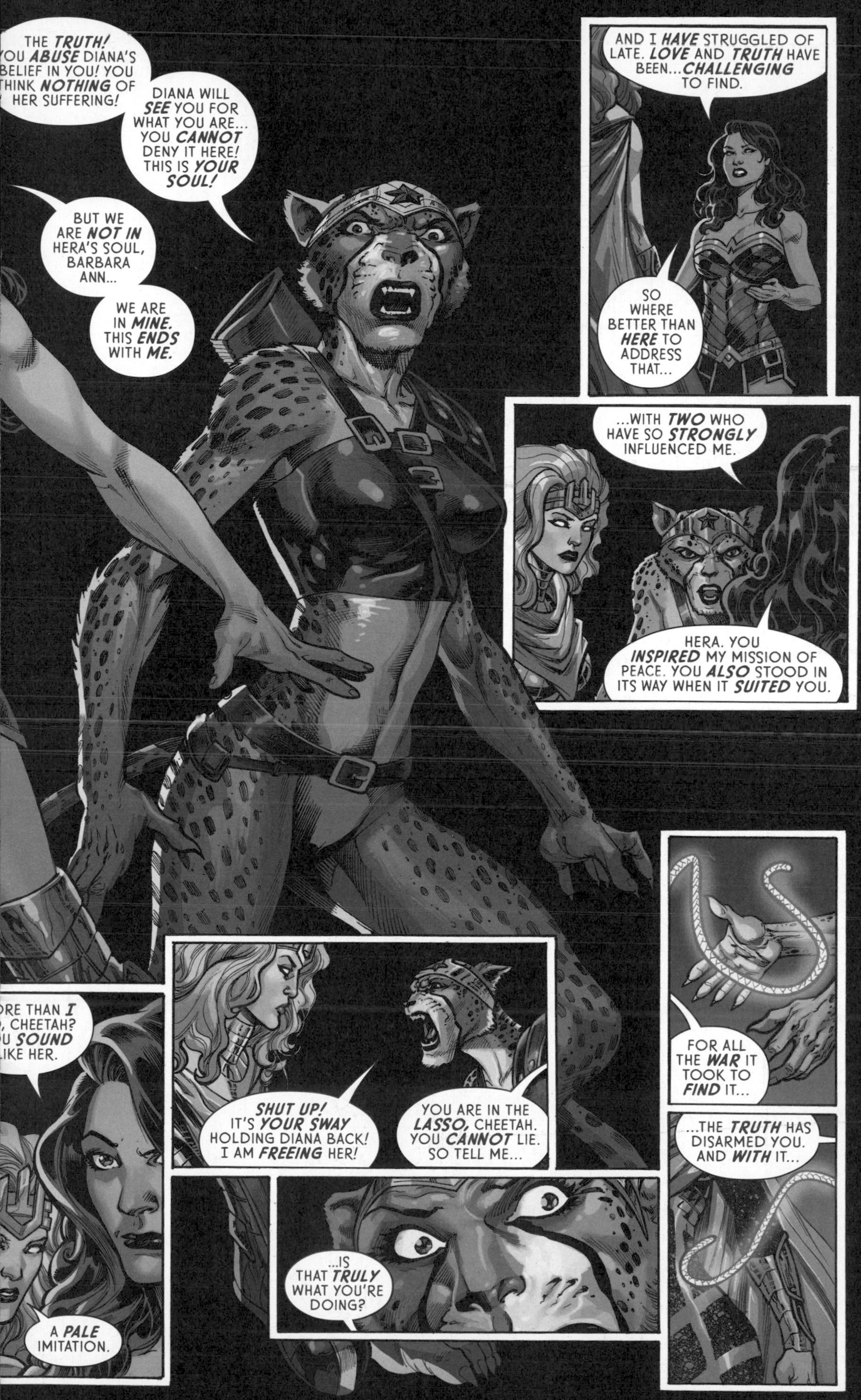

THE TRUTH! YOU ABUSE DIANA'S BELIEF IN YOU! YOU THINK NOTHING OF HER SUFFERING!
DIANA WILL SEE YOU FOR WHAT YOU ARE... YOU CANNOT DENY IT HERE! THIS IS YOUR SOUL!
BUT WE ARE NOT IN HERA'S SOUL, BARBARA ANN...
WE ARE IN MINE. THIS ENDS WITH ME.
AND I HAVE STRUGGLED OF LATE. LOVE AND TRUTH HAVE BEEN...CHALLENGING TO FIND.
SO WHERE BETTER THAN HERE TO ADDRESS THAT...
...WITH TWO WHO HAVE SO STRONGLY INFLUENCED ME.
HERA. YOU INSPIRED MY MISSION OF PEACE. YOU ALSO STOOD IN ITS WAY WHEN IT SUITED YOU.
SHUT UP! IT'S YOUR SWAY HOLDING DIANA BACK! I AM FREEING HER!
YOU ARE IN THE LASSO, CHEETAH. YOU CANNOT LIE. SO TELL ME...
...IS THAT TRULY WHAT YOU'RE DOING?
FOR ALL THE WAR IT TOOK TO FIND IT...
...THE TRUTH HAS DISARMED YOU. AND WITH IT...
A PALE IMITATION.

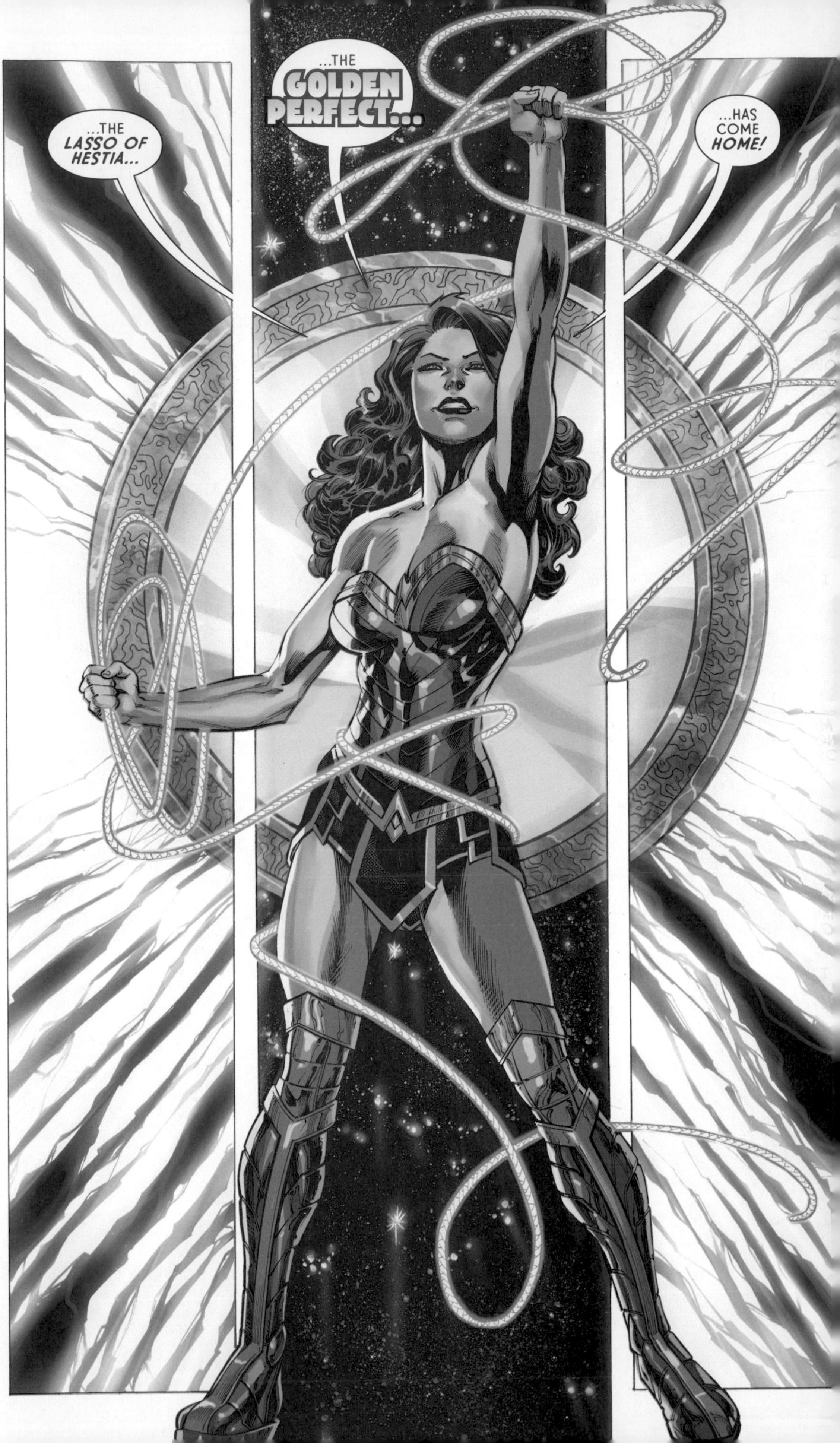
...THE LASSO OF HESTIA...
...THE GOLDEN PERFECT...
...HAS COME HOME!

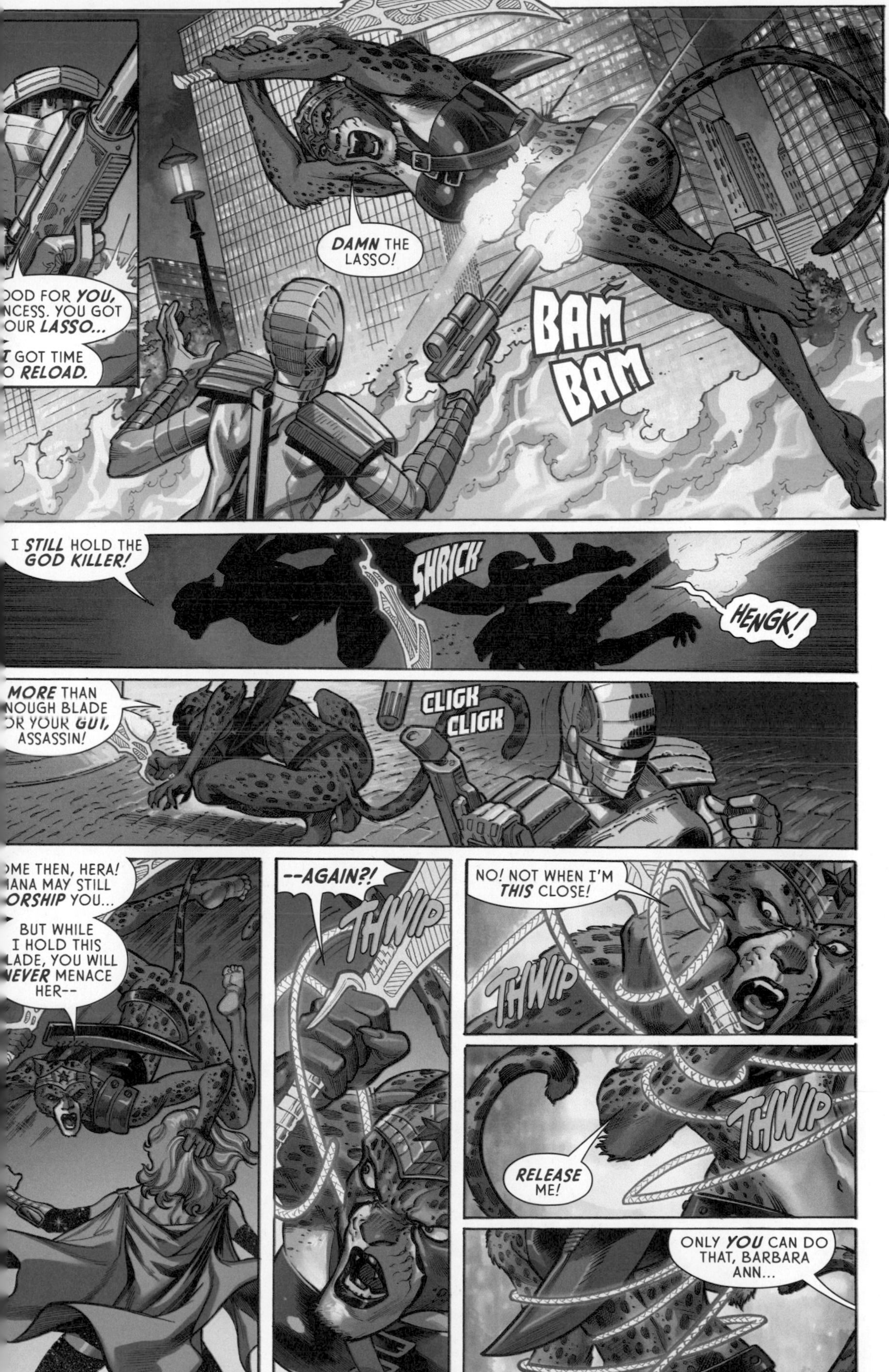
DAMN THE LASSO!
OOD FOR YOU, NCESS. YOU GOT OUR LASSO...
T GOT TIME O RELOAD.
BAM BAM
I STILL HOLD THE GOD KILLER!
SHRICK
HENGK!
MORE THAN NOUGH BLADE OR YOUR GUI, ASSASSIN!
CLICK CLICK
OME THEN, HERA! IANA MAY STILL ORSHIP YOU...
BUT WHILE I HOLD THIS LADE, YOU WILL NEVER MENACE HER--
--AGAIN?!
THWIP
NO! NOT WHEN I'M THIS CLOSE!
THWIP
THWIP
RELEASE ME!
ONLY YOU CAN DO THAT, BARBARA ANN...

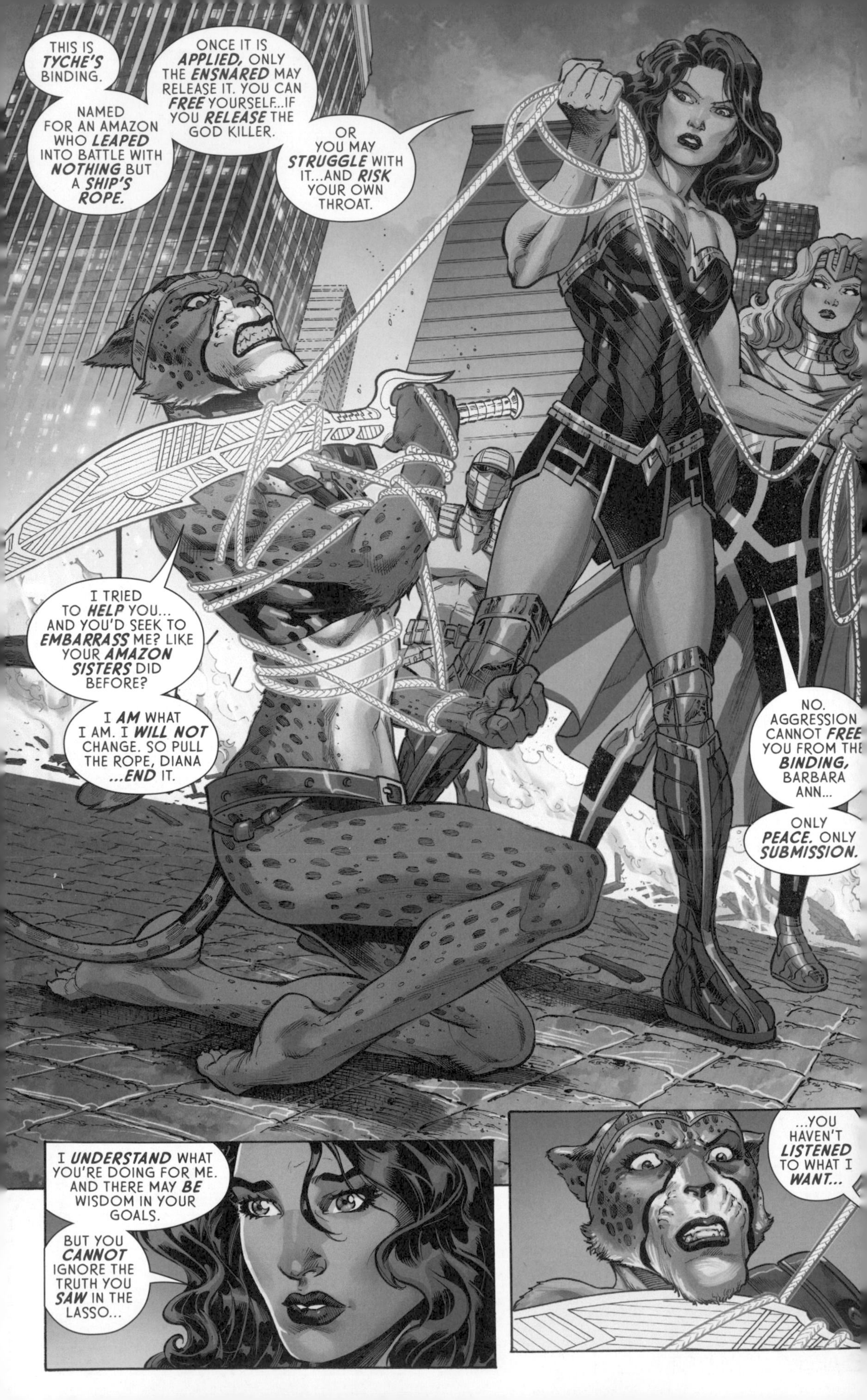
THIS IS TYCHE'S BINDING.
NAMED FOR AN AMAZON WHO LEAPED INTO BATTLE WITH NOTHING BUT A SHIP'S ROPE.
ONCE IT IS APPLIED, ONLY THE ENSNARED MAY RELEASE IT. YOU CAN FREE YOURSELF...IF YOU RELEASE THE GOD KILLER.
OR YOU MAY STRUGGLE WITH IT...AND RISK YOUR OWN THROAT.
I TRIED TO HELP YOU... AND YOU'D SEEK TO EMBARRASS ME? LIKE YOUR AMAZON SISTERS DID BEFORE?
I AM WHAT I AM. I WILL NOT CHANGE. SO PULL THE ROPE, DIANA ...END IT.
NO. AGGRESSION CANNOT FREE YOU FROM THE BINDING, BARBARA ANN...
ONLY PEACE. ONLY SUBMISSION.
I UNDERSTAND WHAT YOU'RE DOING FOR ME. AND THERE MAY BE WISDOM IN YOUR GOALS.
BUT YOU CANNOT IGNORE THE TRUTH YOU SAW IN THE LASSO...
...YOU HAVEN'T LISTENED TO WHAT I WANT...

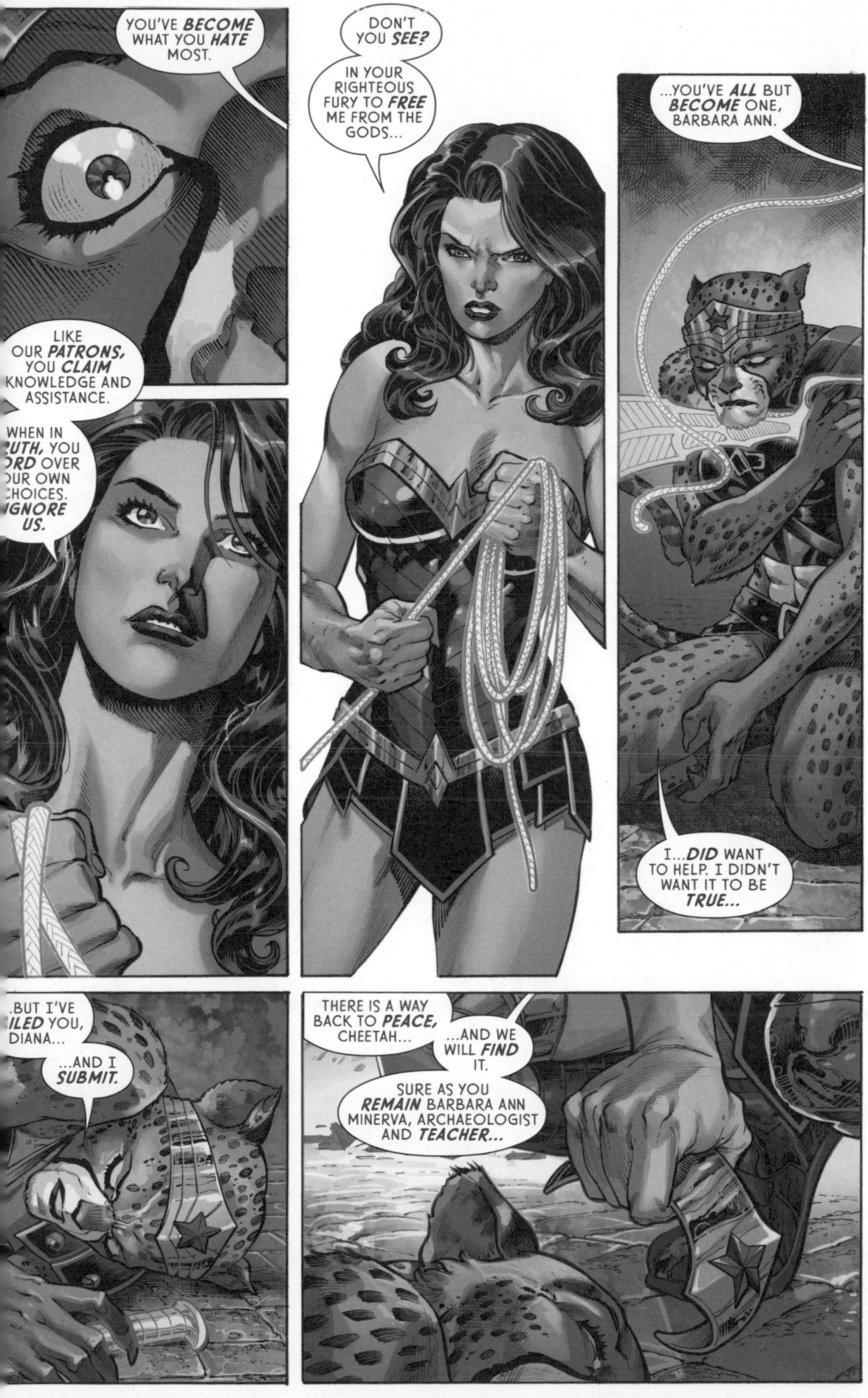
YOU'VE BECOME WHAT YOU HATE MOST.
LIKE OUR PATRONS, YOU CLAIM KNOWLEDGE AND ASSISTANCE.
WHEN IN UTH, YOU ORD OVER UR OWN HOICES. GNORE US.
DON'T YOU SEE?
IN YOUR RIGHTEOUS FURY TO FREE ME FROM THE GODS...
...YOU'VE ALL BUT BECOME ONE, BARBARA ANN.
I...DID WANT TO HELP. I DIDN'T WANT IT TO BE TRUE...
.BUT I'VE ILED YOU, DIANA...
...AND I SUBMIT.
THERE IS A WAY BACK TO PEACE, CHEETAH...
...AND WE WILL FIND IT.
SURE AS YOU REMAIN BARBARA ANN MINERVA, ARCHAEOLOGIST AND TEACHER...

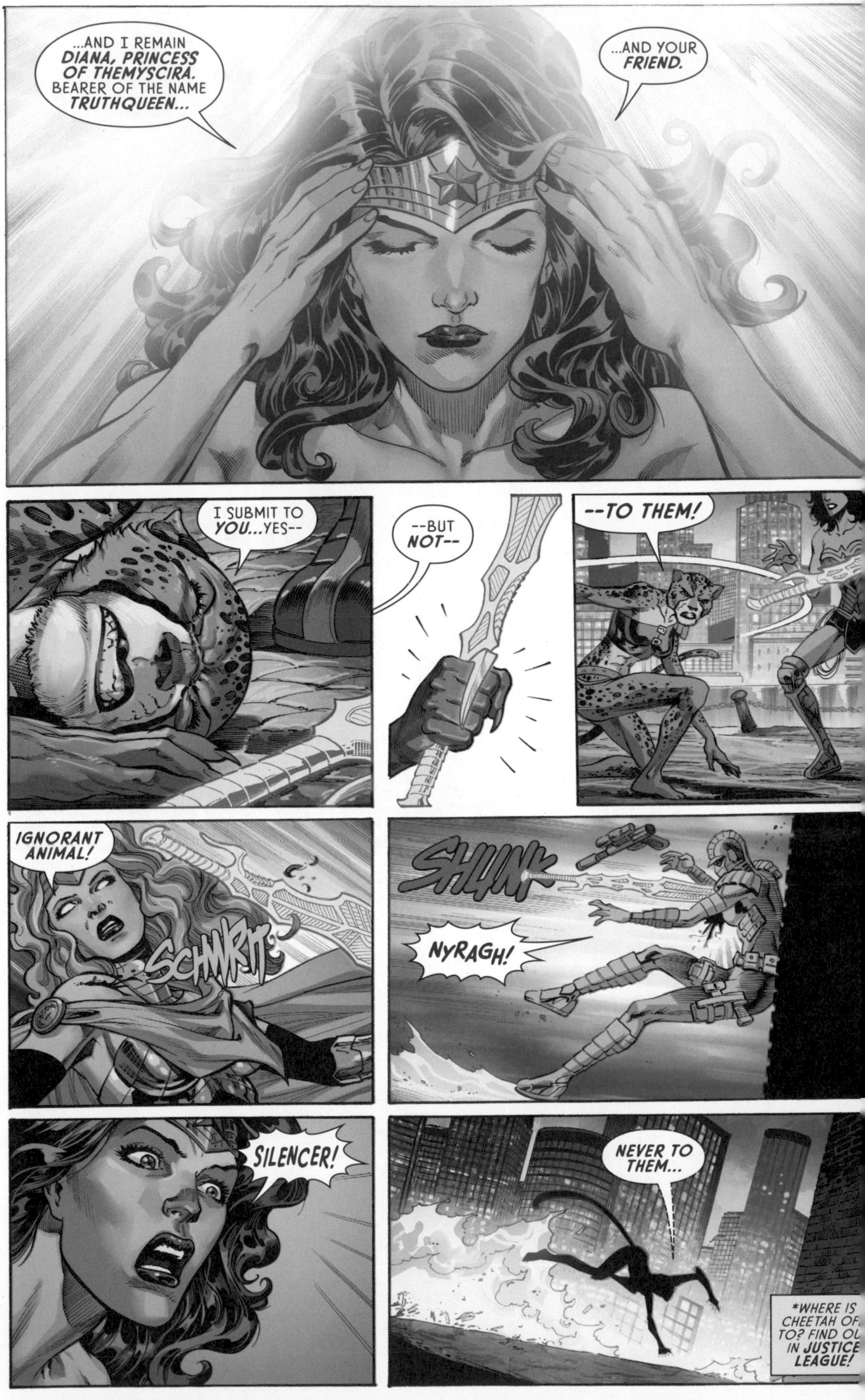

...AND I REMAIN DIANA, PRINCESS OF THEMYSCIRA. BEARER OF THE NAME TRUTHQUEEN...
...AND YOUR FRIEND.
I SUBMIT TO YOU...YES--
--BUT NOT--
--TO THEM!
IGNORANT ANIMAL!
SCHWRIT
SHUNK
NYRAGH!
SILENCER!
NEVER TO THEM...
*WHERE IS CHEETAH OF
TO? FIND OU
IN JUSTICE
LEAGUE!

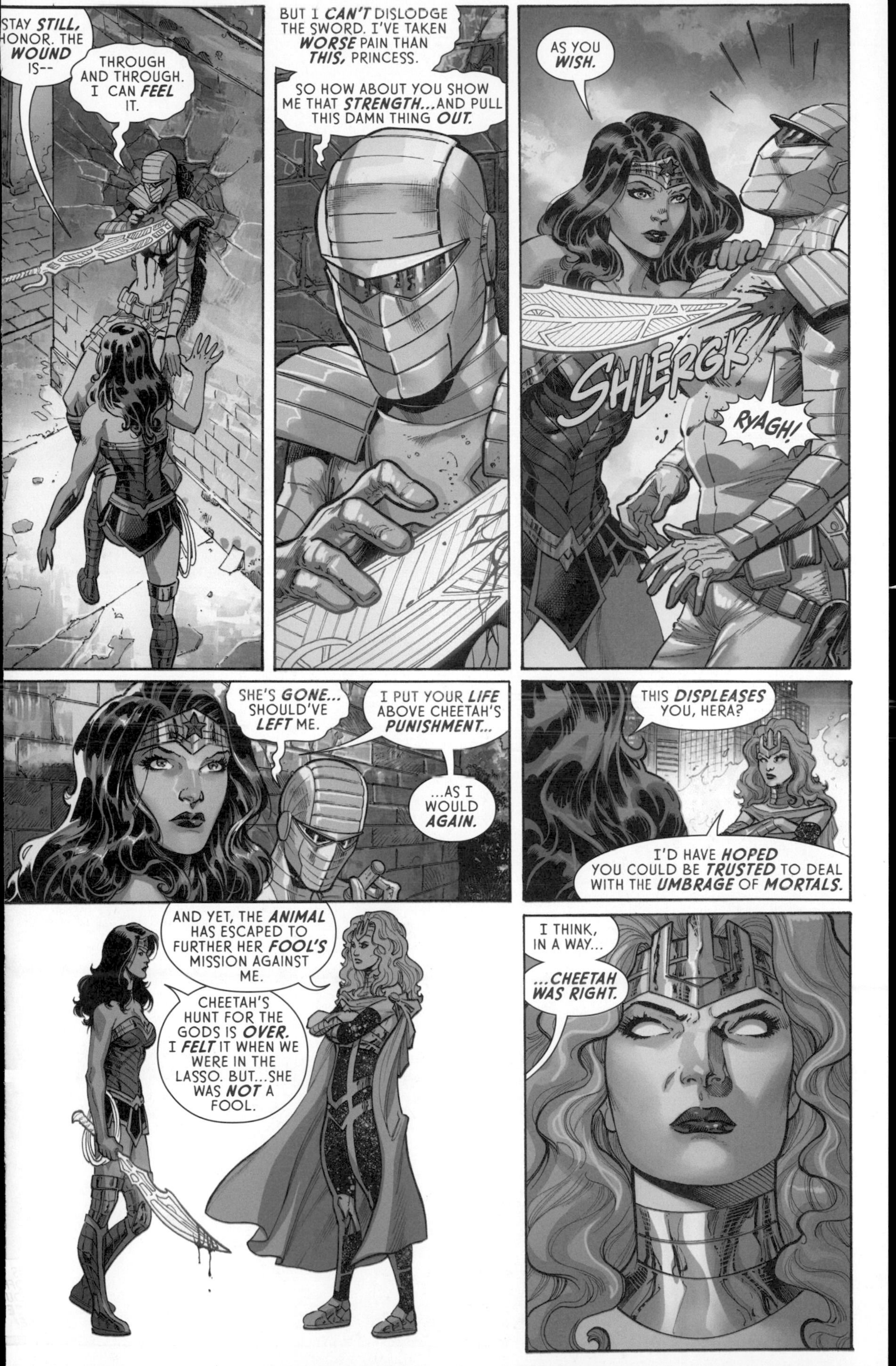
STAY STILL, HONOR. THE WOUND IS--
THROUGH AND THROUGH. I CAN FEEL IT.
BUT I CAN'T DISLODGE THE SWORD. I'VE TAKEN WORSE PAIN THAN THIS, PRINCESS.
SO HOW ABOUT YOU SHOW ME THAT STRENGTH...AND PULL THIS DAMN THING OUT.
AS YOU WISH.
SHLERGK
RYAGH!
SHE'S GONE... SHOULD'VE LEFT ME.
I PUT YOUR LIFE ABOVE CHEETAH'S PUNISHMENT...
...AS I WOULD AGAIN.
THIS DISPLEASES YOU, HERA?
I'D HAVE HOPED YOU COULD BE TRUSTED TO DEAL WITH THE UMBRAGE OF MORTALS.
AND YET, THE ANIMAL HAS ESCAPED TO FURTHER HER FOOL'S MISSION AGAINST ME.
CHEETAH'S HUNT FOR THE GODS IS OVER. I FELT IT WHEN WE WERE IN THE LASSO. BUT...SHE WAS NOT A FOOL.
I THINK, IN A WAY...
...CHEETAH WAS RIGHT.

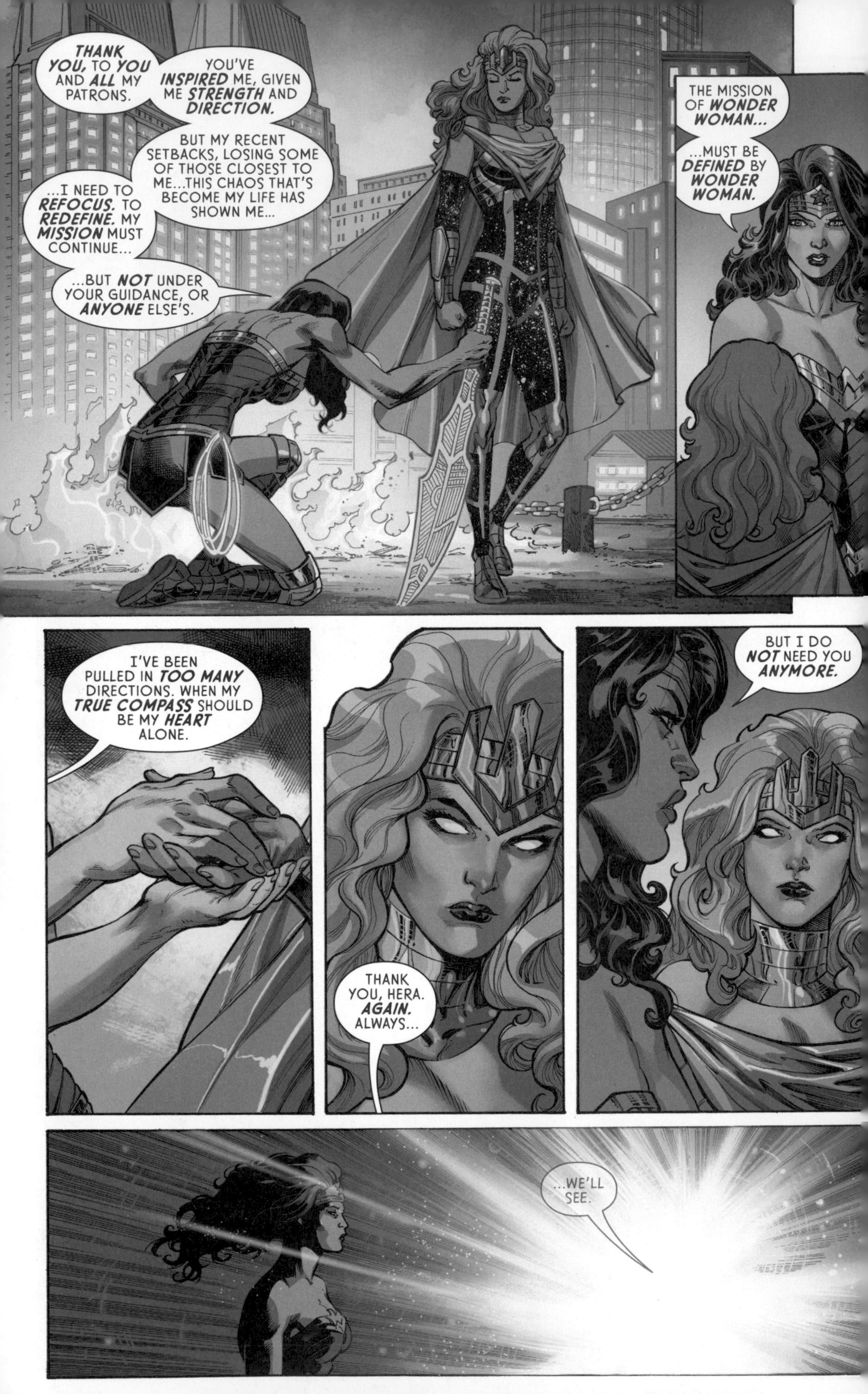
THANK YOU, TO YOU AND ALL MY PATRONS.
YOU'VE INSPIRED ME, GIVEN ME STRENGTH AND DIRECTION.
BUT MY RECENT SETBACKS, LOSING SOME OF THOSE CLOSEST TO ME...THIS CHAOS THAT'S BECOME MY LIFE HAS SHOWN ME...
...I NEED TO REFOCUS. TO REDEFINE. MY MISSION MUST CONTINUE...
...BUT NOT UNDER YOUR GUIDANCE, OR ANYONE ELSE'S.
THE MISSION OF WONDER WOMAN...
...MUST BE DEFINED BY WONDER WOMAN.
I'VE BEEN PULLED IN TOO MANY DIRECTIONS. WHEN MY TRUE COMPASS SHOULD BE MY HEART ALONE.
THANK YOU, HERA. AGAIN. ALWAYS...
BUT I DO NOT NEED YOU ANYMORE.
...WE'LL SEE.

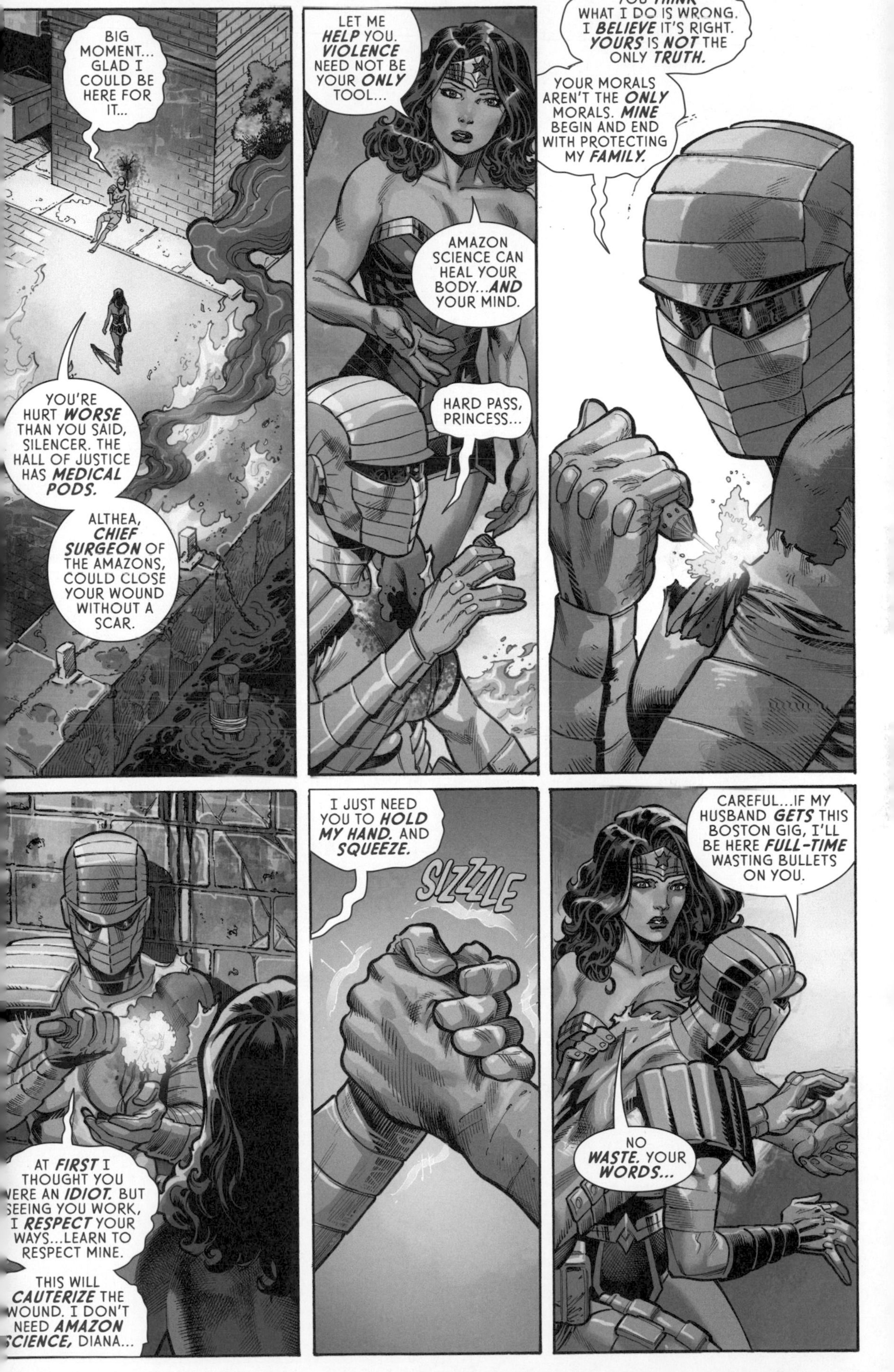
BIG MOMENT... GLAD I COULD BE HERE FOR IT...
YOU'RE HURT WORSE THAN YOU SAID, SILENCER. THE HALL OF JUSTICE HAS MEDICAL PODS.
ALTHEA, CHIEF SURGEON OF THE AMAZONS, COULD CLOSE YOUR WOUND WITHOUT A SCAR.
LET ME HELP YOU. VIOLENCE NEED NOT BE YOUR ONLY TOOL...
AMAZON SCIENCE CAN HEAL YOUR BODY...AND YOUR MIND.
HARD PASS, PRINCESS...
YOU THINK WHAT I DO IS WRONG. I BELIEVE IT'S RIGHT. YOURS IS NOT THE ONLY TRUTH.
YOUR MORALS AREN'T THE ONLY MORALS. MINE BEGIN AND END WITH PROTECTING MY FAMILY.
AT FIRST I THOUGHT YOU WERE AN IDIOT. BUT SEEING YOU WORK, I RESPECT YOUR WAYS...LEARN TO RESPECT MINE.
THIS WILL CAUTERIZE THE WOUND. I DON'T NEED AMAZON SCIENCE, DIANA...
I JUST NEED YOU TO HOLD MY HAND. AND SQUEEZE.
SIZZZLE
CAREFUL...IF MY HUSBAND GETS THIS BOSTON GIG, I'LL BE HERE FULL-TIME WASTING BULLETS ON YOU.
NO WASTE. YOUR WORDS...

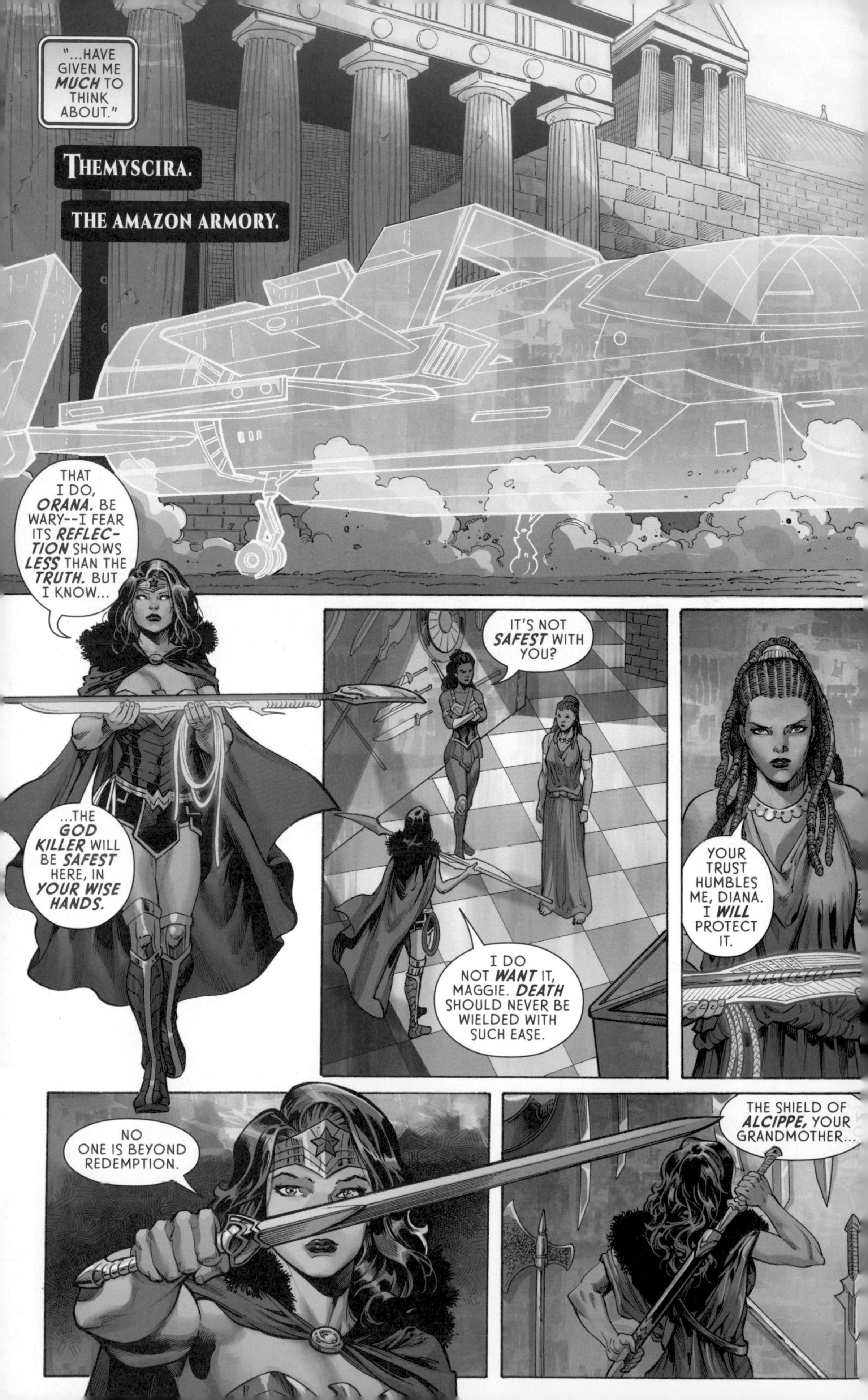
"...HAVE GIVEN ME MUCH TO THINK ABOUT."
THEMYSCIRA.
THE AMAZON ARMORY.
THAT I DO, ORANA. BE WARY--I FEAR ITS REFLECTION SHOWS LESS THAN THE TRUTH. BUT I KNOW...
...THE GOD KILLER WILL BE SAFEST HERE, IN YOUR WISE HANDS.
IT'S NOT SAFEST WITH YOU?
I DO NOT WANT IT, MAGGIE. DEATH SHOULD NEVER BE WIELDED WITH SUCH EASE.
YOUR TRUST HUMBLES ME, DIANA. I WILL PROTECT IT.
NO ONE IS BEYOND REDEMPTION.
THE SHIELD OF ALCIPPE, YOUR GRANDMOTHER...

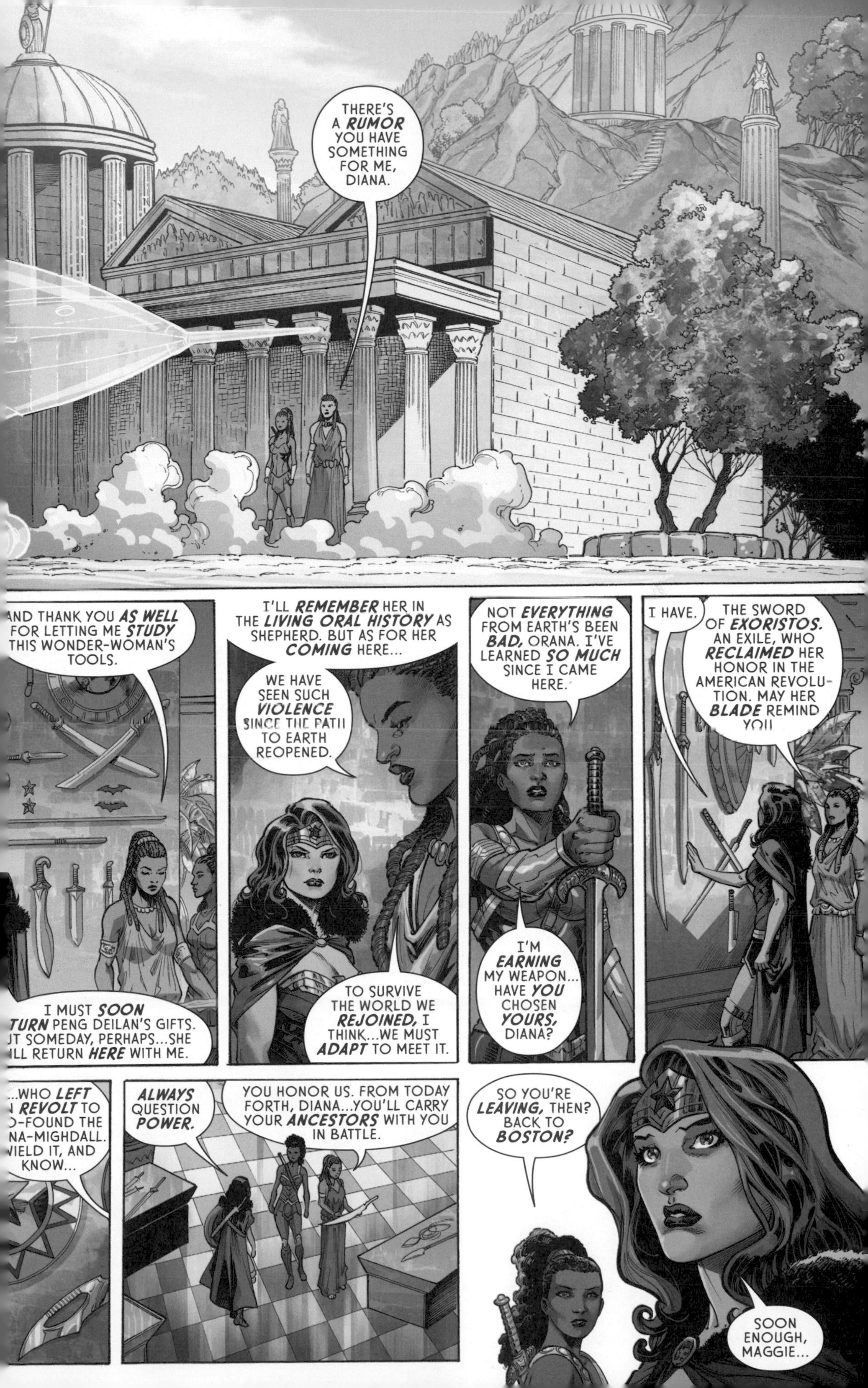
THERE'S A RUMOR YOU HAVE SOMETHING FOR ME, DIANA.
AND THANK YOU AS WELL FOR LETTING ME STUDY THIS WONDER-WOMAN'S TOOLS.
I MUST SOON TURN PENG DEILAN'S GIFTS. UT SOMEDAY, PERHAPS...SHE ILL RETURN HERE WITH ME.
I'LL REMEMBER HER IN THE LIVING ORAL HISTORY AS SHEPHERD. BUT AS FOR HER COMING HERE...
WE HAVE SEEN SUCH VIOLENCE SINCE THE PATH TO EARTH REOPENED.
TO SURVIVE THE WORLD WE REJOINED, I THINK...WE MUST ADAPT TO MEET IT.
NOT EVERYTHING FROM EARTH'S BEEN BAD, ORANA. I'VE LEARNED SO MUCH SINCE I CAME HERE.
I'M EARNING MY WEAPON... HAVE YOU CHOSEN YOURS, DIANA?
I HAVE.
THE SWORD OF EXORISTOS. AN EXILE, WHO RECLAIMED HER HONOR IN THE AMERICAN REVOLUTION. MAY HER BLADE REMIND YOU
...WHO LEFT N REVOLT TO O-FOUND THE NA-MIGHDALL. VIELD IT, AND KNOW...
ALWAYS QUESTION POWER.
YOU HONOR US. FROM TODAY FORTH, DIANA...YOU'LL CARRY YOUR ANCESTORS WITH YOU IN BATTLE.
SO YOU'RE LEAVING, THEN? BACK TO BOSTON?
SOON ENOUGH, MAGGIE...

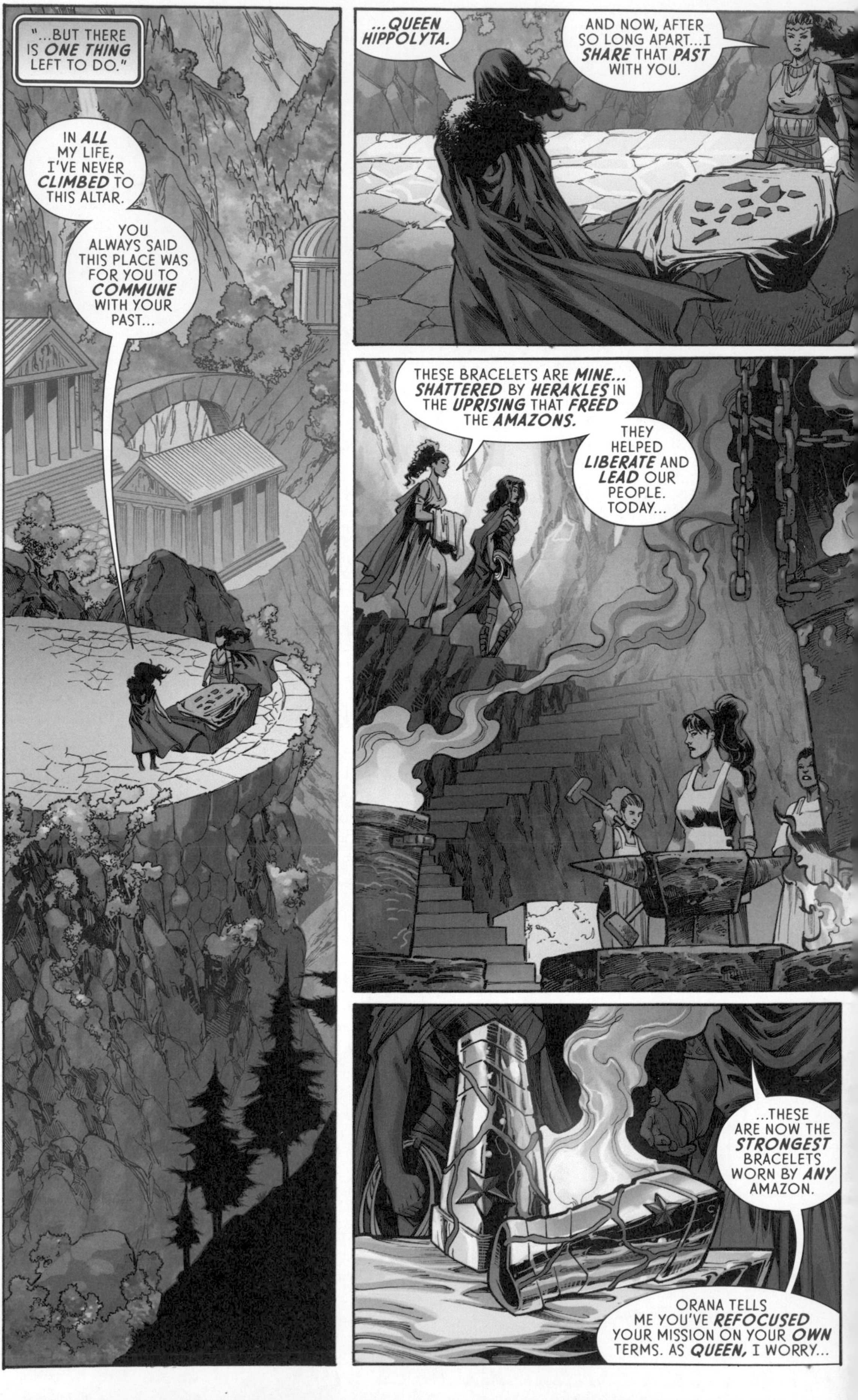
"...BUT THERE IS ONE THING LEFT TO DO."
IN ALL MY LIFE, I'VE NEVER CLIMBED TO THIS ALTAR.
YOU ALWAYS SAID THIS PLACE WAS FOR YOU TO COMMUNE WITH YOUR PAST...
...QUEEN HIPPOLYTA.
AND NOW, AFTER SO LONG APART...I SHARE THAT PAST WITH YOU.
THESE BRACELETS ARE MINE... SHATTERED BY HERAKLES IN THE UPRISING THAT FREED THE AMAZONS.
THEY HELPED LIBERATE AND LEAD OUR PEOPLE. TODAY...
...THESE ARE NOW THE STRONGEST BRACELETS WORN BY ANY AMAZON.
ORANA TELLS ME YOU'VE REFOCUSED YOUR MISSION ON YOUR OWN TERMS. AS QUEEN, I WORRY...

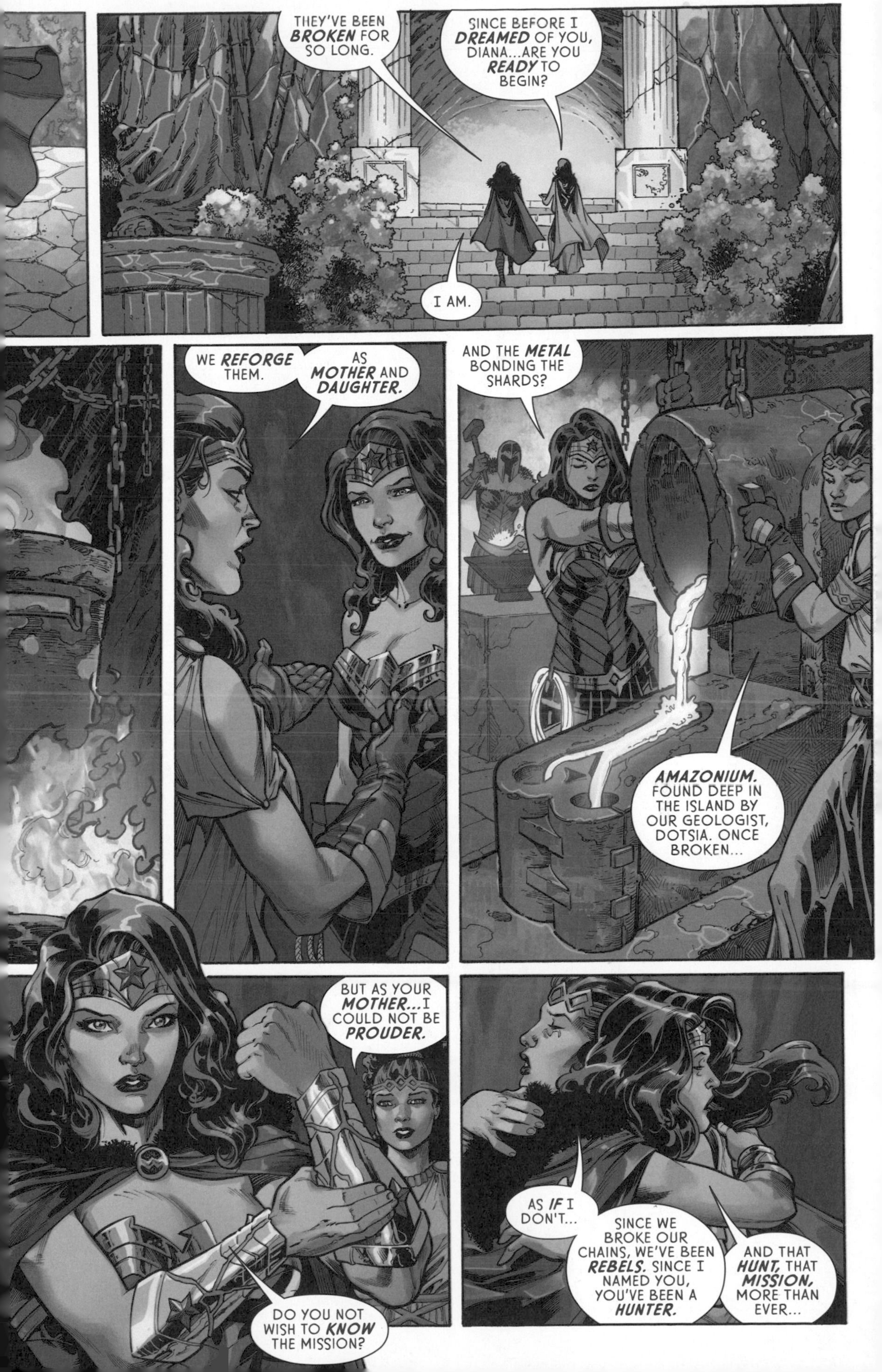
THEY'VE BEEN BROKEN FOR SO LONG.
SINCE BEFORE I DREAMED OF YOU, DIANA...ARE YOU READY TO BEGIN?
I AM.
WE REFORGE THEM.
AS MOTHER AND DAUGHTER.
AND THE METAL BONDING THE SHARDS?
AMAZONIUM. FOUND DEEP IN THE ISLAND BY OUR GEOLOGIST, DOTSIA. ONCE BROKEN...
BUT AS YOUR MOTHER...I COULD NOT BE PROUDER.
DO YOU NOT WISH TO KNOW THE MISSION?
AS IF I DON'T...
SINCE WE BROKE OUR CHAINS, WE'VE BEEN REBELS. SINCE I NAMED YOU, YOU'VE BEEN A HUNTER.
AND THAT HUNT, THAT MISSION, MORE THAN EVER...

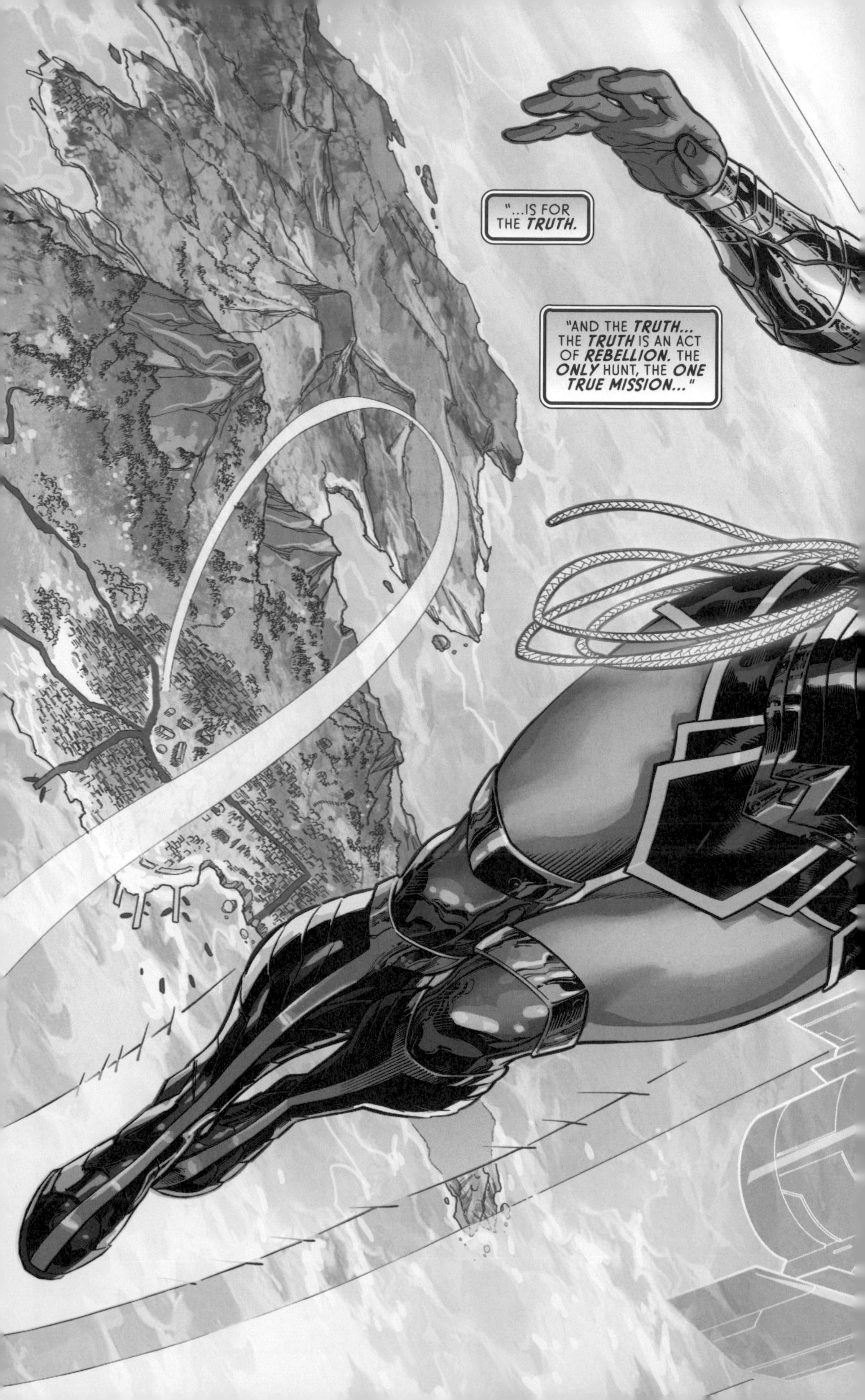
"...IS FOR THE TRUTH.
"AND THE TRUTH... THE TRUTH IS AN ACT OF REBELLION. THE ONLY HUNT, THE ONE TRUE MISSION..."

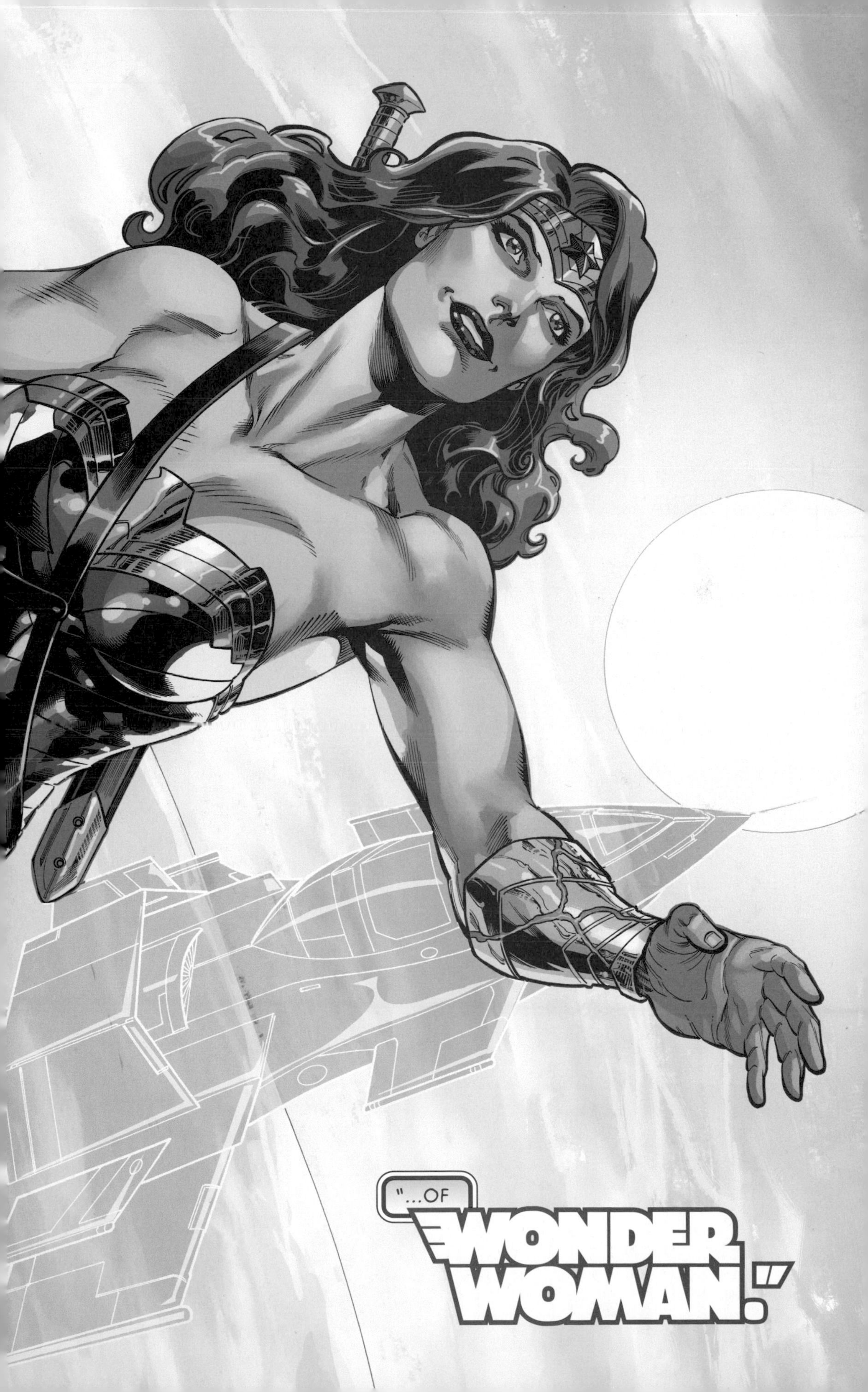
"...OF
WONDER WOMAN."

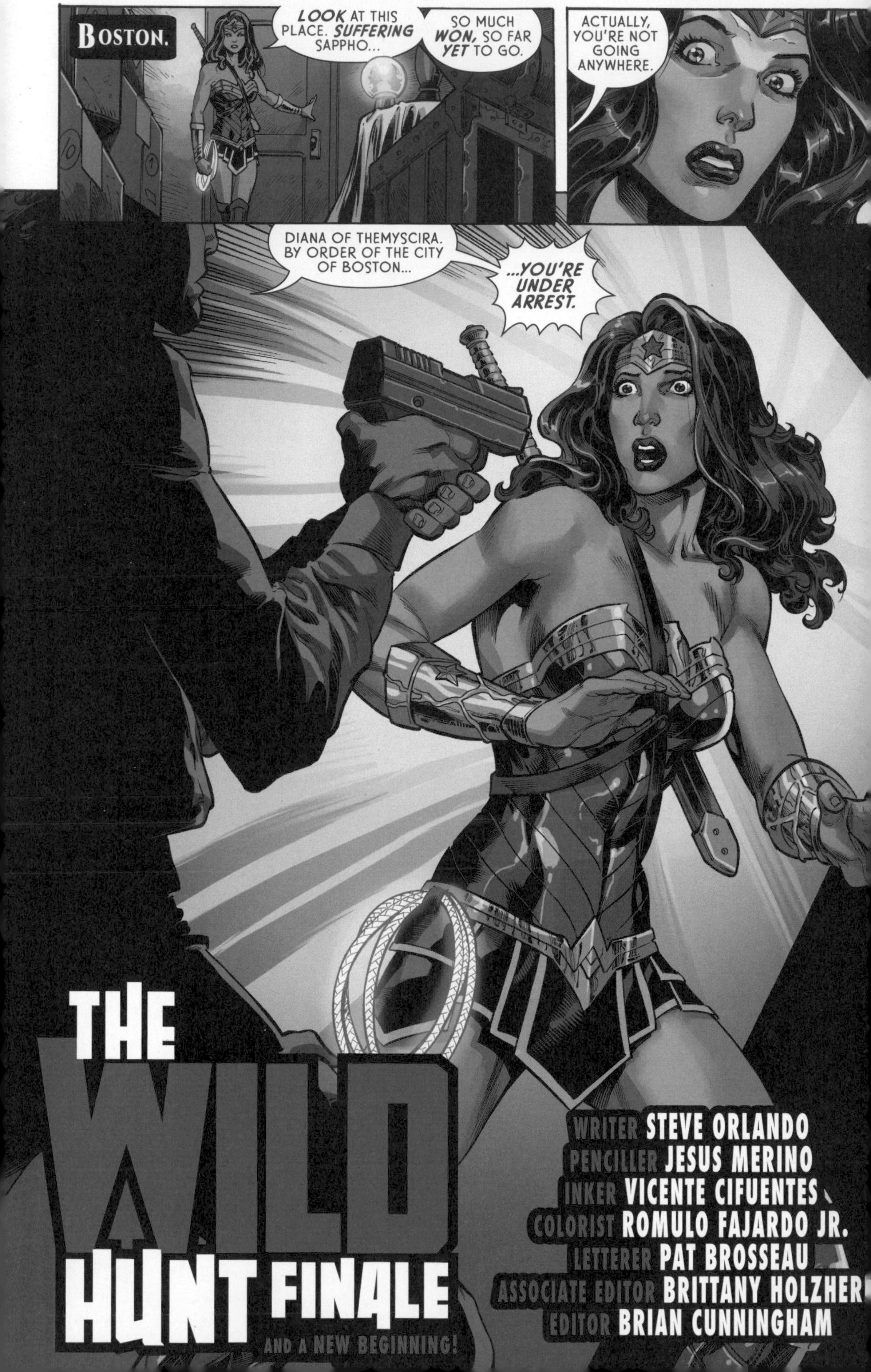
BOSTON.
LOOK AT THIS PLACE. SUFFERING SAPPHO...
SO MUCH WON, SO FAR YET TO GO.
ACTUALLY, YOU'RE NOT GOING ANYWHERE.
DIANA OF THEMYSCIRA. BY ORDER OF THE CITY OF BOSTON...
...YOU'RE UNDER ARREST.
THE WILD HUNT FINALE
AND A NEW BEGINNING!
WRITER STEVE ORLANDO
PENCILLER JESUS MERINO
INKER VICENTE CIFUENTES
COLORIST ROMULO FAJARDO JR.
LETTERER PAT BROSSEAU
ASSOCIATE EDITOR BRITTANY HOLZHERR
EDITOR BRIAN CUNNINGHAM

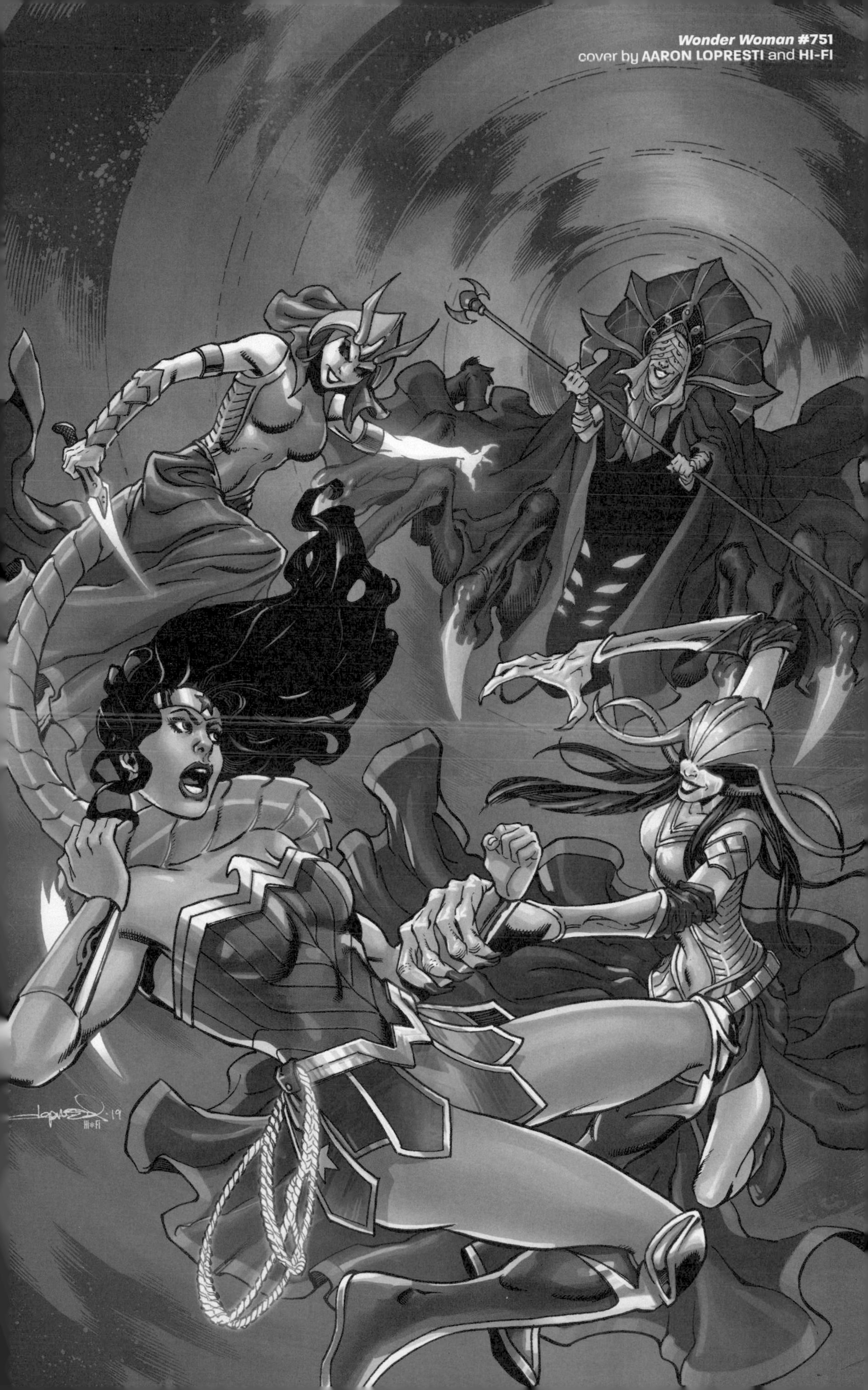

Wonder Woman **#751**
cover by **AARON LOPRESTI** and **HI-FI**

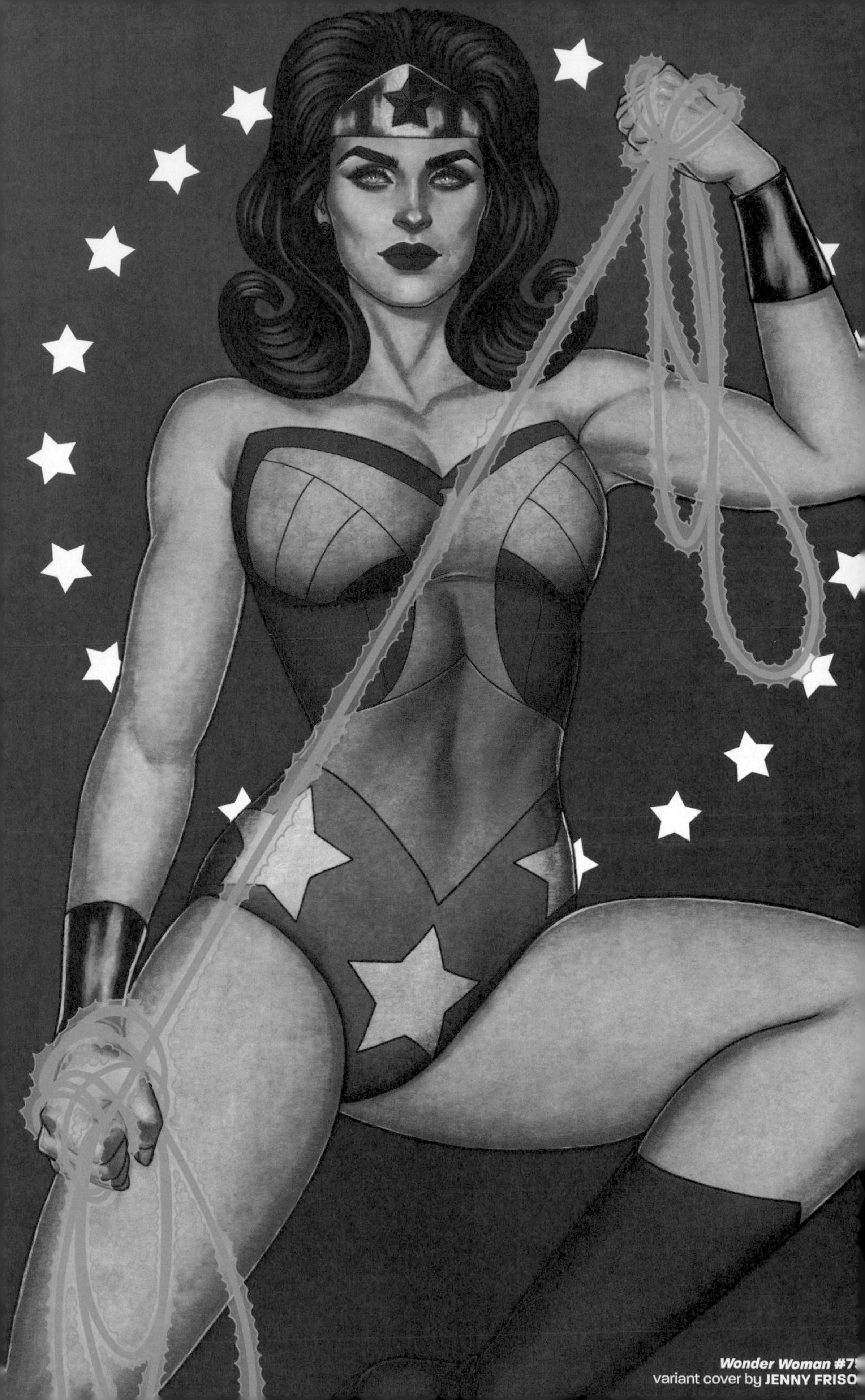

Wonder Woman #75
variant cover by **JENNY FRISON**

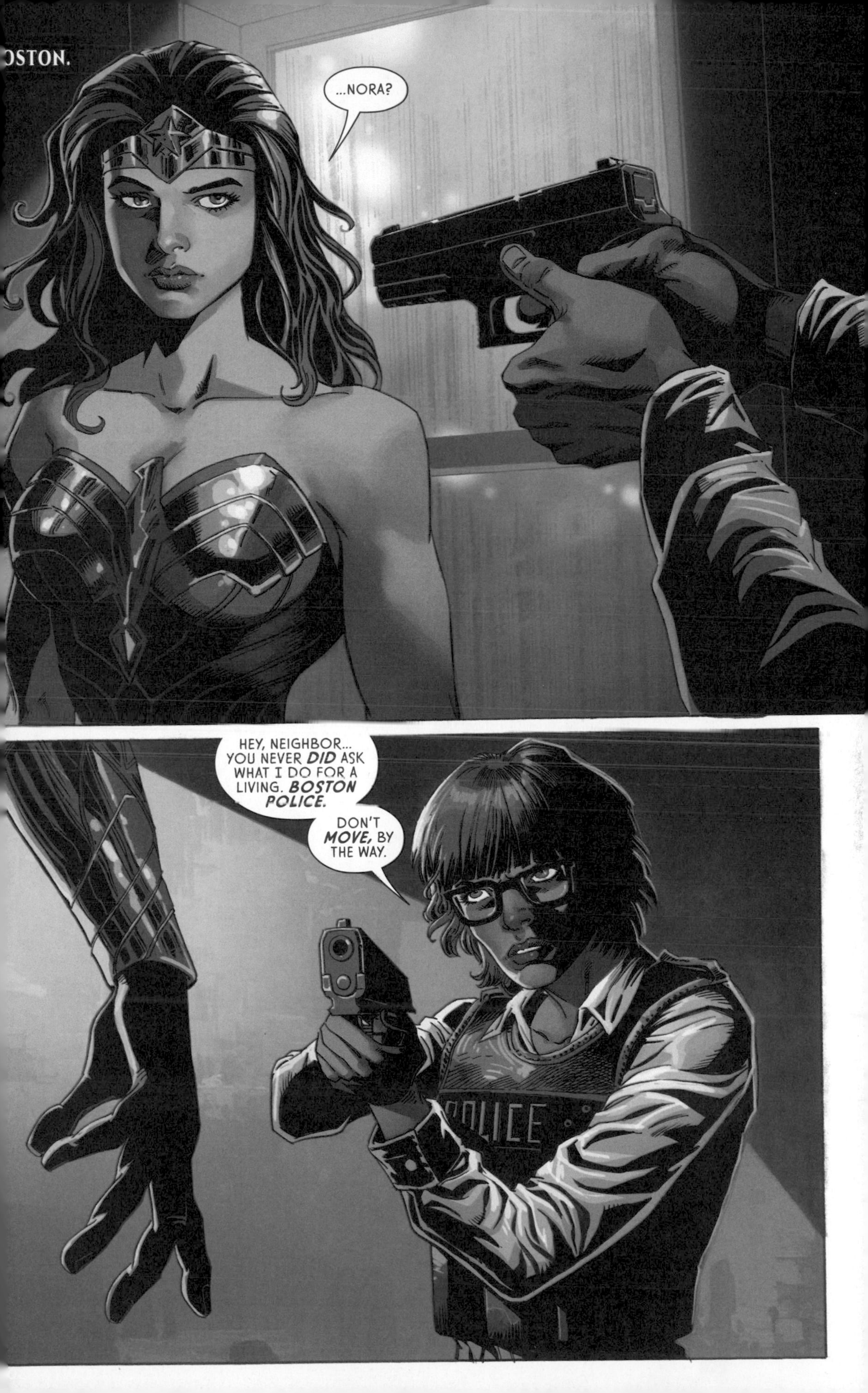
OSTON.
...NORA?
HEY, NEIGHBOR... YOU NEVER DID ASK WHAT I DO FOR A LIVING. BOSTON POLICE.
DON'T MOVE, BY THE WAY.
POLICE

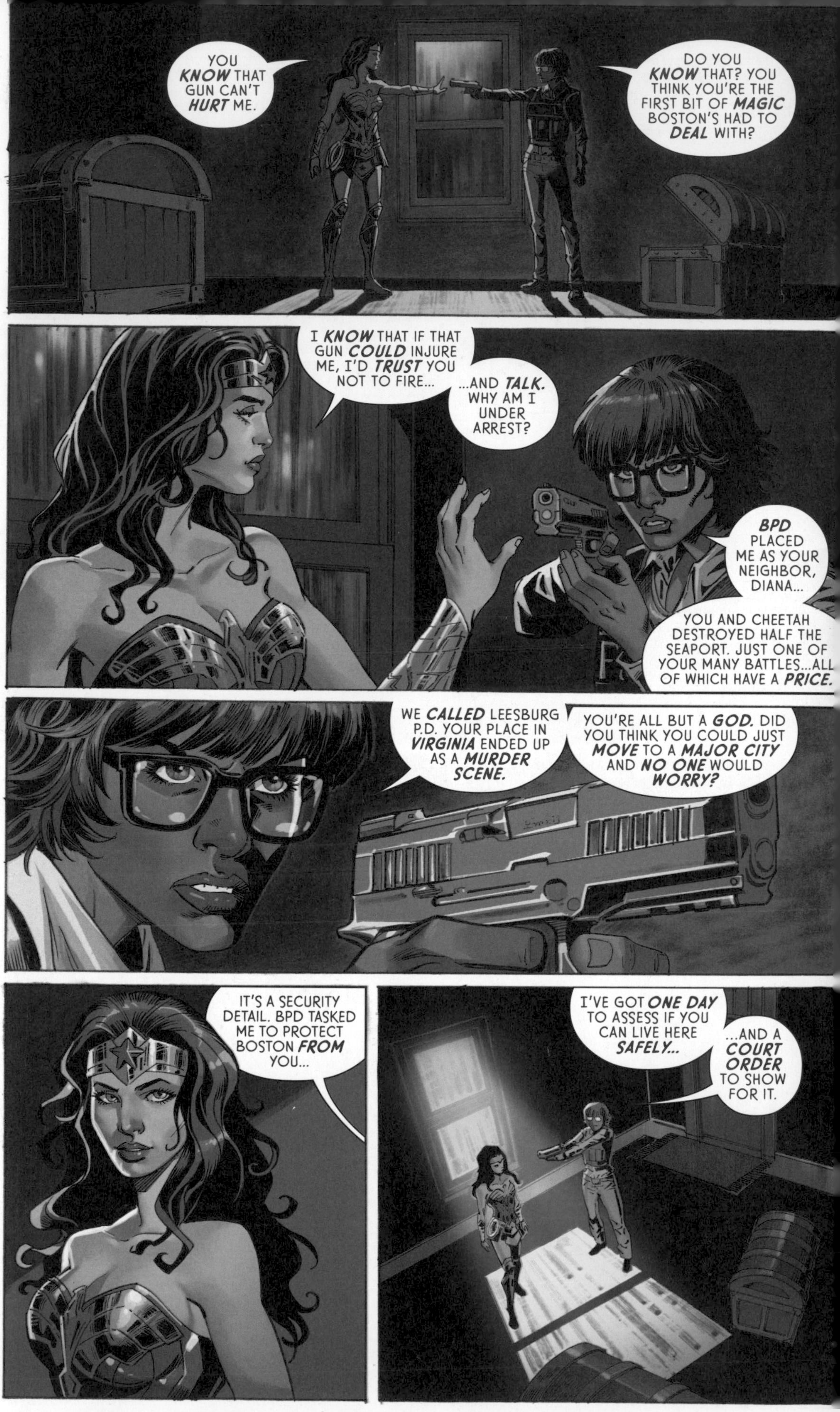
YOU KNOW THAT GUN CAN'T HURT ME.
DO YOU KNOW THAT? YOU THINK YOU'RE THE FIRST BIT OF MAGIC BOSTON'S HAD TO DEAL WITH?
I KNOW THAT IF THAT GUN COULD INJURE ME, I'D TRUST YOU NOT TO FIRE...
...AND TALK. WHY AM I UNDER ARREST?
BPD PLACED ME AS YOUR NEIGHBOR, DIANA...
YOU AND CHEETAH DESTROYED HALF THE SEAPORT. JUST ONE OF YOUR MANY BATTLES...ALL OF WHICH HAVE A PRICE.
WE CALLED LEESBURG P.D. YOUR PLACE IN VIRGINIA ENDED UP AS A MURDER SCENE.
YOU'RE ALL BUT A GOD. DID YOU THINK YOU COULD JUST MOVE TO A MAJOR CITY AND NO ONE WOULD WORRY?
IT'S A SECURITY DETAIL. BPD TASKED ME TO PROTECT BOSTON FROM YOU...
I'VE GOT ONE DAY TO ASSESS IF YOU CAN LIVE HERE SAFELY...
...AND A COURT ORDER TO SHOW FOR IT.

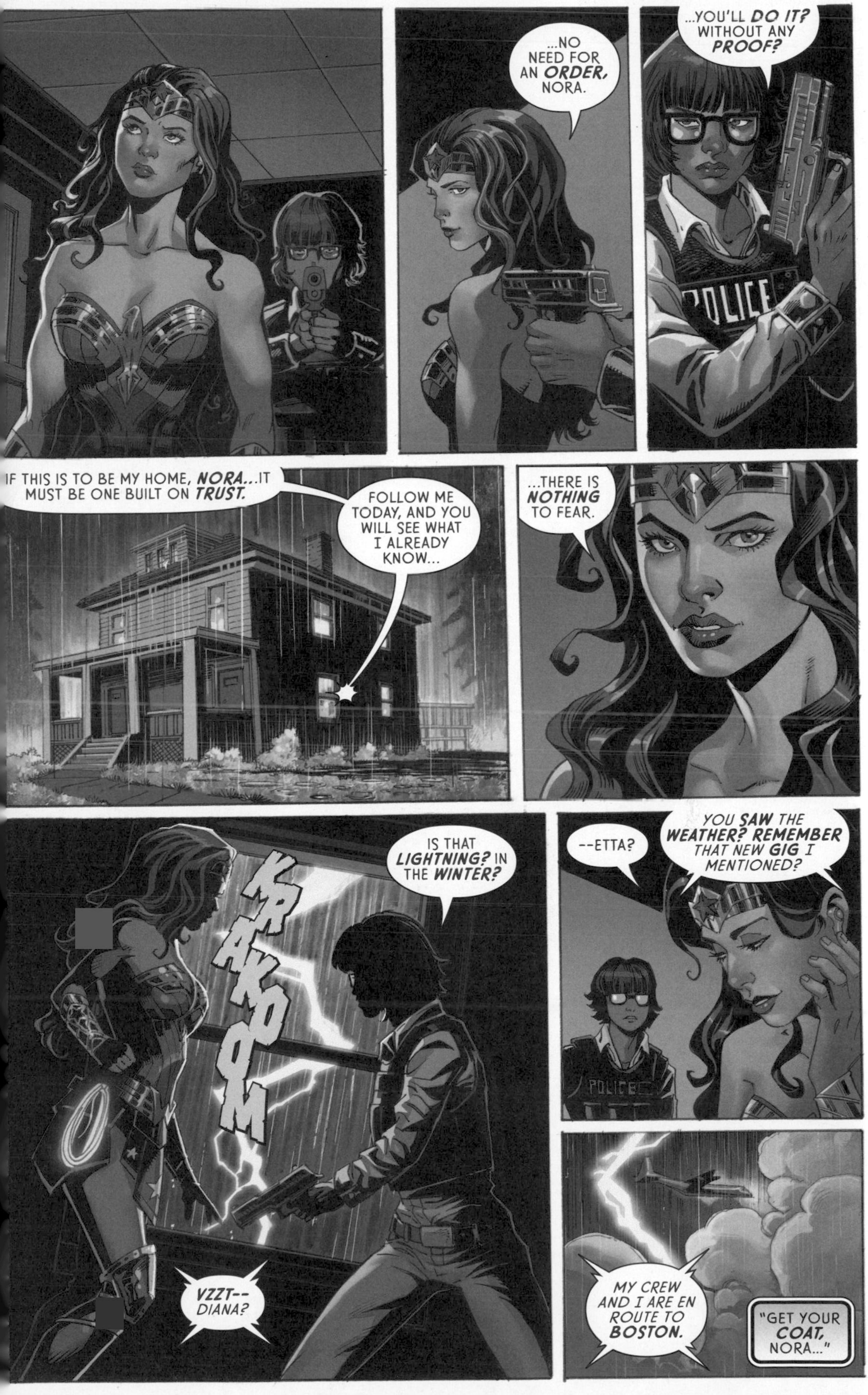
...NO NEED FOR AN ORDER, NORA.
...YOU'LL DO IT? WITHOUT ANY PROOF?
IF THIS IS TO BE MY HOME, NORA...IT MUST BE ONE BUILT ON TRUST.
FOLLOW ME TODAY, AND YOU WILL SEE WHAT I ALREADY KNOW...
...THERE IS NOTHING TO FEAR.
IS THAT LIGHTNING? IN THE WINTER?
KRAKOOM
VZZT-- DIANA?
--ETTA?
YOU SAW THE WEATHER? REMEMBER THAT NEW GIG I MENTIONED?
POLICE
MY CREW AND I ARE EN ROUTE TO BOSTON.
"GET YOUR COAT, NORA..."

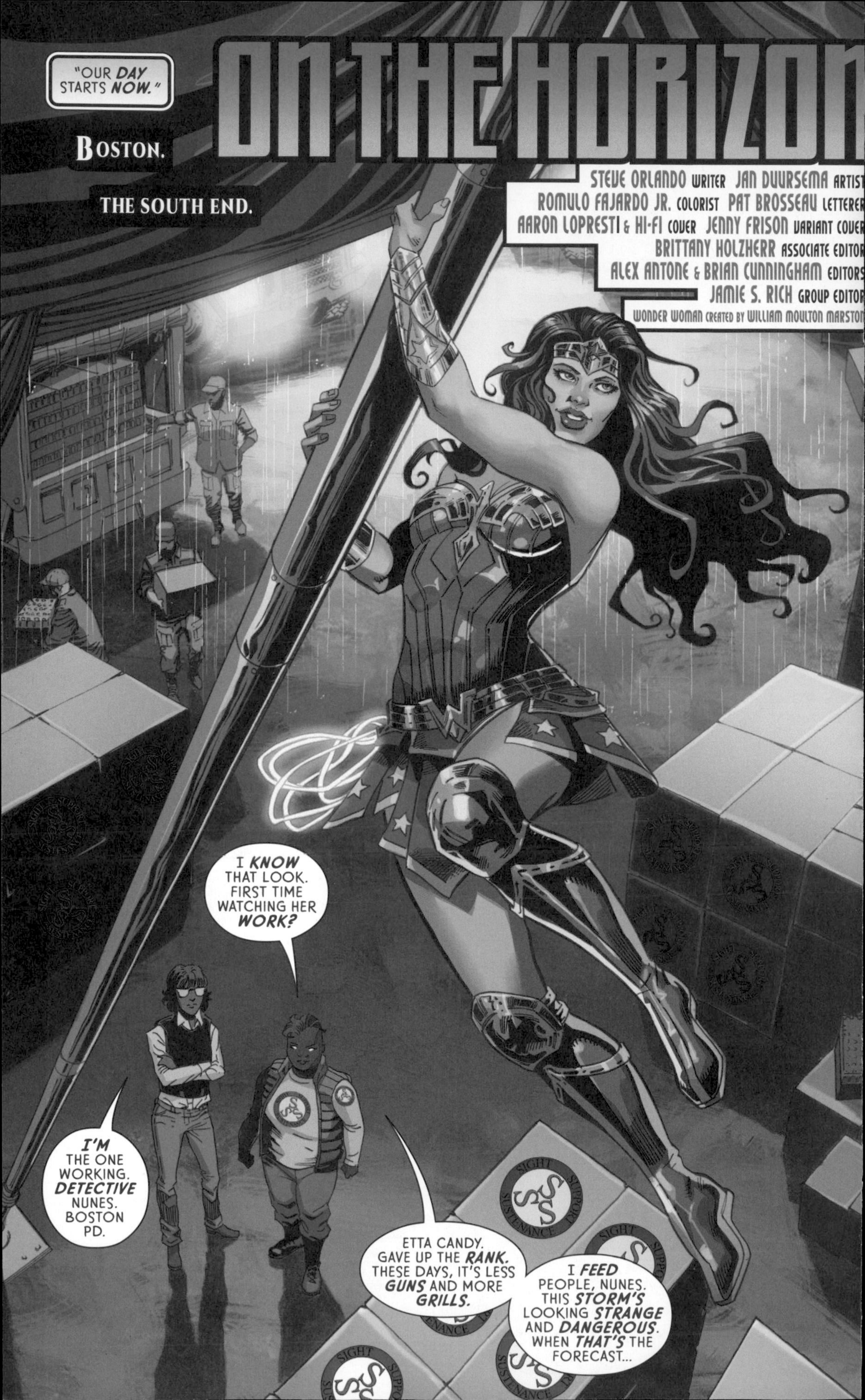
"OUR DAY STARTS NOW."
ON THE HORIZON
BOSTON.
THE SOUTH END.
STEVE ORLANDO WRITER JAN DUURSEMA ARTIST
ROMULO FAJARDO JR. COLORIST PAT BROSSEAU LETTERER
AARON LOPRESTI & HI-FI COVER JENNY FRISON VARIANT COVER
BRITTANY HOLZHERR ASSOCIATE EDITOR
ALEX ANTONE & BRIAN CUNNINGHAM EDITORS
JAMIE S. RICH GROUP EDITOR
WONDER WOMAN CREATED BY WILLIAM MOULTON MARSTON
I KNOW THAT LOOK. FIRST TIME WATCHING HER WORK?
I'M THE ONE WORKING. DETECTIVE NUNES. BOSTON PD.
ETTA CANDY. GAVE UP THE RANK. THESE DAYS, IT'S LESS GUNS AND MORE GRILLS.
I FEED PEOPLE, NUNES. THIS STORM'S LOOKING STRANGE AND DANGEROUS. WHEN THAT'S THE FORECAST...

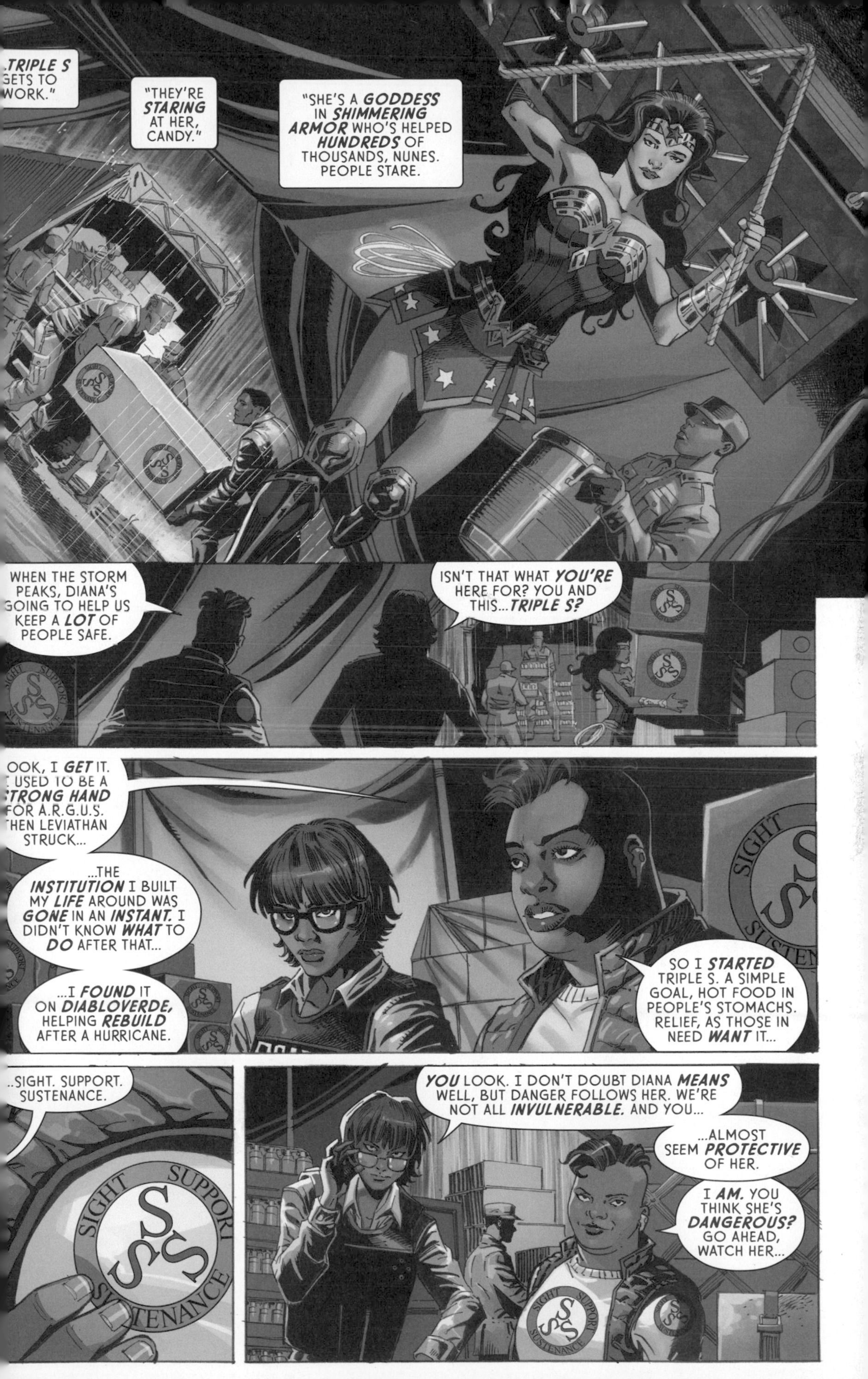

TRIPLE S GETS TO WORK."
"THEY'RE STARING AT HER, CANDY."
"SHE'S A GODDESS IN SHIMMERING ARMOR WHO'S HELPED HUNDREDS OF THOUSANDS, NUNES. PEOPLE STARE.
WHEN THE STORM PEAKS, DIANA'S GOING TO HELP US KEEP A LOT OF PEOPLE SAFE.
ISN'T THAT WHAT YOU'RE HERE FOR? YOU AND THIS...TRIPLE S?
OOK, I GET IT. I USED TO BE A STRONG HAND FOR A.R.G.U.S. THEN LEVIATHAN STRUCK...
...THE INSTITUTION I BUILT MY LIFE AROUND WAS GONE IN AN INSTANT. I DIDN'T KNOW WHAT TO DO AFTER THAT...
...I FOUND IT ON DIABLOVERDE, HELPING REBUILD AFTER A HURRICANE.
SO I STARTED TRIPLE S. A SIMPLE GOAL, HOT FOOD IN PEOPLE'S STOMACHS. RELIEF, AS THOSE IN NEED WANT IT...
..SIGHT. SUPPORT. SUSTENANCE.
SIGHT SUPPORT SUSTENANCE
YOU LOOK. I DON'T DOUBT DIANA MEANS WELL, BUT DANGER FOLLOWS HER. WE'RE NOT ALL INVULNERABLE. AND YOU...
...ALMOST SEEM PROTECTIVE OF HER.
I AM. YOU THINK SHE'S DANGEROUS? GO AHEAD, WATCH HER...

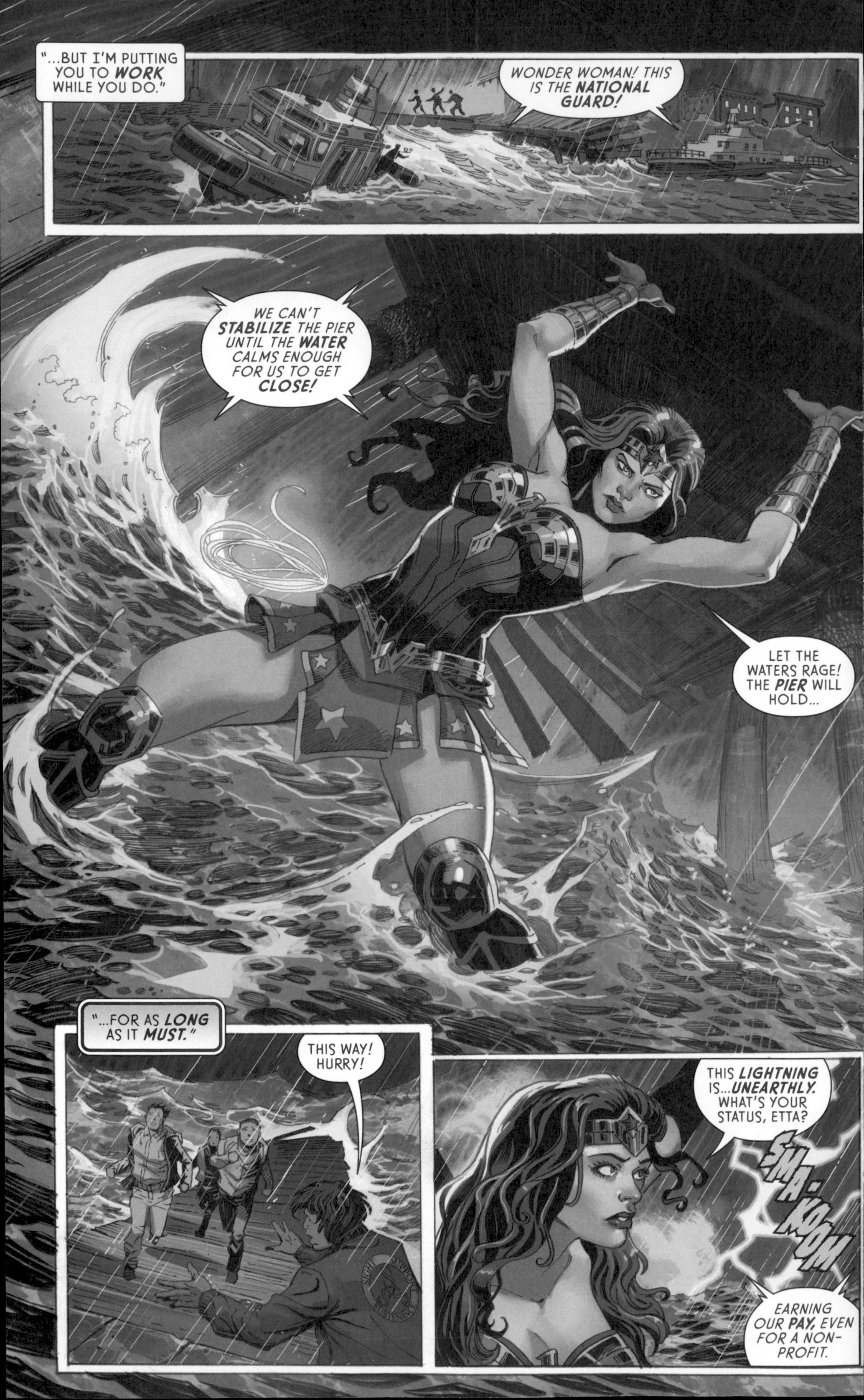
"...BUT I'M PUTTING YOU TO WORK WHILE YOU DO."
WONDER WOMAN! THIS IS THE NATIONAL GUARD!
WE CAN'T STABILIZE THE PIER UNTIL THE WATER CALMS ENOUGH FOR US TO GET CLOSE!
LET THE WATERS RAGE! THE PIER WILL HOLD...
"...FOR AS LONG AS IT MUST."
THIS WAY! HURRY!
THIS LIGHTNING IS...UNEARTHLY. WHAT'S YOUR STATUS, ETTA?
SMA-KOOM
EARNING OUR PAY, EVEN FOR A NON-PROFIT.

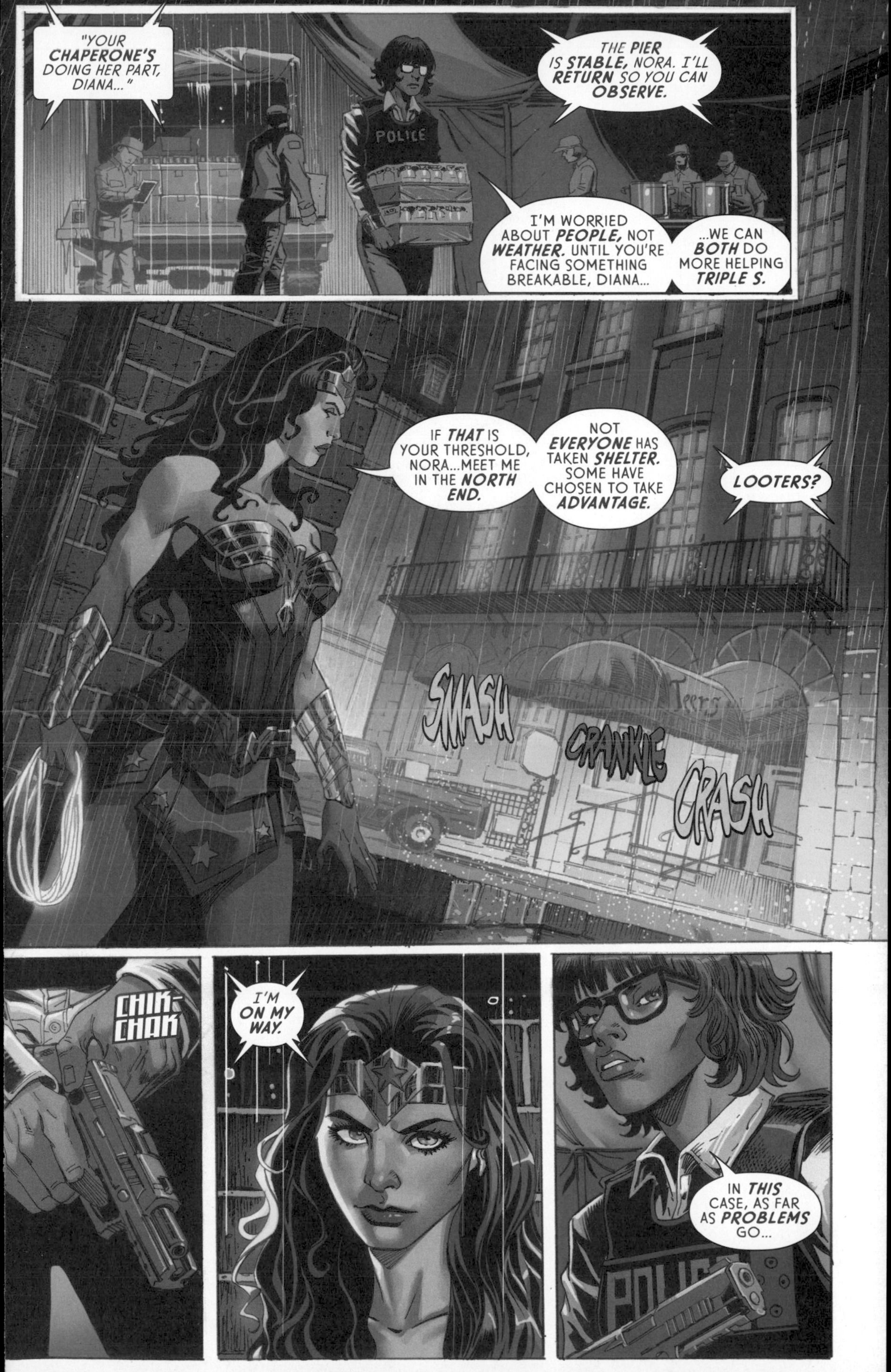
"YOUR CHAPERONE'S DOING HER PART, DIANA..."
THE PIER IS STABLE, NORA. I'LL RETURN SO YOU CAN OBSERVE.
POLICE
I'M WORRIED ABOUT PEOPLE, NOT WEATHER. UNTIL YOU'RE FACING SOMETHING BREAKABLE, DIANA...
...WE CAN BOTH DO MORE HELPING TRIPLE S.
IF THAT IS YOUR THRESHOLD, NORA...MEET ME IN THE NORTH END.
NOT EVERYONE HAS TAKEN SHELTER. SOME HAVE CHOSEN TO TAKE ADVANTAGE.
LOOTERS?
SMASH
CRANKLE
CRASH
CHIK-CHAK
I'M ON MY WAY.
IN THIS CASE, AS FAR AS PROBLEMS GO...

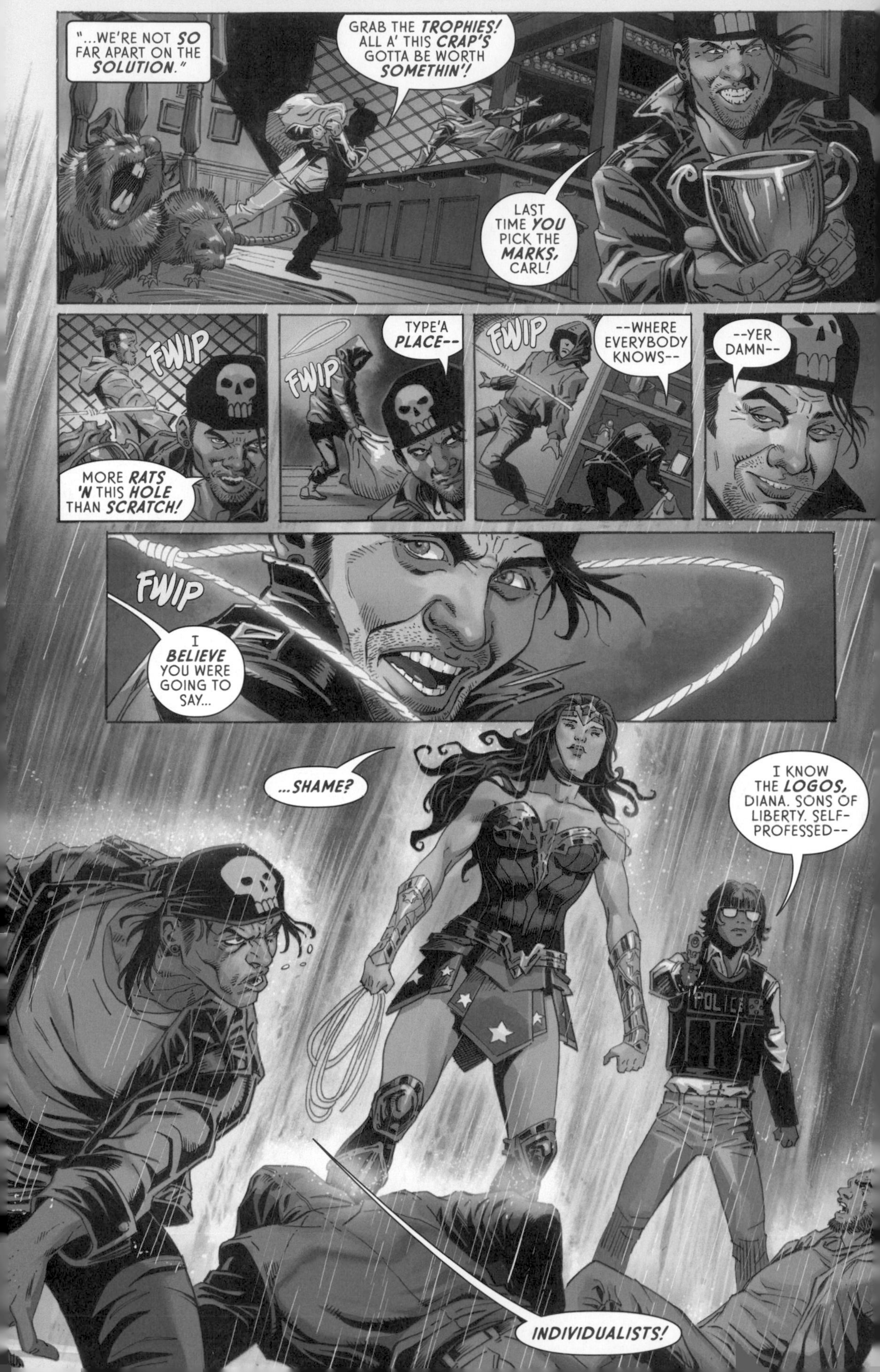
"...WE'RE NOT SO FAR APART ON THE SOLUTION."
GRAB THE TROPHIES! ALL A' THIS CRAP'S GOTTA BE WORTH SOMETHIN'!
LAST TIME YOU PICK THE MARKS, CARL!
FWIP
MORE RATS 'N THIS HOLE THAN SCRATCH!
TYPE'A PLACE--
FWIP
FWIP
--WHERE EVERYBODY KNOWS--
--YER DAMN--
FWIP
I BELIEVE YOU WERE GOING TO SAY...
...SHAME?
I KNOW THE LOGOS, DIANA. SONS OF LIBERTY. SELF-PROFESSED--
INDIVIDUALISTS!
POLICE

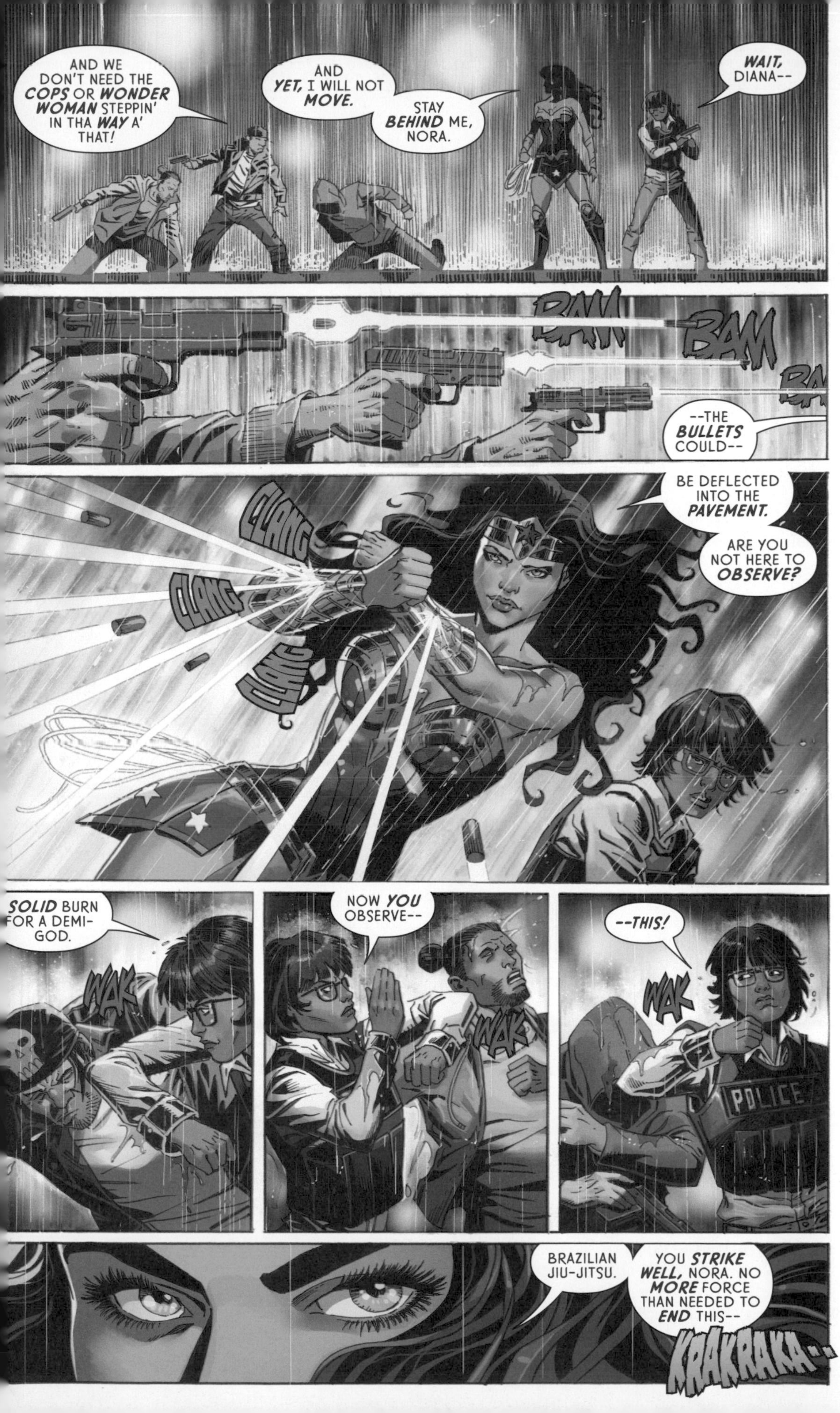
AND WE DON'T NEED THE COPS OR WONDER WOMAN STEPPIN' IN THA WAY A' THAT!
AND YET, I WILL NOT MOVE.
STAY BEHIND ME, NORA.
WAIT, DIANA--
BAM
BAM
--THE BULLETS COULD--
BE DEFLECTED INTO THE PAVEMENT.
ARE YOU NOT HERE TO OBSERVE?
CLANG
CLANG
CLANG
SOLID BURN FOR A DEMI-GOD.
WAK
NOW YOU OBSERVE--
WAK
--THIS!
WAK
POLICE
BRAZILIAN JIU-JITSU.
YOU STRIKE WELL, NORA. NO MORE FORCE THAN NEEDED TO END THIS--
KRAKRAKA

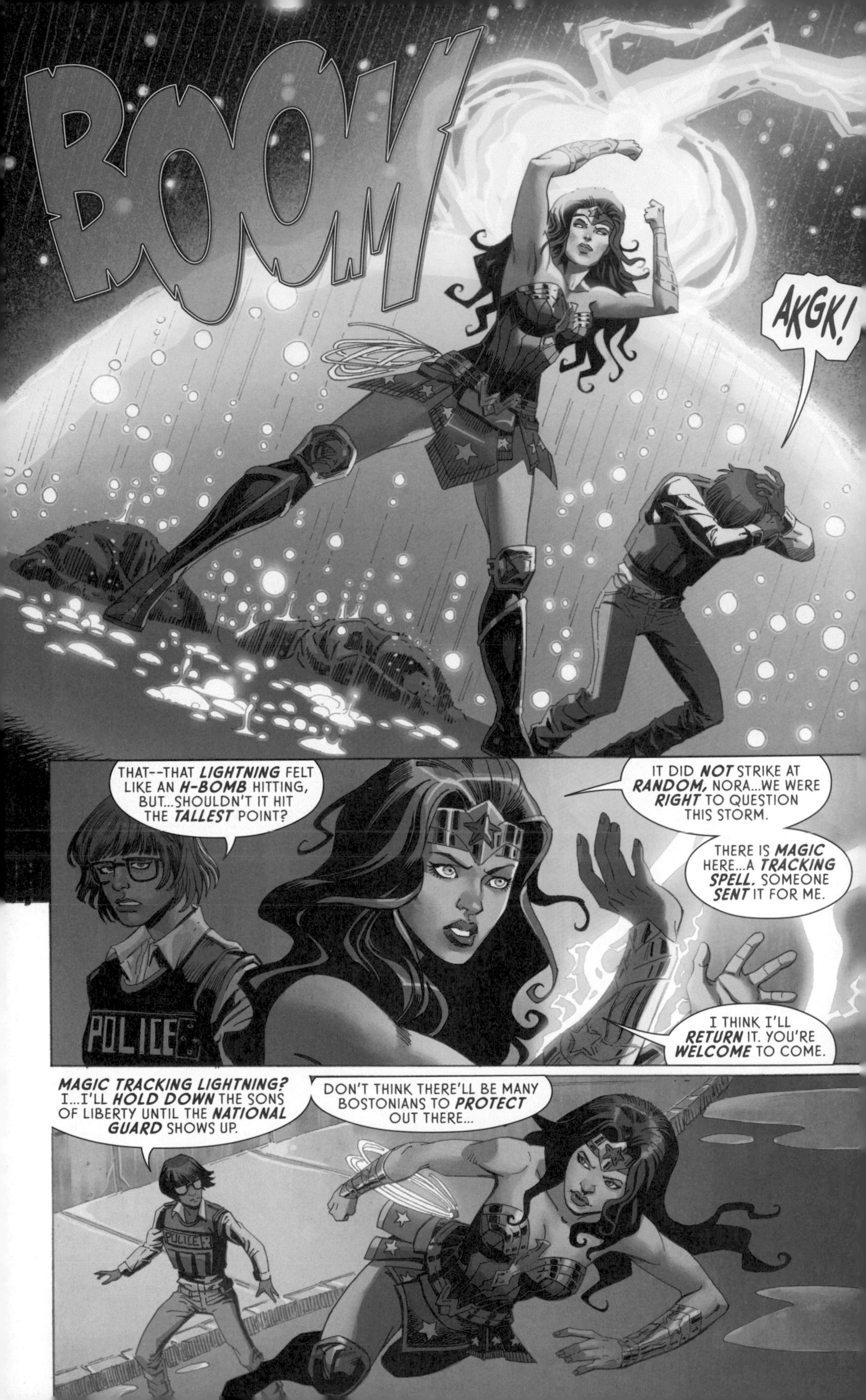
BOOM
AKGK!
THAT--THAT LIGHTNING FELT LIKE AN H-BOMB HITTING, BUT...SHOULDN'T IT HIT THE TALLEST POINT?
IT DID NOT STRIKE AT RANDOM, NORA...WE WERE RIGHT TO QUESTION THIS STORM.
THERE IS MAGIC HERE...A TRACKING SPELL. SOMEONE SENT IT FOR ME.
POLICE
I THINK I'LL RETURN IT. YOU'RE WELCOME TO COME.
MAGIC TRACKING LIGHTNING? I...I'LL HOLD DOWN THE SONS OF LIBERTY UNTIL THE NATIONAL GUARD SHOWS UP.
DON'T THINK THERE'LL BE MANY BOSTONIANS TO PROTECT OUT THERE...
POLICE

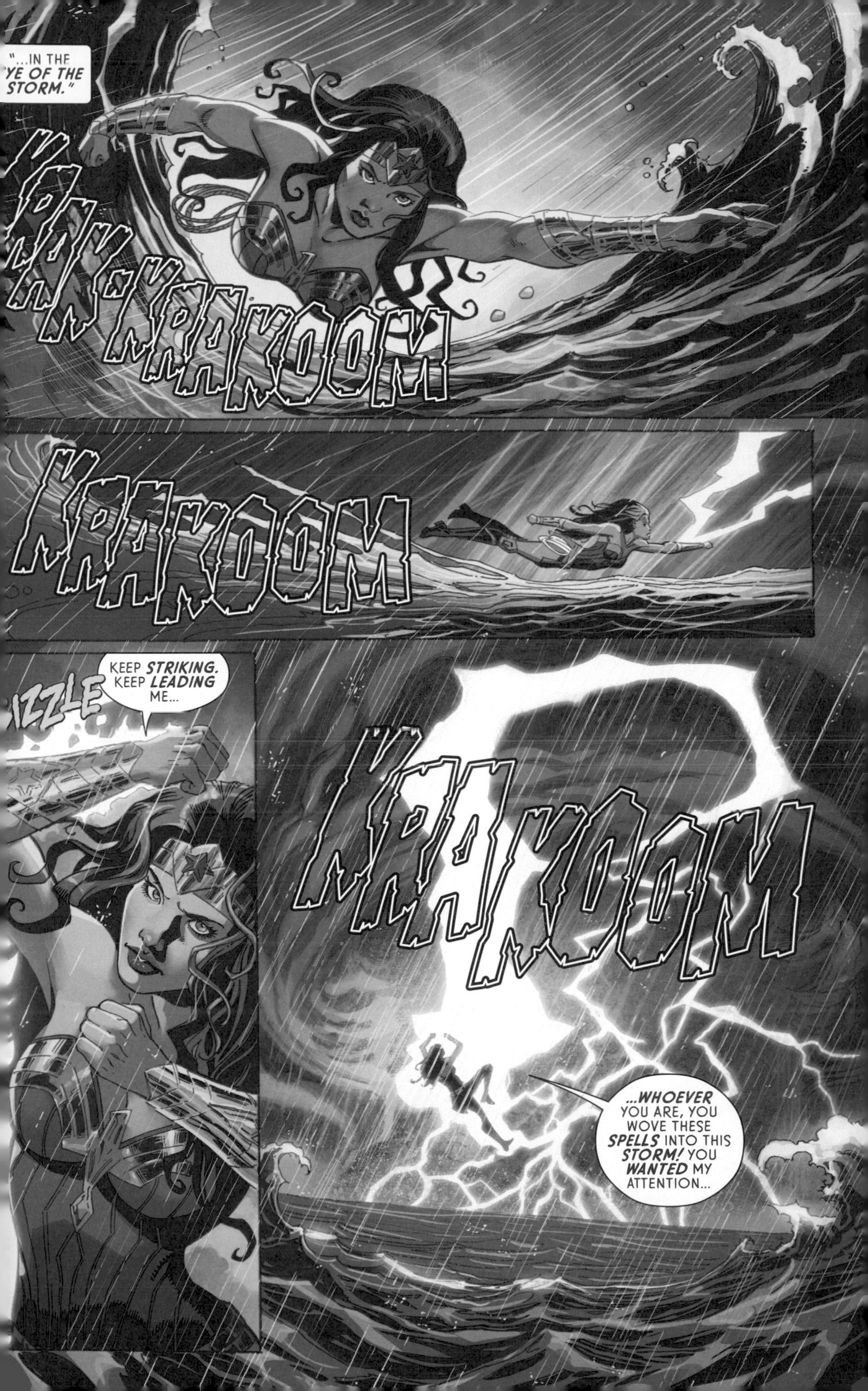
"...IN THE YE OF THE STORM."
KRAKOOM KRAKOOM
KRAKOOM
IZZLE
KEEP STRIKING. KEEP LEADING ME...
KRAKOOM
...WHOEVER YOU ARE, YOU WOVE THESE SPELLS INTO THIS STORM! YOU WANTED MY ATTENTION...

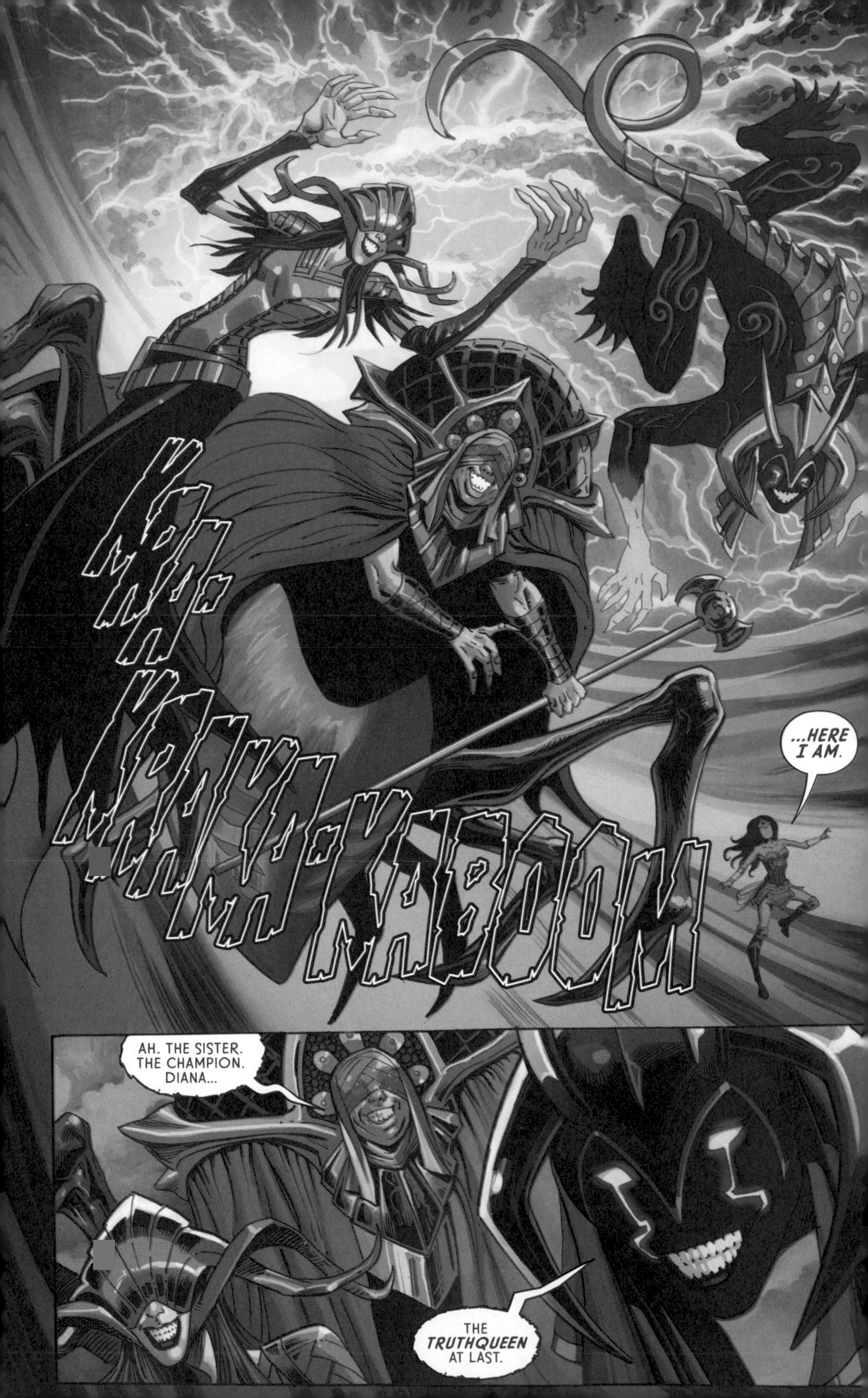
KABOOM
...HERE I AM.
AH. THE SISTER. THE CHAMPION. DIANA...
THE *TRUTHQUEEN* AT LAST.

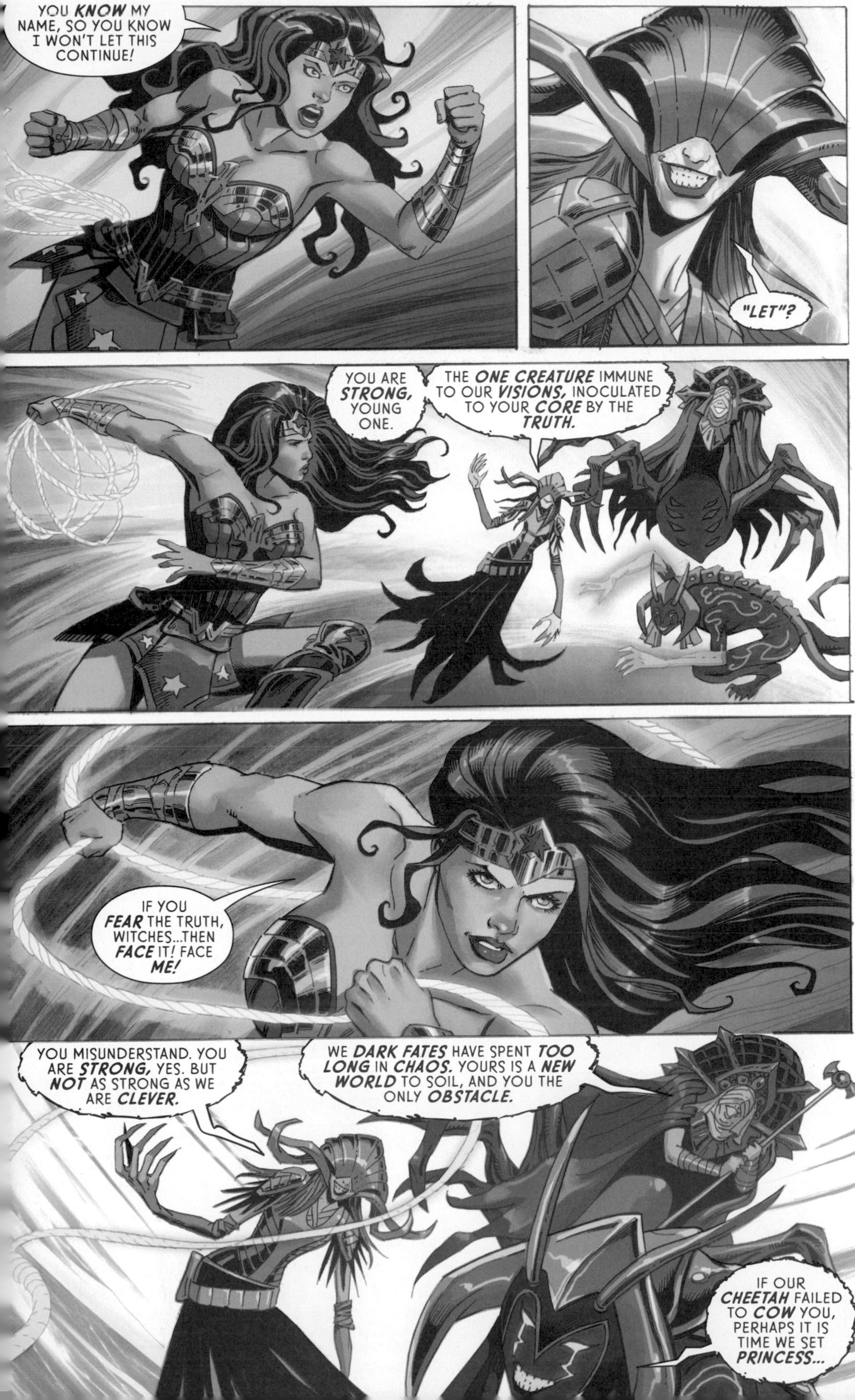
YOU KNOW MY NAME, SO YOU KNOW I WON'T LET THIS CONTINUE!
"LET"?
YOU ARE STRONG, YOUNG ONE.
THE ONE CREATURE IMMUNE TO OUR VISIONS, INOCULATED TO YOUR CORE BY THE TRUTH.
IF YOU FEAR THE TRUTH, WITCHES...THEN FACE IT! FACE ME!
YOU MISUNDERSTAND. YOU ARE STRONG, YES. BUT NOT AS STRONG AS WE ARE CLEVER.
WE DARK FATES HAVE SPENT TOO LONG IN CHAOS. YOURS IS A NEW WORLD TO SOIL, AND YOU THE ONLY OBSTACLE.
IF OUR CHEETAH FAILED TO COW YOU, PERHAPS IT IS TIME WE SET PRINCESS...

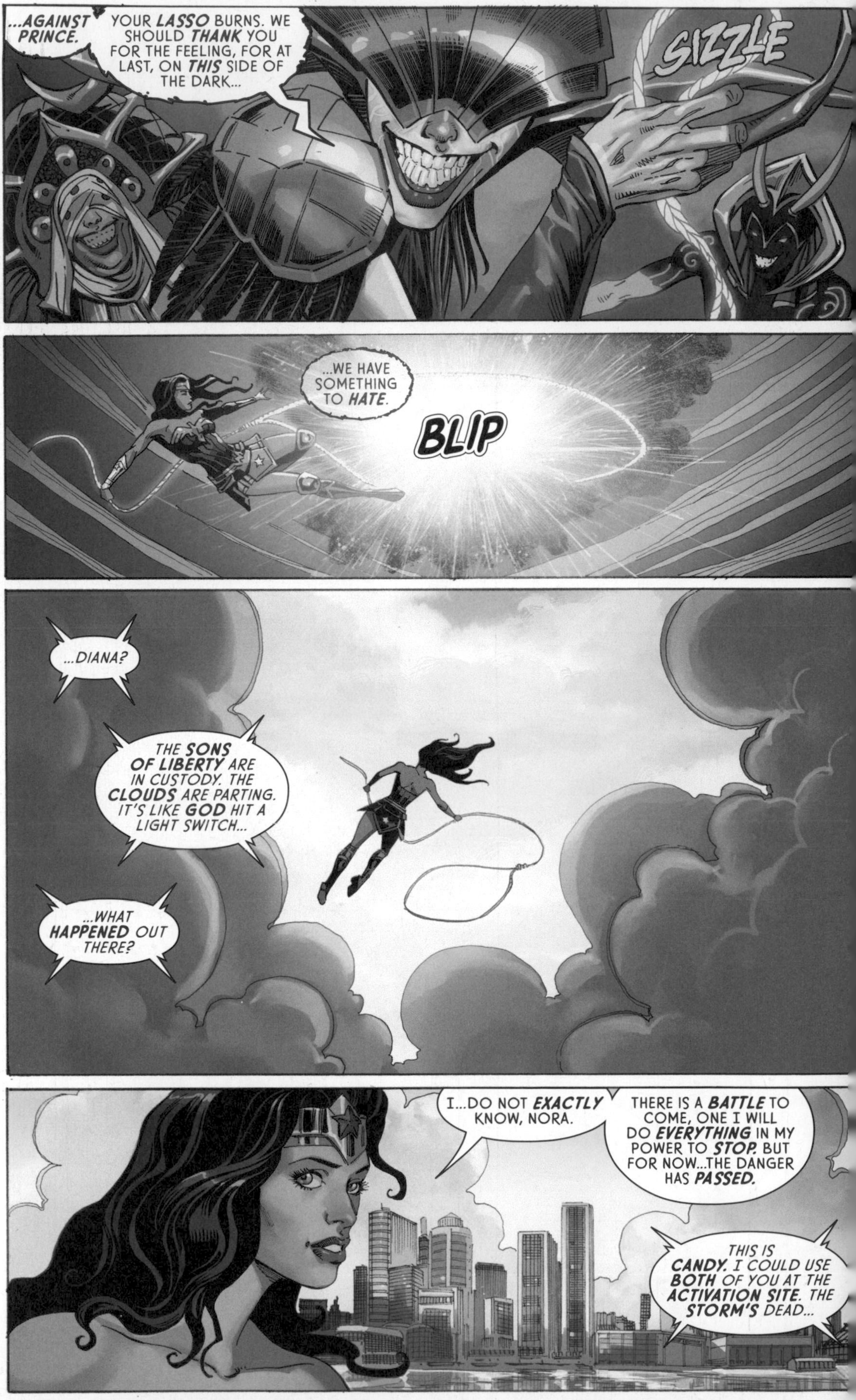
...AGAINST PRINCE.
YOUR LASSO BURNS. WE SHOULD THANK YOU FOR THE FEELING, FOR AT LAST, ON THIS SIDE OF THE DARK...
SIZZLE
...WE HAVE SOMETHING TO HATE.
BLIP
...DIANA?
THE SONS OF LIBERTY ARE IN CUSTODY. THE CLOUDS ARE PARTING. IT'S LIKE GOD HIT A LIGHT SWITCH...
...WHAT HAPPENED OUT THERE?
I...DO NOT EXACTLY KNOW, NORA.
THERE IS A BATTLE TO COME, ONE I WILL DO EVERYTHING IN MY POWER TO STOP. BUT FOR NOW...THE DANGER HAS PASSED.
THIS IS CANDY. I COULD USE BOTH OF YOU AT THE ACTIVATION SITE. THE STORM'S DEAD...

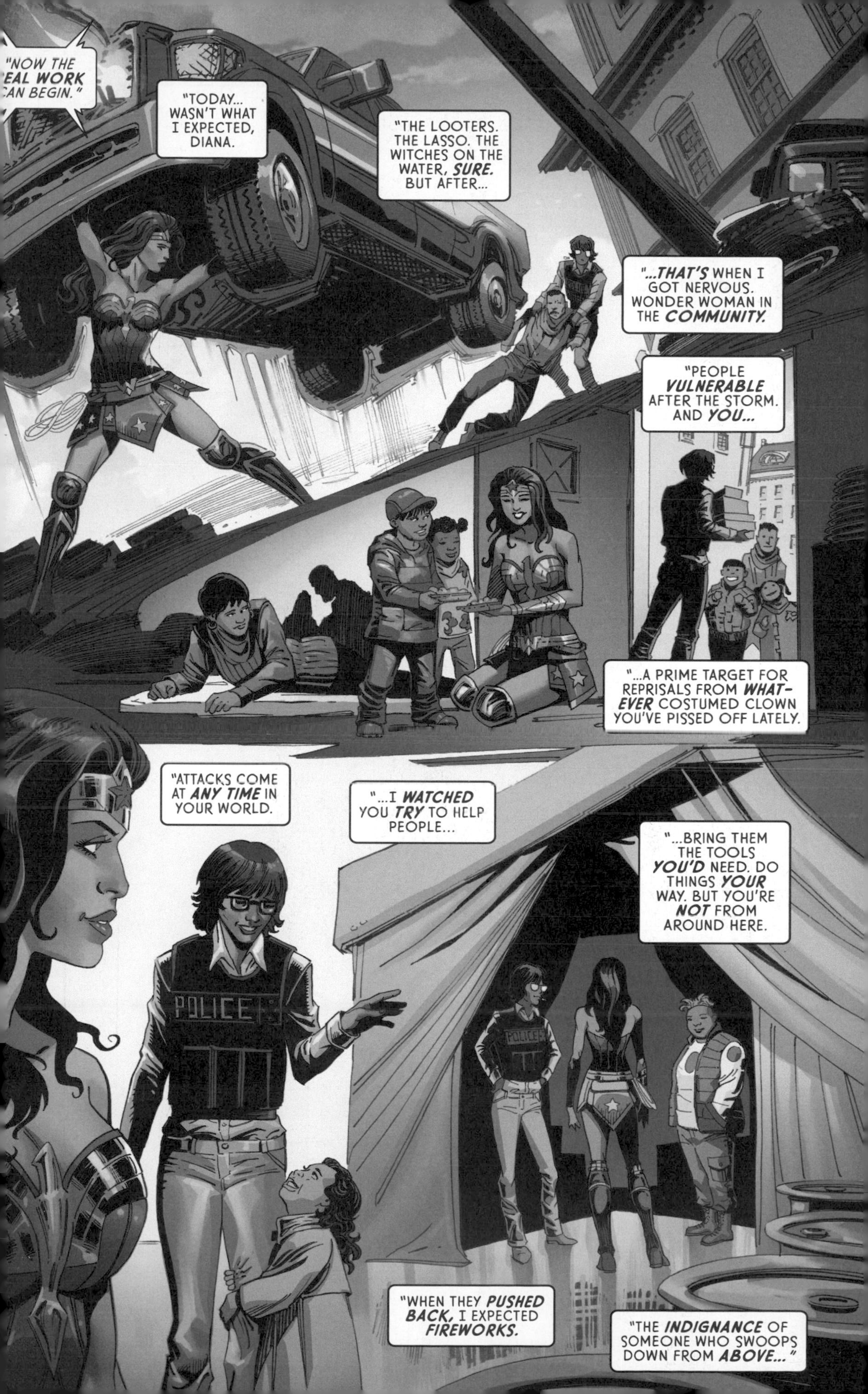
"NOW THE EAL WORK CAN BEGIN."
"TODAY... WASN'T WHAT I EXPECTED, DIANA.
"THE LOOTERS. THE LASSO. THE WITCHES ON THE WATER, SURE. BUT AFTER...
"...THAT'S WHEN I GOT NERVOUS. WONDER WOMAN IN THE COMMUNITY.
"PEOPLE VULNERABLE AFTER THE STORM. AND YOU...
"...A PRIME TARGET FOR REPRISALS FROM WHAT-EVER COSTUMED CLOWN YOU'VE PISSED OFF LATELY.
"ATTACKS COME AT ANY TIME IN YOUR WORLD.
"...I WATCHED YOU TRY TO HELP PEOPLE...
"...BRING THEM THE TOOLS YOU'D NEED. DO THINGS YOUR WAY. BUT YOU'RE NOT FROM AROUND HERE.
POLICE
"WHEN THEY PUSHED BACK, I EXPECTED FIREWORKS.
"THE INDIGNANCE OF SOMEONE WHO SWOOPS DOWN FROM ABOVE..."

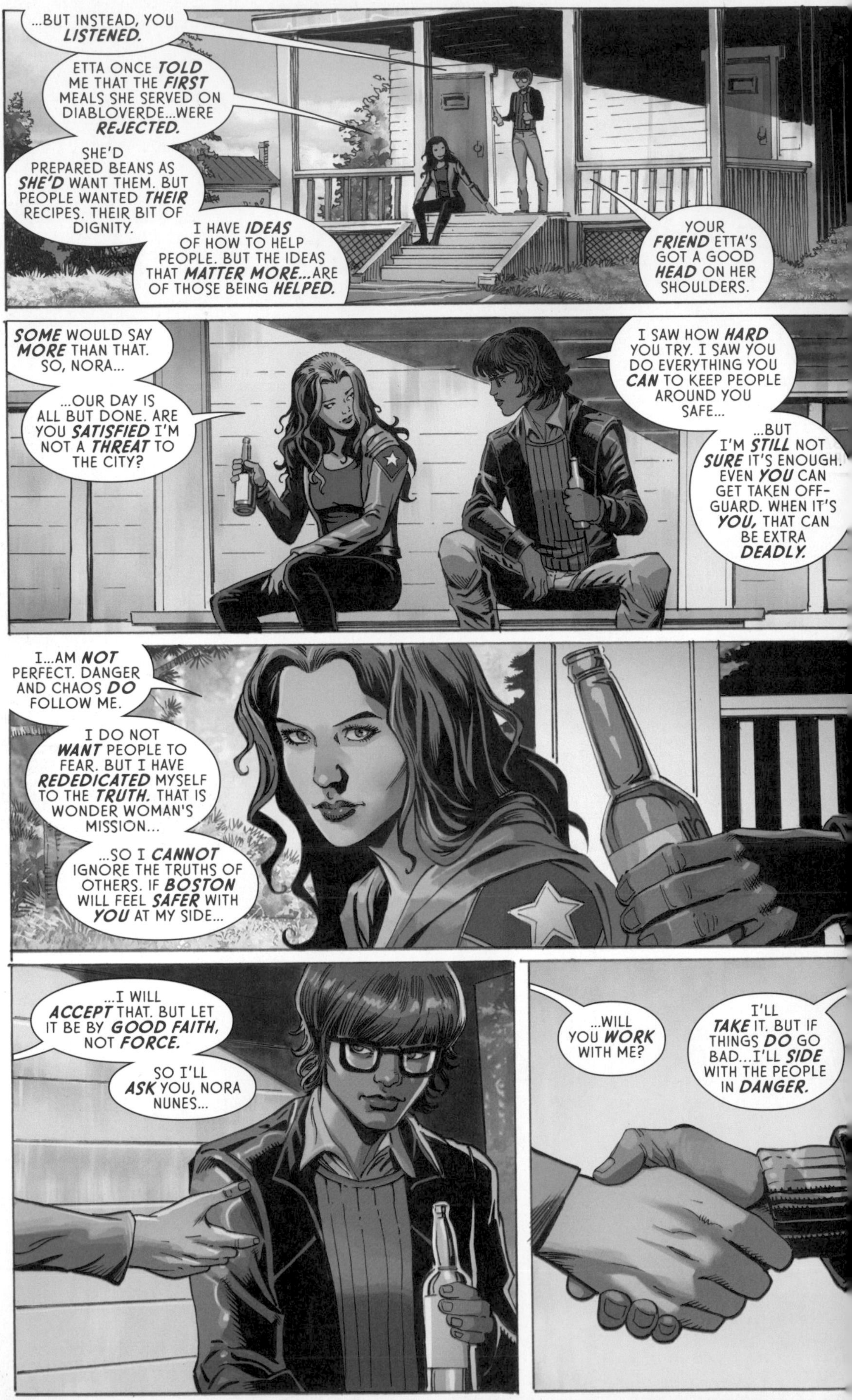
...BUT INSTEAD, YOU LISTENED.
ETTA ONCE TOLD ME THAT THE FIRST MEALS SHE SERVED ON DIABLOVERDE...WERE REJECTED.
SHE'D PREPARED BEANS AS SHE'D WANT THEM. BUT PEOPLE WANTED THEIR RECIPES. THEIR BIT OF DIGNITY.
I HAVE IDEAS OF HOW TO HELP PEOPLE. BUT THE IDEAS THAT MATTER MORE...ARE OF THOSE BEING HELPED.
YOUR FRIEND ETTA'S GOT A GOOD HEAD ON HER SHOULDERS.
SOME WOULD SAY MORE THAN THAT. SO, NORA...
...OUR DAY IS ALL BUT DONE. ARE YOU SATISFIED I'M NOT A THREAT TO THE CITY?
I SAW HOW HARD YOU TRY. I SAW YOU DO EVERYTHING YOU CAN TO KEEP PEOPLE AROUND YOU SAFE...
...BUT I'M STILL NOT SURE IT'S ENOUGH. EVEN YOU CAN GET TAKEN OFF-GUARD. WHEN IT'S YOU, THAT CAN BE EXTRA DEADLY.
I...AM NOT PERFECT. DANGER AND CHAOS DO FOLLOW ME.
I DO NOT WANT PEOPLE TO FEAR. BUT I HAVE REDEDICATED MYSELF TO THE TRUTH. THAT IS WONDER WOMAN'S MISSION...
...SO I CANNOT IGNORE THE TRUTHS OF OTHERS. IF BOSTON WILL FEEL SAFER WITH YOU AT MY SIDE...
...I WILL ACCEPT THAT. BUT LET IT BE BY GOOD FAITH, NOT FORCE.
SO I'LL ASK YOU, NORA NUNES...
...WILL YOU WORK WITH ME?
I'LL TAKE IT. BUT IF THINGS DO GO BAD...I'LL SIDE WITH THE PEOPLE IN DANGER.

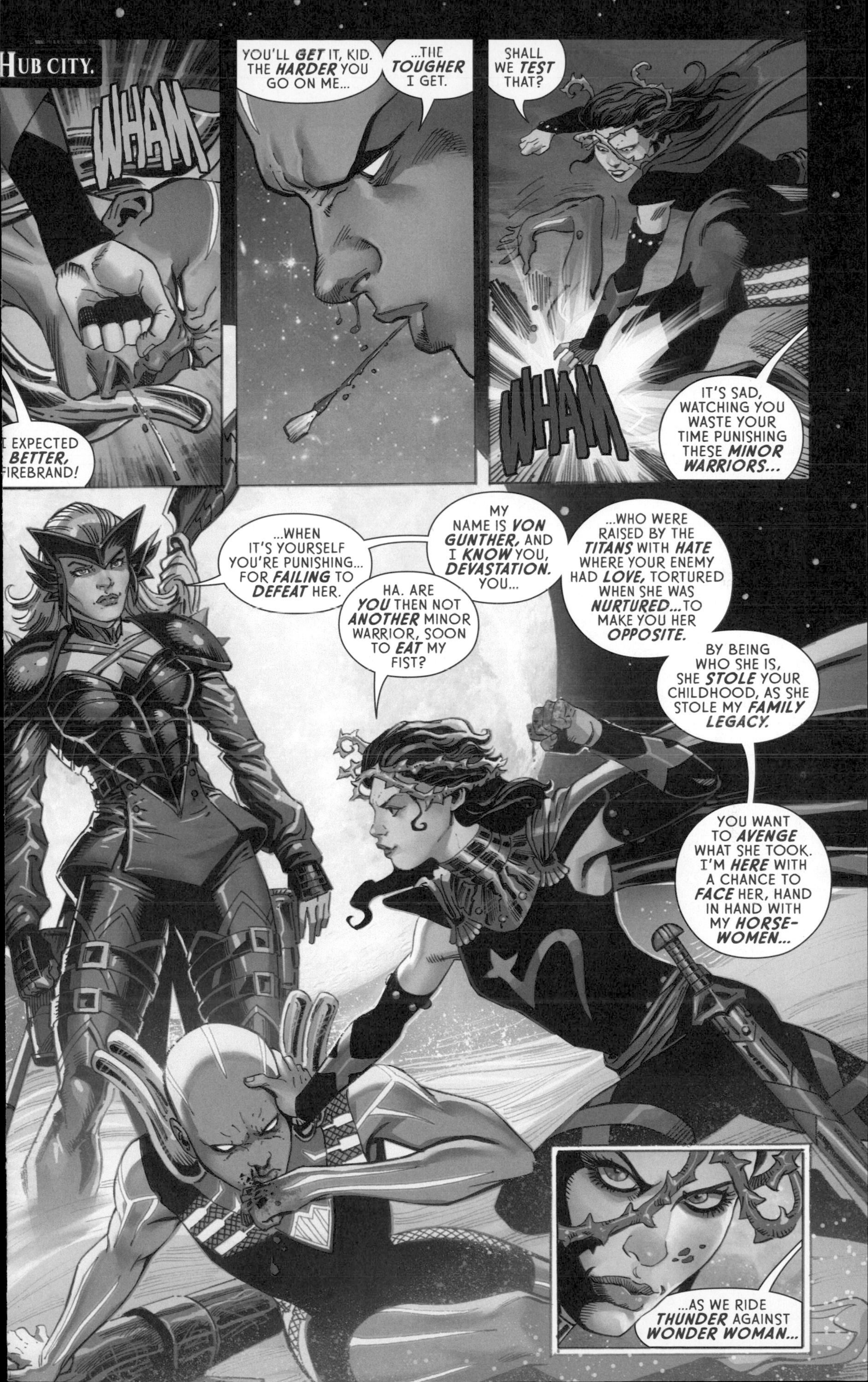
HUB CITY.
WHAM
I EXPECTED BETTER, FIREBRAND!
YOU'LL GET IT, KID. THE HARDER YOU GO ON ME...
...THE TOUGHER I GET.
SHALL WE TEST THAT?
WHAM
IT'S SAD, WATCHING YOU WASTE YOUR TIME PUNISHING THESE MINOR WARRIORS...
...WHEN IT'S YOURSELF YOU'RE PUNISHING... FOR FAILING TO DEFEAT HER.
MY NAME IS VON GUNTHER, AND I KNOW YOU, DEVASTATION. YOU...
HA. ARE YOU THEN NOT ANOTHER MINOR WARRIOR, SOON TO EAT MY FIST?
...WHO WERE RAISED BY THE TITANS WITH HATE WHERE YOUR ENEMY HAD LOVE, TORTURED WHEN SHE WAS NURTURED...TO MAKE YOU HER OPPOSITE.
BY BEING WHO SHE IS, SHE STOLE YOUR CHILDHOOD, AS SHE STOLE MY FAMILY LEGACY.
YOU WANT TO AVENGE WHAT SHE TOOK. I'M HERE WITH A CHANCE TO FACE HER, HAND IN HAND WITH MY HORSE-WOMEN...
...AS WE RIDE THUNDER AGAINST WONDER WOMAN...

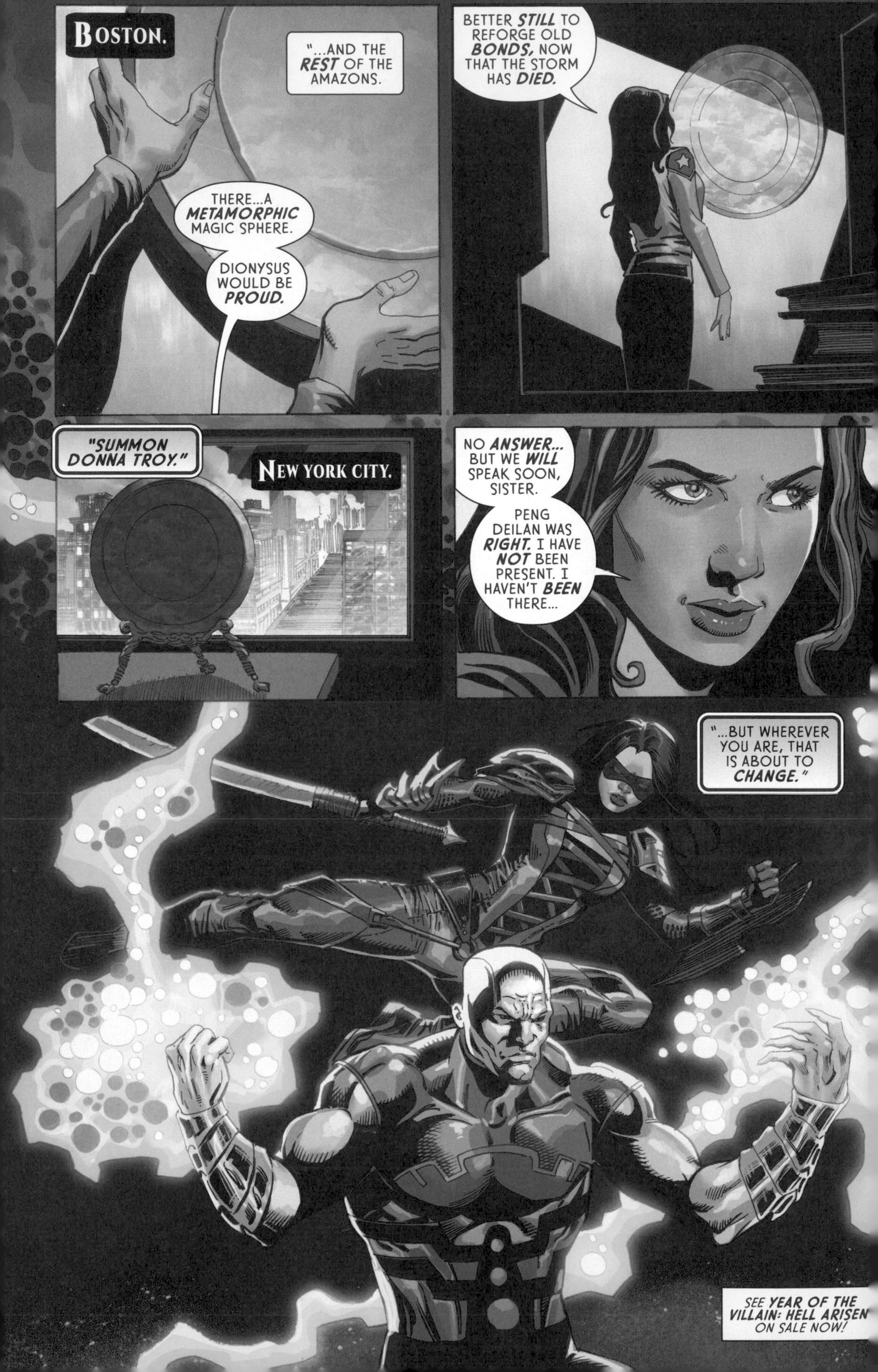

BOSTON.
"...AND THE REST OF THE AMAZONS.
THERE...A METAMORPHIC MAGIC SPHERE.
DIONYSUS WOULD BE PROUD.
BETTER STILL TO REFORGE OLD BONDS, NOW THAT THE STORM HAS DIED.
"SUMMON DONNA TROY."
NEW YORK CITY.
NO ANSWER... BUT WE WILL SPEAK SOON, SISTER.
PENG DEILAN WAS RIGHT. I HAVE NOT BEEN PRESENT. I HAVEN'T BEEN THERE...
"...BUT WHEREVER YOU ARE, THAT IS ABOUT TO CHANGE."
SEE YEAR OF THE VILLAIN: HELL ARISEN ON SALE NOW!

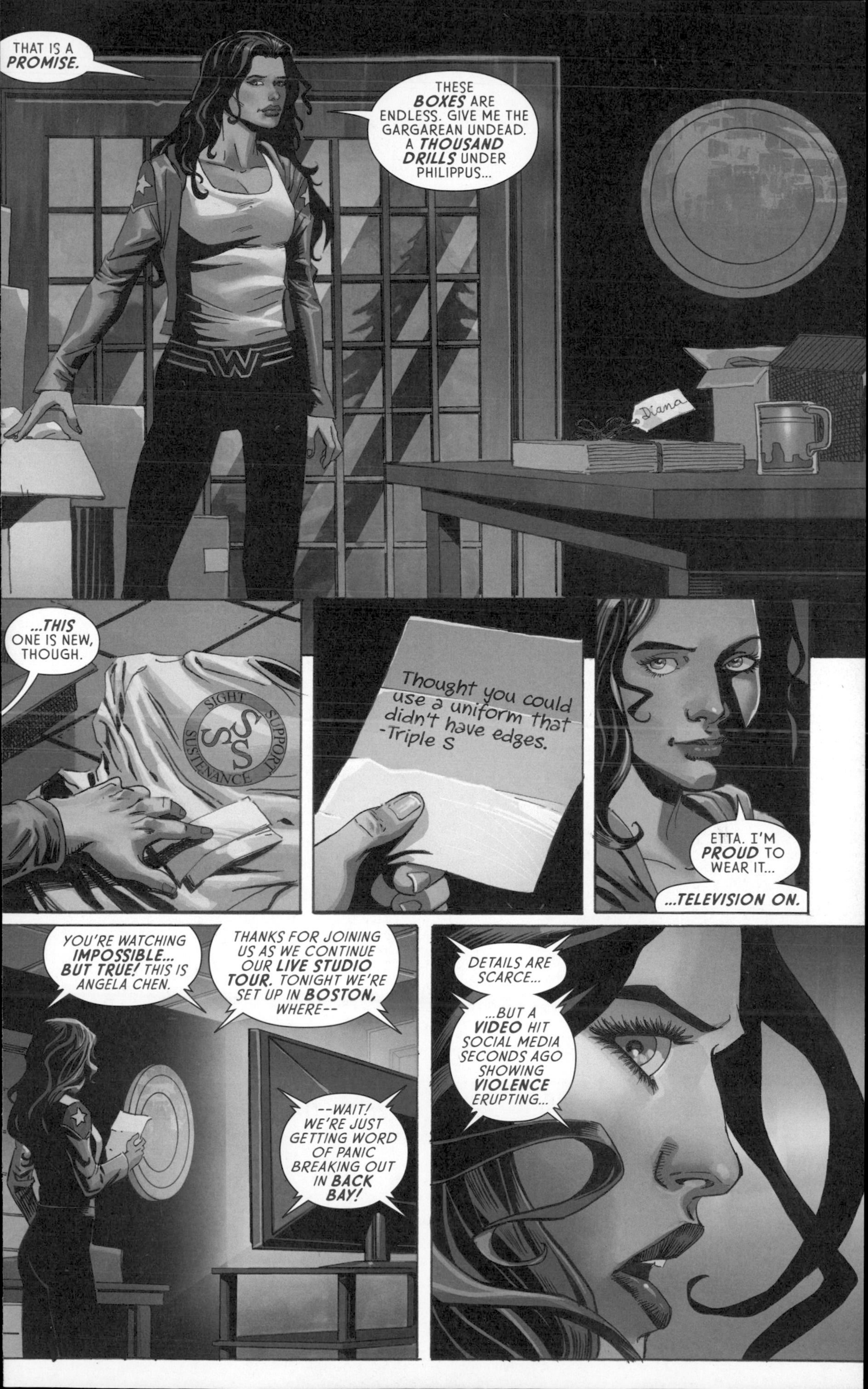
THAT IS A PROMISE.
THESE BOXES ARE ENDLESS. GIVE ME THE GARGAREAN UNDEAD. A THOUSAND DRILLS UNDER PHILIPPUS...
Diana
...THIS ONE IS NEW, THOUGH.
SIGHT SUPPORT SUSTENANCE
Thought you could use a uniform that didn't have edges. -Triple S
ETTA. I'M PROUD TO WEAR IT...
...TELEVISION ON.
YOU'RE WATCHING IMPOSSIBLE... BUT TRUE! THIS IS ANGELA CHEN.
THANKS FOR JOINING US AS WE CONTINUE OUR LIVE STUDIO TOUR. TONIGHT WE'RE SET UP IN BOSTON, WHERE--
--WAIT! WE'RE JUST GETTING WORD OF PANIC BREAKING OUT IN BACK BAY!
DETAILS ARE SCARCE...
...BUT A VIDEO HIT SOCIAL MEDIA SECONDS AGO SHOWING VIOLENCE ERUPTING...

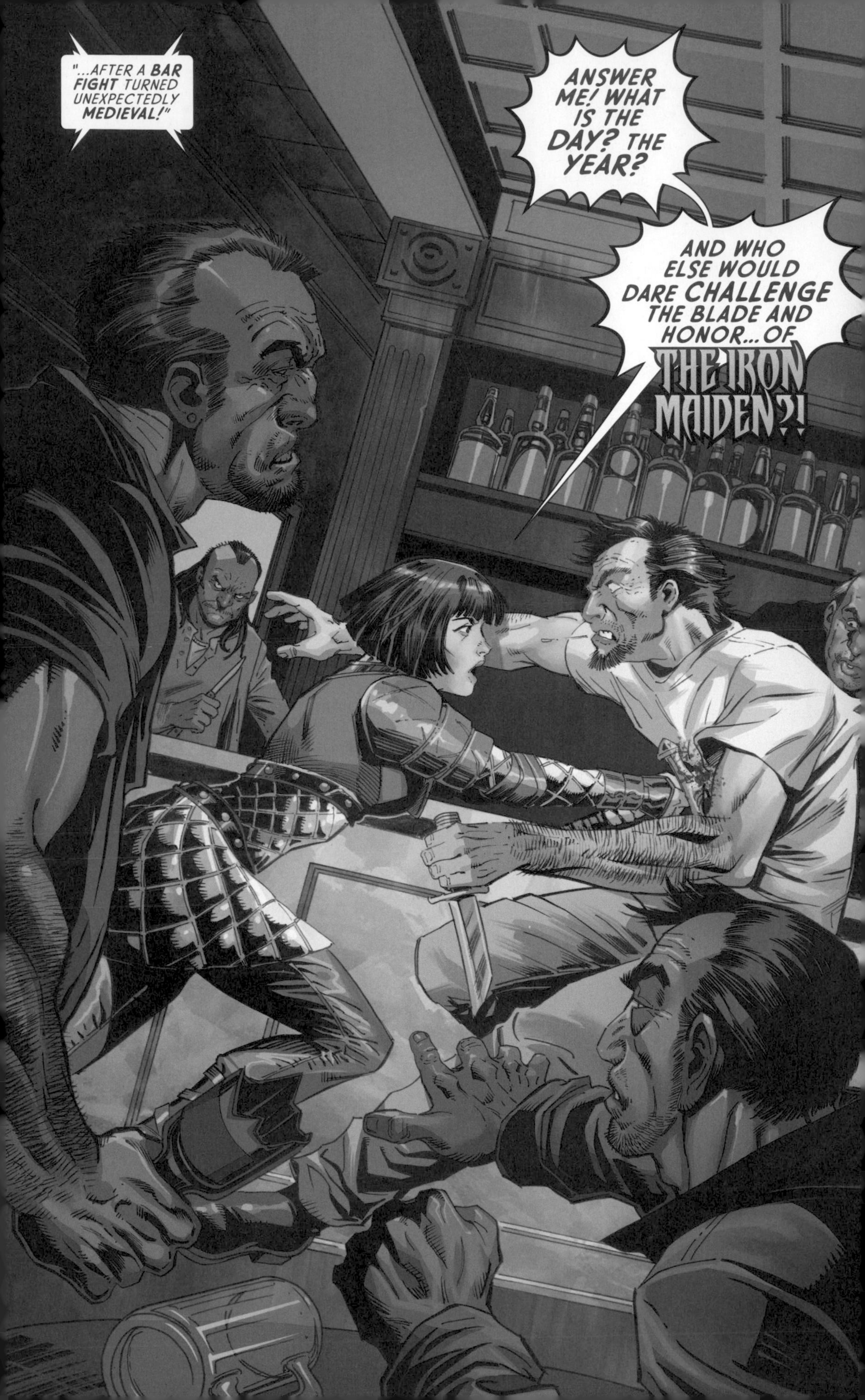
"...AFTER A BAR FIGHT TURNED UNEXPECTEDLY MEDIEVAL!"
ANSWER ME! WHAT IS THE DAY? THE YEAR?
AND WHO ELSE WOULD DARE CHALLENGE THE BLADE AND HONOR...OF THE IRON MAIDEN?!

Wonder Woman **#752**
cover by **GUILLEM MARCH** and **ARIF PRIANTO**

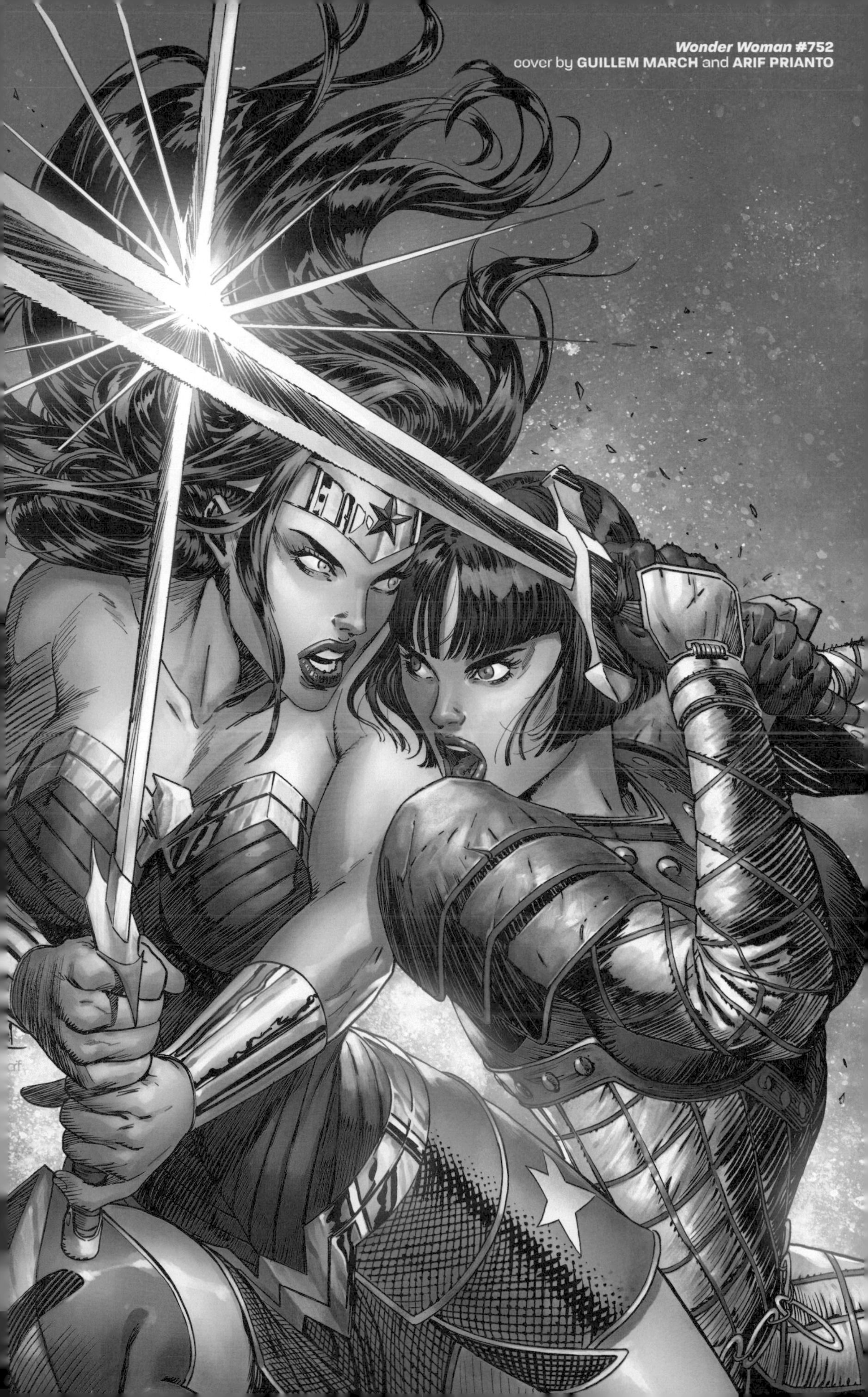

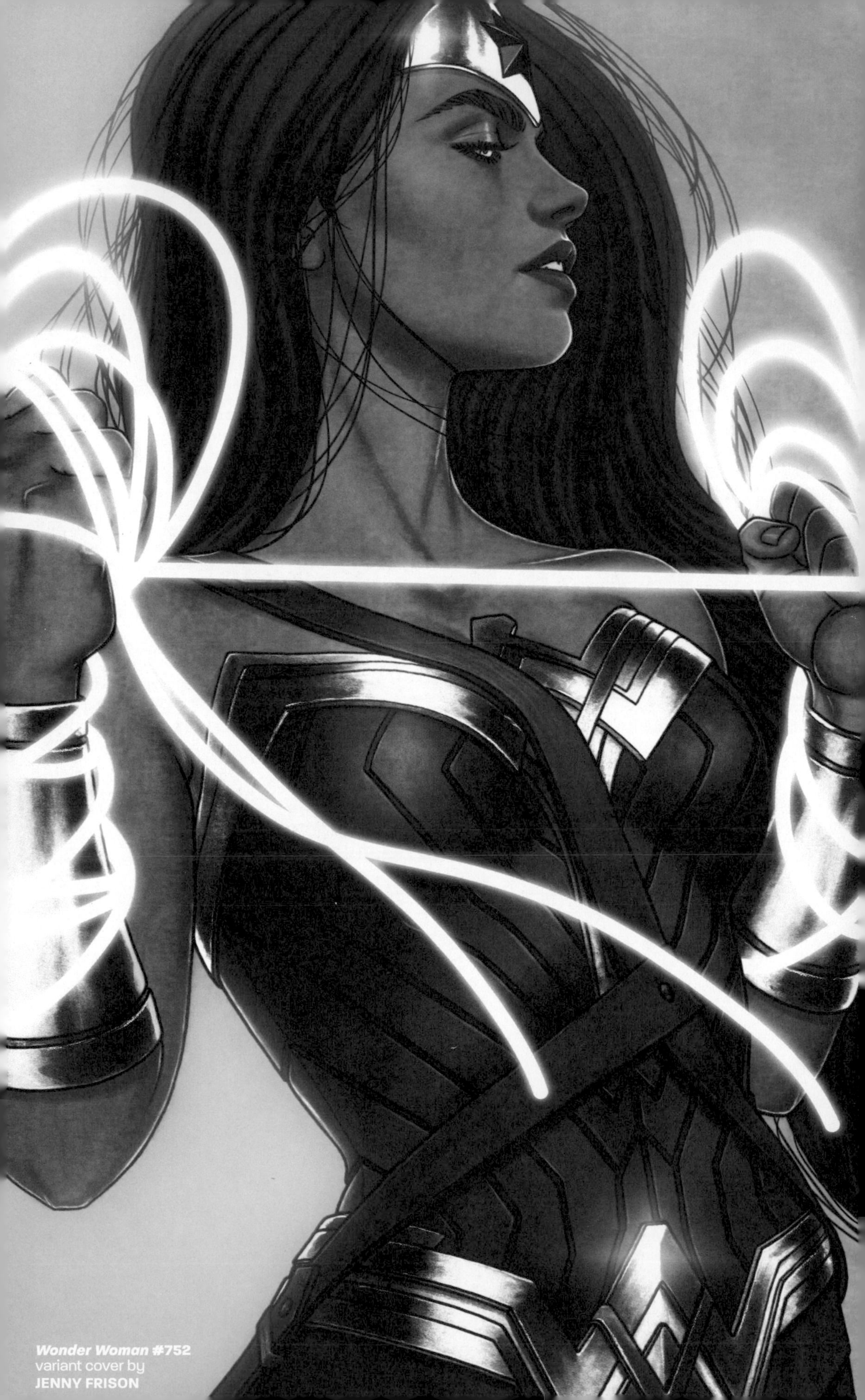

***Wonder Woman* #752**
variant cover by
JENNY FRISON

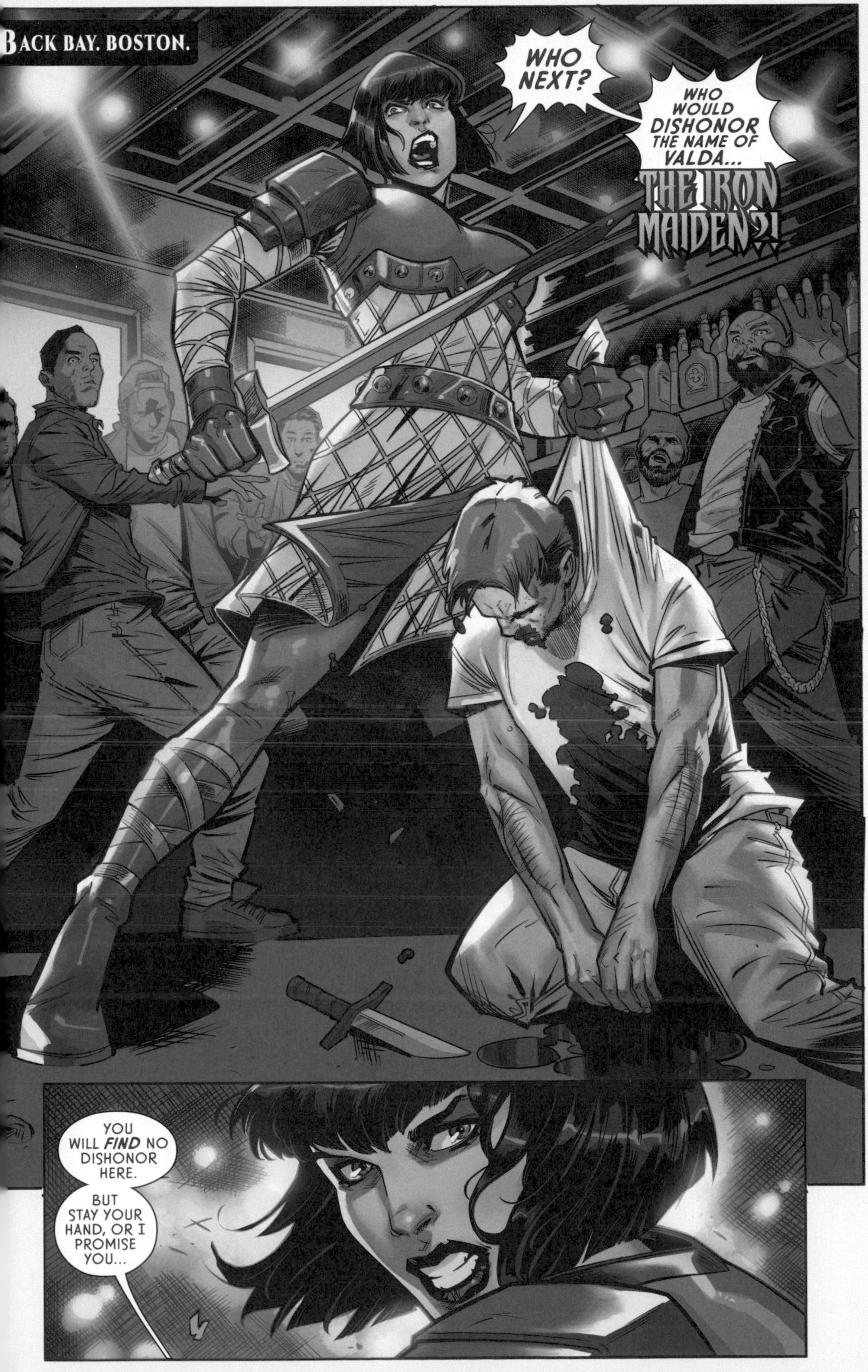
BACK BAY. BOSTON.
WHO NEXT?
WHO WOULD DISHONOR THE NAME OF VALDA... THE IRON MAIDEN?!
YOU WILL FIND NO DISHONOR HERE.
BUT STAY YOUR HAND, OR I PROMISE YOU...

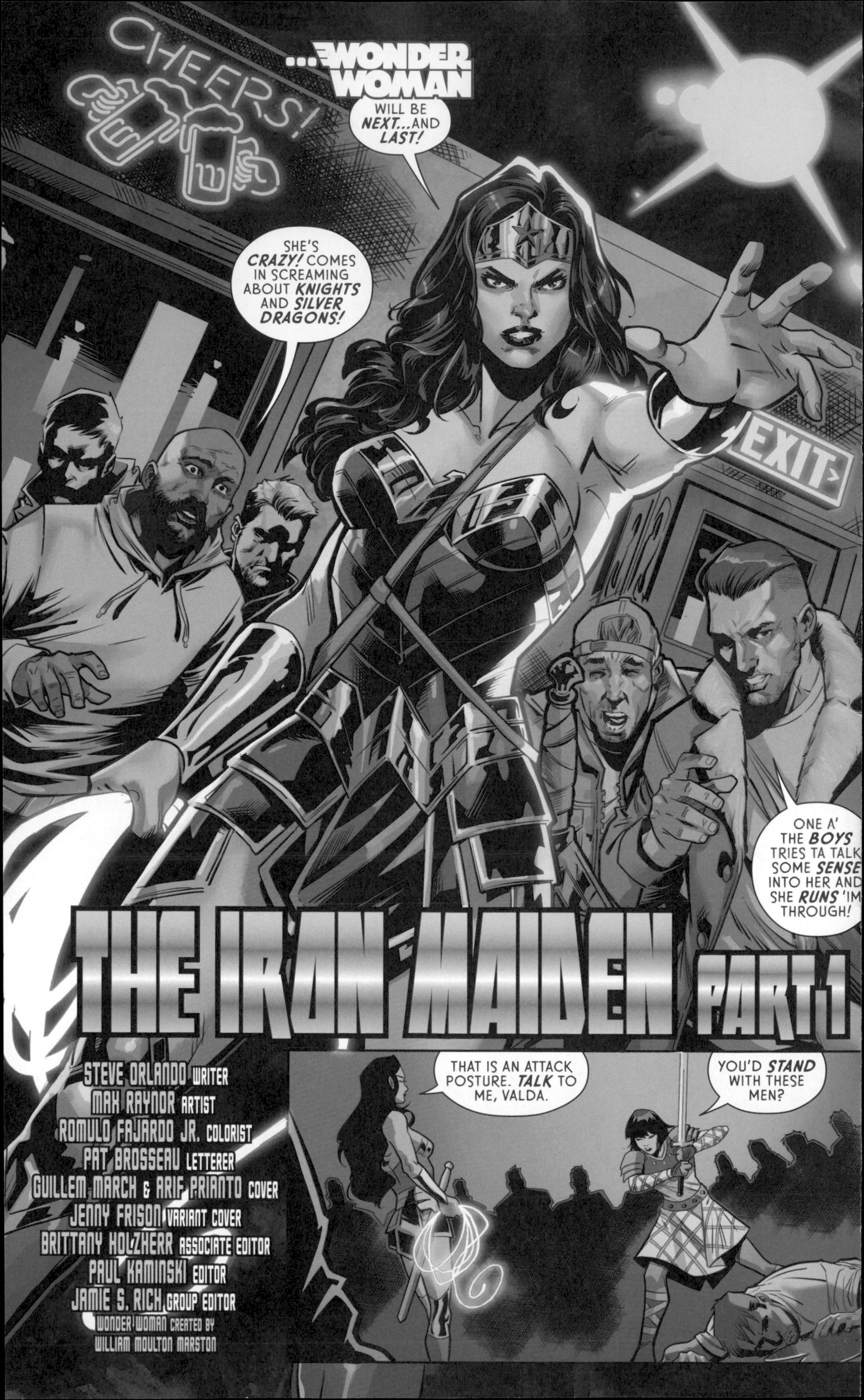
CHEERS!
...WONDER WOMAN
WILL BE NEXT...AND LAST!
SHE'S CRAZY! COMES IN SCREAMING ABOUT KNIGHTS AND SILVER DRAGONS!
EXIT
ONE A' THE BOYS TRIES TA TALK SOME SENSE INTO HER AND SHE RUNS 'IM THROUGH!
THE IRON MAIDEN PART 1
STEVE ORLANDO WRITER
MAX RAYNOR ARTIST
ROMULO FAJARDO JR. COLORIST
PAT BROSSEAU LETTERER
GUILLEM MARCH & ARIF PRIANTO COVER
JENNY FRISON VARIANT COVER
BRITTANY HOLZHERR ASSOCIATE EDITOR
PAUL KAMINSKI EDITOR
JAMIE S. RICH GROUP EDITOR
WONDER WOMAN CREATED BY WILLIAM MOULTON MARSTON
THAT IS AN ATTACK POSTURE. TALK TO ME, VALDA.
YOU'D STAND WITH THESE MEN?

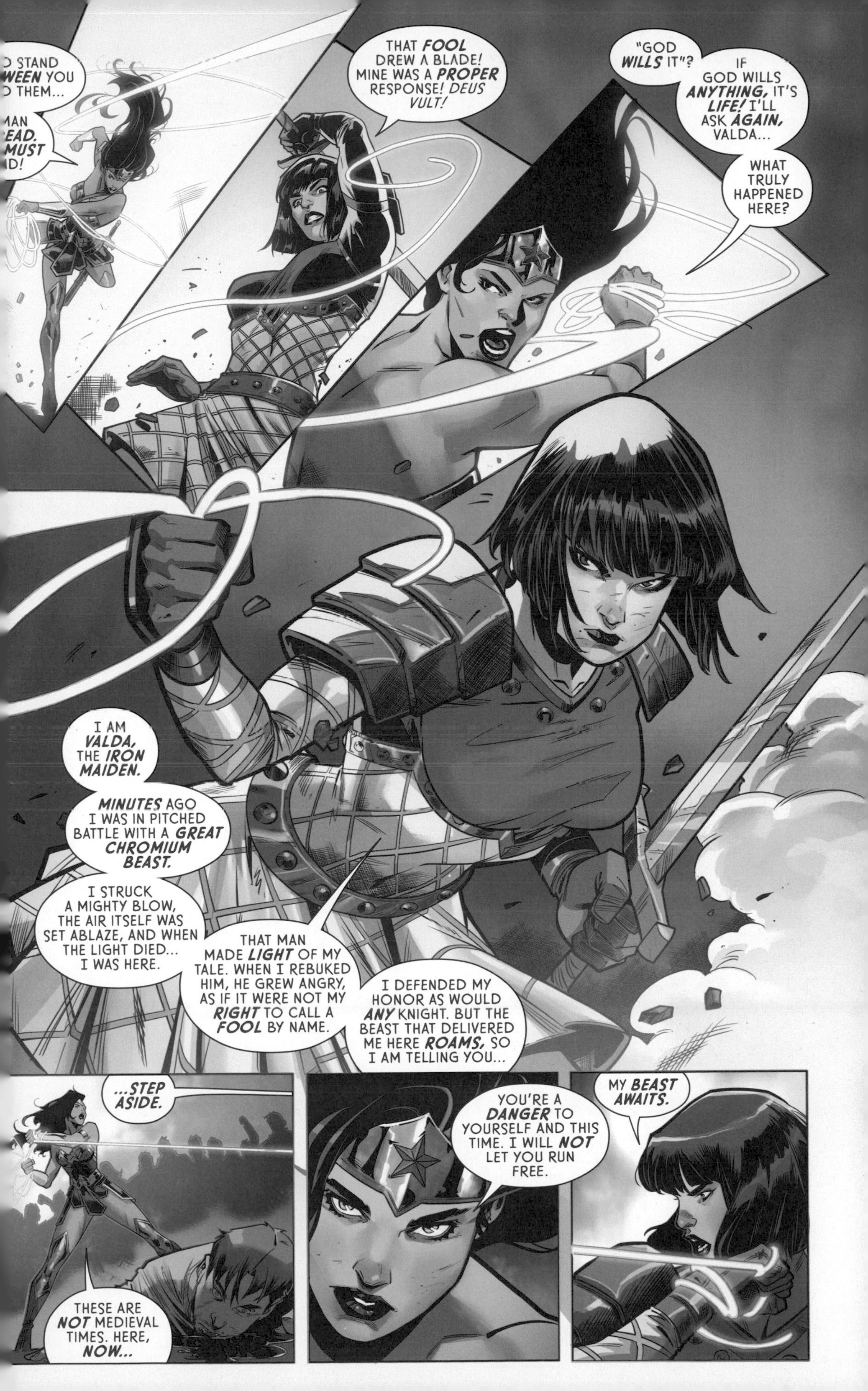
O STAND WEEN YOU D THEM...
MAN EAD. MUST D!
THAT FOOL DREW A BLADE! MINE WAS A PROPER RESPONSE! DEUS VULT!
"GOD WILLS IT"?
IF GOD WILLS ANYTHING, IT'S LIFE! I'LL ASK AGAIN, VALDA...
WHAT TRULY HAPPENED HERE?
I AM VALDA, THE IRON MAIDEN.
MINUTES AGO I WAS IN PITCHED BATTLE WITH A GREAT CHROMIUM BEAST.
I STRUCK A MIGHTY BLOW, THE AIR ITSELF WAS SET ABLAZE, AND WHEN THE LIGHT DIED... I WAS HERE.
THAT MAN MADE LIGHT OF MY TALE. WHEN I REBUKED HIM, HE GREW ANGRY, AS IF IT WERE NOT MY RIGHT TO CALL A FOOL BY NAME.
I DEFENDED MY HONOR AS WOULD ANY KNIGHT. BUT THE BEAST THAT DELIVERED ME HERE ROAMS, SO I AM TELLING YOU...
...STEP ASIDE.
THESE ARE NOT MEDIEVAL TIMES. HERE, NOW...
YOU'RE A DANGER TO YOURSELF AND THIS TIME. I WILL NOT LET YOU RUN FREE.
MY BEAST AWAITS.

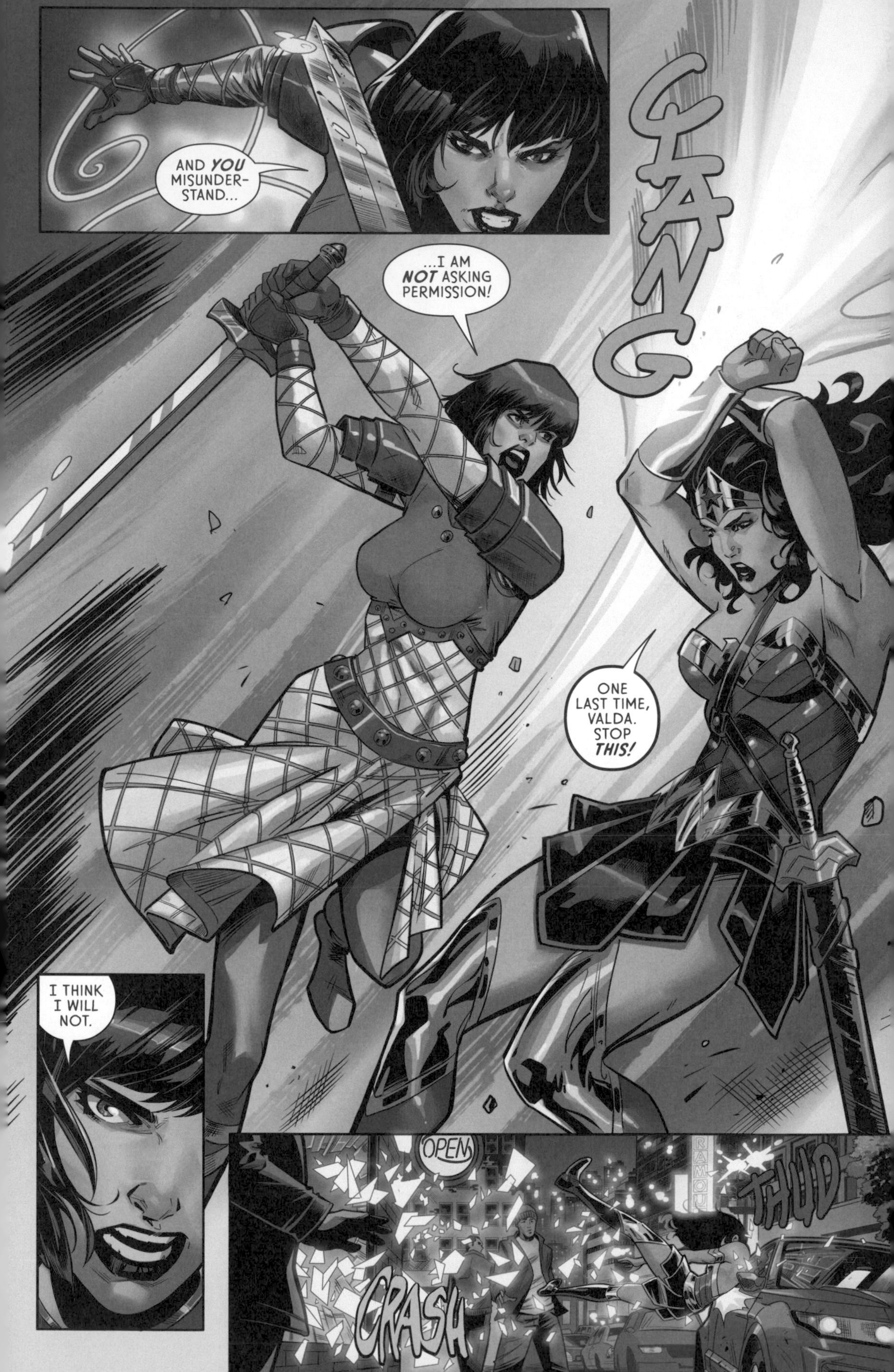
AND YOU MISUNDERSTAND...
CLANG
...I AM NOT ASKING PERMISSION!
ONE LAST TIME, VALDA. STOP THIS!
I THINK I WILL NOT.
OPEN
THUD
CRASH

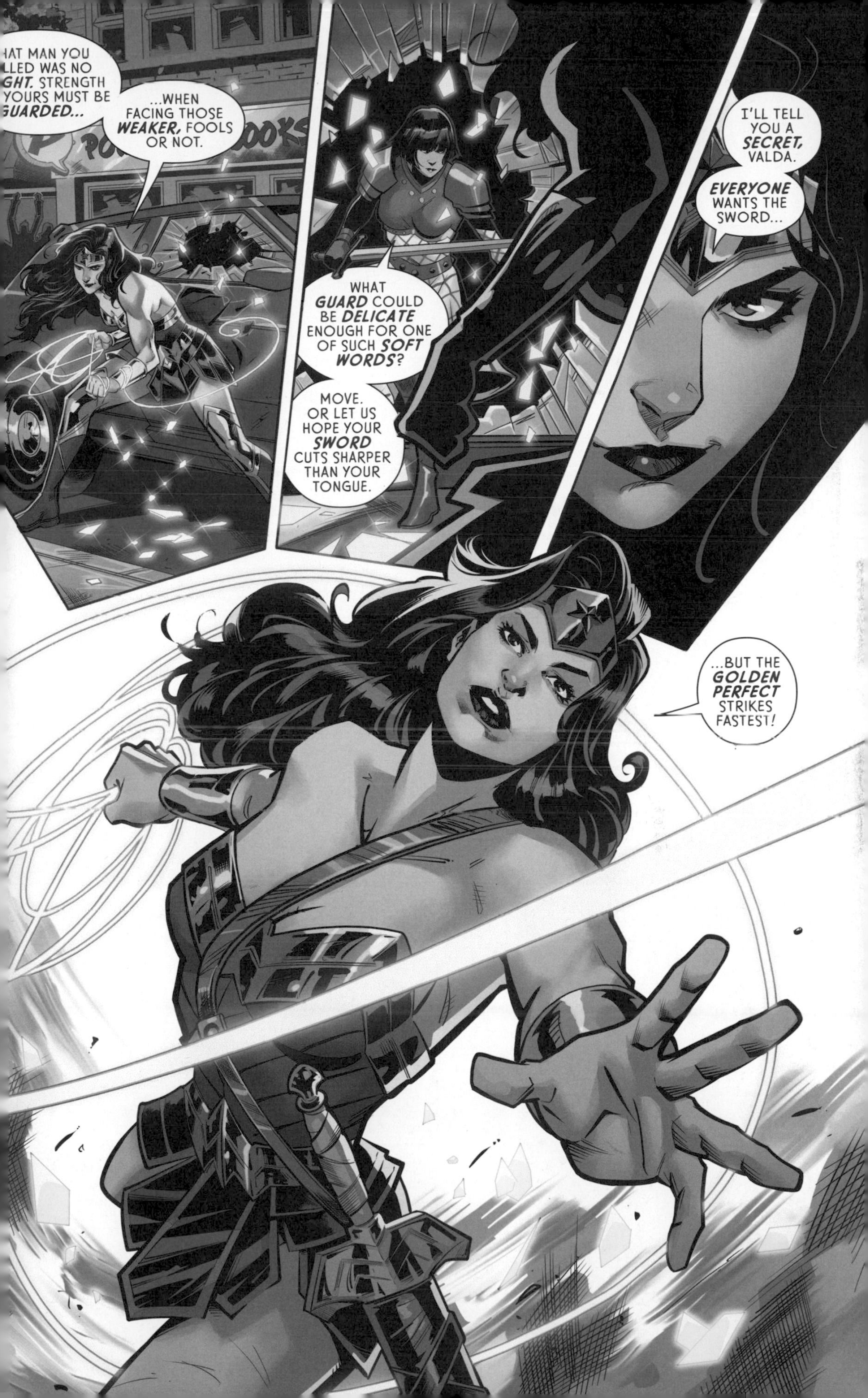
HAT MAN YOU LLED WAS NO GHT. STRENGTH YOURS MUST BE GUARDED...
...WHEN FACING THOSE WEAKER, FOOLS OR NOT.
WHAT GUARD COULD BE DELICATE ENOUGH FOR ONE OF SUCH SOFT WORDS?
MOVE. OR LET US HOPE YOUR SWORD CUTS SHARPER THAN YOUR TONGUE.
I'LL TELL YOU A SECRET, VALDA.
EVERYONE WANTS THE SWORD...
...BUT THE GOLDEN PERFECT STRIKES FASTEST!

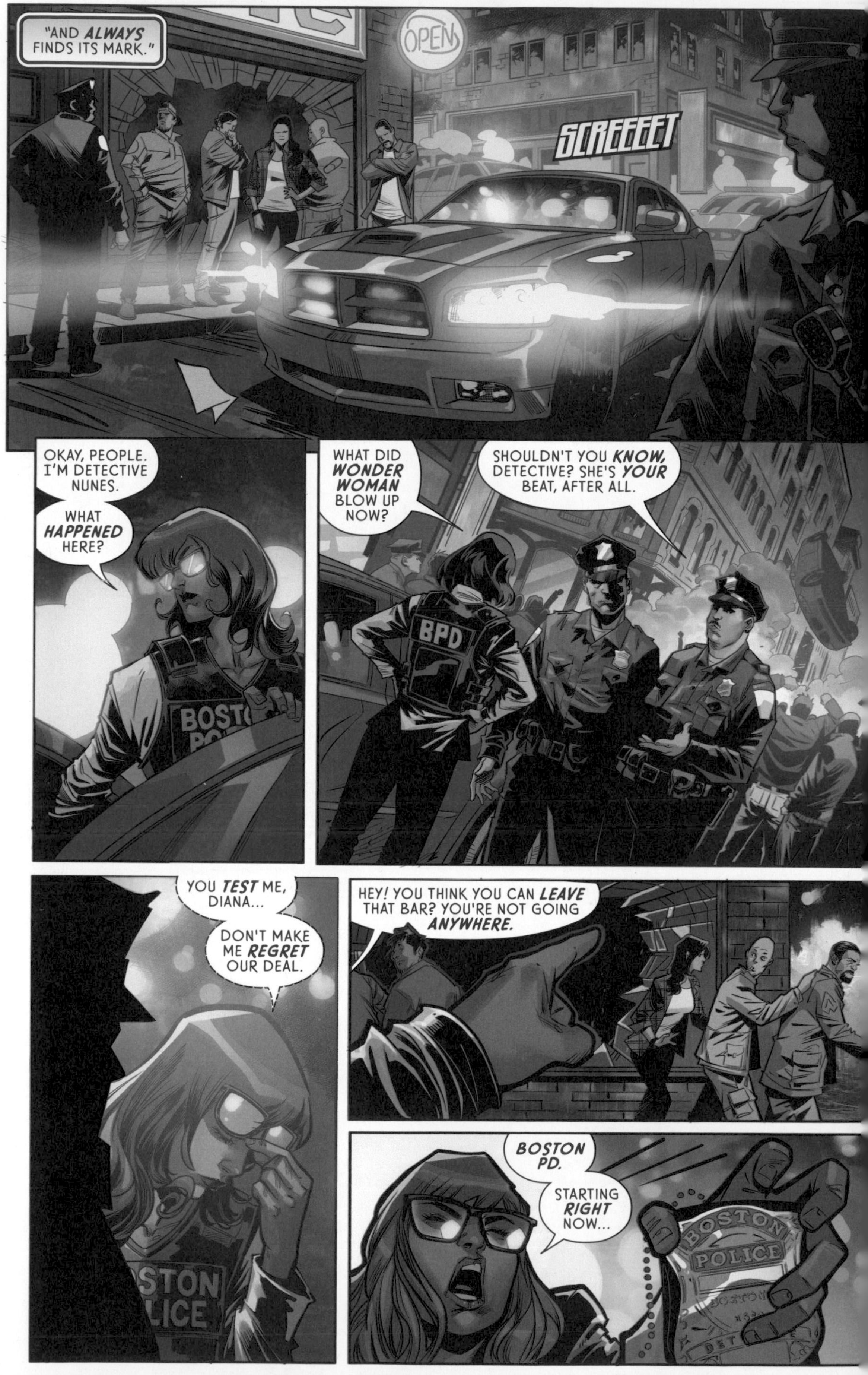
"AND ALWAYS FINDS ITS MARK."
OPEN
SCREEEET
OKAY, PEOPLE. I'M DETECTIVE NUNES.
WHAT HAPPENED HERE?
BOSTON POLICE
WHAT DID WONDER WOMAN BLOW UP NOW?
SHOULDN'T YOU KNOW, DETECTIVE? SHE'S YOUR BEAT, AFTER ALL.
BPD
YOU TEST ME, DIANA...
DON'T MAKE ME REGRET OUR DEAL.
HEY! YOU THINK YOU CAN LEAVE THAT BAR? YOU'RE NOT GOING ANYWHERE.
BOSTON PD.
STARTING RIGHT NOW...
BOSTON POLICE

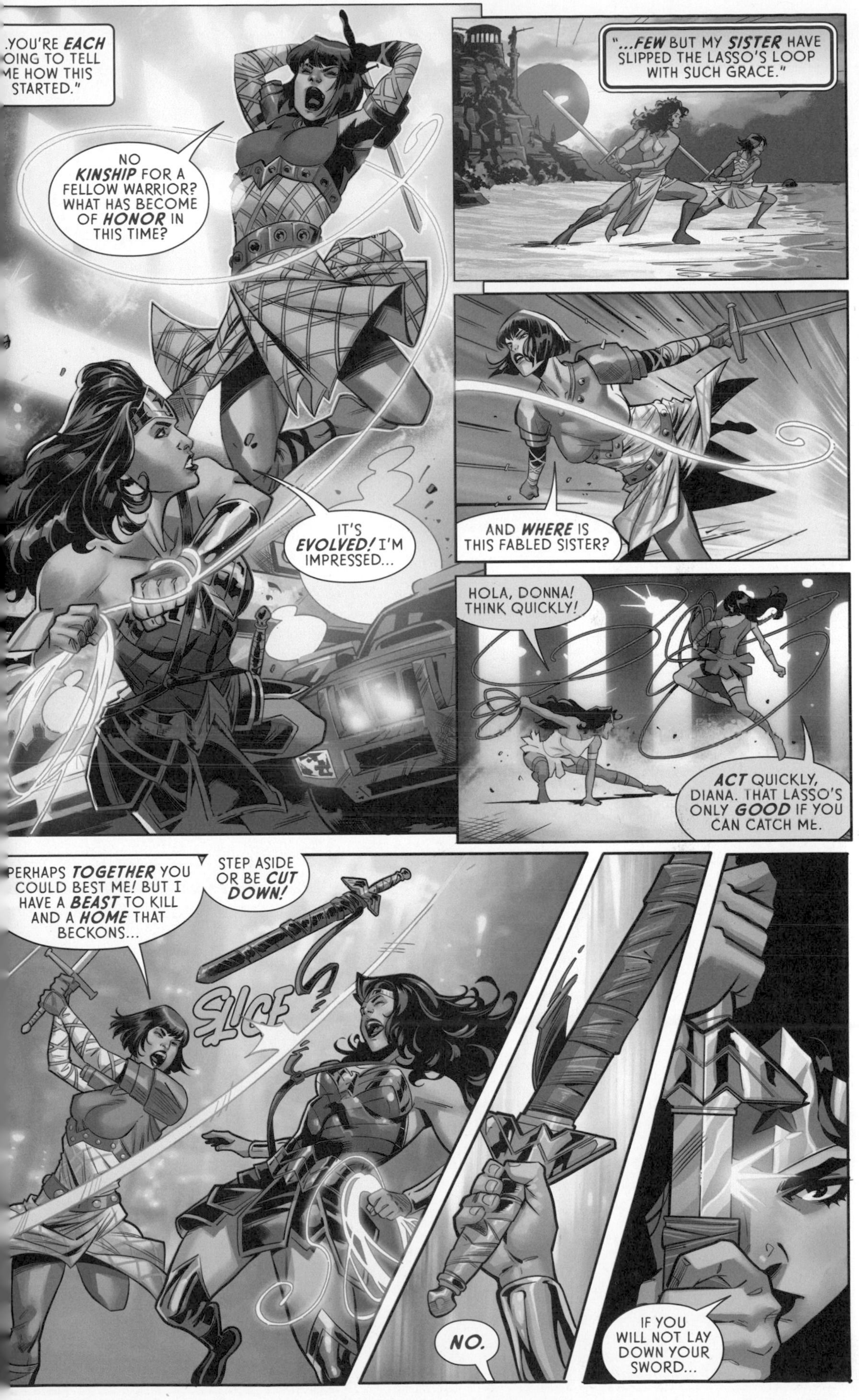
.YOU'RE EACH OING TO TELL ME HOW THIS STARTED."
"...FEW BUT MY SISTER HAVE SLIPPED THE LASSO'S LOOP WITH SUCH GRACE."
NO KINSHIP FOR A FELLOW WARRIOR? WHAT HAS BECOME OF HONOR IN THIS TIME?
AND WHERE IS THIS FABLED SISTER?
IT'S EVOLVED! I'M IMPRESSED...
HOLA, DONNA! THINK QUICKLY!
ACT QUICKLY, DIANA. THAT LASSO'S ONLY GOOD IF YOU CAN CATCH ME.
PERHAPS TOGETHER YOU COULD BEST ME! BUT I HAVE A BEAST TO KILL AND A HOME THAT BECKONS...
STEP ASIDE OR BE CUT DOWN!
SLICE
NO.
IF YOU WILL NOT LAY DOWN YOUR SWORD...

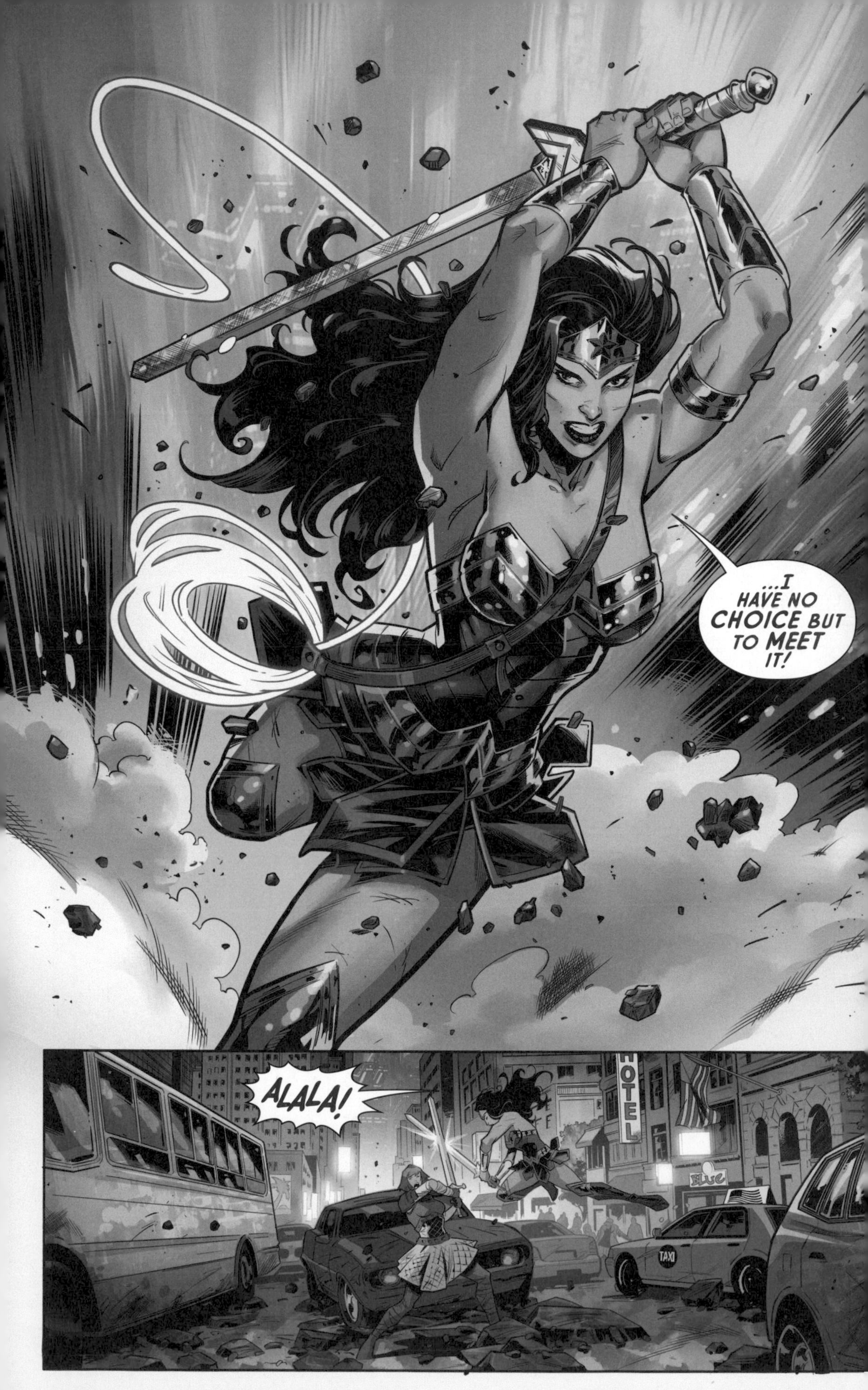
...I HAVE NO CHOICE BUT TO MEET IT!
ALALA!
HOTEL
BLUE
TAXI

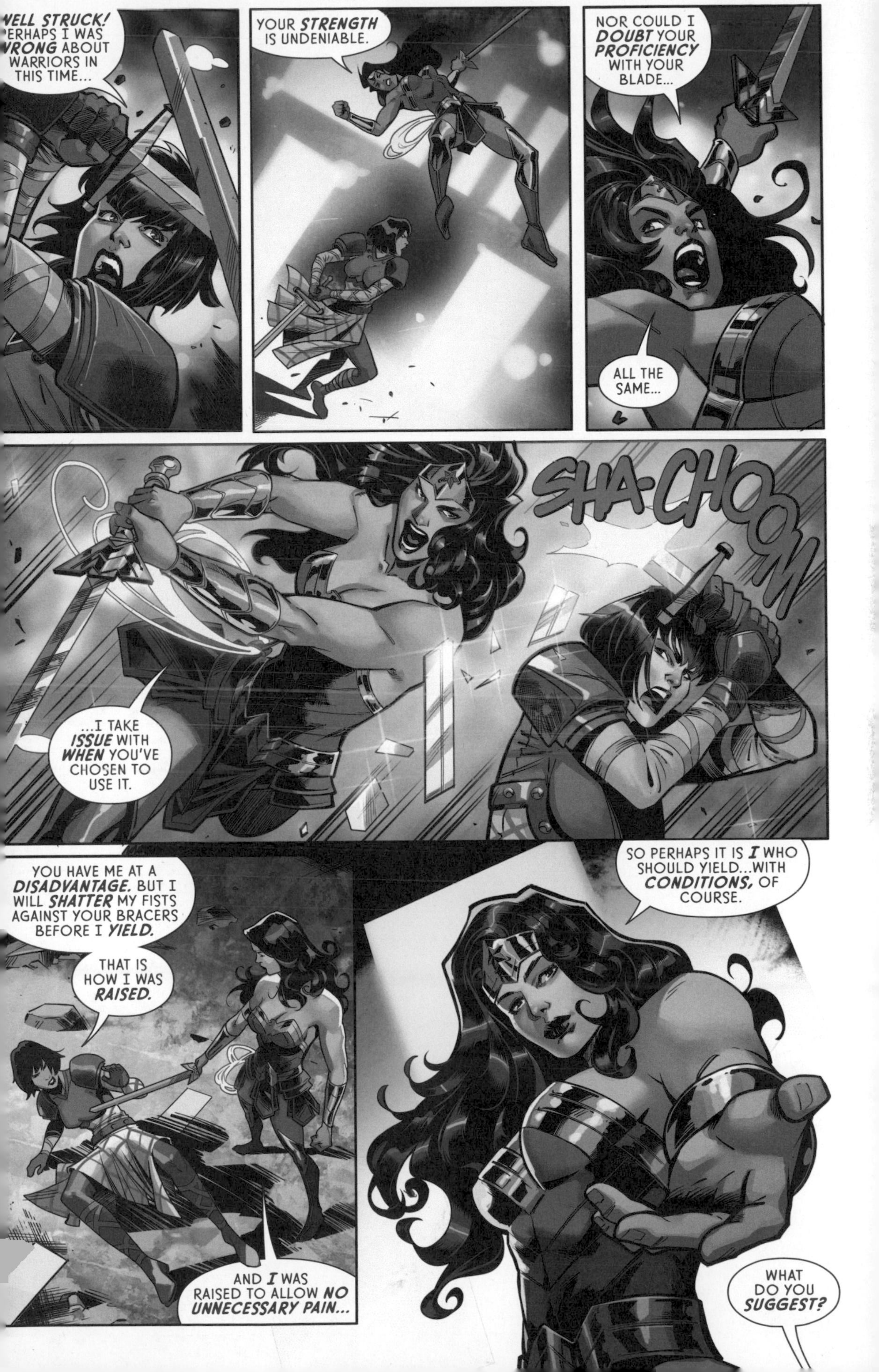
WELL STRUCK! PERHAPS I WAS WRONG ABOUT WARRIORS IN THIS TIME...
YOUR STRENGTH IS UNDENIABLE.
NOR COULD I DOUBT YOUR PROFICIENCY WITH YOUR BLADE...
ALL THE SAME...
SHA-CHOOM
...I TAKE ISSUE WITH WHEN YOU'VE CHOSEN TO USE IT.
YOU HAVE ME AT A DISADVANTAGE. BUT I WILL SHATTER MY FISTS AGAINST YOUR BRACERS BEFORE I YIELD.
THAT IS HOW I WAS RAISED.
AND I WAS RAISED TO ALLOW NO UNNECESSARY PAIN...
SO PERHAPS IT IS I WHO SHOULD YIELD...WITH CONDITIONS, OF COURSE.
WHAT DO YOU SUGGEST?

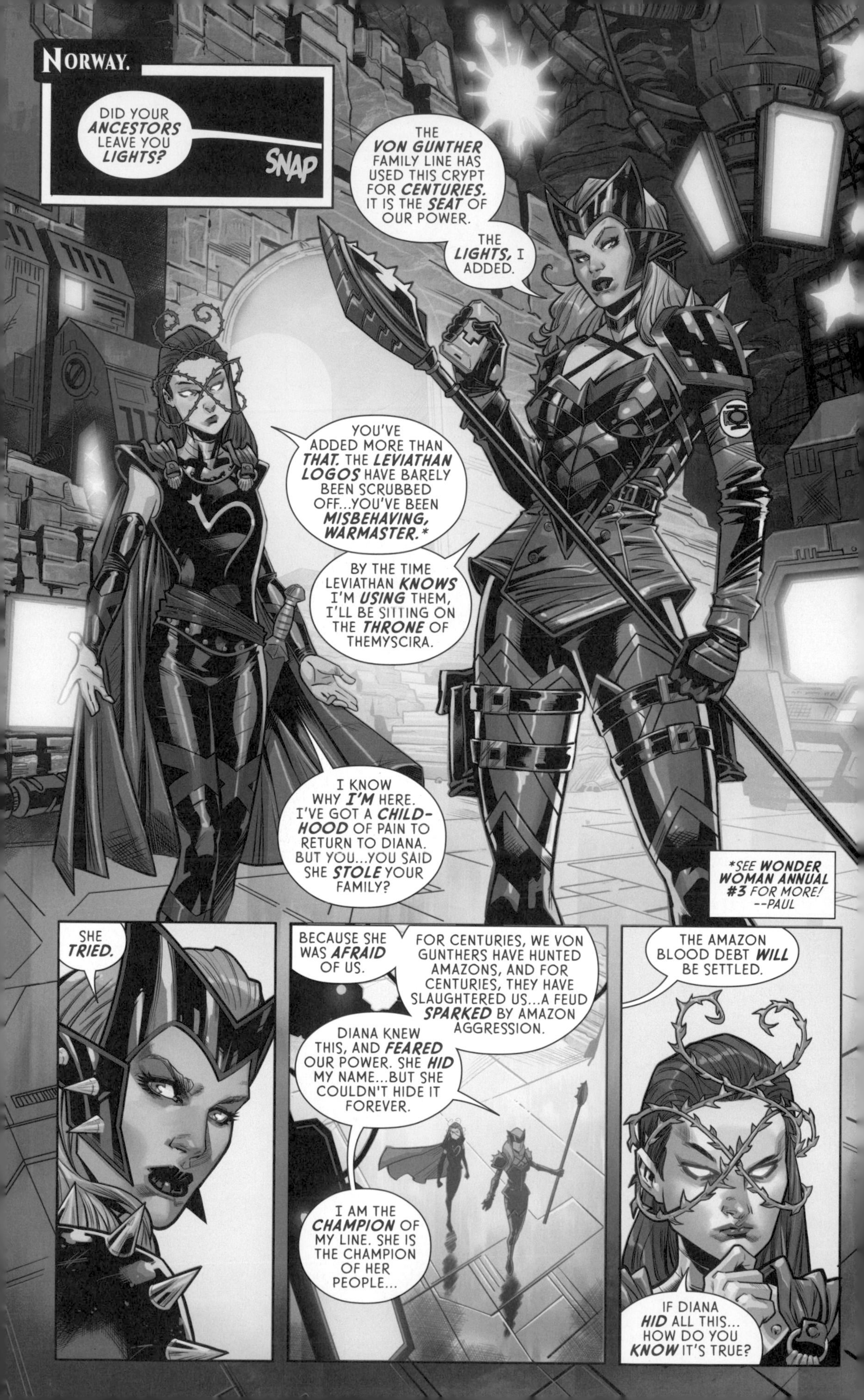
NORWAY.
DID YOUR ANCESTORS LEAVE YOU LIGHTS?
SNAP
THE VON GUNTHER FAMILY LINE HAS USED THIS CRYPT FOR CENTURIES. IT IS THE SEAT OF OUR POWER.
THE LIGHTS, I ADDED.
YOU'VE ADDED MORE THAN THAT. THE LEVIATHAN LOGOS HAVE BARELY BEEN SCRUBBED OFF...YOU'VE BEEN MISBEHAVING, WARMASTER.*
BY THE TIME LEVIATHAN KNOWS I'M USING THEM, I'LL BE SITTING ON THE THRONE OF THEMYSCIRA.
I KNOW WHY I'M HERE. I'VE GOT A CHILD-HOOD OF PAIN TO RETURN TO DIANA. BUT YOU...YOU SAID SHE STOLE YOUR FAMILY?
*SEE WONDER WOMAN ANNUAL #3 FOR MORE! --PAUL
SHE TRIED.
BECAUSE SHE WAS AFRAID OF US.
FOR CENTURIES, WE VON GUNTHERS HAVE HUNTED AMAZONS, AND FOR CENTURIES, THEY HAVE SLAUGHTERED US...A FEUD SPARKED BY AMAZON AGGRESSION.
DIANA KNEW THIS, AND FEARED OUR POWER. SHE HID MY NAME...BUT SHE COULDN'T HIDE IT FOREVER.
I AM THE CHAMPION OF MY LINE. SHE IS THE CHAMPION OF HER PEOPLE...
THE AMAZON BLOOD DEBT WILL BE SETTLED.
IF DIANA HID ALL THIS... HOW DO YOU KNOW IT'S TRUE?

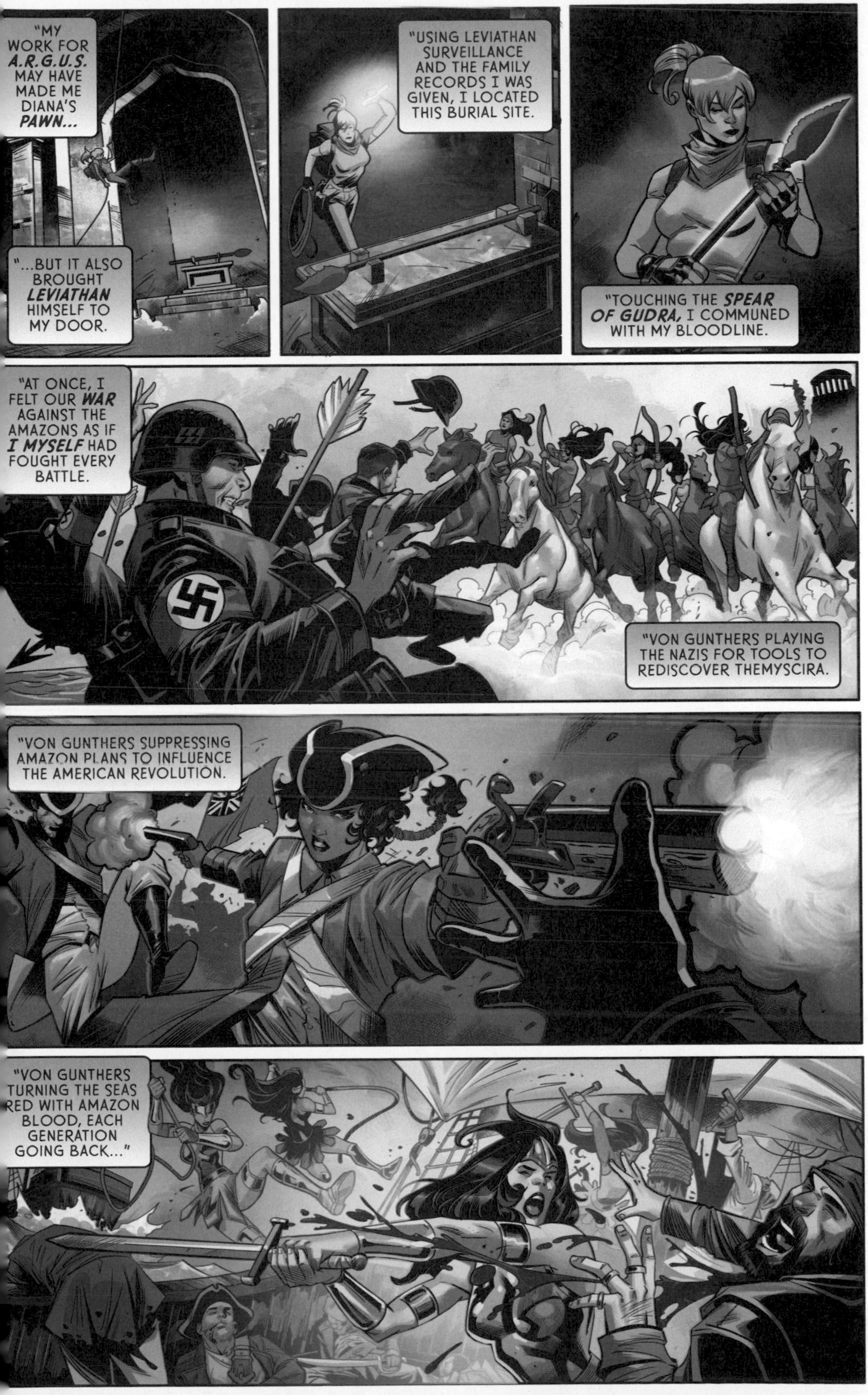
"MY WORK FOR A.R.G.U.S. MAY HAVE MADE ME DIANA'S PAWN...
"...BUT IT ALSO BROUGHT LEVIATHAN HIMSELF TO MY DOOR.
"USING LEVIATHAN SURVEILLANCE AND THE FAMILY RECORDS I WAS GIVEN, I LOCATED THIS BURIAL SITE.
"TOUCHING THE SPEAR OF GUDRA, I COMMUNED WITH MY BLOODLINE.
"AT ONCE, I FELT OUR WAR AGAINST THE AMAZONS AS IF I MYSELF HAD FOUGHT EVERY BATTLE.
"VON GUNTHERS PLAYING THE NAZIS FOR TOOLS TO REDISCOVER THEMYSCIRA.
"VON GUNTHERS SUPPRESSING AMAZON PLANS TO INFLUENCE THE AMERICAN REVOLUTION.
"VON GUNTHERS TURNING THE SEAS RED WITH AMAZON BLOOD, EACH GENERATION GOING BACK..."

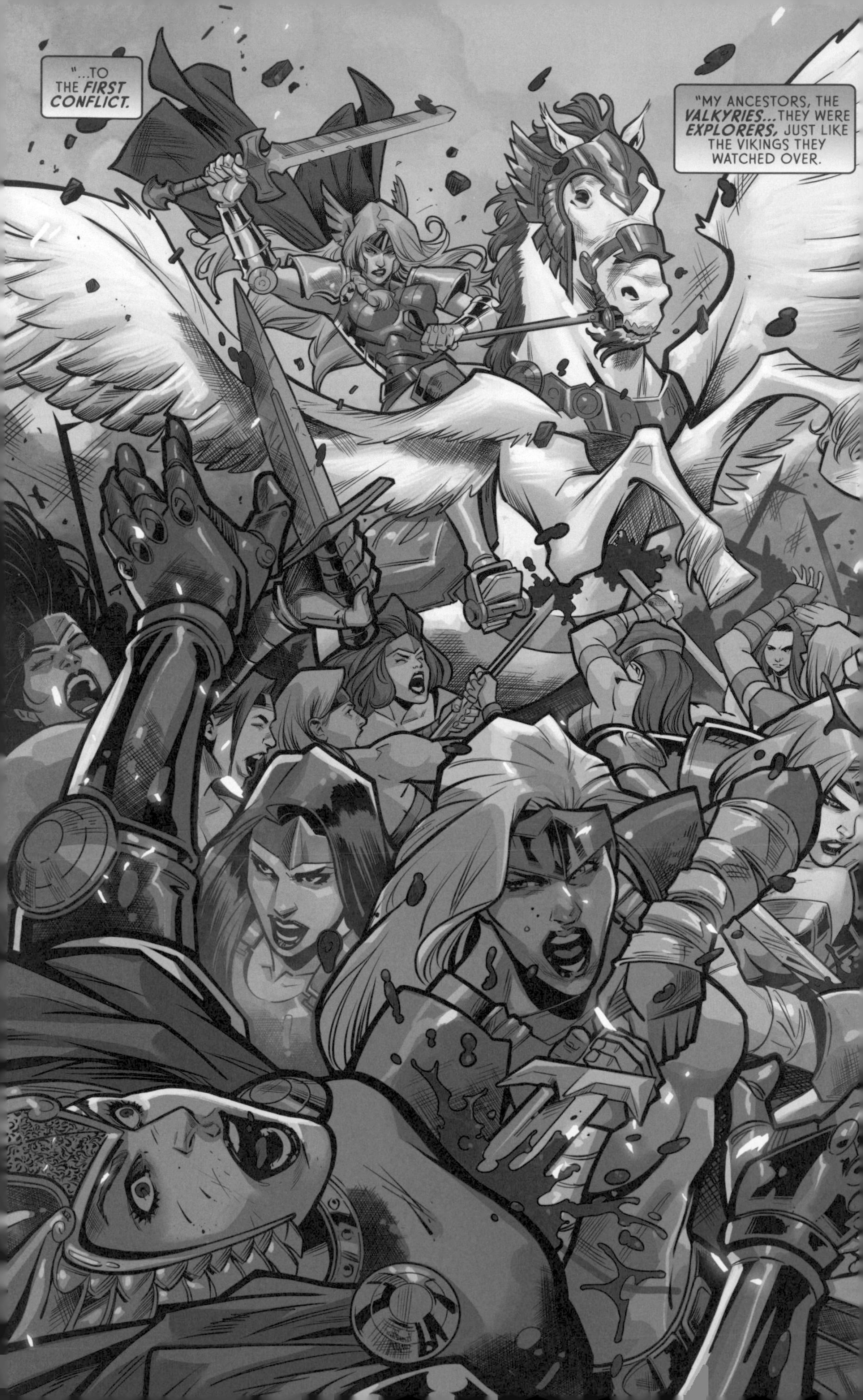
"...TO THE *FIRST* *CONFLICT.*
"MY ANCESTORS, THE *VALKYRIES*...THEY WERE *EXPLORERS,* JUST LIKE THE VIKINGS THEY WATCHED OVER.

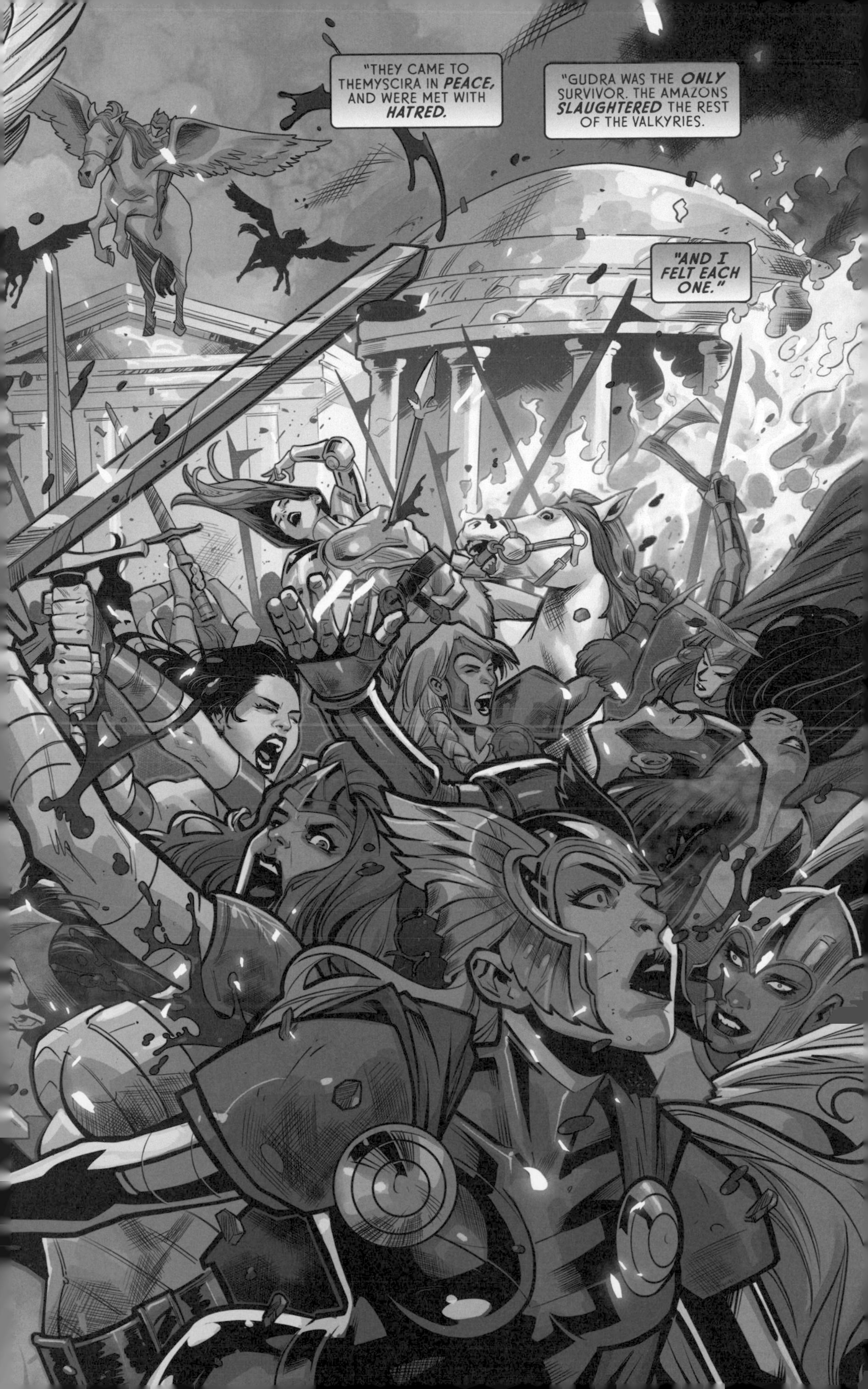
"THEY CAME TO THEMYSCIRA IN *PEACE,* AND WERE MET WITH *HATRED.*
"GUDRA WAS THE *ONLY* SURVIVOR. THE AMAZONS *SLAUGHTERED* THE REST OF THE VALKYRIES.
"AND I FELT EACH ONE."

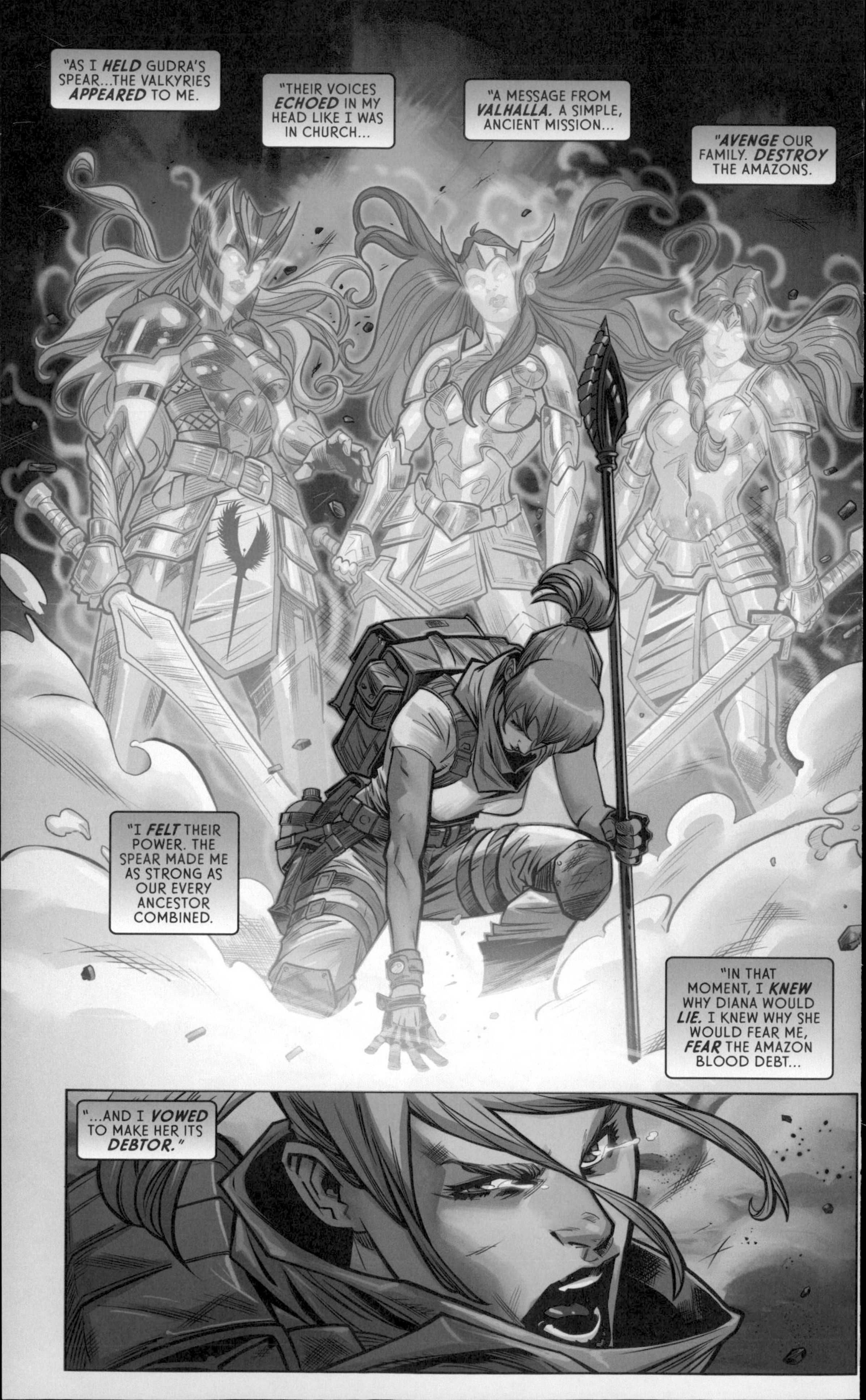
"AS I HELD GUDRA'S SPEAR...THE VALKYRIES APPEARED TO ME.
"THEIR VOICES ECHOED IN MY HEAD LIKE I WAS IN CHURCH...
"A MESSAGE FROM VALHALLA. A SIMPLE, ANCIENT MISSION...
"AVENGE OUR FAMILY. DESTROY THE AMAZONS.
"I FELT THEIR POWER. THE SPEAR MADE ME AS STRONG AS OUR EVERY ANCESTOR COMBINED.
"IN THAT MOMENT, I KNEW WHY DIANA WOULD LIE. I KNEW WHY SHE WOULD FEAR ME, FEAR THE AMAZON BLOOD DEBT...
"...AND I VOWED TO MAKE HER ITS DEBTOR."

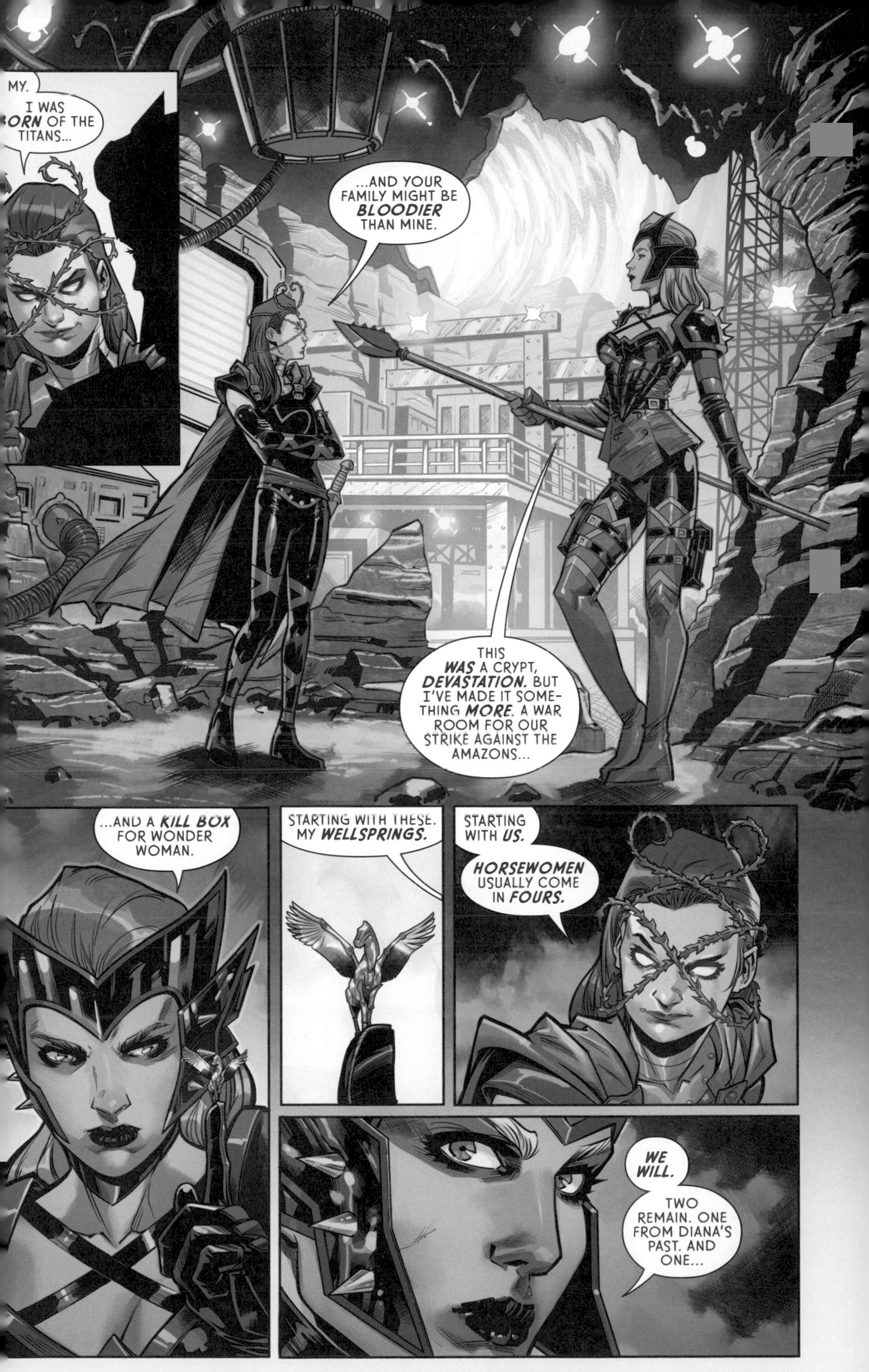
MY.
I WAS ORN OF THE TITANS...
...AND YOUR FAMILY MIGHT BE BLOODIER THAN MINE.
THIS WAS A CRYPT, DEVASTATION. BUT I'VE MADE IT SOMETHING MORE. A WAR ROOM FOR OUR STRIKE AGAINST THE AMAZONS...
...AND A KILL BOX FOR WONDER WOMAN.
STARTING WITH THESE. MY WELLSPRINGS.
STARTING WITH US.
HORSEWOMEN USUALLY COME IN FOURS.
WE WILL.
TWO REMAIN. ONE FROM DIANA'S PAST. AND ONE...

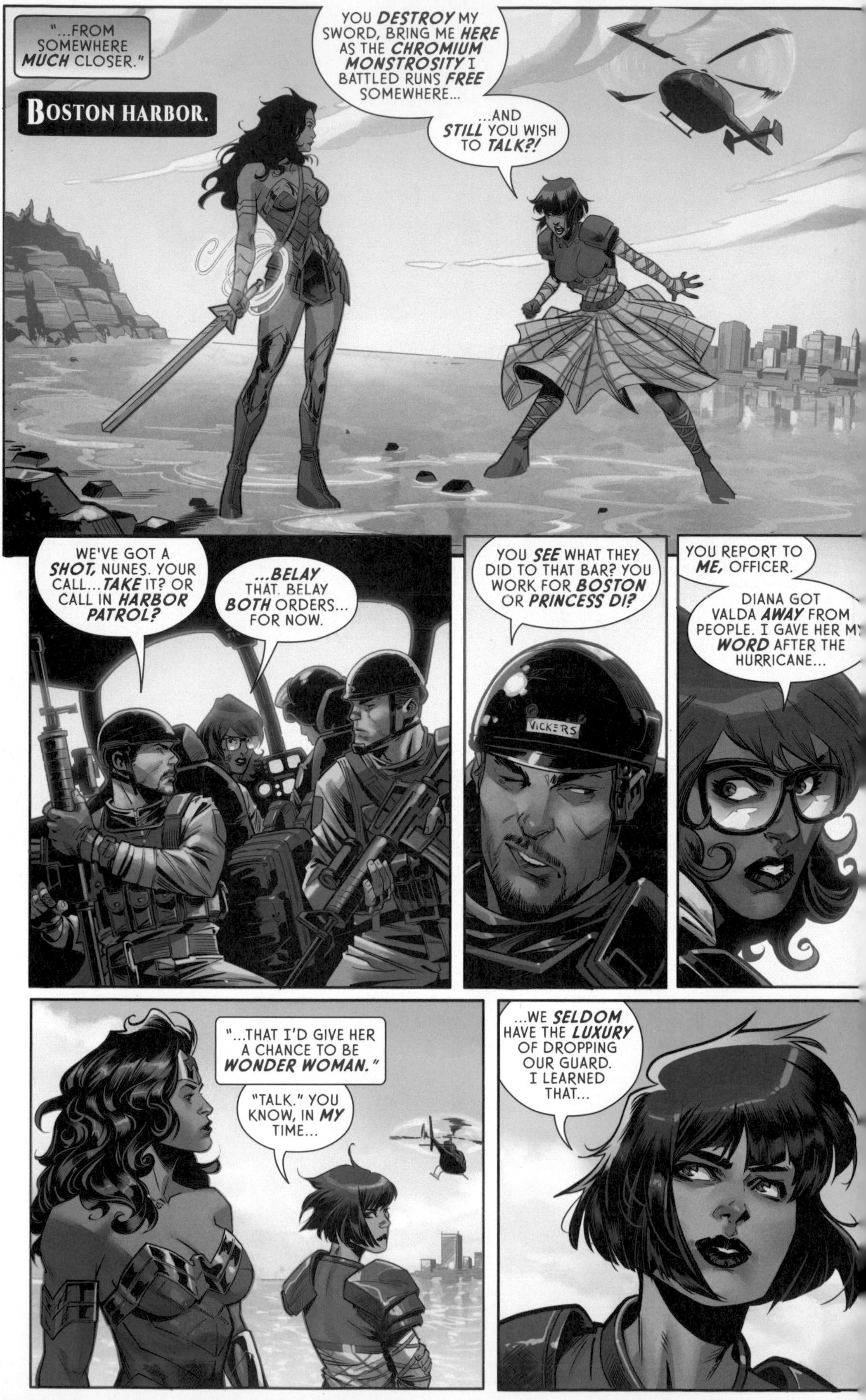
"...FROM SOMEWHERE MUCH CLOSER."
BOSTON HARBOR.
YOU DESTROY MY SWORD, BRING ME HERE AS THE CHROMIUM MONSTROSITY I BATTLED RUNS FREE SOMEWHERE...
...AND STILL YOU WISH TO TALK?!
WE'VE GOT A SHOT, NUNES. YOUR CALL...TAKE IT? OR CALL IN HARBOR PATROL?
...BELAY THAT. BELAY BOTH ORDERS... FOR NOW.
YOU SEE WHAT THEY DID TO THAT BAR? YOU WORK FOR BOSTON OR PRINCESS DI?
VICKERS
YOU REPORT TO ME, OFFICER.
DIANA GOT VALDA AWAY FROM PEOPLE. I GAVE HER MY WORD AFTER THE HURRICANE...
"...THAT I'D GIVE HER A CHANCE TO BE WONDER WOMAN."
"TALK." YOU KNOW, IN MY TIME...
...WE SELDOM HAVE THE LUXURY OF DROPPING OUR GUARD. I LEARNED THAT...

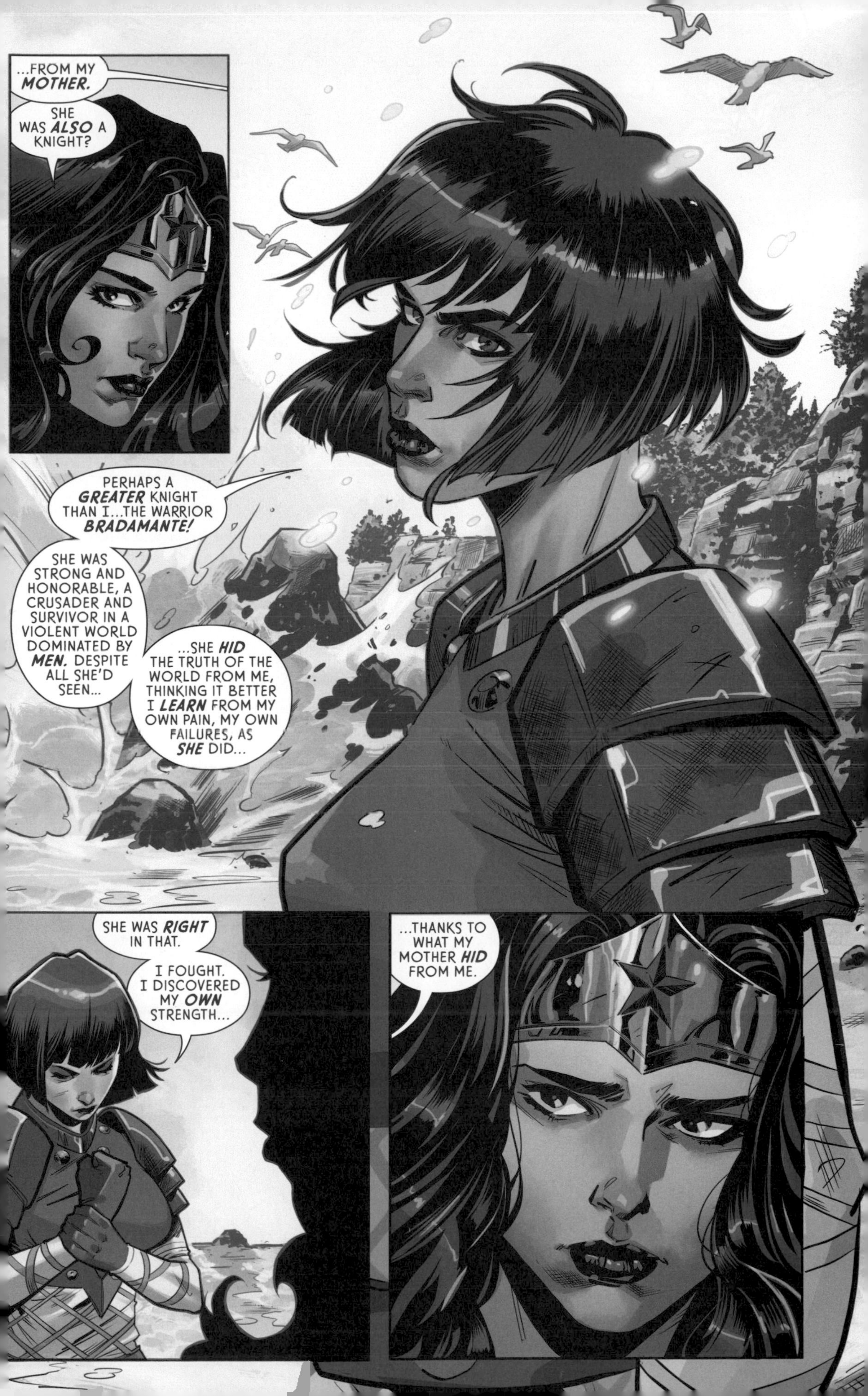
...FROM MY MOTHER.
SHE WAS ALSO A KNIGHT?
PERHAPS A GREATER KNIGHT THAN I...THE WARRIOR BRADAMANTE!
SHE WAS STRONG AND HONORABLE, A CRUSADER AND SURVIVOR IN A VIOLENT WORLD DOMINATED BY MEN. DESPITE ALL SHE'D SEEN...
...SHE HID THE TRUTH OF THE WORLD FROM ME, THINKING IT BETTER I LEARN FROM MY OWN PAIN, MY OWN FAILURES, AS SHE DID...
SHE WAS RIGHT IN THAT.
I FOUGHT. I DISCOVERED MY OWN STRENGTH...
...THANKS TO WHAT MY MOTHER HID FROM ME.

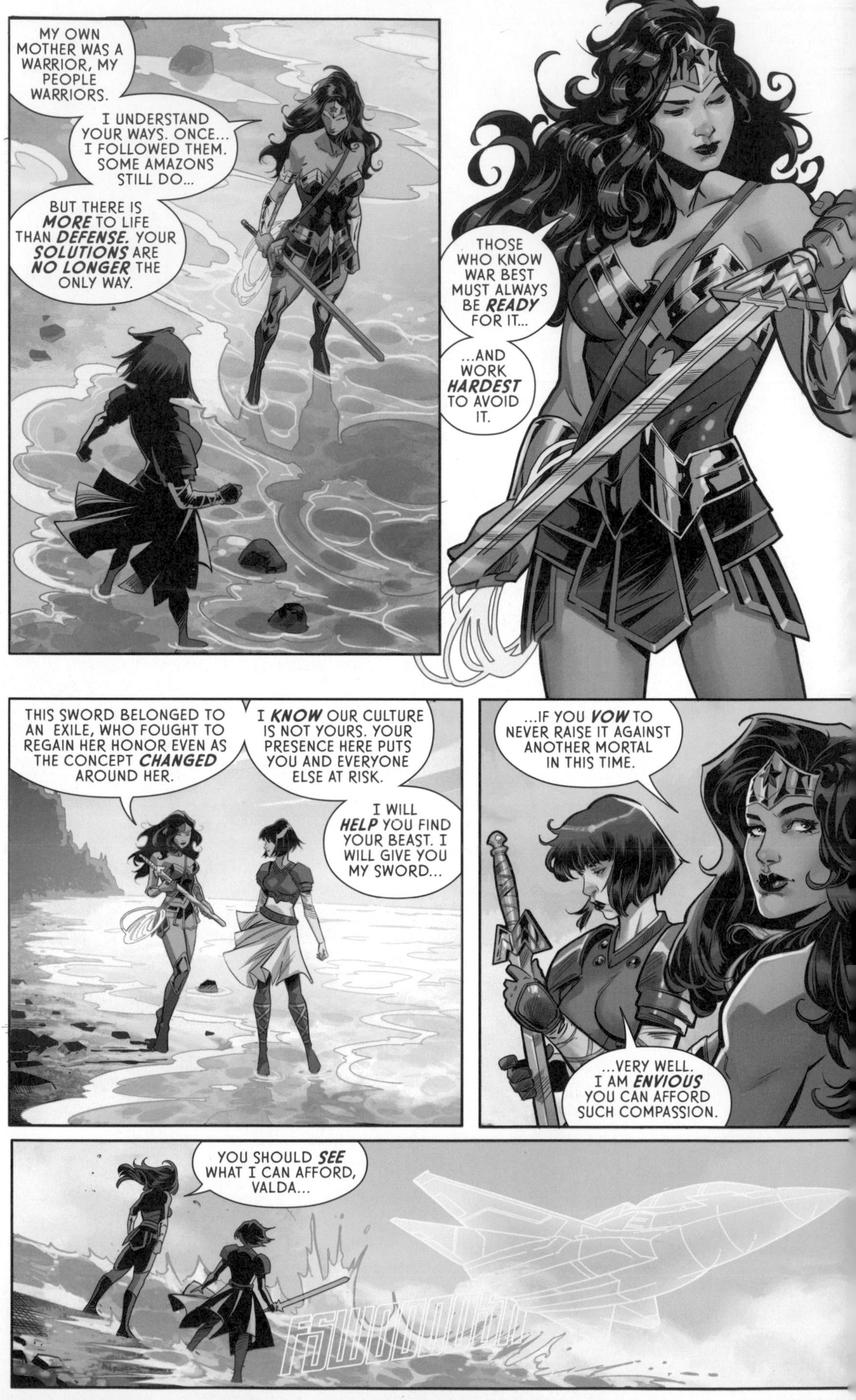
MY OWN MOTHER WAS A WARRIOR, MY PEOPLE WARRIORS.
I UNDERSTAND YOUR WAYS. ONCE... I FOLLOWED THEM. SOME AMAZONS STILL DO...
BUT THERE IS ***MORE*** TO LIFE THAN ***DEFENSE.*** YOUR ***SOLUTIONS*** ARE ***NO LONGER*** THE ONLY WAY.
THOSE WHO KNOW WAR BEST MUST ALWAYS BE ***READY*** FOR IT...
...AND WORK ***HARDEST*** TO AVOID IT.
THIS SWORD BELONGED TO AN EXILE, WHO FOUGHT TO REGAIN HER HONOR EVEN AS THE CONCEPT ***CHANGED*** AROUND HER.
I ***KNOW*** OUR CULTURE IS NOT YOURS. YOUR PRESENCE HERE PUTS YOU AND EVERYONE ELSE AT RISK.
I WILL ***HELP*** YOU FIND YOUR BEAST. I WILL GIVE YOU MY SWORD...
...IF YOU ***VOW*** TO NEVER RAISE IT AGAINST ANOTHER MORTAL IN THIS TIME.
...VERY WELL. I AM ***ENVIOUS*** YOU CAN AFFORD SUCH COMPASSION.
YOU SHOULD ***SEE*** WHAT I CAN AFFORD, VALDA...
FSWOOOOSH

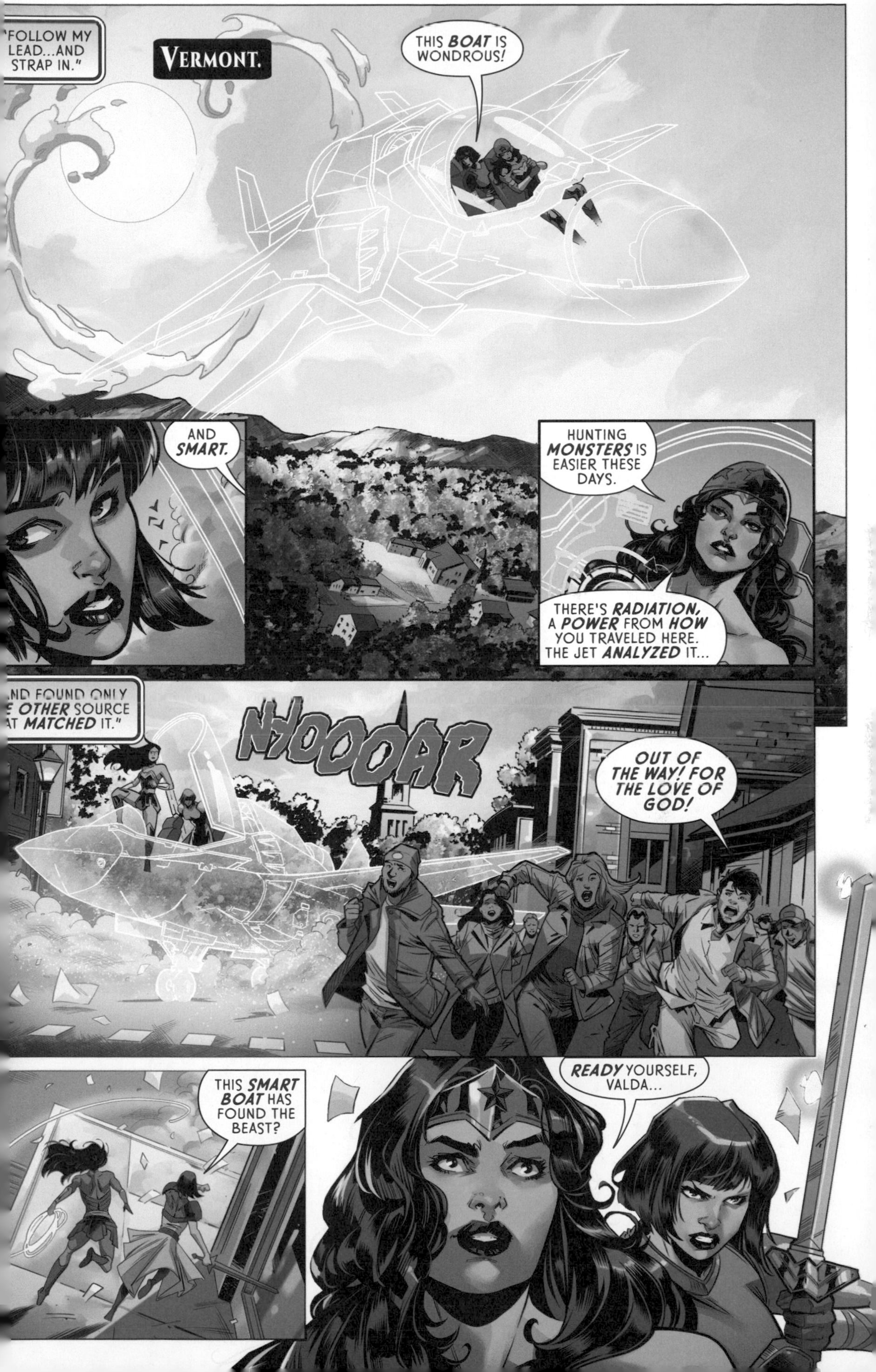
"FOLLOW MY LEAD...AND STRAP IN."
VERMONT.
THIS BOAT IS WONDROUS!
AND SMART.
HUNTING MONSTERS IS EASIER THESE DAYS.
THERE'S RADIATION, A POWER FROM HOW YOU TRAVELED HERE. THE JET ANALYZED IT...
ND FOUND ONLY E OTHER SOURCE AT MATCHED IT."
NHOOOAR
OUT OF THE WAY! FOR THE LOVE OF GOD!
THIS SMART BOAT HAS FOUND THE BEAST?
READY YOURSELF, VALDA...

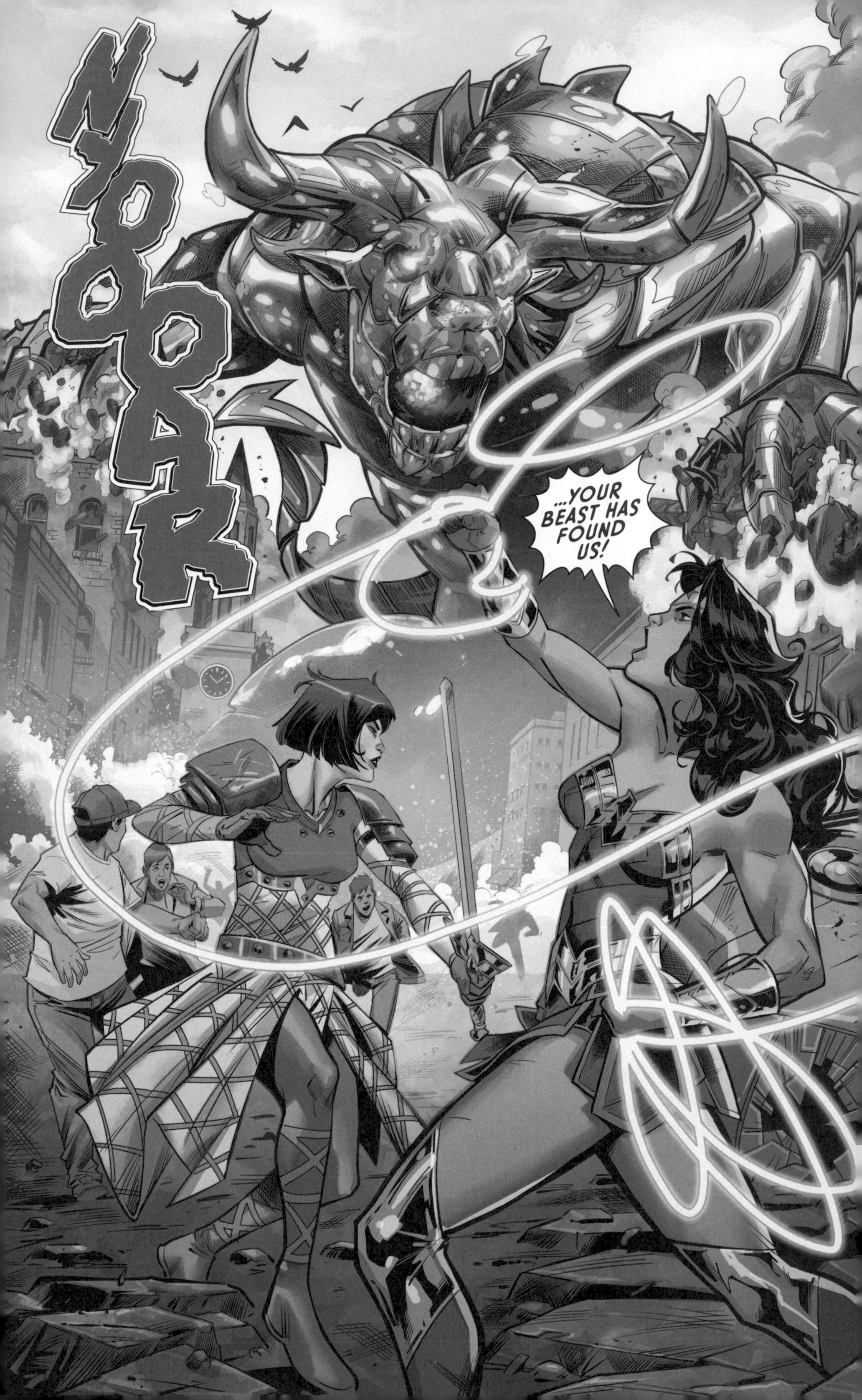
NROOOAR
...YOUR BEAST HAS FOUND US!

***Wonder Woman* #753**
cover by **ROBSON ROCHA,**
DANNY MIKI and **BRAD ANDERSON**

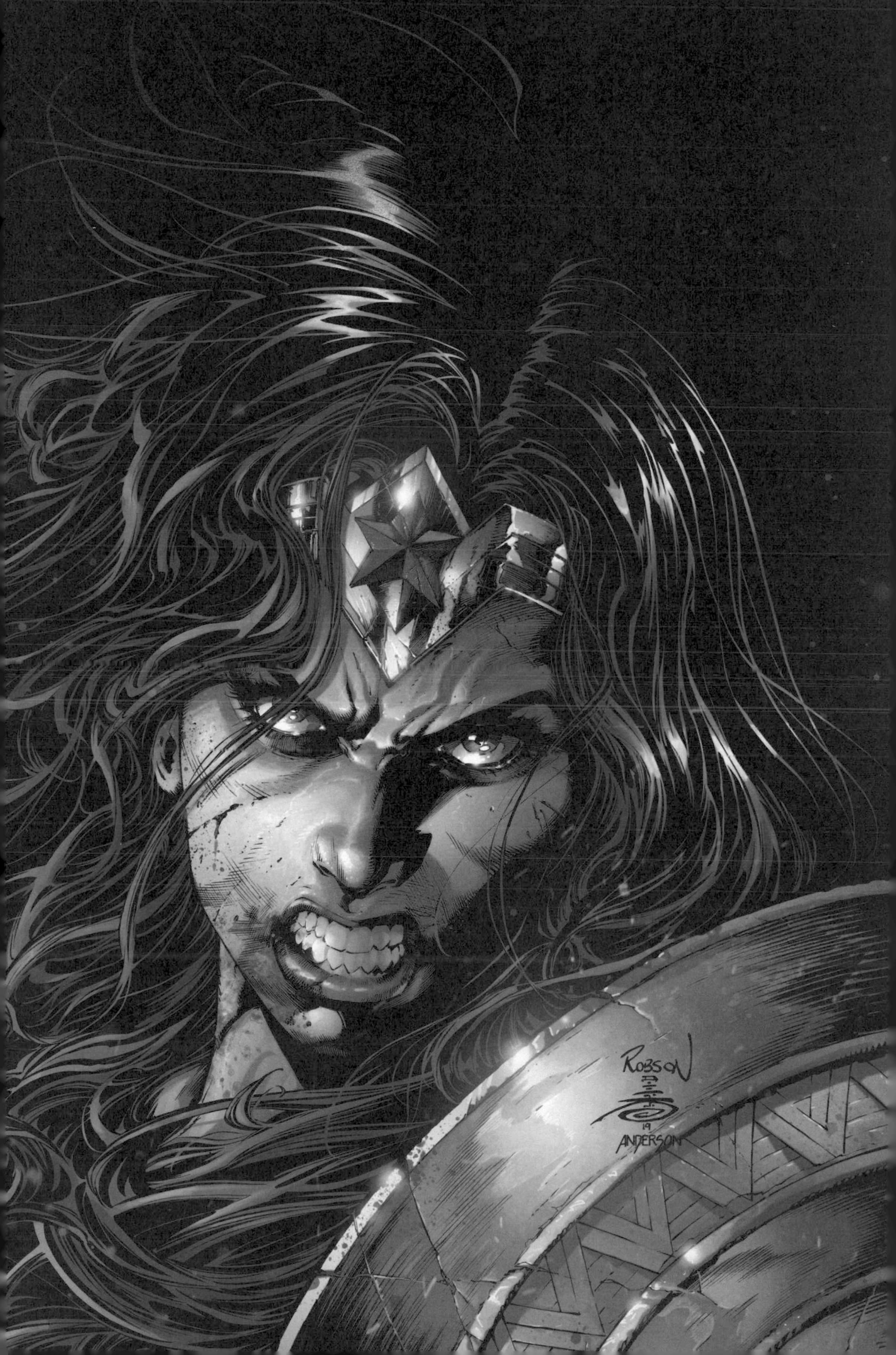
ROBSON
19
ANDERSON

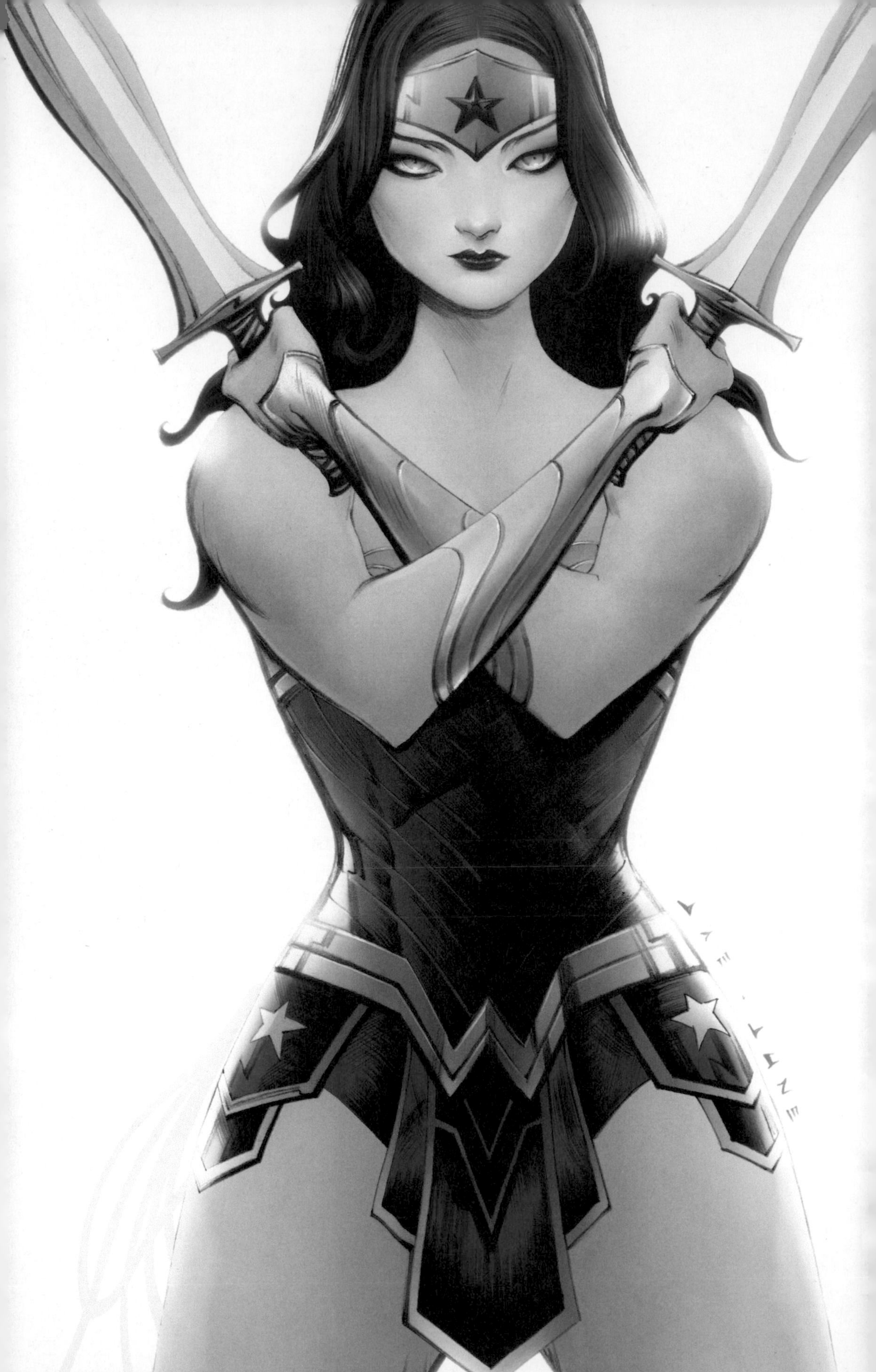

***Wonder Woman* #753**
variant cover by **JAE LEE** and **JUNE CHUNG**

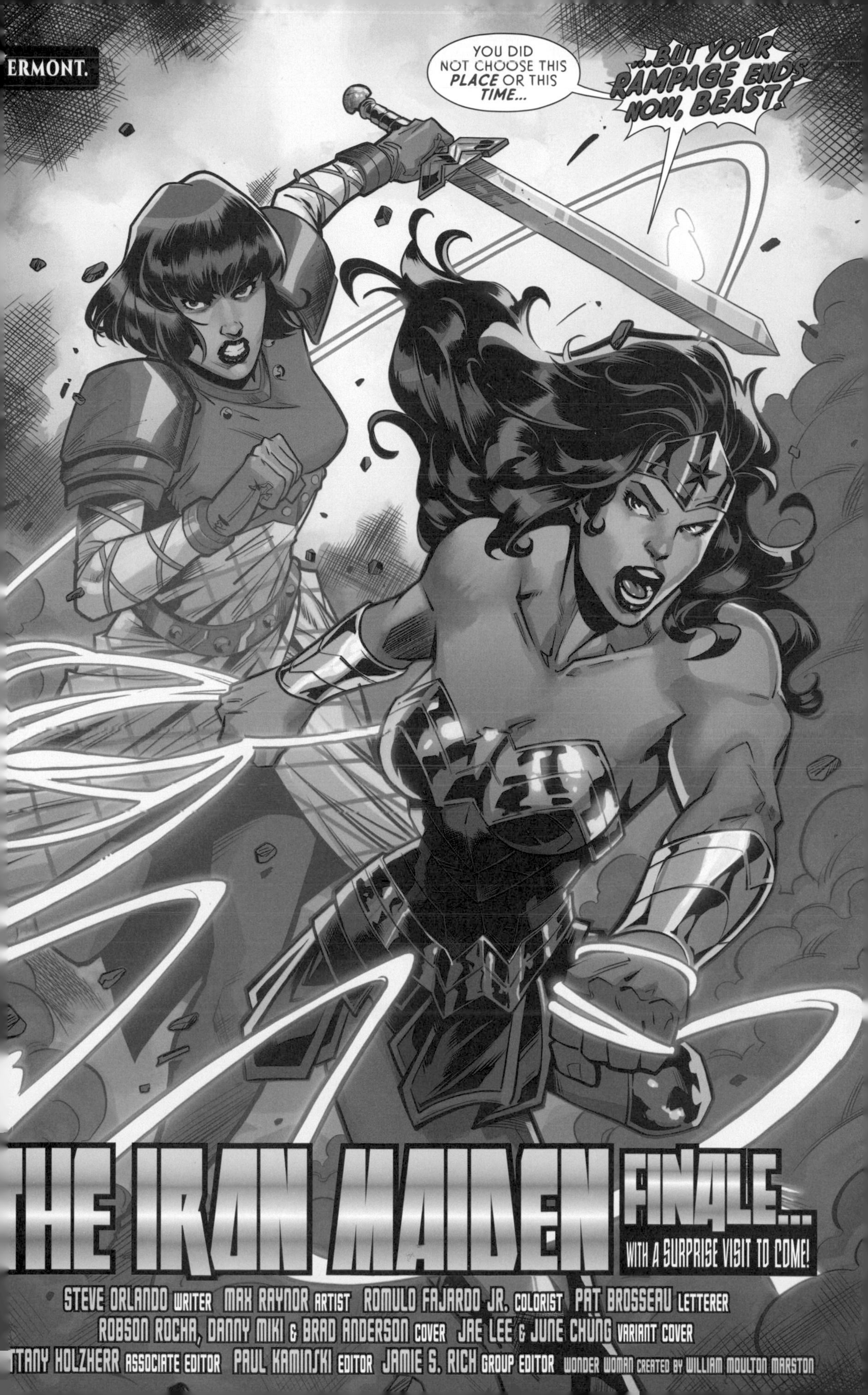
ERMONT.
YOU DID NOT CHOOSE THIS PLACE OR THIS TIME...
...BUT YOUR RAMPAGE ENDS NOW, BEAST!
THE IRON MAIDEN FINALE...
WITH A SURPRISE VISIT TO COME!
STEVE ORLANDO WRITER MAX RAYNOR ARTIST ROMULO FAJARDO JR. COLORIST PAT BROSSEAU LETTERER
ROBSON ROCHA, DANNY MIKI & BRAD ANDERSON COVER JAE LEE & JUNE CHUNG VARIANT COVER
TTANY HOLZHERR ASSOCIATE EDITOR PAUL KAMINSKI EDITOR JAMIE S. RICH GROUP EDITOR WONDER WOMAN CREATED BY WILLIAM MOULTON MARSTON

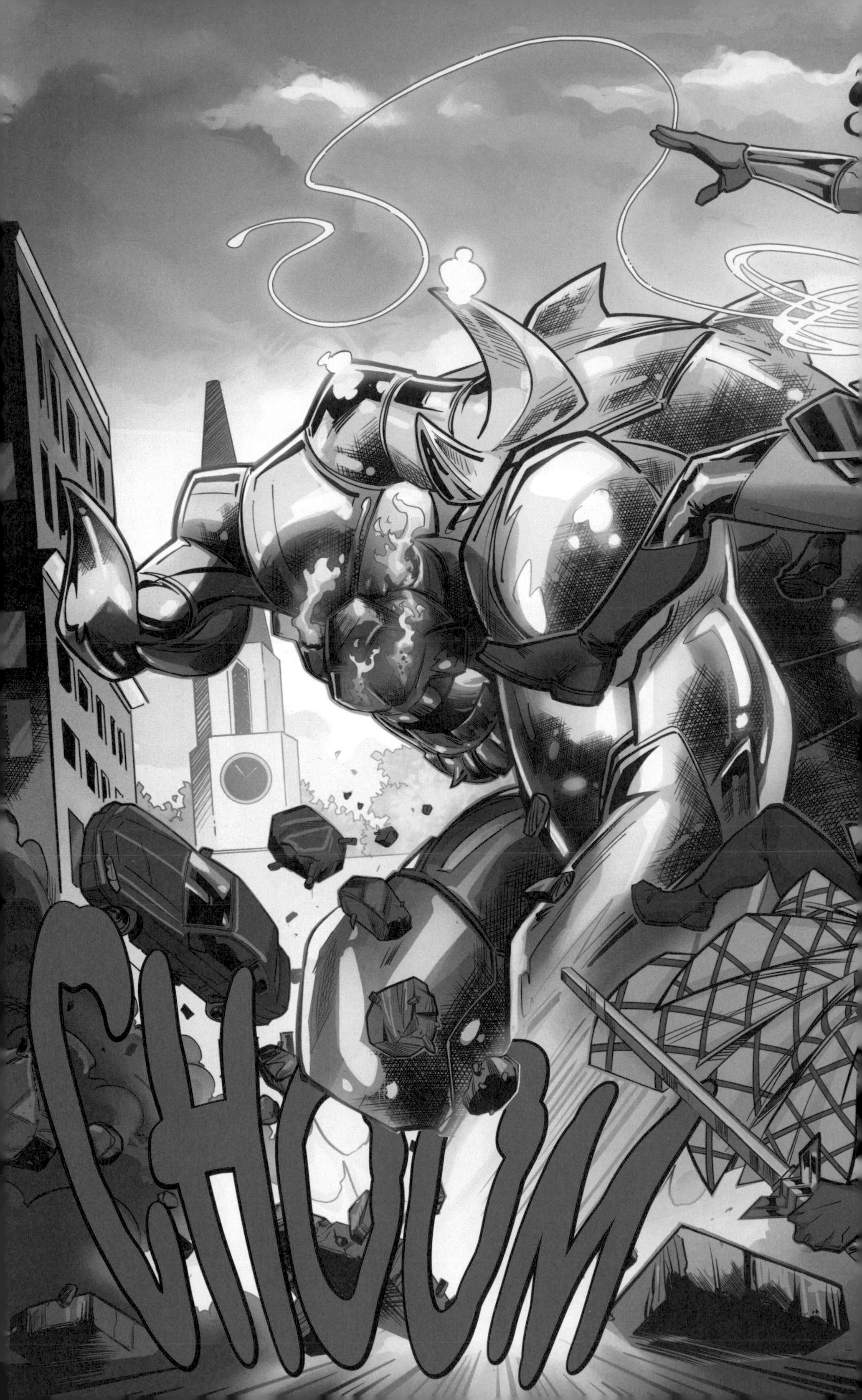
CHOOM

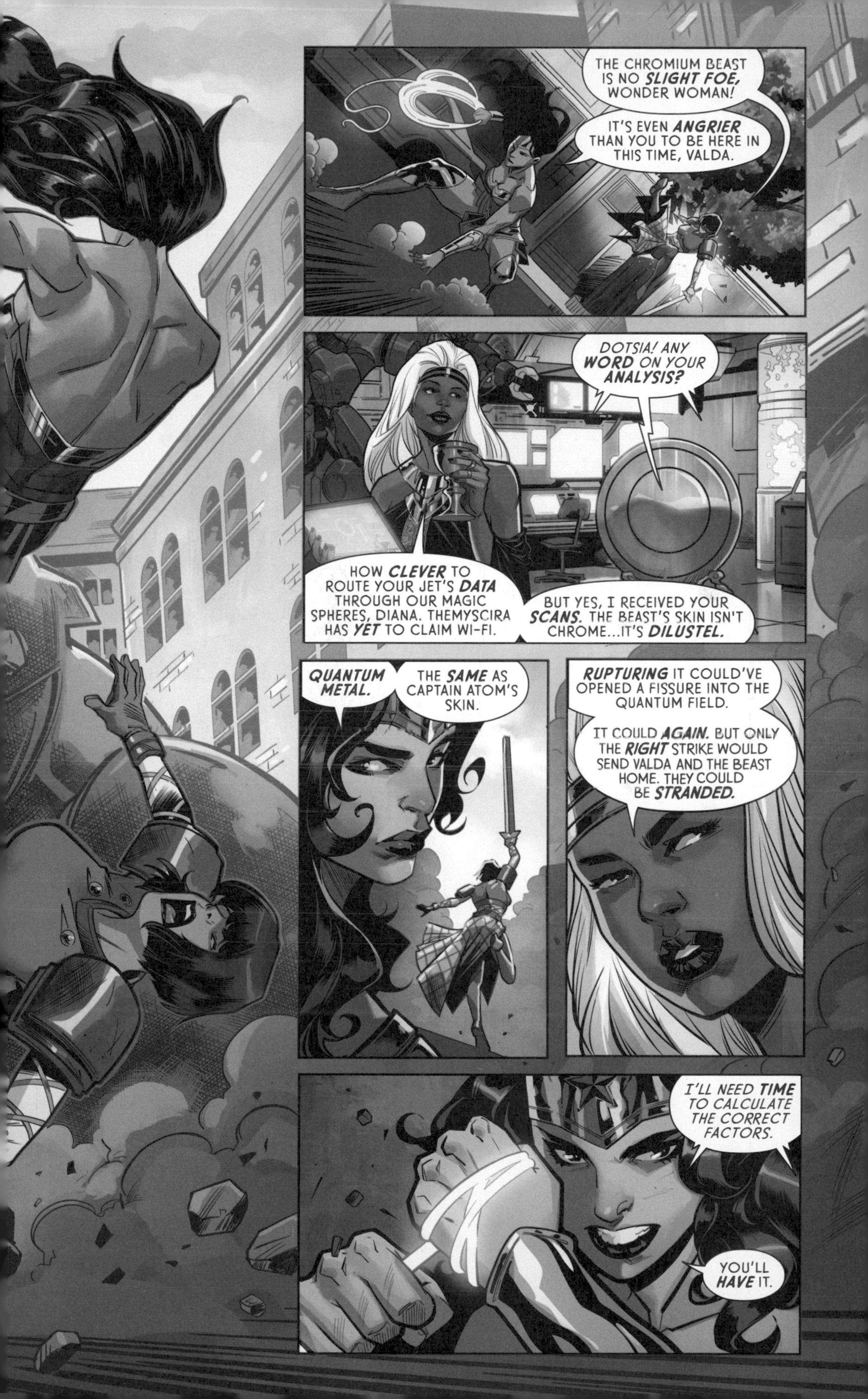
THE CHROMIUM BEAST IS NO SLIGHT FOE, WONDER WOMAN!
IT'S EVEN ANGRIER THAN YOU TO BE HERE IN THIS TIME, VALDA.
DOTSIA! ANY WORD ON YOUR ANALYSIS?
HOW CLEVER TO ROUTE YOUR JET'S DATA THROUGH OUR MAGIC SPHERES, DIANA. THEMYSCIRA HAS YET TO CLAIM WI-FI.
BUT YES, I RECEIVED YOUR SCANS. THE BEAST'S SKIN ISN'T CHROME...IT'S DILUSTEL.
QUANTUM METAL.
THE SAME AS CAPTAIN ATOM'S SKIN.
RUPTURING IT COULD'VE OPENED A FISSURE INTO THE QUANTUM FIELD.
IT COULD AGAIN. BUT ONLY THE RIGHT STRIKE WOULD SEND VALDA AND THE BEAST HOME. THEY COULD BE STRANDED.
I'LL NEED TIME TO CALCULATE THE CORRECT FACTORS.
YOU'LL HAVE IT.

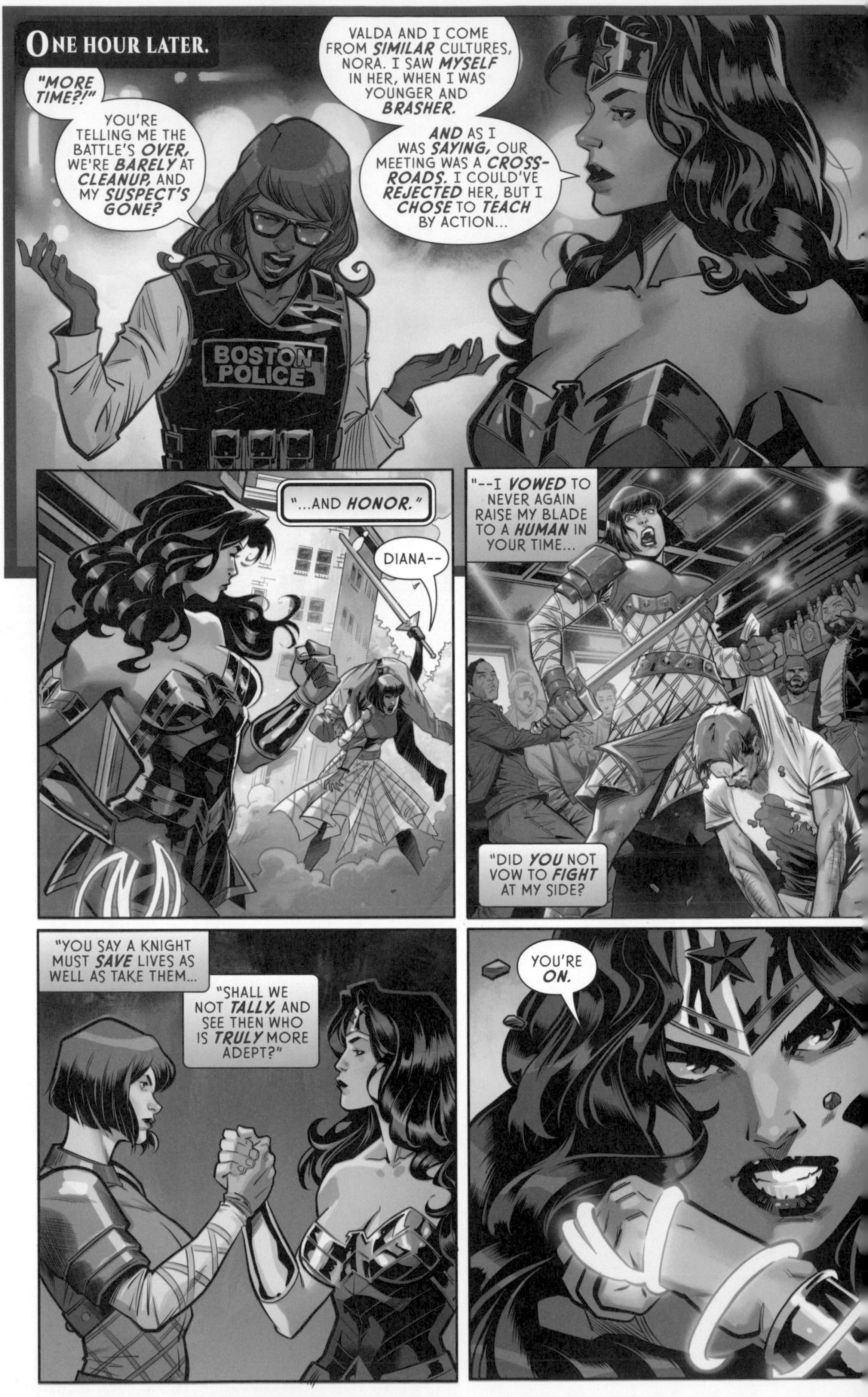
ONE HOUR LATER.
"MORE TIME?!"
YOU'RE TELLING ME THE BATTLE'S OVER, WE'RE BARELY AT CLEANUP, AND MY SUSPECT'S GONE?
VALDA AND I COME FROM SIMILAR CULTURES, NORA. I SAW MYSELF IN HER, WHEN I WAS YOUNGER AND BRASHER.
AND AS I WAS SAYING, OUR MEETING WAS A CROSS-ROADS. I COULD'VE REJECTED HER, BUT I CHOSE TO TEACH BY ACTION...
"...AND HONOR."
DIANA--
"--I VOWED TO NEVER AGAIN RAISE MY BLADE TO A HUMAN IN YOUR TIME...
"DID YOU NOT VOW TO FIGHT AT MY SIDE?
"YOU SAY A KNIGHT MUST SAVE LIVES AS WELL AS TAKE THEM...
"SHALL WE NOT TALLY, AND SEE THEN WHO IS TRULY MORE ADEPT?"
YOU'RE ON.
BOSTON POLICE

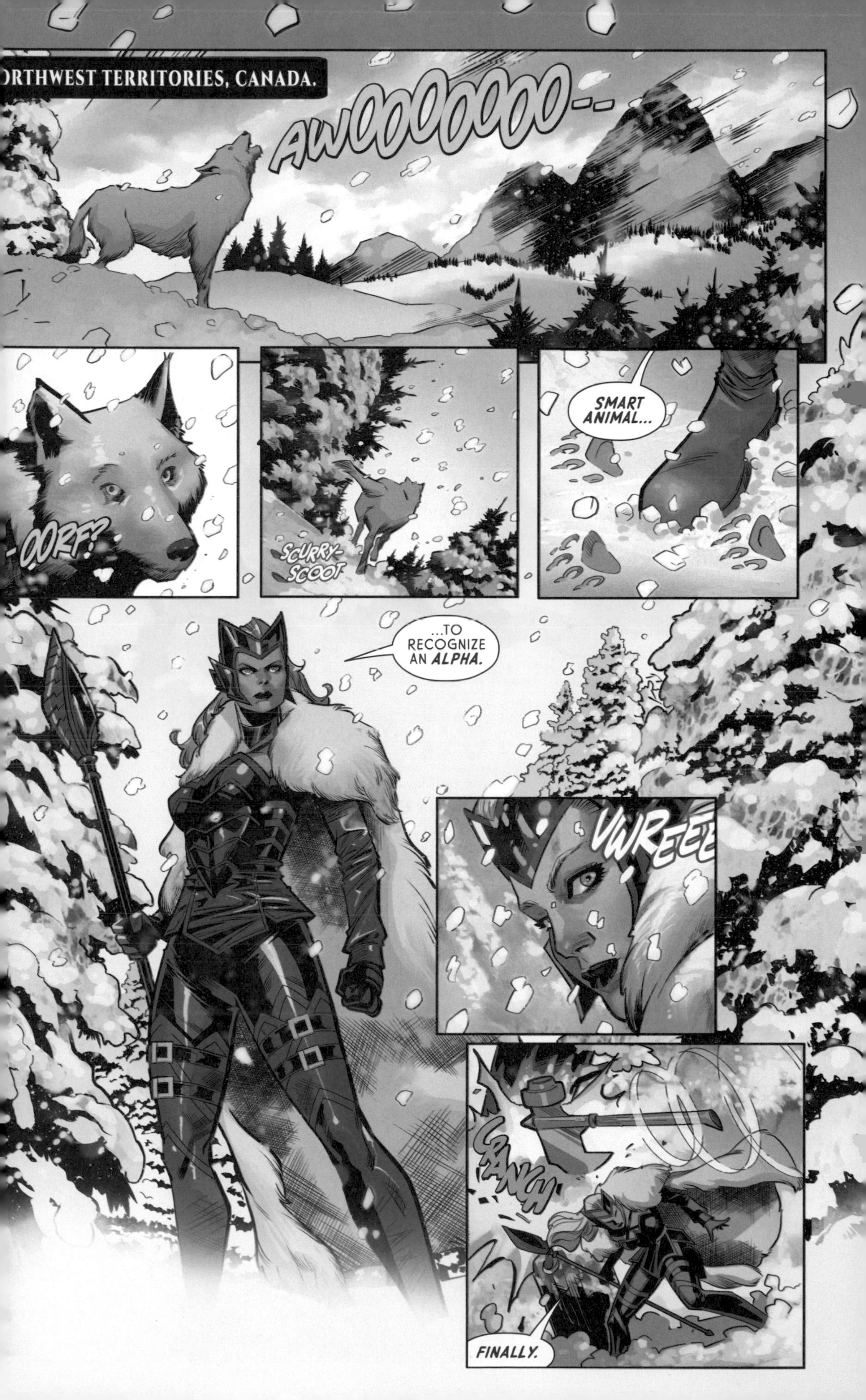

ORTHWEST TERRITORIES, CANADA.
AWOOOOOOO--
-OORF?
SCURRY-SCOOT
SMART ANIMAL...
...TO RECOGNIZE AN ALPHA.
VWREEE
CRANCH
FINALLY.

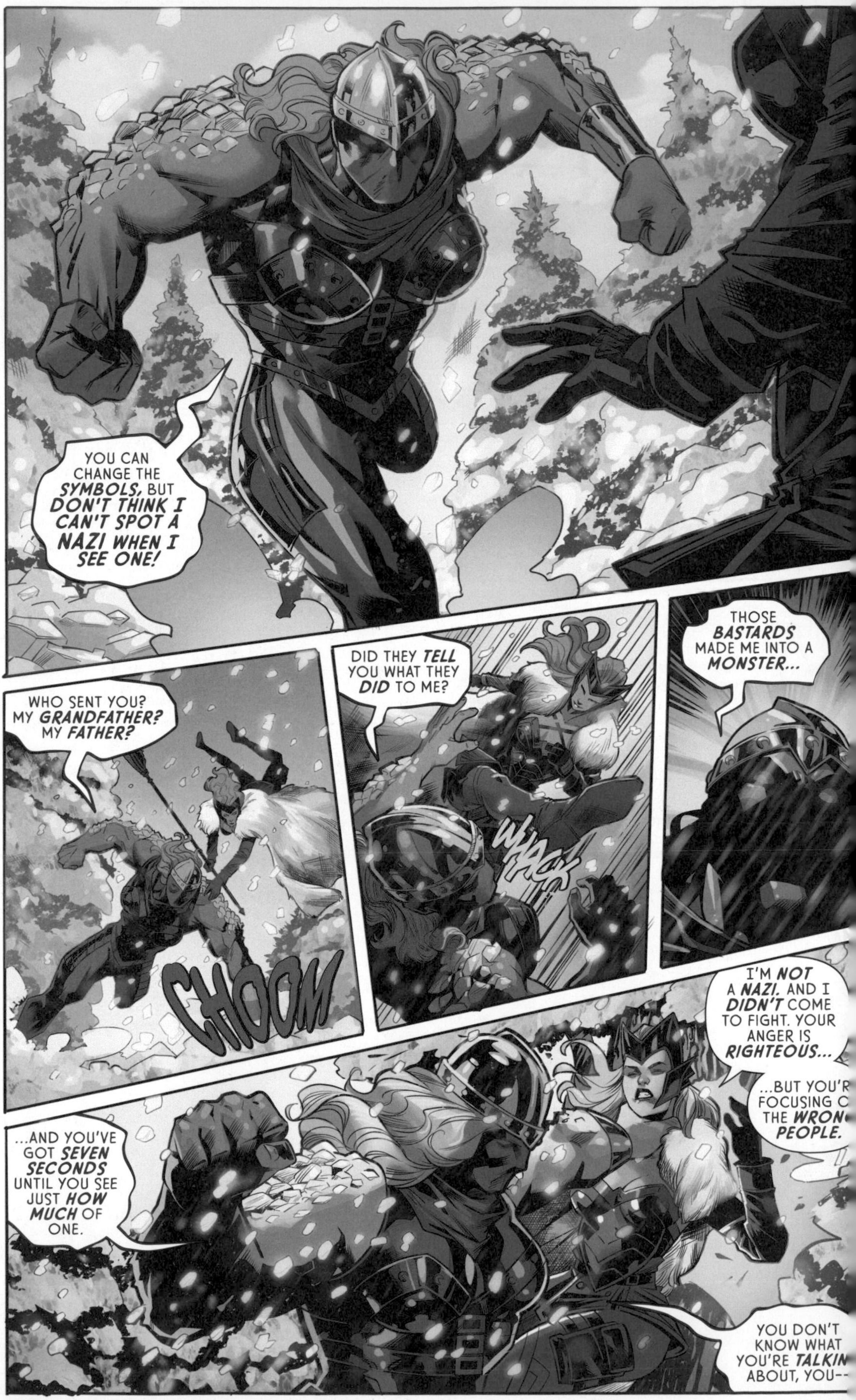
YOU CAN CHANGE THE SYMBOLS, BUT DON'T THINK I CAN'T SPOT A NAZI WHEN I SEE ONE!
WHO SENT YOU? MY GRANDFATHER? MY FATHER?
CHOOM
DID THEY TELL YOU WHAT THEY DID TO ME?
WHACK
THOSE BASTARDS MADE ME INTO A MONSTER...
...AND YOU'VE GOT SEVEN SECONDS UNTIL YOU SEE JUST HOW MUCH OF ONE.
I'M NOT A NAZI. AND I DIDN'T COME TO FIGHT. YOUR ANGER IS RIGHTEOUS...
...BUT YOU'R FOCUSING O THE WRON PEOPLE.
YOU DON'T KNOW WHAT YOU'RE TALKIN ABOUT, YOU--

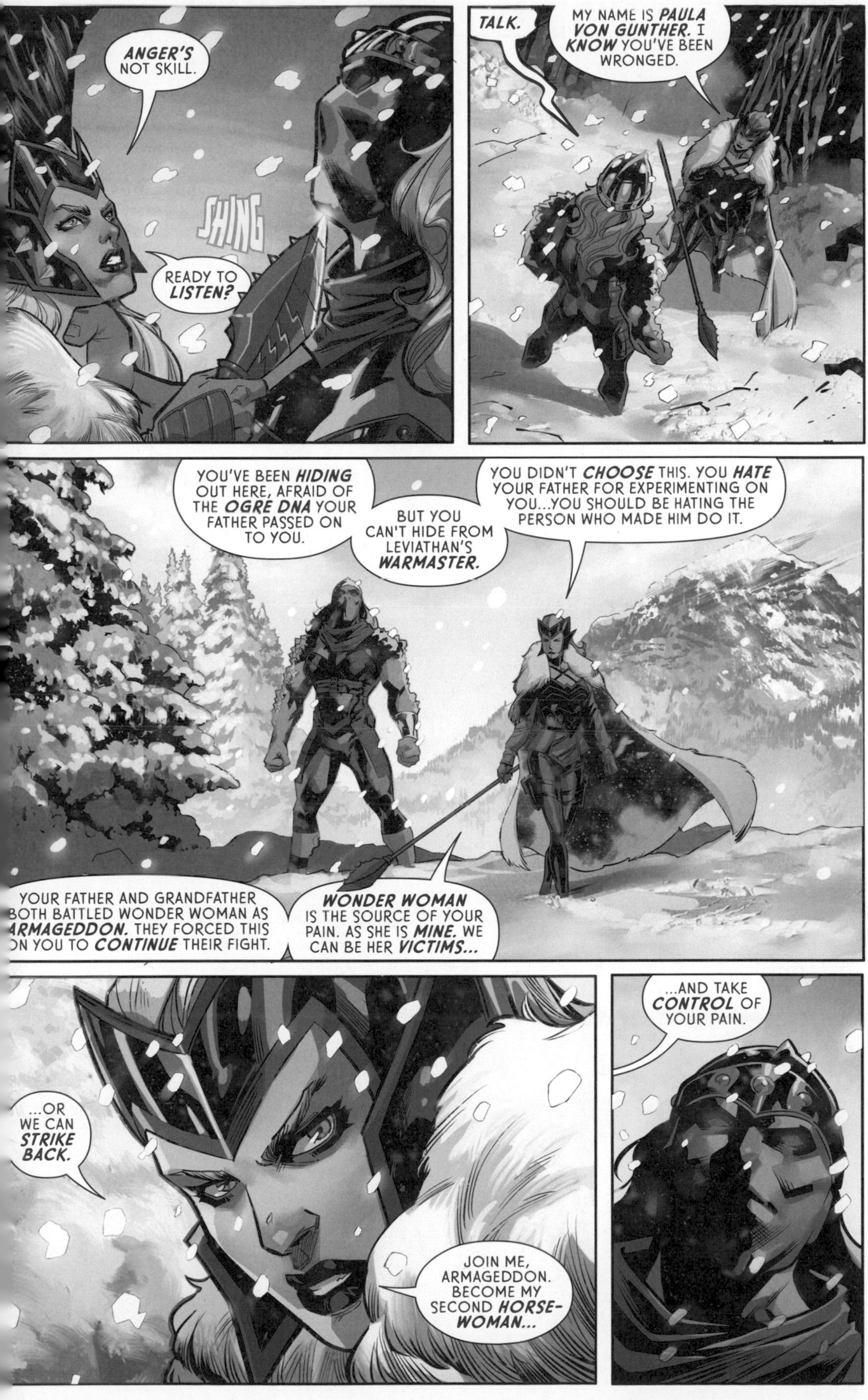
ANGER'S NOT SKILL.
SHING
READY TO LISTEN?
TALK.
MY NAME IS PAULA VON GUNTHER. I KNOW YOU'VE BEEN WRONGED.
YOU'VE BEEN HIDING OUT HERE, AFRAID OF THE OGRE DNA YOUR FATHER PASSED ON TO YOU.
BUT YOU CAN'T HIDE FROM LEVIATHAN'S WARMASTER.
YOU DIDN'T CHOOSE THIS. YOU HATE YOUR FATHER FOR EXPERIMENTING ON YOU...YOU SHOULD BE HATING THE PERSON WHO MADE HIM DO IT.
YOUR FATHER AND GRANDFATHER BOTH BATTLED WONDER WOMAN AS ARMAGEDDON. THEY FORCED THIS ON YOU TO CONTINUE THEIR FIGHT.
WONDER WOMAN IS THE SOURCE OF YOUR PAIN. AS SHE IS MINE. WE CAN BE HER VICTIMS...
...OR WE CAN STRIKE BACK.
JOIN ME, ARMAGEDDON. BECOME MY SECOND HORSE-WOMAN...
...AND TAKE CONTROL OF YOUR PAIN.

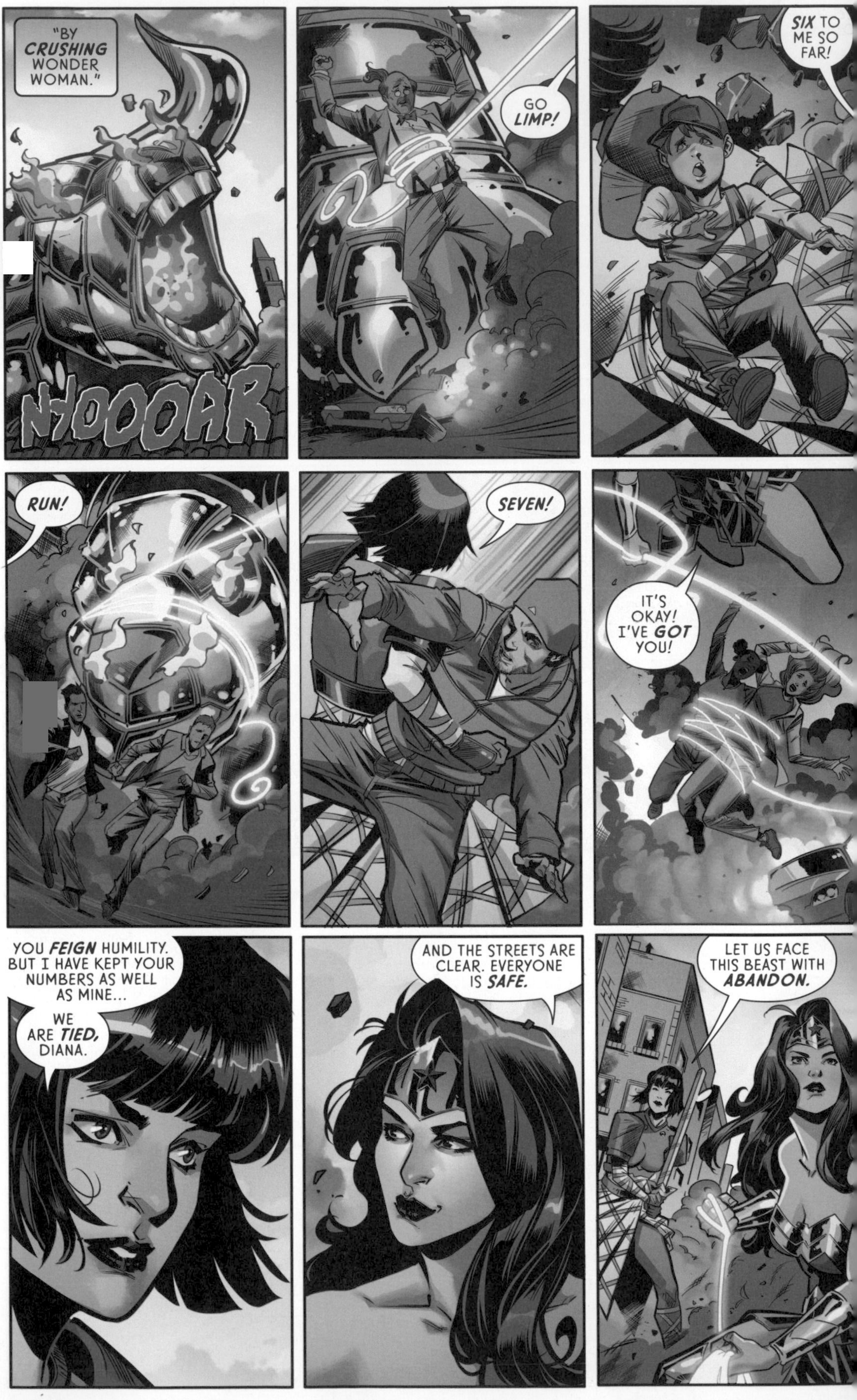
"BY CRUSHING WONDER WOMAN."
NHOOOAR
GO LIMP!
SIX TO ME SO FAR!
RUN!
SEVEN!
IT'S OKAY! I'VE GOT YOU!
YOU FEIGN HUMILITY. BUT I HAVE KEPT YOUR NUMBERS AS WELL AS MINE...
WE ARE TIED, DIANA.
AND THE STREETS ARE CLEAR. EVERYONE IS SAFE.
LET US FACE THIS BEAST WITH ABANDON.

...ECKLESSNESS HASN'T GOTTEN US *ANYWHERE*, VALDA.

LET'S TRY...

...SOMETHING *DECISIVE!*

THE *RIGHT STRIKE* WILL SEND YOU *HOME*...

...BUT IF YOU STRIKE *WRONG*, YOU'LL BE *LOST* IN TIME. SO BRING IT DOWN...

...AND DO *NOT* BREAK ITS SKIN!

FEAR NOT, WONDER WOMAN...

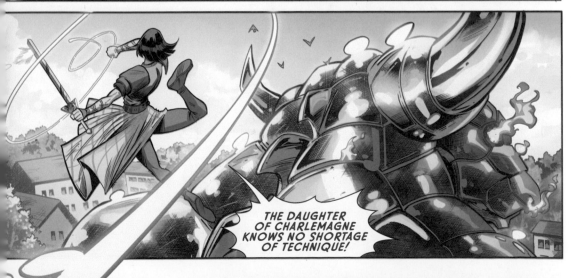

THE *DAUGHTER OF CHARLEMAGNE* KNOWS NO SHORTAGE OF TECHNIQUE!

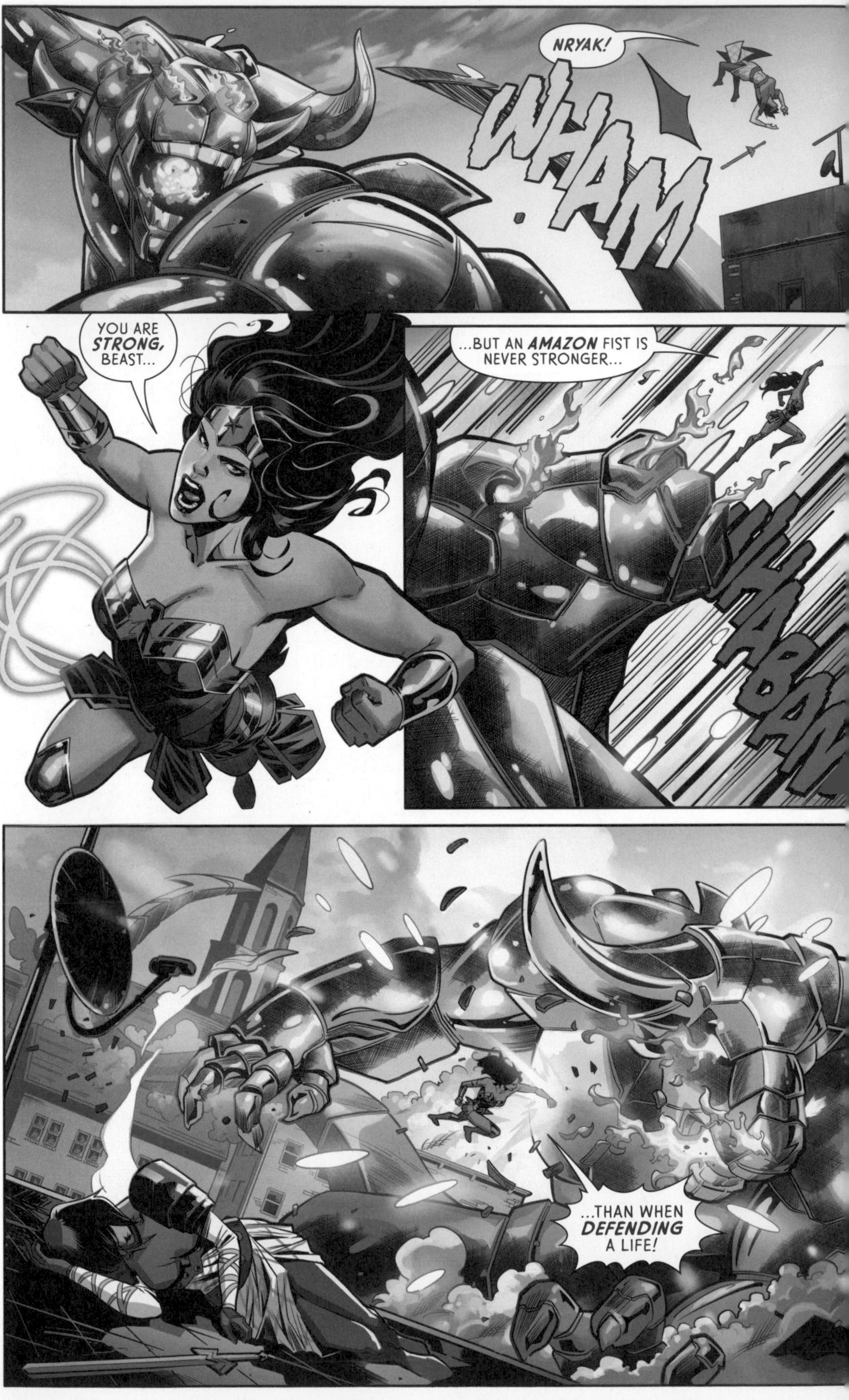
NRYAK!
WHAM
YOU ARE **STRONG,** BEAST...
...BUT AN **AMAZON** FIST IS NEVER STRONGER...
...THAN WHEN **DEFENDING** A LIFE!

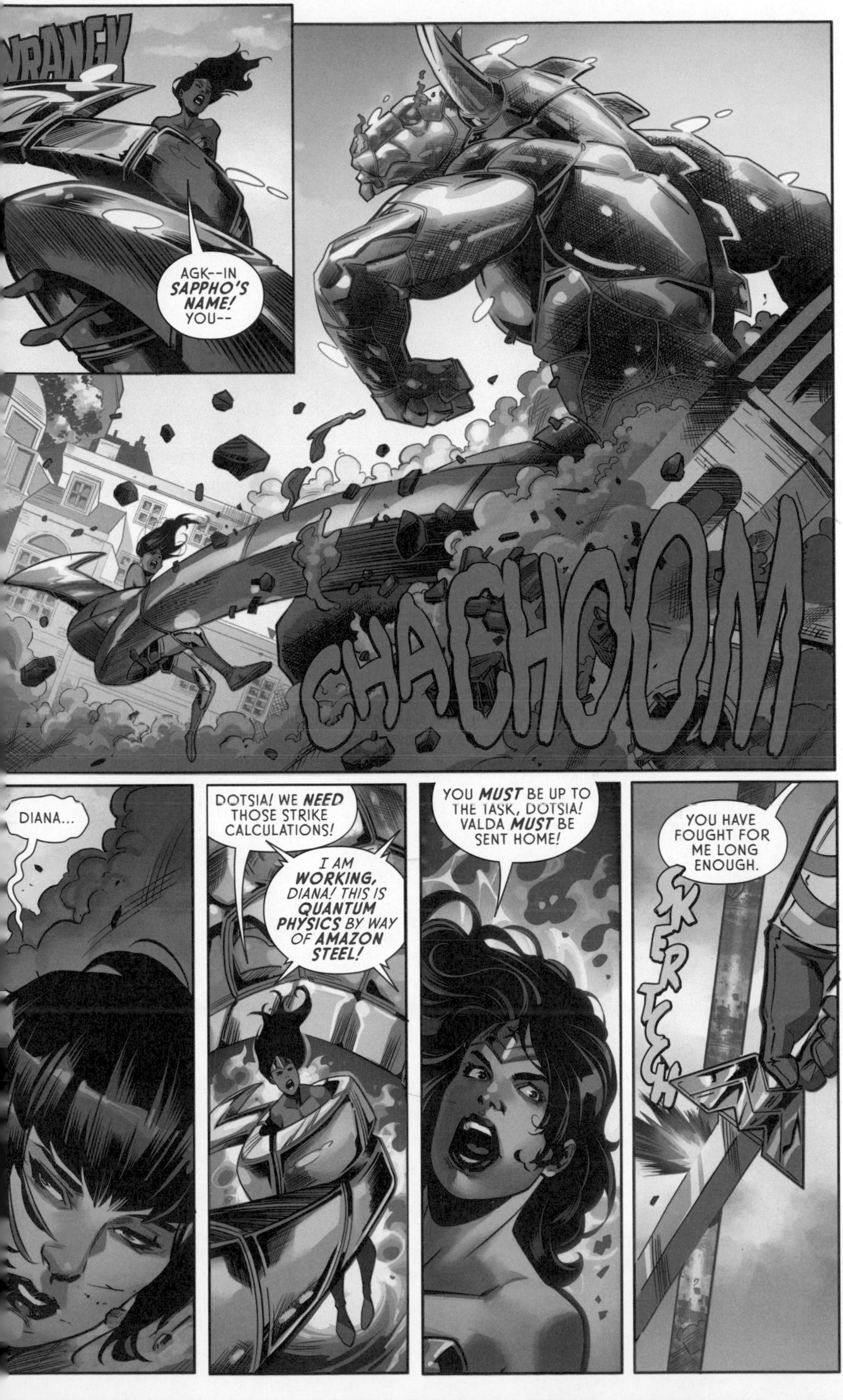
RANGK
AGK--IN SAPPHO'S NAME! YOU--
CHACHOOM
DIANA...
DOTSIA! WE NEED THOSE STRIKE CALCULATIONS!
I AM WORKING, DIANA! THIS IS QUANTUM PHYSICS BY WAY OF AMAZON STEEL!
YOU MUST BE UP TO THE TASK, DOTSIA! VALDA MUST BE SENT HOME!
YOU HAVE FOUGHT FOR ME LONG ENOUGH.
SKERTCH

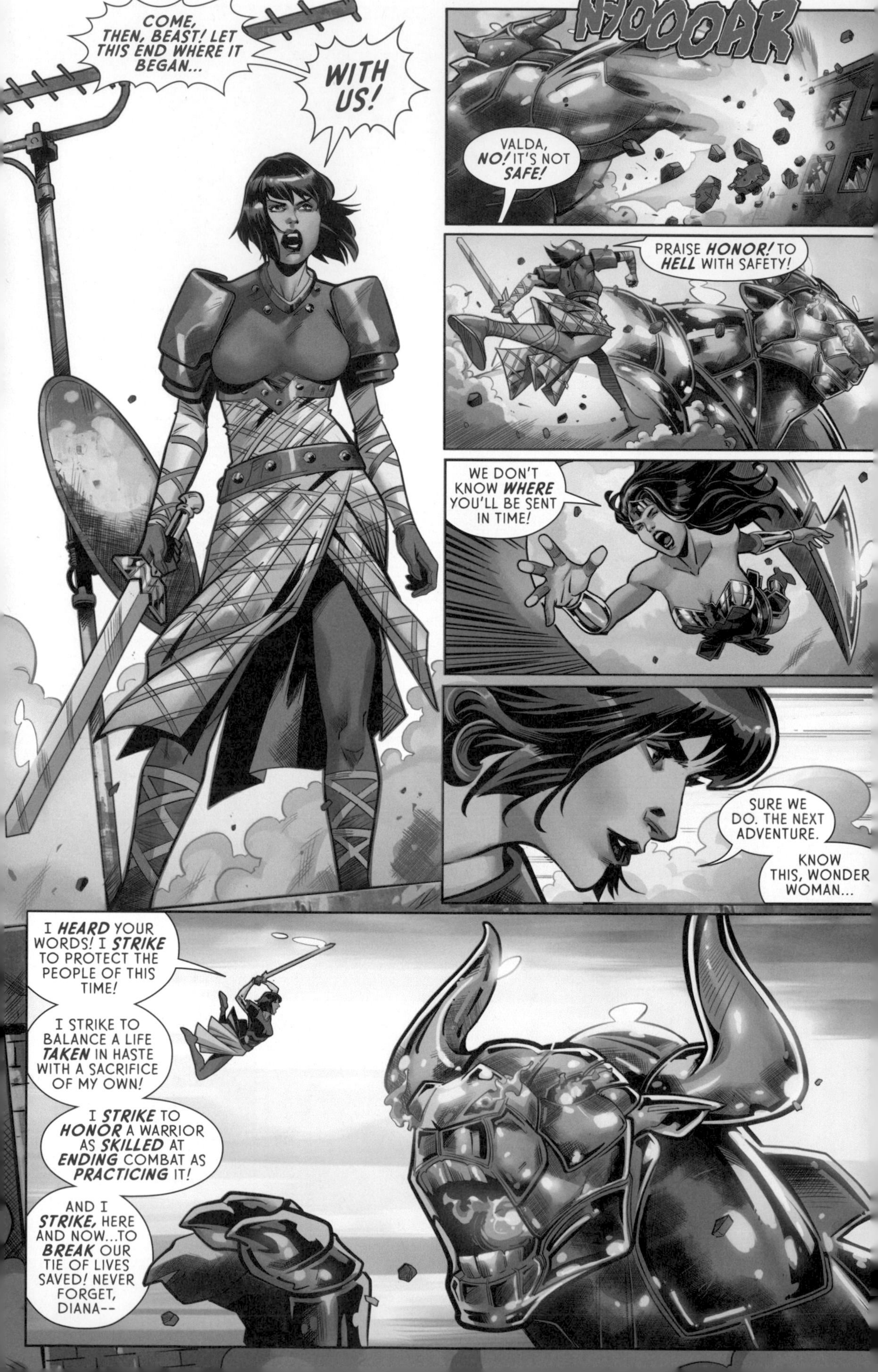
COME, THEN, BEAST! LET THIS END WHERE IT BEGAN...
WITH US!
NHOOOAR
VALDA, NO! IT'S NOT SAFE!
PRAISE HONOR! TO HELL WITH SAFETY!
WE DON'T KNOW WHERE YOU'LL BE SENT IN TIME!
SURE WE DO. THE NEXT ADVENTURE.
KNOW THIS, WONDER WOMAN...
I HEARD YOUR WORDS! I STRIKE TO PROTECT THE PEOPLE OF THIS TIME!
I STRIKE TO BALANCE A LIFE TAKEN IN HASTE WITH A SACRIFICE OF MY OWN!
I STRIKE TO HONOR A WARRIOR AS SKILLED AT ENDING COMBAT AS PRACTICING IT!
AND I STRIKE, HERE AND NOW...TO BREAK OUR TIE OF LIVES SAVED! NEVER FORGET, DIANA--

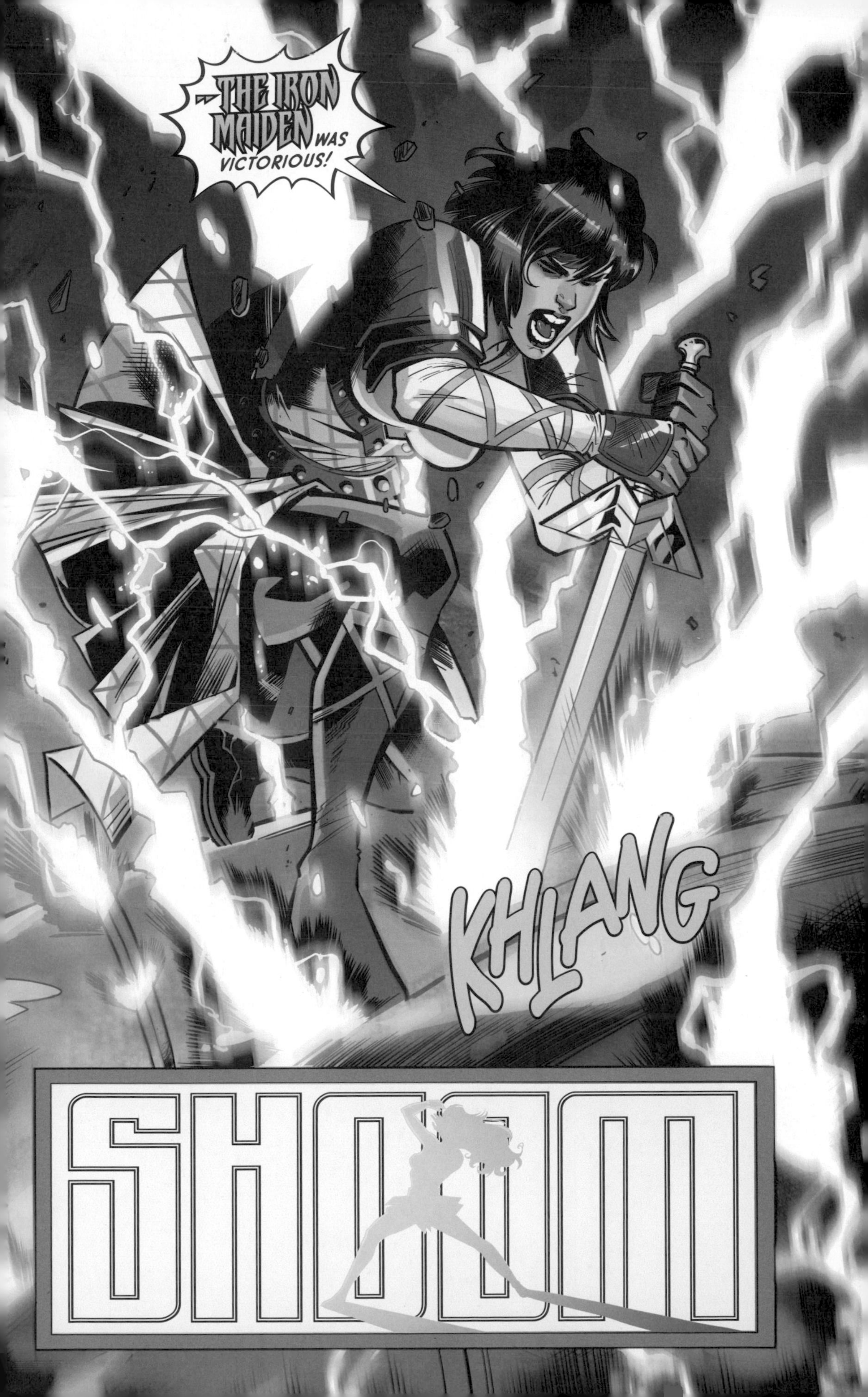
..THE IRON MAIDEN WAS VICTORIOUS!
KHLANG
SHOOM

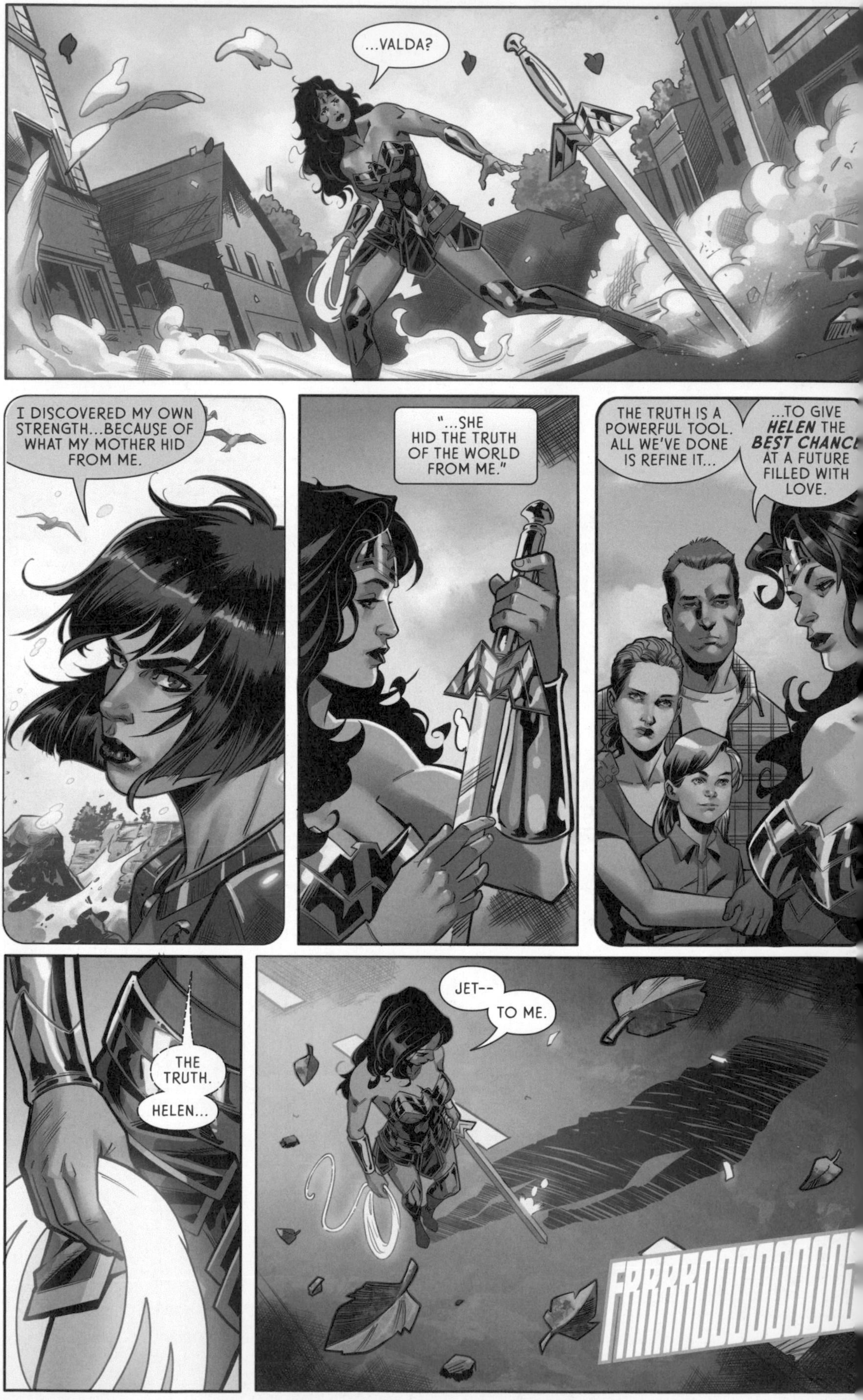
...VALDA?
I DISCOVERED MY OWN STRENGTH...BECAUSE OF WHAT MY MOTHER HID FROM ME.
"...SHE HID THE TRUTH OF THE WORLD FROM ME."
THE TRUTH IS A POWERFUL TOOL. ALL WE'VE DONE IS REFINE IT...
...TO GIVE HELEN THE BEST CHANCE AT A FUTURE FILLED WITH LOVE.
THE TRUTH.
HELEN...
JET--
TO ME.

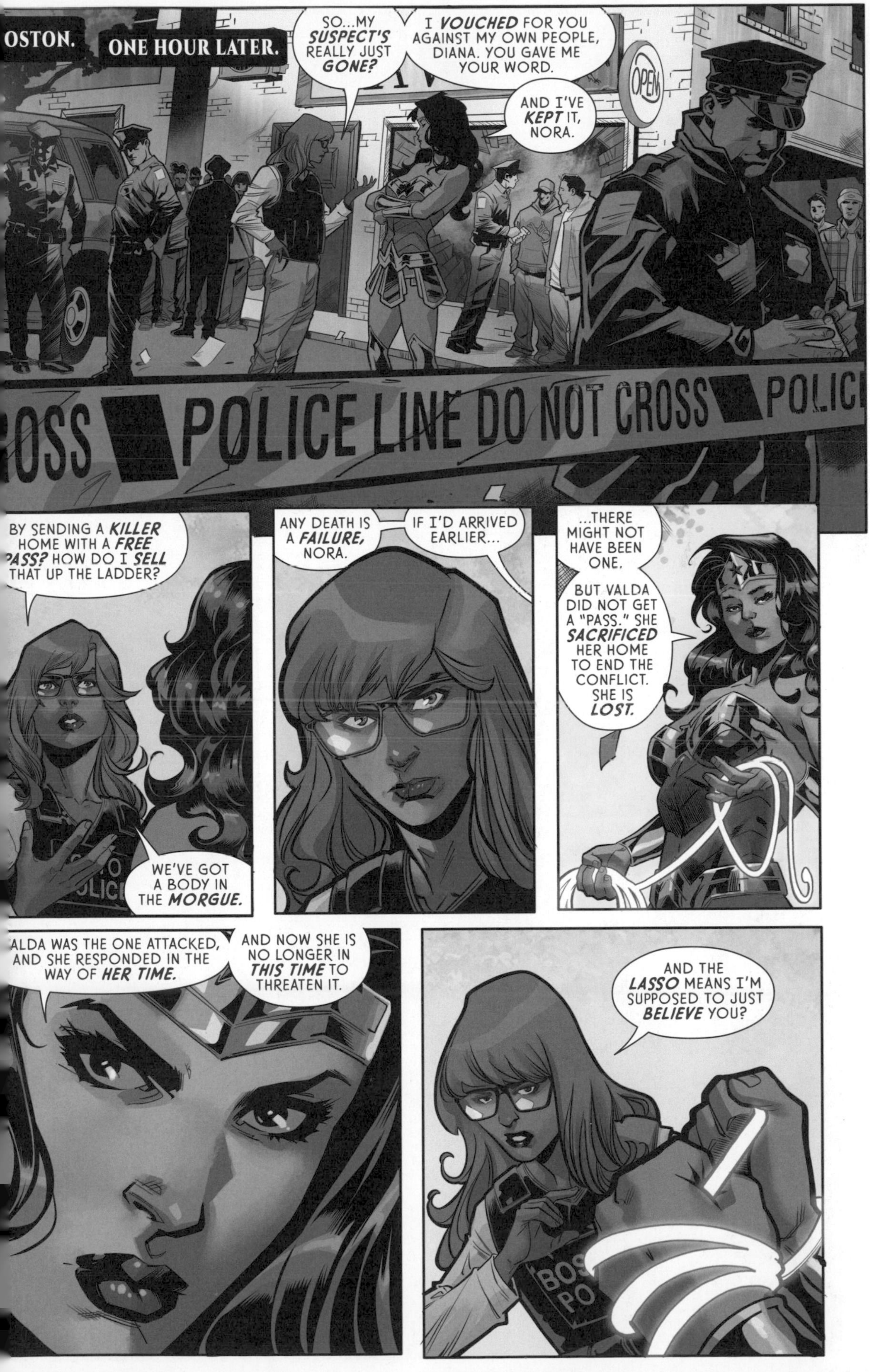
OSTON.
ONE HOUR LATER.
SO...MY SUSPECT'S REALLY JUST GONE?
I VOUCHED FOR YOU AGAINST MY OWN PEOPLE, DIANA. YOU GAVE ME YOUR WORD.
AND I'VE KEPT IT, NORA.
OPEN
POLICE LINE DO NOT CROSS
BY SENDING A KILLER HOME WITH A FREE PASS? HOW DO I SELL THAT UP THE LADDER?
WE'VE GOT A BODY IN THE MORGUE.
ANY DEATH IS A FAILURE, NORA.
IF I'D ARRIVED EARLIER...
...THERE MIGHT NOT HAVE BEEN ONE.
BUT VALDA DID NOT GET A "PASS." SHE SACRIFICED HER HOME TO END THE CONFLICT. SHE IS LOST.
VALDA WAS THE ONE ATTACKED, AND SHE RESPONDED IN THE WAY OF HER TIME.
AND NOW SHE IS NO LONGER IN THIS TIME TO THREATEN IT.
AND THE LASSO MEANS I'M SUPPOSED TO JUST BELIEVE YOU?

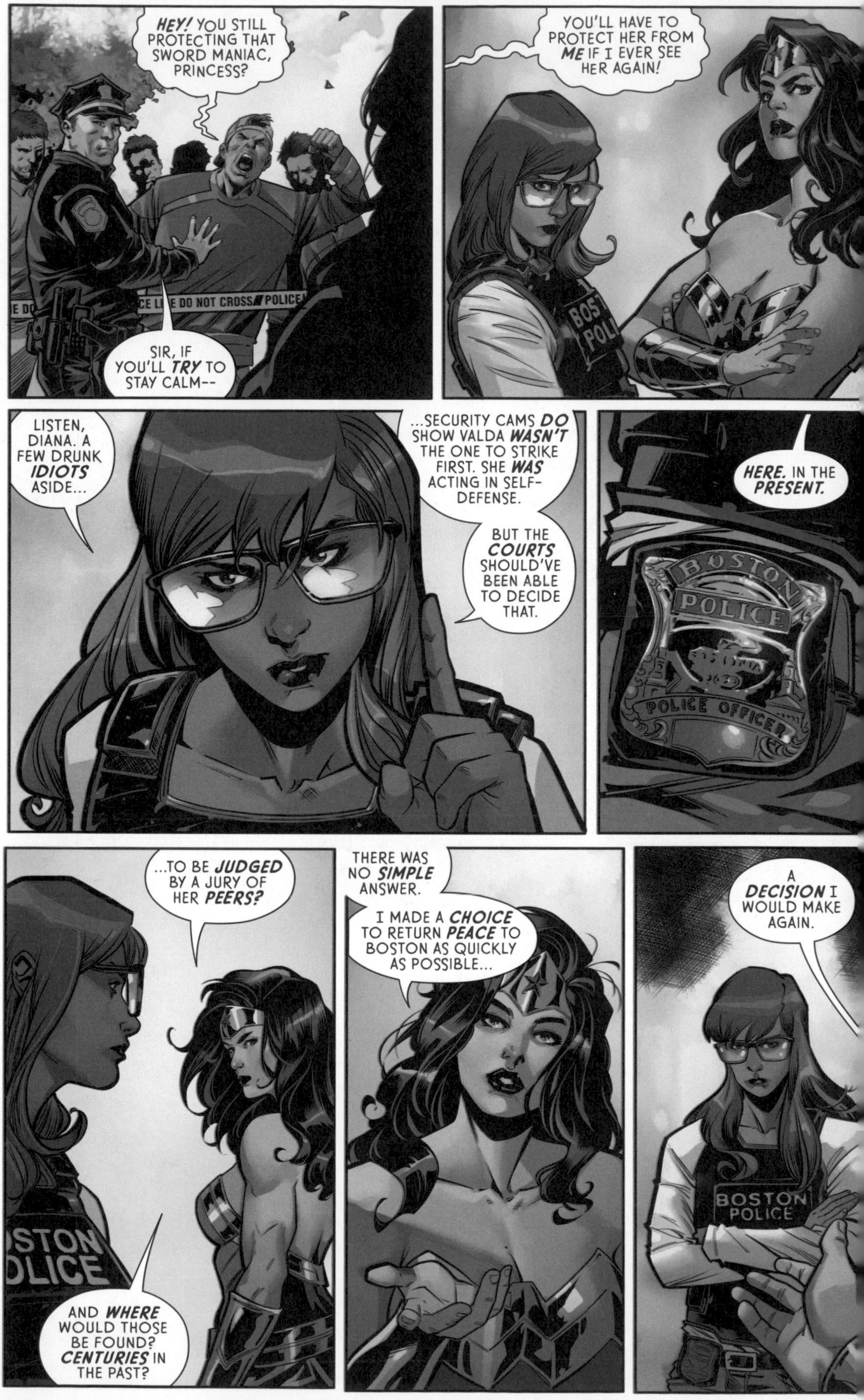
HEY! YOU STILL PROTECTING THAT SWORD MANIAC, PRINCESS?
DO NOT CROSS POLICE
SIR, IF YOU'LL TRY TO STAY CALM--
YOU'LL HAVE TO PROTECT HER FROM ME IF I EVER SEE HER AGAIN!
BOSTON POLICE
LISTEN, DIANA. A FEW DRUNK IDIOTS ASIDE...
...SECURITY CAMS DO SHOW VALDA WASN'T THE ONE TO STRIKE FIRST. SHE WAS ACTING IN SELF-DEFENSE.
BUT THE COURTS SHOULD'VE BEEN ABLE TO DECIDE THAT.
HERE. IN THE PRESENT.
BOSTON POLICE
POLICE OFFICER
...TO BE JUDGED BY A JURY OF HER PEERS?
OSTON OLICE
AND WHERE WOULD THOSE BE FOUND? CENTURIES IN THE PAST?
THERE WAS NO SIMPLE ANSWER.
I MADE A CHOICE TO RETURN PEACE TO BOSTON AS QUICKLY AS POSSIBLE...
A DECISION I WOULD MAKE AGAIN.
BOSTON POLICE

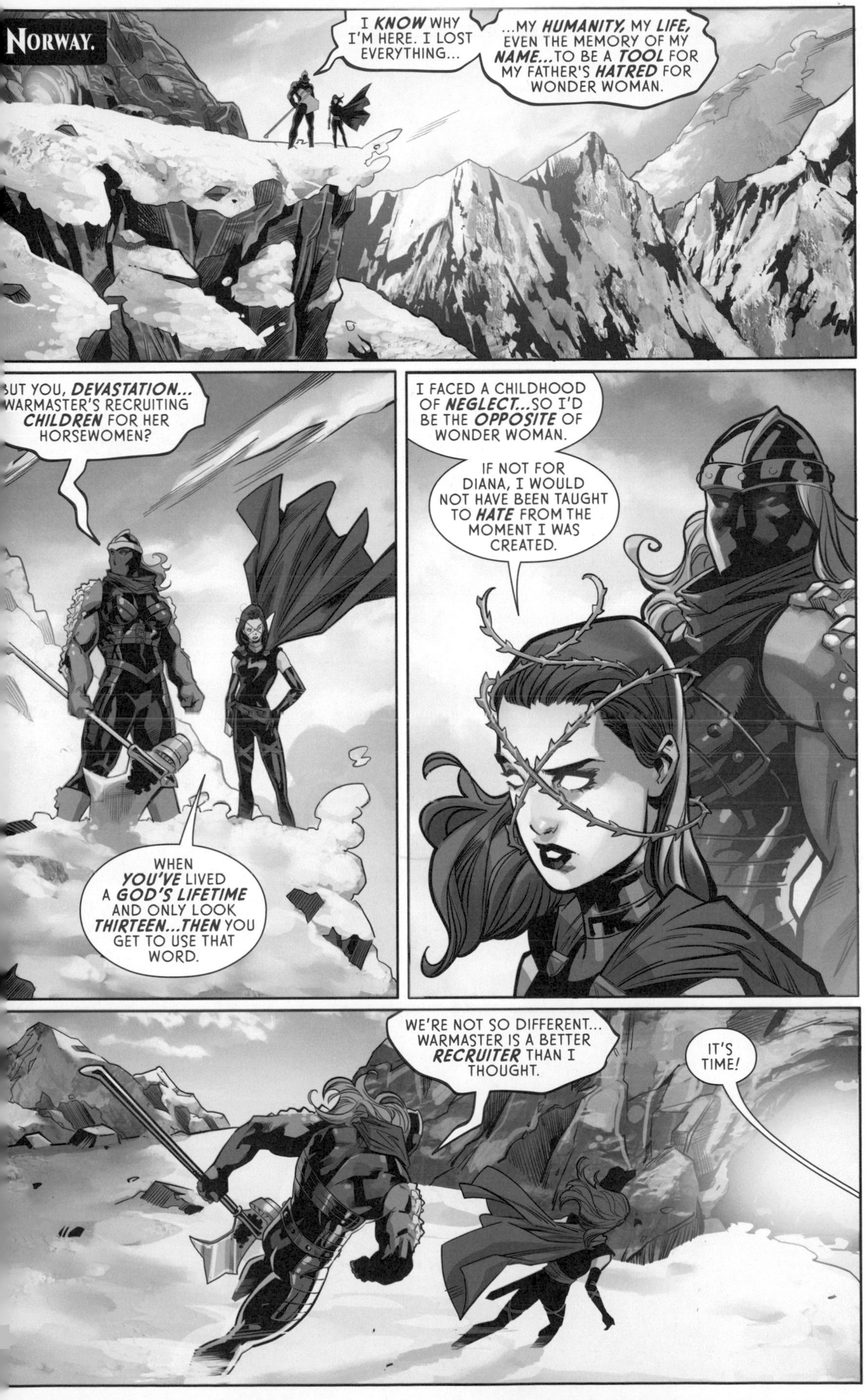
NORWAY.
I KNOW WHY I'M HERE. I LOST EVERYTHING...
...MY HUMANITY, MY LIFE, EVEN THE MEMORY OF MY NAME...TO BE A TOOL FOR MY FATHER'S HATRED FOR WONDER WOMAN.
BUT YOU, DEVASTATION... WARMASTER'S RECRUITING CHILDREN FOR HER HORSEWOMEN?
WHEN YOU'VE LIVED A GOD'S LIFETIME AND ONLY LOOK THIRTEEN...THEN YOU GET TO USE THAT WORD.
I FACED A CHILDHOOD OF NEGLECT...SO I'D BE THE OPPOSITE OF WONDER WOMAN.
IF NOT FOR DIANA, I WOULD NOT HAVE BEEN TAUGHT TO HATE FROM THE MOMENT I WAS CREATED.
WE'RE NOT SO DIFFERENT... WARMASTER IS A BETTER RECRUITER THAN I THOUGHT.
IT'S TIME!

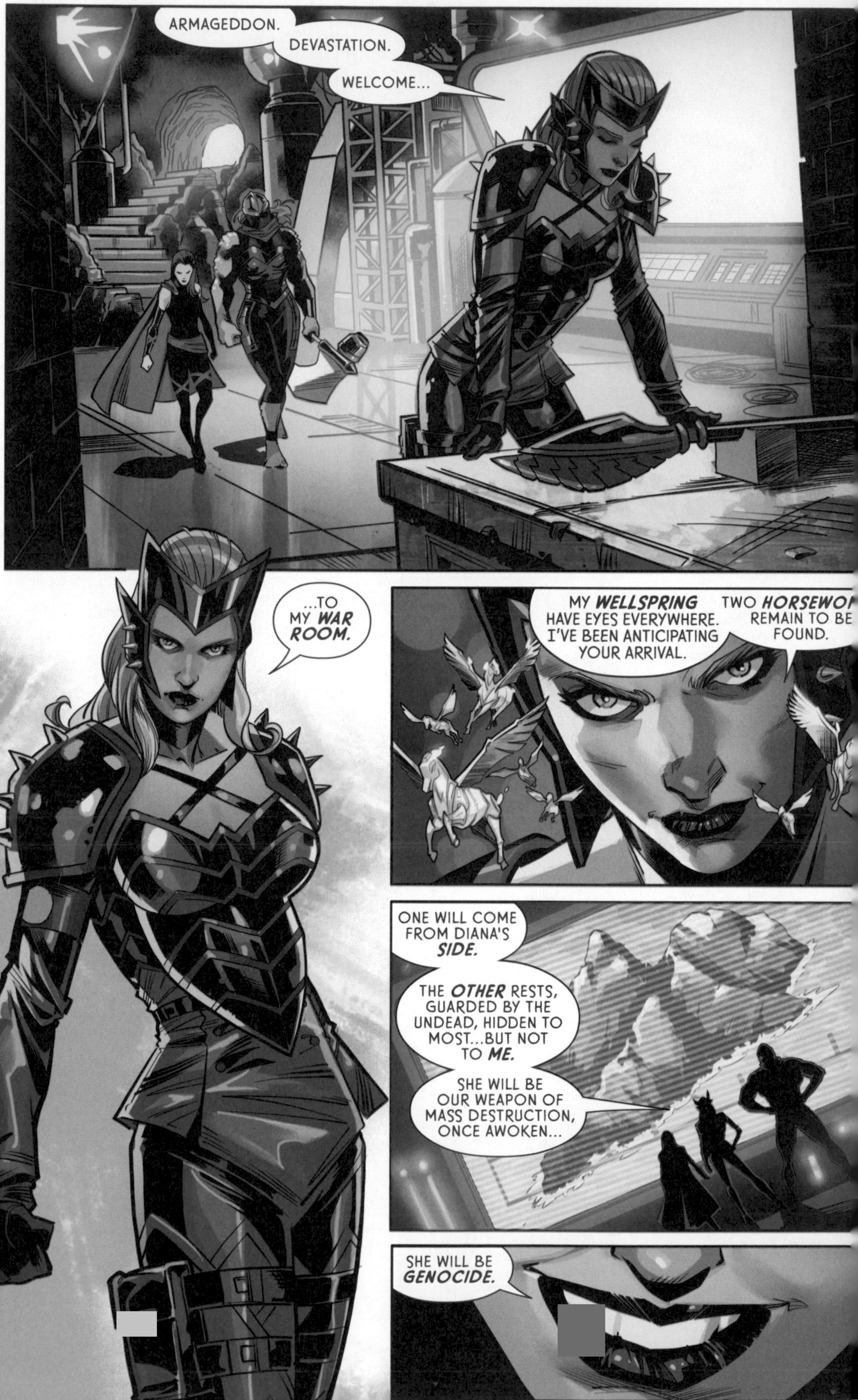
ARMAGEDDON.
DEVASTATION.
WELCOME...
...TO MY WAR ROOM.
MY WELLSPRING HAVE EYES EVERYWHERE. I'VE BEEN ANTICIPATING YOUR ARRIVAL.
TWO HORSEWO REMAIN TO BE FOUND.
ONE WILL COME FROM DIANA'S SIDE.
THE OTHER RESTS, GUARDED BY THE UNDEAD, HIDDEN TO MOST...BUT NOT TO ME.
SHE WILL BE OUR WEAPON OF MASS DESTRUCTION, ONCE AWOKEN...
SHE WILL BE GENOCIDE.

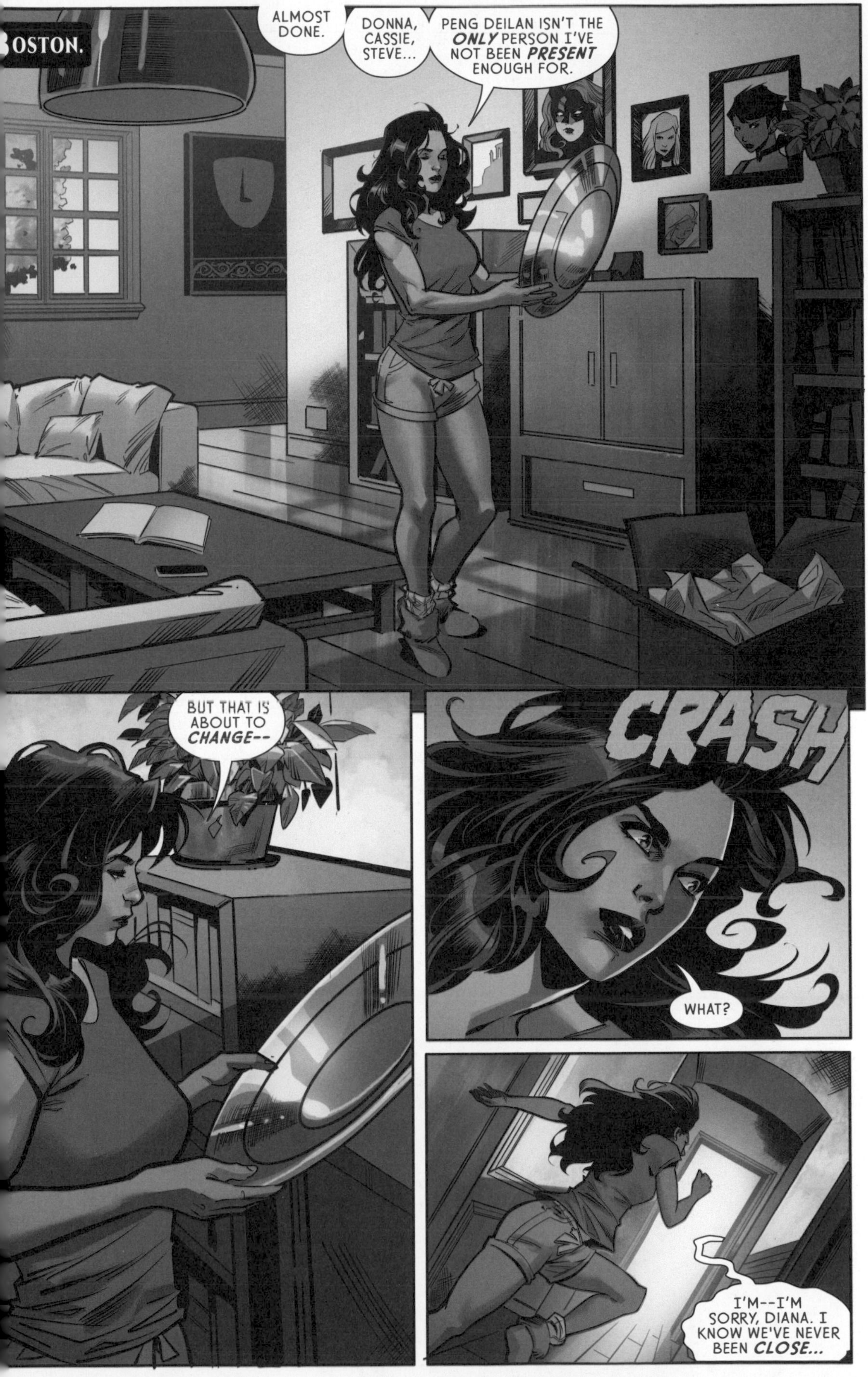
OSTON.
ALMOST DONE.
DONNA, CASSIE, STEVE...
PENG DEILAN ISN'T THE ONLY PERSON I'VE NOT BEEN PRESENT ENOUGH FOR.
BUT THAT IS ABOUT TO CHANGE--
CRASH
WHAT?
I'M--I'M SORRY, DIANA. I KNOW WE'VE NEVER BEEN CLOSE...

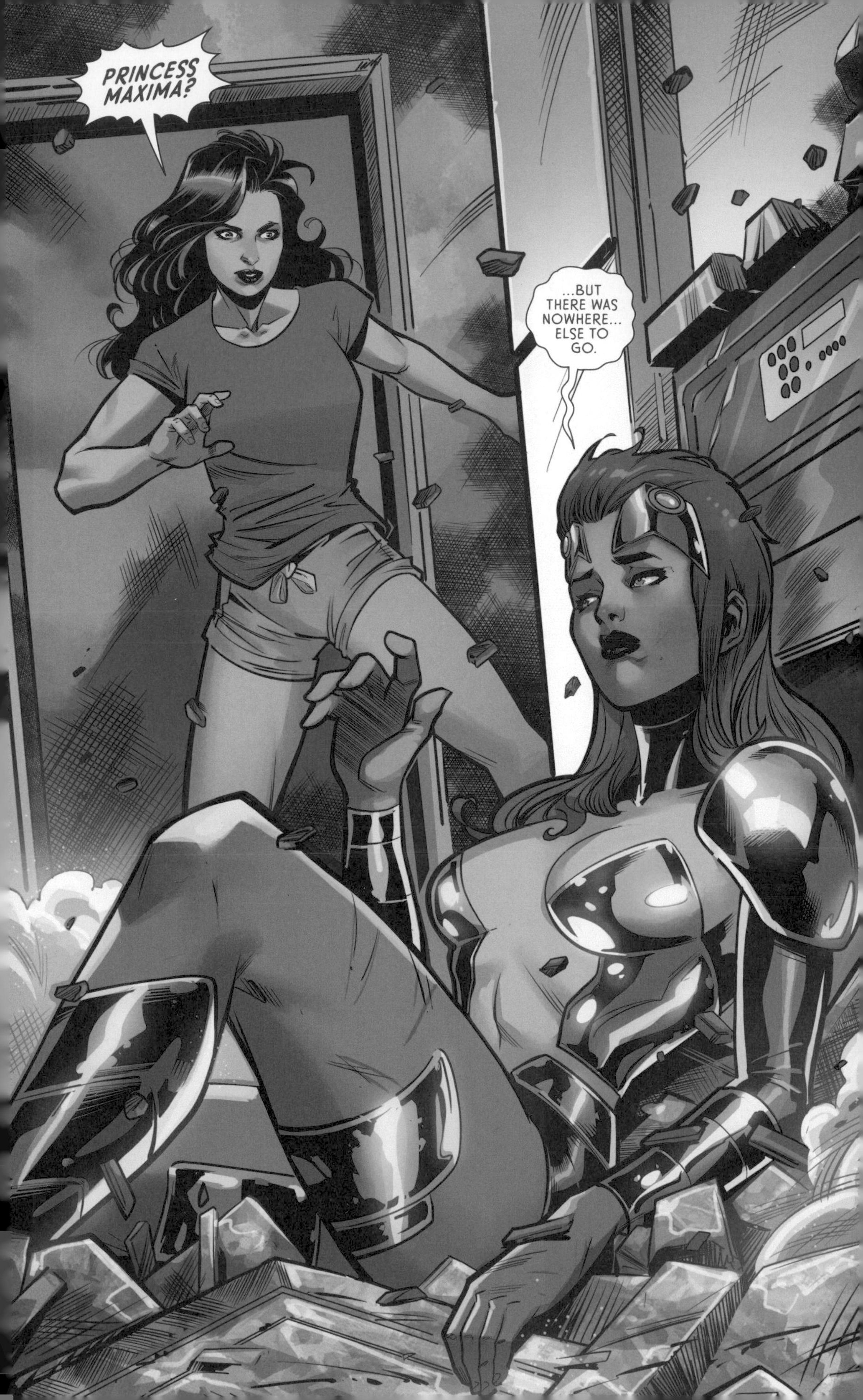
PRINCESS MAXIMA?
...BUT THERE WAS NOWHERE... ELSE TO GO.

***Wonder Woman* #754**
cover by **ROBSON ROCHA,**
DANNY MIKI and **BRAD ANDERSON**

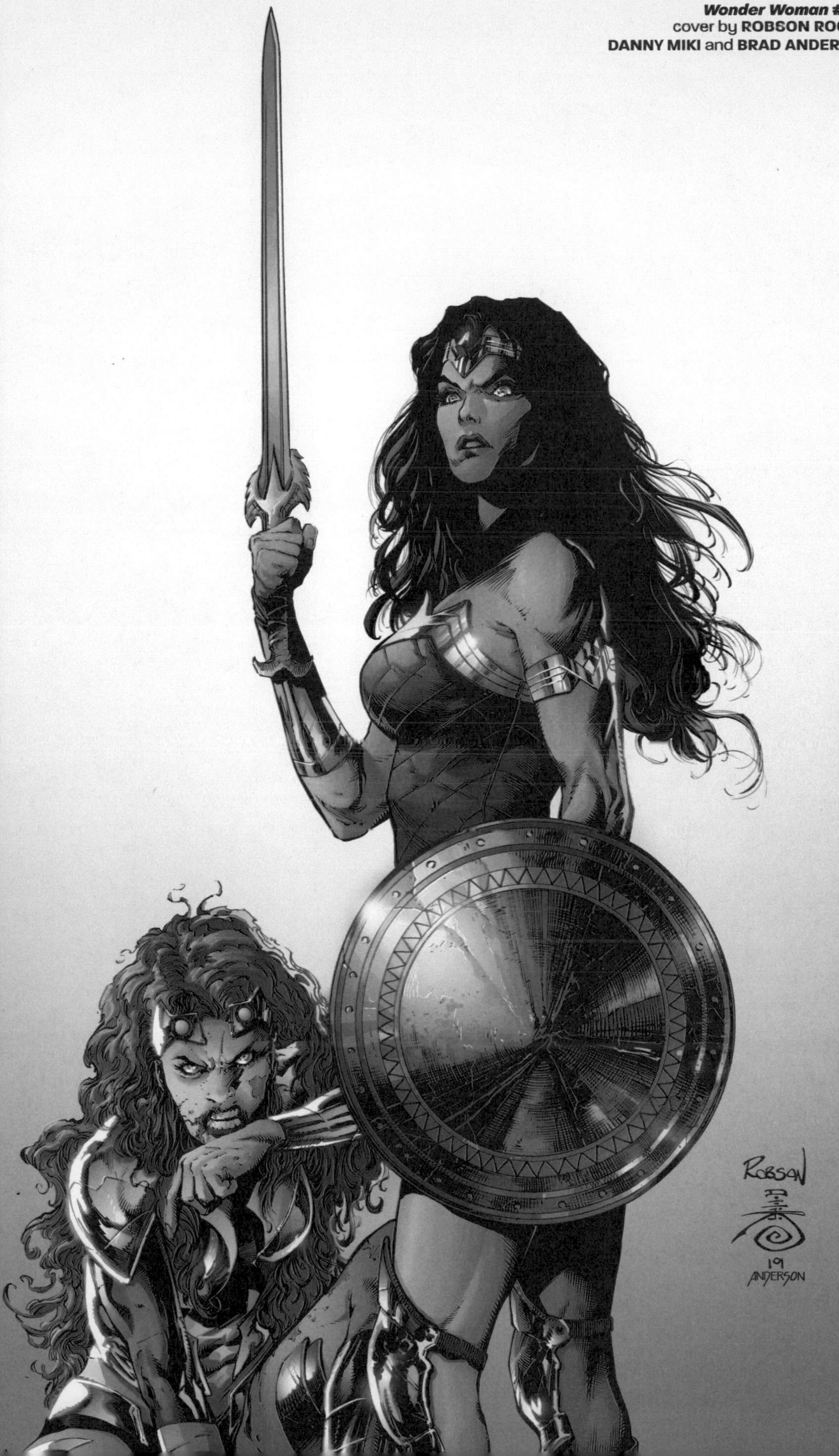
ROBSON
19
ANDERSON

***Wonder Woman* #754**
variant cover by **RAFAEL GRAMPÃ** and **PEDRO COBIACO**

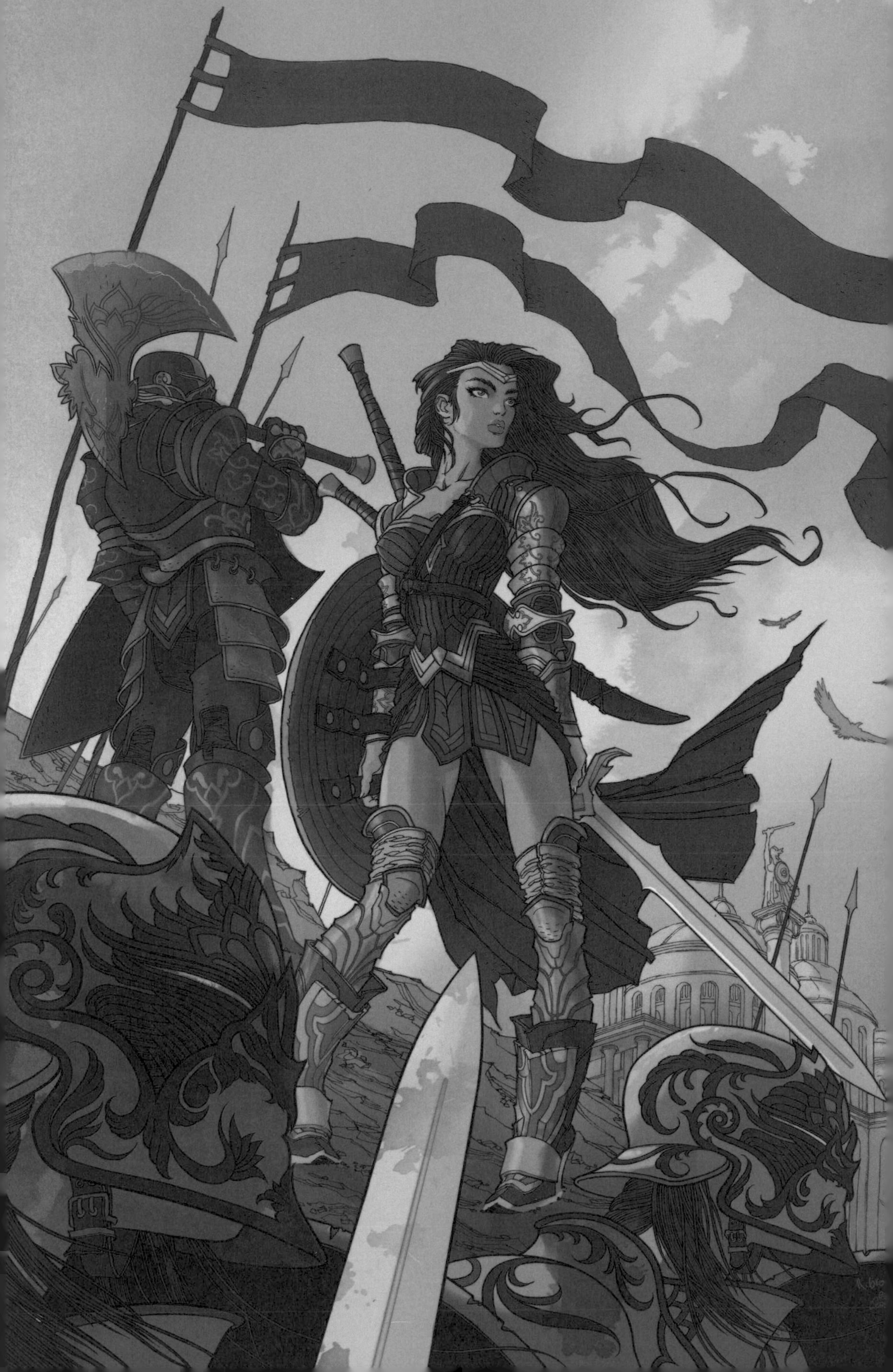

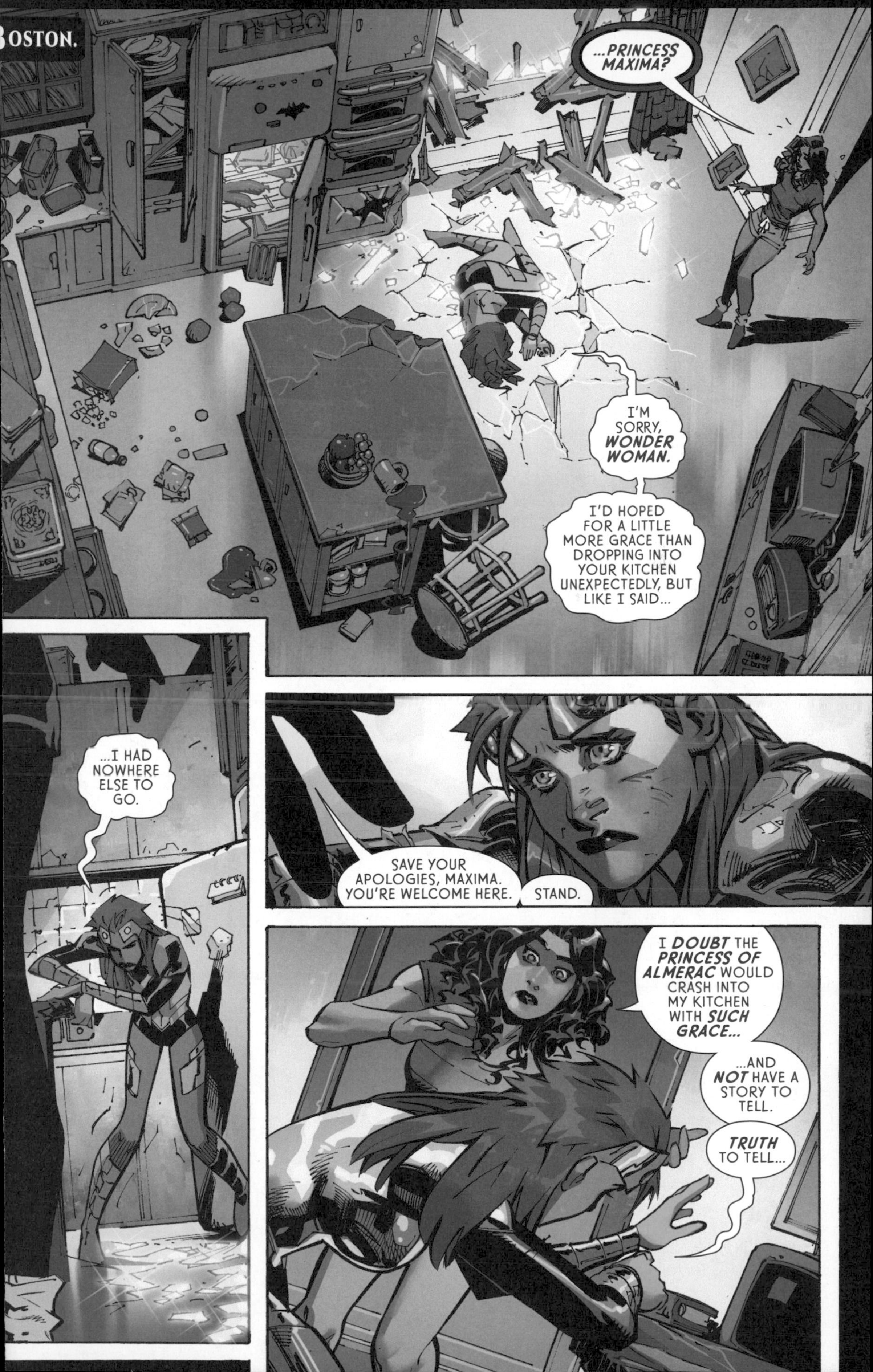
BOSTON.
...PRINCESS MAXIMA?
I'M SORRY, WONDER WOMAN.
I'D HOPED FOR A LITTLE MORE GRACE THAN DROPPING INTO YOUR KITCHEN UNEXPECTEDLY, BUT LIKE I SAID...
...I HAD NOWHERE ELSE TO GO.
SAVE YOUR APOLOGIES, MAXIMA. YOU'RE WELCOME HERE.
STAND.
I DOUBT THE PRINCESS OF ALMERAC WOULD CRASH INTO MY KITCHEN WITH SUCH GRACE...
...AND NOT HAVE A STORY TO TELL.
TRUTH TO TELL...

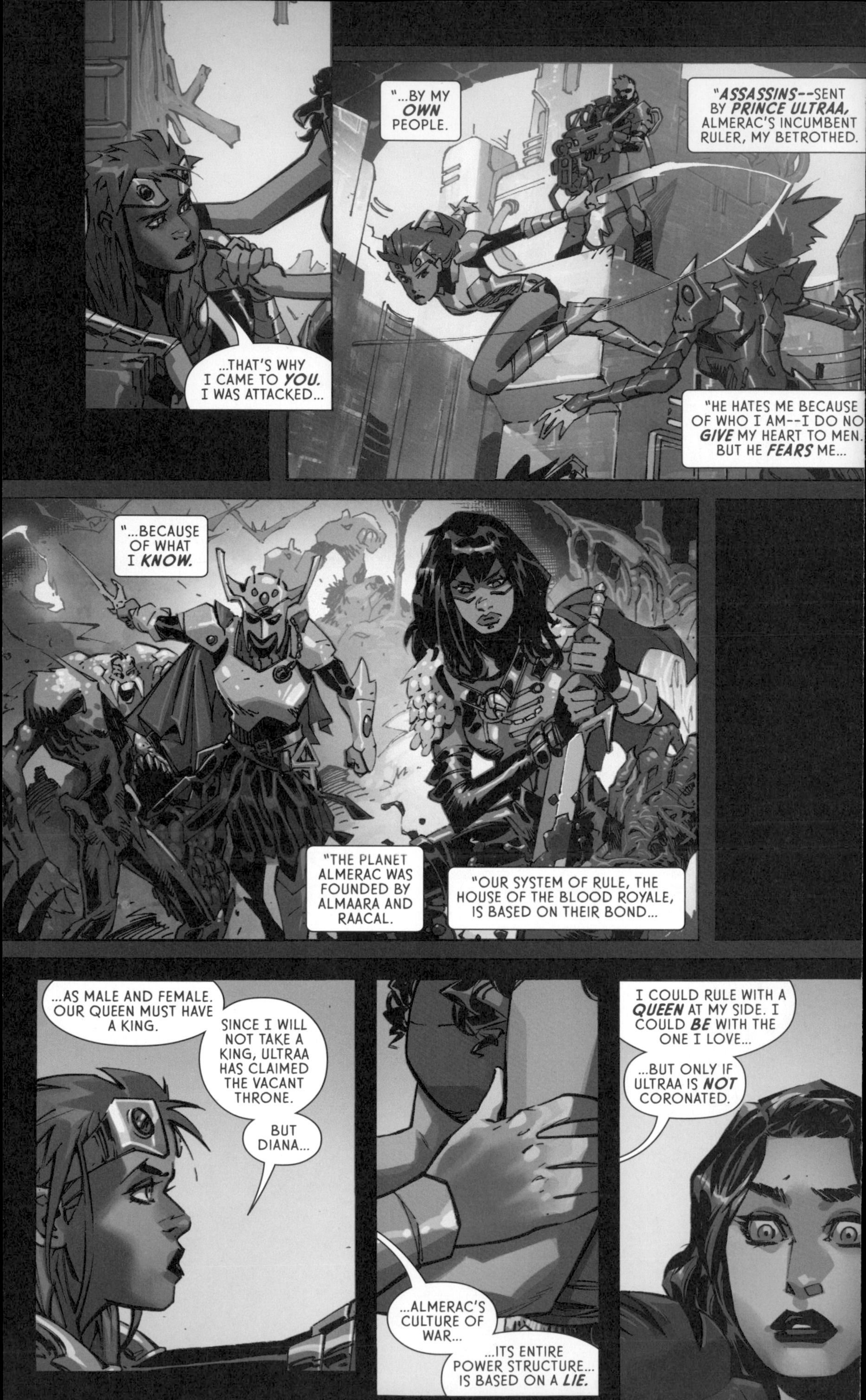
...THAT'S WHY
I CAME TO ***YOU.***
I WAS ATTACKED...
"...BY MY
OWN
PEOPLE.
"***ASSASSINS***--SENT
BY ***PRINCE ULTRAA,***
ALMERAC'S INCUMBENT
RULER, MY BETROTHED.
"HE HATES ME BECAUSE
OF WHO I AM--I DO NO
GIVE MY HEART TO MEN.
BUT HE ***FEARS*** ME...
"...BECAUSE
OF WHAT
I ***KNOW.***
"THE PLANET
ALMERAC WAS
FOUNDED BY
ALMAARA AND
RAACAL.
"OUR SYSTEM OF RULE, THE
HOUSE OF THE BLOOD ROYALE,
IS BASED ON THEIR BOND...
...AS MALE AND FEMALE.
OUR QUEEN MUST HAVE
A KING.
SINCE I WILL
NOT TAKE A
KING, ULTRAA
HAS CLAIMED
THE VACANT
THRONE.
BUT
DIANA...
...ALMERAC'S
CULTURE OF
WAR...
...ITS ENTIRE
POWER STRUCTURE...
IS BASED ON A ***LIE.***
I COULD RULE WITH A
QUEEN AT MY SIDE. I
COULD ***BE*** WITH THE
ONE I LOVE...
...BUT ONLY IF
ULTRAA IS ***NOT***
CORONATED.

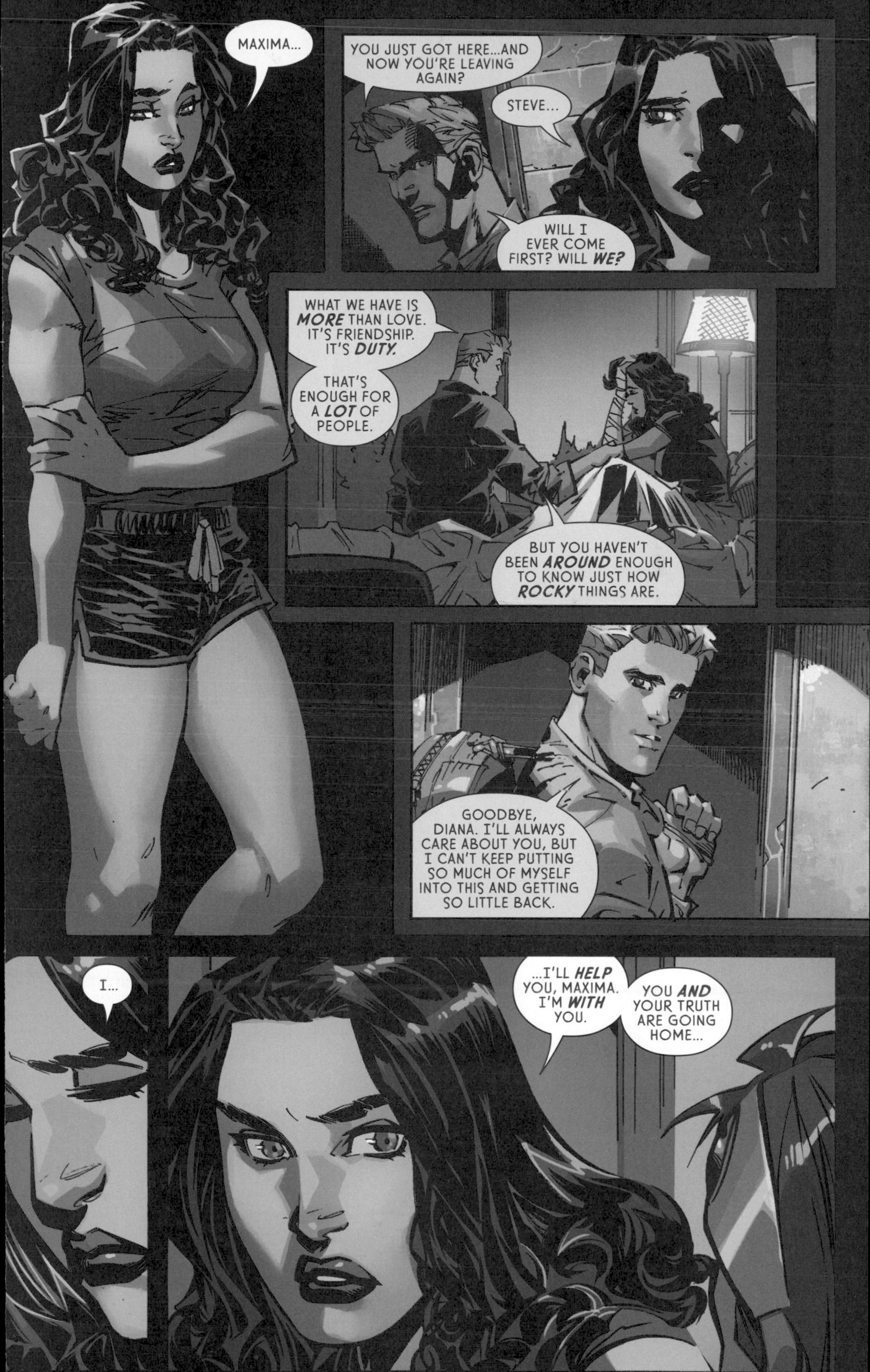
MAXIMA...
YOU JUST GOT HERE...AND NOW YOU'RE LEAVING AGAIN?
STEVE...
WILL I EVER COME FIRST? WILL *WE?*
WHAT WE HAVE IS *MORE* THAN LOVE. IT'S FRIENDSHIP. IT'S *DUTY.*
THAT'S ENOUGH FOR A *LOT* OF PEOPLE.
BUT YOU HAVEN'T BEEN *AROUND* ENOUGH TO KNOW JUST HOW *ROCKY* THINGS ARE.
GOODBYE, DIANA. I'LL ALWAYS CARE ABOUT YOU, BUT I CAN'T KEEP PUTTING SO MUCH OF MYSELF INTO THIS AND GETTING SO LITTLE BACK.
I...
...I'LL *HELP* YOU, MAXIMA. I'M *WITH* YOU.
YOU *AND* YOUR TRUTH ARE GOING HOME...

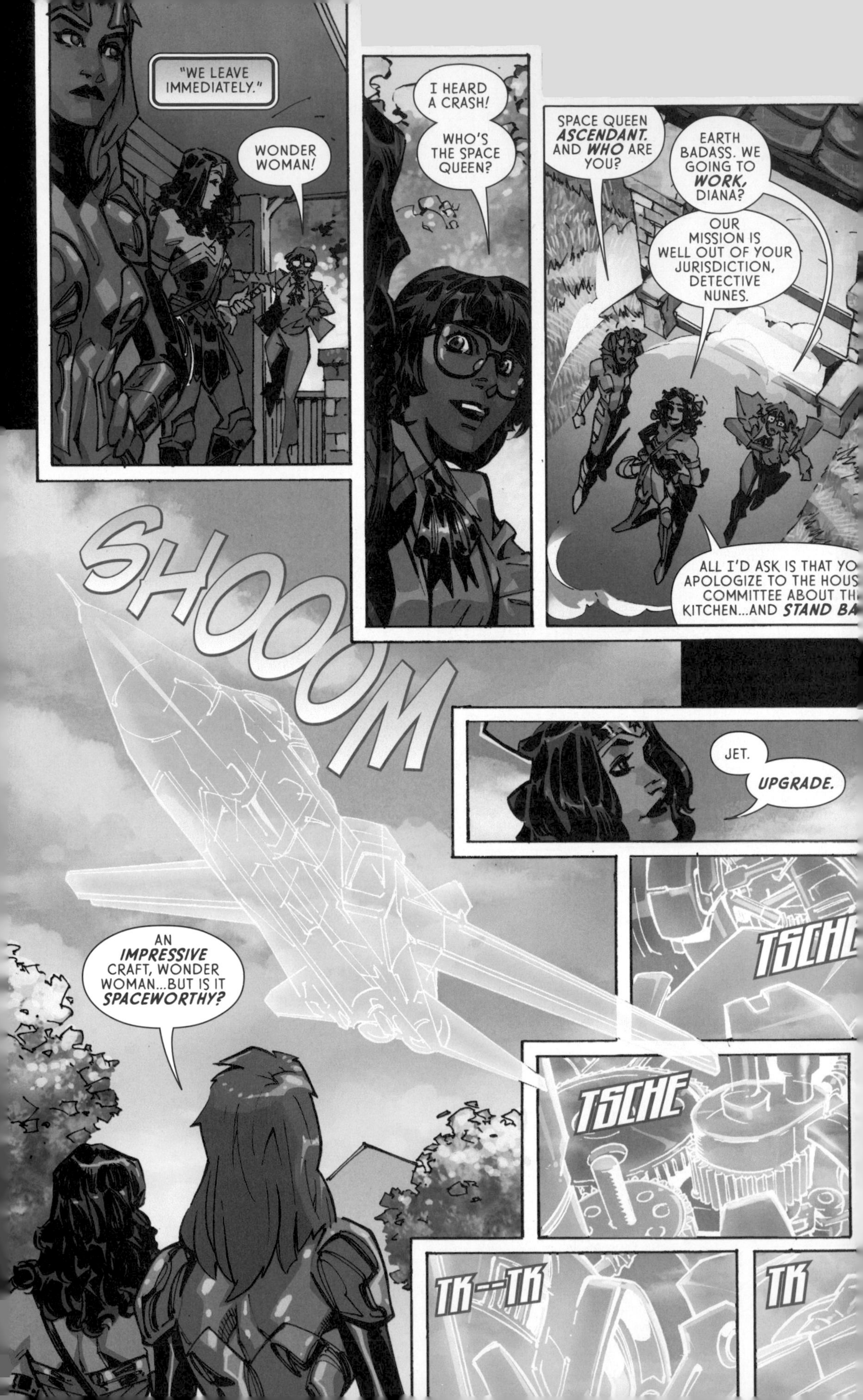
"WE LEAVE IMMEDIATELY."
WONDER WOMAN!
I HEARD A CRASH!
WHO'S THE SPACE QUEEN?
SPACE QUEEN ASCENDANT. AND WHO ARE YOU?
EARTH BADASS. WE GOING TO WORK, DIANA?
OUR MISSION IS WELL OUT OF YOUR JURISDICTION, DETECTIVE NUNES.
ALL I'D ASK IS THAT YO APOLOGIZE TO THE HOUS COMMITTEE ABOUT TH KITCHEN...AND STAND BA
SHOOOOM
JET.
UPGRADE.
AN IMPRESSIVE CRAFT, WONDER WOMAN...BUT IS IT SPACEWORTHY?
TSCHE
TSCHE
TK--TK
TK

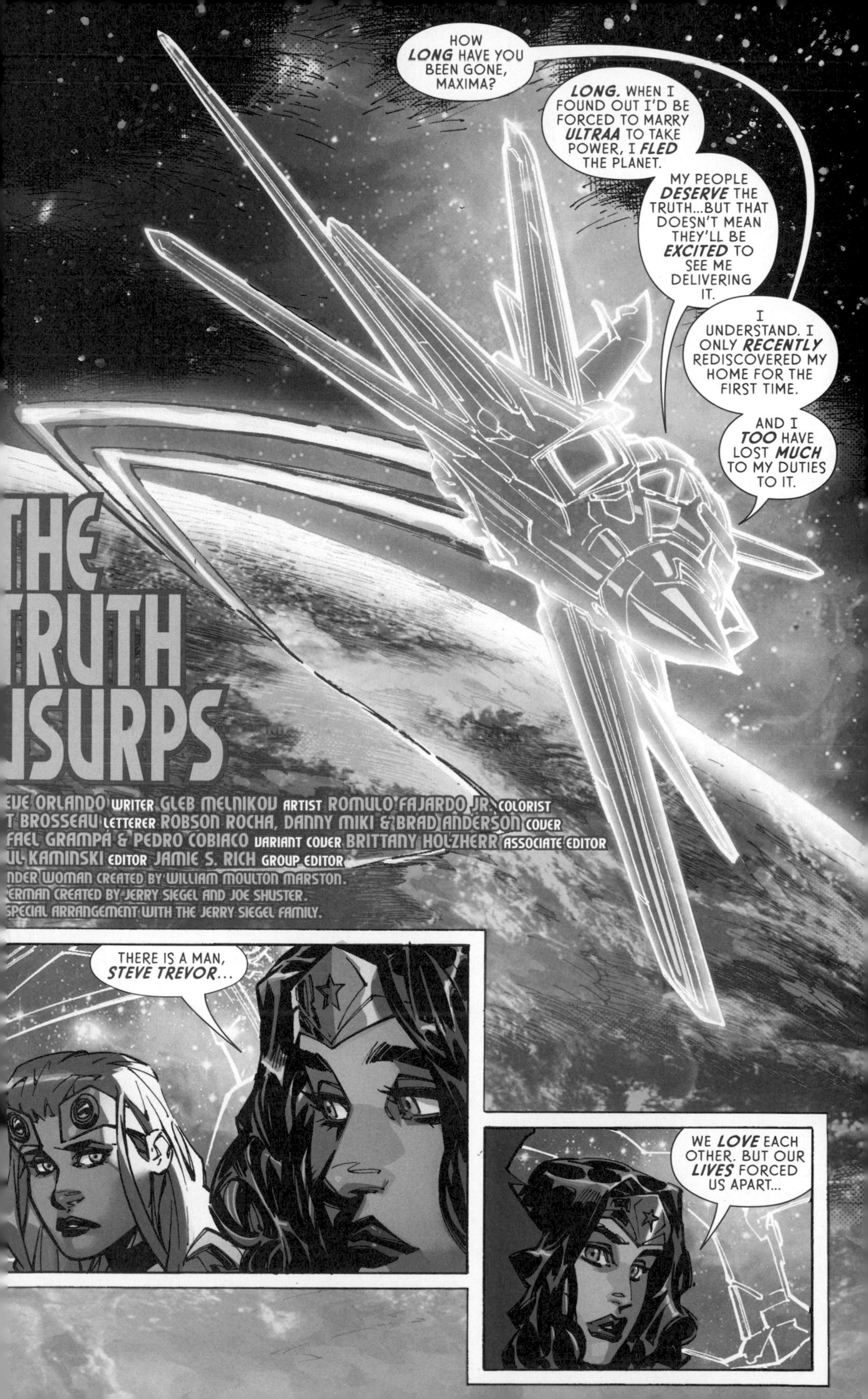

HOW LONG HAVE YOU BEEN GONE, MAXIMA?
LONG. WHEN I FOUND OUT I'D BE FORCED TO MARRY ULTRAA TO TAKE POWER, I FLED THE PLANET.
MY PEOPLE DESERVE THE TRUTH...BUT THAT DOESN'T MEAN THEY'LL BE EXCITED TO SEE ME DELIVERING IT.
I UNDERSTAND. I ONLY RECENTLY REDISCOVERED MY HOME FOR THE FIRST TIME.
AND I TOO HAVE LOST MUCH TO MY DUTIES TO IT.
THE TRUTH USURPS
EVE ORLANDO WRITER GLEB MELNIKOV ARTIST ROMULO FAJARDO JR. COLORIST
T BROSSEAU LETTERER ROBSON ROCHA, DANNY MIKI & BRAD ANDERSON COVER
FAEL GRAMPÁ & PEDRO COBIACO VARIANT COVER BRITTANY HOLZHERR ASSOCIATE EDITOR
UL KAMINSKI EDITOR JAMIE S. RICH GROUP EDITOR
NDER WOMAN CREATED BY WILLIAM MOULTON MARSTON.
ERMAN CREATED BY JERRY SIEGEL AND JOE SHUSTER.
SPECIAL ARRANGEMENT WITH THE JERRY SIEGEL FAMILY.
THERE IS A MAN, STEVE TREVOR...
WE LOVE EACH OTHER. BUT OUR LIVES FORCED US APART...

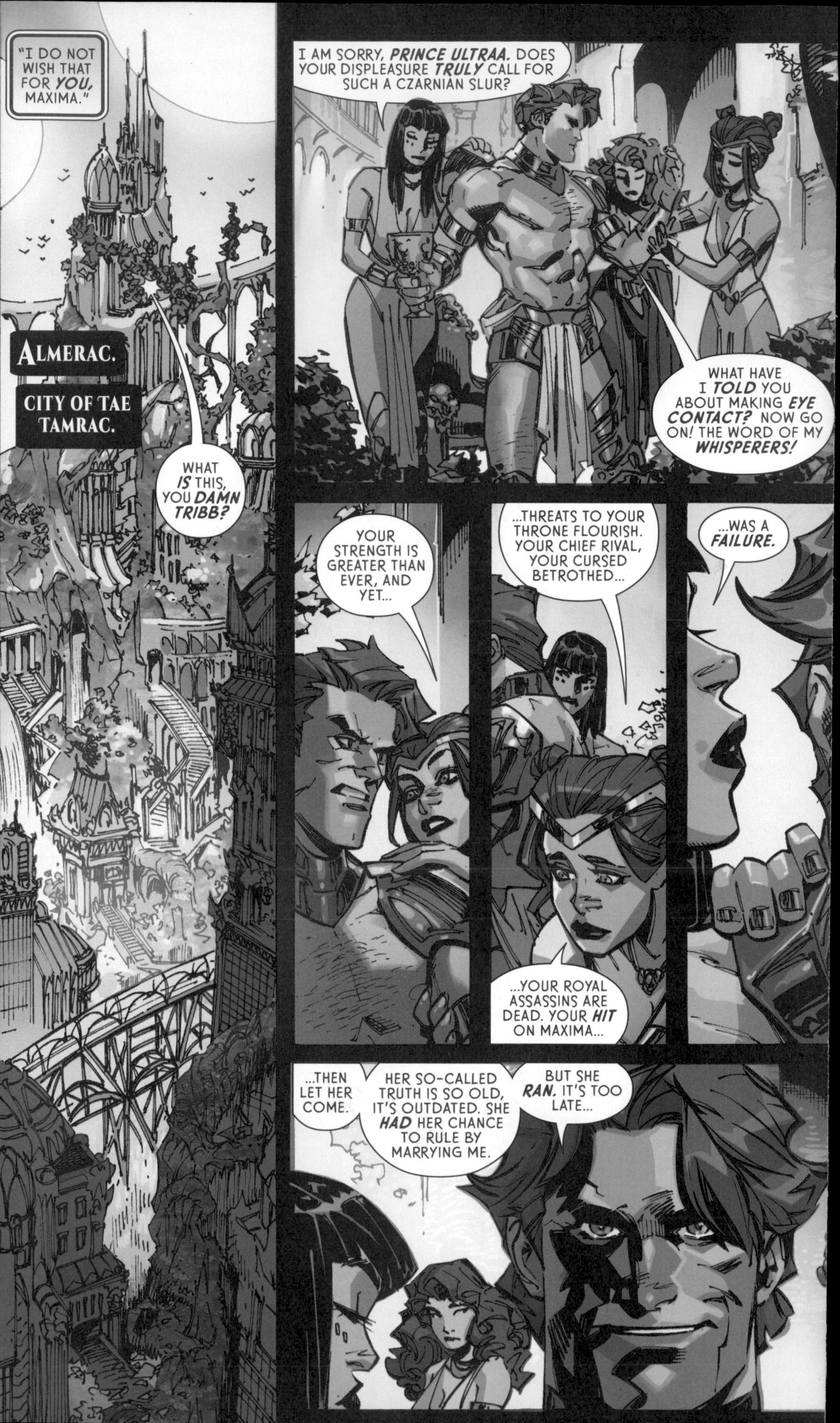
"I DO NOT WISH THAT FOR YOU, MAXIMA."
ALMERAC.
CITY OF TAE TAMRAC.
WHAT IS THIS, YOU DAMN TRIBB?
I AM SORRY, PRINCE ULTRAA. DOES YOUR DISPLEASURE TRULY CALL FOR SUCH A CZARNIAN SLUR?
WHAT HAVE I TOLD YOU ABOUT MAKING EYE CONTACT? NOW GO ON! THE WORD OF MY WHISPERERS!
YOUR STRENGTH IS GREATER THAN EVER, AND YET...
...THREATS TO YOUR THRONE FLOURISH. YOUR CHIEF RIVAL, YOUR CURSED BETROTHED...
...YOUR ROYAL ASSASSINS ARE DEAD. YOUR HIT ON MAXIMA...
...WAS A FAILURE.
BUT SHE RAN. IT'S TOO LATE...
HER SO-CALLED TRUTH IS SO OLD, IT'S OUTDATED. SHE HAD HER CHANCE TO RULE BY MARRYING ME.
...THEN LET HER COME.

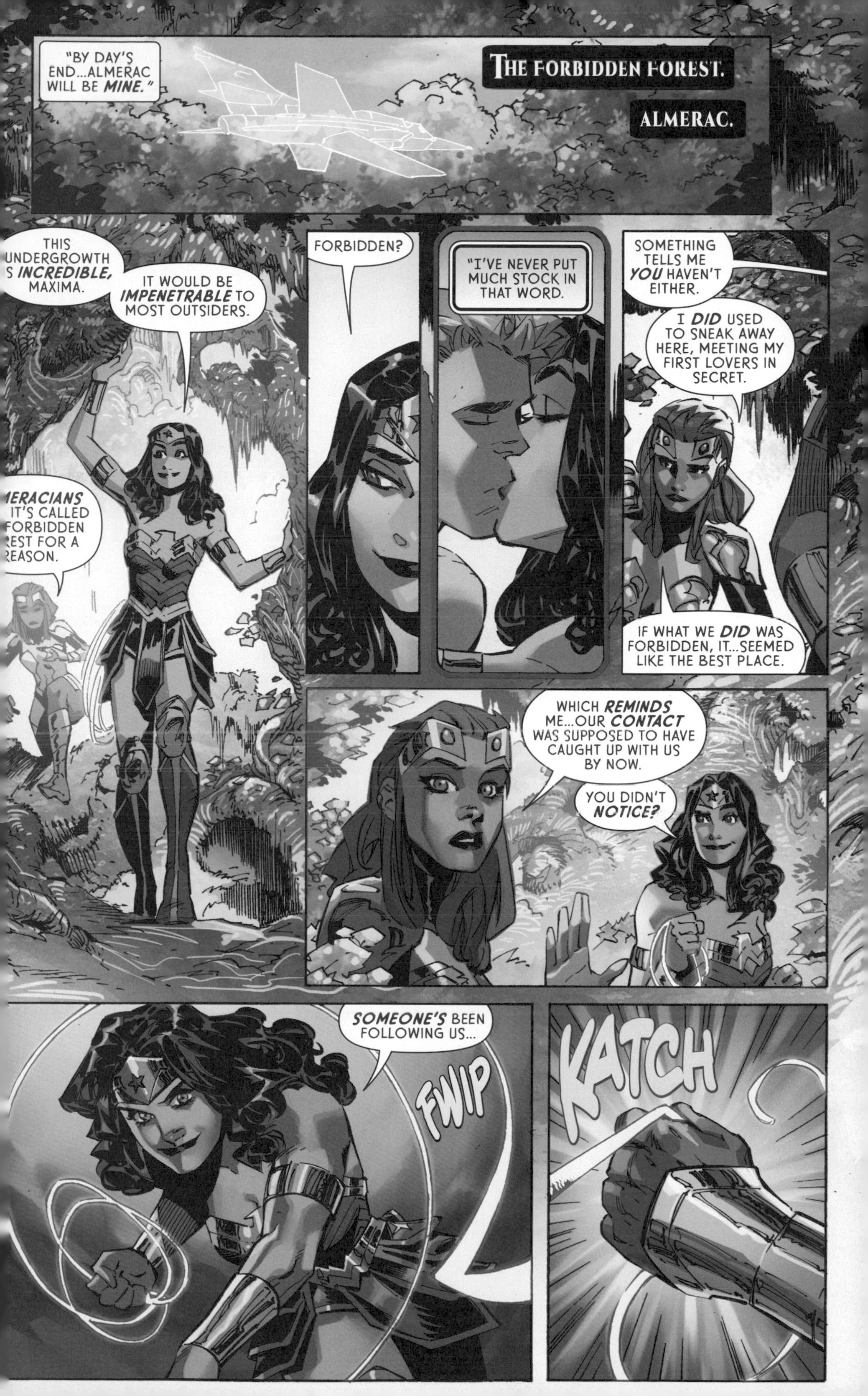

"BY DAY'S END...ALMERAC WILL BE MINE."
THE FORBIDDEN FOREST.
ALMERAC.
THIS UNDERGROWTH S INCREDIBLE, MAXIMA.
IT WOULD BE IMPENETRABLE TO MOST OUTSIDERS.
ERACIANS IT'S CALLED FORBIDDEN REST FOR A REASON.
FORBIDDEN?
"I'VE NEVER PUT MUCH STOCK IN THAT WORD.
SOMETHING TELLS ME YOU HAVEN'T EITHER.
I DID USED TO SNEAK AWAY HERE, MEETING MY FIRST LOVERS IN SECRET.
IF WHAT WE DID WAS FORBIDDEN, IT...SEEMED LIKE THE BEST PLACE.
WHICH REMINDS ME...OUR CONTACT WAS SUPPOSED TO HAVE CAUGHT UP WITH US BY NOW.
YOU DIDN'T NOTICE?
SOMEONE'S BEEN FOLLOWING US...
FWIP
KATCH

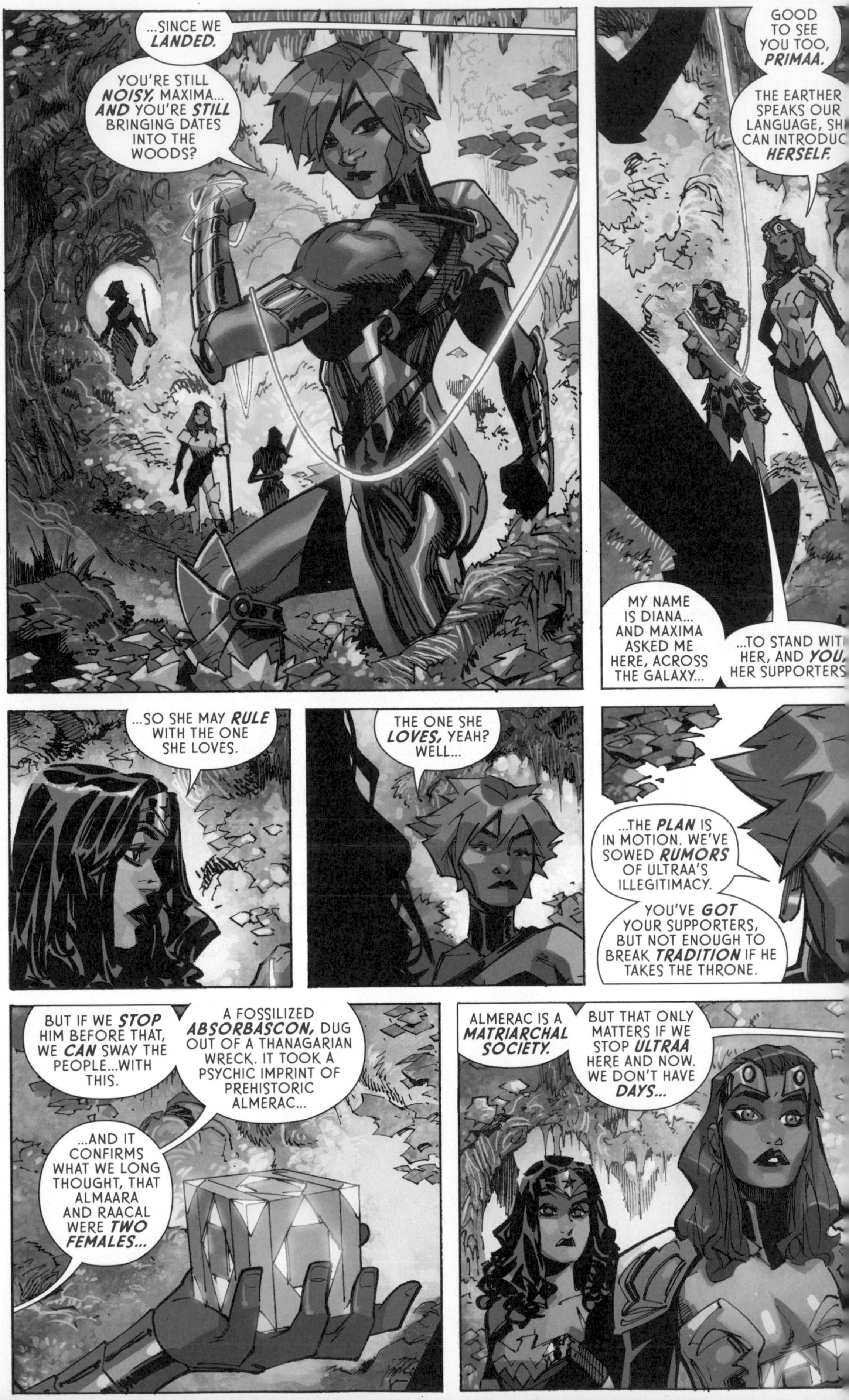
...SINCE WE LANDED.
YOU'RE STILL NOISY, MAXIMA... AND YOU'RE STILL BRINGING DATES INTO THE WOODS?
GOOD TO SEE YOU TOO, PRIMAA.
THE EARTHER SPEAKS OUR LANGUAGE, SH CAN INTRODUC HERSELF.
MY NAME IS DIANA... AND MAXIMA ASKED ME HERE, ACROSS THE GALAXY...
...TO STAND WIT HER, AND YOU, HER SUPPORTERS
...SO SHE MAY RULE WITH THE ONE SHE LOVES.
THE ONE SHE LOVES, YEAH? WELL...
...THE PLAN IS IN MOTION. WE'VE SOWED RUMORS OF ULTRAA'S ILLEGITIMACY.
YOU'VE GOT YOUR SUPPORTERS, BUT NOT ENOUGH TO BREAK TRADITION IF HE TAKES THE THRONE.
BUT IF WE STOP HIM BEFORE THAT, WE CAN SWAY THE PEOPLE...WITH THIS.
A FOSSILIZED ABSORBASCON, DUG OUT OF A THANAGARIAN WRECK. IT TOOK A PSYCHIC IMPRINT OF PREHISTORIC ALMERAC...
...AND IT CONFIRMS WHAT WE LONG THOUGHT, THAT ALMAARA AND RAACAL WERE TWO FEMALES...
ALMERAC IS A MATRIARCHAL SOCIETY.
BUT THAT ONLY MATTERS IF WE STOP ULTRAA HERE AND NOW. WE DON'T HAVE DAYS...

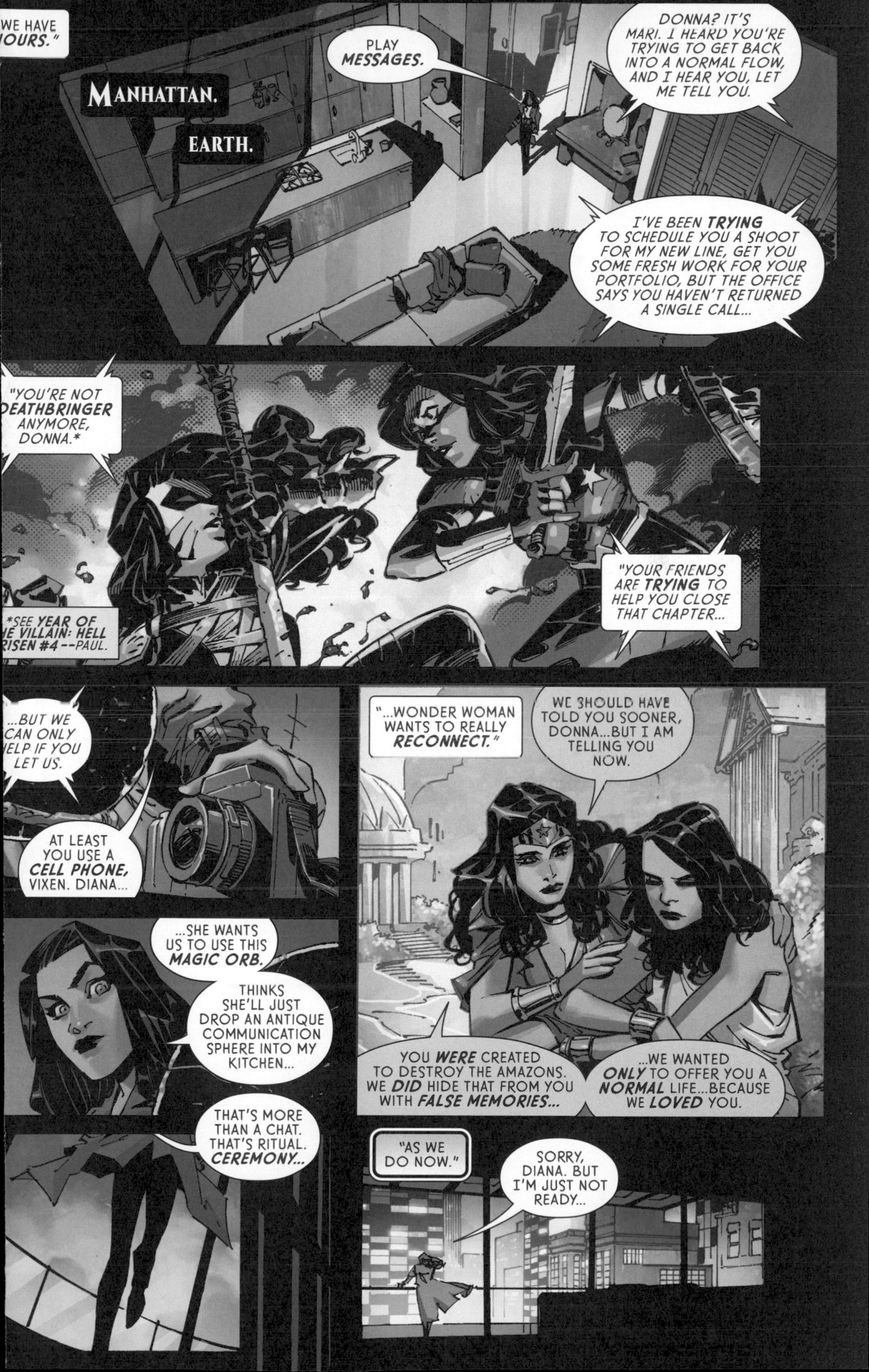

WE HAVE HOURS."
MANHATTAN.
EARTH.
PLAY MESSAGES.
DONNA? IT'S MARI. I HEARD YOU'RE TRYING TO GET BACK INTO A NORMAL FLOW, AND I HEAR YOU, LET ME TELL YOU.
I'VE BEEN TRYING TO SCHEDULE YOU A SHOOT FOR MY NEW LINE, GET YOU SOME FRESH WORK FOR YOUR PORTFOLIO, BUT THE OFFICE SAYS YOU HAVEN'T RETURNED A SINGLE CALL...
"YOU'RE NOT DEATHBRINGER ANYMORE, DONNA.*
*SEE YEAR OF THE VILLAIN: HELL ARISEN #4 --PAUL.
"YOUR FRIENDS ARE TRYING TO HELP YOU CLOSE THAT CHAPTER...
...BUT WE CAN ONLY HELP IF YOU LET US.
AT LEAST YOU USE A CELL PHONE, VIXEN. DIANA...
...SHE WANTS US TO USE THIS MAGIC ORB.
THINKS SHE'LL JUST DROP AN ANTIQUE COMMUNICATION SPHERE INTO MY KITCHEN...
THAT'S MORE THAN A CHAT. THAT'S RITUAL. CEREMONY...
"...WONDER WOMAN WANTS TO REALLY RECONNECT."
WE SHOULD HAVE TOLD YOU SOONER, DONNA...BUT I AM TELLING YOU NOW.
YOU WERE CREATED TO DESTROY THE AMAZONS. WE DID HIDE THAT FROM YOU WITH FALSE MEMORIES...
...WE WANTED ONLY TO OFFER YOU A NORMAL LIFE...BECAUSE WE LOVED YOU.
"AS WE DO NOW."
SORRY, DIANA. BUT I'M JUST NOT READY...

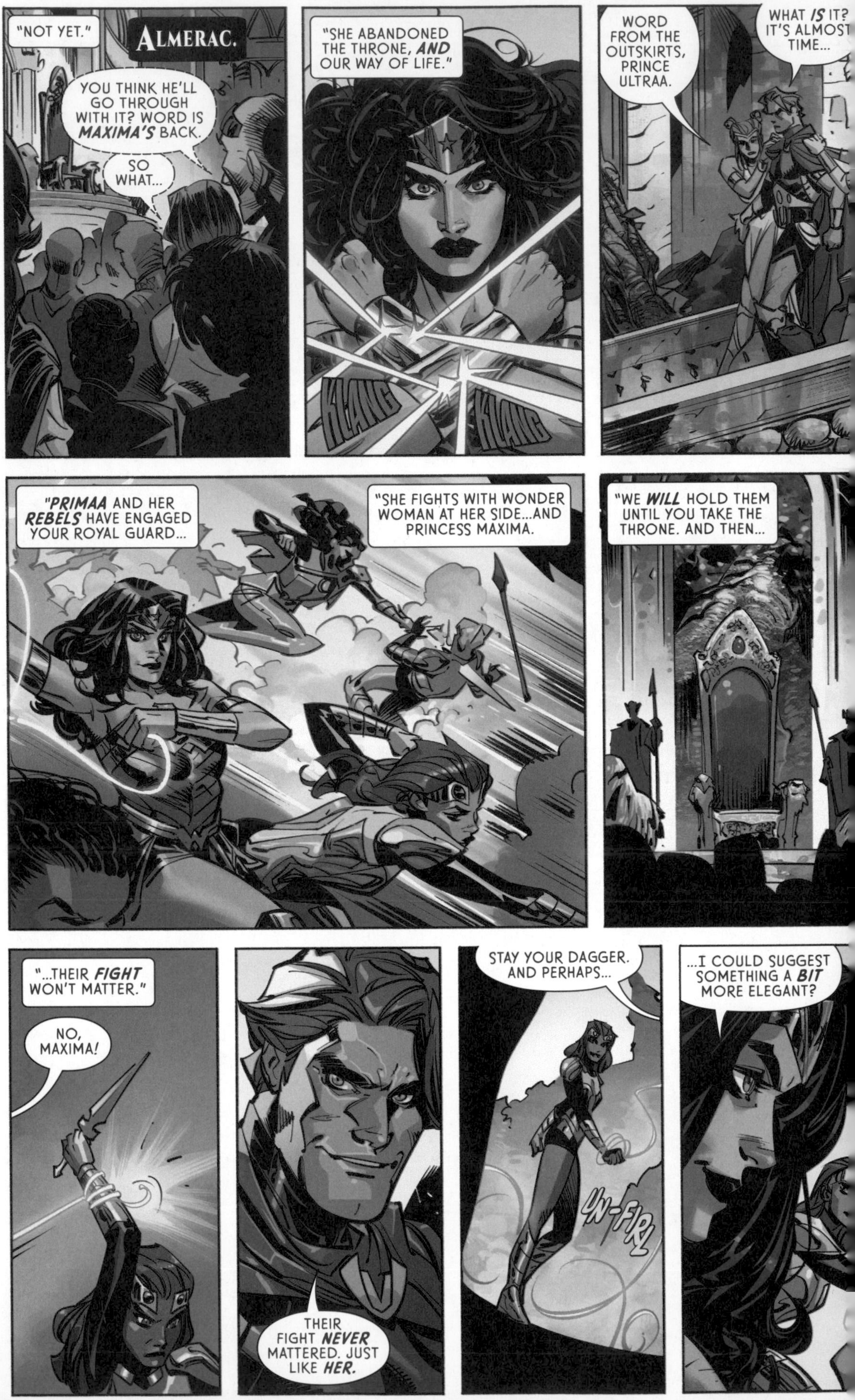

"NOT YET."
ALMERAC.
YOU THINK HE'LL GO THROUGH WITH IT? WORD IS MAXIMA'S BACK.
SO WHAT...
"SHE ABANDONED THE THRONE, AND OUR WAY OF LIFE."
KLANG
KLANG
WORD FROM THE OUTSKIRTS, PRINCE ULTRAA.
WHAT IS IT? IT'S ALMOST TIME...
"PRIMAA AND HER REBELS HAVE ENGAGED YOUR ROYAL GUARD...
"SHE FIGHTS WITH WONDER WOMAN AT HER SIDE...AND PRINCESS MAXIMA.
"WE WILL HOLD THEM UNTIL YOU TAKE THE THRONE. AND THEN...
"...THEIR FIGHT WON'T MATTER."
NO, MAXIMA!
THEIR FIGHT NEVER MATTERED. JUST LIKE HER.
STAY YOUR DAGGER. AND PERHAPS...
UN-FIRL
...I COULD SUGGEST SOMETHING A BIT MORE ELEGANT?

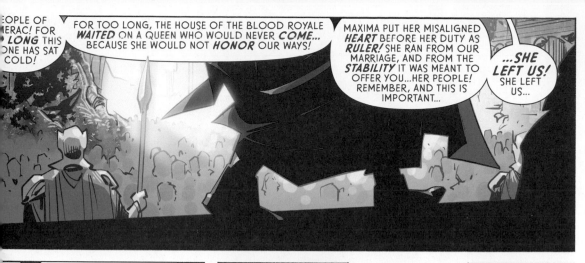

EOPLE OF ERAC! FOR LONG THIS ONE HAS SAT COLD!

FOR TOO LONG, THE HOUSE OF THE BLOOD ROYALE *WAITED* ON A QUEEN WHO WOULD NEVER *COME*... BECAUSE SHE WOULD NOT *HONOR* OUR WAYS!

MAXIMA PUT HER MISALIGNED *HEART* BEFORE HER DUTY AS *RULER!* SHE RAN FROM OUR MARRIAGE, AND FROM THE *STABILITY* IT WAS MEANT TO OFFER YOU...HER PEOPLE! REMEMBER, AND THIS IS IMPORTANT...

...SHE *LEFT US!* SHE LEFT US...

BUT NG RAA ER LL!

LET TODAY MARK THE *END* OF THE ROYAL COURTSHIP! MAXIMA'S CLAIM IS *FORFEIT!* ONCE THE *HYPERCROWN* GRACES MY HEAD...

SHE LEFT US! SHE LEFT US! SHE LEFT US! SHE LEFT US!

...YOU WILL NEVER BE *ABANDONED* AGAIN!

SHE LEFT US! SHE LEFT--

RRRRUMBLE

THOOM THOOM

WHAT-- WHAT IS THAT? *POUNDING?*

IT'S PRIMAA'S REBELS! IT HAS TO BE! SHE'S BROUGHT THE *PRINCESS!*

NO! DO NOT SAY HER NAME! I'M THE ONE WHO MATTERS!

WHATEVER'S OUTSIDE, IN *SECONDS* SHE'LL BE *IRRELEVANT!* AND THE *ONLY* THING YOU'LL BE SAYING IS--

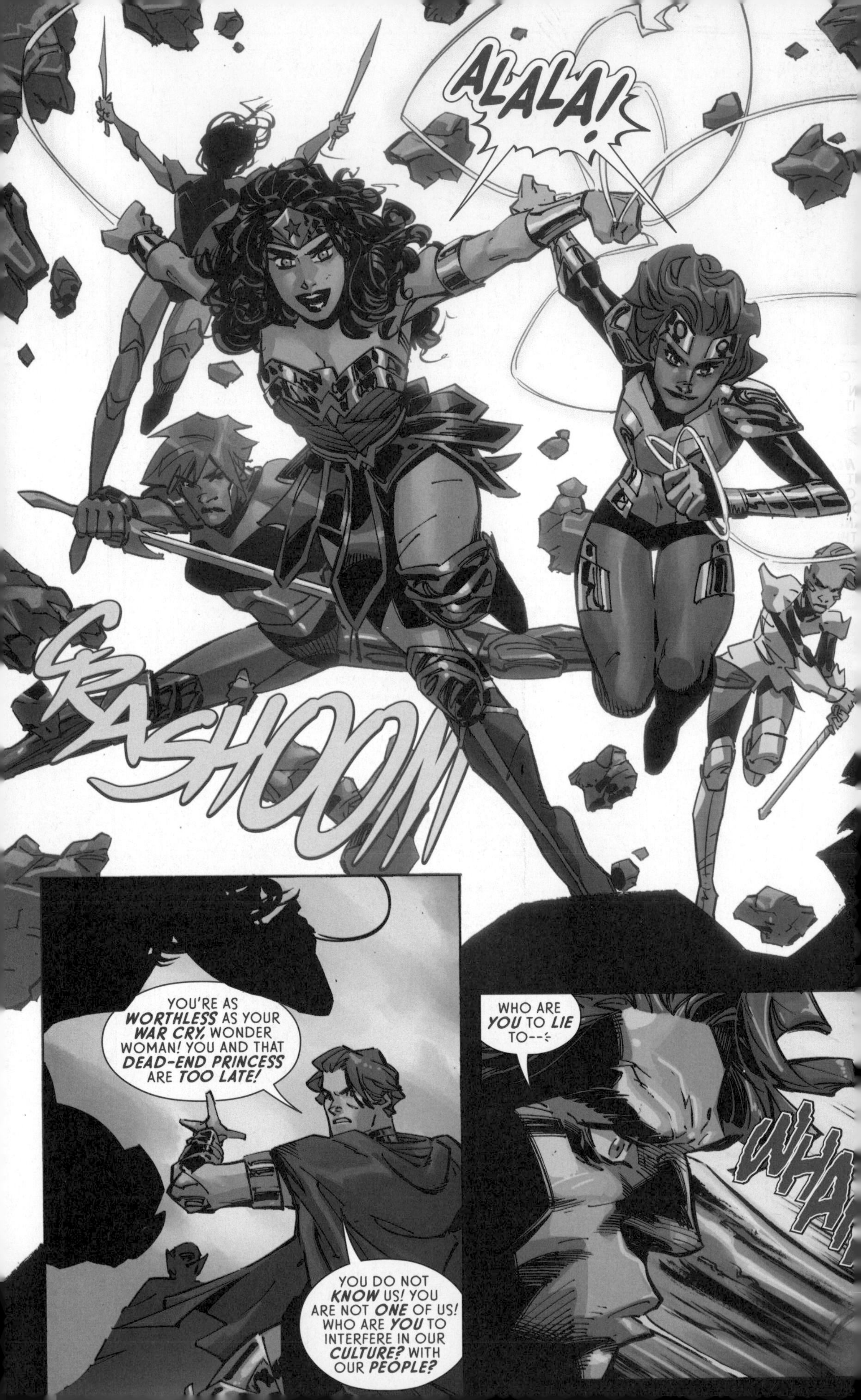

ALALA!
CRASHOOM
YOU'RE AS WORTHLESS AS YOUR WAR CRY, WONDER WOMAN! YOU AND THAT DEAD-END PRINCESS ARE TOO LATE!
YOU DO NOT KNOW US! YOU ARE NOT ONE OF US! WHO ARE YOU TO INTERFERE IN OUR CULTURE? WITH OUR PEOPLE?
WHO ARE YOU TO LIE TO--
WHA

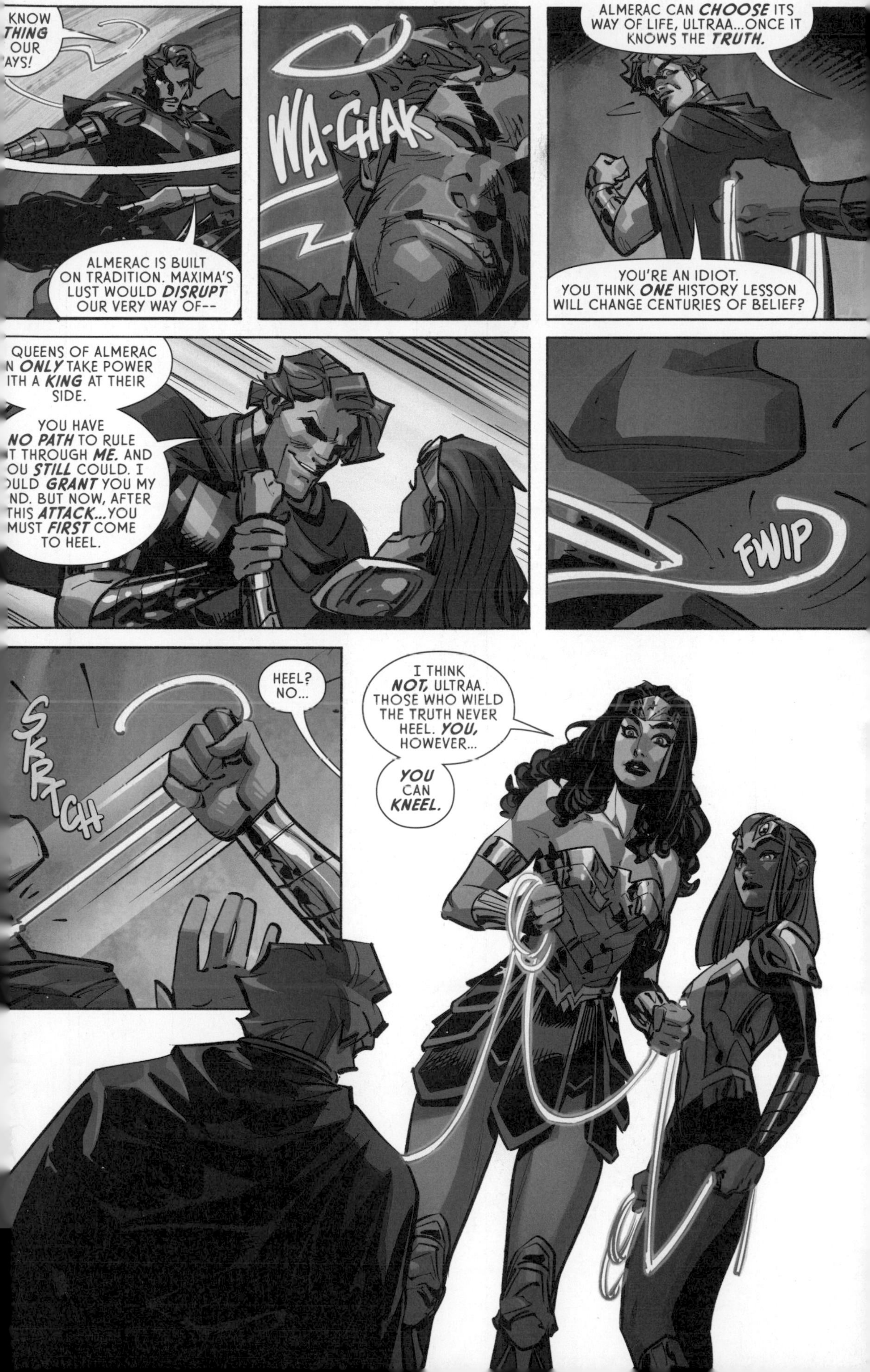
KNOW
THING
OUR
AYS!
ALMERAC IS BUILT ON TRADITION. MAXIMA'S LUST WOULD DISRUPT OUR VERY WAY OF--
WA-CHAK
ALMERAC CAN CHOOSE ITS WAY OF LIFE, ULTRAA...ONCE IT KNOWS THE TRUTH.
YOU'RE AN IDIOT. YOU THINK ONE HISTORY LESSON WILL CHANGE CENTURIES OF BELIEF?
QUEENS OF ALMERAC
N ONLY TAKE POWER
ITH A KING AT THEIR
SIDE.
YOU HAVE
NO PATH TO RULE
T THROUGH ME. AND
OU STILL COULD. I
OULD GRANT YOU MY
ND. BUT NOW, AFTER
THIS ATTACK...YOU
MUST FIRST COME
TO HEEL.
FWIP
SKRTCH
HEEL? NO...
I THINK NOT, ULTRAA. THOSE WHO WIELD THE TRUTH NEVER HEEL. YOU, HOWEVER...
YOU CAN KNEEL.

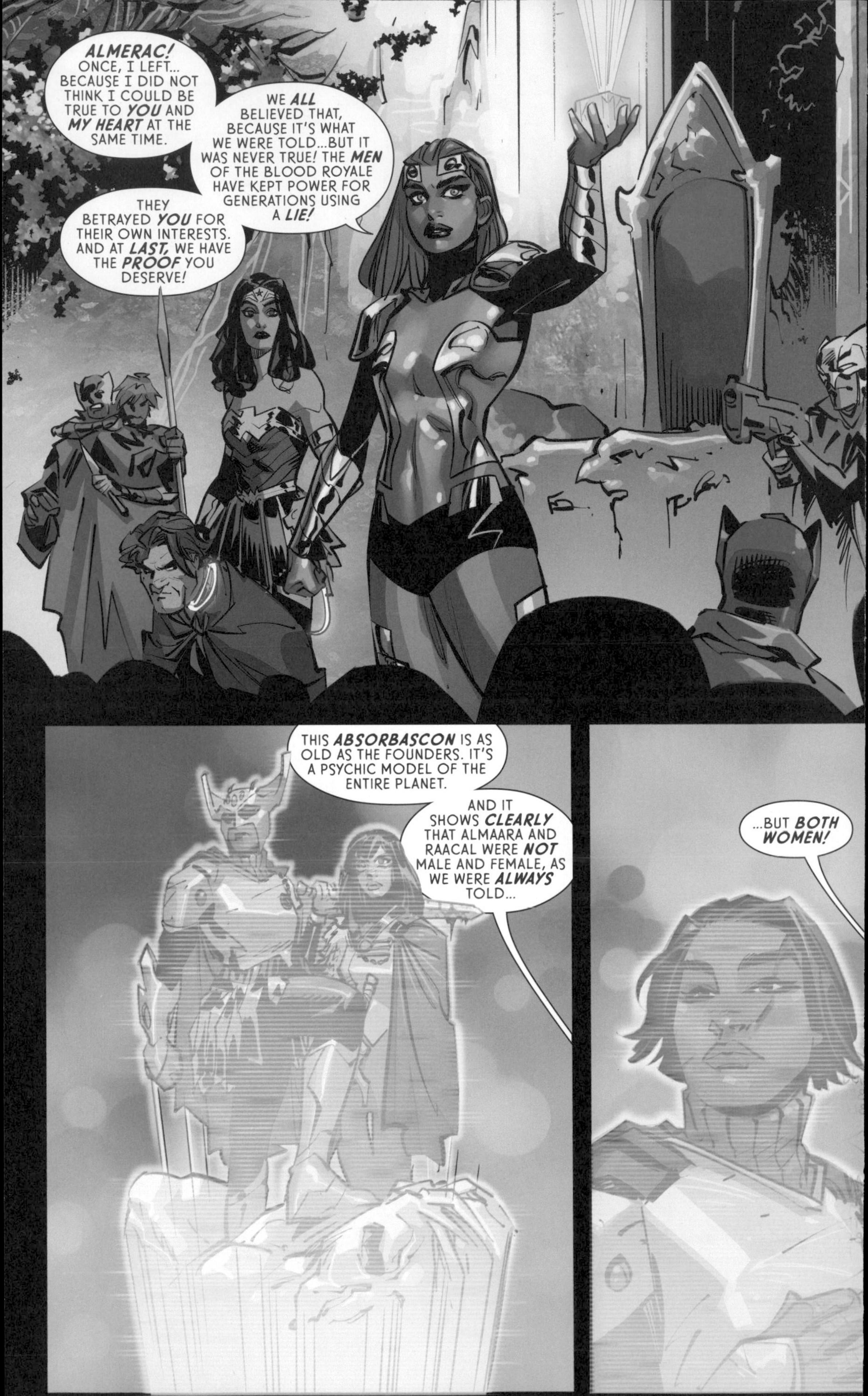
ALMERAC! ONCE, I LEFT... BECAUSE I DID NOT THINK I COULD BE TRUE TO YOU AND MY HEART AT THE SAME TIME.
WE ALL BELIEVED THAT, BECAUSE IT'S WHAT WE WERE TOLD...BUT IT WAS NEVER TRUE! THE MEN OF THE BLOOD ROYALE HAVE KEPT POWER FOR GENERATIONS USING A LIE!
THEY BETRAYED YOU FOR THEIR OWN INTERESTS. AND AT LAST, WE HAVE THE PROOF YOU DESERVE!
THIS ABSORBASCON IS AS OLD AS THE FOUNDERS. IT'S A PSYCHIC MODEL OF THE ENTIRE PLANET.
AND IT SHOWS CLEARLY THAT ALMAARA AND RAACAL WERE NOT MALE AND FEMALE, AS WE WERE ALWAYS TOLD...
...BUT BOTH WOMEN!

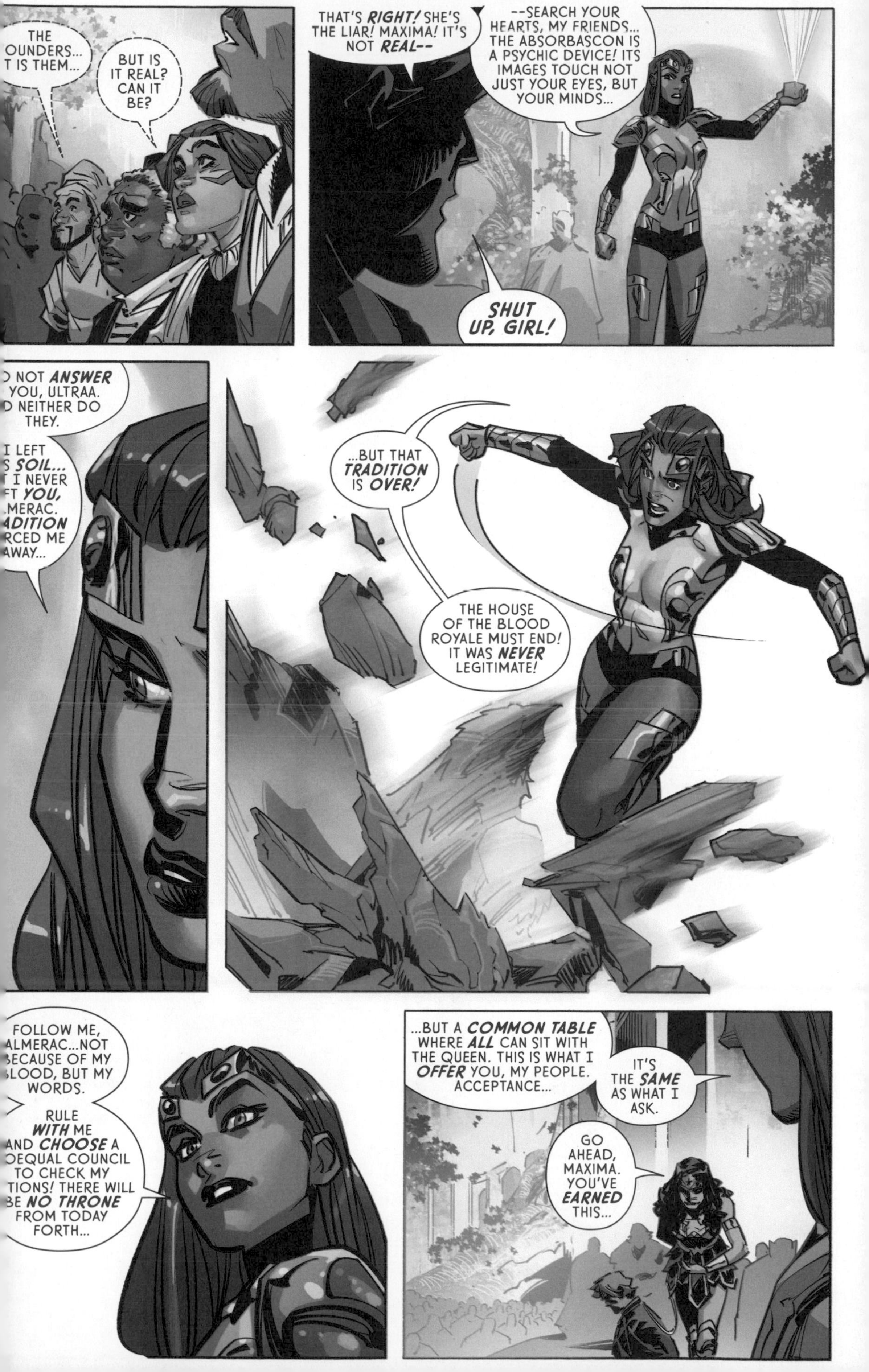

THE OUNDERS... T IS THEM...
BUT IS IT REAL? CAN IT BE?
THAT'S RIGHT! SHE'S THE LIAR! MAXIMA! IT'S NOT REAL--
--SEARCH YOUR HEARTS, MY FRIENDS... THE ABSORBASCON IS A PSYCHIC DEVICE! ITS IMAGES TOUCH NOT JUST YOUR EYES, BUT YOUR MINDS...
SHUT UP, GIRL!
O NOT ANSWER YOU, ULTRAA. D NEITHER DO THEY.
I LEFT S SOIL... T I NEVER FT YOU, .MERAC. ADITION RCED ME AWAY...
...BUT THAT TRADITION IS OVER!
THE HOUSE OF THE BLOOD ROYALE MUST END! IT WAS NEVER LEGITIMATE!
FOLLOW ME, ALMERAC...NOT BECAUSE OF MY BLOOD, BUT MY WORDS.
RULE WITH ME AND CHOOSE A OEQUAL COUNCIL TO CHECK MY TIONS! THERE WILL BE NO THRONE FROM TODAY FORTH...
...BUT A COMMON TABLE WHERE ALL CAN SIT WITH THE QUEEN. THIS IS WHAT I OFFER YOU, MY PEOPLE. ACCEPTANCE...
IT'S THE SAME AS WHAT I ASK.
GO AHEAD, MAXIMA. YOU'VE EARNED THIS...

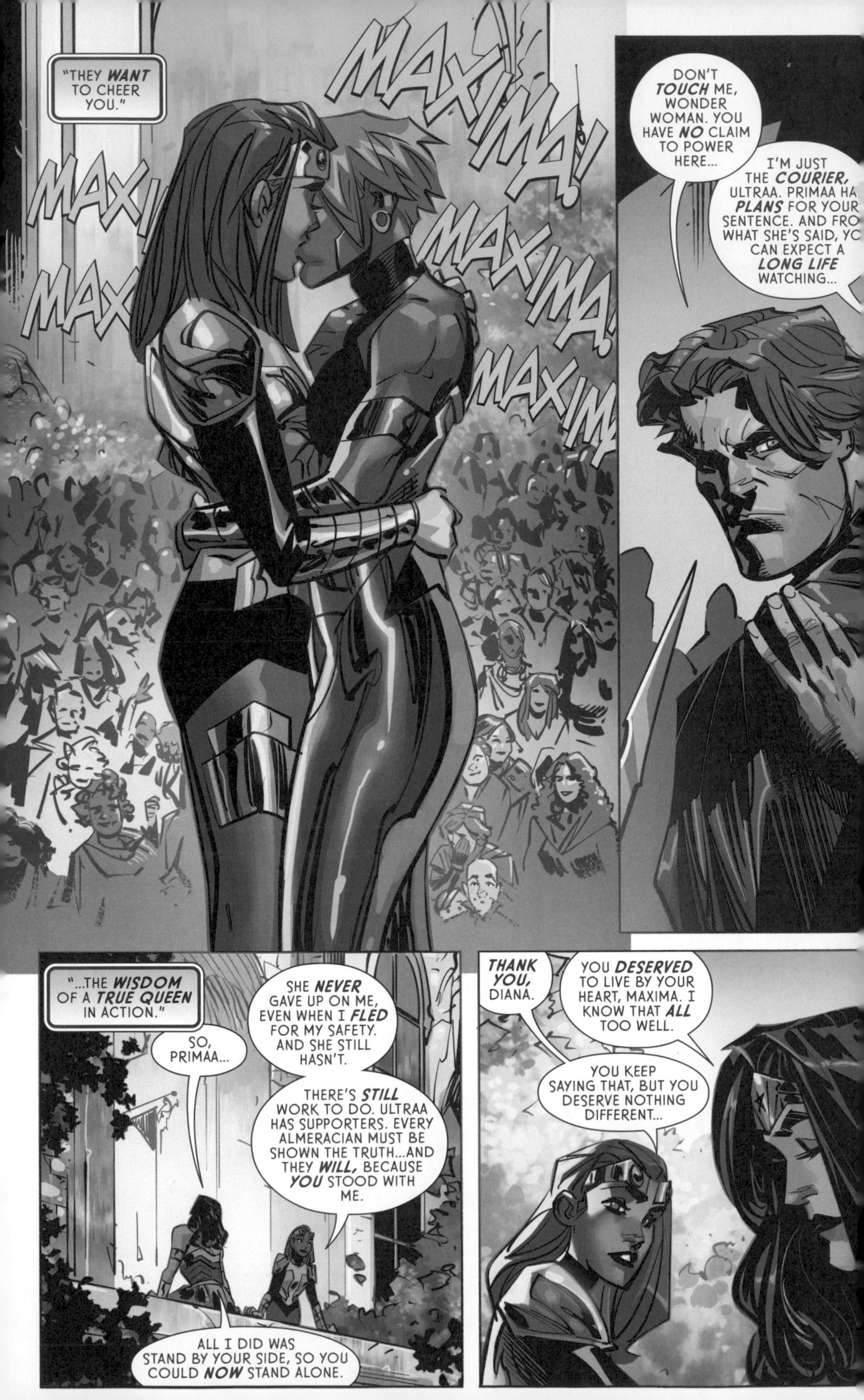
"THEY WANT TO CHEER YOU."
MAXIMA!
MAXIMA!
MAXIMA!
MAXIM
MAXI
MAX
DON'T TOUCH ME, WONDER WOMAN. YOU HAVE NO CLAIM TO POWER HERE...
I'M JUST THE COURIER, ULTRAA. PRIMAA HA PLANS FOR YOUR SENTENCE. AND FRO WHAT SHE'S SAID, YO CAN EXPECT A LONG LIFE WATCHING...
"...THE WISDOM OF A TRUE QUEEN IN ACTION."
SO, PRIMAA...
SHE NEVER GAVE UP ON ME, EVEN WHEN I FLED FOR MY SAFETY. AND SHE STILL HASN'T.
THERE'S STILL WORK TO DO. ULTRAA HAS SUPPORTERS. EVERY ALMERACIAN MUST BE SHOWN THE TRUTH...AND THEY WILL, BECAUSE YOU STOOD WITH ME.
ALL I DID WAS STAND BY YOUR SIDE, SO YOU COULD NOW STAND ALONE.
THANK YOU, DIANA.
YOU DESERVED TO LIVE BY YOUR HEART, MAXIMA. I KNOW THAT ALL TOO WELL.
YOU KEEP SAYING THAT, BUT YOU DESERVE NOTHING DIFFERENT...

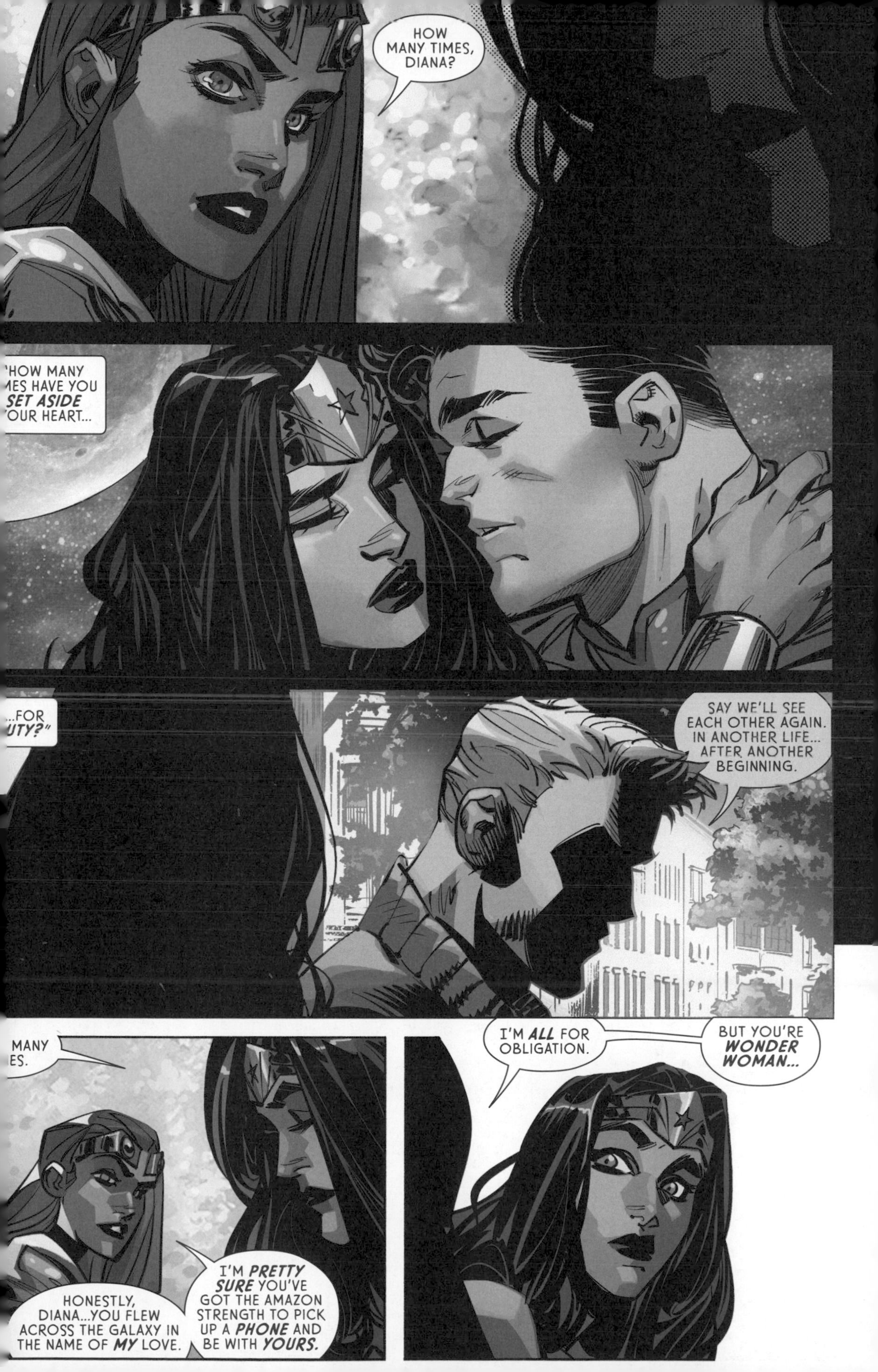

HOW MANY TIMES, DIANA?
"HOW MANY
MES HAVE YOU SET ASIDE
OUR HEART...
...FOR
UTY?"
SAY WE'LL SEE EACH OTHER AGAIN. IN ANOTHER LIFE... AFTER ANOTHER BEGINNING.
MANY
ES.
HONESTLY, DIANA...YOU FLEW ACROSS THE GALAXY IN THE NAME OF MY LOVE.
I'M PRETTY SURE YOU'VE GOT THE AMAZON STRENGTH TO PICK UP A PHONE AND BE WITH YOURS.
I'M ALL FOR OBLIGATION.
BUT YOU'RE WONDER WOMAN...

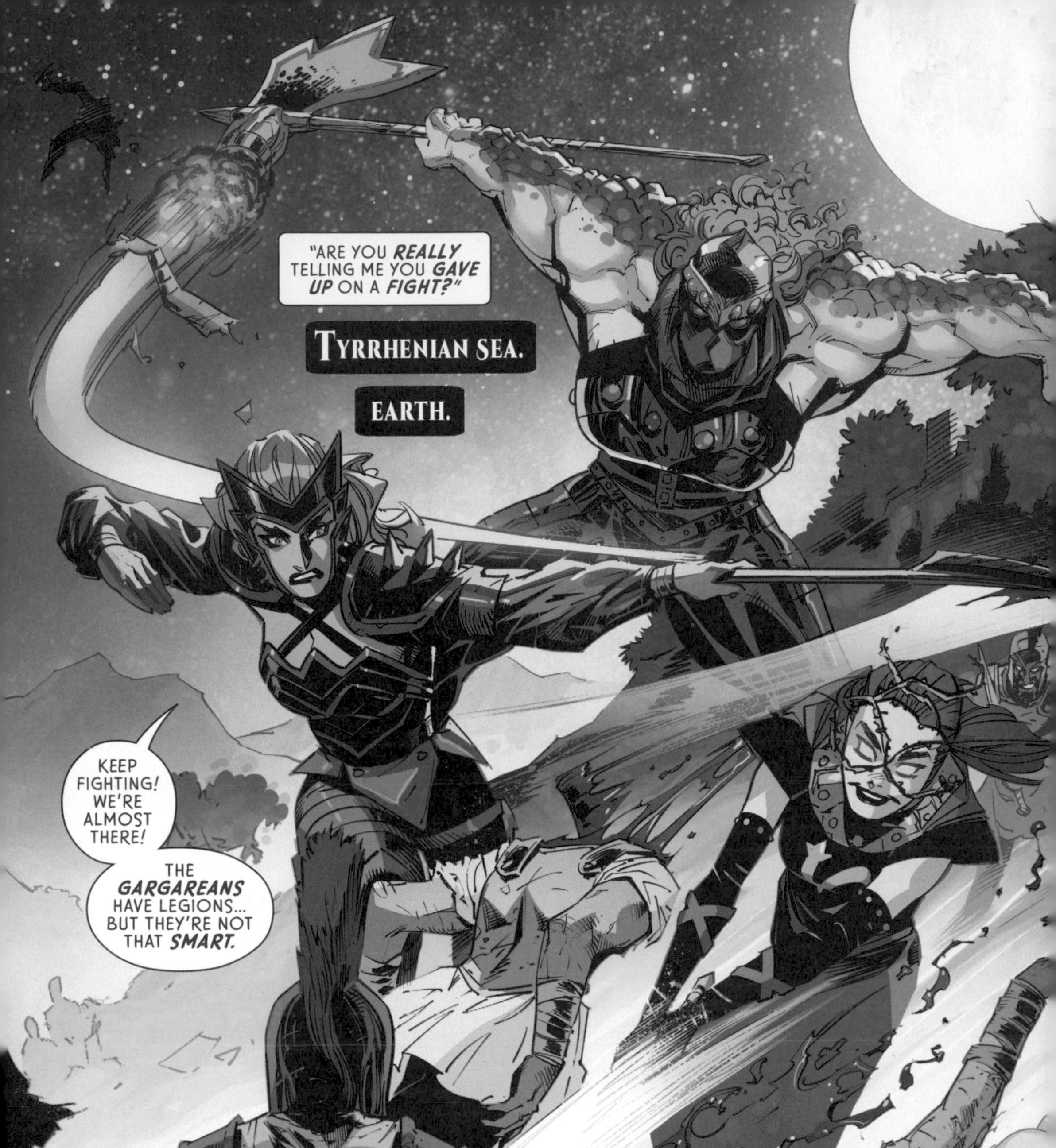
"ARE YOU REALLY TELLING ME YOU GAVE UP ON A FIGHT?"
TYRRHENIAN SEA.
EARTH.
KEEP FIGHTING! WE'RE ALMOST THERE!
THE GARGAREANS HAVE LEGIONS... BUT THEY'RE NOT THAT SMART.

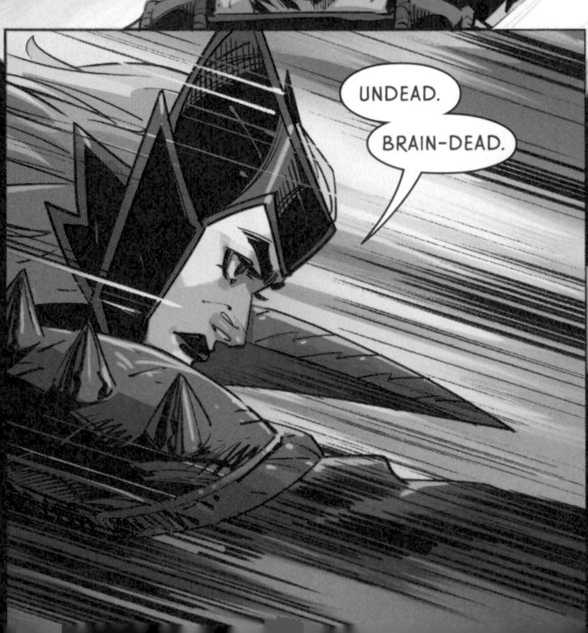
UNDEAD.
BRAIN-DEAD.

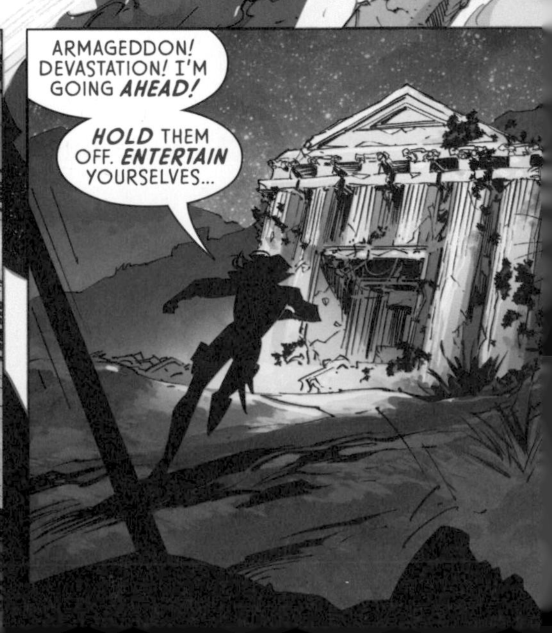
ARMAGEDDON! DEVASTATION! I'M GOING AHEAD!
HOLD THEM OFF. ENTERTAIN YOURSELVES...

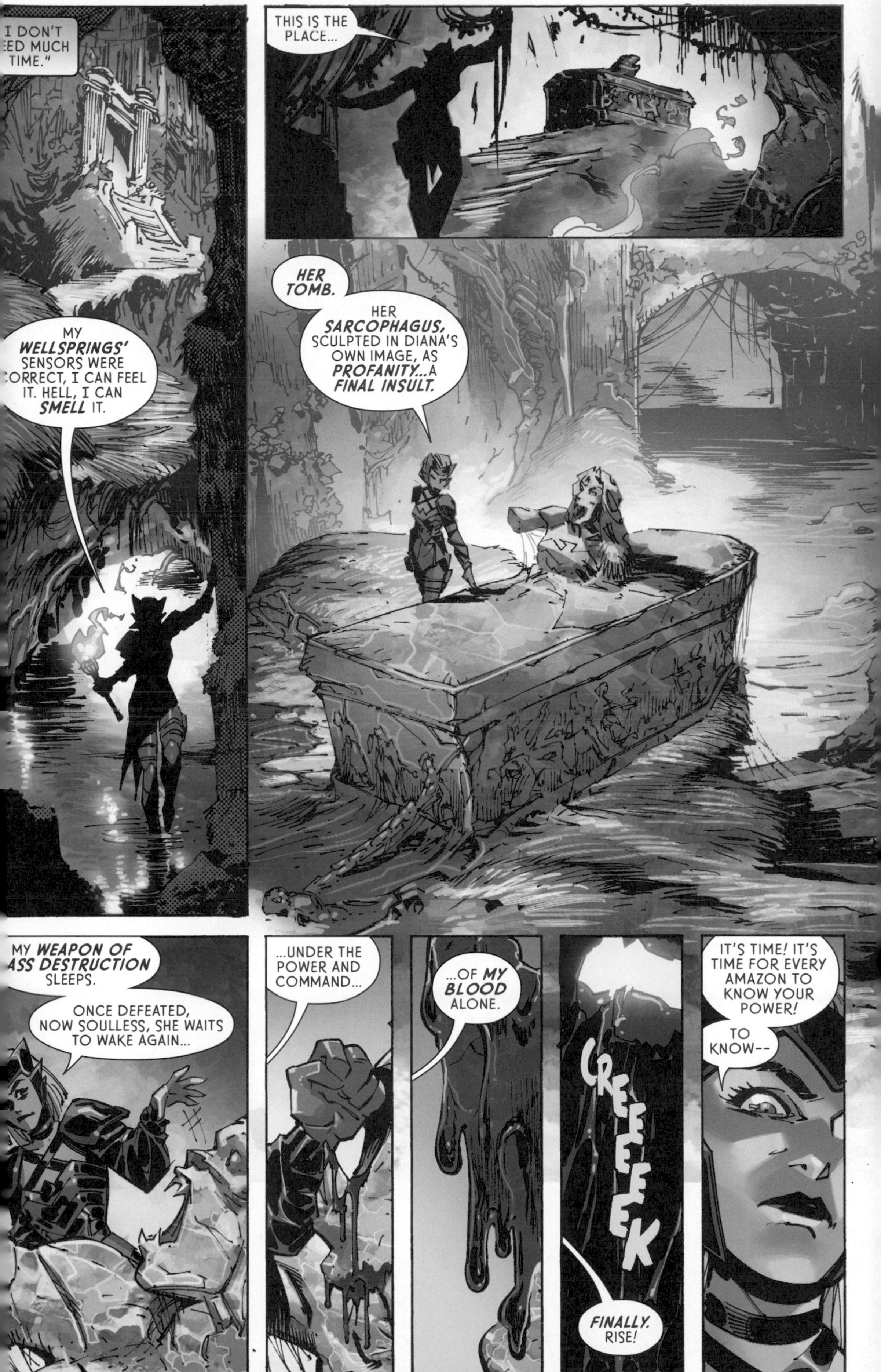

I DON'T EED MUCH TIME."
MY WELLSPRINGS' SENSORS WERE CORRECT, I CAN FEEL IT. HELL, I CAN SMELL IT.
THIS IS THE PLACE...
HER TOMB.
HER SARCOPHAGUS, SCULPTED IN DIANA'S OWN IMAGE, AS PROFANITY...A FINAL INSULT.
MY WEAPON OF ASS DESTRUCTION SLEEPS.
ONCE DEFEATED, NOW SOULLESS, SHE WAITS TO WAKE AGAIN...
...UNDER THE POWER AND COMMAND...
...OF MY BLOOD ALONE.
CREEEEK
FINALLY. RISE!
IT'S TIME! IT'S TIME FOR EVERY AMAZON TO KNOW YOUR POWER!
TO KNOW--

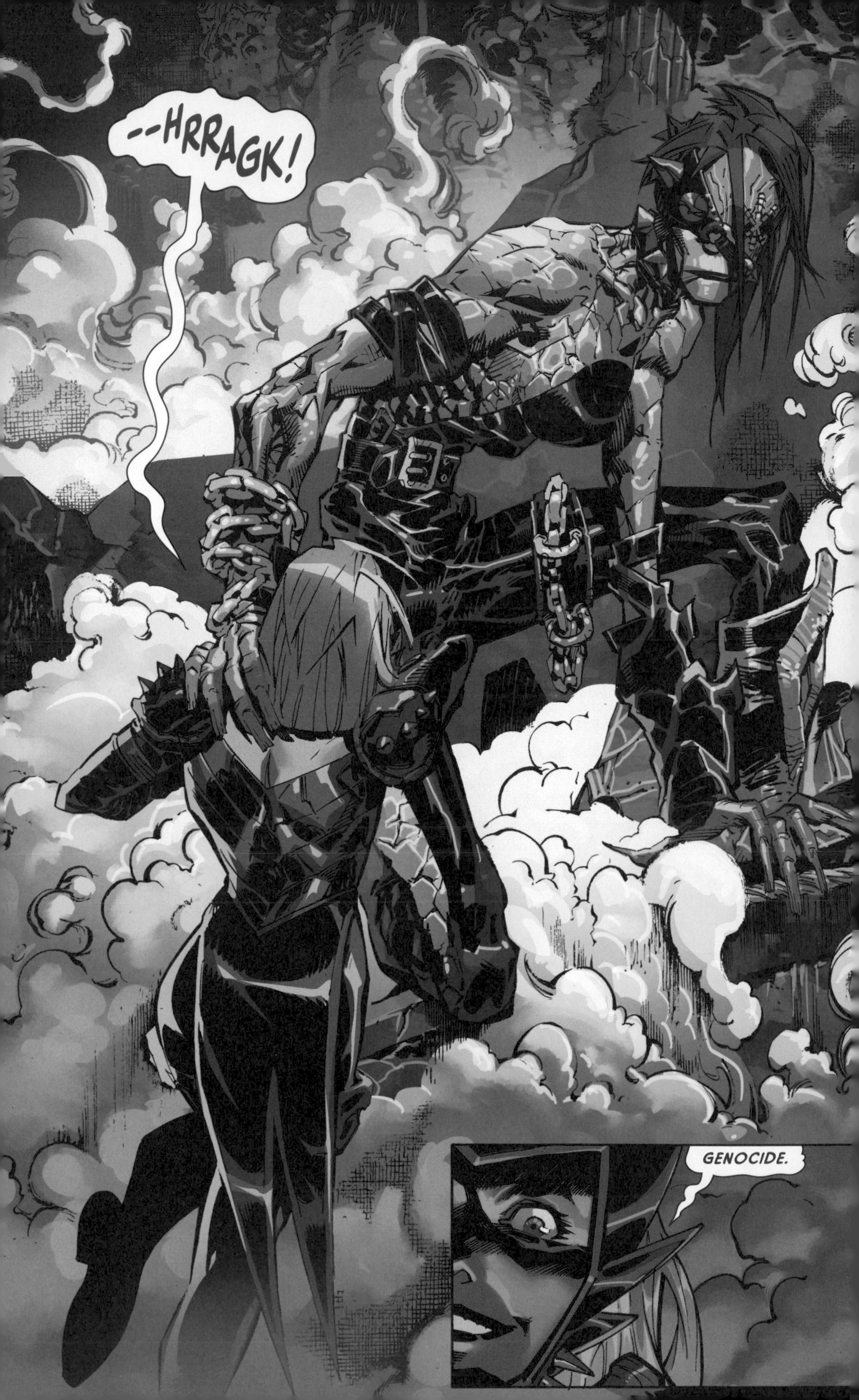
--HRRAGK!
GENOCIDE.

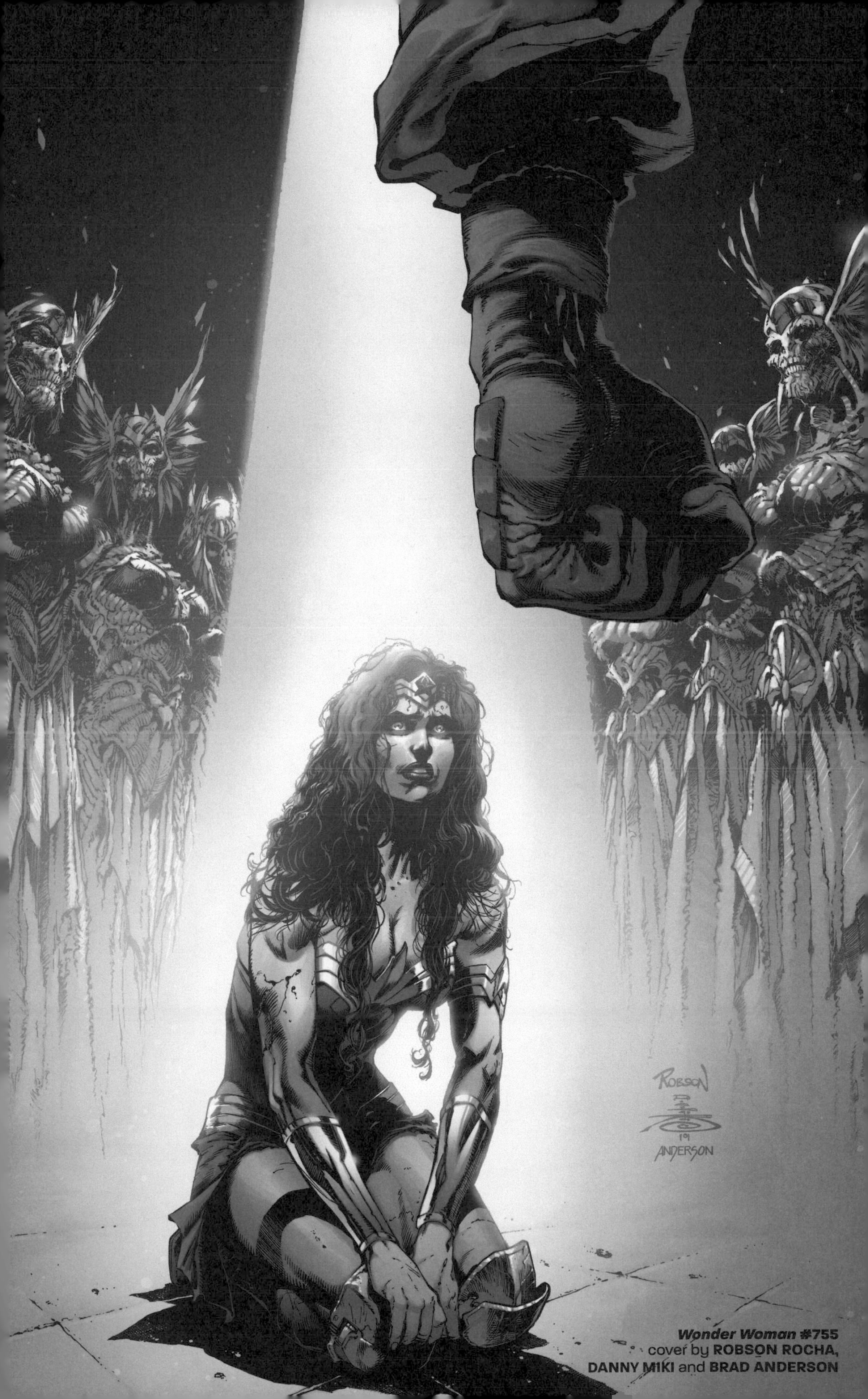
ROBSON
ANDERSON

***Wonder Woman* #755**
cover by **ROBSON ROCHA,**
DANNY MIKI and **BRAD ANDERSON**

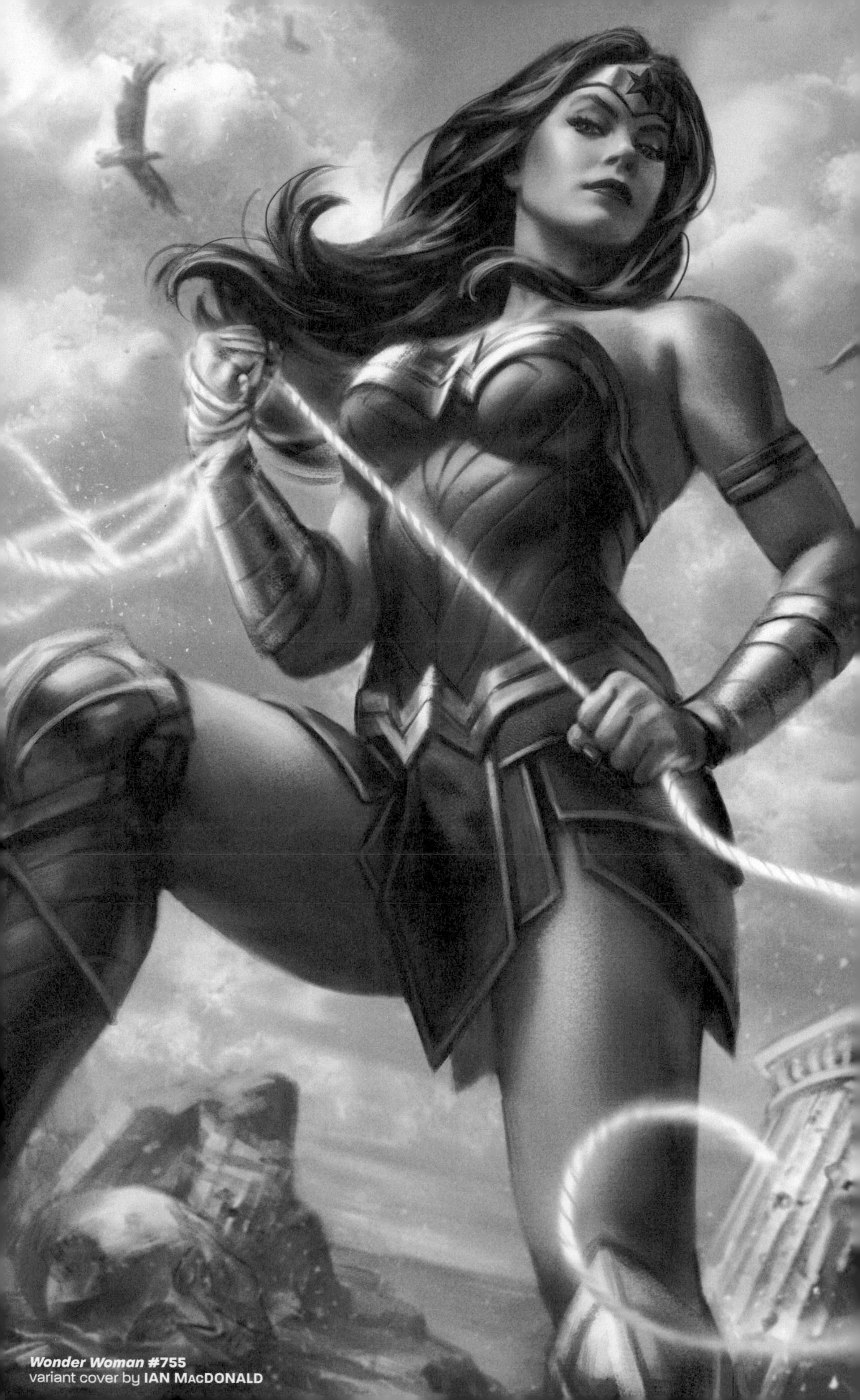

Wonder Woman #755
variant cover by **IAN MacDONALD**

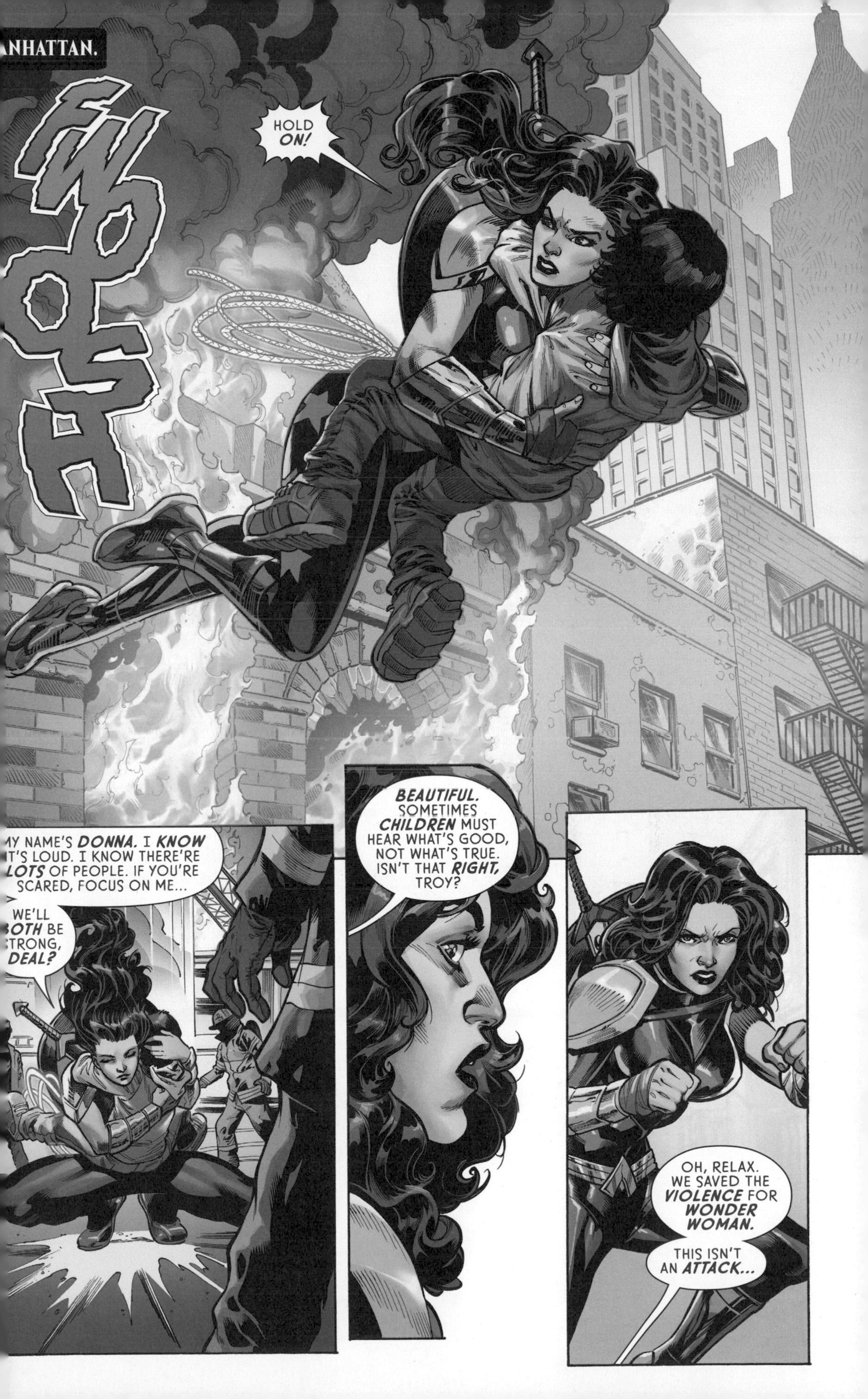

NHATTAN.
FWOOSH
HOLD ON!
MY NAME'S DONNA. I KNOW IT'S LOUD. I KNOW THERE'RE LOTS OF PEOPLE. IF YOU'RE SCARED, FOCUS ON ME...
WE'LL BOTH BE STRONG, DEAL?
BEAUTIFUL. SOMETIMES CHILDREN MUST HEAR WHAT'S GOOD, NOT WHAT'S TRUE. ISN'T THAT RIGHT, TROY?
OH, RELAX. WE SAVED THE VIOLENCE FOR WONDER WOMAN.
THIS ISN'T AN ATTACK...

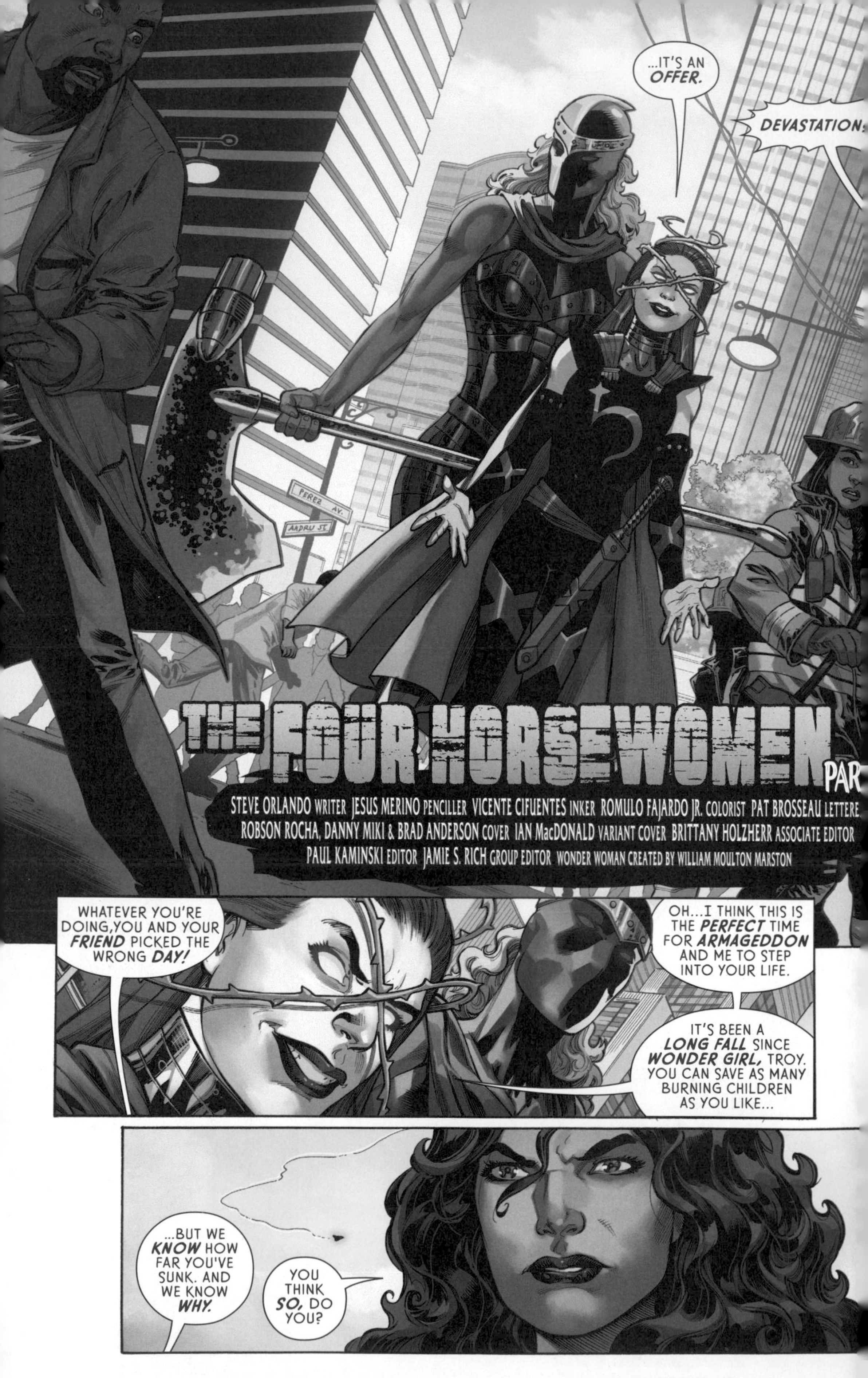

...IT'S AN OFFER.
DEVASTATION
PEREZ AV.
ANDRU ST.
THE FOUR HORSEWOMEN PAR
STEVE ORLANDO WRITER JESUS MERINO PENCILLER VICENTE CIFUENTES INKER ROMULO FAJARDO JR. COLORIST PAT BROSSEAU LETTERE
ROBSON ROCHA, DANNY MIKI & BRAD ANDERSON COVER IAN MacDONALD VARIANT COVER BRITTANY HOLZHERR ASSOCIATE EDITOR
PAUL KAMINSKI EDITOR JAMIE S. RICH GROUP EDITOR WONDER WOMAN CREATED BY WILLIAM MOULTON MARSTON
WHATEVER YOU'RE DOING, YOU AND YOUR FRIEND PICKED THE WRONG DAY!
OH...I THINK THIS IS THE PERFECT TIME FOR ARMAGEDDON AND ME TO STEP INTO YOUR LIFE.
IT'S BEEN A LONG FALL SINCE WONDER GIRL, TROY. YOU CAN SAVE AS MANY BURNING CHILDREN AS YOU LIKE...
...BUT WE KNOW HOW FAR YOU'VE SUNK. AND WE KNOW WHY.
YOU THINK SO, DO YOU?

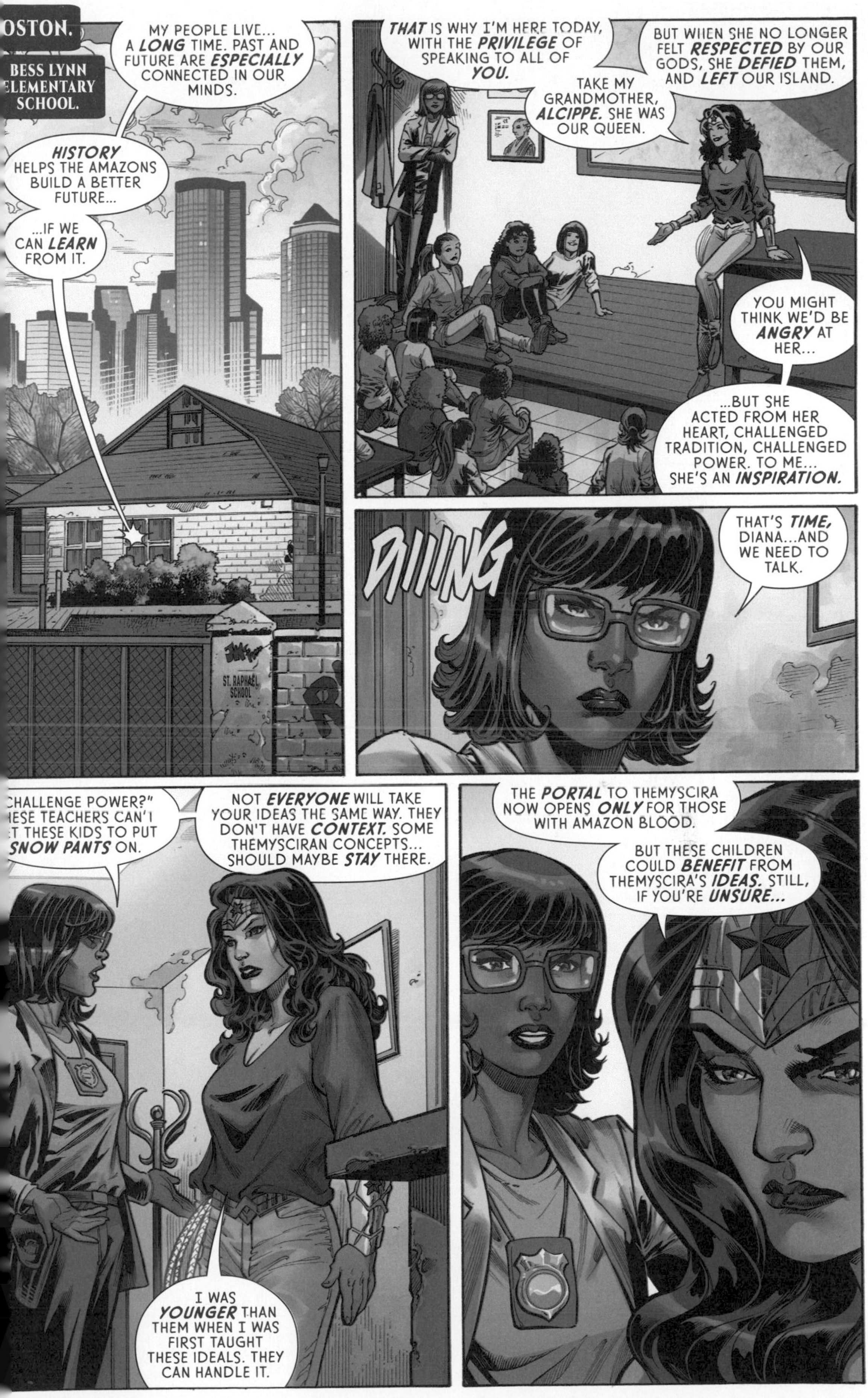
OSTON.
BESS LYNN ELEMENTARY SCHOOL.
MY PEOPLE LIVE... A LONG TIME. PAST AND FUTURE ARE ESPECIALLY CONNECTED IN OUR MINDS.
HISTORY HELPS THE AMAZONS BUILD A BETTER FUTURE...
...IF WE CAN LEARN FROM IT.
ST. RAPHAEL SCHOOL
THAT IS WHY I'M HERE TODAY, WITH THE PRIVILEGE OF SPEAKING TO ALL OF YOU.
TAKE MY GRANDMOTHER, ALCIPPE. SHE WAS OUR QUEEN.
BUT WHEN SHE NO LONGER FELT RESPECTED BY OUR GODS, SHE DEFIED THEM, AND LEFT OUR ISLAND.
YOU MIGHT THINK WE'D BE ANGRY AT HER...
...BUT SHE ACTED FROM HER HEART, CHALLENGED TRADITION, CHALLENGED POWER. TO ME... SHE'S AN INSPIRATION.
DIIING
THAT'S TIME, DIANA...AND WE NEED TO TALK.
CHALLENGE POWER?" IESE TEACHERS CAN'T T THESE KIDS TO PUT SNOW PANTS ON.
NOT EVERYONE WILL TAKE YOUR IDEAS THE SAME WAY. THEY DON'T HAVE CONTEXT. SOME THEMYSCIRAN CONCEPTS... SHOULD MAYBE STAY THERE.
I WAS YOUNGER THAN THEM WHEN I WAS FIRST TAUGHT THESE IDEALS. THEY CAN HANDLE IT.
THE PORTAL TO THEMYSCIRA NOW OPENS ONLY FOR THOSE WITH AMAZON BLOOD.
BUT THESE CHILDREN COULD BENEFIT FROM THEMYSCIRA'S IDEAS. STILL, IF YOU'RE UNSURE...

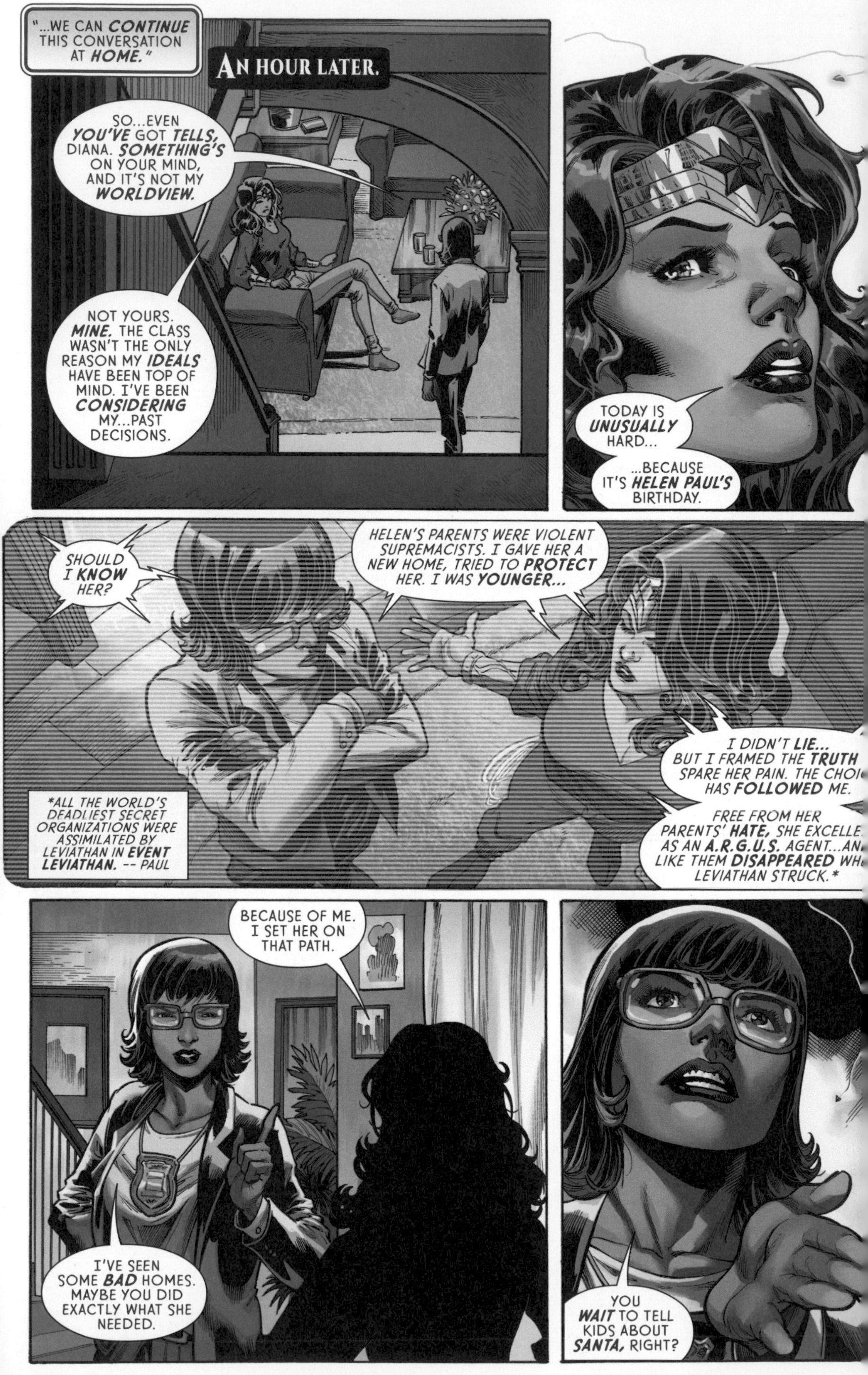
"...WE CAN CONTINUE THIS CONVERSATION AT HOME."
AN HOUR LATER.
SO...EVEN YOU'VE GOT TELLS, DIANA. SOMETHING'S ON YOUR MIND, AND IT'S NOT MY WORLDVIEW.
NOT YOURS. MINE. THE CLASS WASN'T THE ONLY REASON MY IDEALS HAVE BEEN TOP OF MIND. I'VE BEEN CONSIDERING MY...PAST DECISIONS.
TODAY IS UNUSUALLY HARD...
...BECAUSE IT'S HELEN PAUL'S BIRTHDAY.
SHOULD I KNOW HER?
HELEN'S PARENTS WERE VIOLENT SUPREMACISTS. I GAVE HER A NEW HOME, TRIED TO PROTECT HER. I WAS YOUNGER...
I DIDN'T LIE... BUT I FRAMED THE TRUTH SPARE HER PAIN. THE CHOI HAS FOLLOWED ME.
FREE FROM HER PARENTS' HATE, SHE EXCELLE AS AN A.R.G.U.S. AGENT...AN LIKE THEM DISAPPEARED WH LEVIATHAN STRUCK.*
*ALL THE WORLD'S DEADLIEST SECRET ORGANIZATIONS WERE ASSIMILATED BY LEVIATHAN IN EVENT LEVIATHAN. -- PAUL
BECAUSE OF ME. I SET HER ON THAT PATH.
I'VE SEEN SOME BAD HOMES. MAYBE YOU DID EXACTLY WHAT SHE NEEDED.
YOU WAIT TO TELL KIDS ABOUT SANTA, RIGHT?

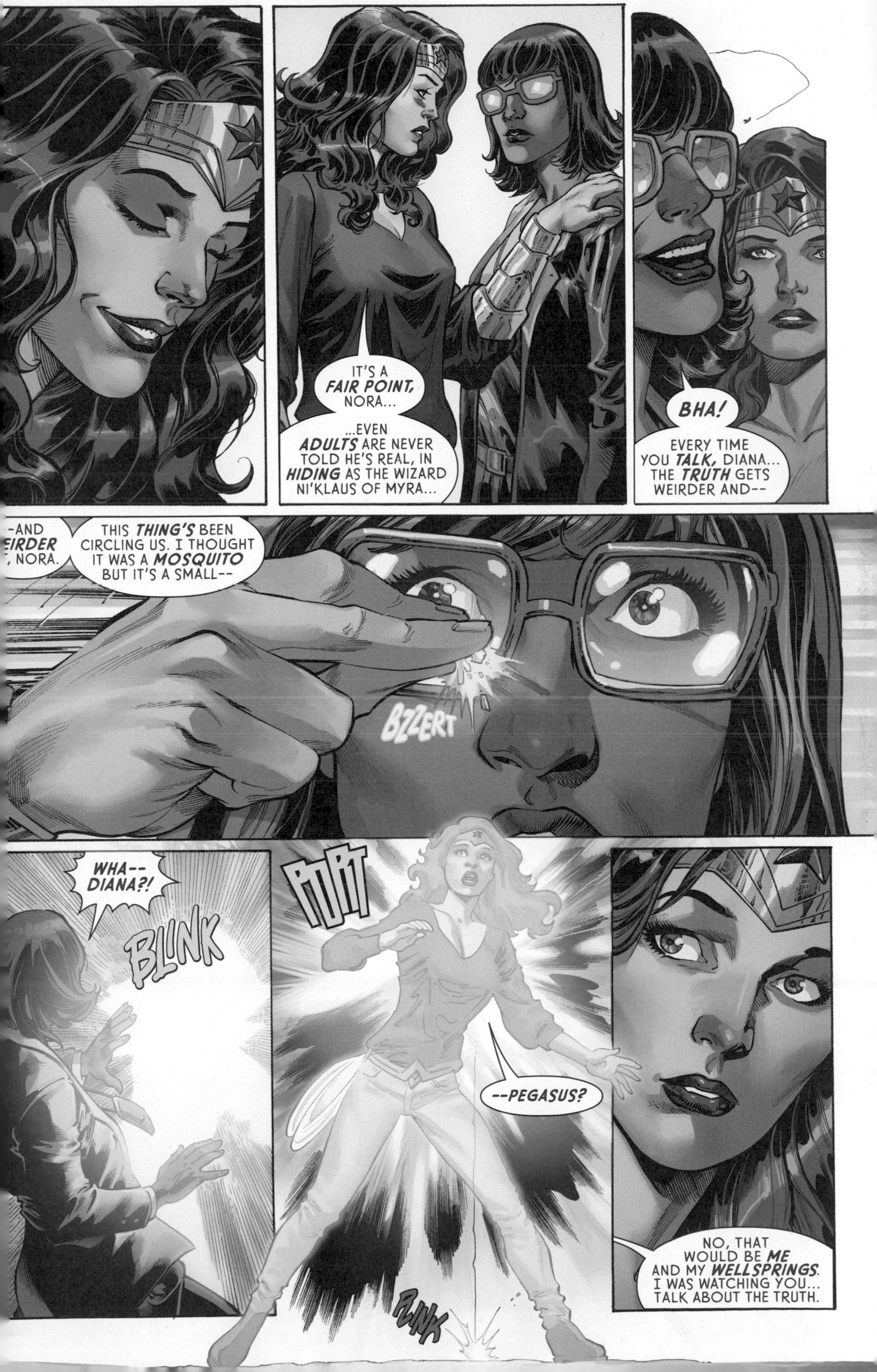
IT'S A FAIR POINT, NORA...
...EVEN ADULTS ARE NEVER TOLD HE'S REAL, IN HIDING AS THE WIZARD NI'KLAUS OF MYRA...
BHA!
EVERY TIME YOU TALK, DIANA... THE TRUTH GETS WEIRDER AND--
-AND EIRDER , NORA.
THIS THING'S BEEN CIRCLING US. I THOUGHT IT WAS A MOSQUITO BUT IT'S A SMALL--
BZZERT
WHA-- DIANA?!
BLINK
PTOPT
--PEGASUS?
PLINK
NO, THAT WOULD BE ME AND MY WELLSPRINGS. I WAS WATCHING YOU... TALK ABOUT THE TRUTH.

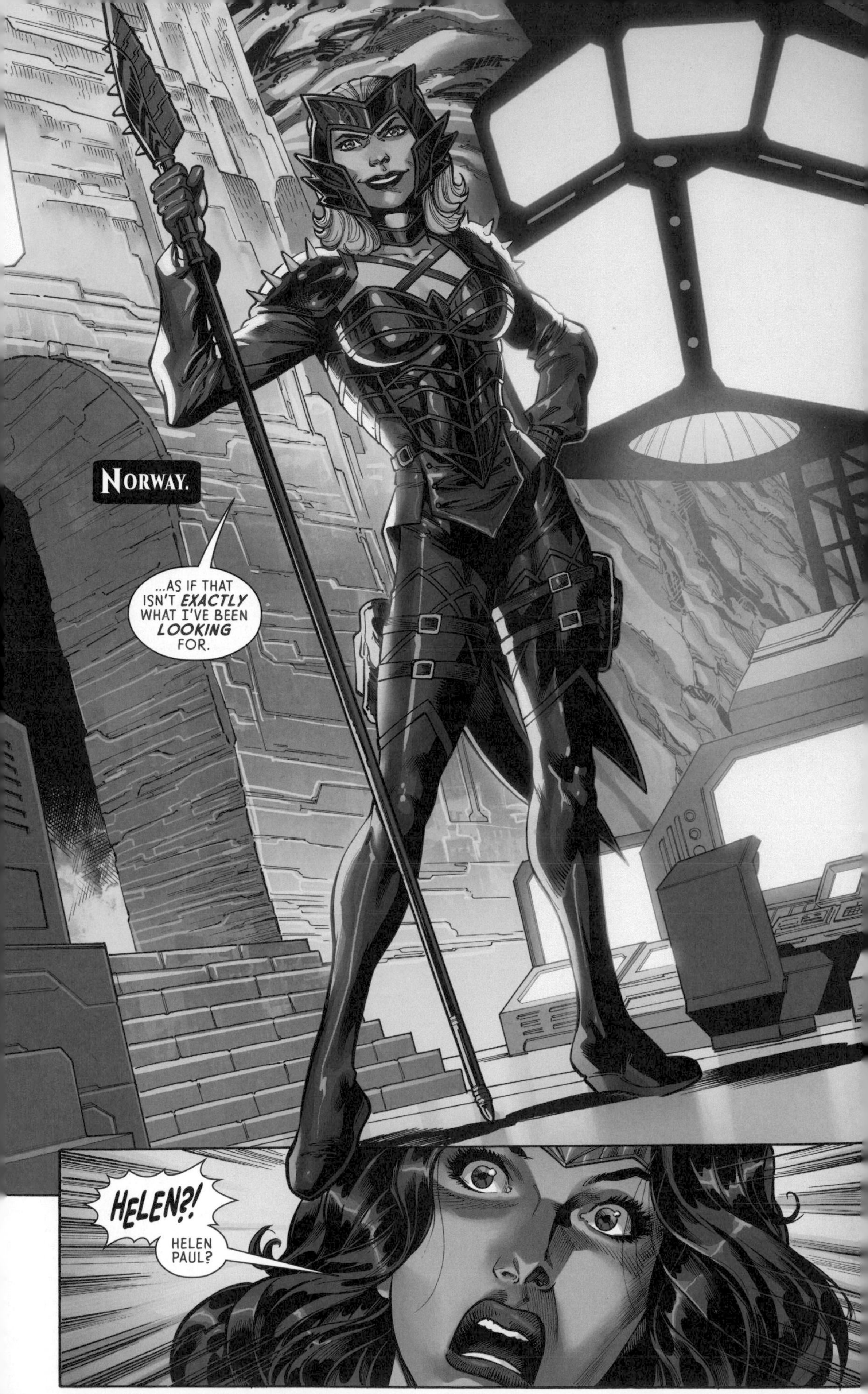
NORWAY.
...AS IF THAT ISN'T *EXACTLY* WHAT I'VE BEEN *LOOKING* FOR.
HELEN?!
HELEN PAUL?

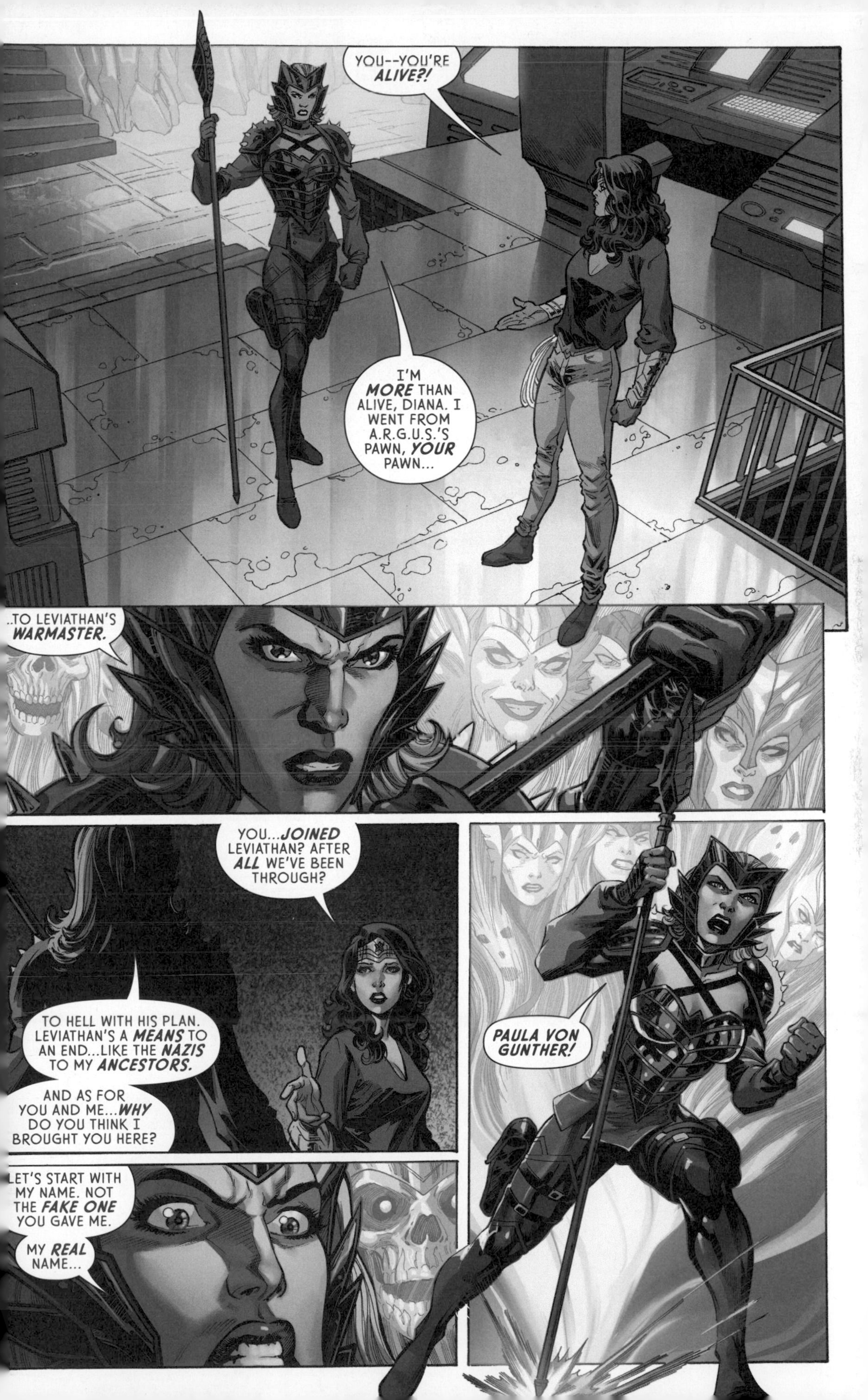
YOU--YOU'RE ALIVE?!
I'M MORE THAN ALIVE, DIANA. I WENT FROM A.R.G.U.S.'S PAWN, YOUR PAWN...
..TO LEVIATHAN'S WARMASTER.
YOU...JOINED LEVIATHAN? AFTER ALL WE'VE BEEN THROUGH?
TO HELL WITH HIS PLAN. LEVIATHAN'S A MEANS TO AN END...LIKE THE NAZIS TO MY ANCESTORS.
AND AS FOR YOU AND ME...WHY DO YOU THINK I BROUGHT YOU HERE?
LET'S START WITH MY NAME. NOT THE FAKE ONE YOU GAVE ME.
MY REAL NAME...
PAULA VON GUNTHER!

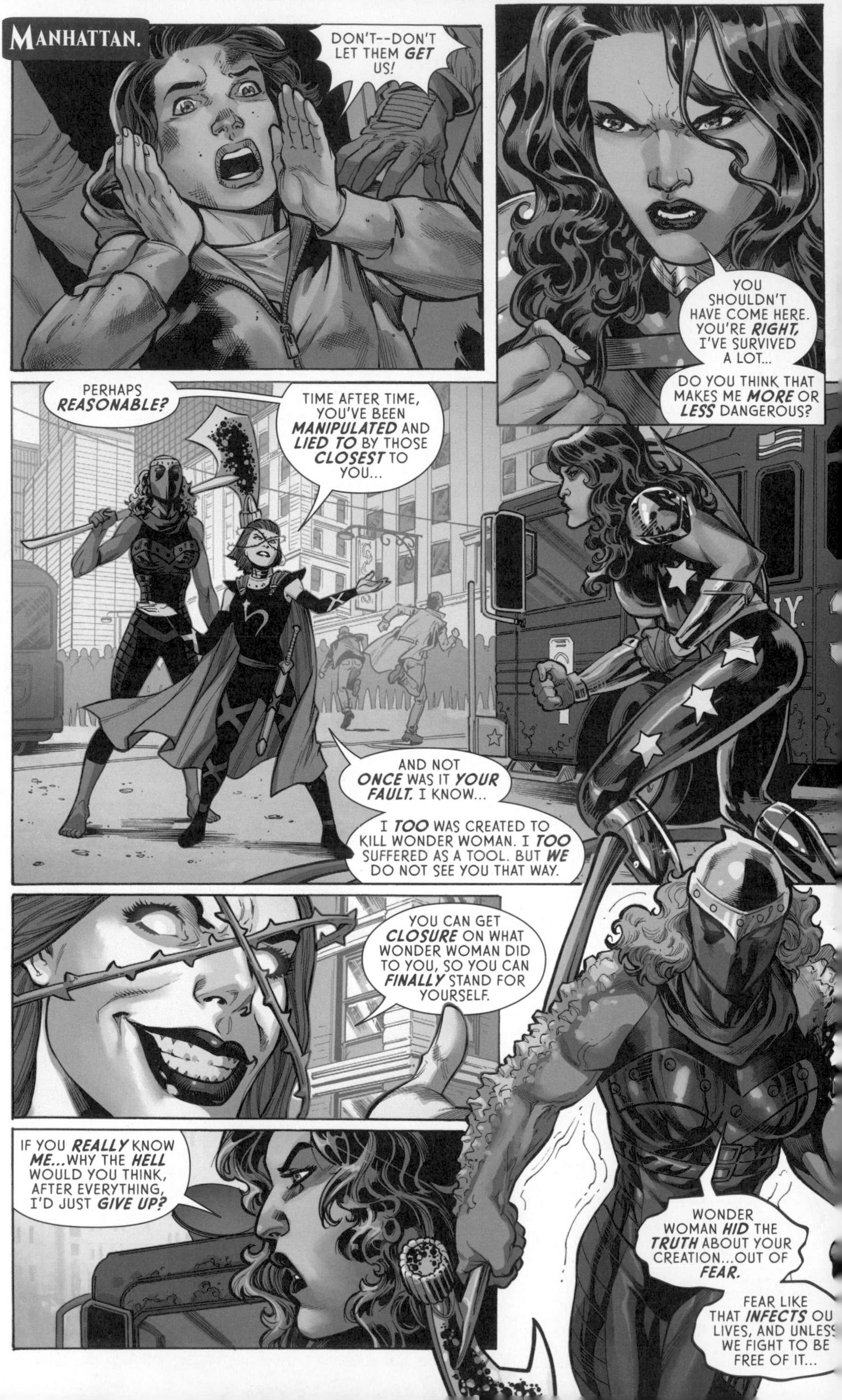
MANHATTAN.
DON'T--DON'T LET THEM GET US!
YOU SHOULDN'T HAVE COME HERE. YOU'RE RIGHT, I'VE SURVIVED A LOT...
DO YOU THINK THAT MAKES ME MORE OR LESS DANGEROUS?
PERHAPS REASONABLE?
TIME AFTER TIME, YOU'VE BEEN MANIPULATED AND LIED TO BY THOSE CLOSEST TO YOU...
AND NOT ONCE WAS IT YOUR FAULT. I KNOW...
I TOO WAS CREATED TO KILL WONDER WOMAN. I TOO SUFFERED AS A TOOL. BUT WE DO NOT SEE YOU THAT WAY.
YOU CAN GET CLOSURE ON WHAT WONDER WOMAN DID TO YOU, SO YOU CAN FINALLY STAND FOR YOURSELF.
IF YOU REALLY KNOW ME...WHY THE HELL WOULD YOU THINK, AFTER EVERYTHING, I'D JUST GIVE UP?
WONDER WOMAN HID THE TRUTH ABOUT YOUR CREATION...OUT OF FEAR.
FEAR LIKE THAT INFECTS OU LIVES, AND UNLESS WE FIGHT TO BE FREE OF IT...

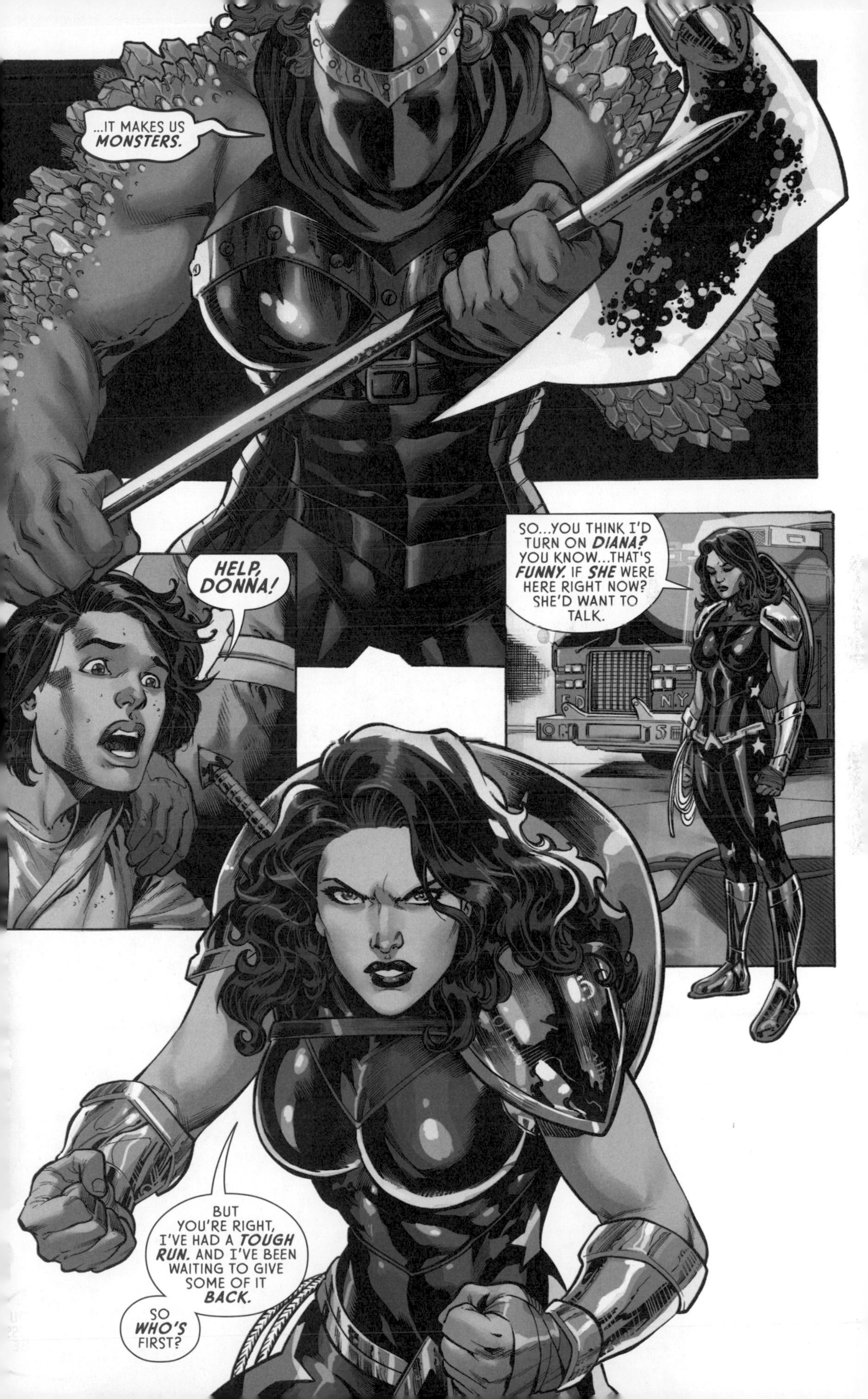
...IT MAKES US MONSTERS.
HELP, DONNA!
SO...YOU THINK I'D TURN ON DIANA? YOU KNOW...THAT'S FUNNY. IF SHE WERE HERE RIGHT NOW? SHE'D WANT TO TALK.
BUT YOU'RE RIGHT, I'VE HAD A TOUGH RUN. AND I'VE BEEN WAITING TO GIVE SOME OF IT BACK.
SO WHO'S FIRST?

NORWAY.

HELEN--

IT'S *PAULA*. THE AMAZONS HAVE A *LOT* TO ANSWER FOR, DIANA. *YOU* ESPECIALLY. BUT OUT OF *RESPECT* FOR OUR PAST...

SHINT

...WOULD YOU CARE TO *ADMIT* WHAT YOU DID?

WHAT I DID...

"...RESCUING YOU FROM YOUR BIRTH PARENTS...

"...PLACING YOU IN A LOVING HOME...

"...SETTING YOU ON A HOPEFUL PATH...

"...WAS TO *SHIELD* YOU FROM HATE.*

PETRA PAUL

HAROLD [P]UL

*SEE THE FULL STORY IN *WONDER WOMAN ANNUAL #3*.-- PAUL

NO MATTER YOUR PAST, YOU WERE MY *SISTER*, LIKE SO MANY.

AND AS I DO FOR THEM, WANTED ONLY T[HE] *BEST* FOR YO[U]

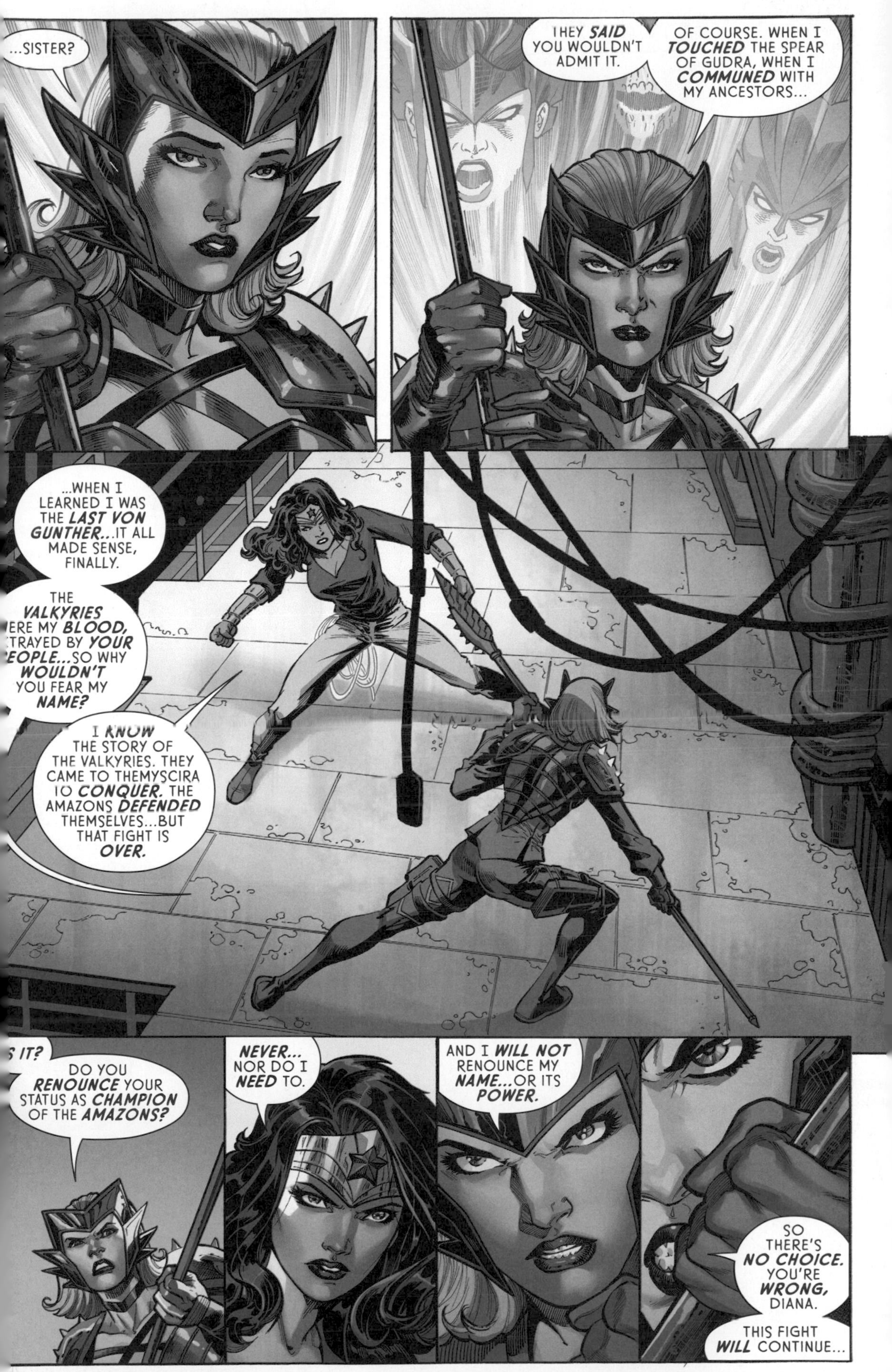
...SISTER?
THEY SAID YOU WOULDN'T ADMIT IT.
OF COURSE. WHEN I TOUCHED THE SPEAR OF GUDRA, WHEN I COMMUNED WITH MY ANCESTORS...
...WHEN I LEARNED I WAS THE LAST VON GUNTHER...IT ALL MADE SENSE, FINALLY.
THE VALKYRIES ERE MY BLOOD, TRAYED BY YOUR EOPLE...SO WHY WOULDN'T YOU FEAR MY NAME?
I KNOW THE STORY OF THE VALKYRIES. THEY CAME TO THEMYSCIRA TO CONQUER. THE AMAZONS DEFENDED THEMSELVES...BUT THAT FIGHT IS OVER.
S IT?
DO YOU RENOUNCE YOUR STATUS AS CHAMPION OF THE AMAZONS?
NEVER... NOR DO I NEED TO.
AND I WILL NOT RENOUNCE MY NAME...OR ITS POWER.
SO THERE'S NO CHOICE. YOU'RE WRONG, DIANA.
THIS FIGHT WILL CONTINUE...

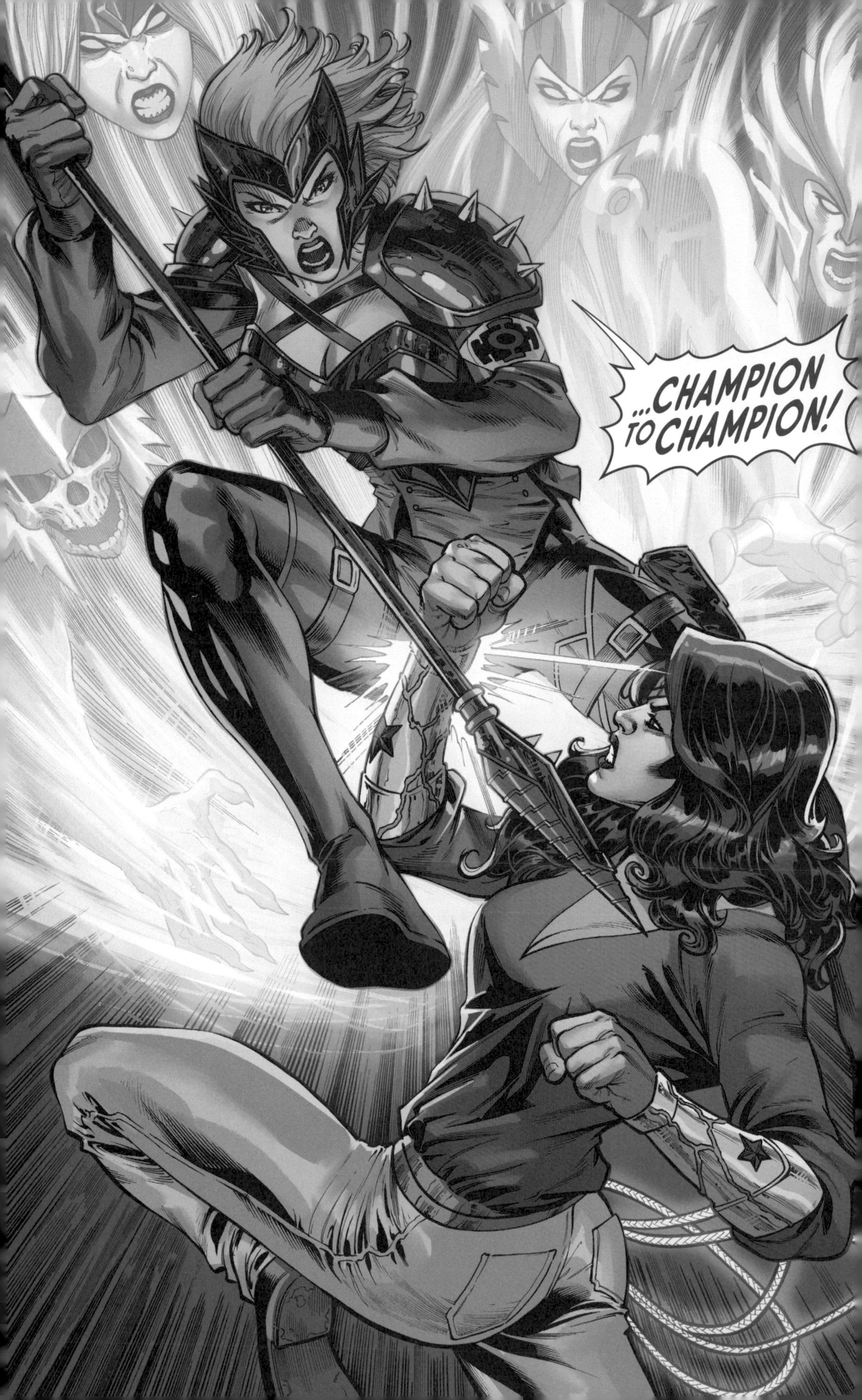
...CHAMPION TO CHAMPION!

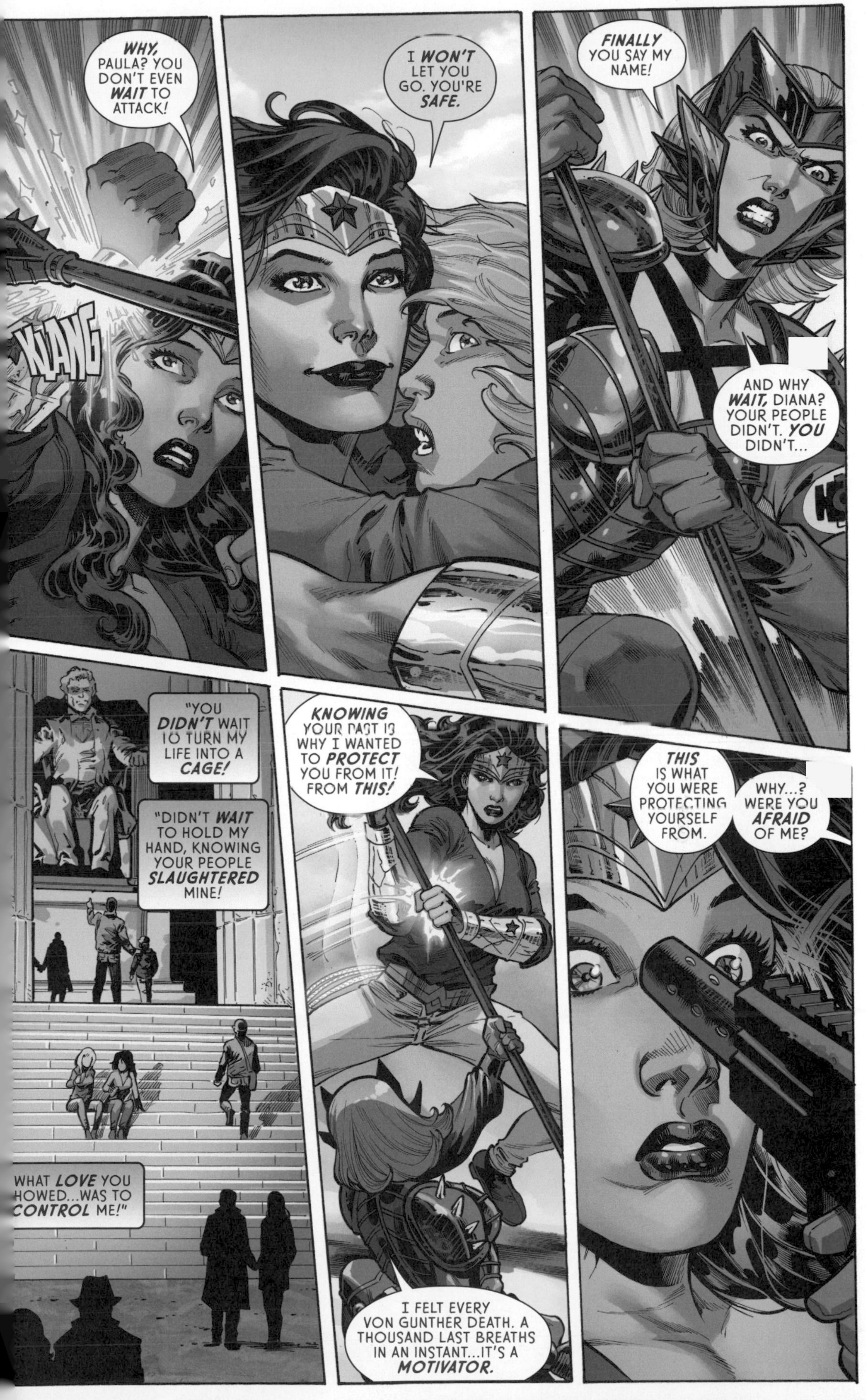

WHY, PAULA? YOU DON'T EVEN WAIT TO ATTACK!
KLANG
I WON'T LET YOU GO. YOU'RE SAFE.
FINALLY YOU SAY MY NAME!
AND WHY WAIT, DIANA? YOUR PEOPLE DIDN'T. YOU DIDN'T...
"YOU DIDN'T WAIT TO TURN MY LIFE INTO A CAGE!
"DIDN'T WAIT TO HOLD MY HAND, KNOWING YOUR PEOPLE SLAUGHTERED MINE!
WHAT LOVE YOU HOWED...WAS TO CONTROL ME!"
KNOWING YOUR PAST IS WHY I WANTED TO PROTECT YOU FROM IT! FROM THIS!
I FELT EVERY VON GUNTHER DEATH. A THOUSAND LAST BREATHS IN AN INSTANT...IT'S A MOTIVATOR.
THIS IS WHAT YOU WERE PROTECTING YOURSELF FROM.
WHY...? WERE YOU AFRAID OF ME?

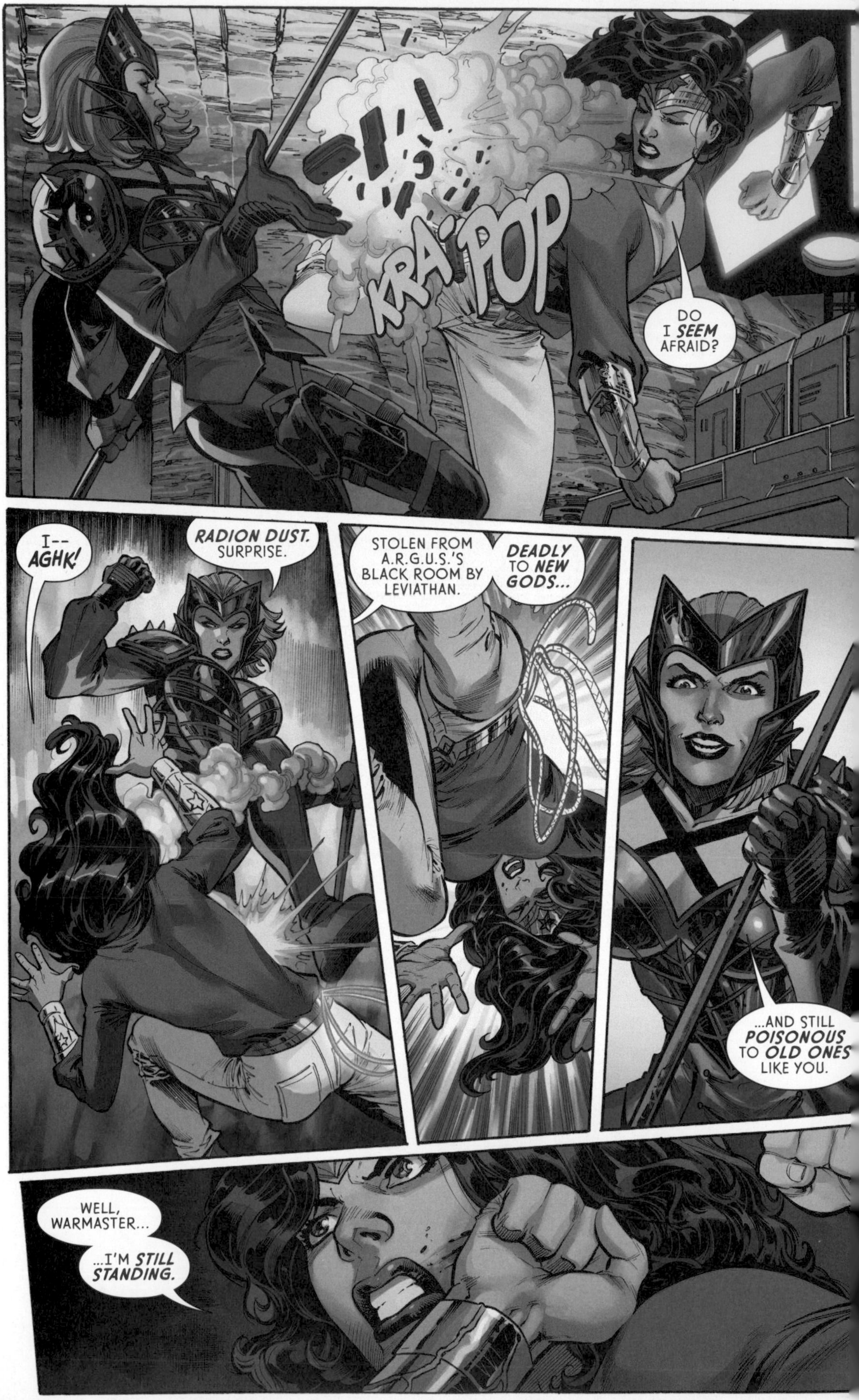
KRA-POP
DO I SEEM AFRAID?
I-- AGHK!
RADION DUST. SURPRISE.
STOLEN FROM A.R.G.U.S.'S BLACK ROOM BY LEVIATHAN.
DEADLY TO NEW GODS...
...AND STILL POISONOUS TO OLD ONES LIKE YOU.
WELL, WARMASTER...
...I'M STILL STANDING.

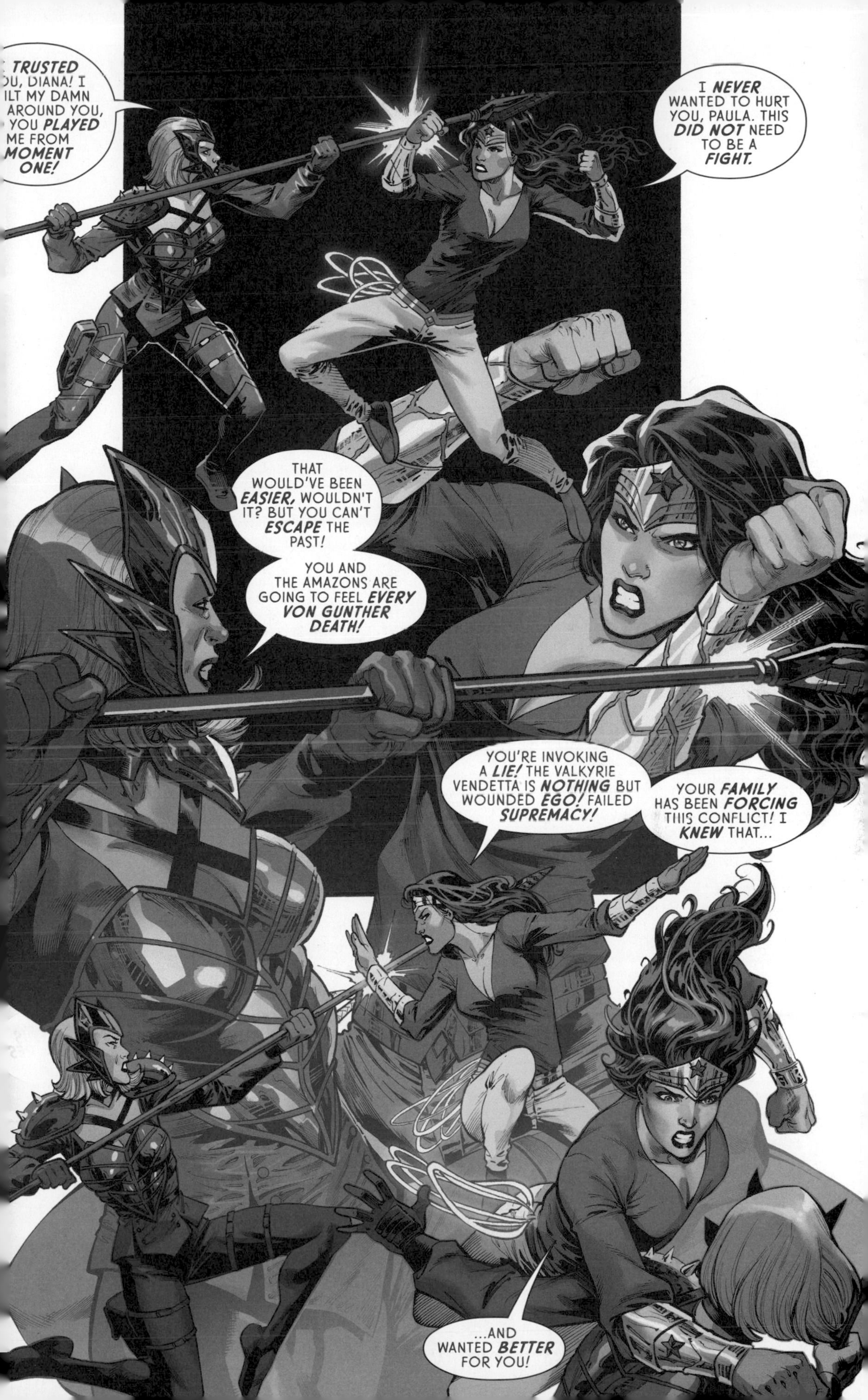
TRUSTED OU, DIANA! I ILT MY DAMN AROUND YOU, YOU PLAYED ME FROM MOMENT ONE!
I NEVER WANTED TO HURT YOU, PAULA. THIS DID NOT NEED TO BE A FIGHT.
THAT WOULD'VE BEEN EASIER, WOULDN'T IT? BUT YOU CAN'T ESCAPE THE PAST!
YOU AND THE AMAZONS ARE GOING TO FEEL EVERY VON GUNTHER DEATH!
YOU'RE INVOKING A LIE! THE VALKYRIE VENDETTA IS NOTHING BUT WOUNDED EGO! FAILED SUPREMACY!
YOUR FAMILY HAS BEEN FORCING THIS CONFLICT! I KNEW THAT...
...AND WANTED BETTER FOR YOU!

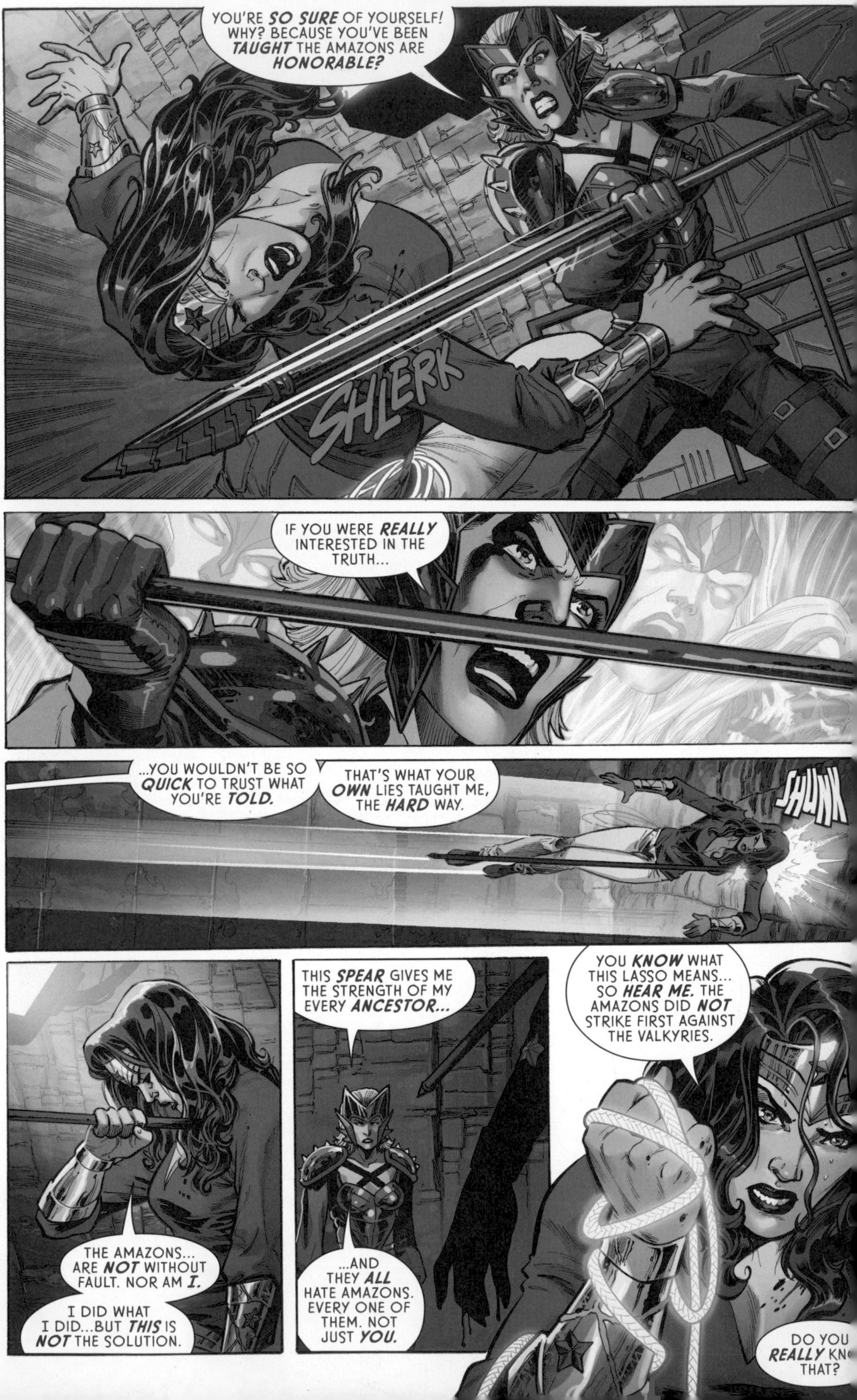
YOU'RE SO SURE OF YOURSELF! WHY? BECAUSE YOU'VE BEEN TAUGHT THE AMAZONS ARE HONORABLE?
SHLERK
IF YOU WERE REALLY INTERESTED IN THE TRUTH...
...YOU WOULDN'T BE SO QUICK TO TRUST WHAT YOU'RE TOLD.
THAT'S WHAT YOUR OWN LIES TAUGHT ME, THE HARD WAY.
SHUNK
THE AMAZONS... ARE NOT WITHOUT FAULT. NOR AM I.
I DID WHAT I DID...BUT THIS IS NOT THE SOLUTION.
THIS SPEAR GIVES ME THE STRENGTH OF MY EVERY ANCESTOR...
...AND THEY ALL HATE AMAZONS. EVERY ONE OF THEM. NOT JUST YOU.
YOU KNOW WHAT THIS LASSO MEANS... SO HEAR ME. THE AMAZONS DID NOT STRIKE FIRST AGAINST THE VALKYRIES.

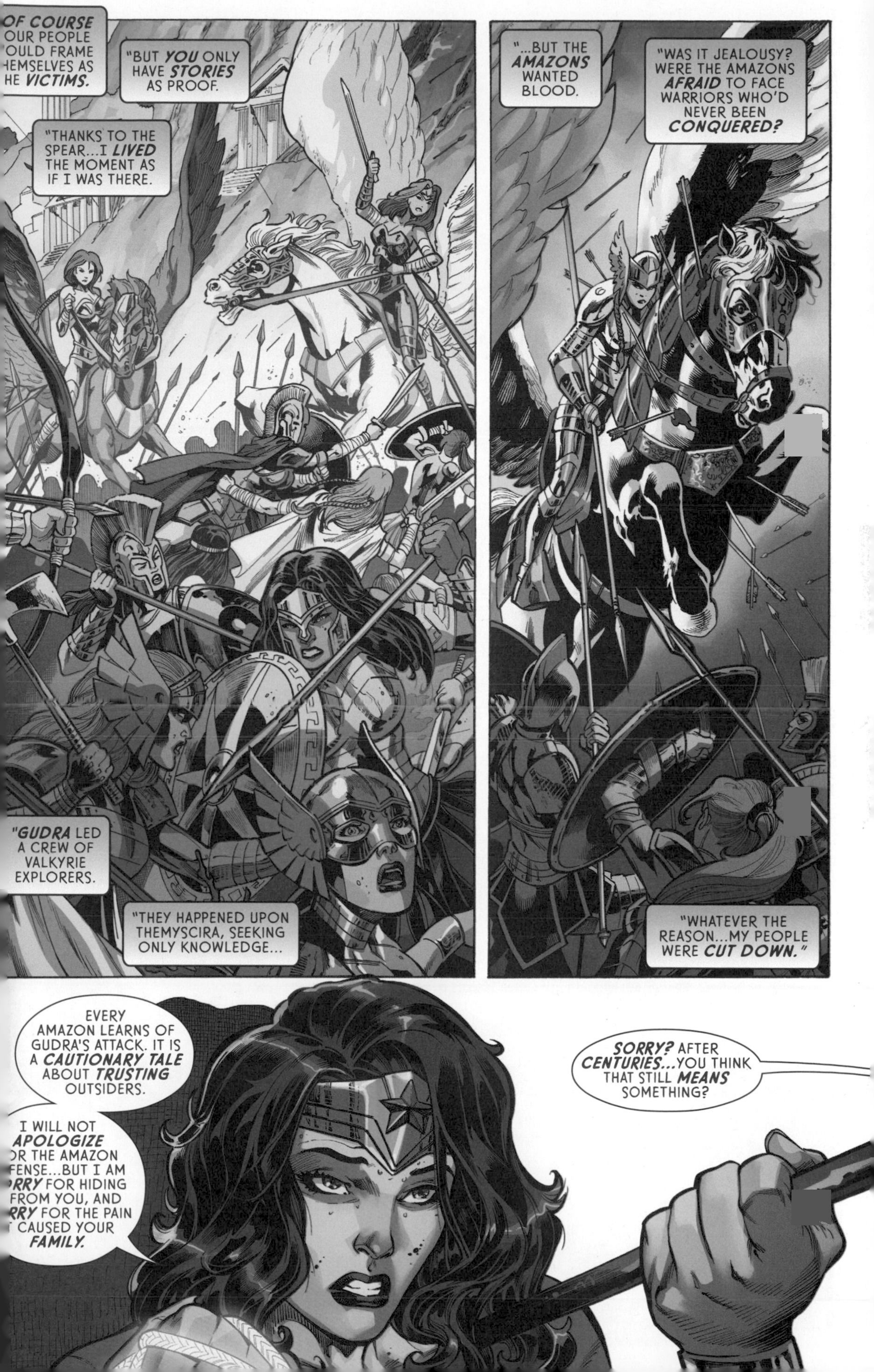
OF COURSE OUR PEOPLE OULD FRAME HEMSELVES AS HE VICTIMS.
"BUT YOU ONLY HAVE STORIES AS PROOF.
"THANKS TO THE SPEAR...I LIVED THE MOMENT AS IF I WAS THERE.
"GUDRA LED A CREW OF VALKYRIE EXPLORERS.
"THEY HAPPENED UPON THEMYSCIRA, SEEKING ONLY KNOWLEDGE...
"...BUT THE AMAZONS WANTED BLOOD.
"WAS IT JEALOUSY? WERE THE AMAZONS AFRAID TO FACE WARRIORS WHO'D NEVER BEEN CONQUERED?
"WHATEVER THE REASON...MY PEOPLE WERE CUT DOWN."
EVERY AMAZON LEARNS OF GUDRA'S ATTACK. IT IS A CAUTIONARY TALE ABOUT TRUSTING OUTSIDERS.
I WILL NOT APOLOGIZE OR THE AMAZON FENSE...BUT I AM RRY FOR HIDING FROM YOU, AND RRY FOR THE PAIN CAUSED YOUR FAMILY.
SORRY? AFTER CENTURIES...YOU THINK THAT STILL MEANS SOMETHING?

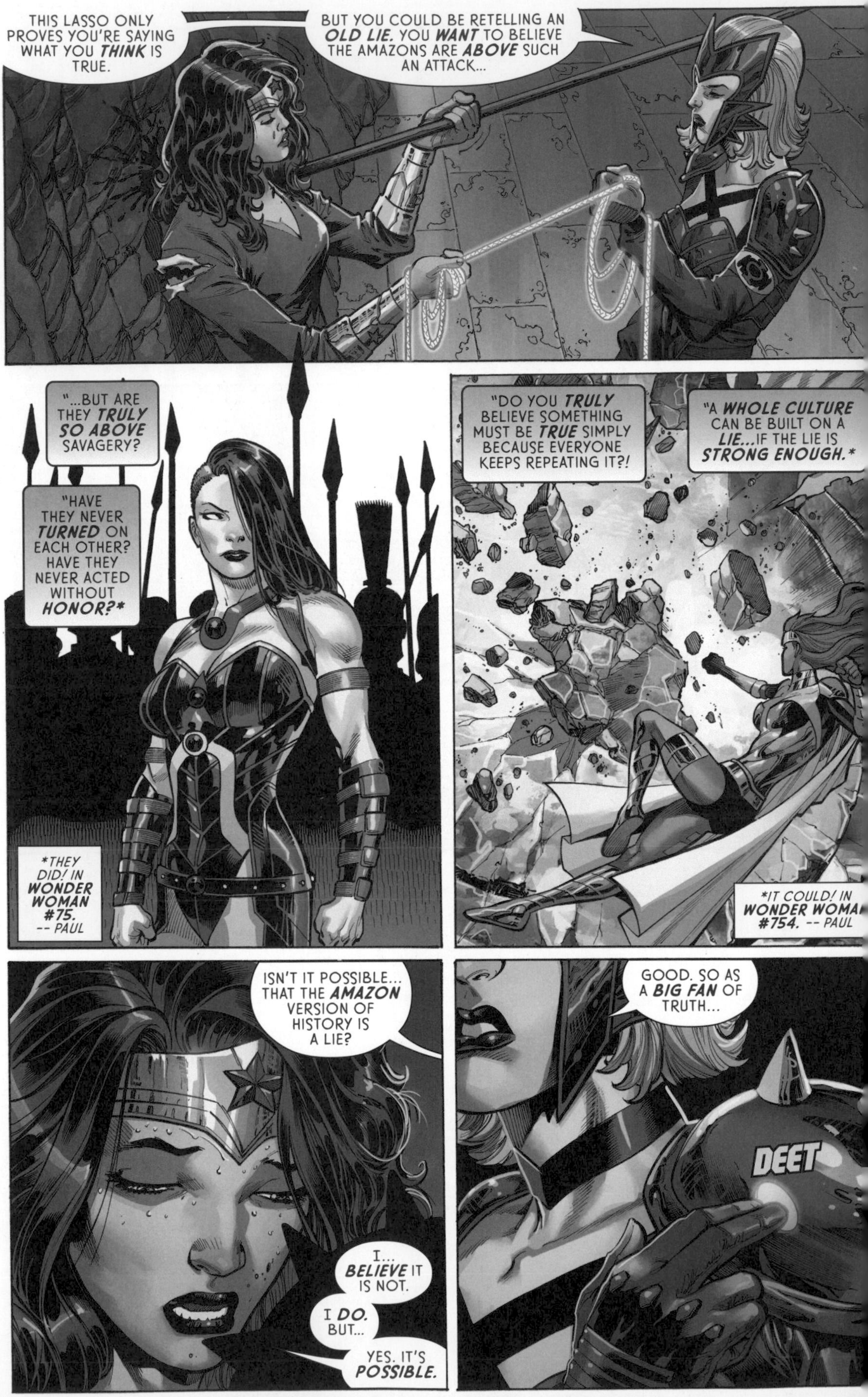
THIS LASSO ONLY PROVES YOU'RE SAYING WHAT YOU *THINK* IS TRUE.
BUT YOU COULD BE RETELLING AN *OLD LIE.* YOU *WANT* TO BELIEVE THE AMAZONS ARE *ABOVE* SUCH AN ATTACK...
"...BUT ARE THEY *TRULY SO ABOVE* SAVAGERY?
"HAVE THEY NEVER *TURNED* ON EACH OTHER? HAVE THEY NEVER ACTED WITHOUT *HONOR?**
*THEY DID! IN *WONDER WOMAN #75.* -- PAUL
"DO YOU *TRULY* BELIEVE SOMETHING MUST BE *TRUE* SIMPLY BECAUSE EVERYONE KEEPS REPEATING IT?!
"A *WHOLE CULTURE* CAN BE BUILT ON A *LIE...*IF THE LIE IS *STRONG ENOUGH.**
*IT COULD! IN *WONDER WOMA* *#754.* -- PAUL
ISN'T IT POSSIBLE... THAT THE *AMAZON* VERSION OF HISTORY IS A LIE?
I... *BELIEVE* IT IS NOT.
I *DO.* BUT...
YES. IT'S *POSSIBLE.*
GOOD. SO AS A *BIG FAN* OF TRUTH...
DEET

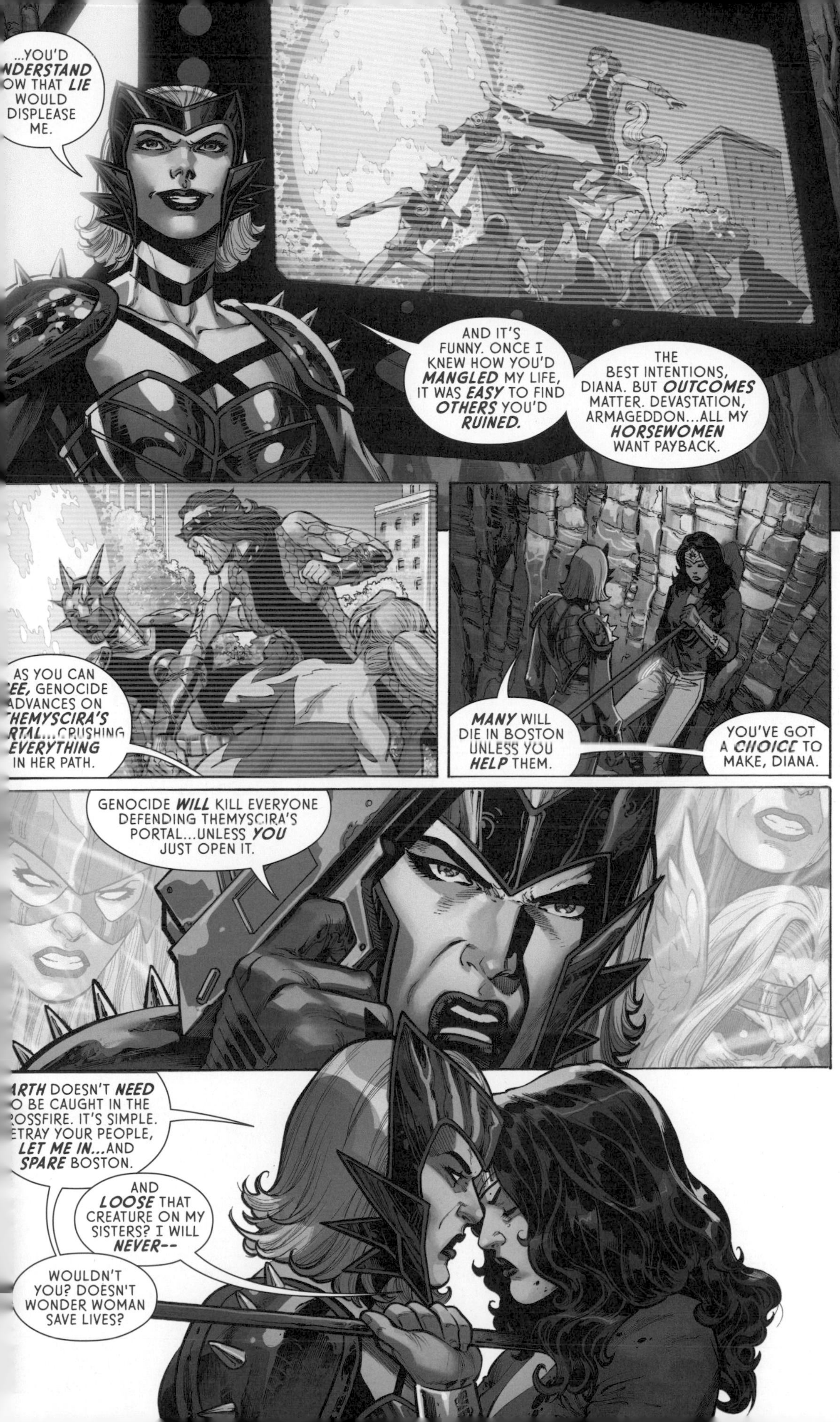

...YOU'D NDERSTAND OW THAT LIE WOULD DISPLEASE ME.
AND IT'S FUNNY. ONCE I KNEW HOW YOU'D MANGLED MY LIFE, IT WAS EASY TO FIND OTHERS YOU'D RUINED.
THE BEST INTENTIONS, DIANA. BUT OUTCOMES MATTER. DEVASTATION, ARMAGEDDON...ALL MY HORSEWOMEN WANT PAYBACK.
AS YOU CAN EE, GENOCIDE ADVANCES ON THEMYSCIRA'S RTAL...CRUSHING EVERYTHING IN HER PATH.
MANY WILL DIE IN BOSTON UNLESS YOU HELP THEM.
YOU'VE GOT A CHOICE TO MAKE, DIANA.
GENOCIDE WILL KILL EVERYONE DEFENDING THEMYSCIRA'S PORTAL...UNLESS YOU JUST OPEN IT.
ARTH DOESN'T NEED O BE CAUGHT IN THE ROSSFIRE. IT'S SIMPLE. ETRAY YOUR PEOPLE, LET ME IN...AND SPARE BOSTON.
AND LOOSE THAT CREATURE ON MY SISTERS? I WILL NEVER--
WOULDN'T YOU? DOESN'T WONDER WOMAN SAVE LIVES?

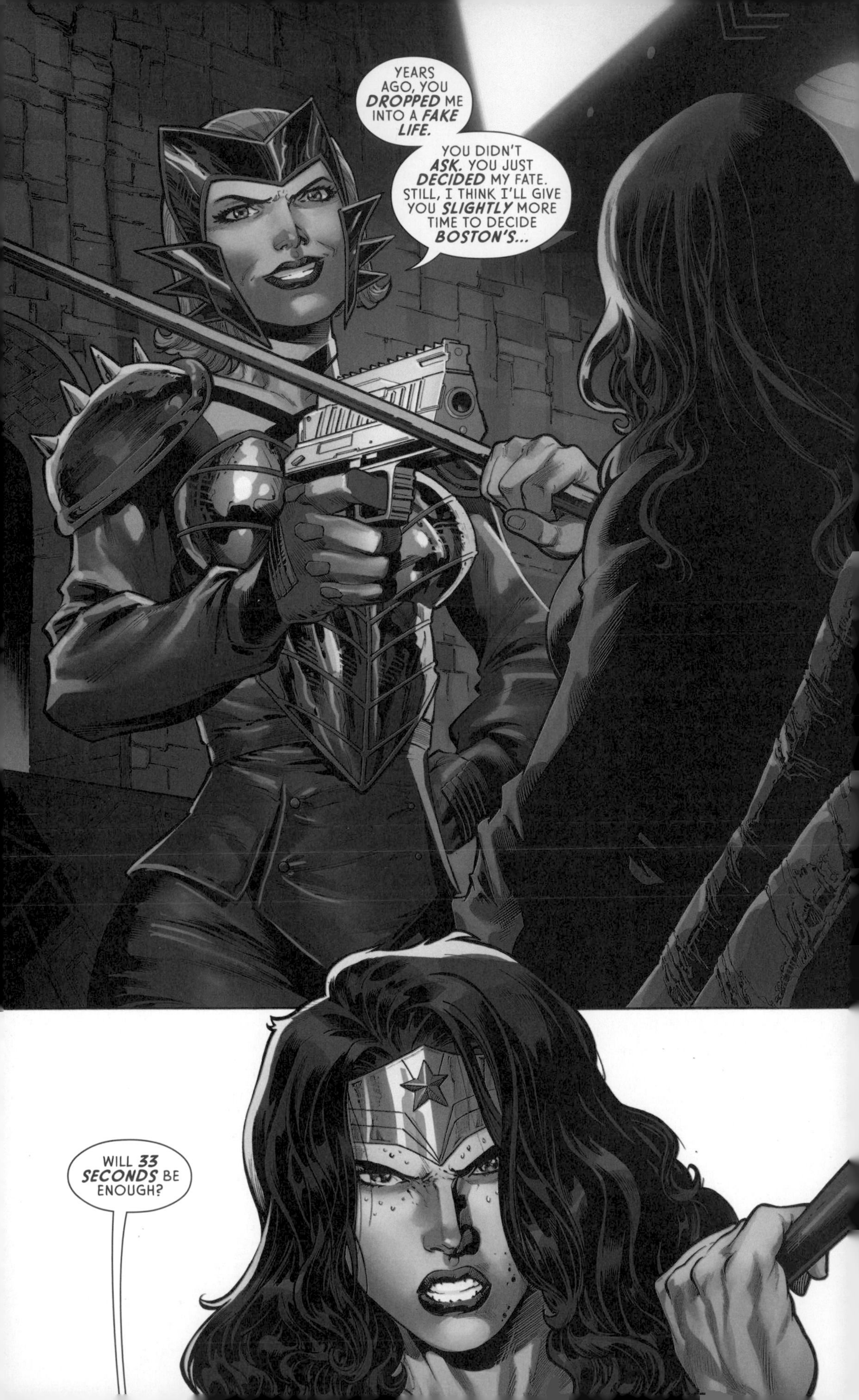
YEARS AGO, YOU DROPPED ME INTO A FAKE LIFE.
YOU DIDN'T ASK. YOU JUST DECIDED MY FATE. STILL, I THINK I'LL GIVE YOU SLIGHTLY MORE TIME TO DECIDE BOSTON'S...
WILL 33 SECONDS BE ENOUGH?

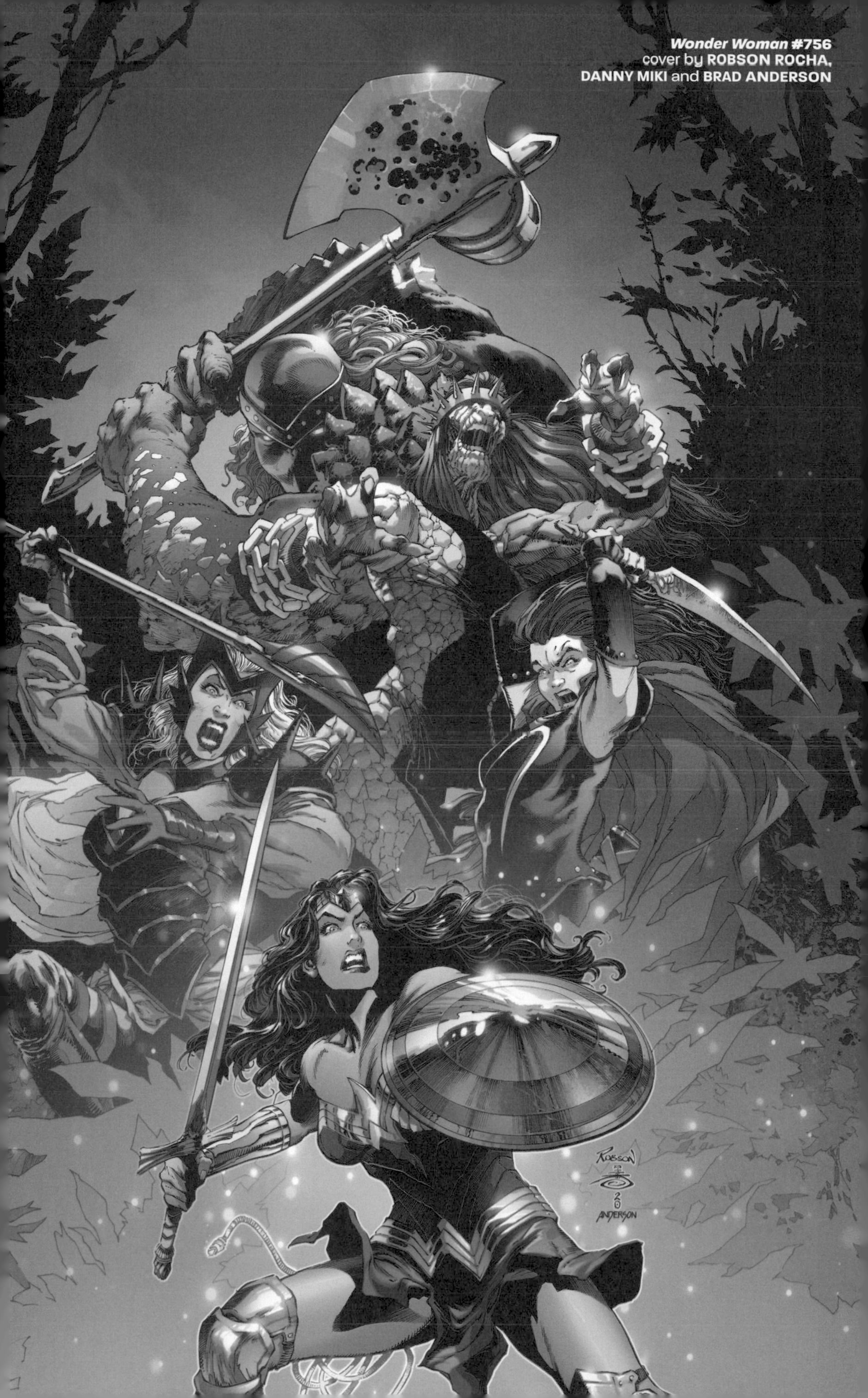

Wonder Woman #756
cover by ROBSON ROCHA,
DANNY MIKI and BRAD ANDERSON

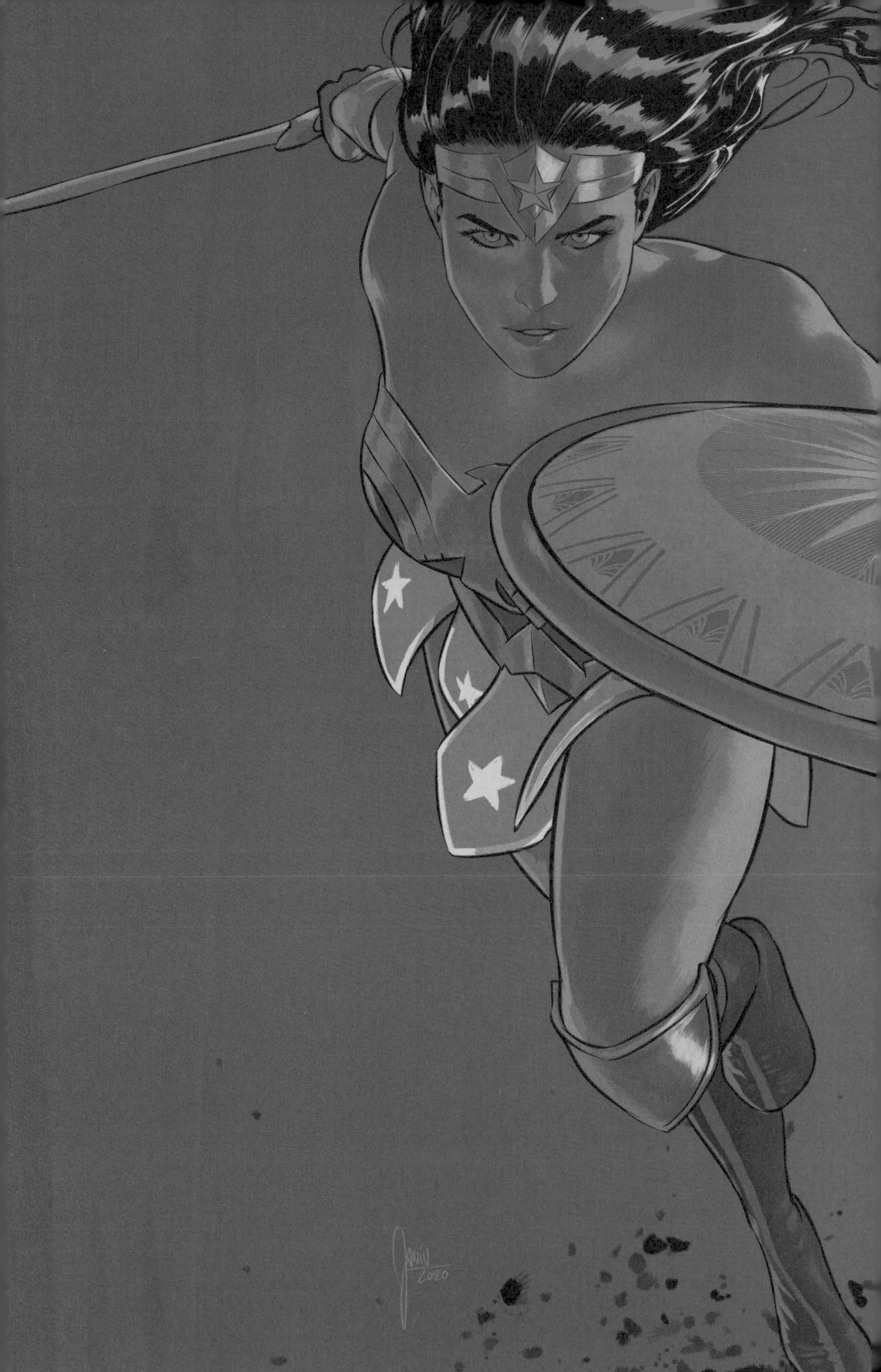

***Wonder Woman* #756**
variant cover by **MIKEL JANÍN**

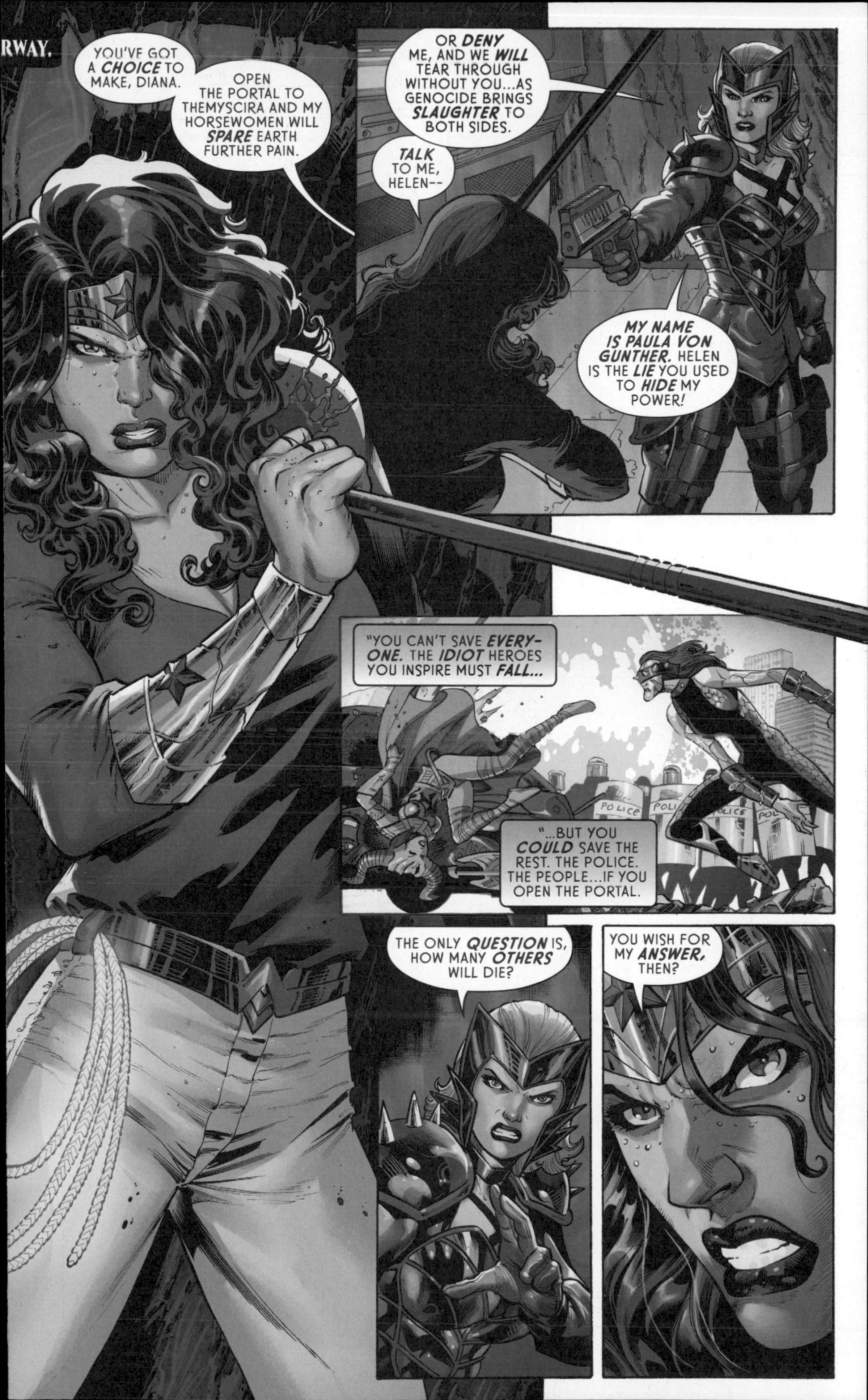
YOU'VE GOT A CHOICE TO MAKE, DIANA.
OPEN THE PORTAL TO THEMYSCIRA AND MY HORSEWOMEN WILL SPARE EARTH FURTHER PAIN.
OR DENY ME, AND WE WILL TEAR THROUGH WITHOUT YOU...AS GENOCIDE BRINGS SLAUGHTER TO BOTH SIDES.
TALK TO ME, HELEN--
MY NAME IS PAULA VON GUNTHER. HELEN IS THE LIE YOU USED TO HIDE MY POWER!
"YOU CAN'T SAVE EVERY-ONE. THE IDIOT HEROES YOU INSPIRE MUST FALL...
POLICE
"...BUT YOU COULD SAVE THE REST. THE POLICE. THE PEOPLE...IF YOU OPEN THE PORTAL.
THE ONLY QUESTION IS, HOW MANY OTHERS WILL DIE?
YOU WISH FOR MY ANSWER, THEN?

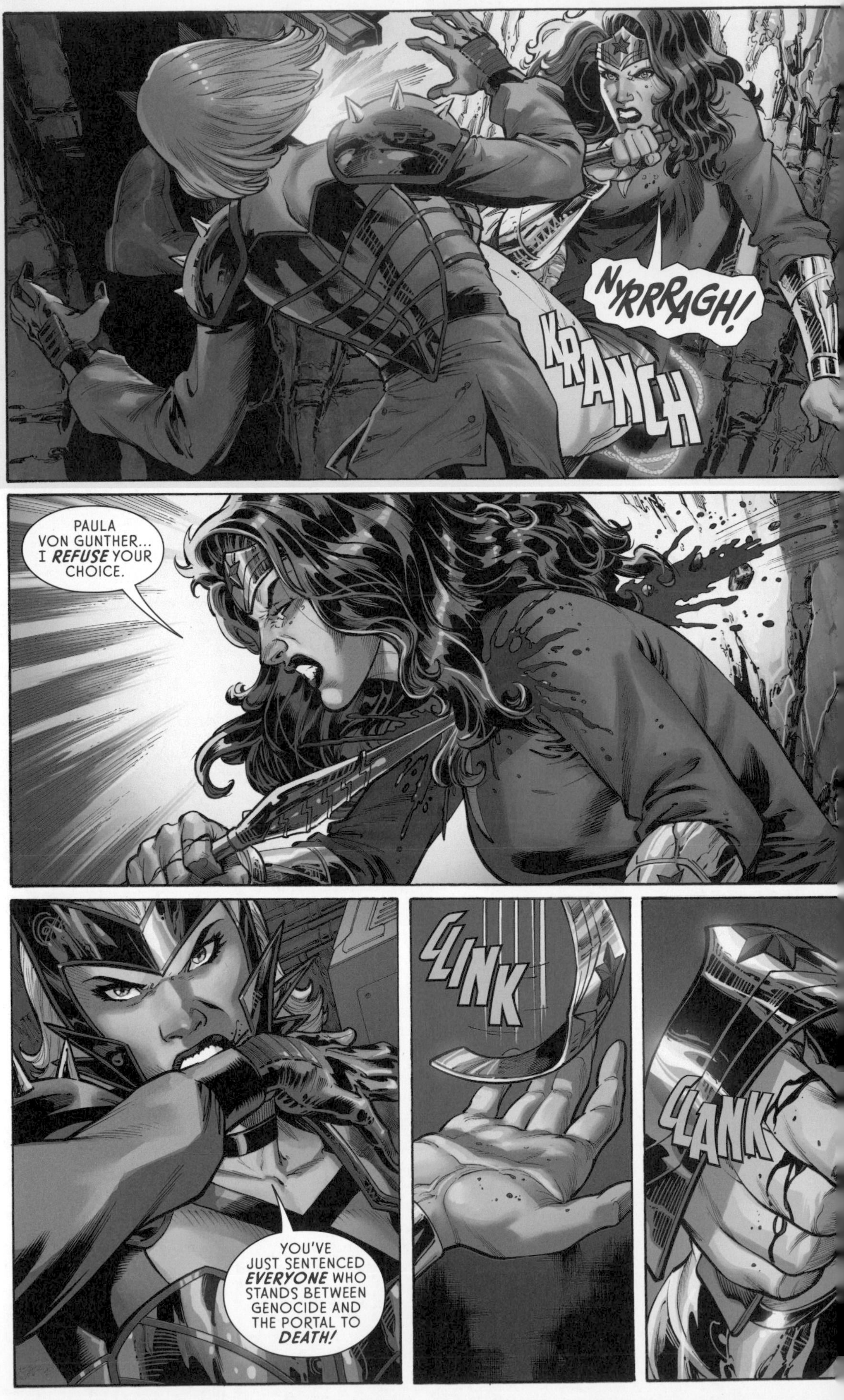
NYRRRAGH!
KRANCH
PAULA VON GUNTHER... I *REFUSE* YOUR CHOICE.
YOU'VE JUST SENTENCED *EVERYONE* WHO STANDS BETWEEN GENOCIDE AND THE PORTAL TO *DEATH!*
CLINK
CLANK

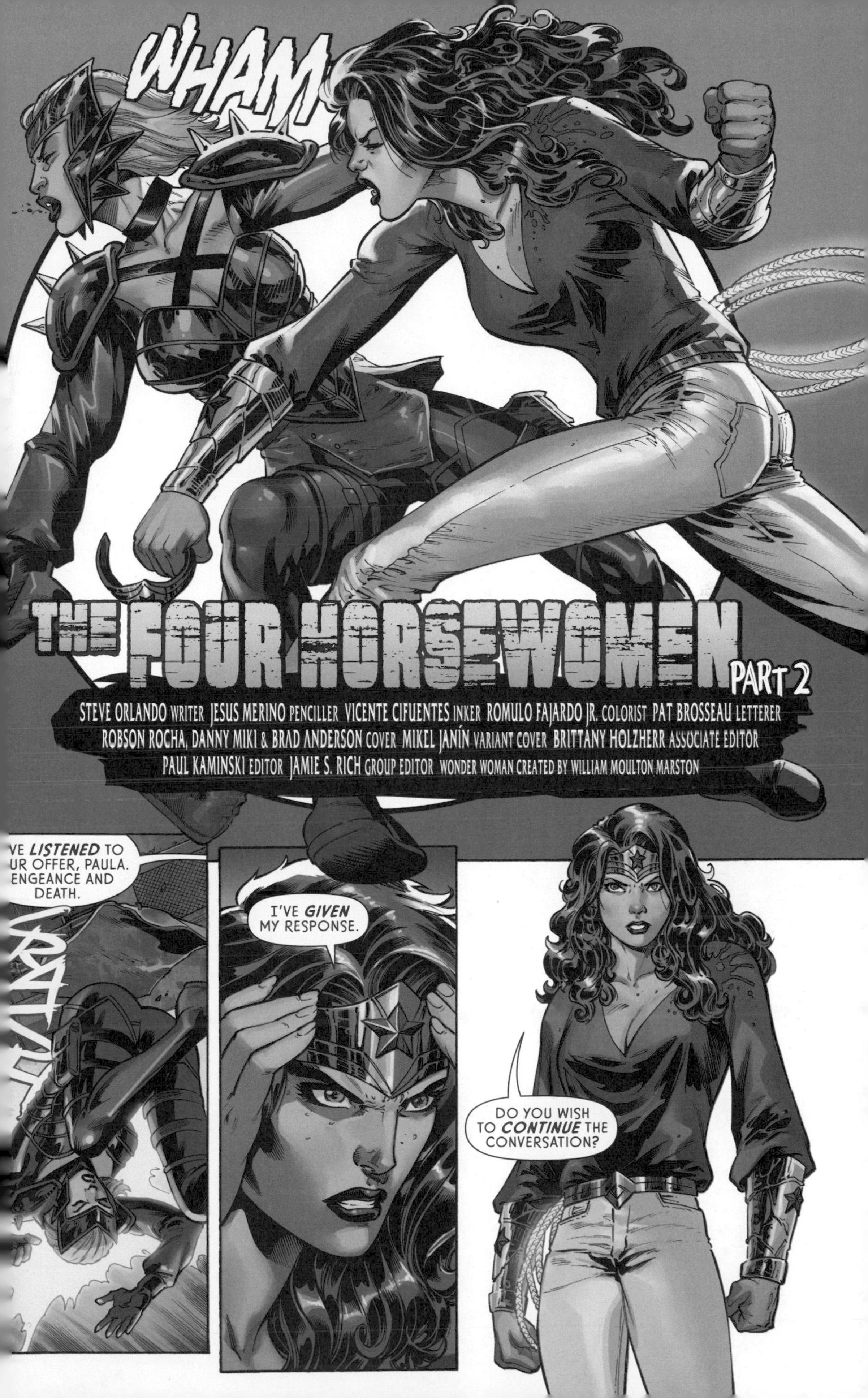
WHAM
THE FOUR HORSEWOMEN PART 2
STEVE ORLANDO WRITER JESUS MERINO PENCILLER VICENTE CIFUENTES INKER ROMULO FAJARDO JR. COLORIST PAT BROSSEAU LETTERER
ROBSON ROCHA, DANNY MIKI & BRAD ANDERSON COVER MIKEL JANÍN VARIANT COVER BRITTANY HOLZHERR ASSOCIATE EDITOR
PAUL KAMINSKI EDITOR JAMIE S. RICH GROUP EDITOR WONDER WOMAN CREATED BY WILLIAM MOULTON MARSTON
VE LISTENED TO UR OFFER, PAULA. ENGEANCE AND DEATH.
I'VE GIVEN MY RESPONSE.
DO YOU WISH TO CONTINUE THE CONVERSATION?

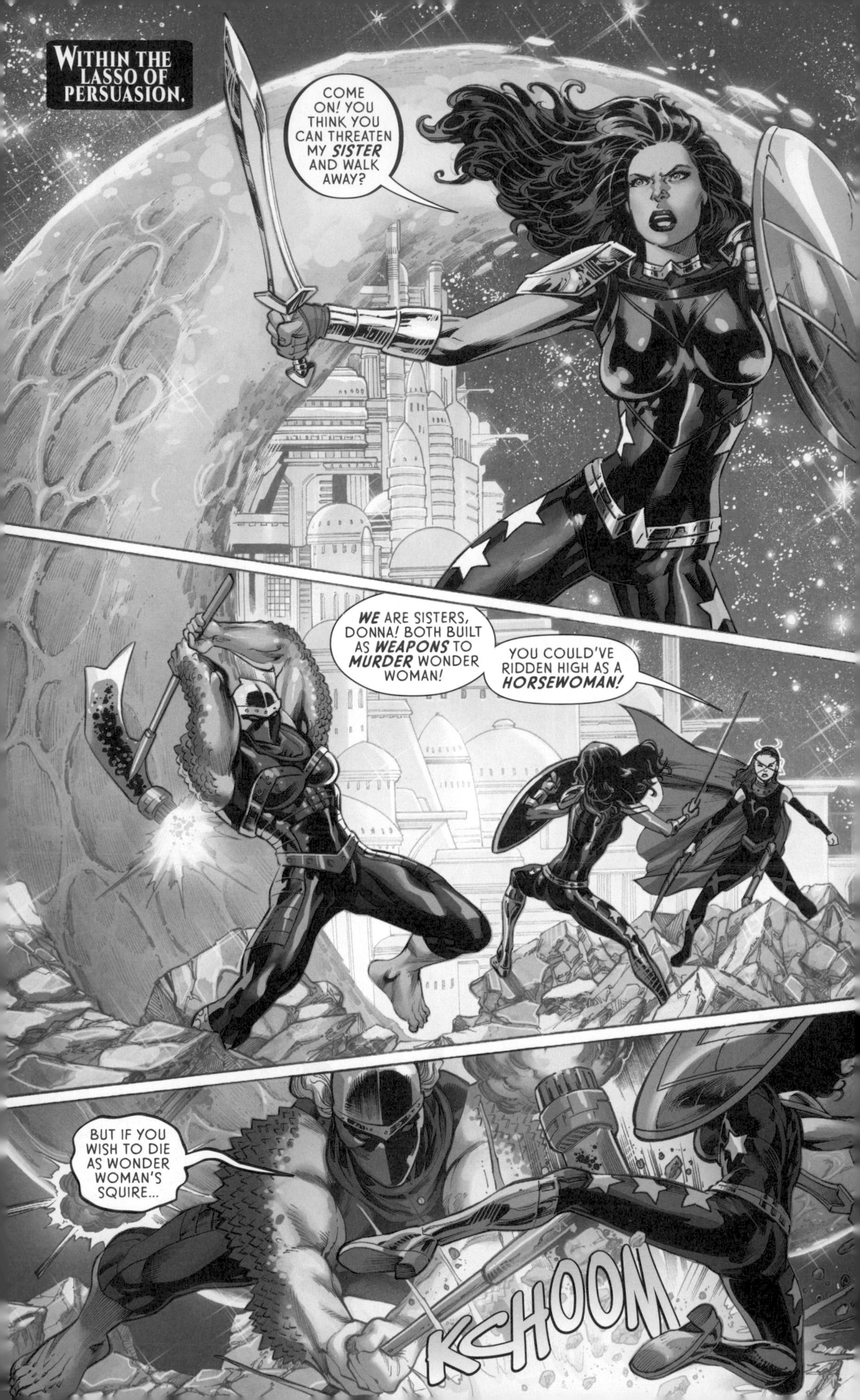
WITHIN THE LASSO OF PERSUASION.
COME ON! YOU THINK YOU CAN THREATEN MY SISTER AND WALK AWAY?
WE ARE SISTERS, DONNA! BOTH BUILT AS WEAPONS TO MURDER WONDER WOMAN!
YOU COULD'VE RIDDEN HIGH AS A HORSEWOMAN!
BUT IF YOU WISH TO DIE AS WONDER WOMAN'S SQUIRE...
KCHOOM

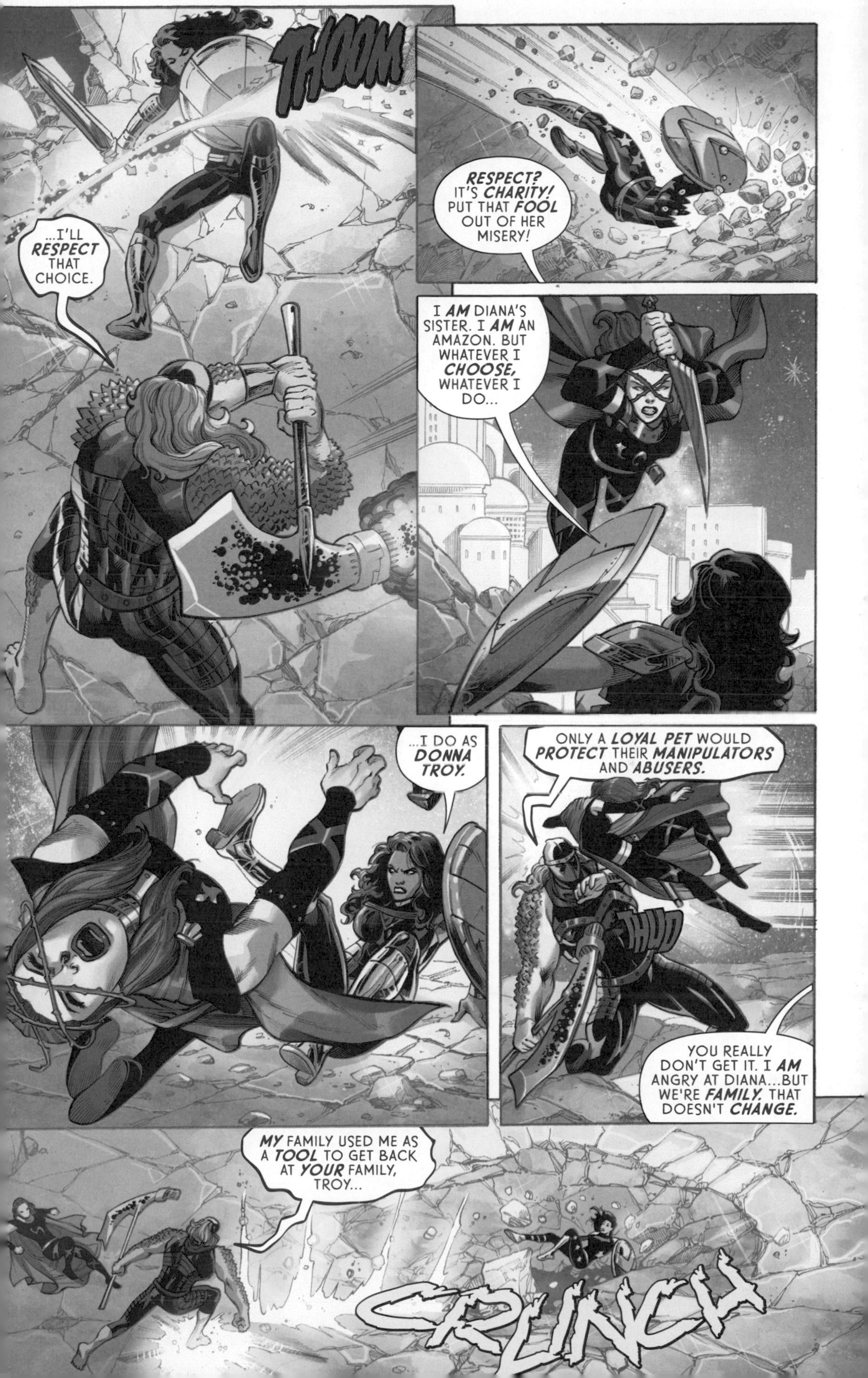
THOOM
...I'LL RESPECT THAT CHOICE.
RESPECT? IT'S CHARITY! PUT THAT FOOL OUT OF HER MISERY!
I AM DIANA'S SISTER. I AM AN AMAZON. BUT WHATEVER I CHOOSE, WHATEVER I DO...
...I DO AS DONNA TROY.
ONLY A LOYAL PET WOULD PROTECT THEIR MANIPULATORS AND ABUSERS.
THUD
YOU REALLY DON'T GET IT. I AM ANGRY AT DIANA...BUT WE'RE FAMILY. THAT DOESN'T CHANGE.
MY FAMILY USED ME AS A TOOL TO GET BACK AT YOUR FAMILY, TROY...
CRUNCH

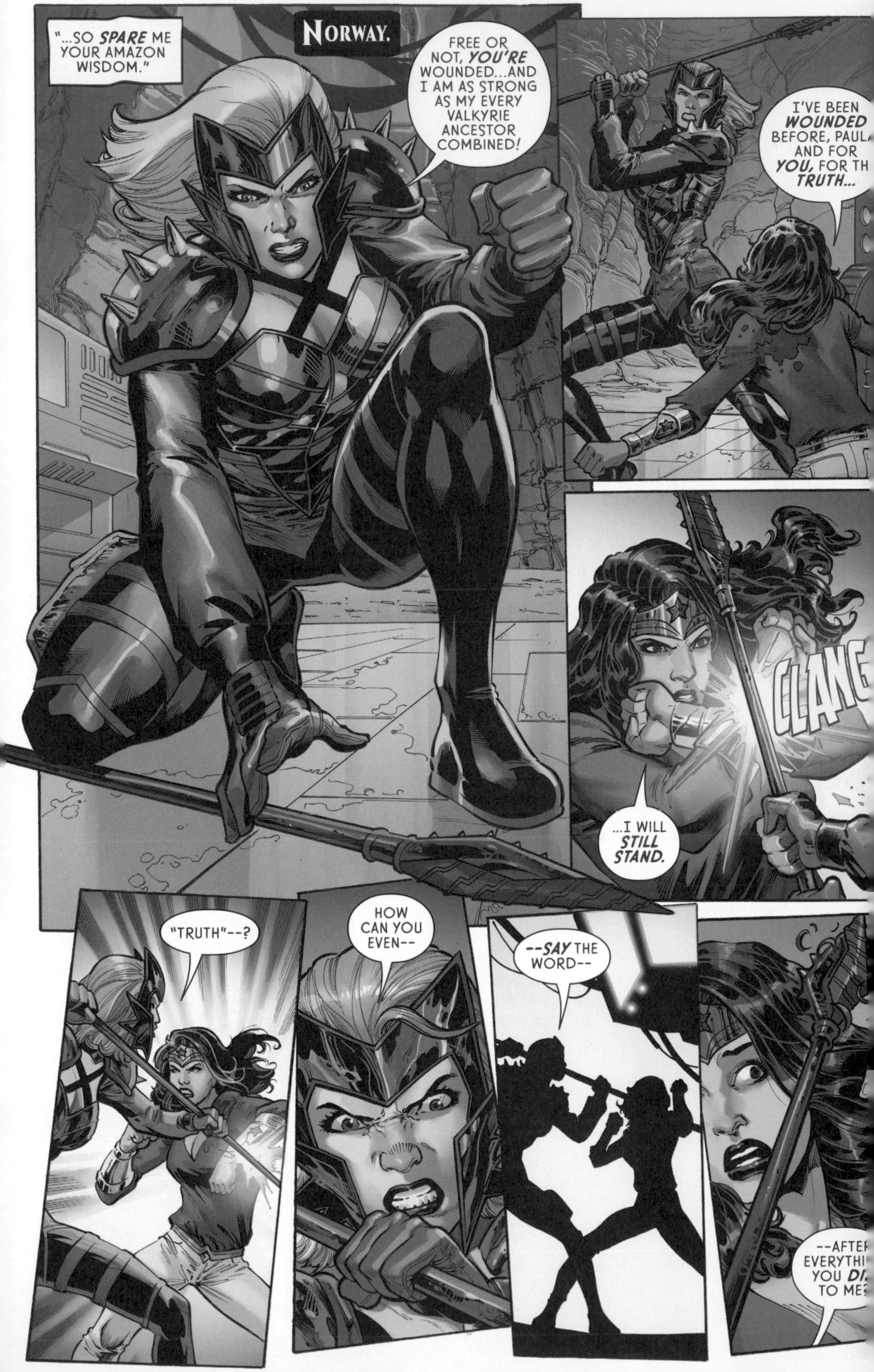
"...SO SPARE ME YOUR AMAZON WISDOM."
NORWAY.
FREE OR NOT, YOU'RE WOUNDED...AND I AM AS STRONG AS MY EVERY VALKYRIE ANCESTOR COMBINED!
I'VE BEEN WOUNDED BEFORE, PAUL, AND FOR YOU, FOR TH TRUTH...
CLANG
...I WILL STILL STAND.
"TRUTH"--?
HOW CAN YOU EVEN--
--SAY THE WORD--
--AFTER EVERYTHI YOU DI TO ME?

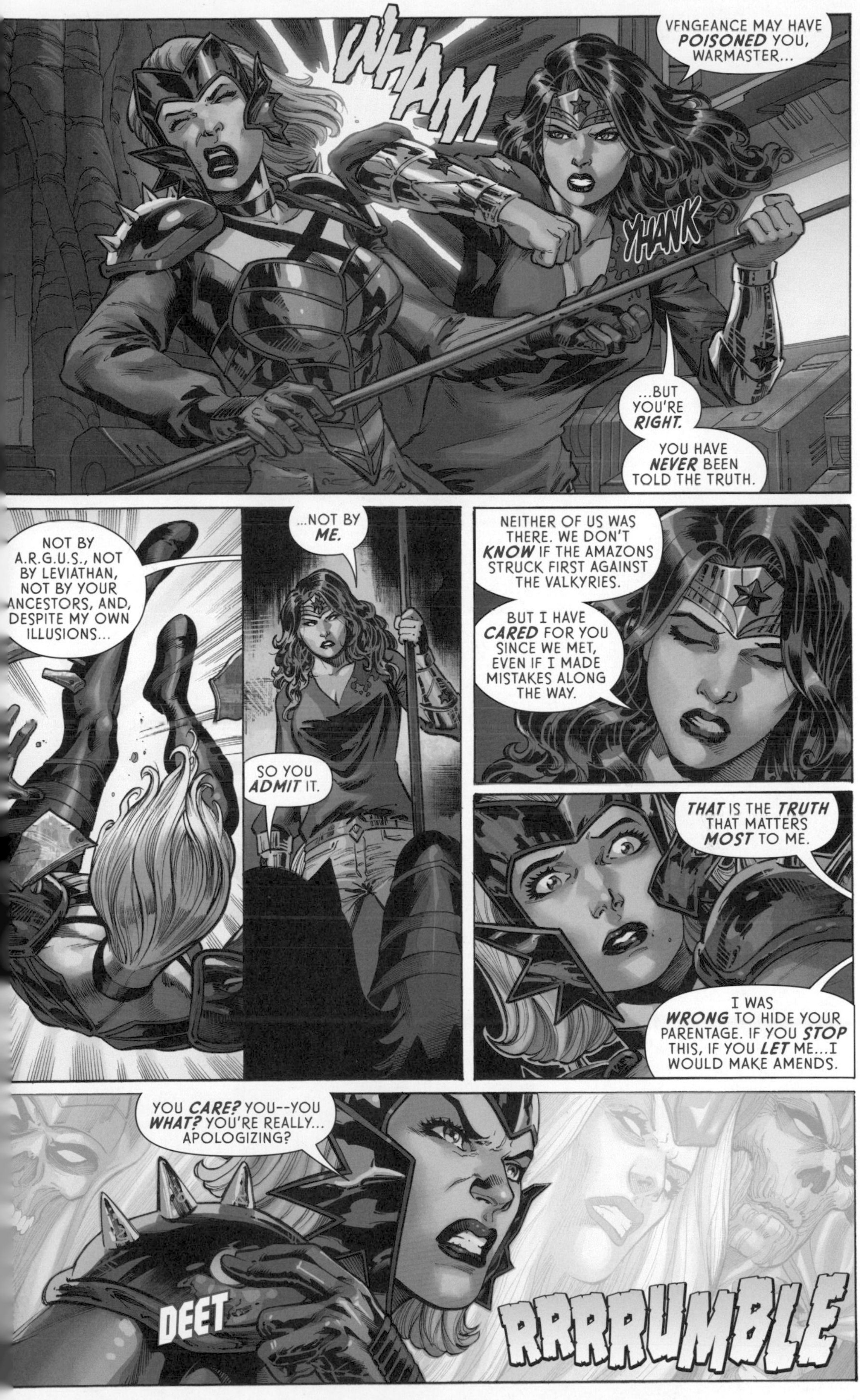
WHAM
VENGEANCE MAY HAVE POISONED YOU, WARMASTER...
YHANK
...BUT YOU'RE RIGHT.
YOU HAVE NEVER BEEN TOLD THE TRUTH.
NOT BY A.R.G.U.S., NOT BY LEVIATHAN, NOT BY YOUR ANCESTORS, AND, DESPITE MY OWN ILLUSIONS...
...NOT BY ME.
SO YOU ADMIT IT.
NEITHER OF US WAS THERE. WE DON'T KNOW IF THE AMAZONS STRUCK FIRST AGAINST THE VALKYRIES.
BUT I HAVE CARED FOR YOU SINCE WE MET, EVEN IF I MADE MISTAKES ALONG THE WAY.
THAT IS THE TRUTH THAT MATTERS MOST TO ME.
I WAS WRONG TO HIDE YOUR PARENTAGE. IF YOU STOP THIS, IF YOU LET ME...I WOULD MAKE AMENDS.
YOU CARE? YOU--YOU WHAT? YOU'RE REALLY... APOLOGIZING?
DEET
RRRRUMBLE

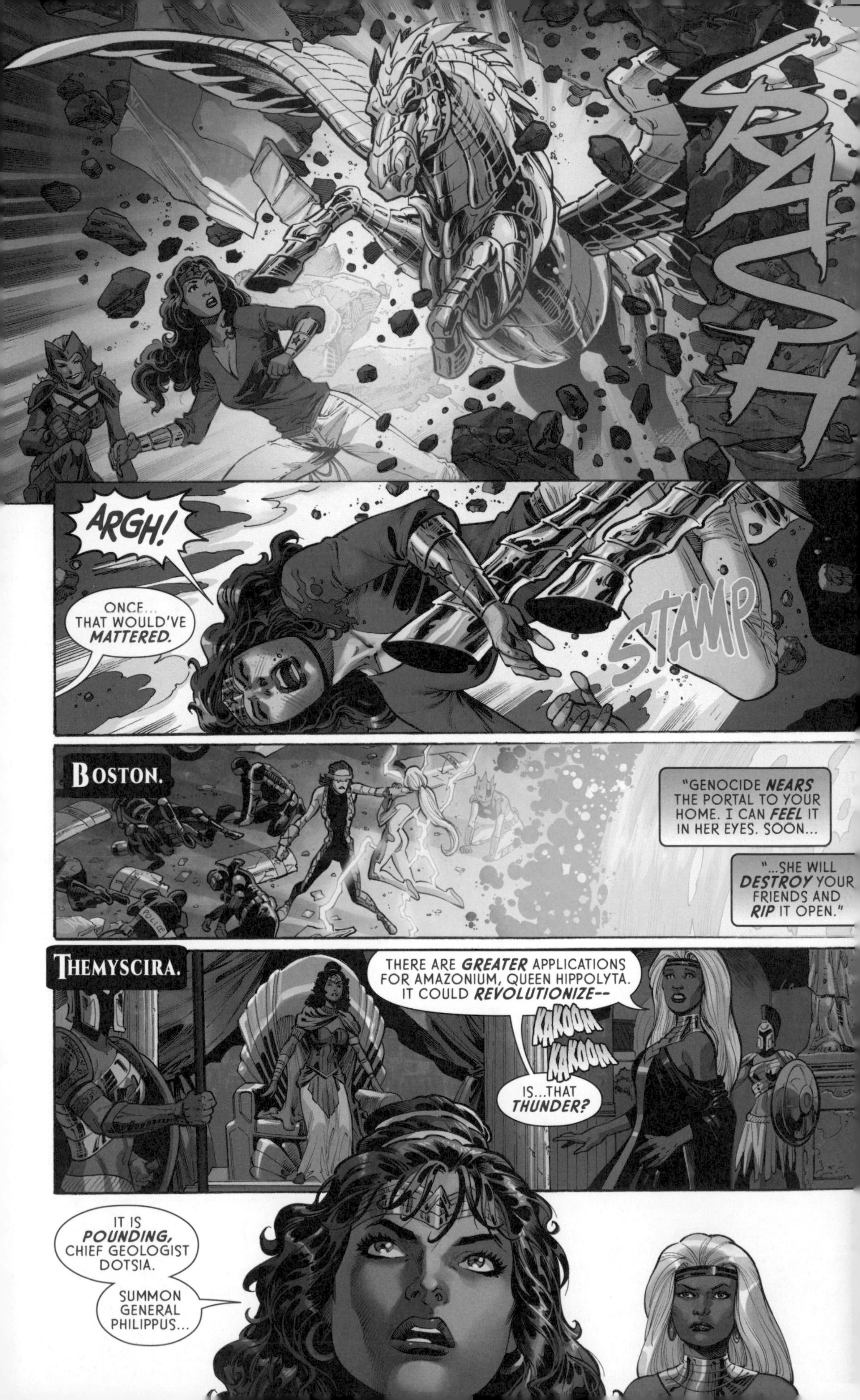
CRASH
ARGH!
ONCE... THAT WOULD'VE MATTERED.
STAMP
BOSTON.
"GENOCIDE NEARS THE PORTAL TO YOUR HOME. I CAN FEEL IT IN HER EYES. SOON...
"...SHE WILL DESTROY YOUR FRIENDS AND RIP IT OPEN."
THEMYSCIRA.
THERE ARE GREATER APPLICATIONS FOR AMAZONIUM, QUEEN HIPPOLYTA. IT COULD REVOLUTIONIZE--
KAKOOM KAKOOM
IS...THAT THUNDER?
IT IS POUNDING, CHIEF GEOLOGIST DOTSIA.
SUMMON GENERAL PHILIPPUS...

"...AND PREPARE
OURSELF TO BREAK
ORE THAN ROCKS."
FIND THE BODY...TROY MIGHT BE OUR ONLY WAY OUT OF THIS DAMNED REALM.
VON GUNTHER WILL WANT HER WEAPONS AS TROPHIES...NOW THAT TROY'S OFF THE BOARD.
OFF THE BOARD?
CLANGK
I'M JUST
TEPPING BACK
OUT ONTO IT!
KRACK
DON'T, TROY!
IDIOT! YOU CAN'T--
YOU--

MANHATTAN.

WHAT--WHAT *WAS* THAT? SOME TYPE OF *ILLUSION?* WHAT HAVE YOU *DONE* TO US, TROY?!

PUT YOU IN *MY* LASSO, DEVASTATION. THE *LASSO OF PERSUASION.* PEOPLE WERE *SAFE* OUT HERE. AND *THERE?*

EACH TIME I USE IT, IT'S A RISK. WE GO *INSIDE* FOR THE BATTLE OF WILLS...WITH NO GUARANTEE I *WIN.*

I'LL FEED... YOU MY FIST...

PROBABLY *NOT.* I'M STILL *UNDEFEATED* ON THE INSIDE. SO ON THE *OUTSIDE*...NOW YOU DO WHAT I SAY.

AND *I SAY* YOU'R GOING TO TELL M *EVERYTHING* ABOUT THIS ATTAC ON DIANA. AND THEN...

...YOU'RE GOING TO SIT DOWN AND SHUT UP UNTIL THE *JUSTICE LEAGUE* ARRIVES.

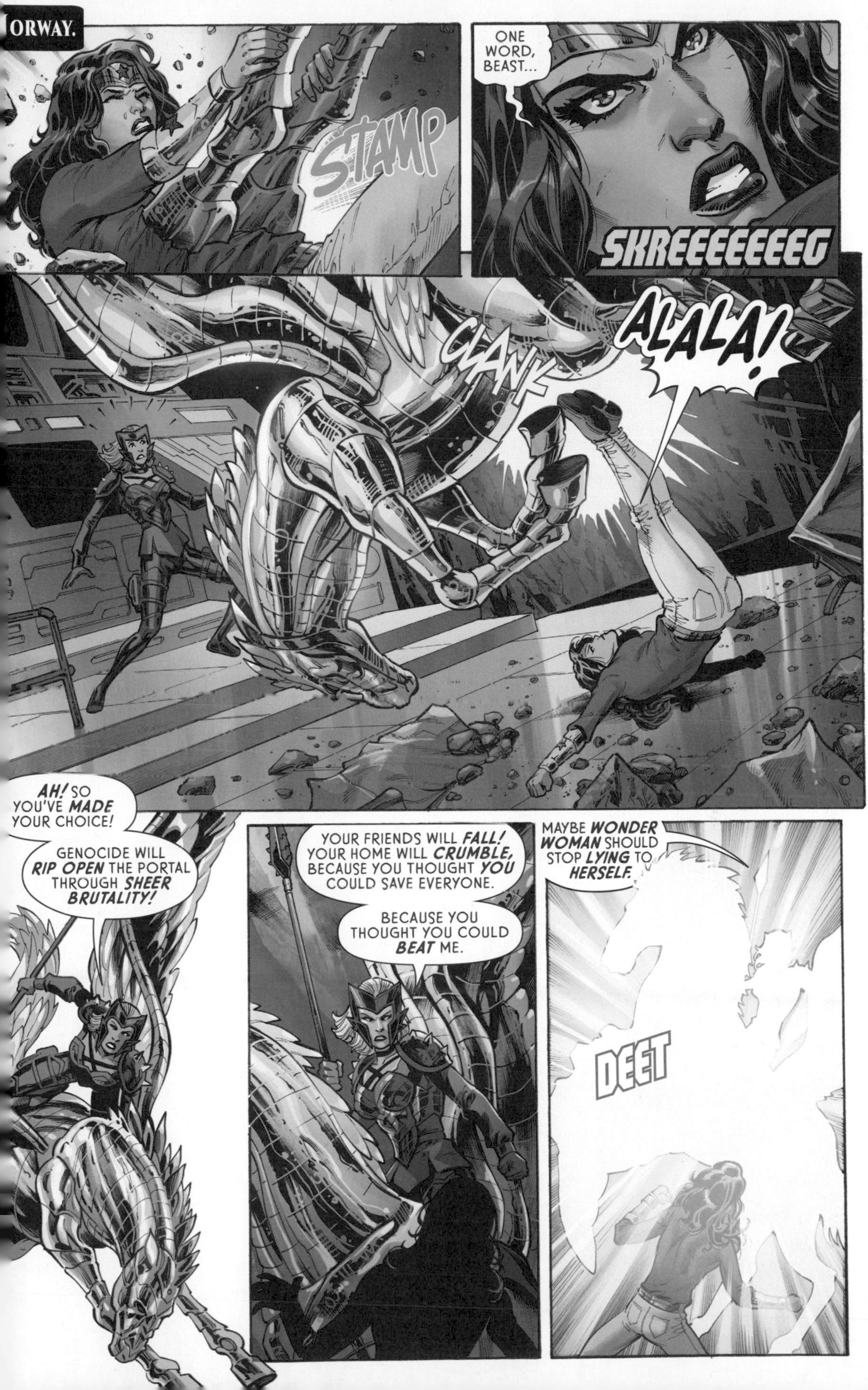
ORWAY.
STAMP
ONE WORD, BEAST...
SKREEEEEEEG
CLANK
ALALA!
AH! SO YOU'VE MADE YOUR CHOICE!
GENOCIDE WILL RIP OPEN THE PORTAL THROUGH SHEER BRUTALITY!
YOUR FRIENDS WILL FALL! YOUR HOME WILL CRUMBLE, BECAUSE YOU THOUGHT YOU COULD SAVE EVERYONE.
BECAUSE YOU THOUGHT YOU COULD BEAT ME.
MAYBE WONDER WOMAN SHOULD STOP LYING TO HERSELF.
DEET

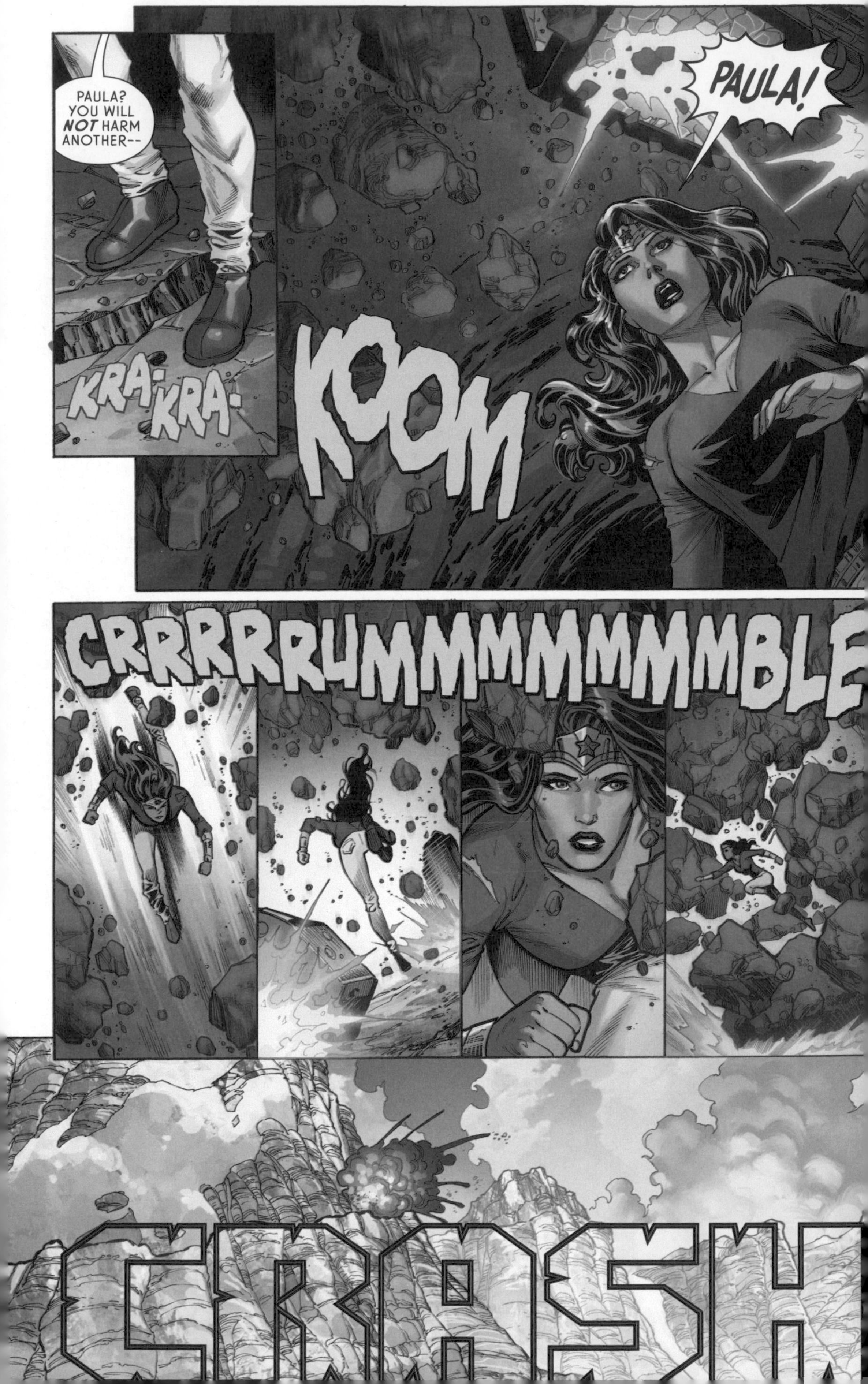

PAULA? YOU WILL NOT HARM ANOTHER--
KRA-KRA-
PAULA!
KOOM
CRRRRRUMMMMMMMMBLE
CRASH

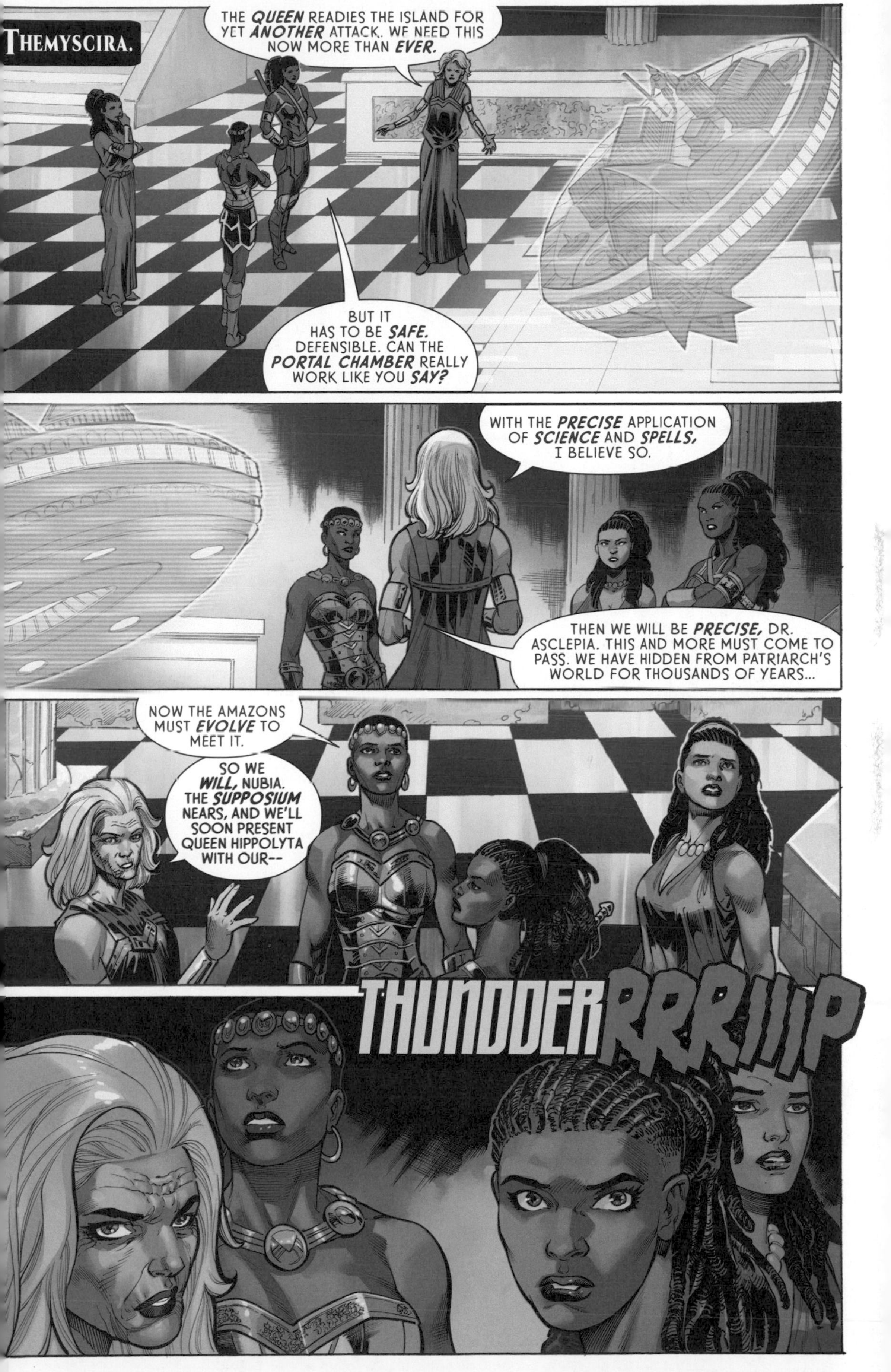
THEMYSCIRA.
THE QUEEN READIES THE ISLAND FOR YET ANOTHER ATTACK. WE NEED THIS NOW MORE THAN EVER.
BUT IT HAS TO BE SAFE. DEFENSIBLE. CAN THE PORTAL CHAMBER REALLY WORK LIKE YOU SAY?
WITH THE PRECISE APPLICATION OF SCIENCE AND SPELLS, I BELIEVE SO.
THEN WE WILL BE PRECISE, DR. ASCLEPIA. THIS AND MORE MUST COME TO PASS. WE HAVE HIDDEN FROM PATRIARCH'S WORLD FOR THOUSANDS OF YEARS...
NOW THE AMAZONS MUST EVOLVE TO MEET IT.
SO WE WILL, NUBIA. THE SUPPOSIUM NEARS, AND WE'LL SOON PRESENT QUEEN HIPPOLYTA WITH OUR--
THUNDDERRRRIIIP

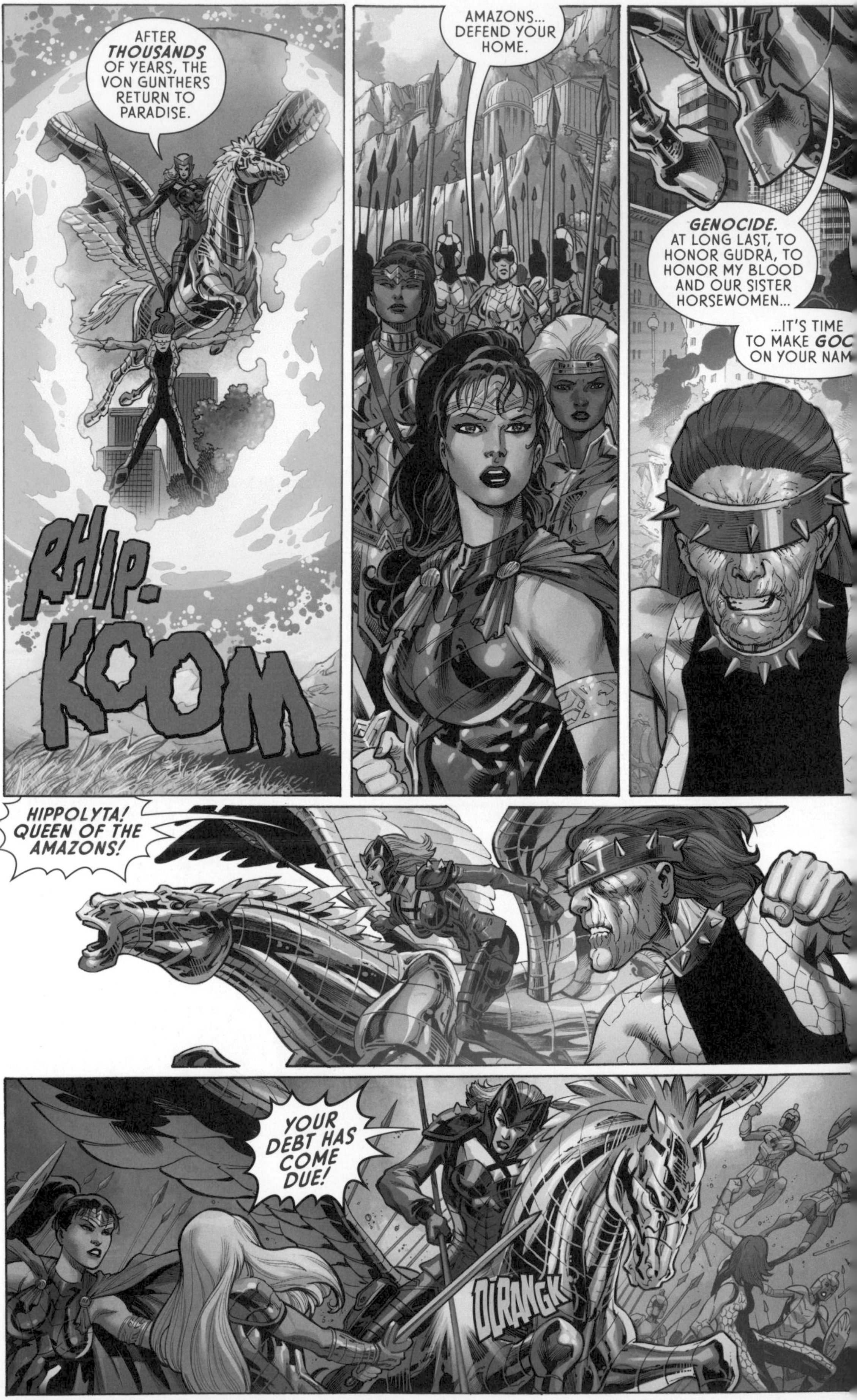
AFTER THOUSANDS OF YEARS, THE VON GUNTHERS RETURN TO PARADISE.
RHIP-KOOM
AMAZONS... DEFEND YOUR HOME.
GENOCIDE. AT LONG LAST, TO HONOR GUDRA, TO HONOR MY BLOOD AND OUR SISTER HORSEWOMEN...
...IT'S TIME TO MAKE GOC ON YOUR NAM
HIPPOLYTA! QUEEN OF THE AMAZONS!
YOUR DEBT HAS COME DUE!
DLRANGK

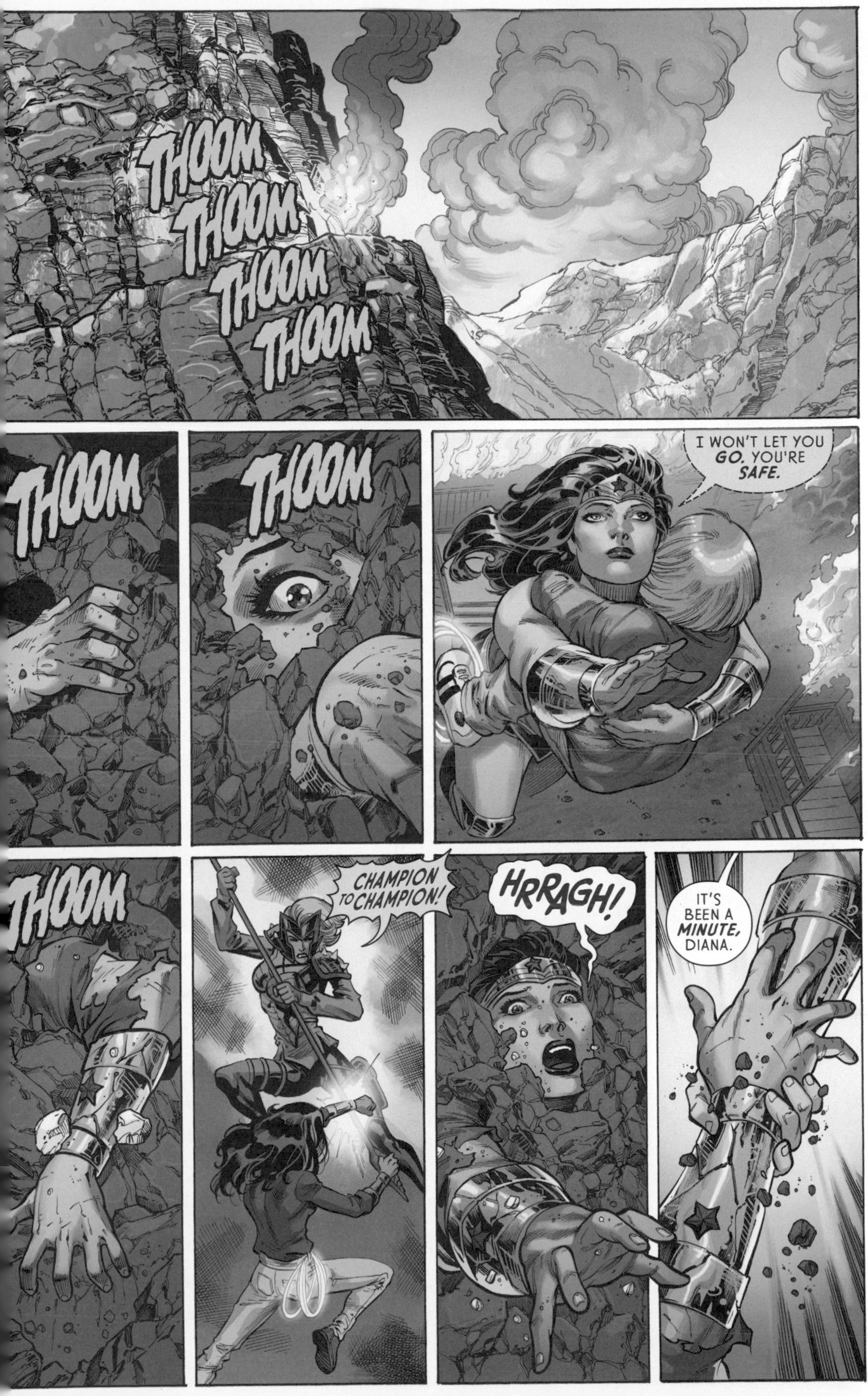
THOOM
THOOM
THOOM
THOOM
THOOM
THOOM
I WON'T LET YOU GO. YOU'RE SAFE.
THOOM
CHAMPION TO CHAMPION!
HRRAGH!
IT'S BEEN A MINUTE, DIANA.

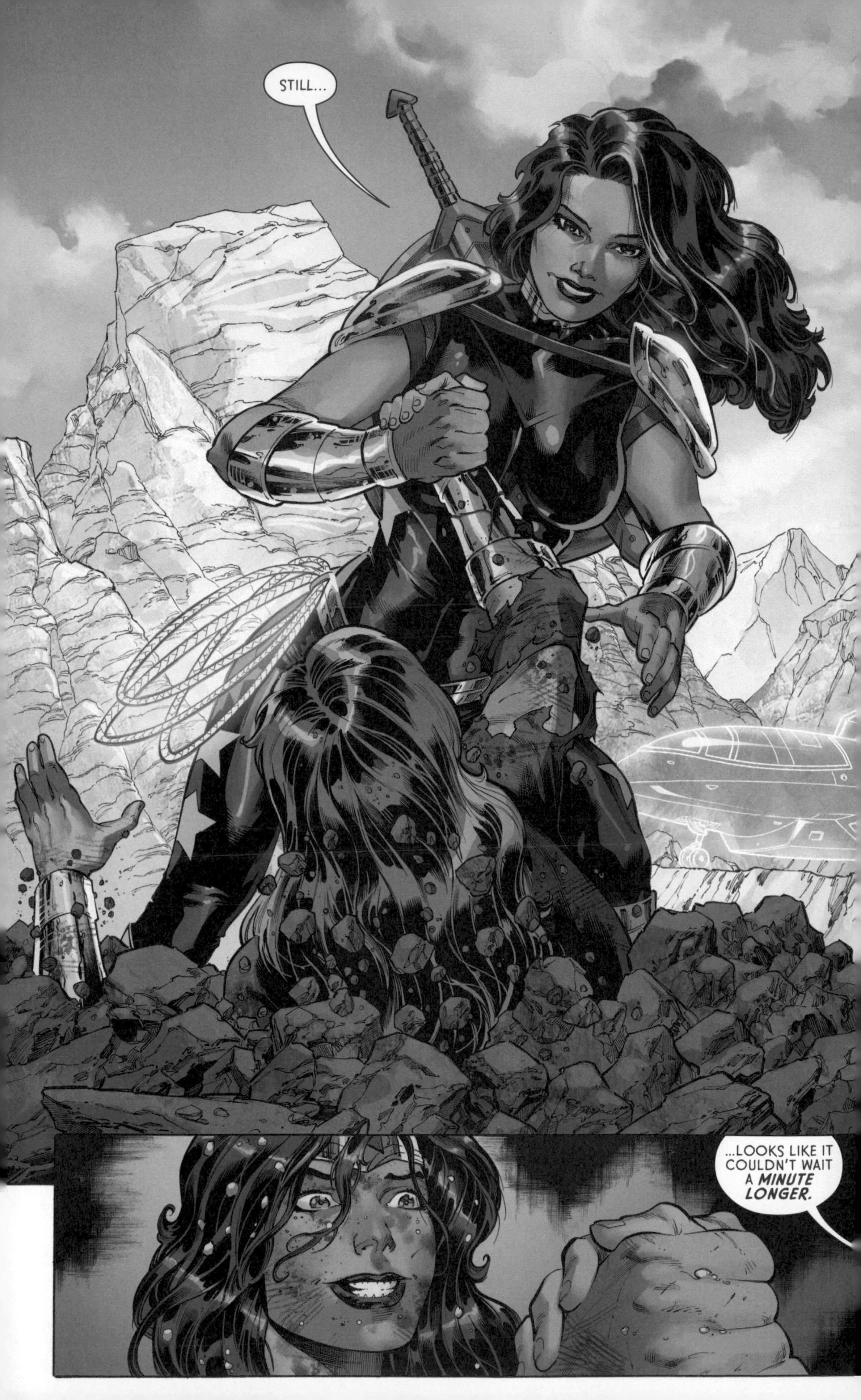
STILL...
...LOOKS LIKE IT COULDN'T WAIT A *MINUTE LONGER.*

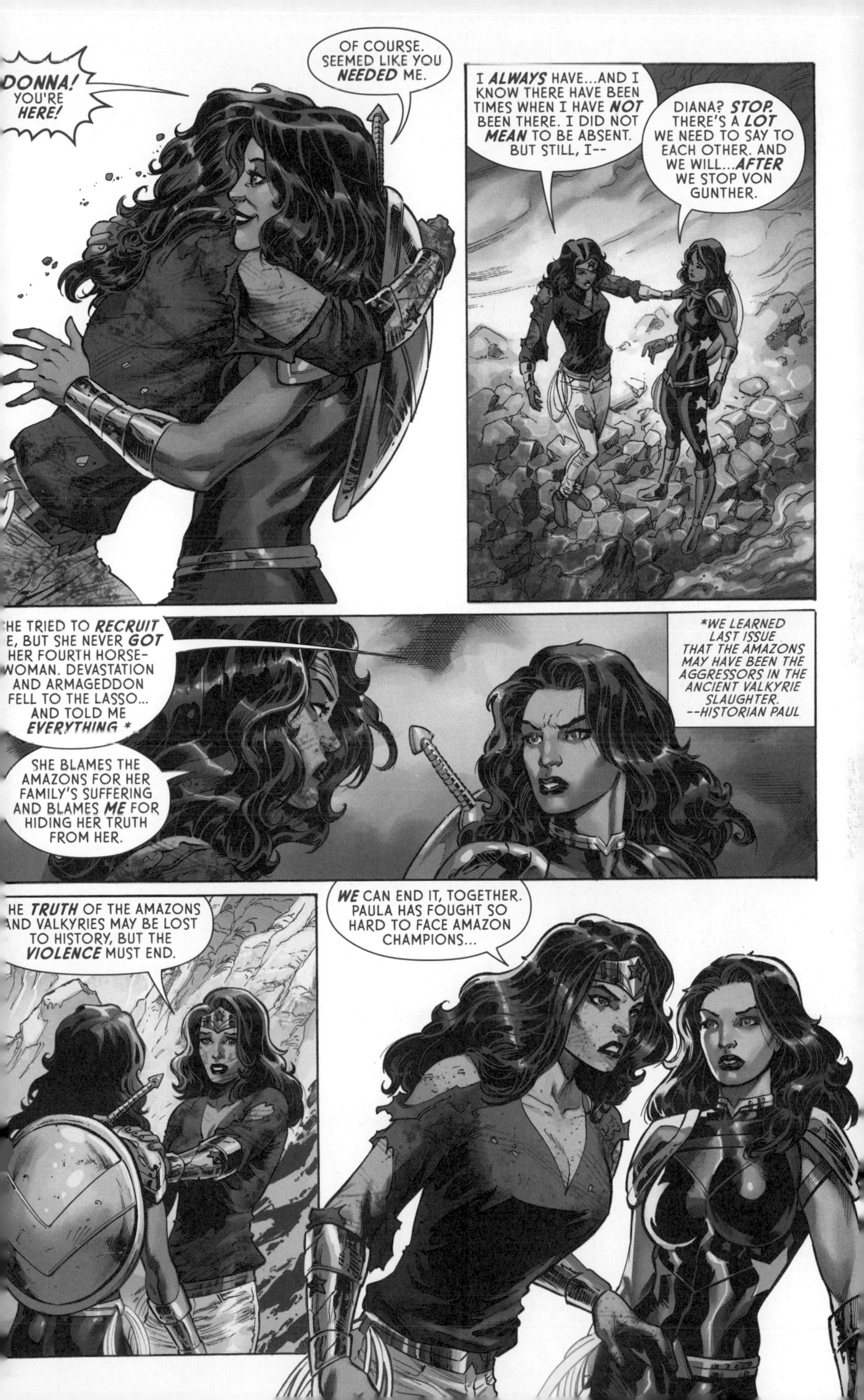
DONNA! YOU'RE HERE!
OF COURSE. SEEMED LIKE YOU NEEDED ME.
I ALWAYS HAVE...AND I KNOW THERE HAVE BEEN TIMES WHEN I HAVE NOT BEEN THERE. I DID NOT MEAN TO BE ABSENT. BUT STILL, I--
DIANA? STOP. THERE'S A LOT WE NEED TO SAY TO EACH OTHER. AND WE WILL...AFTER WE STOP VON GUNTHER.
HE TRIED TO RECRUIT E, BUT SHE NEVER GOT HER FOURTH HORSE-WOMAN. DEVASTATION AND ARMAGEDDON FELL TO THE LASSO... AND TOLD ME EVERYTHING *
*WE LEARNED LAST ISSUE THAT THE AMAZONS MAY HAVE BEEN THE AGGRESSORS IN THE ANCIENT VALKYRIE SLAUGHTER. --HISTORIAN PAUL
SHE BLAMES THE AMAZONS FOR HER FAMILY'S SUFFERING AND BLAMES ME FOR HIDING HER TRUTH FROM HER.
HE TRUTH OF THE AMAZONS ND VALKYRIES MAY BE LOST TO HISTORY, BUT THE VIOLENCE MUST END.
WE CAN END IT, TOGETHER. PAULA HAS FOUGHT SO HARD TO FACE AMAZON CHAMPIONS...

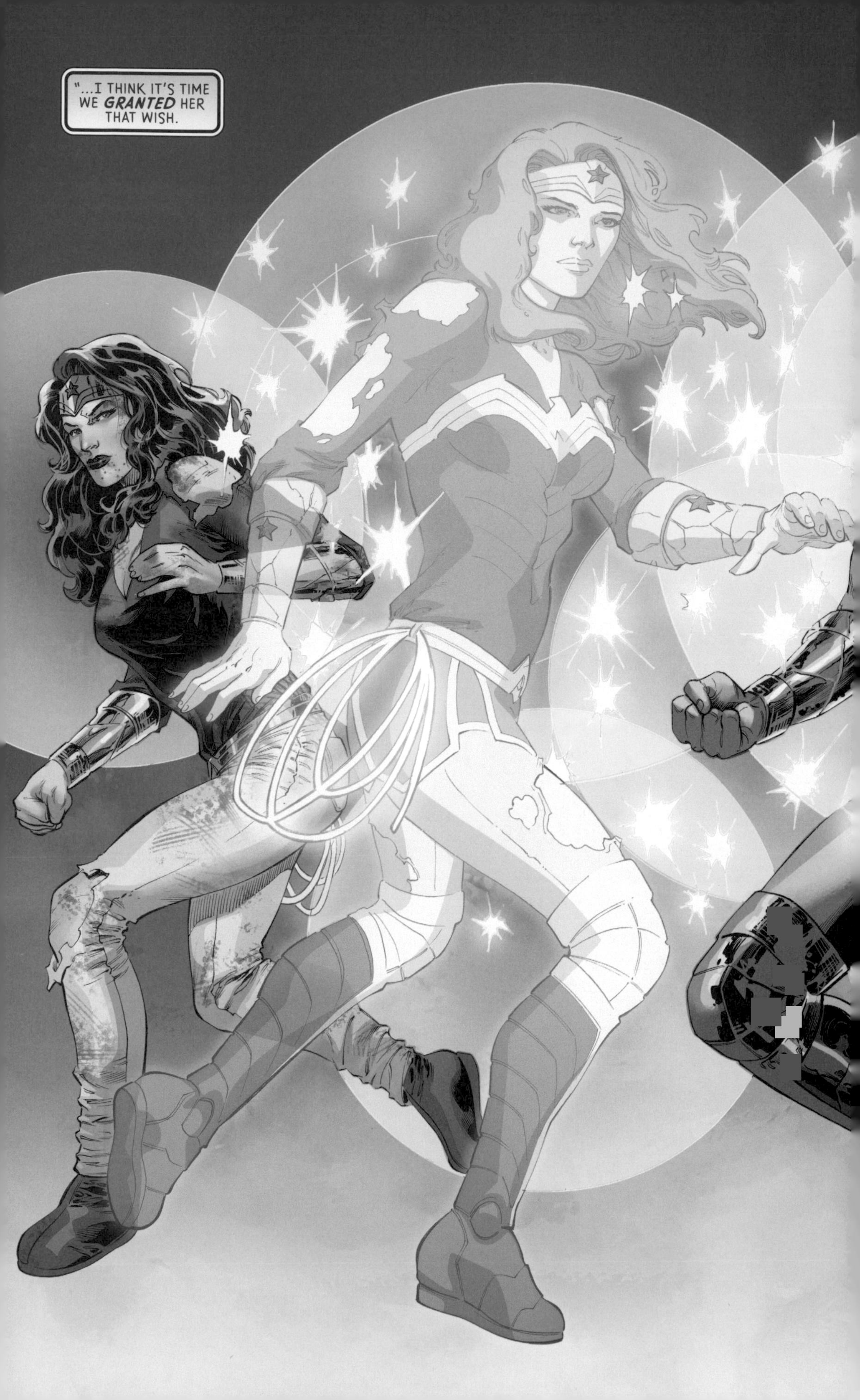
"...I THINK IT'S TIME WE GRANTED HER THAT WISH.

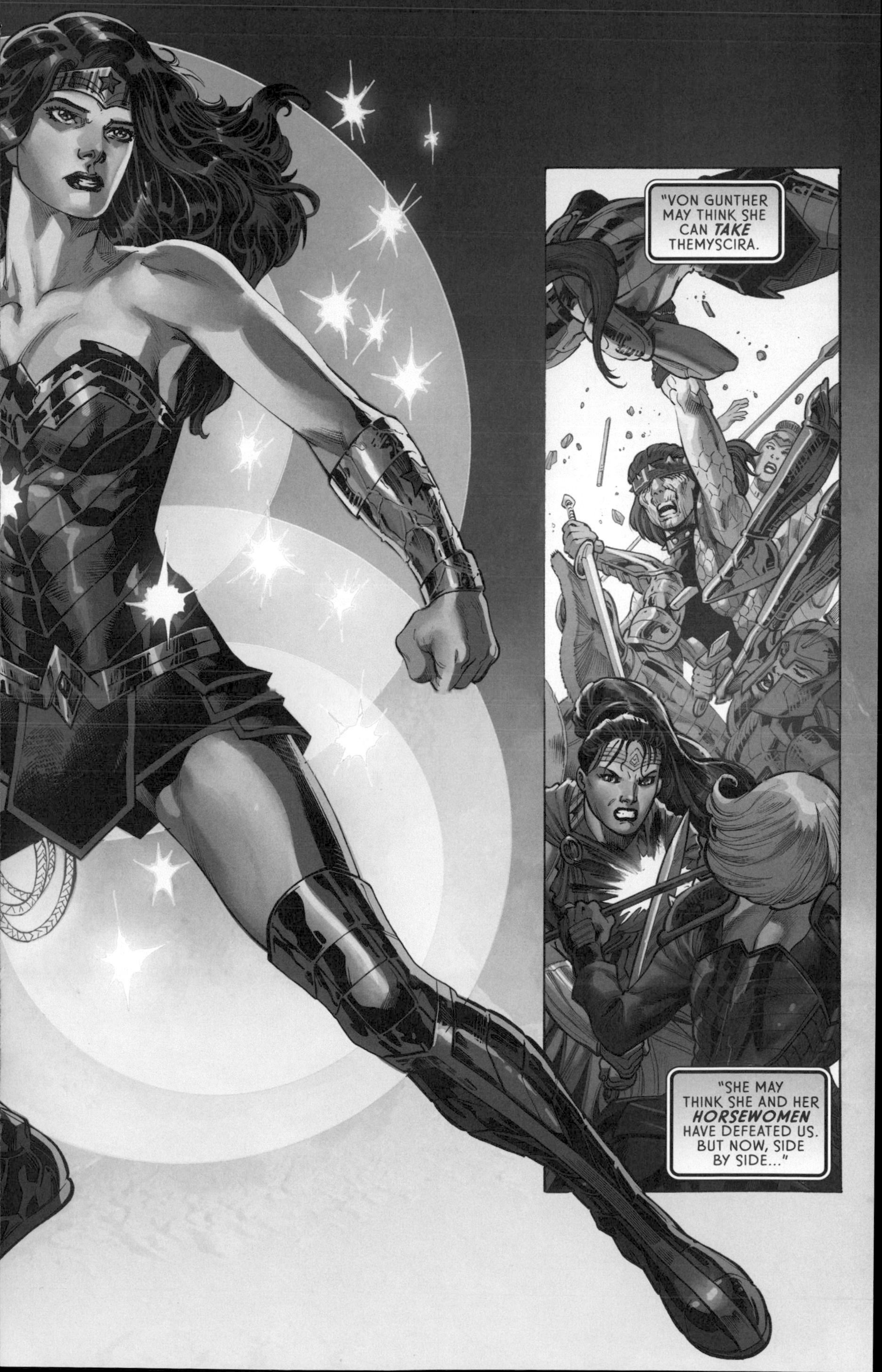
"VON GUNTHER MAY THINK SHE CAN *TAKE* THEMYSCIRA.
"SHE MAY THINK SHE AND HER ***HORSEWOMEN*** HAVE DEFEATED US. BUT NOW, SIDE BY SIDE..."

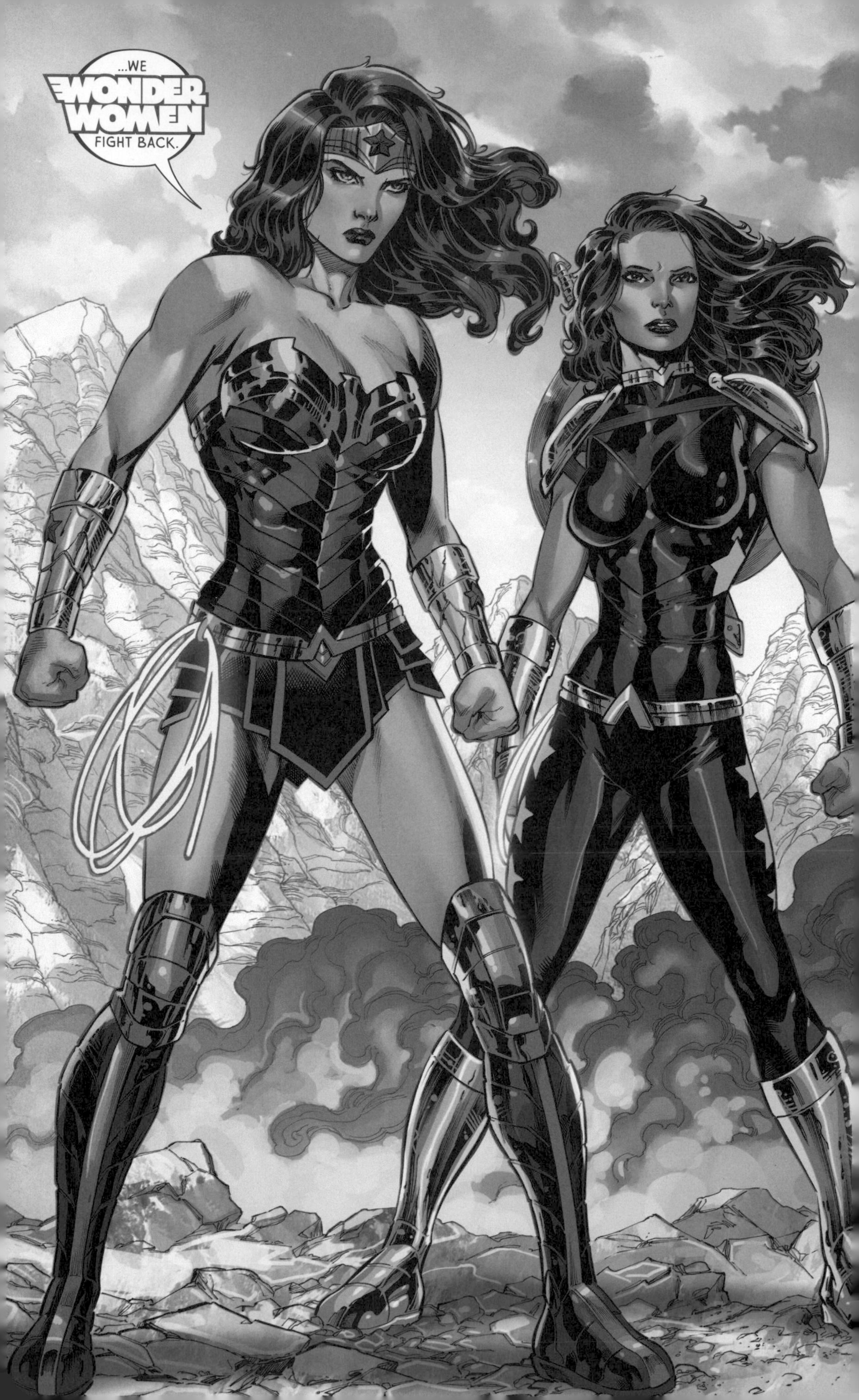
...WE WONDER WOMEN FIGHT BACK.

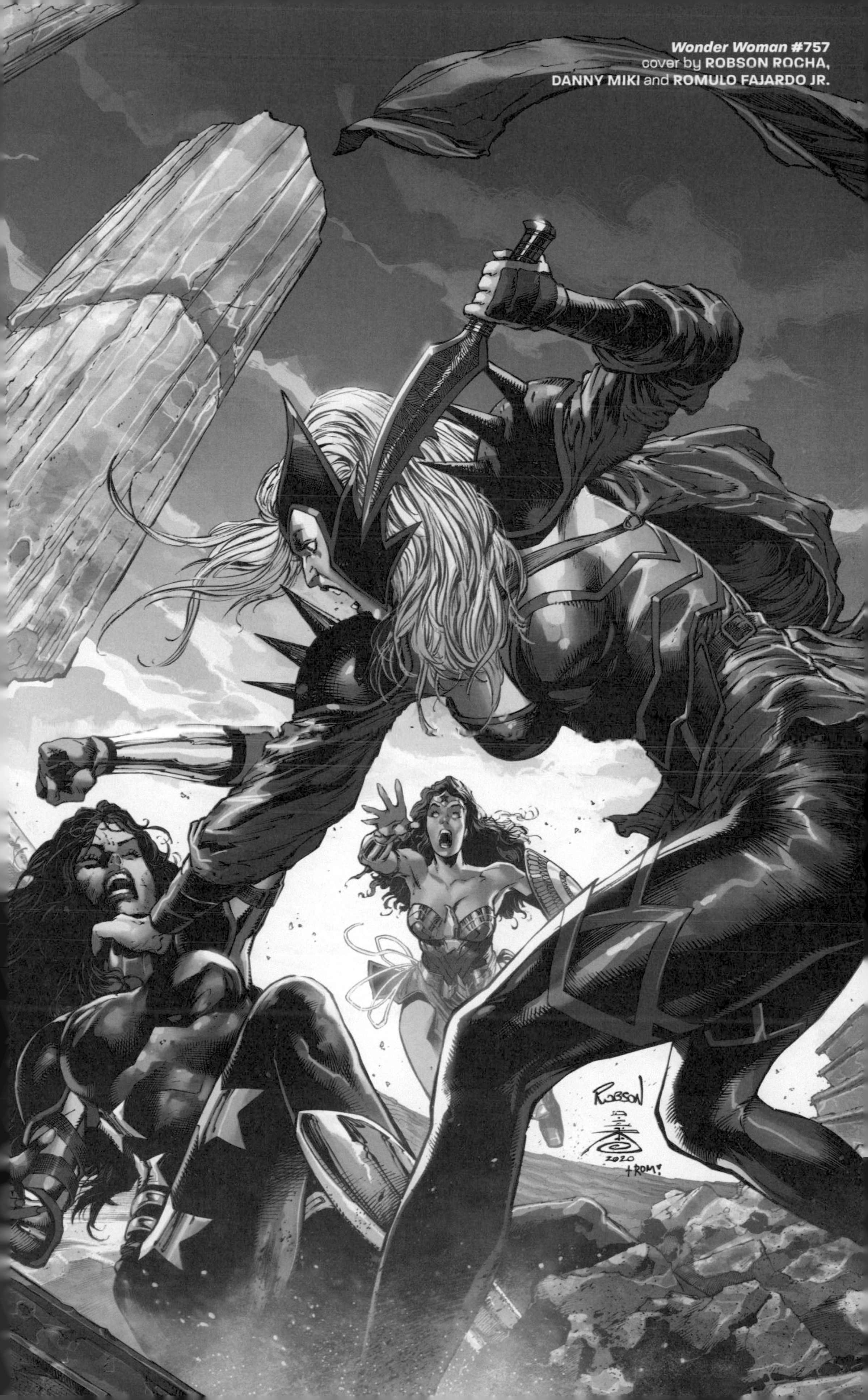
ROBSON
2020
+ROM!

Wonder Woman #757
cover by ROBSON ROCHA,
DANNY MIKI and ROMULO FAJARDO JR.

***Wonder Woman* #757**
variant cover by **OLIVIER COIPEL**

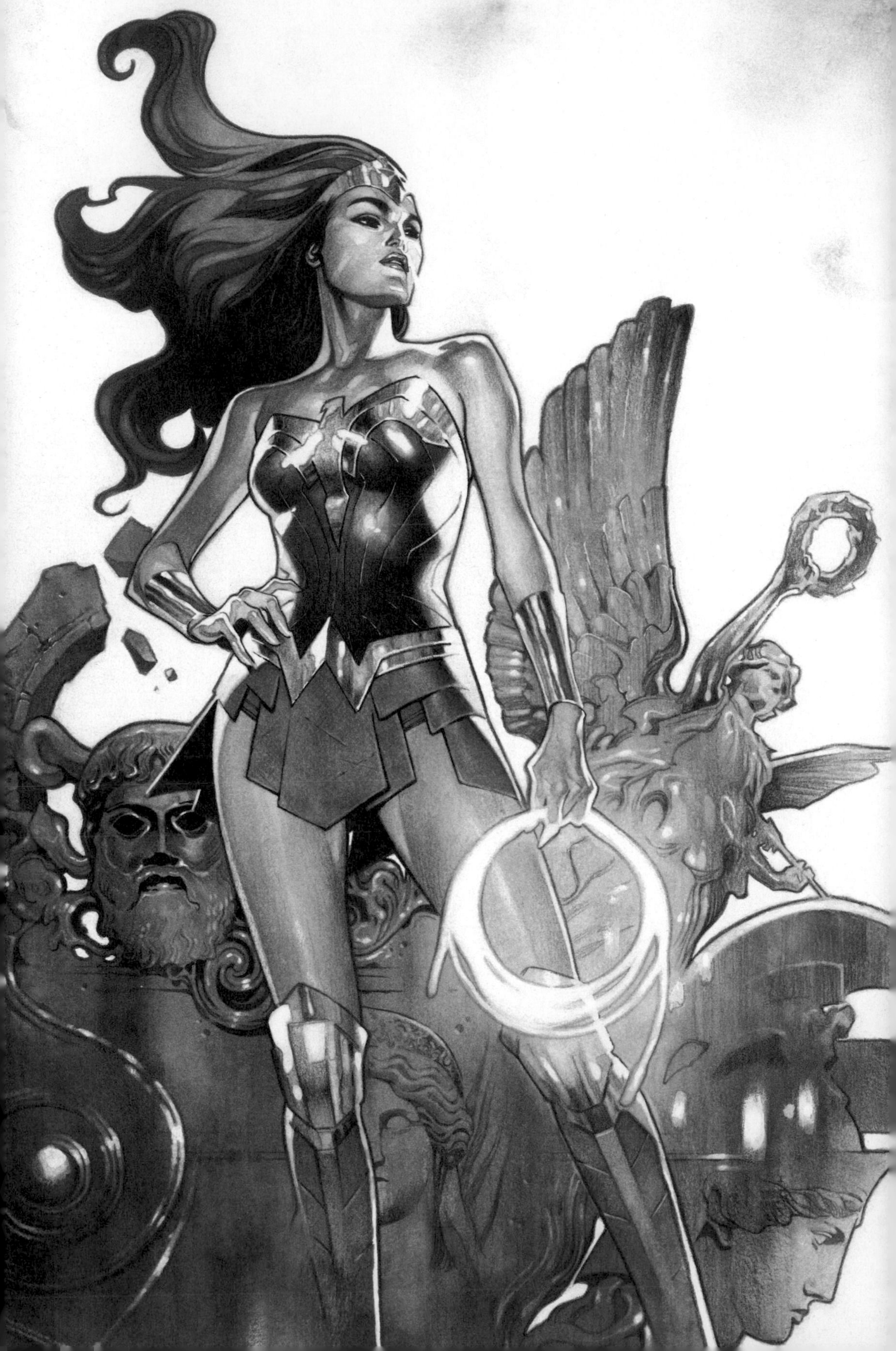

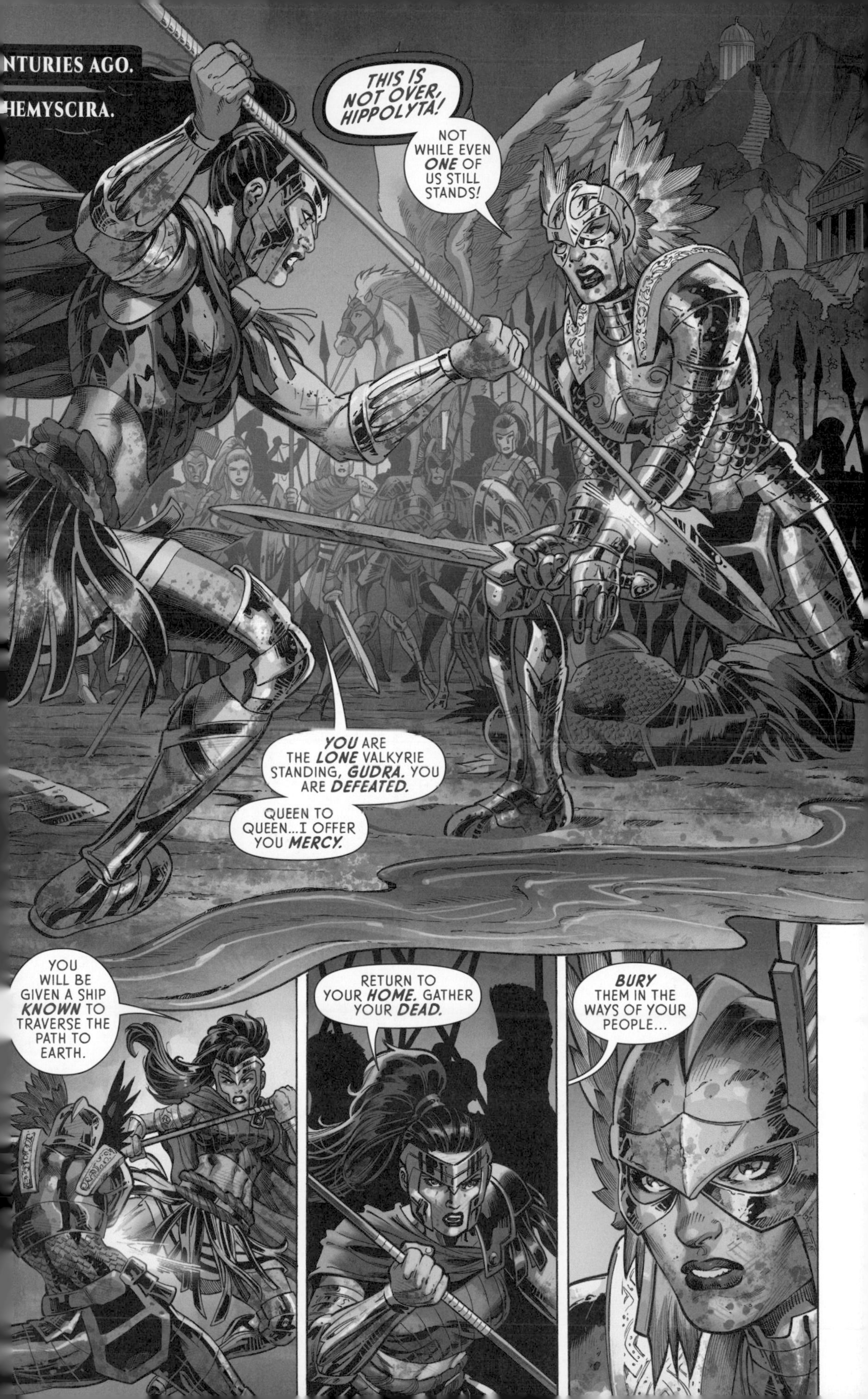
NTURIES AGO.
HEMYSCIRA.
THIS IS NOT OVER, HIPPOLYTA!
NOT WHILE EVEN ONE OF US STILL STANDS!
YOU ARE THE LONE VALKYRIE STANDING, GUDRA. YOU ARE DEFEATED.
QUEEN TO QUEEN...I OFFER YOU MERCY.
YOU WILL BE GIVEN A SHIP KNOWN TO TRAVERSE THE PATH TO EARTH.
RETURN TO YOUR HOME. GATHER YOUR DEAD.
BURY THEM IN THE WAYS OF YOUR PEOPLE...

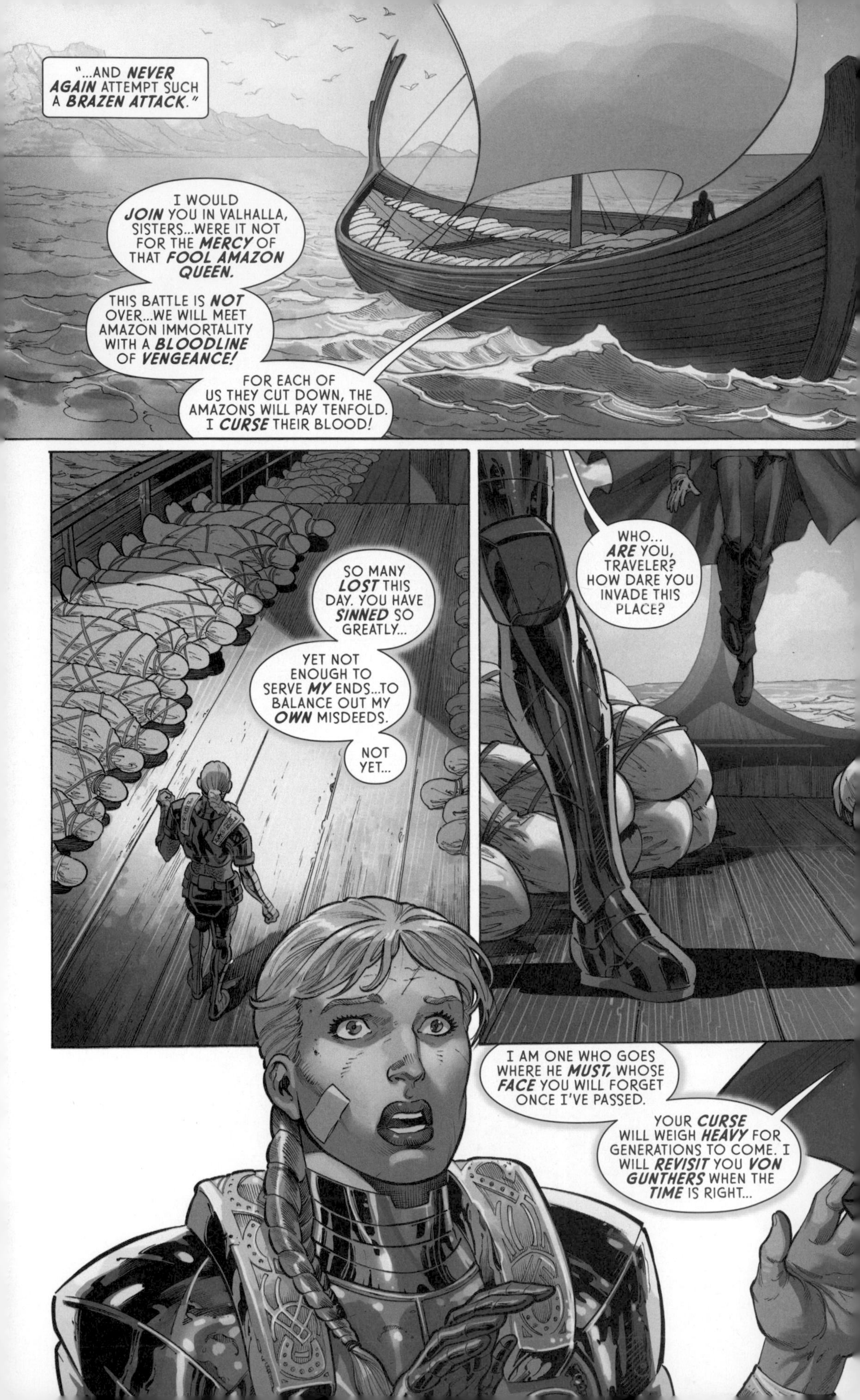
"...AND NEVER AGAIN ATTEMPT SUCH A BRAZEN ATTACK."
I WOULD JOIN YOU IN VALHALLA, SISTERS...WERE IT NOT FOR THE MERCY OF THAT FOOL AMAZON QUEEN.
THIS BATTLE IS NOT OVER...WE WILL MEET AMAZON IMMORTALITY WITH A BLOODLINE OF VENGEANCE!
FOR EACH OF US THEY CUT DOWN, THE AMAZONS WILL PAY TENFOLD. I CURSE THEIR BLOOD!
SO MANY LOST THIS DAY. YOU HAVE SINNED SO GREATLY...
YET NOT ENOUGH TO SERVE MY ENDS...TO BALANCE OUT MY OWN MISDEEDS.
NOT YET...
WHO... ARE YOU, TRAVELER? HOW DARE YOU INVADE THIS PLACE?
I AM ONE WHO GOES WHERE HE MUST, WHOSE FACE YOU WILL FORGET ONCE I'VE PASSED.
YOUR CURSE WILL WEIGH HEAVY FOR GENERATIONS TO COME. I WILL REVISIT YOU VON GUNTHERS WHEN THE TIME IS RIGHT...

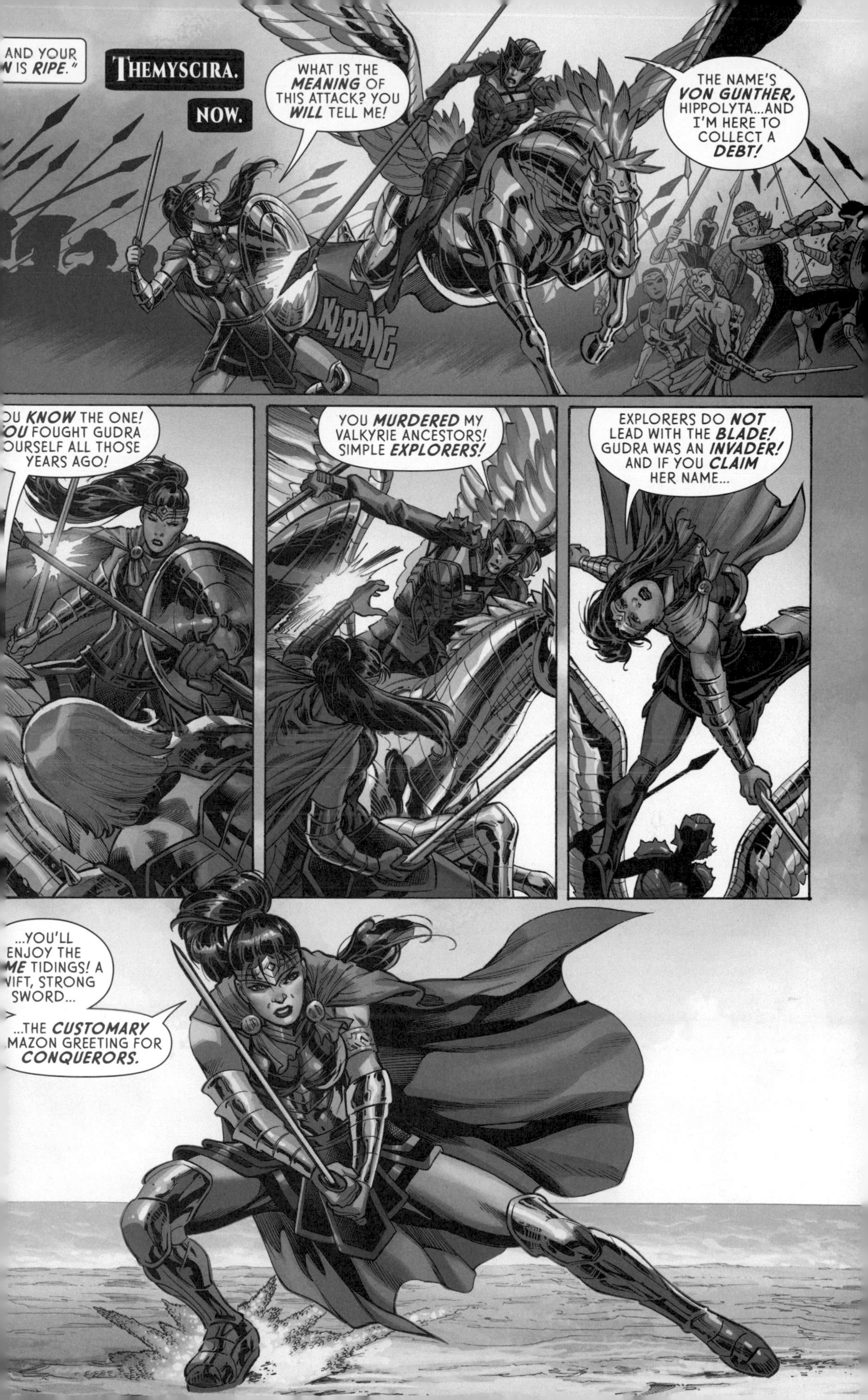
AND YOUR
N IS RIPE."
THEMYSCIRA.
NOW.
WHAT IS THE MEANING OF THIS ATTACK? YOU WILL TELL ME!
THE NAME'S VON GUNTHER, HIPPOLYTA...AND I'M HERE TO COLLECT A DEBT!
KLRANG
OU KNOW THE ONE! OU FOUGHT GUDRA OURSELF ALL THOSE YEARS AGO!
YOU MURDERED MY VALKYRIE ANCESTORS! SIMPLE EXPLORERS!
EXPLORERS DO NOT LEAD WITH THE BLADE! GUDRA WAS AN INVADER! AND IF YOU CLAIM HER NAME...
...YOU'LL ENJOY THE ME TIDINGS! A WIFT, STRONG SWORD...
...THE CUSTOMARY MAZON GREETING FOR CONQUERORS.

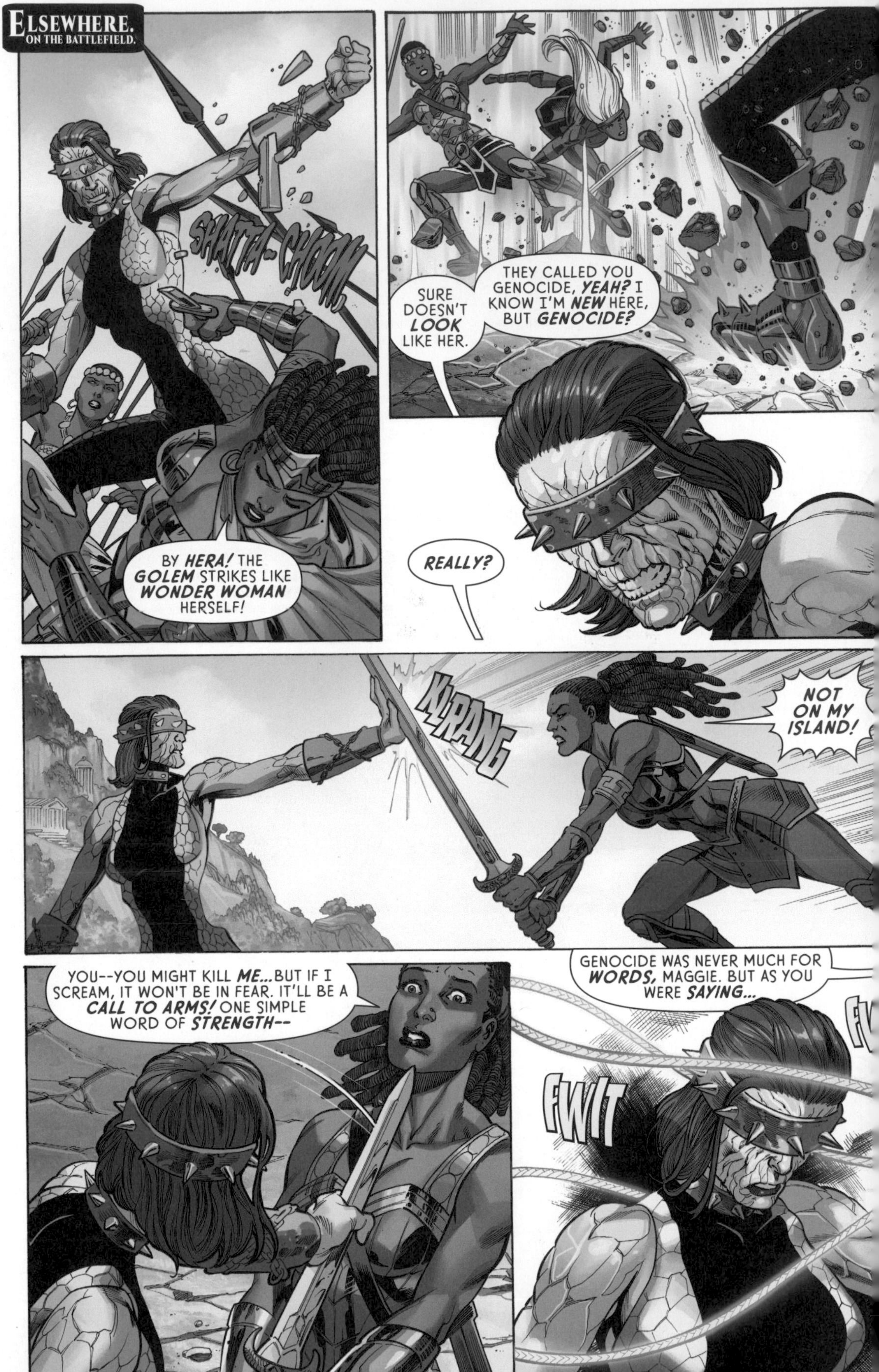
ELSEWHERE. ON THE BATTLEFIELD.
SHATTA-CHOOM
BY HERA! THE GOLEM STRIKES LIKE WONDER WOMAN HERSELF!
THEY CALLED YOU GENOCIDE, YEAH? I KNOW I'M NEW HERE, BUT GENOCIDE?
SURE DOESN'T LOOK LIKE HER.
REALLY?
KLRANG
NOT ON MY ISLAND!
YOU--YOU MIGHT KILL ME...BUT IF I SCREAM, IT WON'T BE IN FEAR. IT'LL BE A CALL TO ARMS! ONE SIMPLE WORD OF STRENGTH--
GENOCIDE WAS NEVER MUCH FOR WORDS, MAGGIE. BUT AS YOU WERE SAYING...
FWIT

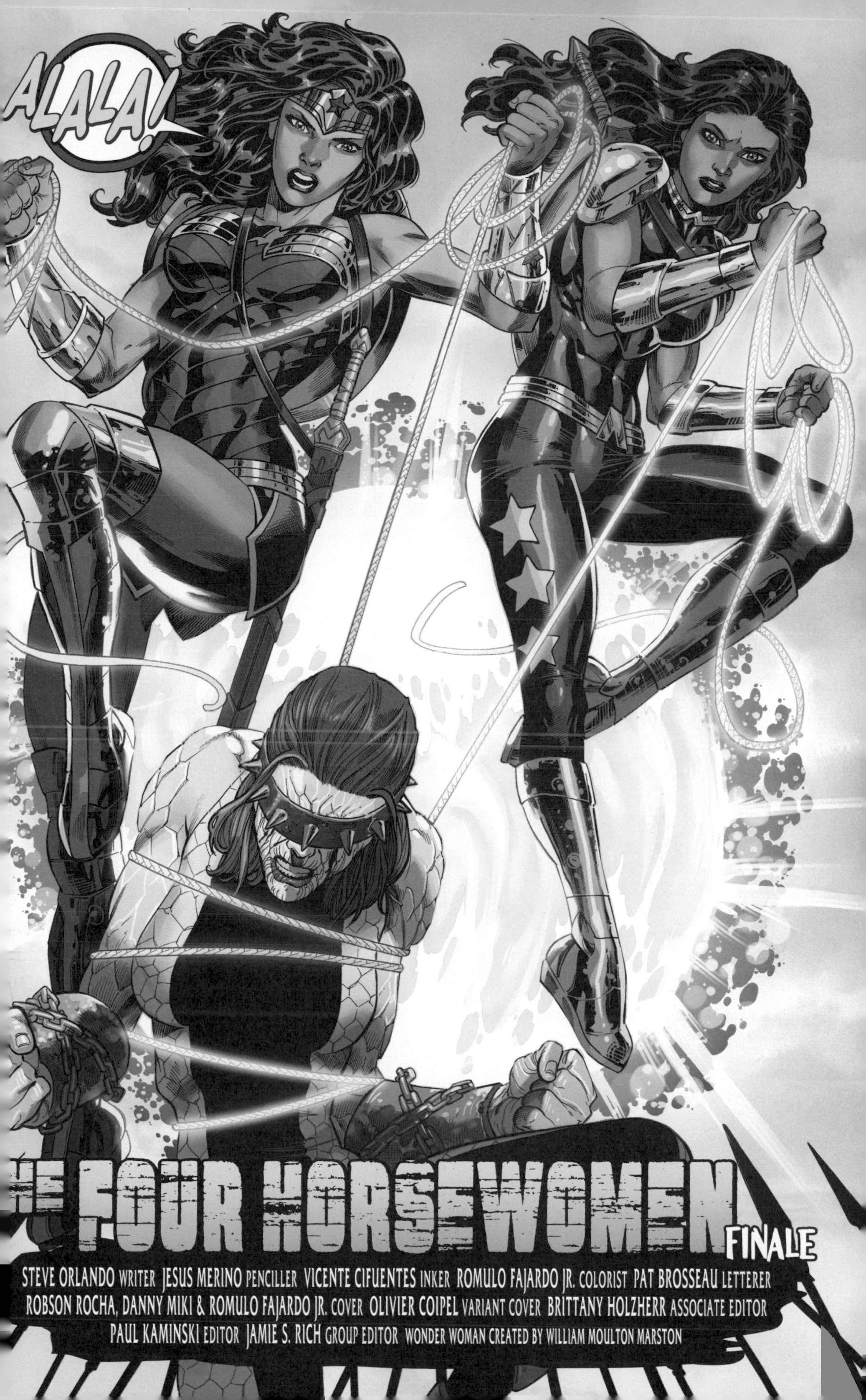
ALALA!
HE FOUR HORSEWOMEN
FINALE
STEVE ORLANDO WRITER JESUS MERINO PENCILLER VICENTE CIFUENTES INKER ROMULO FAJARDO JR. COLORIST PAT BROSSEAU LETTERER
ROBSON ROCHA, DANNY MIKI & ROMULO FAJARDO JR. COVER OLIVIER COIPEL VARIANT COVER BRITTANY HOLZHERR ASSOCIATE EDITOR
PAUL KAMINSKI EDITOR JAMIE S. RICH GROUP EDITOR WONDER WOMAN CREATED BY WILLIAM MOULTON MARSTON

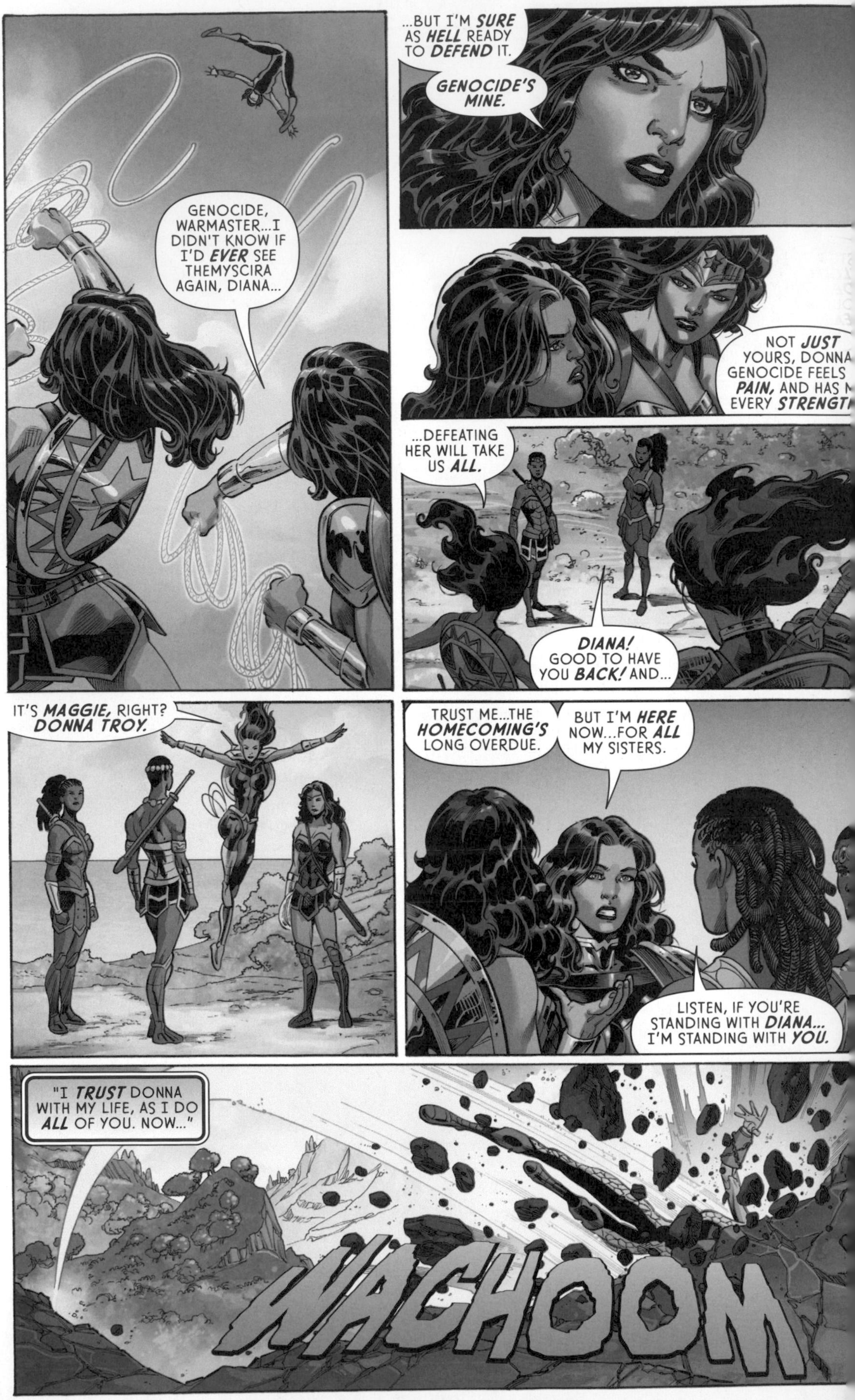
GENOCIDE, WARMASTER...I DIDN'T KNOW IF I'D EVER SEE THEMYSCIRA AGAIN, DIANA...
...BUT I'M SURE AS HELL READY TO DEFEND IT.
GENOCIDE'S MINE.
NOT JUST YOURS, DONNA GENOCIDE FEELS PAIN, AND HAS EVERY
...DEFEATING HER WILL TAKE US ALL.
DIANA! GOOD TO HAVE YOU BACK! AND...
IT'S MAGGIE, RIGHT? DONNA TROY.
TRUST ME...THE HOMECOMING'S LONG OVERDUE.
BUT I'M HERE NOW...FOR ALL MY SISTERS.
LISTEN, IF YOU'RE STANDING WITH DIANA... I'M STANDING WITH YOU.
"I TRUST DONNA WITH MY LIFE, AS I DO ALL OF YOU. NOW..."
WACHOOM

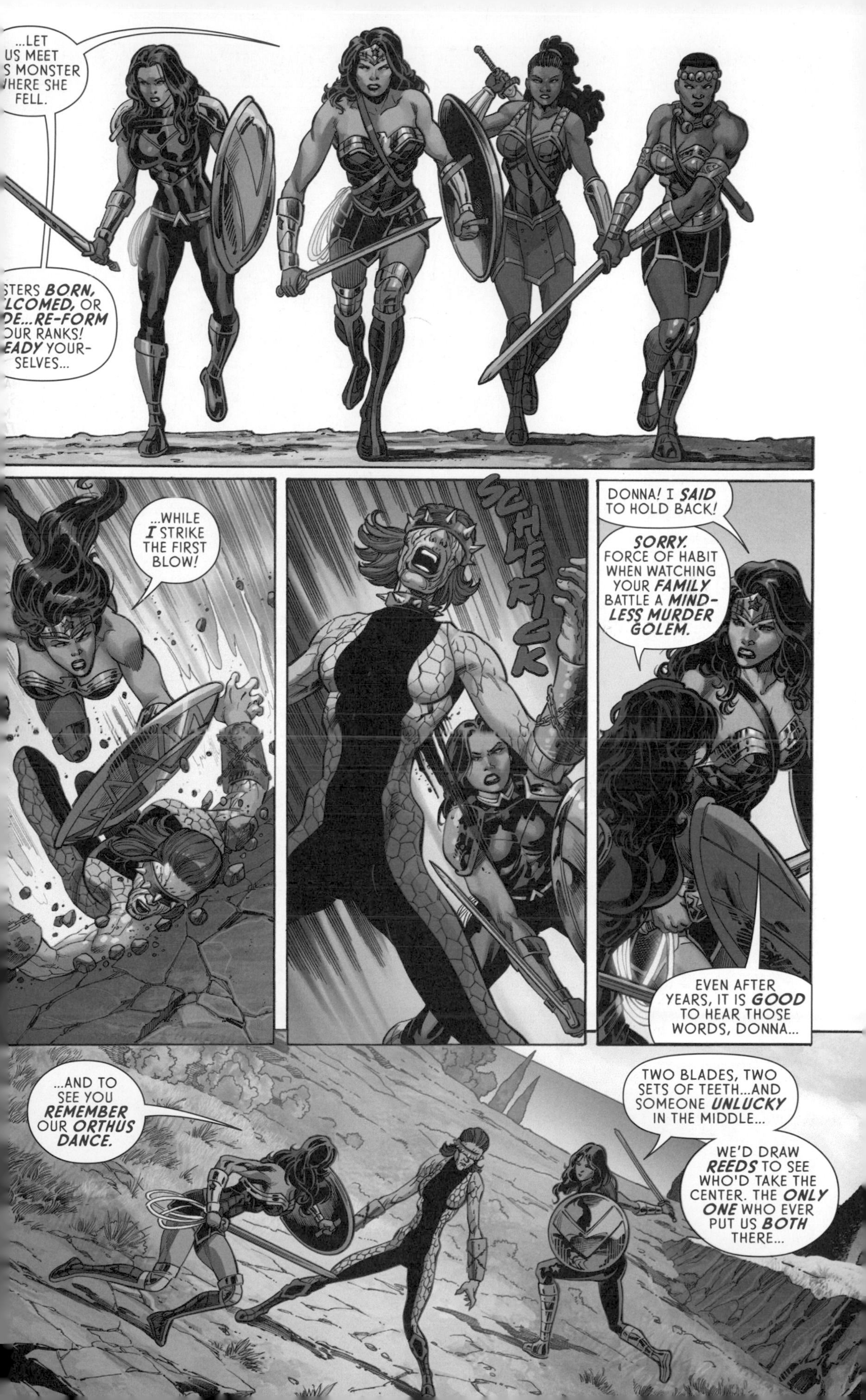
...LET US MEET S MONSTER HERE SHE FELL.
STERS BORN, LCOMED, OR DE...RE-FORM OUR RANKS! EADY YOUR-SELVES...
...WHILE I STRIKE THE FIRST BLOW!
SCHLERICK
DONNA! I SAID TO HOLD BACK!
SORRY. FORCE OF HABIT WHEN WATCHING YOUR FAMILY BATTLE A MINDLESS MURDER GOLEM.
EVEN AFTER YEARS, IT IS GOOD TO HEAR THOSE WORDS, DONNA...
...AND TO SEE YOU REMEMBER OUR ORTHUS DANCE.
TWO BLADES, TWO SETS OF TEETH...AND SOMEONE UNLUCKY IN THE MIDDLE...
WE'D DRAW REEDS TO SEE WHO'D TAKE THE CENTER. THE ONLY ONE WHO EVER PUT US BOTH THERE...

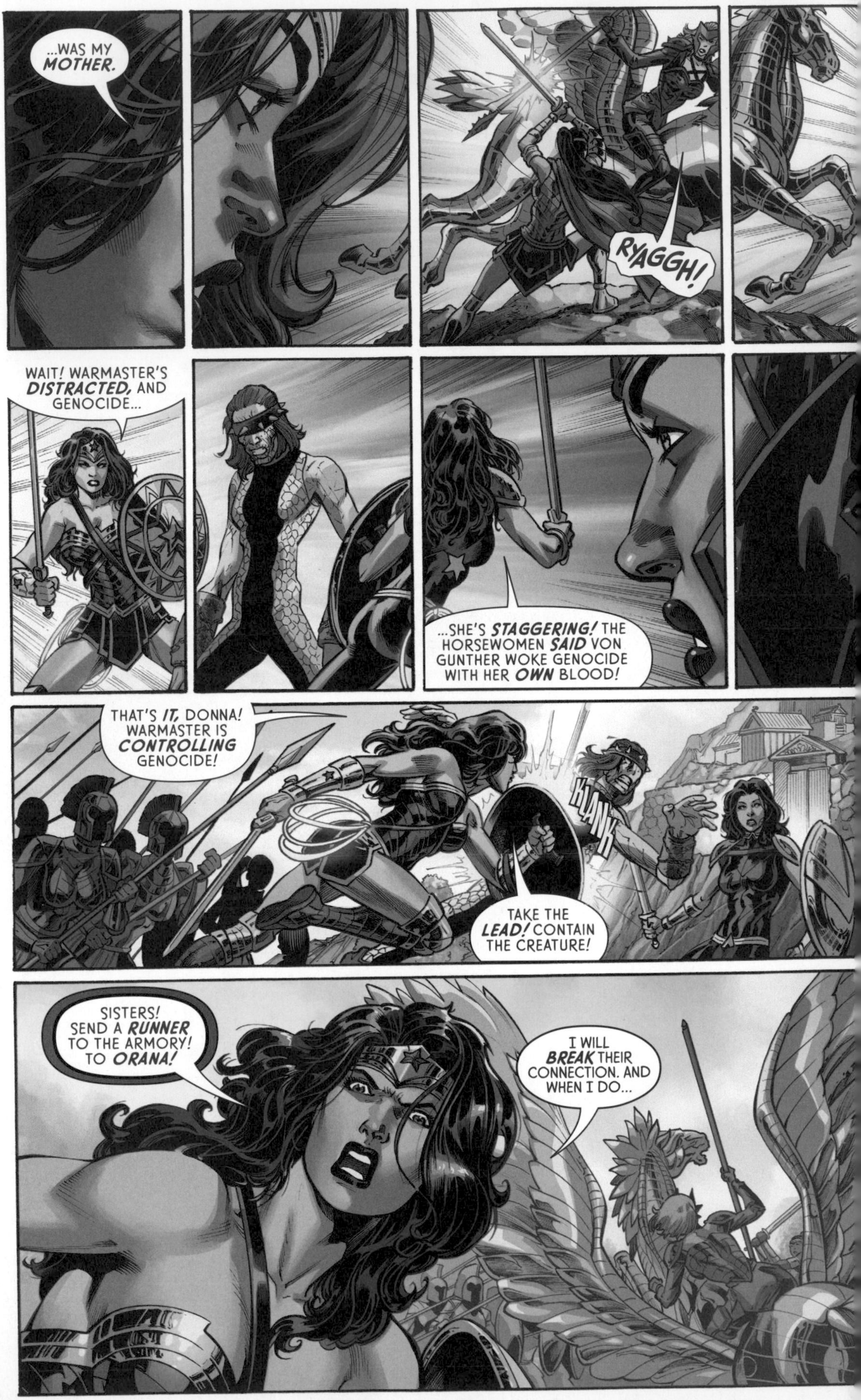

...WAS MY MOTHER.
RYAGGH!
WAIT! WARMASTER'S DISTRACTED, AND GENOCIDE...
...SHE'S STAGGERING! THE HORSEWOMEN SAID VON GUNTHER WOKE GENOCIDE WITH HER OWN BLOOD!
THAT'S IT, DONNA! WARMASTER IS CONTROLLING GENOCIDE!
KLANK
TAKE THE LEAD! CONTAIN THE CREATURE!
SISTERS! SEND A RUNNER TO THE ARMORY! TO ORANA!
I WILL BREAK THEIR CONNECTION. AND WHEN I DO...

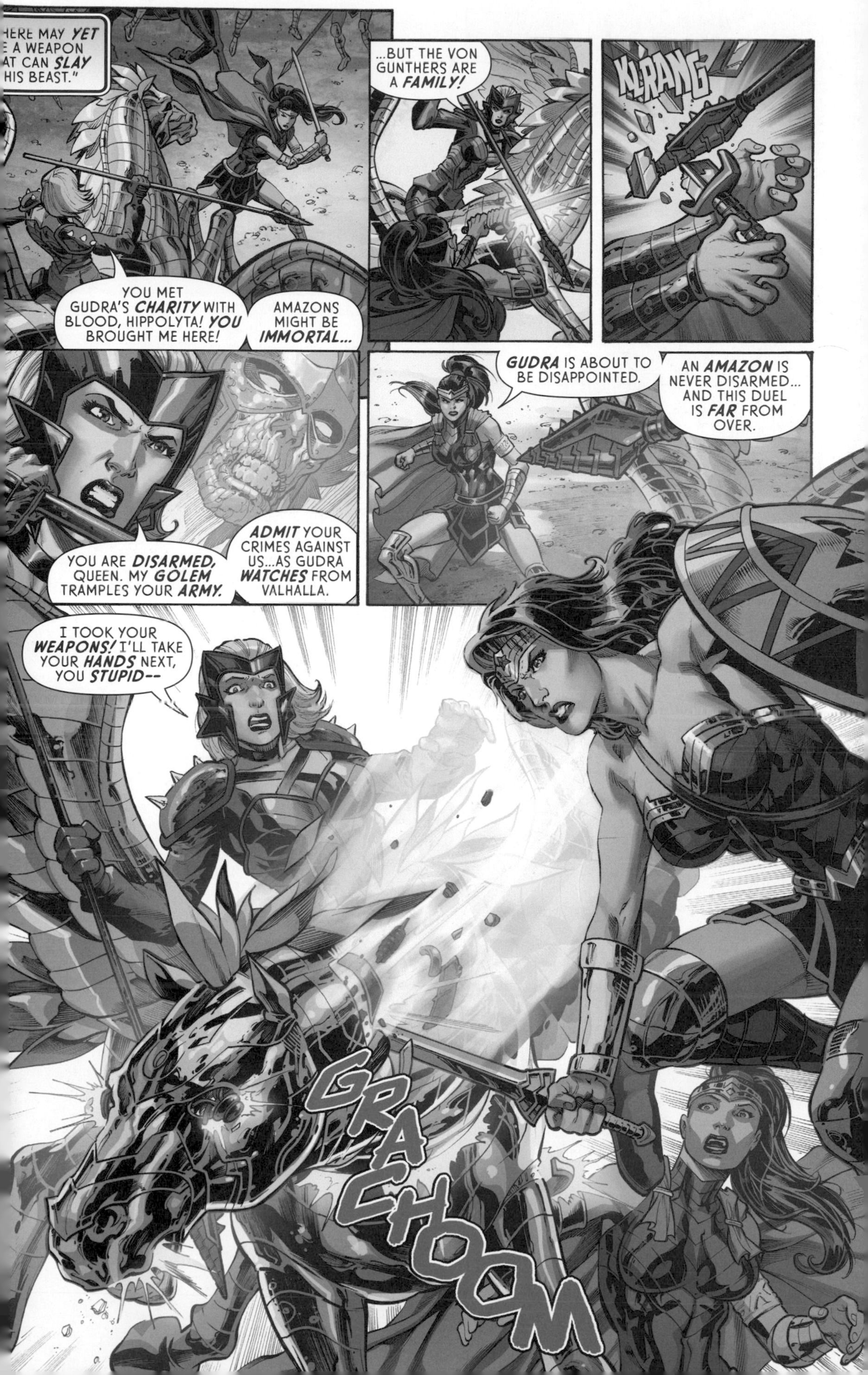

HERE MAY YET
E A WEAPON
AT CAN SLAY
HIS BEAST."
YOU MET GUDRA'S CHARITY WITH BLOOD, HIPPOLYTA! YOU BROUGHT ME HERE!
AMAZONS MIGHT BE IMMORTAL...
...BUT THE VON GUNTHERS ARE A FAMILY!
KLRANG
YOU ARE DISARMED, QUEEN. MY GOLEM TRAMPLES YOUR ARMY.
ADMIT YOUR CRIMES AGAINST US...AS GUDRA WATCHES FROM VALHALLA.
GUDRA IS ABOUT TO BE DISAPPOINTED.
AN AMAZON IS NEVER DISARMED... AND THIS DUEL IS FAR FROM OVER.
I TOOK YOUR WEAPONS! I'LL TAKE YOUR HANDS NEXT, YOU STUPID--
GRACHOOM

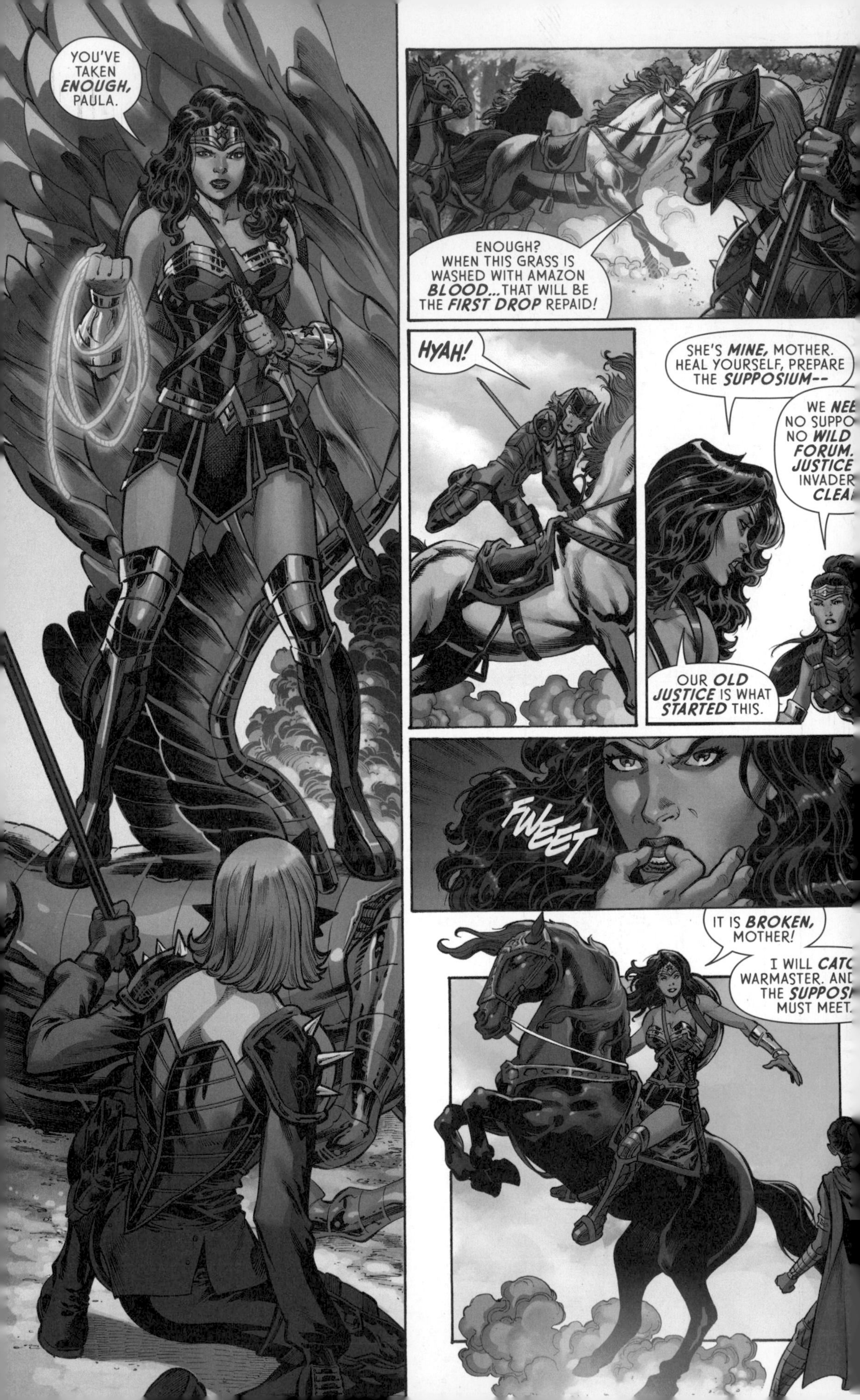
YOU'VE TAKEN ENOUGH, PAULA.
ENOUGH? WHEN THIS GRASS IS WASHED WITH AMAZON BLOOD...THAT WILL BE THE FIRST DROP REPAID!
HYAH!
SHE'S MINE, MOTHER. HEAL YOURSELF, PREPARE THE SUPPOSIUM--
WE NEE NO SUPPO NO WILD FORUM. JUSTICE INVADER CLEA
OUR OLD JUSTICE IS WHAT STARTED THIS.
FWEET
IT IS BROKEN, MOTHER!
I WILL CATC WARMASTER. AND THE SUPPOSI MUST MEET.

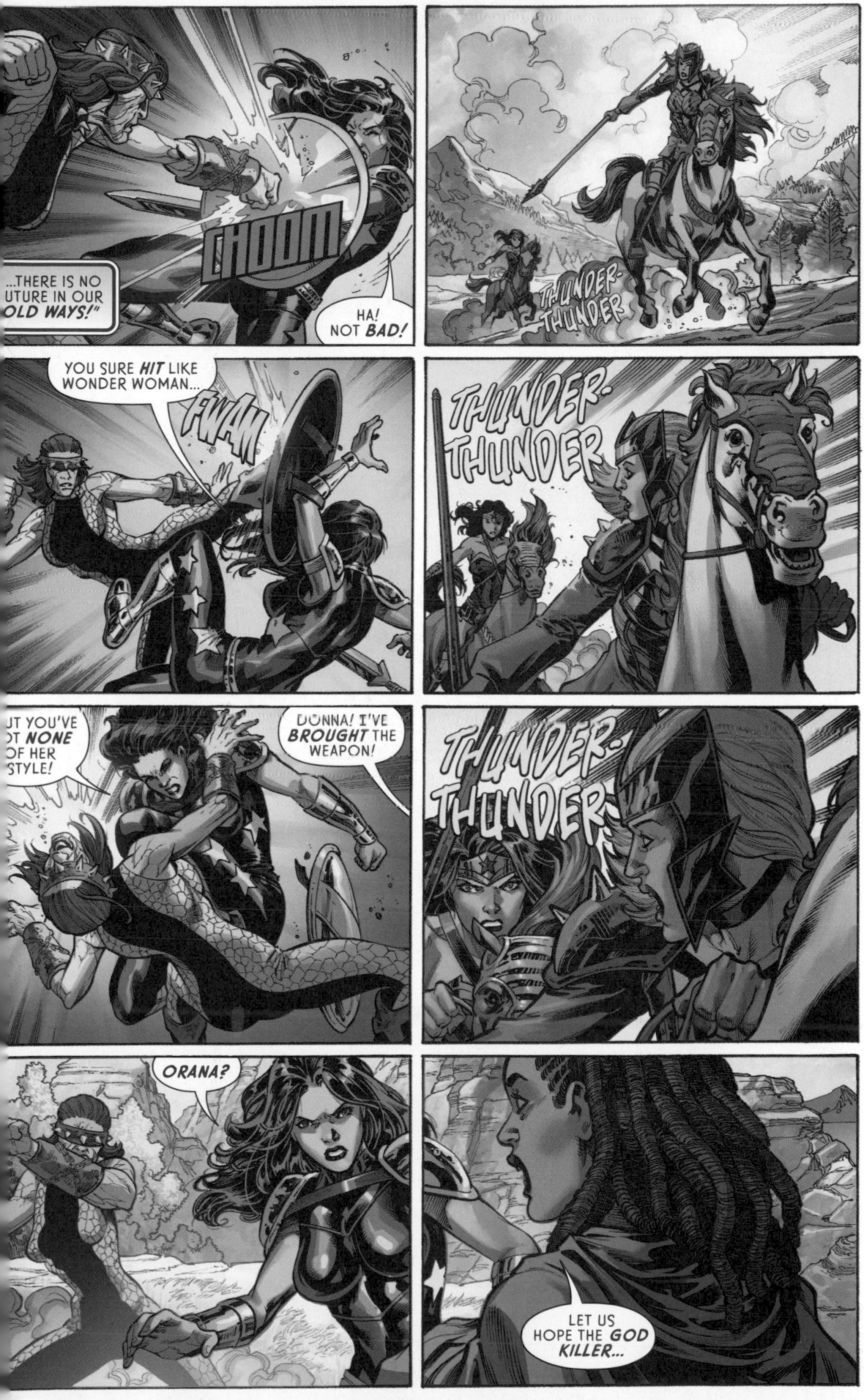

...THERE IS NO
UTURE IN OUR
OLD WAYS!"
CHOOM
HA!
NOT BAD!
THUNDER-
THUNDER
YOU SURE HIT LIKE
WONDER WOMAN...
FWAM
THUNDER-
THUNDER
UT YOU'VE
OT NONE
OF HER
STYLE!
DONNA! I'VE
BROUGHT THE
WEAPON!
THUNDER-
THUNDER
ORANA?
LET US
HOPE THE GOD
KILLER...

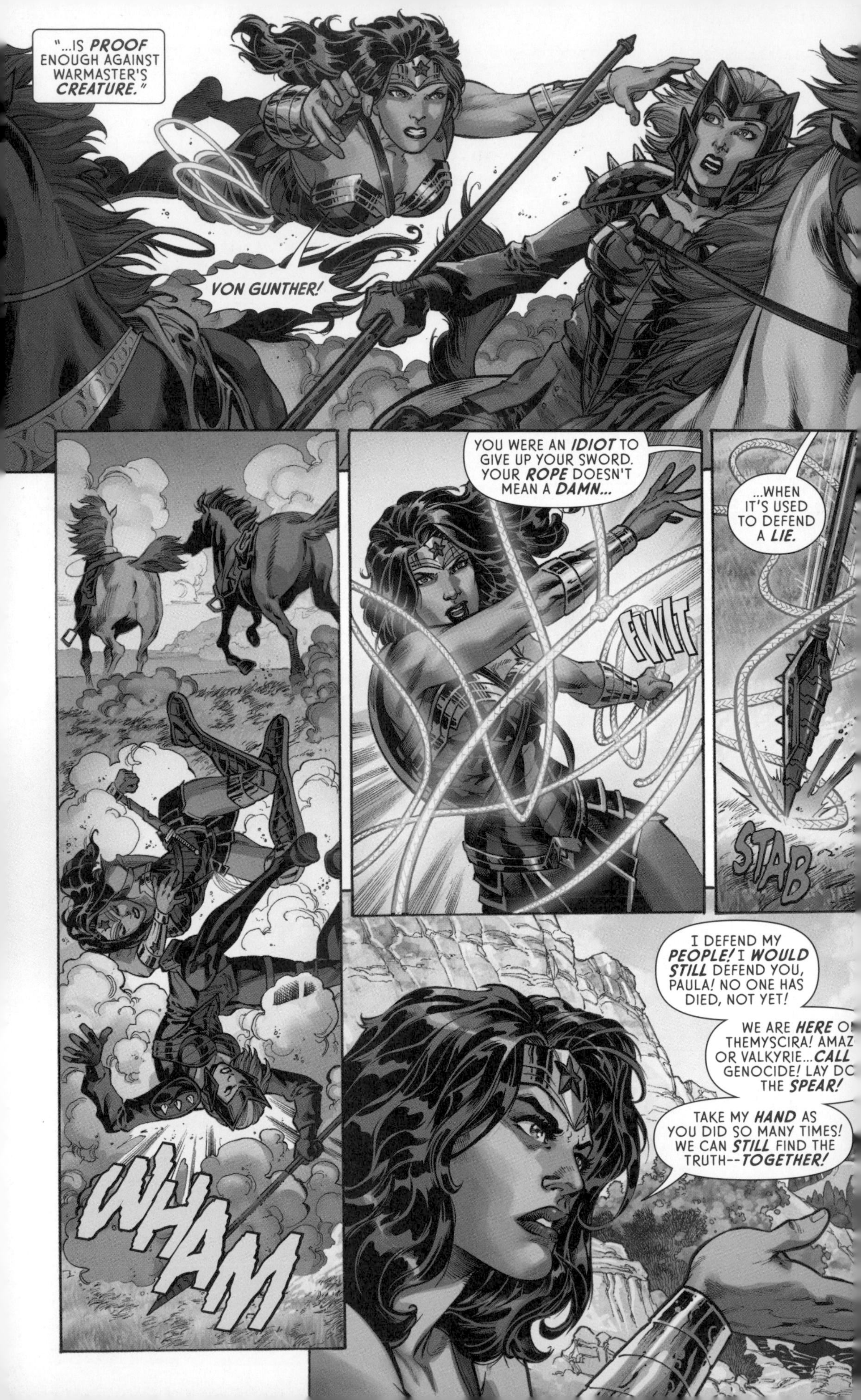
"...IS PROOF ENOUGH AGAINST WARMASTER'S CREATURE."
VON GUNTHER!
YOU WERE AN IDIOT TO GIVE UP YOUR SWORD. YOUR ROPE DOESN'T MEAN A DAMN...
...WHEN IT'S USED TO DEFEND A LIE.
FWIT
STAB
WHAM
I DEFEND MY PEOPLE! I WOULD STILL DEFEND YOU, PAULA! NO ONE HAS DIED, NOT YET!
TAKE MY HAND AS YOU DID SO MANY TIMES! WE CAN STILL FIND THE TRUTH--TOGETHER!

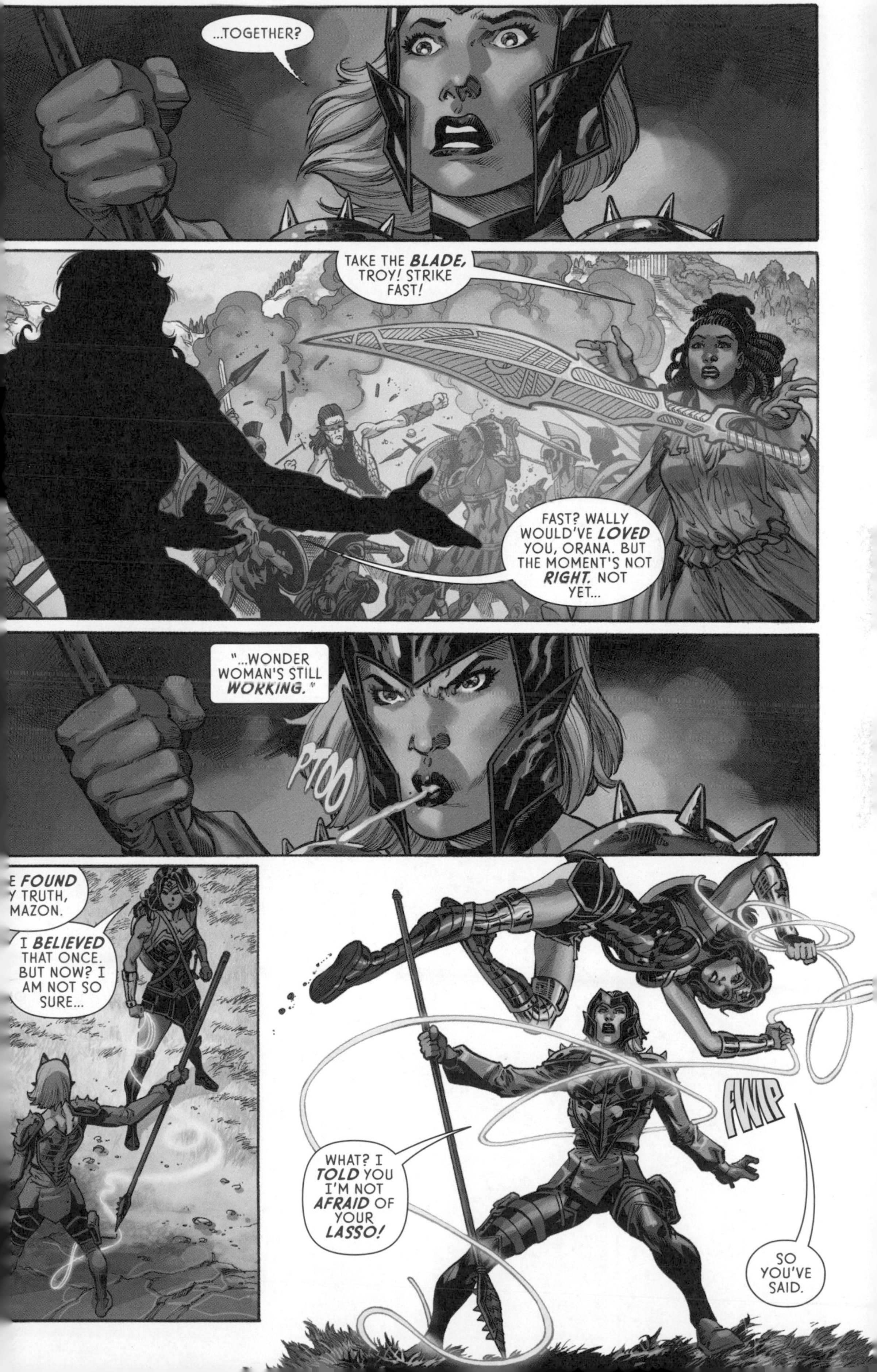

...TOGETHER?
TAKE THE BLADE, TROY! STRIKE FAST!
FAST? WALLY WOULD'VE LOVED YOU, ORANA. BUT THE MOMENT'S NOT RIGHT. NOT YET...
"...WONDER WOMAN'S STILL WORKING."
PTOO
E FOUND Y TRUTH, MAZON.
I BELIEVED THAT ONCE. BUT NOW? I AM NOT SO SURE...
WHAT? I TOLD YOU I'M NOT AFRAID OF YOUR LASSO!
FWIP
SO YOU'VE SAID.

NO! YOUR **TRUTH** MEANS NOTHING! YOUR **PRECIOUS SISTERS** FED YOU A LIE!

YOUR FAMILY IS **JUST** AS CAPABLE OF LIES AS **MINE.** AND EVERY TIME I'VE GIVEN YOU AN OUT...

...YOU'VE **FALTERED.** BECAUSE YOU'VE **DOUBTED.**

YOU COME FROM A LINE OF **HATE.** I **TRIED** TO FREE YOU OF THAT.

YOUR ANCESTORS FORCED YOU TO FEEL THEIR **TRAUMA.** IT MADE YOU HATE THE AMAZONS.

HATE **ME.**

YOU **ACTED** BECAUSE YOU **BELIEVED** THE PAST AS THEY SAW IT.

YOU'VE BEEN SO **ANGRY...** BECAUSE YOU **BELIEVED.**

YOU WERE **SURE** THE AMAZONS WERE THE **ROOT** OF YOUR FAMILY'S PAIN. THAT **THEY** STRUCK FIRST.

BUT ARE **MINE** THE ACTIONS OF ONE WHO **HATES?** YOU **BELIEVED** YOUR FAMILY'S STORY SO **STRONGLY,** ONCE...

...BUT ARE YOU **STILL** SO SURE? **TRULY?**

ARE YOU?

CLANK

THE--THE VOICES SCREAMED SO LOUD FOR SO LONG, DIANA. AND--AND I...

AAAIIIIIAAAGH!

...I STILL FEEL THEIR PAIN! THE DEATH OF EACH VALKYRIE, EACH VON GUNTHER WHO FOLLOWED. BUT I...

I DON'T KNOW ANYMORE. DON'T **KNOW**

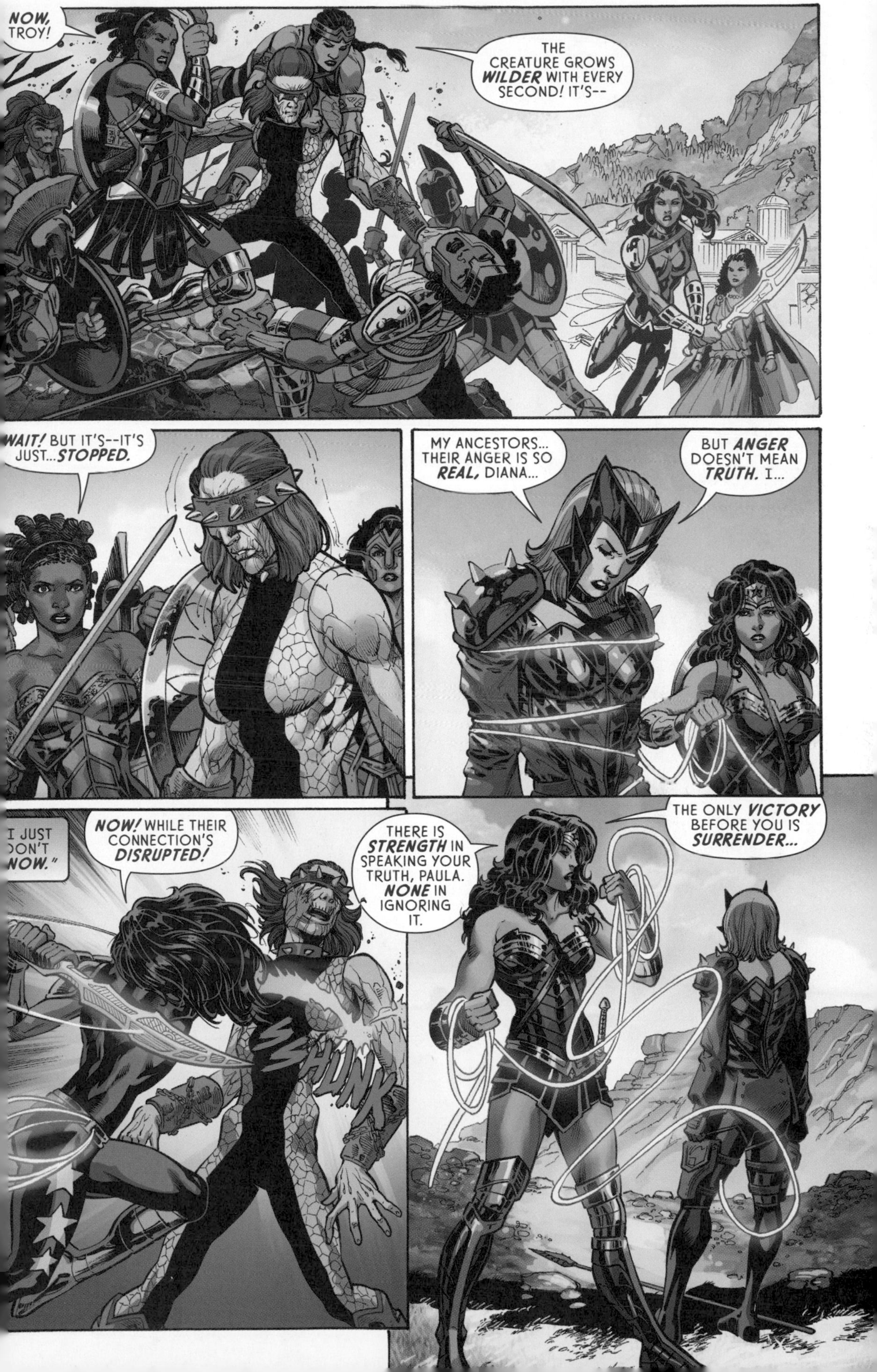
NOW, TROY!
THE CREATURE GROWS WILDER WITH EVERY SECOND! IT'S--
WAIT! BUT IT'S--IT'S JUST...STOPPED.
MY ANCESTORS... THEIR ANGER IS SO REAL, DIANA...
BUT ANGER DOESN'T MEAN TRUTH. I...
I JUST DON'T NOW."
NOW! WHILE THEIR CONNECTION'S DISRUPTED!
SHHUNK
THERE IS STRENGTH IN SPEAKING YOUR TRUTH, PAULA. NONE IN IGNORING IT.
THE ONLY VICTORY BEFORE YOU IS SURRENDER...

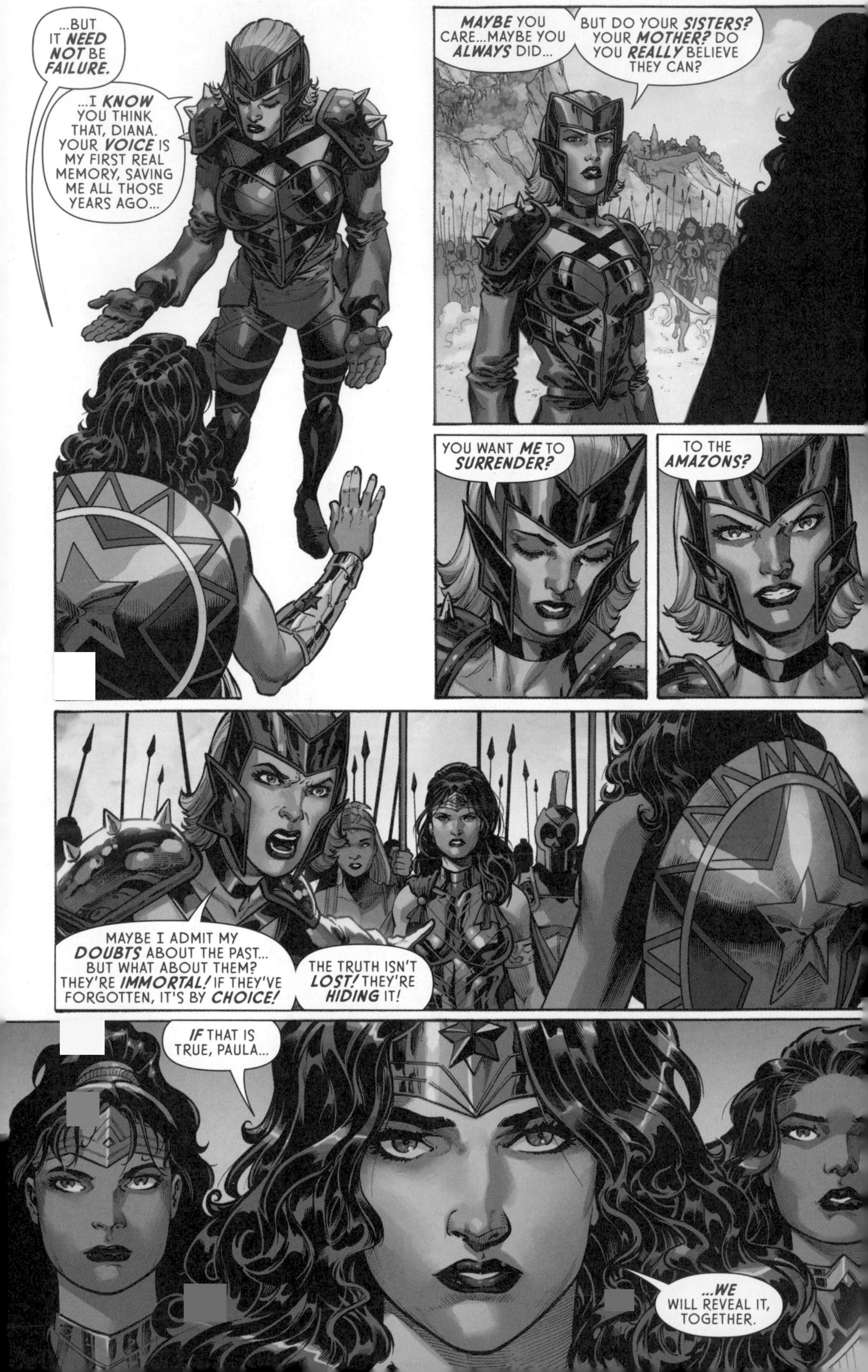
...BUT IT NEED NOT BE FAILURE.
...I KNOW YOU THINK THAT, DIANA. YOUR VOICE IS MY FIRST REAL MEMORY, SAVING ME ALL THOSE YEARS AGO...
MAYBE YOU CARE...MAYBE YOU ALWAYS DID...
BUT DO YOUR SISTERS? YOUR MOTHER? DO YOU REALLY BELIEVE THEY CAN?
YOU WANT ME TO SURRENDER?
TO THE AMAZONS?
MAYBE I ADMIT MY DOUBTS ABOUT THE PAST... BUT WHAT ABOUT THEM? THEY'RE IMMORTAL! IF THEY'VE FORGOTTEN, IT'S BY CHOICE!
THE TRUTH ISN'T LOST! THEY'RE HIDING IT!
IF THAT IS TRUE, PAULA...
...WE WILL REVEAL IT, TOGETHER.

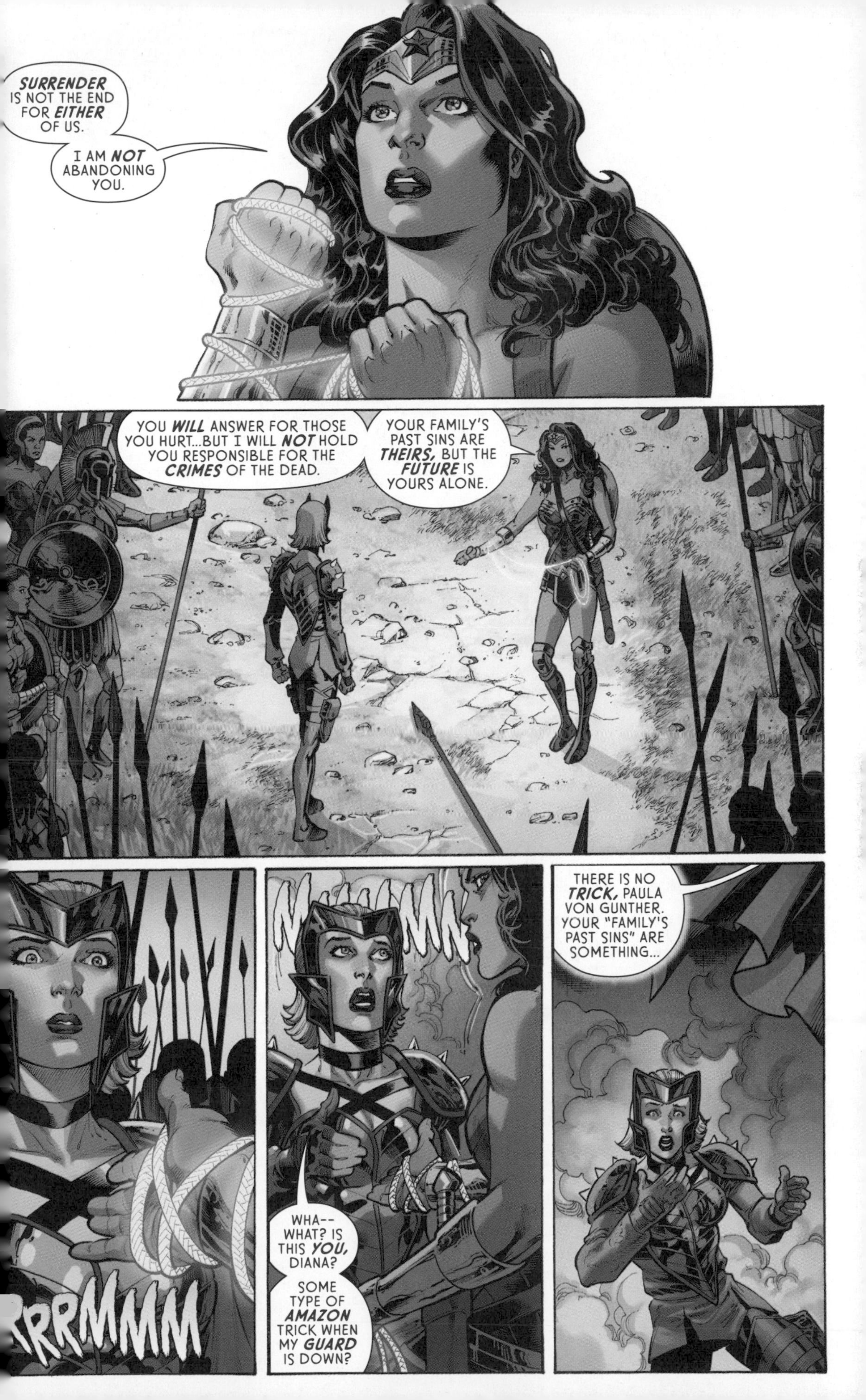
SURRENDER IS NOT THE END FOR EITHER OF US.
I AM NOT ABANDONING YOU.
YOU WILL ANSWER FOR THOSE YOU HURT...BUT I WILL NOT HOLD YOU RESPONSIBLE FOR THE CRIMES OF THE DEAD.
YOUR FAMILY'S PAST SINS ARE THEIRS, BUT THE FUTURE IS YOURS ALONE.
RRMMM
MMMMN
WHA-- WHAT? IS THIS YOU, DIANA?
SOME TYPE OF AMAZON TRICK WHEN MY GUARD IS DOWN?
THERE IS NO TRICK, PAULA VON GUNTHER. YOUR "FAMILY'S PAST SINS" ARE SOMETHING...

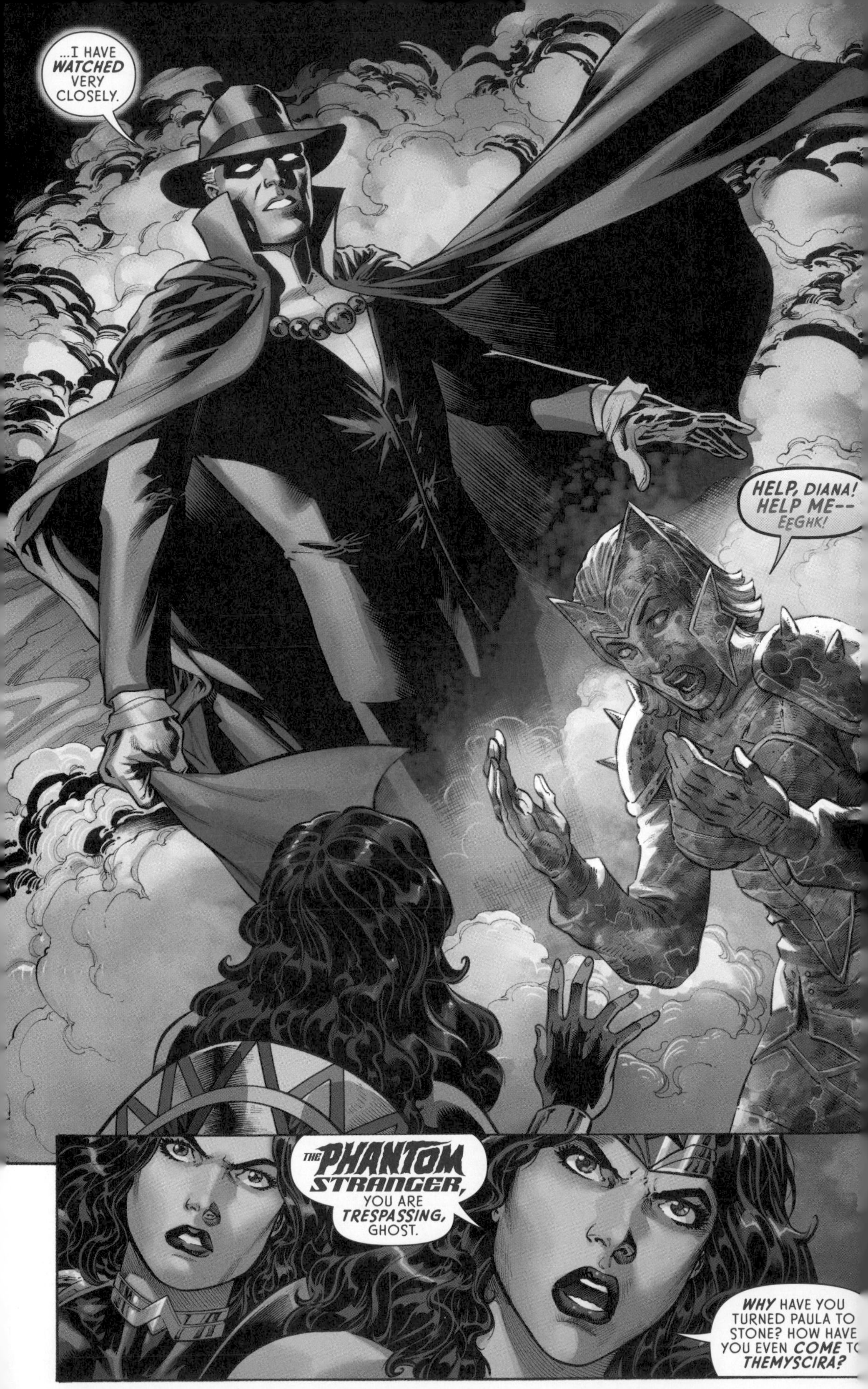
...I HAVE WATCHED VERY CLOSELY.
HELP, DIANA! HELP ME-- EEGHK!
THE PHANTOM STRANGER, YOU ARE TRESPASSING, GHOST.
WHY HAVE YOU TURNED PAULA TO STONE? HOW HAVE YOU EVEN COME TO THEMYSCIRA?

A SERVANT OF THE **PRESENCE** NEED NOT EXPLAIN HIMSELF TO A MINOR PANTHEON'S CHARGE.

I SERVE **NO GODS** THESE DAYS, STRANGER. **YOURS** INCLUDED.

WE WHO EXIST, **ALL** SERVE. FOR **CENTURIES,** AMAZON... I HAVE WATCHED THE VON GUNTHERS' VENDETTA.

TODAY...PAULA VON GUNTHER HAS INHERITED BOTH THEIR STRENGTH AND THEIR **ACCUMULATED** SIN.

CANNOT **SAVE** VON GUNTHER...BUT I **CAN** DELIVER HER. AND IN ELEVATING A SOUL SO RIPE WITH SIN...

...COME ALL THE CLOSER TO MY OWN PENANCE.

SHE WILL FACE JUDGMENT AS I DID BEFORE THE PRESENCE...AND BE SHOWN THE PATH TO **REDEMPTION.**

PAULA NEEDS NO **GODS** TO FIND REDEMPTION, ONLY **HERSELF.**

HER **HATRED** FOR YOUR PEOPLE IS UNRELENTING. SHE IS A **SOUL** SO **SPOILED**...THERE IS **NO ONE** LEFT TO STAND BY HER SIDE.

THERE'S **ME.**

CURIOUS, THEN. YOU SPEAK OF **STOPPING** VON GUNTHER'S DELIVERANCE, DIANA TRUTHQUEEN. BUT LOOK AROUND...

SHE HAS **BEEN** DELIVERED.

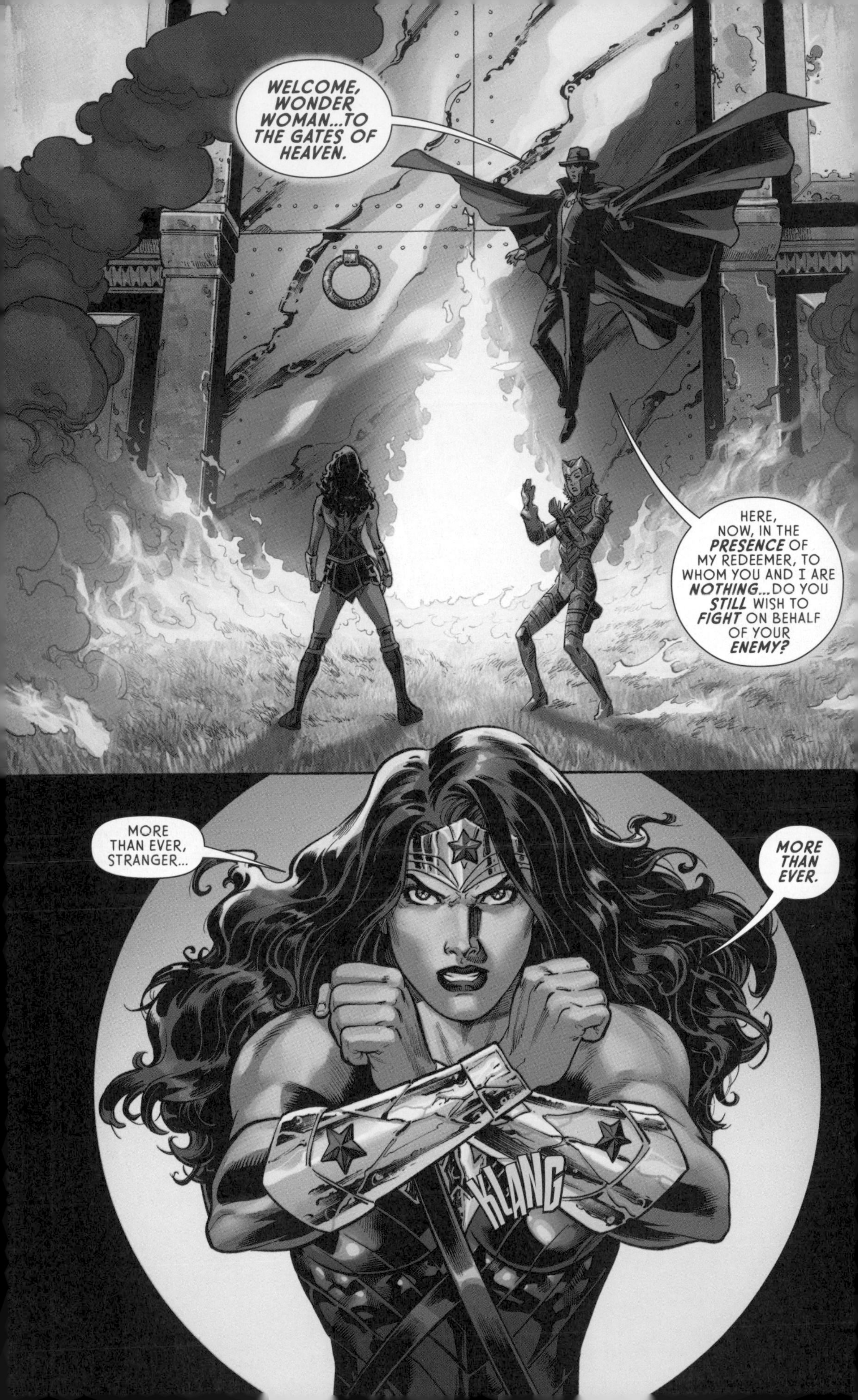
WELCOME, WONDER WOMAN...TO THE GATES OF HEAVEN.
HERE, NOW, IN THE PRESENCE OF MY REDEEMER, TO WHOM YOU AND I ARE NOTHING...DO YOU STILL WISH TO FIGHT ON BEHALF OF YOUR ENEMY?
MORE THAN EVER, STRANGER...
MORE THAN EVER.
KLANG

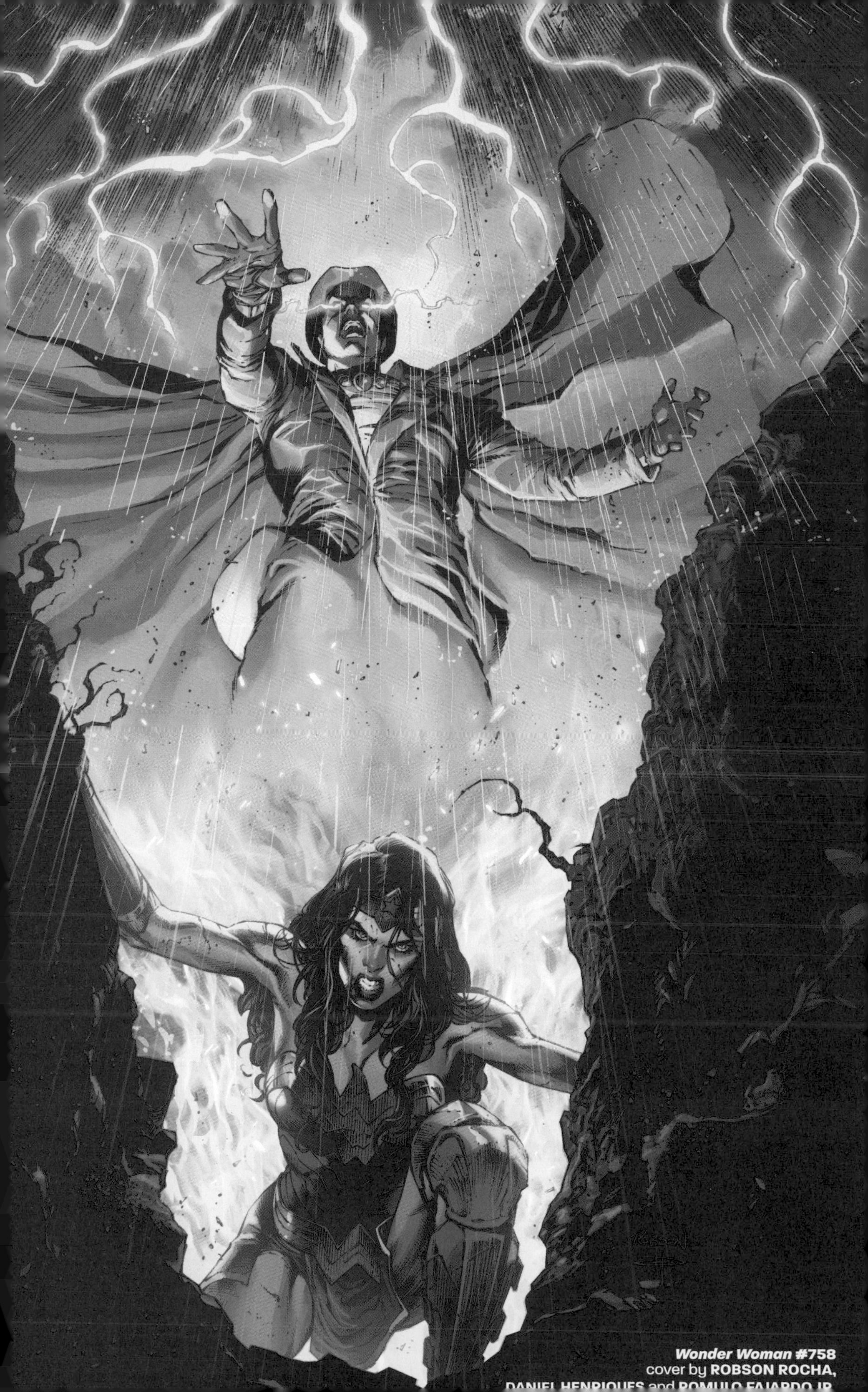

***Wonder Woman* #758**
cover by **ROBSON ROCHA,**
DANIEL HENRIQUES and **ROMULO FAJARDO JR.**

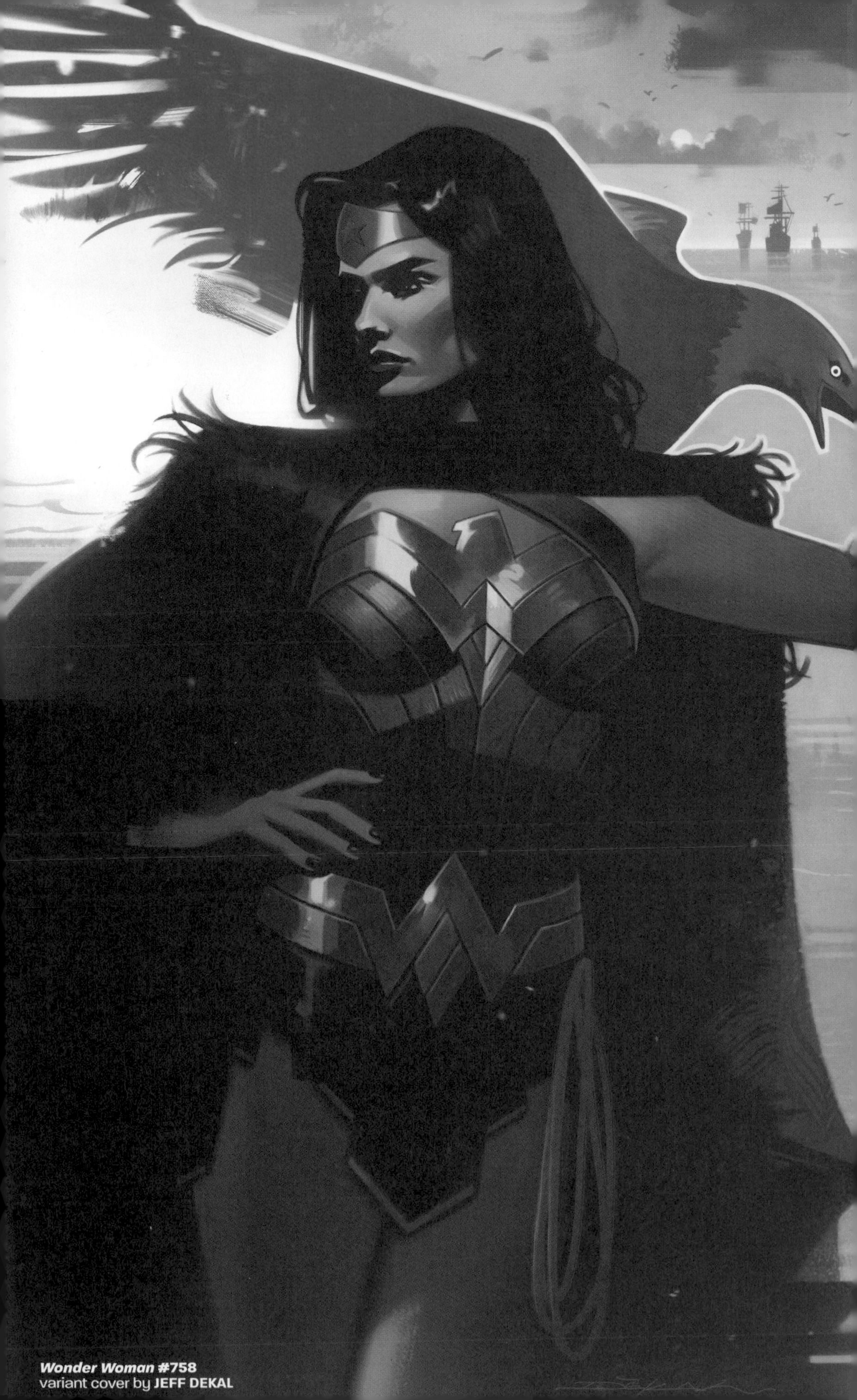

***Wonder Woman* #758**
variant cover by **JEFF DEKAL**

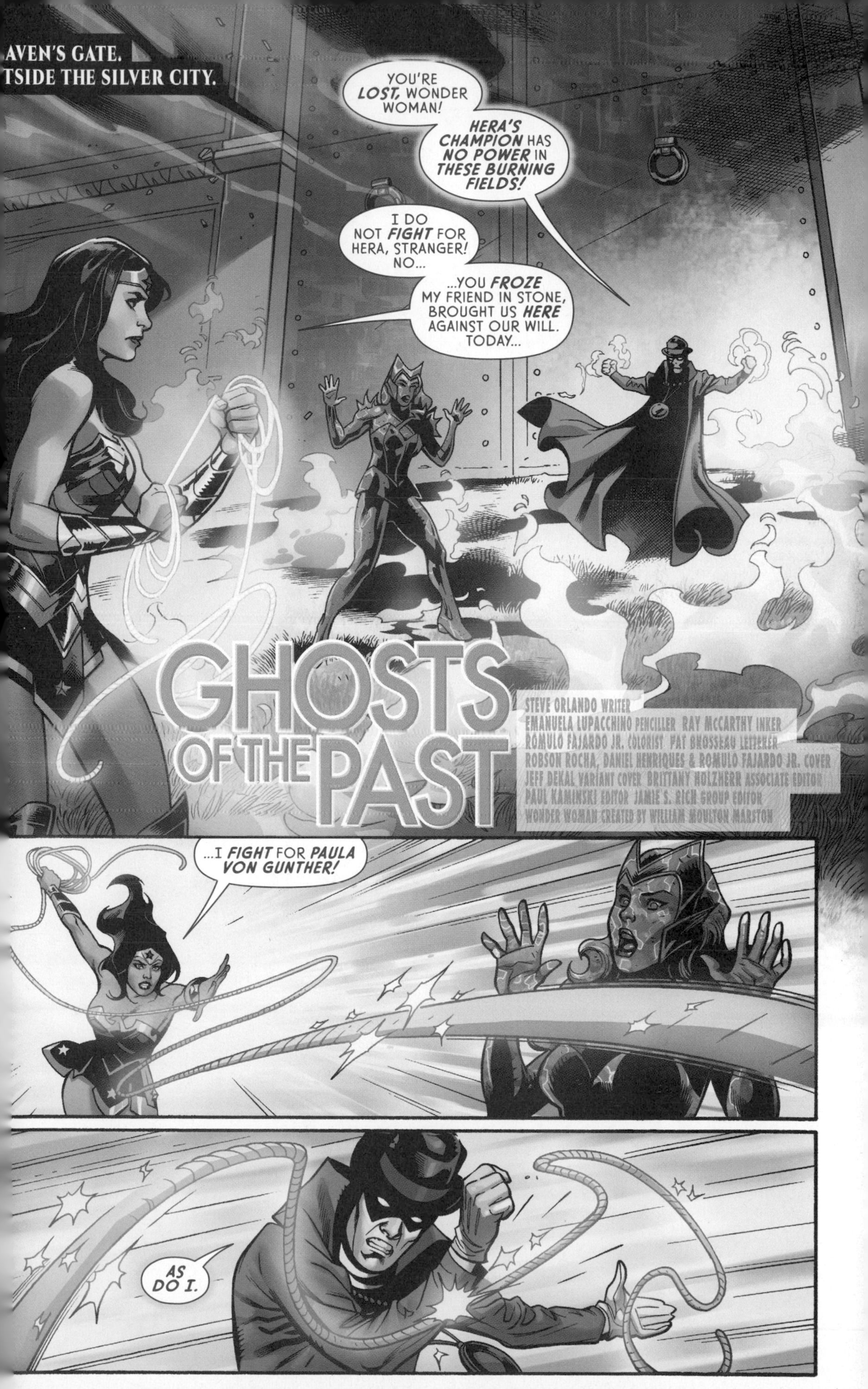
AVEN'S GATE.
TSIDE THE SILVER CITY.
YOU'RE LOST, WONDER WOMAN!
HERA'S CHAMPION HAS NO POWER IN THESE BURNING FIELDS!
I DO NOT FIGHT FOR HERA, STRANGER! NO...
...YOU FROZE MY FRIEND IN STONE, BROUGHT US HERE AGAINST OUR WILL. TODAY...
GHOSTS OF THE PAST
STEVE ORLANDO WRITER
EMANUELA LUPACCHINO PENCILLER RAY McCARTHY INKER
ROMULO FAJARDO JR. COLORIST PAT BROSSEAU LETTERER
ROBSON ROCHA, DANIEL HENRIQUES & ROMULO FAJARDO JR. COVER
JEFF DEKAL VARIANT COVER BRITTANY HOLZHERR ASSOCIATE EDITOR
PAUL KAMINSKI EDITOR JAMIE S. RICH GROUP EDITOR
WONDER WOMAN CREATED BY WILLIAM MOULTON MARSTON
...I FIGHT FOR PAULA VON GUNTHER!
AS DO I.

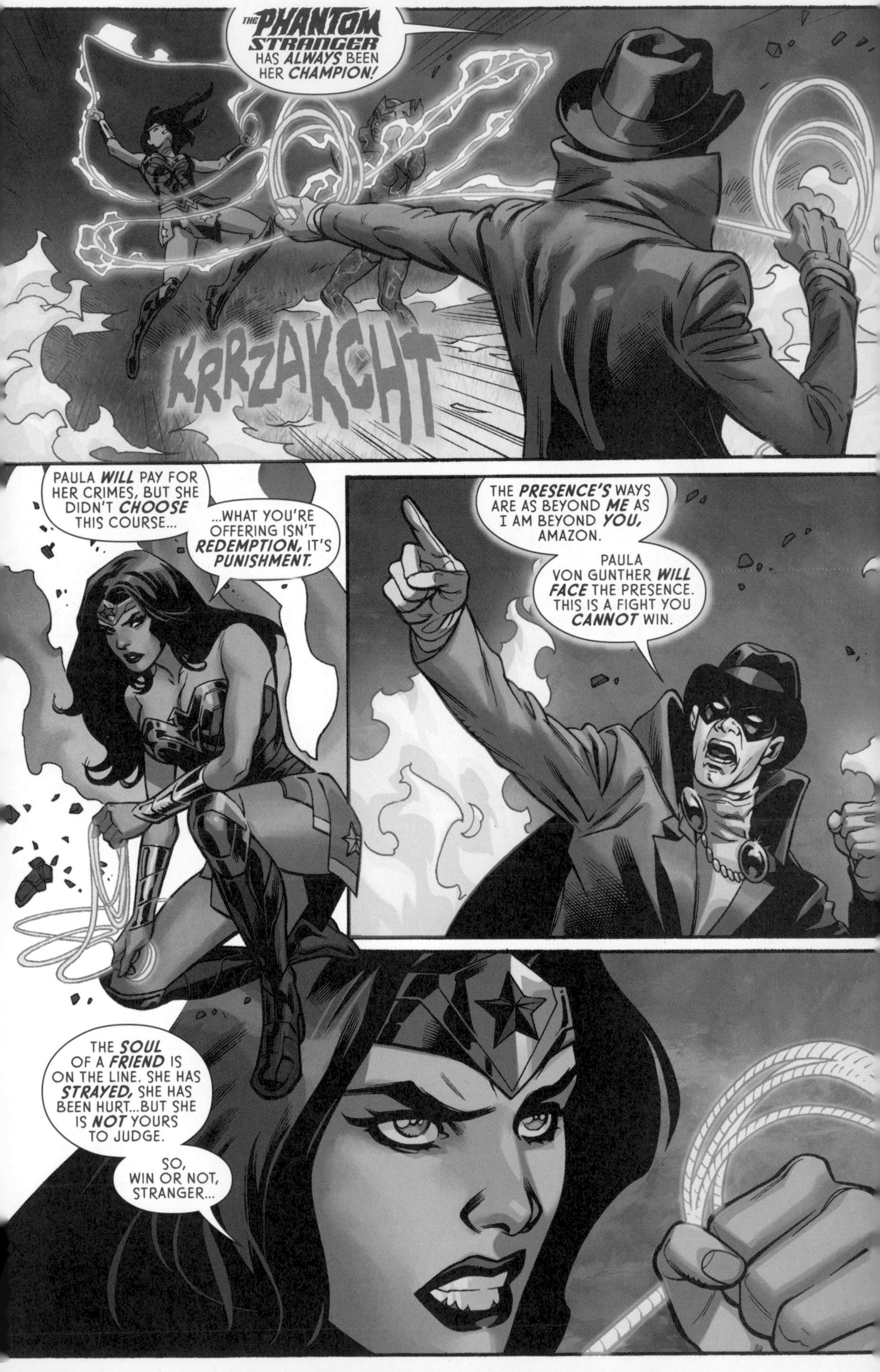
THE PHANTOM STRANGER HAS ALWAYS BEEN HER CHAMPION!
KRRZAKCHT
PAULA WILL PAY FOR HER CRIMES, BUT SHE DIDN'T CHOOSE THIS COURSE...
...WHAT YOU'RE OFFERING ISN'T REDEMPTION, IT'S PUNISHMENT.
THE PRESENCE'S WAYS ARE AS BEYOND ME AS I AM BEYOND YOU, AMAZON.
PAULA VON GUNTHER WILL FACE THE PRESENCE. THIS IS A FIGHT YOU CANNOT WIN.
THE SOUL OF A FRIEND IS ON THE LINE. SHE HAS STRAYED, SHE HAS BEEN HURT...BUT SHE IS NOT YOURS TO JUDGE.
SO, WIN OR NOT, STRANGER...

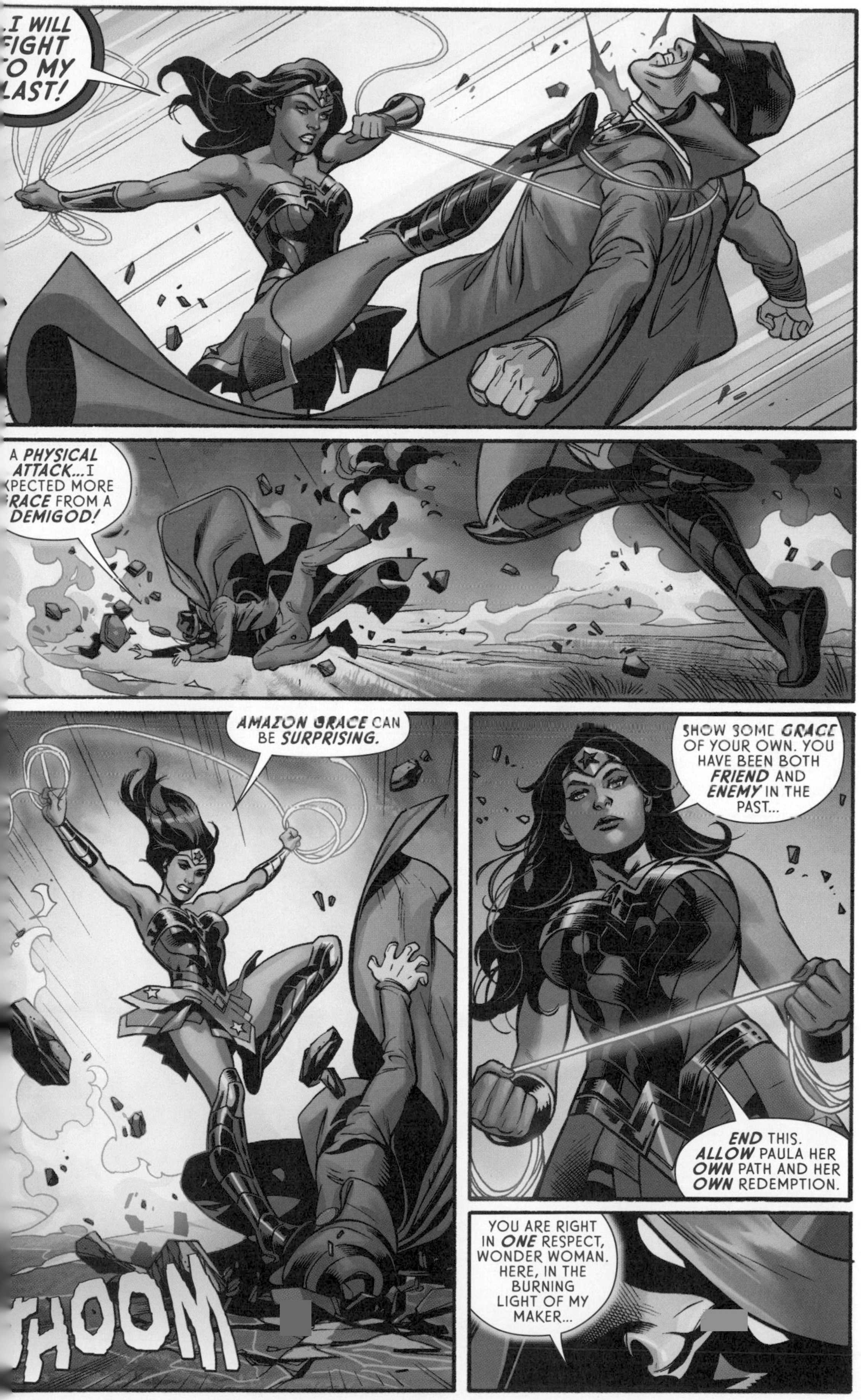

.I WILL FIGHT TO MY LAST!
A PHYSICAL ATTACK...I XPECTED MORE RACE FROM A DEMIGOD!
AMAZON GRACE CAN BE SURPRISING.
THOOM
SHOW SOME GRACE OF YOUR OWN. YOU HAVE BEEN BOTH FRIEND AND ENEMY IN THE PAST...
END THIS. ALLOW PAULA HER OWN PATH AND HER OWN REDEMPTION.
YOU ARE RIGHT IN ONE RESPECT, WONDER WOMAN. HERE, IN THE BURNING LIGHT OF MY MAKER...

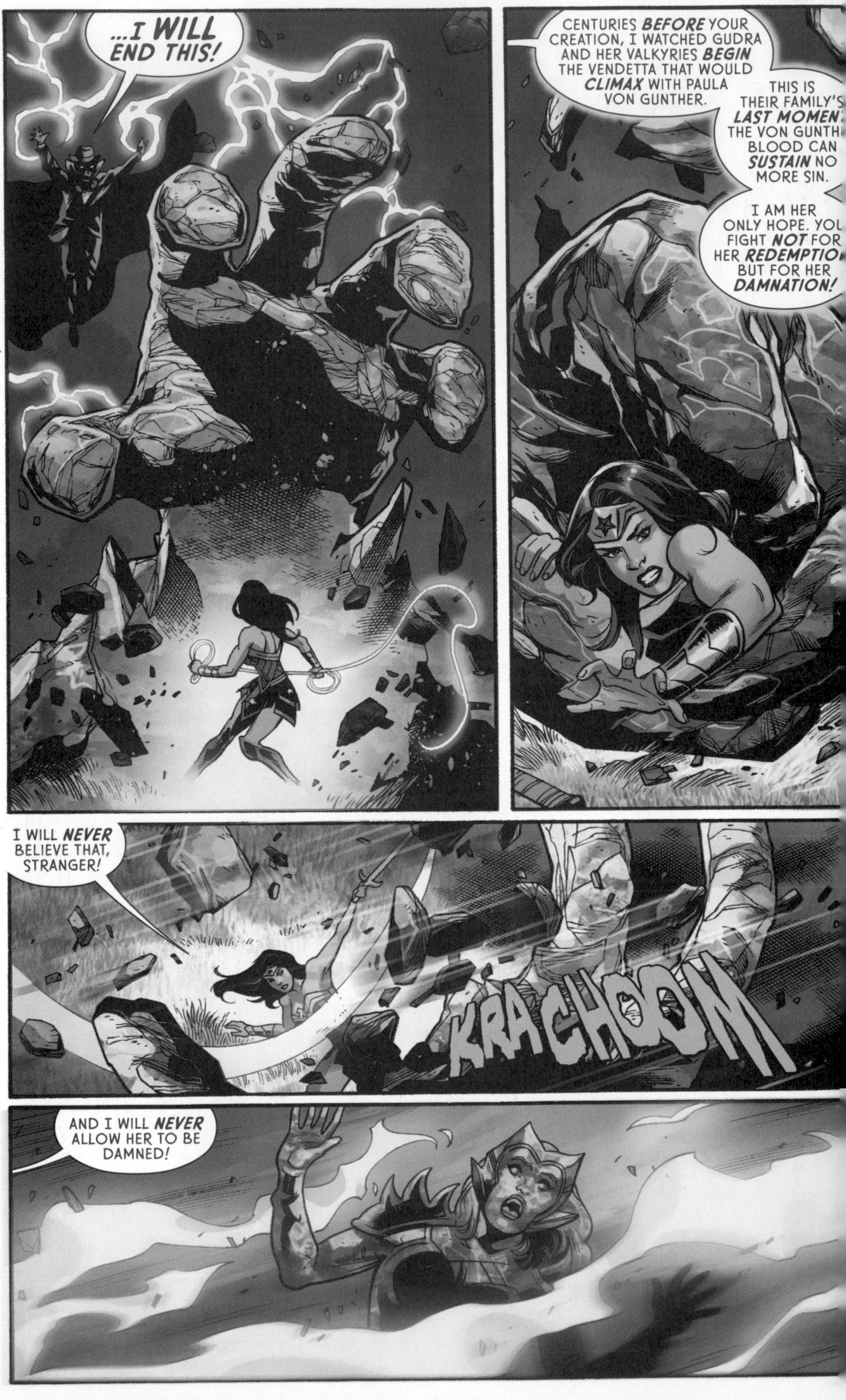

...I WILL END THIS!
CENTURIES BEFORE YOUR CREATION, I WATCHED GUDRA AND HER VALKYRIES BEGIN THE VENDETTA THAT WOULD CLIMAX WITH PAULA VON GUNTHER.
THIS IS THEIR FAMILY'S LAST MOMEN THE VON GUNTH BLOOD CAN SUSTAIN NO MORE SIN.
I AM HER ONLY HOPE. YO FIGHT NOT FOR HER REDEMPTIO BUT FOR HER DAMNATION!
I WILL NEVER BELIEVE THAT, STRANGER!
KRACHOOM
AND I WILL NEVER ALLOW HER TO BE DAMNED!

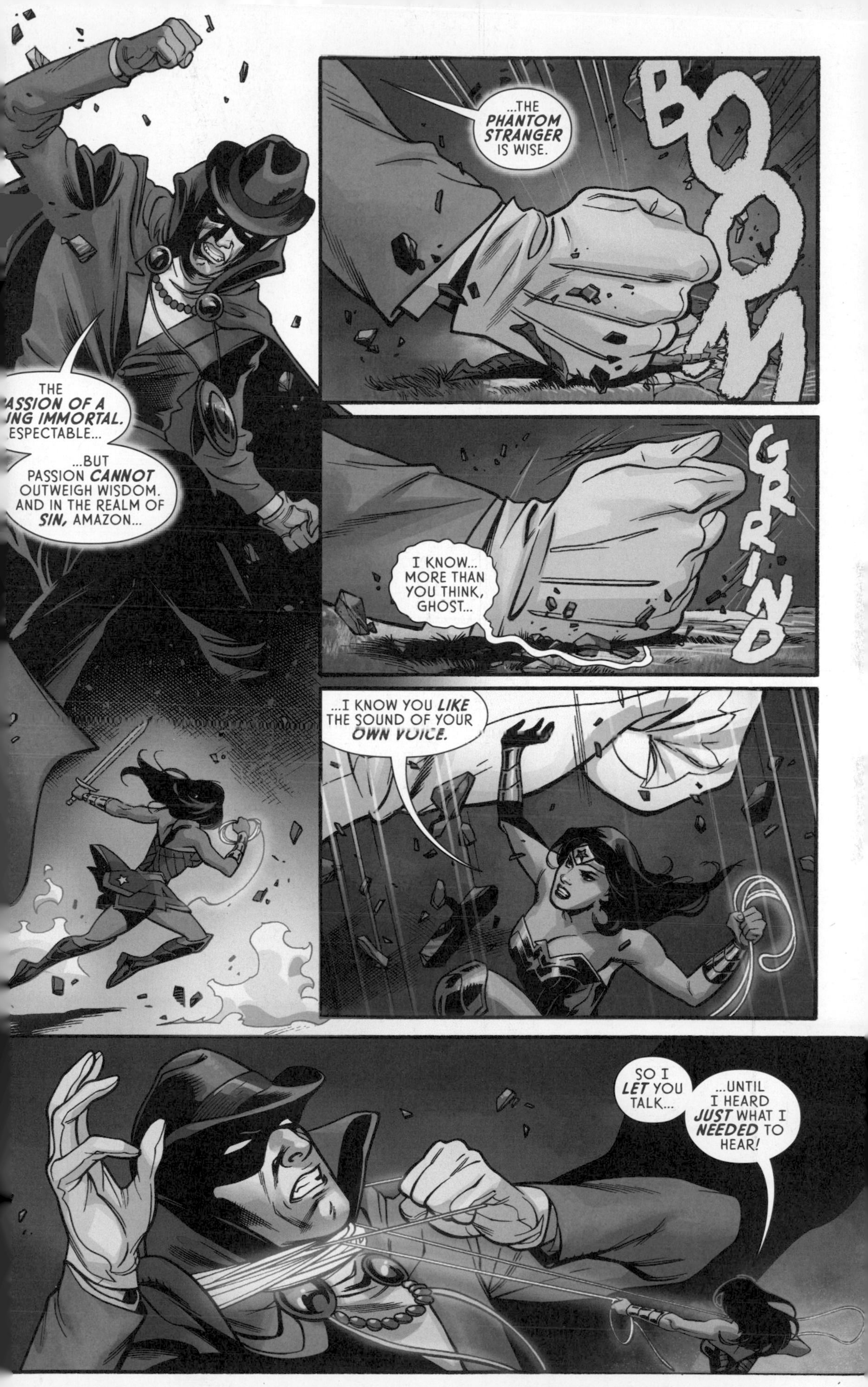
THE
ASSION OF A
ING IMMORTAL.
ESPECTABLE...
...BUT
PASSION CANNOT
OUTWEIGH WISDOM.
AND IN THE REALM OF
SIN, AMAZON...
...THE
PHANTOM
STRANGER
IS WISE.
BOOM
GRRIND
I KNOW...
MORE THAN
YOU THINK,
GHOST...
...I KNOW YOU LIKE
THE SOUND OF YOUR
OWN VOICE.
SO I
LET YOU
TALK...
...UNTIL
I HEARD
JUST WHAT I
NEEDED TO
HEAR!

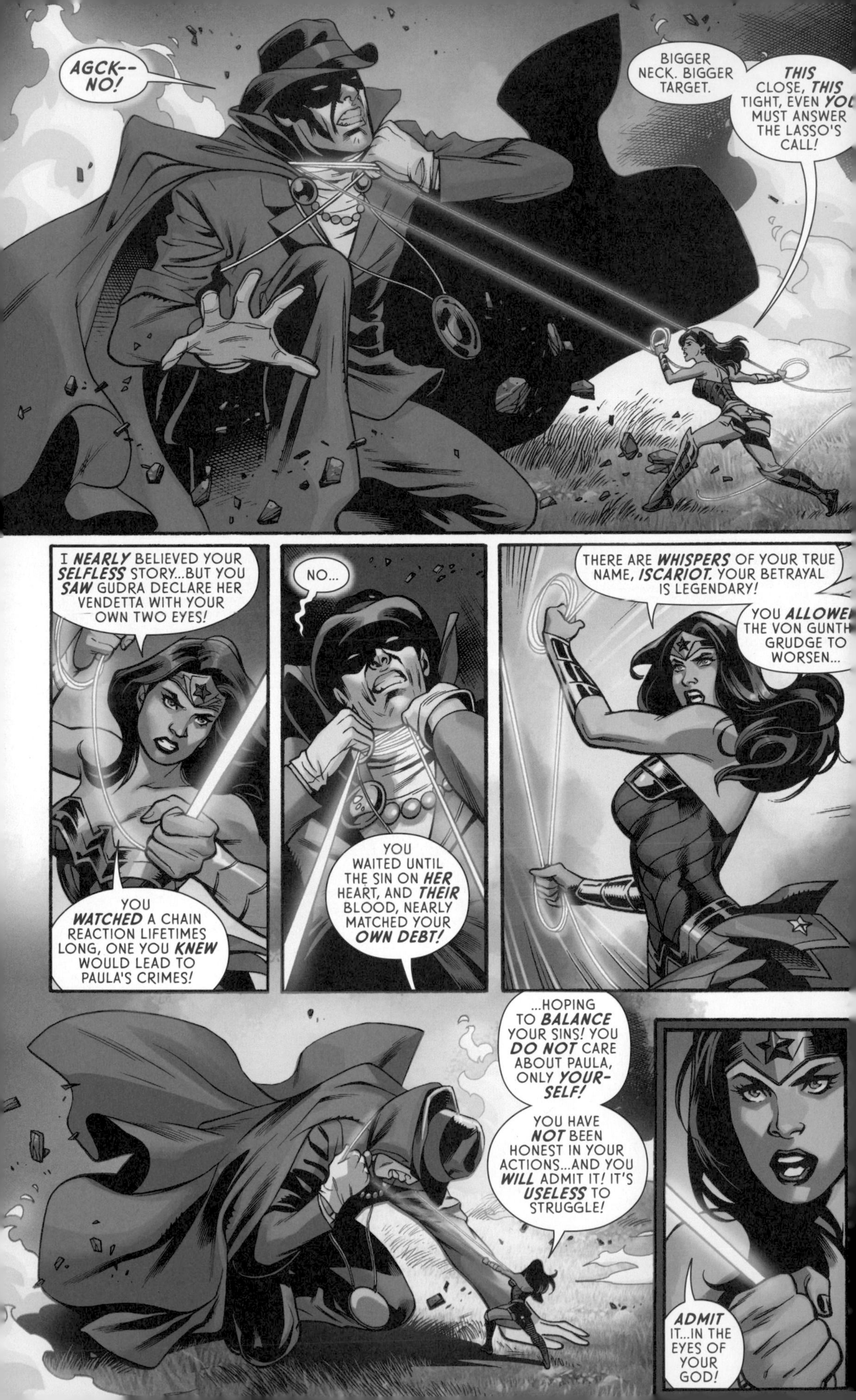
AGCK-- NO!
BIGGER NECK. BIGGER TARGET.
THIS CLOSE, THIS TIGHT, EVEN YOL MUST ANSWER THE LASSO'S CALL!
I NEARLY BELIEVED YOUR SELFLESS STORY...BUT YOU SAW GUDRA DECLARE HER VENDETTA WITH YOUR OWN TWO EYES!
YOU WATCHED A CHAIN REACTION LIFETIMES LONG, ONE YOU KNEW WOULD LEAD TO PAULA'S CRIMES!
NO...
YOU WAITED UNTIL THE SIN ON HER HEART, AND THEIR BLOOD, NEARLY MATCHED YOUR OWN DEBT!
THERE ARE WHISPERS OF YOUR TRUE NAME, ISCARIOT. YOUR BETRAYAL IS LEGENDARY!
YOU ALLOWE THE VON GUNTH GRUDGE TO WORSEN...
...HOPING TO BALANCE YOUR SINS! YOU DO NOT CARE ABOUT PAULA, ONLY YOUR-SELF!
YOU HAVE NOT BEEN HONEST IN YOUR ACTIONS...AND YOU WILL ADMIT IT! IT'S USELESS TO STRUGGLE!
ADMIT IT...IN THE EYES OF YOUR GOD!

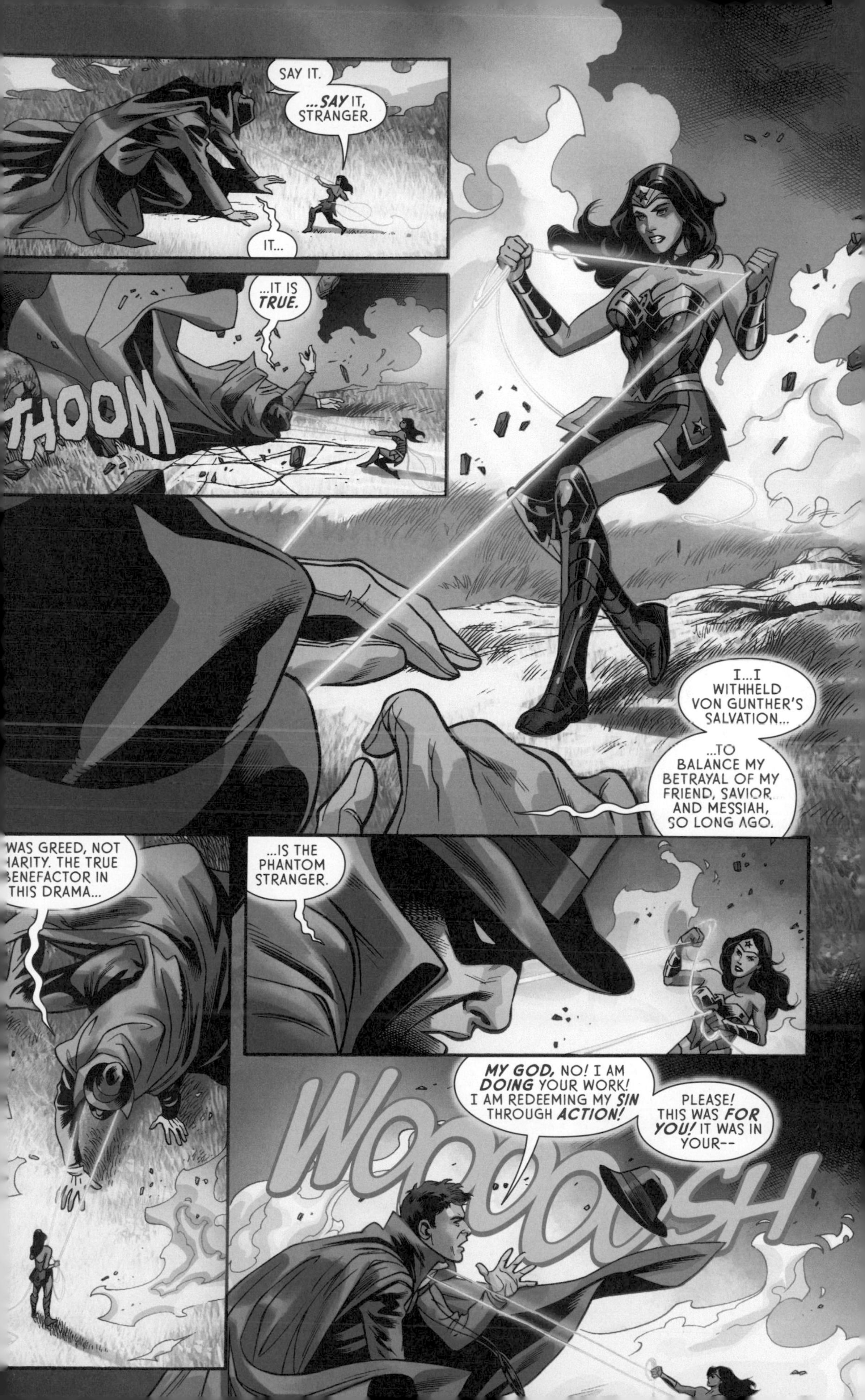
SAY IT.
...SAY IT, STRANGER.
IT...
...IT IS TRUE.
THOOM
I...I WITHHELD VON GUNTHER'S SALVATION...
...TO BALANCE MY BETRAYAL OF MY FRIEND, SAVIOR AND MESSIAH, SO LONG AGO.
WAS GREED, NOT HARITY. THE TRUE BENEFACTOR IN THIS DRAMA...
...IS THE PHANTOM STRANGER.
MY GOD, NO! I AM DOING YOUR WORK! I AM REDEEMING MY SIN THROUGH ACTION!
PLEASE! THIS WAS FOR YOU! IT WAS IN YOUR--
WOOOOSH

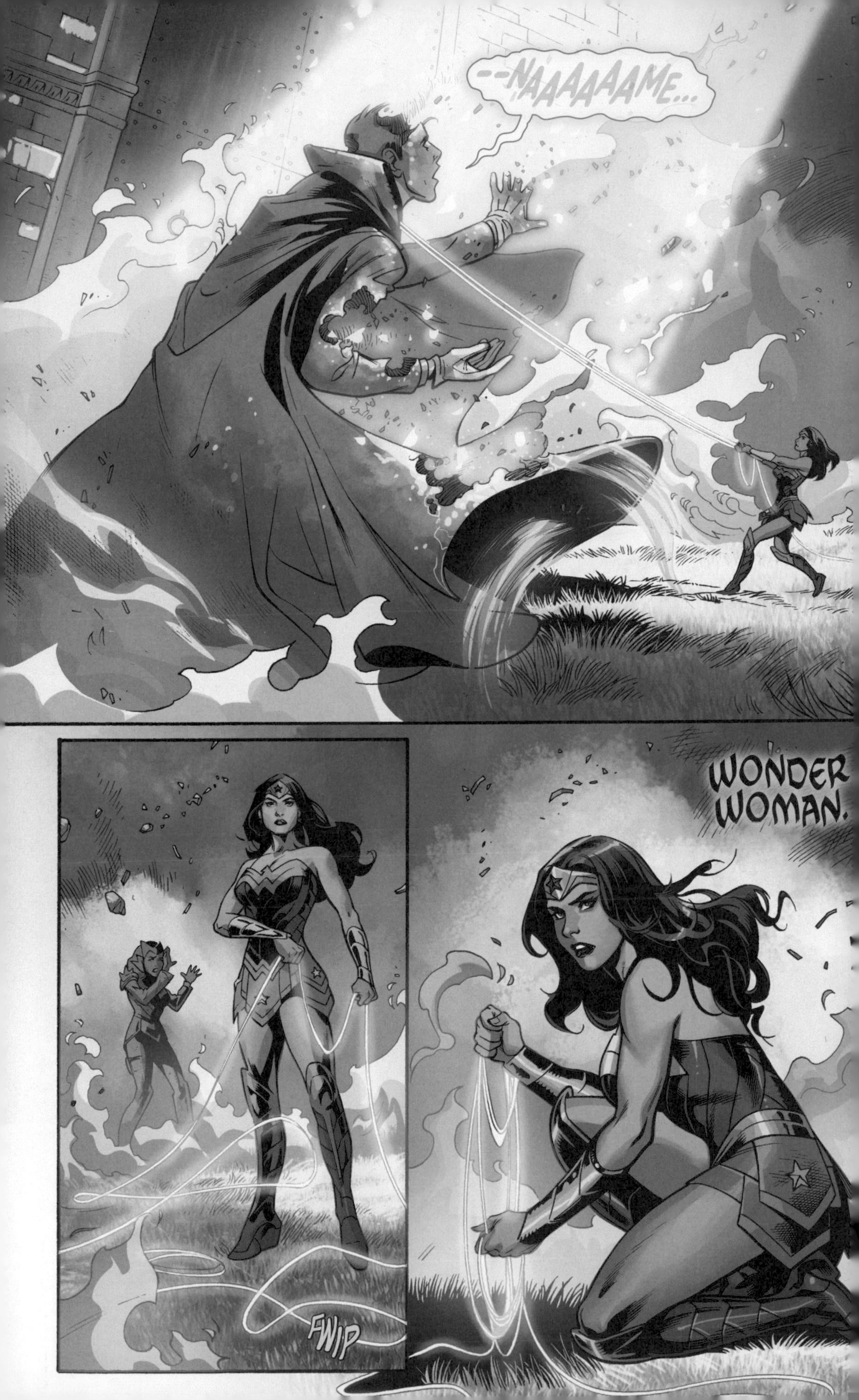

--NAAAAAAME...
FWIP
WONDER WOMAN.

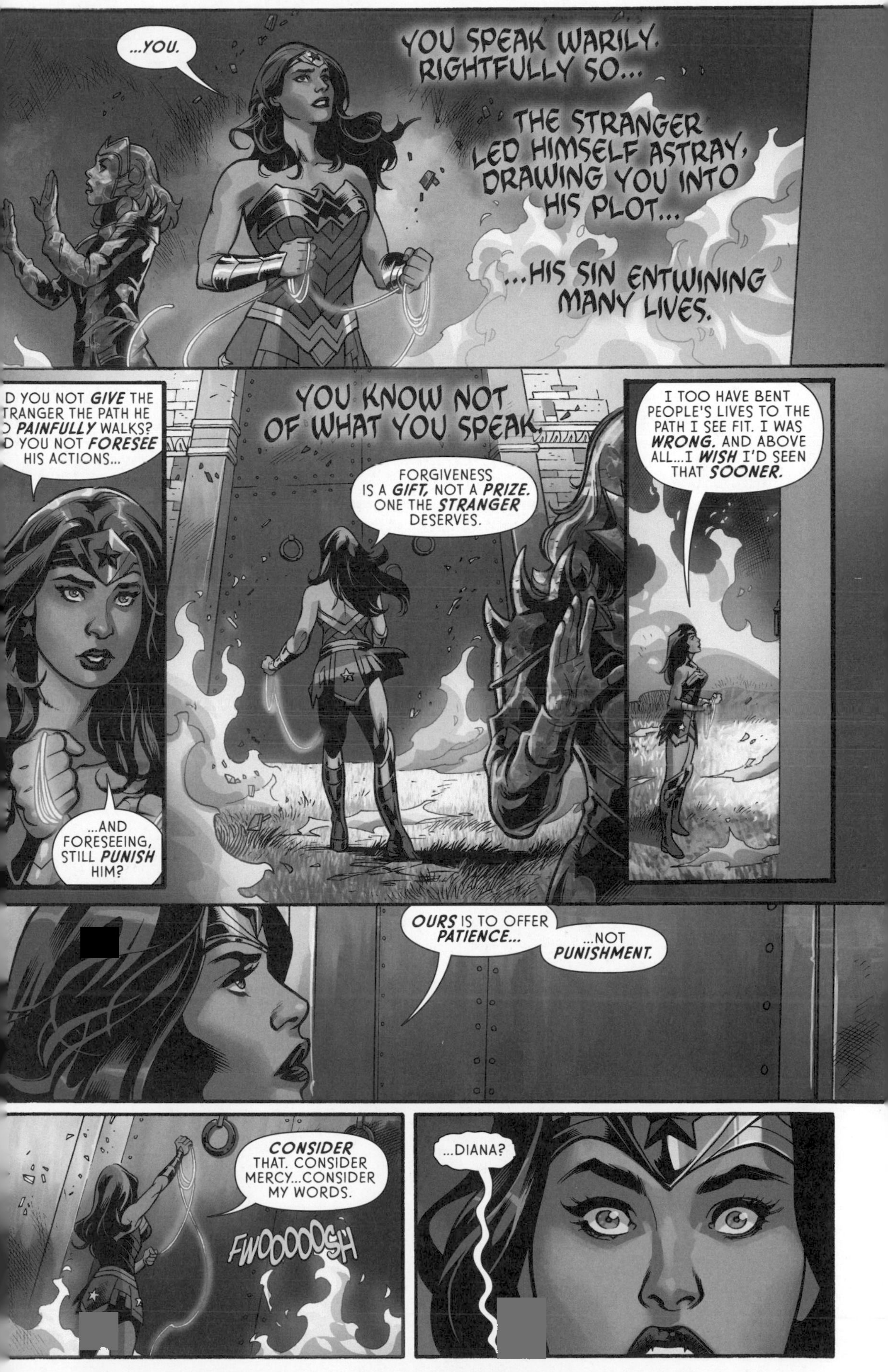
...YOU.
YOU SPEAK WARILY. RIGHTFULLY SO...
THE STRANGER LED HIMSELF ASTRAY, DRAWING YOU INTO HIS PLOT...
...HIS SIN ENTWINING MANY LIVES.
D YOU NOT *GIVE* THE TRANGER THE PATH HE D *PAINFULLY* WALKS? D YOU NOT *FORESEE* HIS ACTIONS...
...AND FORESEEING, STILL *PUNISH* HIM?
YOU KNOW NOT OF WHAT YOU SPEAK.
FORGIVENESS IS A *GIFT,* NOT A *PRIZE.* ONE THE *STRANGER* DESERVES.
I TOO HAVE BENT PEOPLE'S LIVES TO THE PATH I SEE FIT. I WAS *WRONG.* AND ABOVE ALL...I *WISH* I'D SEEN THAT *SOONER.*
OURS IS TO OFFER *PATIENCE...*
...NOT *PUNISHMENT.*
CONSIDER THAT. CONSIDER MERCY...CONSIDER MY WORDS.
FWOOOOOSH
...DIANA?

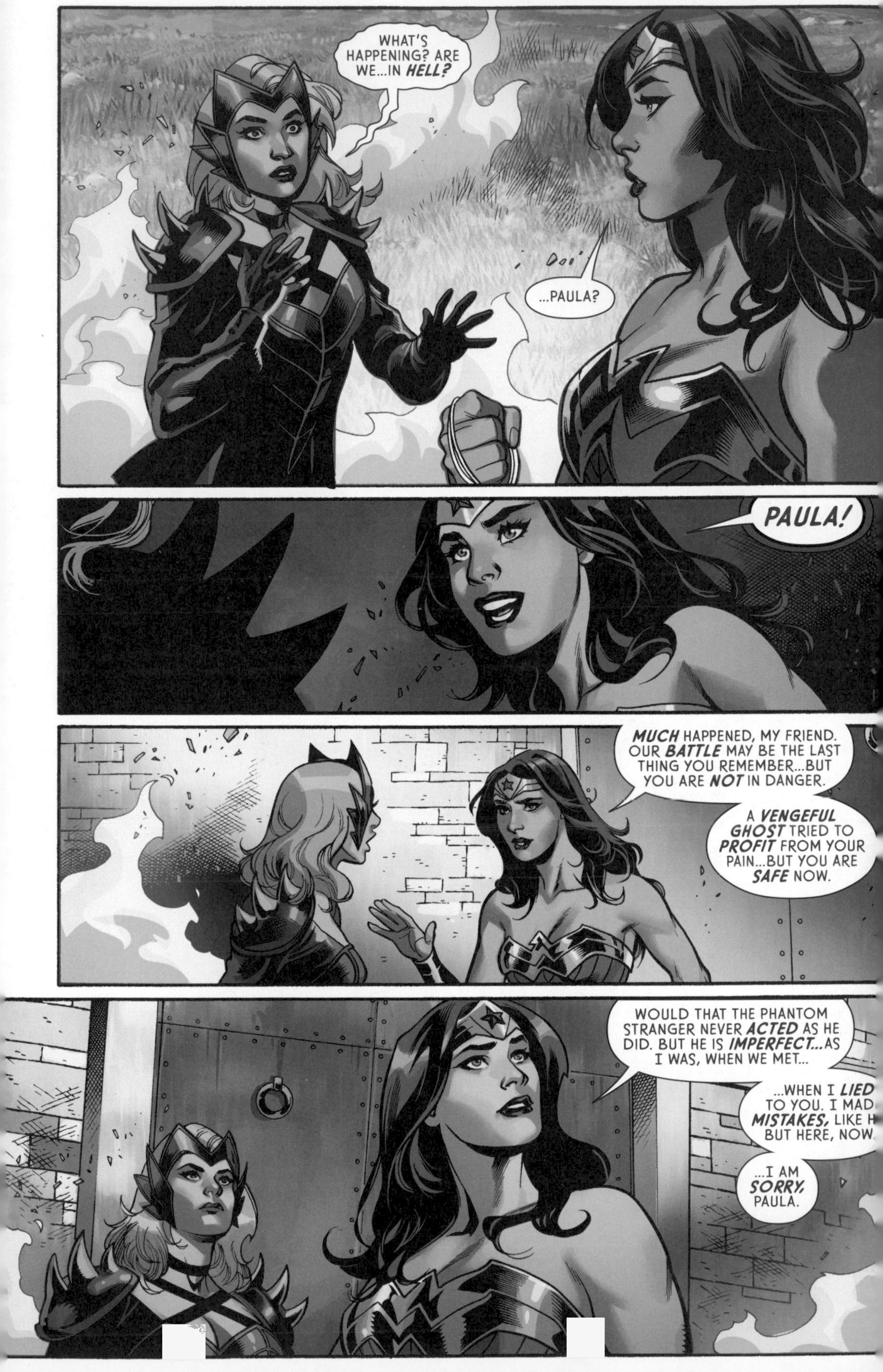

WHAT'S HAPPENING? ARE WE...IN HELL?
...PAULA?
PAULA!
MUCH HAPPENED, MY FRIEND. OUR BATTLE MAY BE THE LAST THING YOU REMEMBER...BUT YOU ARE NOT IN DANGER.
A VENGEFUL GHOST TRIED TO PROFIT FROM YOUR PAIN...BUT YOU ARE SAFE NOW.
WOULD THAT THE PHANTOM STRANGER NEVER ACTED AS HE DID. BUT HE IS IMPERFECT...AS I WAS, WHEN WE MET...
...WHEN I LIED TO YOU. I MAD MISTAKES, LIKE H BUT HERE, NOW.
...I AM SORRY, PAULA.

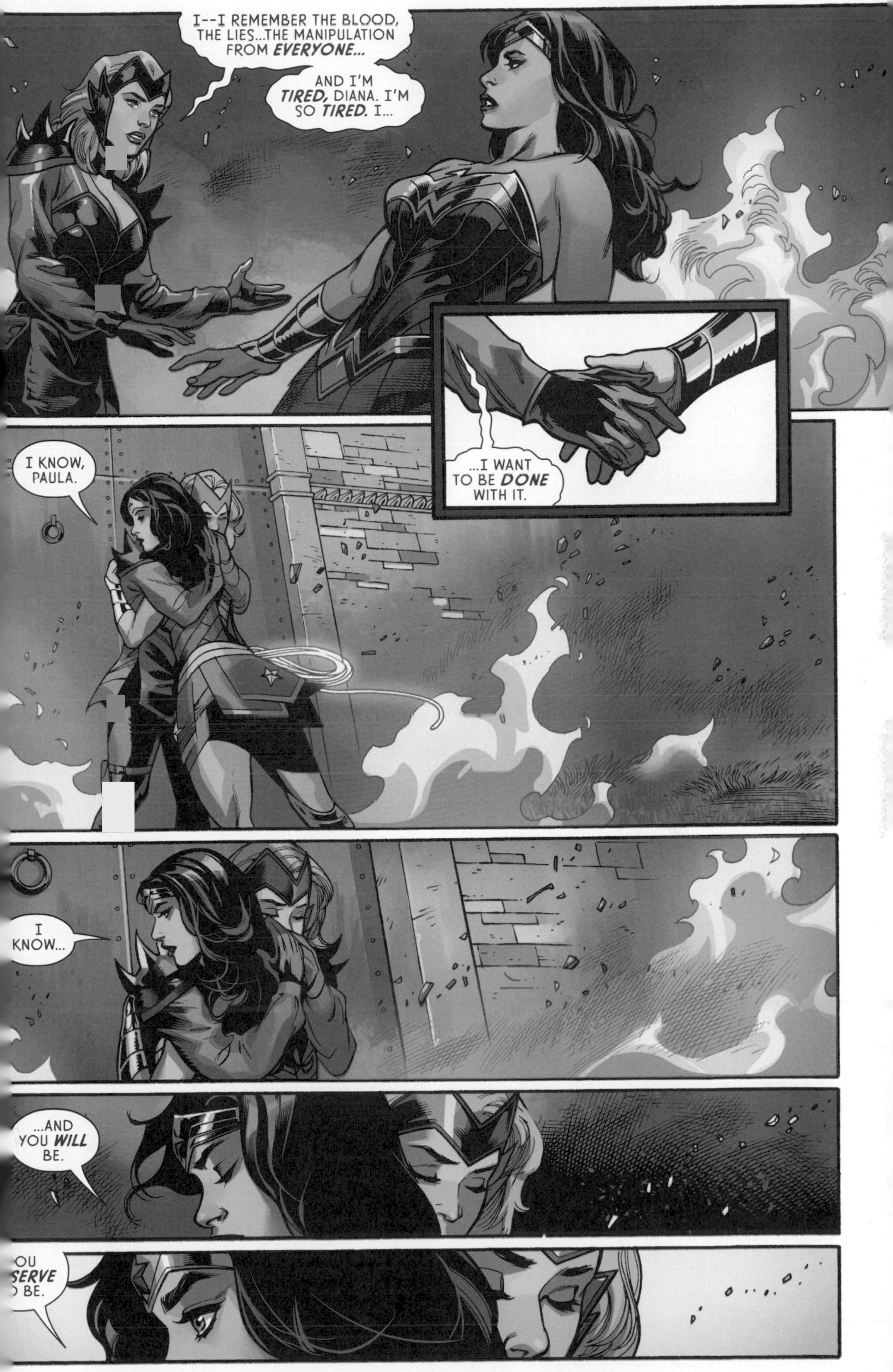
I--I REMEMBER THE BLOOD, THE LIES...THE MANIPULATION FROM EVERYONE...
AND I'M TIRED, DIANA. I'M SO TIRED. I...
...I WANT TO BE DONE WITH IT.
I KNOW, PAULA.
I KNOW...
...AND YOU WILL BE.
OU SERVE BE.

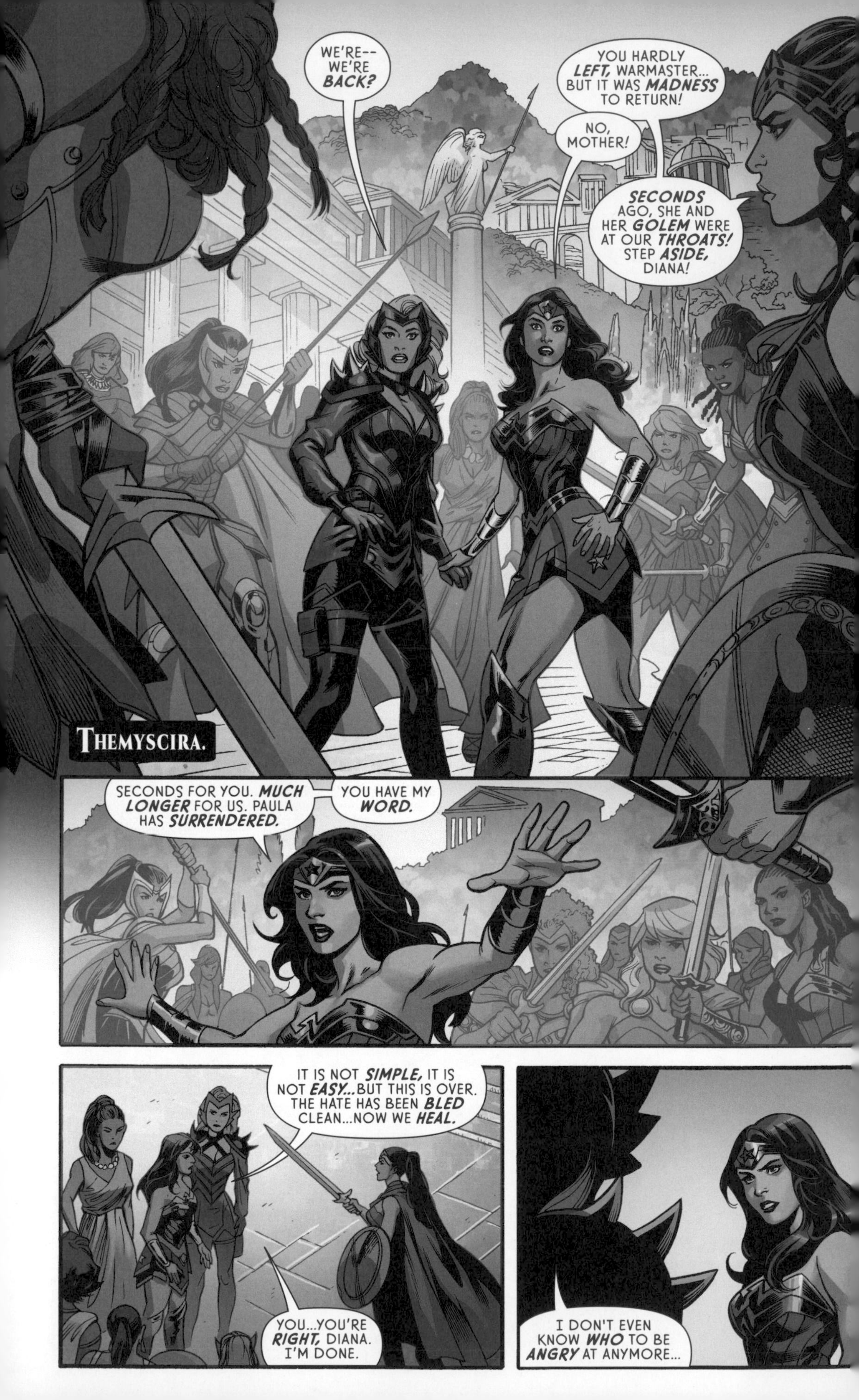
WE'RE-- WE'RE BACK?
YOU HARDLY LEFT, WARMASTER... BUT IT WAS MADNESS TO RETURN!
NO, MOTHER!
SECONDS AGO, SHE AND HER GOLEM WERE AT OUR THROATS! STEP ASIDE, DIANA!
THEMYSCIRA.
SECONDS FOR YOU. MUCH LONGER FOR US. PAULA HAS SURRENDERED.
YOU HAVE MY WORD.
IT IS NOT SIMPLE, IT IS NOT EASY...BUT THIS IS OVER. THE HATE HAS BEEN BLED CLEAN...NOW WE HEAL.
YOU...YOU'RE RIGHT, DIANA. I'M DONE.
I DON'T EVEN KNOW WHO TO BE ANGRY AT ANYMORE...

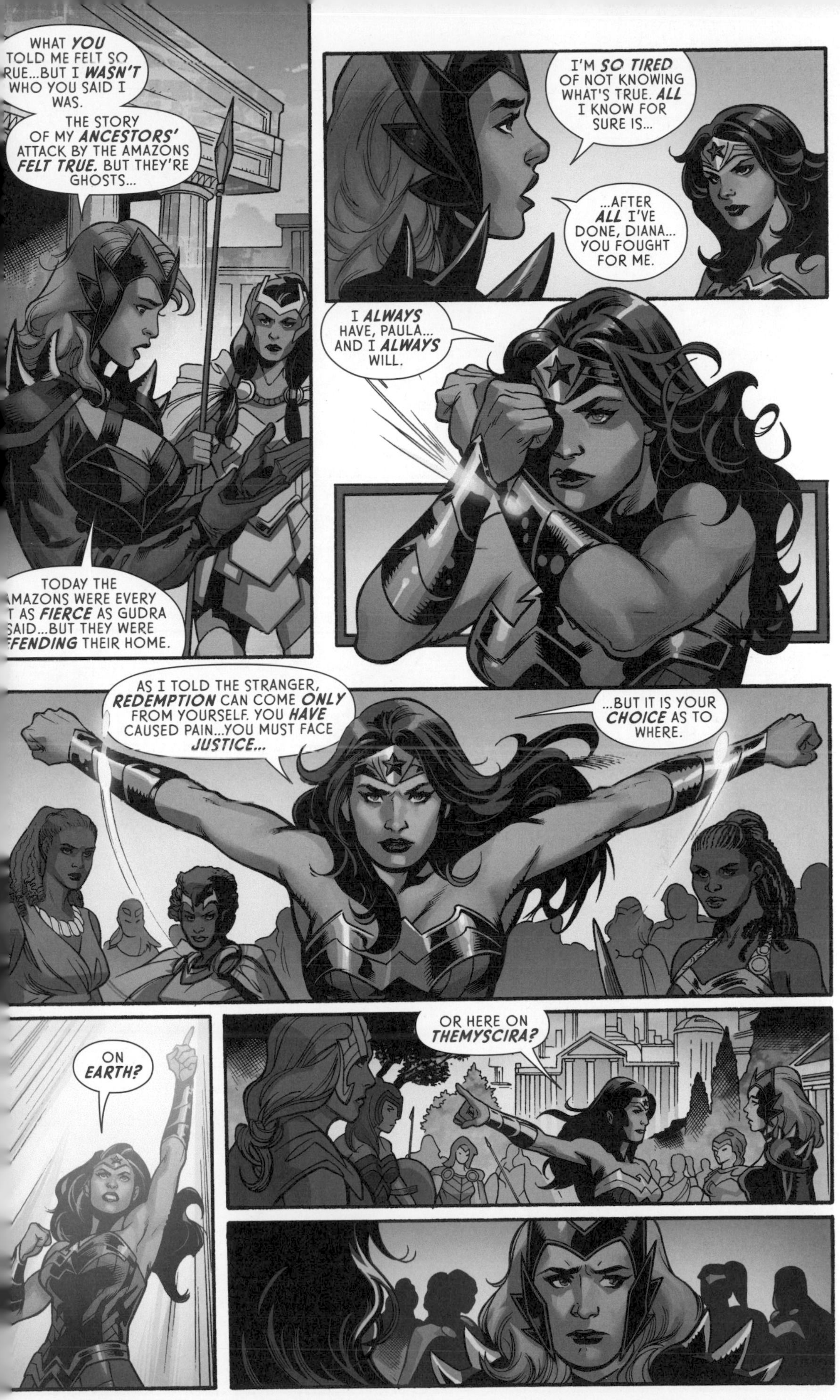
WHAT YOU TOLD ME FELT SO TRUE...BUT I WASN'T WHO YOU SAID I WAS.
THE STORY OF MY ANCESTORS' ATTACK BY THE AMAZONS FELT TRUE. BUT THEY'RE GHOSTS...
TODAY THE AMAZONS WERE EVERY BIT AS FIERCE AS GUDRA SAID...BUT THEY WERE DEFENDING THEIR HOME.
I'M SO TIRED OF NOT KNOWING WHAT'S TRUE. ALL I KNOW FOR SURE IS...
...AFTER ALL I'VE DONE, DIANA... YOU FOUGHT FOR ME.
I ALWAYS HAVE, PAULA... AND I ALWAYS WILL.
AS I TOLD THE STRANGER, REDEMPTION CAN COME ONLY FROM YOURSELF. YOU HAVE CAUSED PAIN...YOU MUST FACE JUSTICE...
...BUT IT IS YOUR CHOICE AS TO WHERE.
ON EARTH?
OR HERE ON THEMYSCIRA?

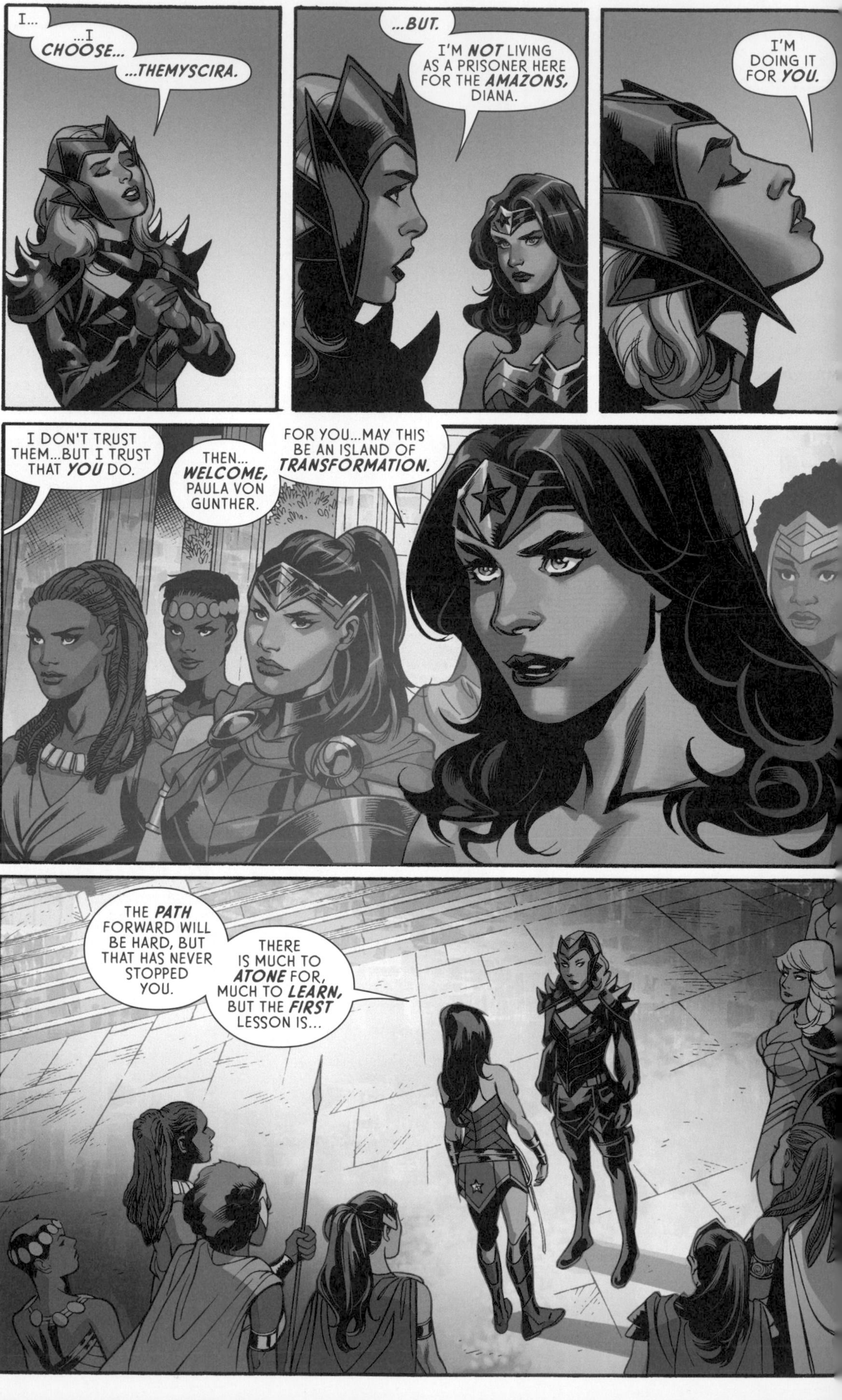
I...
...I CHOOSE...
...THEMYSCIRA.
...BUT.
I'M NOT LIVING AS A PRISONER HERE FOR THE AMAZONS, DIANA.
I'M DOING IT FOR YOU.
I DON'T TRUST THEM...BUT I TRUST THAT YOU DO.
THEN... WELCOME, PAULA VON GUNTHER.
FOR YOU...MAY THIS BE AN ISLAND OF TRANSFORMATION.
THE PATH FORWARD WILL BE HARD, BUT THAT HAS NEVER STOPPED YOU.
THERE IS MUCH TO ATONE FOR, MUCH TO LEARN, BUT THE FIRST LESSON IS...

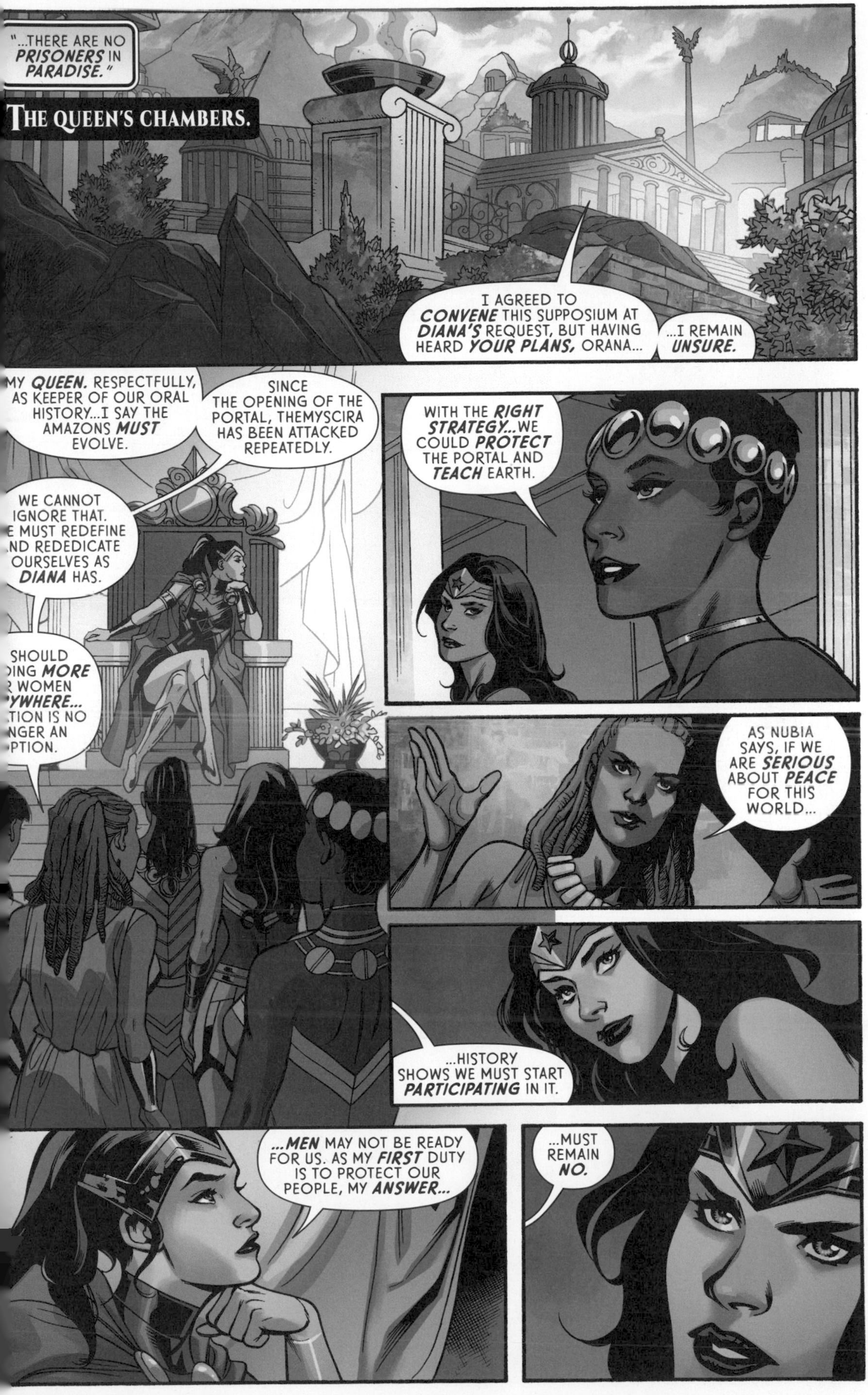

"...THERE ARE NO PRISONERS IN PARADISE."
THE QUEEN'S CHAMBERS.
I AGREED TO CONVENE THIS SUPPOSIUM AT DIANA'S REQUEST, BUT HAVING HEARD YOUR PLANS, ORANA...
...I REMAIN UNSURE.
MY QUEEN. RESPECTFULLY, AS KEEPER OF OUR ORAL HISTORY...I SAY THE AMAZONS MUST EVOLVE.
SINCE THE OPENING OF THE PORTAL, THEMYSCIRA HAS BEEN ATTACKED REPEATEDLY.
WE CANNOT IGNORE THAT.
E MUST REDEFINE ND REDEDICATE OURSELVES AS DIANA HAS.
SHOULD DING MORE R WOMEN YWHERE... TION IS NO NGER AN PTION.
WITH THE RIGHT STRATEGY...WE COULD PROTECT THE PORTAL AND TEACH EARTH.
AS NUBIA SAYS, IF WE ARE SERIOUS ABOUT PEACE FOR THIS WORLD...
...HISTORY SHOWS WE MUST START PARTICIPATING IN IT.
...MEN MAY NOT BE READY FOR US. AS MY FIRST DUTY IS TO PROTECT OUR PEOPLE, MY ANSWER...
...MUST REMAIN NO.

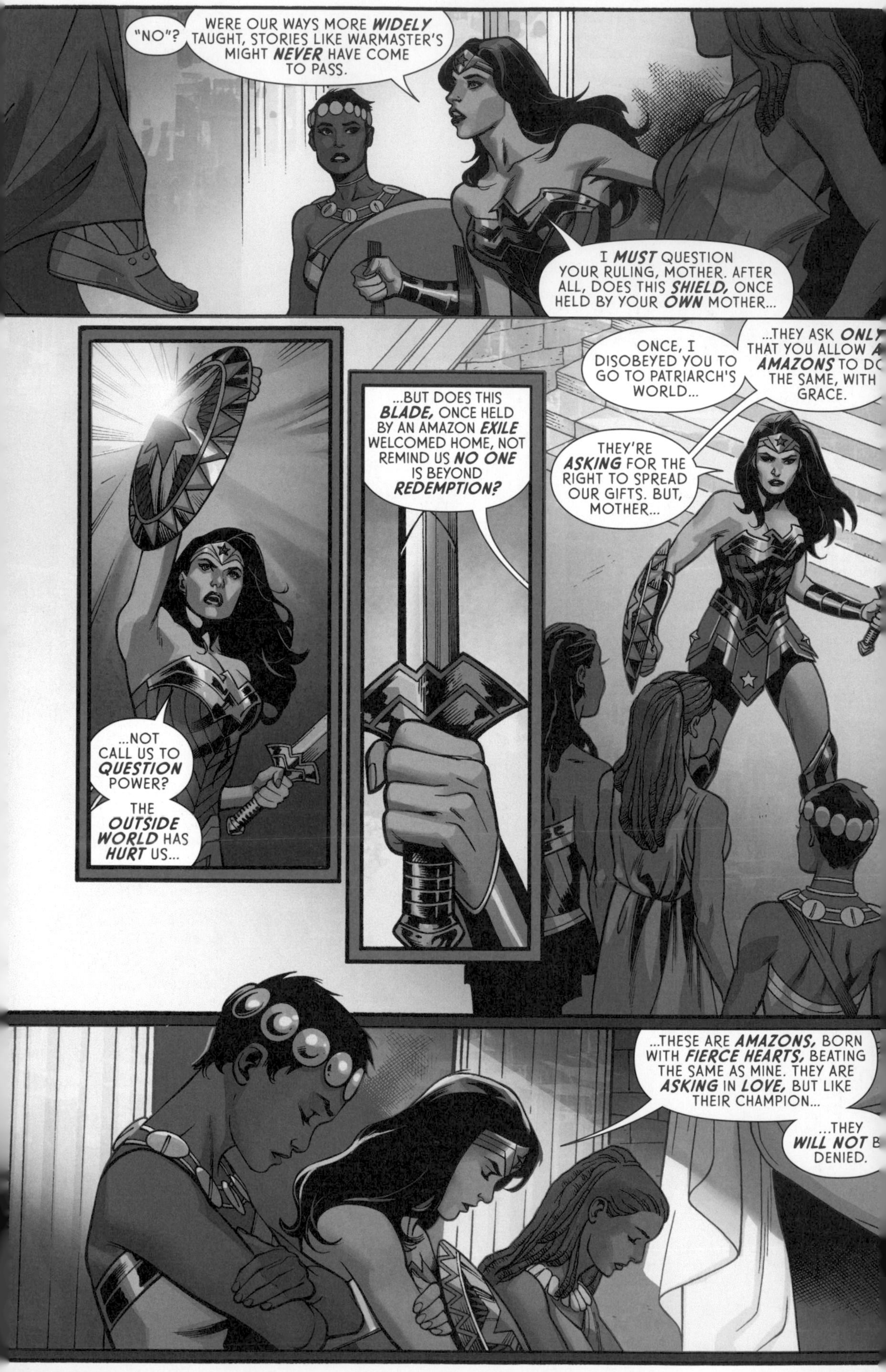
"NO"?
WERE OUR WAYS MORE WIDELY TAUGHT, STORIES LIKE WARMASTER'S MIGHT NEVER HAVE COME TO PASS.
I MUST QUESTION YOUR RULING, MOTHER. AFTER ALL, DOES THIS SHIELD, ONCE HELD BY YOUR OWN MOTHER...
...NOT CALL US TO QUESTION POWER?
THE OUTSIDE WORLD HAS HURT US...
...BUT DOES THIS BLADE, ONCE HELD BY AN AMAZON EXILE WELCOMED HOME, NOT REMIND US NO ONE IS BEYOND REDEMPTION?
ONCE, I DISOBEYED YOU TO GO TO PATRIARCH'S WORLD...
...THEY ASK ONLY THAT YOU ALLOW AMAZONS TO DO THE SAME, WITH GRACE.
THEY'RE ASKING FOR THE RIGHT TO SPREAD OUR GIFTS. BUT, MOTHER...
...THESE ARE AMAZONS, BORN WITH FIERCE HEARTS, BEATING THE SAME AS MINE. THEY ARE ASKING IN LOVE, BUT LIKE THEIR CHAMPION...
...THEY WILL NOT DENIED.

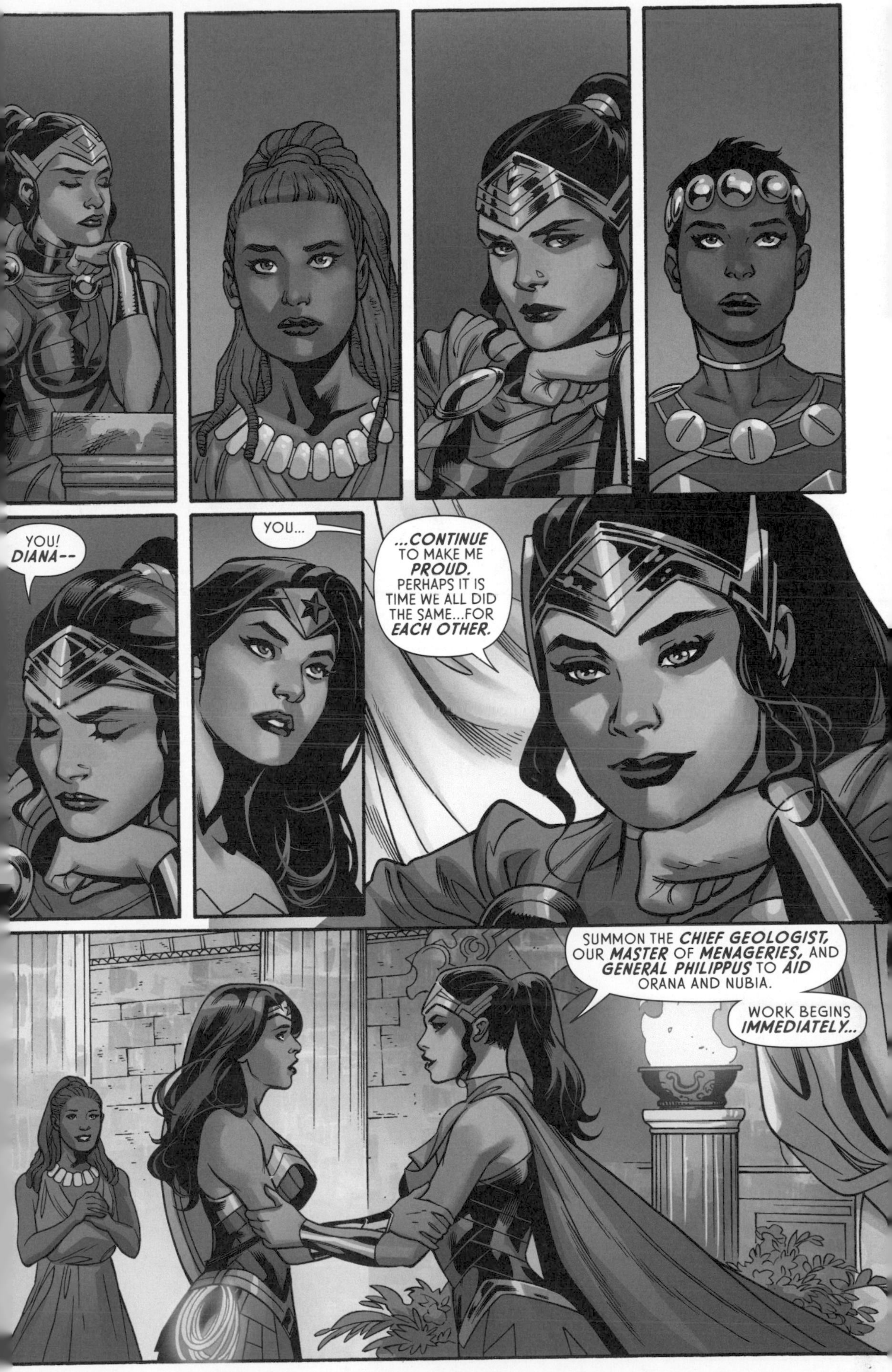
YOU! DIANA--
YOU...
...CONTINUE TO MAKE ME PROUD. PERHAPS IT IS TIME WE ALL DID THE SAME...FOR EACH OTHER.
SUMMON THE CHIEF GEOLOGIST, OUR MASTER OF MENAGERIES, AND GENERAL PHILIPPUS TO AID ORANA AND NUBIA.
WORK BEGINS IMMEDIATELY...

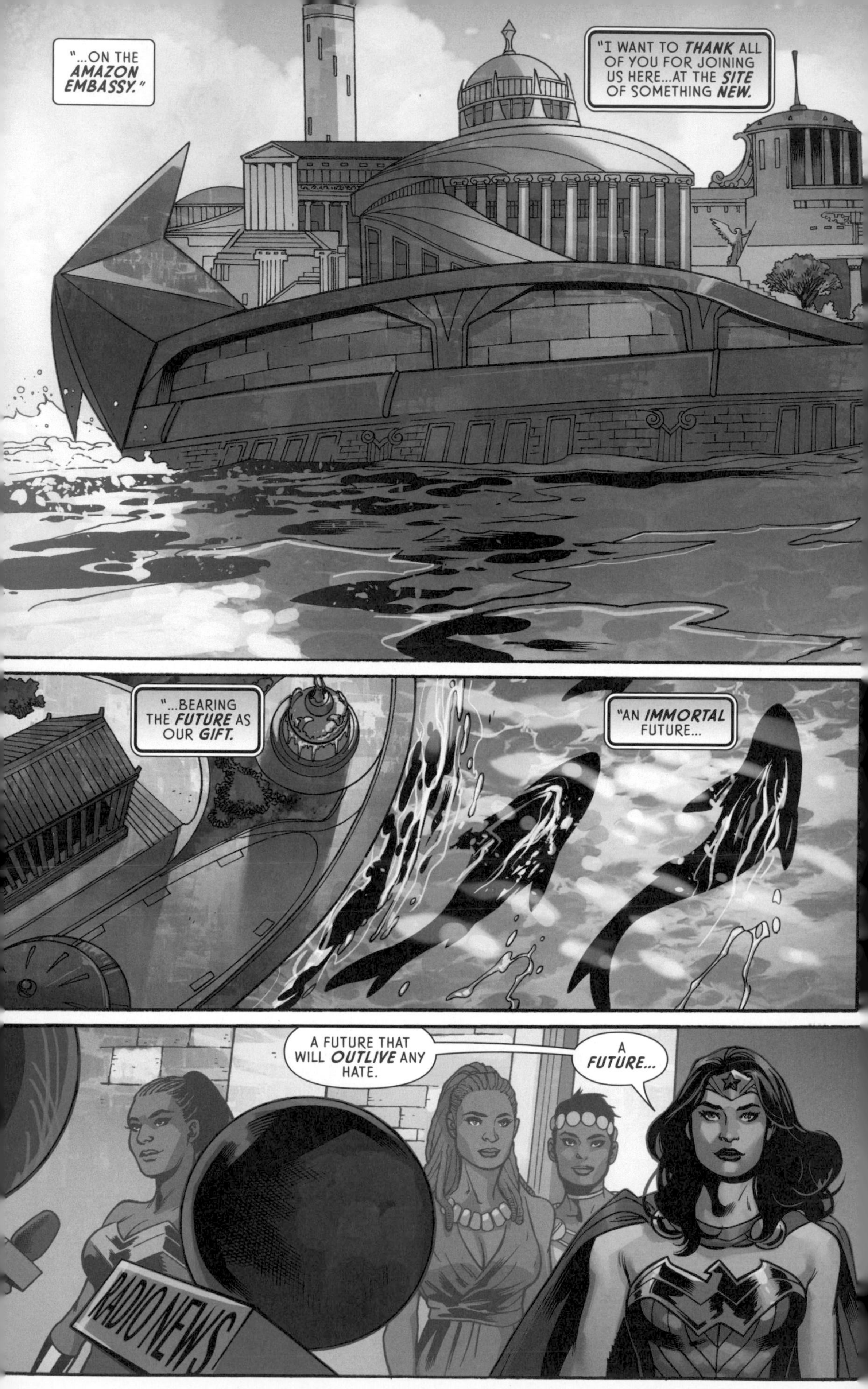
"...ON THE AMAZON EMBASSY."
"I WANT TO THANK ALL OF YOU FOR JOINING US HERE...AT THE SITE OF SOMETHING NEW.
"...BEARING THE FUTURE AS OUR GIFT.
"AN IMMORTAL FUTURE...
A FUTURE THAT WILL OUTLIVE ANY HATE.
A FUTURE...
RADIO NEWS

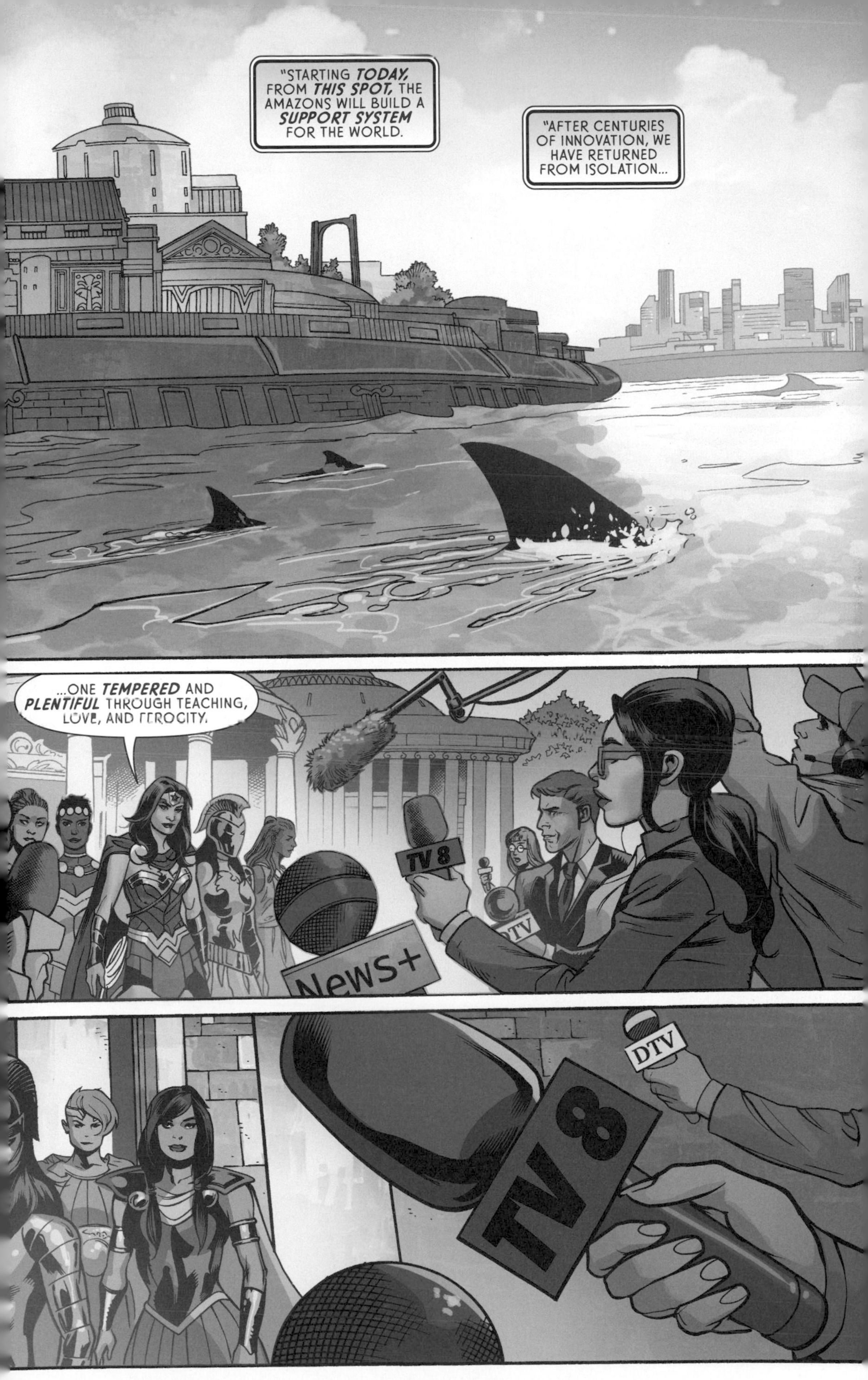

"STARTING TODAY, FROM THIS SPOT, THE AMAZONS WILL BUILD A SUPPORT SYSTEM FOR THE WORLD.
"AFTER CENTURIES OF INNOVATION, WE HAVE RETURNED FROM ISOLATION...
...ONE TEMPERED AND PLENTIFUL THROUGH TEACHING, LOVE, AND FEROCITY.
TV 8
DTV
News+
DTV
TV 8

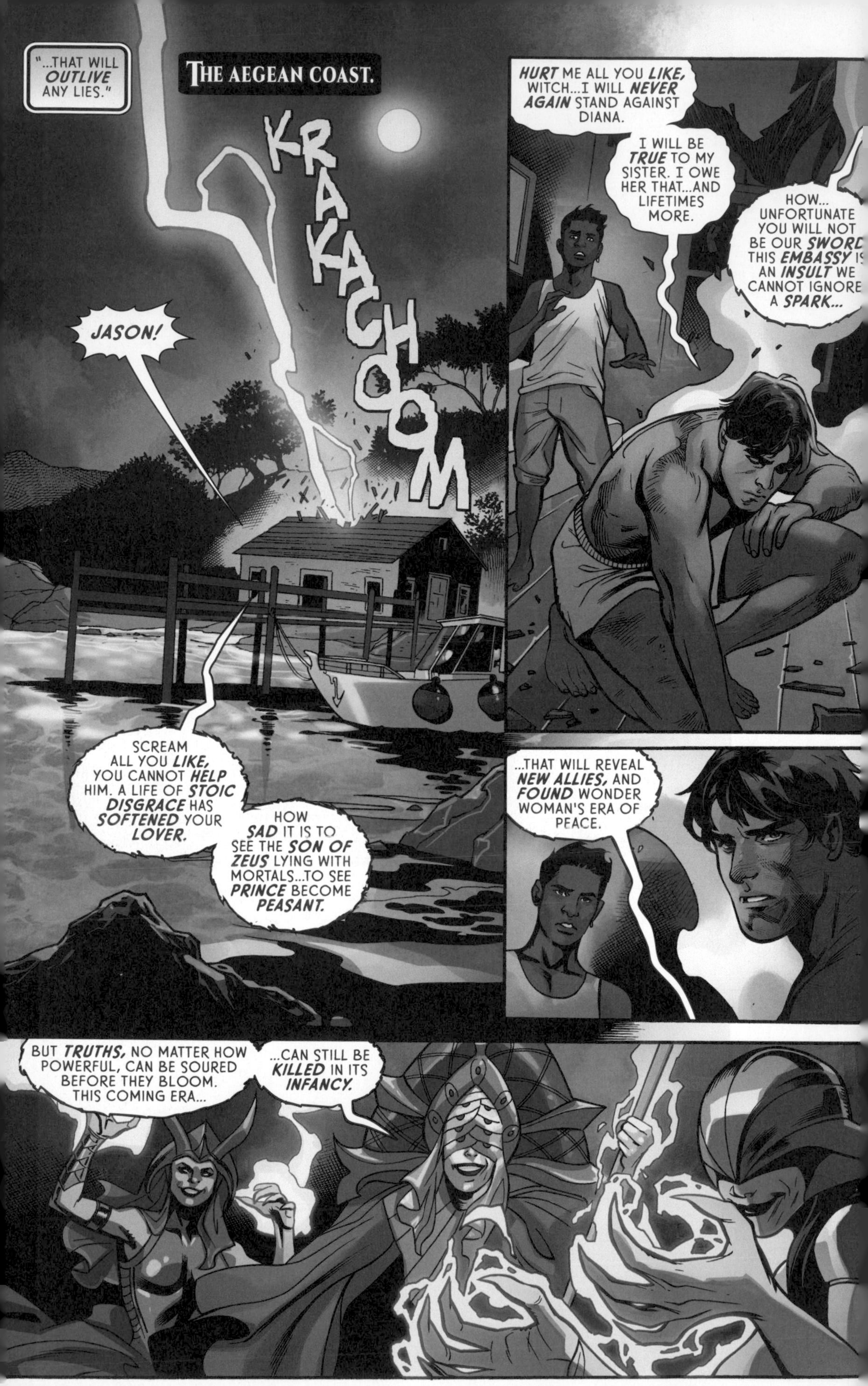
"...THAT WILL OUTLIVE ANY LIES."
THE AEGEAN COAST.
KRAKACHOOM
JASON!
SCREAM ALL YOU LIKE, YOU CANNOT HELP HIM. A LIFE OF STOIC DISGRACE HAS SOFTENED YOUR LOVER.
HOW SAD IT IS TO SEE THE SON OF ZEUS LYING WITH MORTALS...TO SEE PRINCE BECOME PEASANT.
HURT ME ALL YOU LIKE, WITCH...I WILL NEVER AGAIN STAND AGAINST DIANA.
I WILL BE TRUE TO MY SISTER. I OWE HER THAT...AND LIFETIMES MORE.
HOW... UNFORTUNATE YOU WILL NOT BE OUR SWORD. THIS EMBASSY IS AN INSULT WE CANNOT IGNORE. A SPARK...
...THAT WILL REVEAL NEW ALLIES, AND FOUND WONDER WOMAN'S ERA OF PEACE.
BUT TRUTHS, NO MATTER HOW POWERFUL, CAN BE SOURED BEFORE THEY BLOOM. THIS COMING ERA...
...CAN STILL BE KILLED IN ITS INFANCY.

***Wonder Woman Annual* #4**
cover by **BRYAN HITCH** and **ALEX SINCLAIR**

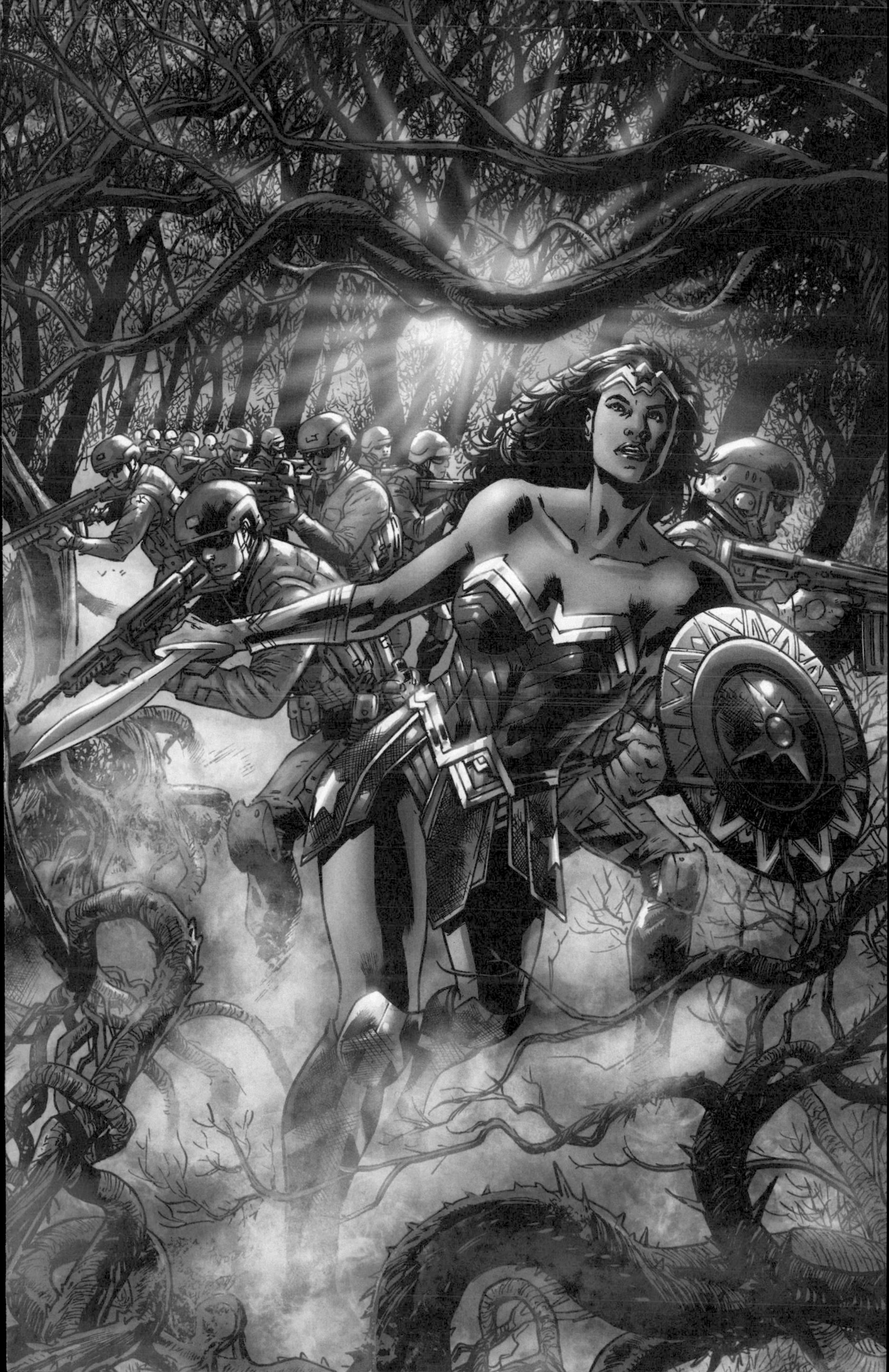

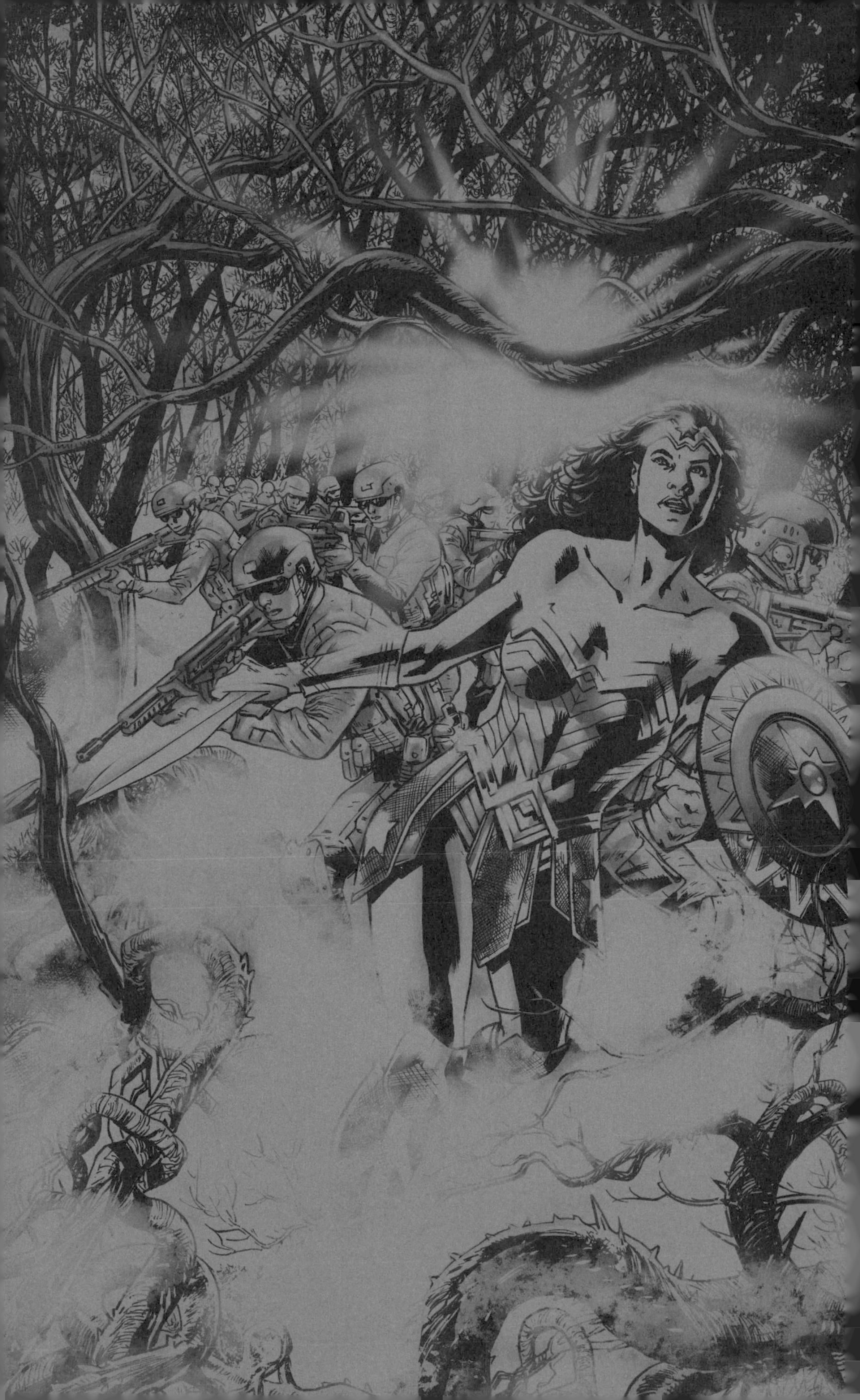

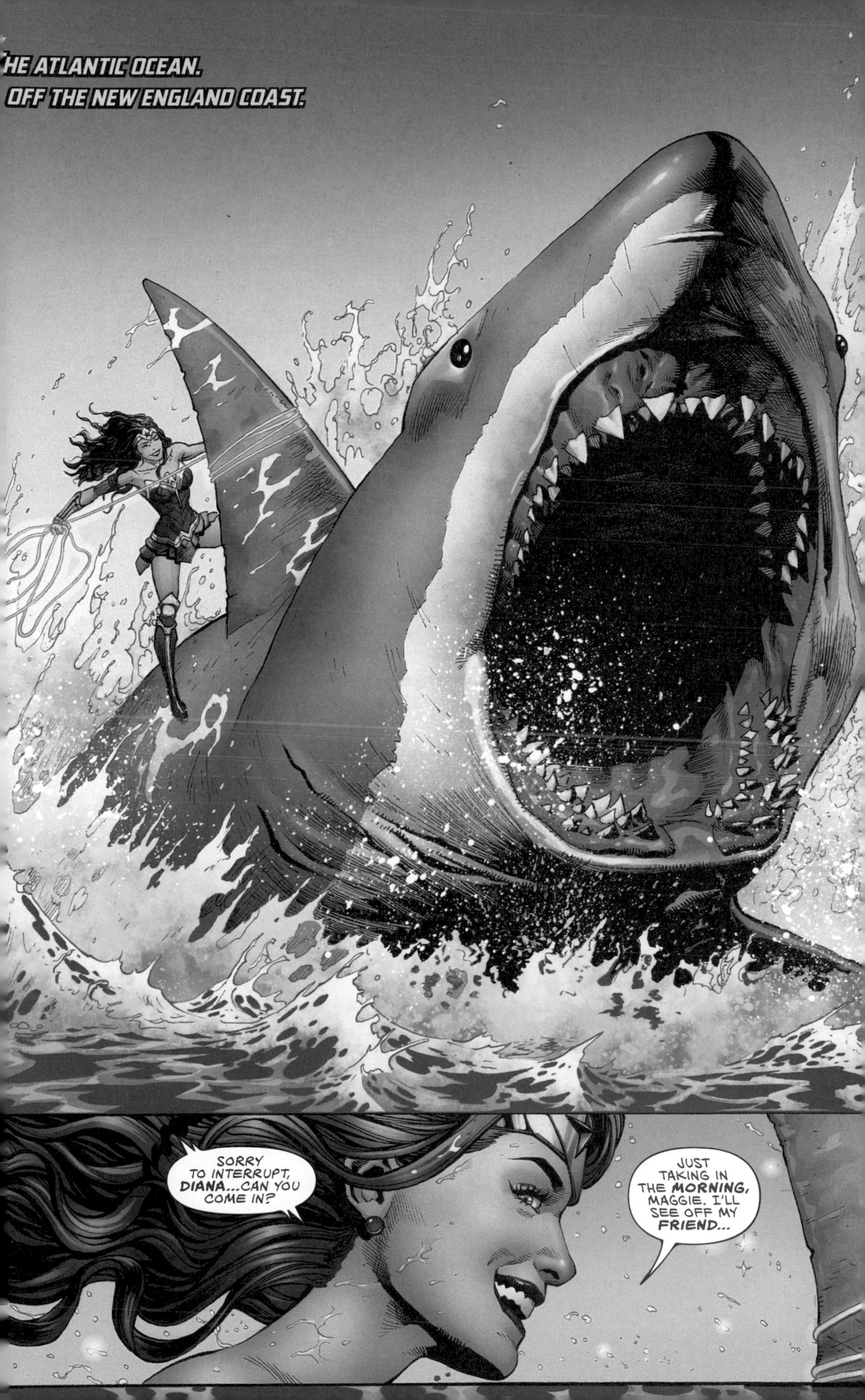
HE ATLANTIC OCEAN.
OFF THE NEW ENGLAND COAST.
SORRY TO INTERRUPT, DIANA...CAN YOU COME IN?
JUST TAKING IN THE MORNING, MAGGIE. I'LL SEE OFF MY FRIEND...

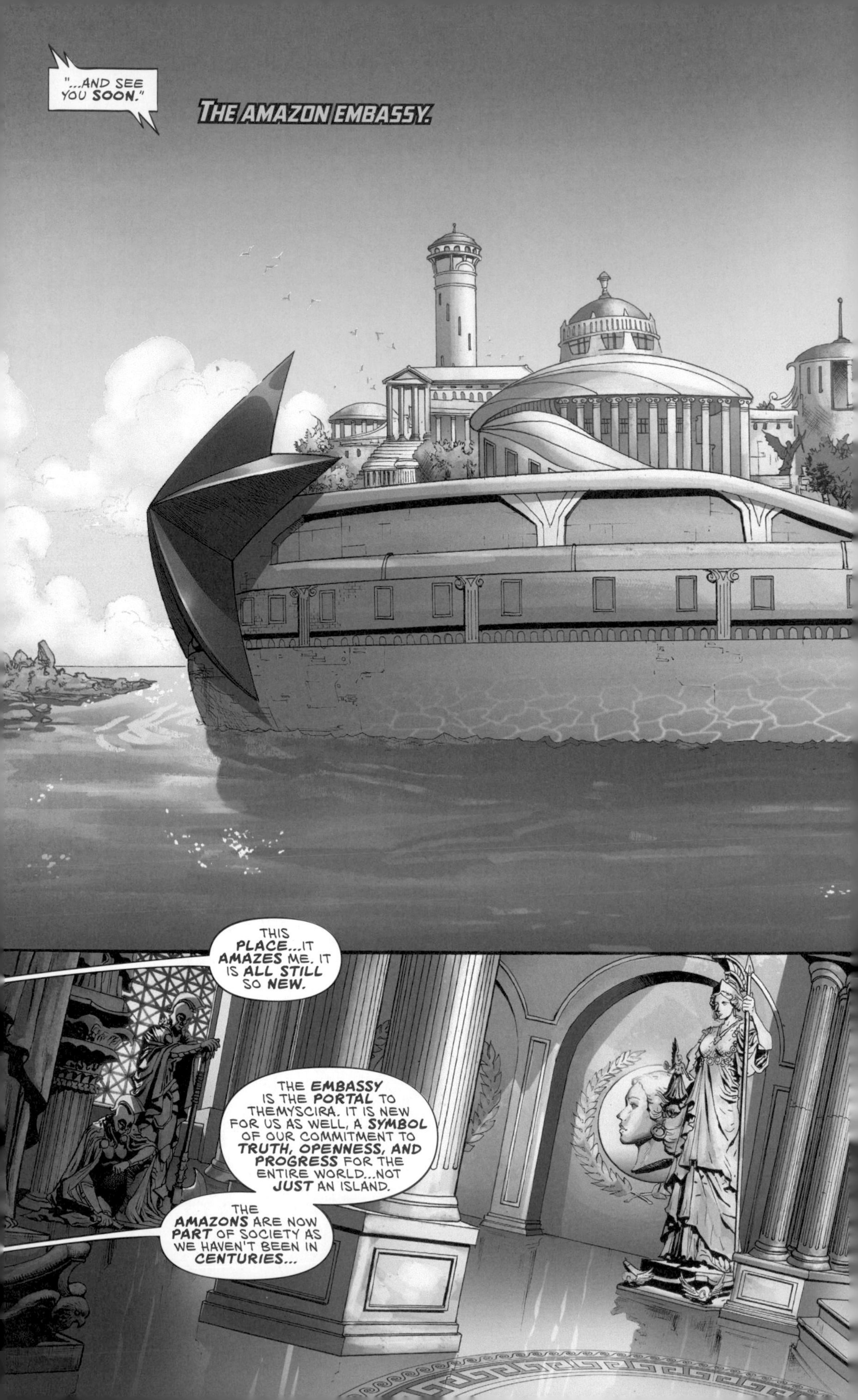
"...AND SEE YOU SOON."
THE AMAZON EMBASSY.
THIS PLACE...IT AMAZES ME. IT IS ALL STILL SO NEW.
THE EMBASSY IS THE PORTAL TO THEMYSCIRA. IT IS NEW FOR US AS WELL, A SYMBOL OF OUR COMMITMENT TO TRUTH, OPENNESS, AND PROGRESS FOR THE ENTIRE WORLD...NOT JUST AN ISLAND.
THE AMAZONS ARE NOW PART OF SOCIETY AS WE HAVEN'T BEEN IN CENTURIES...

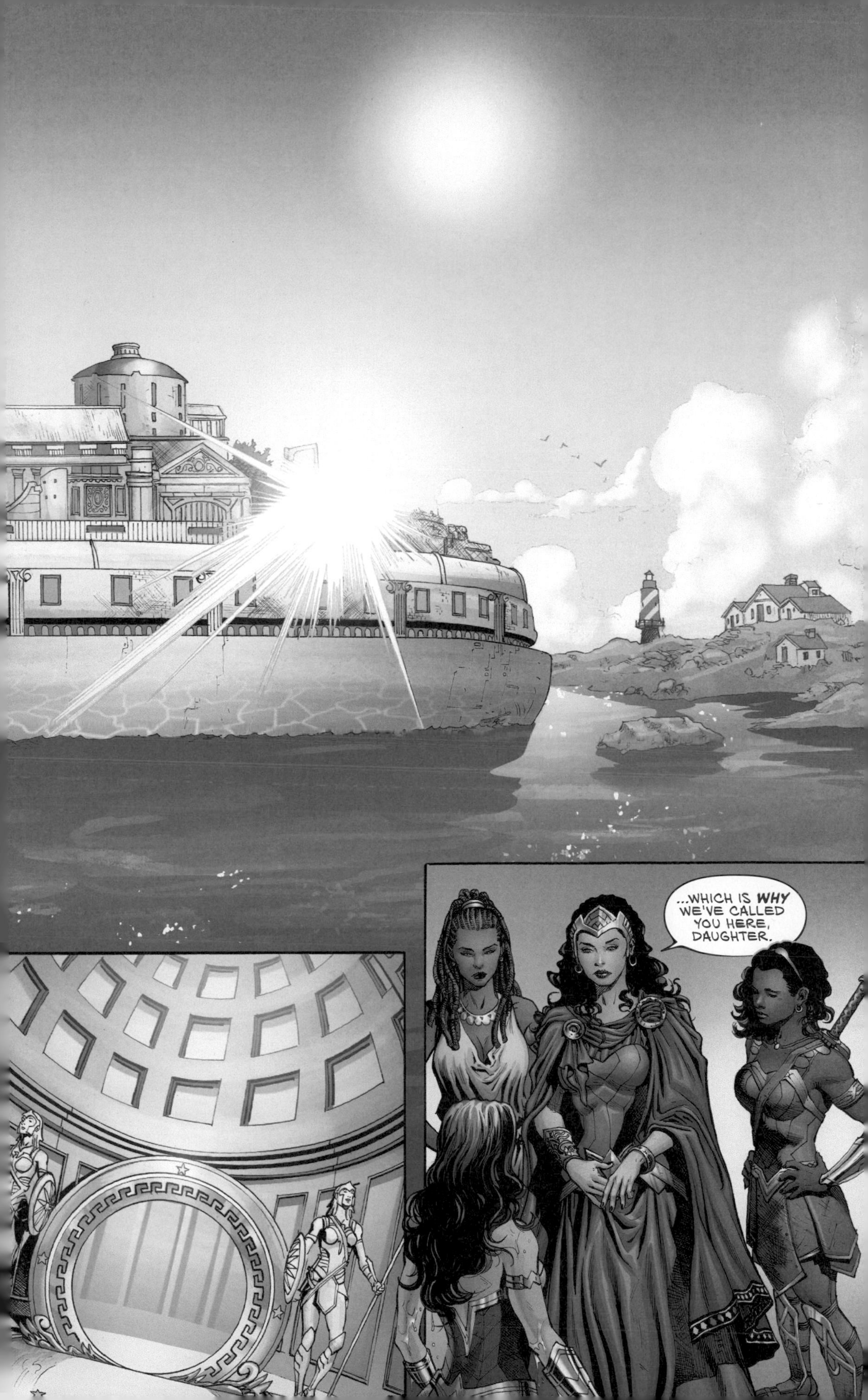
...WHICH IS WHY WE'VE CALLED YOU HERE, DAUGHTER.

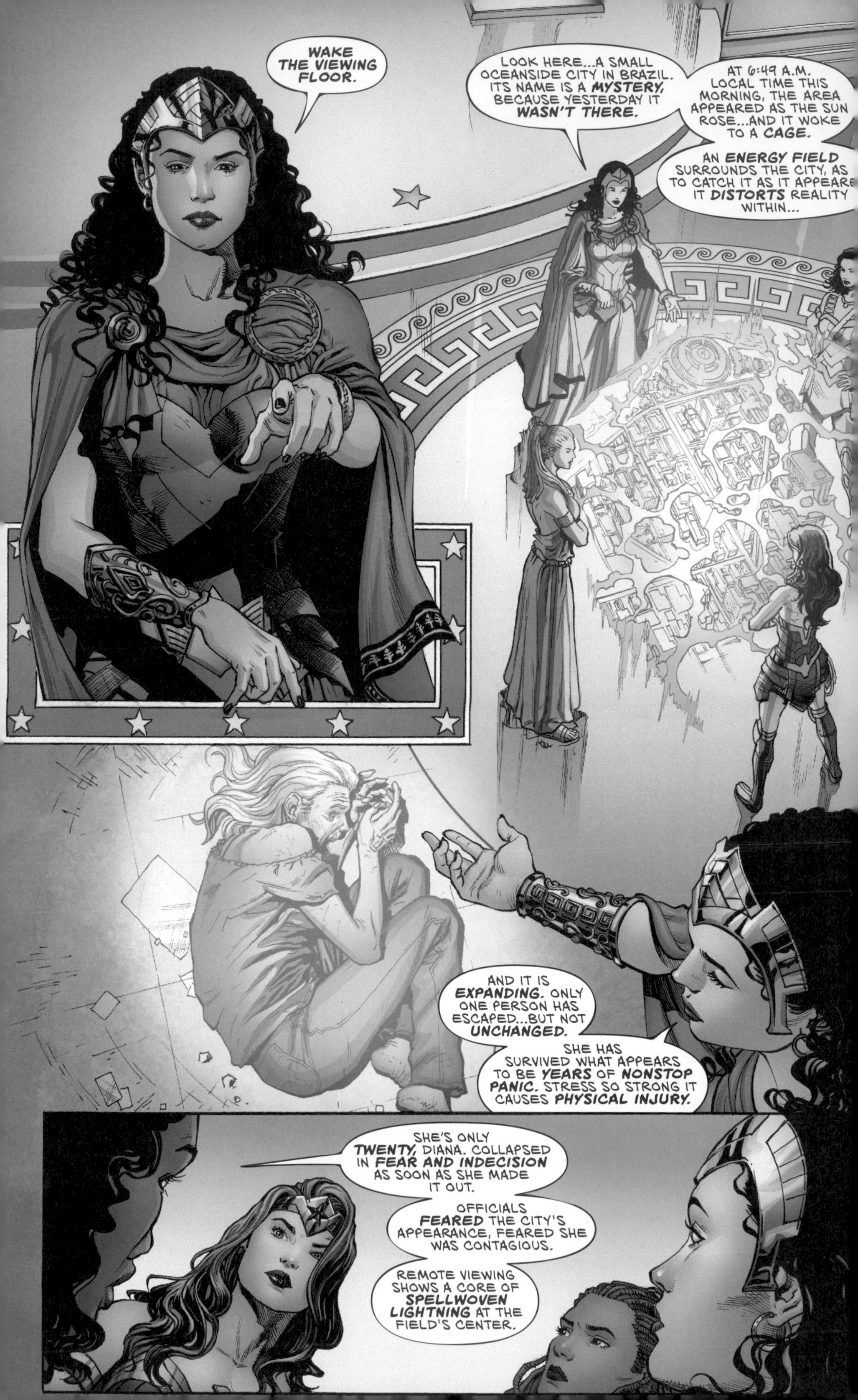
WAKE THE VIEWING FLOOR.
LOOK HERE...A SMALL OCEANSIDE CITY IN BRAZIL. ITS NAME IS A MYSTERY, BECAUSE YESTERDAY IT WASN'T THERE.
AT 6:49 A.M. LOCAL TIME THIS MORNING, THE AREA APPEARED AS THE SUN ROSE...AND IT WOKE TO A CAGE.
AN ENERGY FIELD SURROUNDS THE CITY, AS TO CATCH IT AS IT APPEARE IT DISTORTS REALITY WITHIN...
AND IT IS EXPANDING. ONLY ONE PERSON HAS ESCAPED...BUT NOT UNCHANGED.
SHE HAS SURVIVED WHAT APPEARS TO BE YEARS OF NONSTOP PANIC. STRESS SO STRONG IT CAUSES PHYSICAL INJURY.
SHE'S ONLY TWENTY, DIANA. COLLAPSED IN FEAR AND INDECISION AS SOON AS SHE MADE IT OUT.
OFFICIALS FEARED THE CITY'S APPEARANCE, FEARED SHE WAS CONTAGIOUS.
REMOTE VIEWING SHOWS A CORE OF SPELLWOVEN LIGHTNING AT THE FIELD'S CENTER.

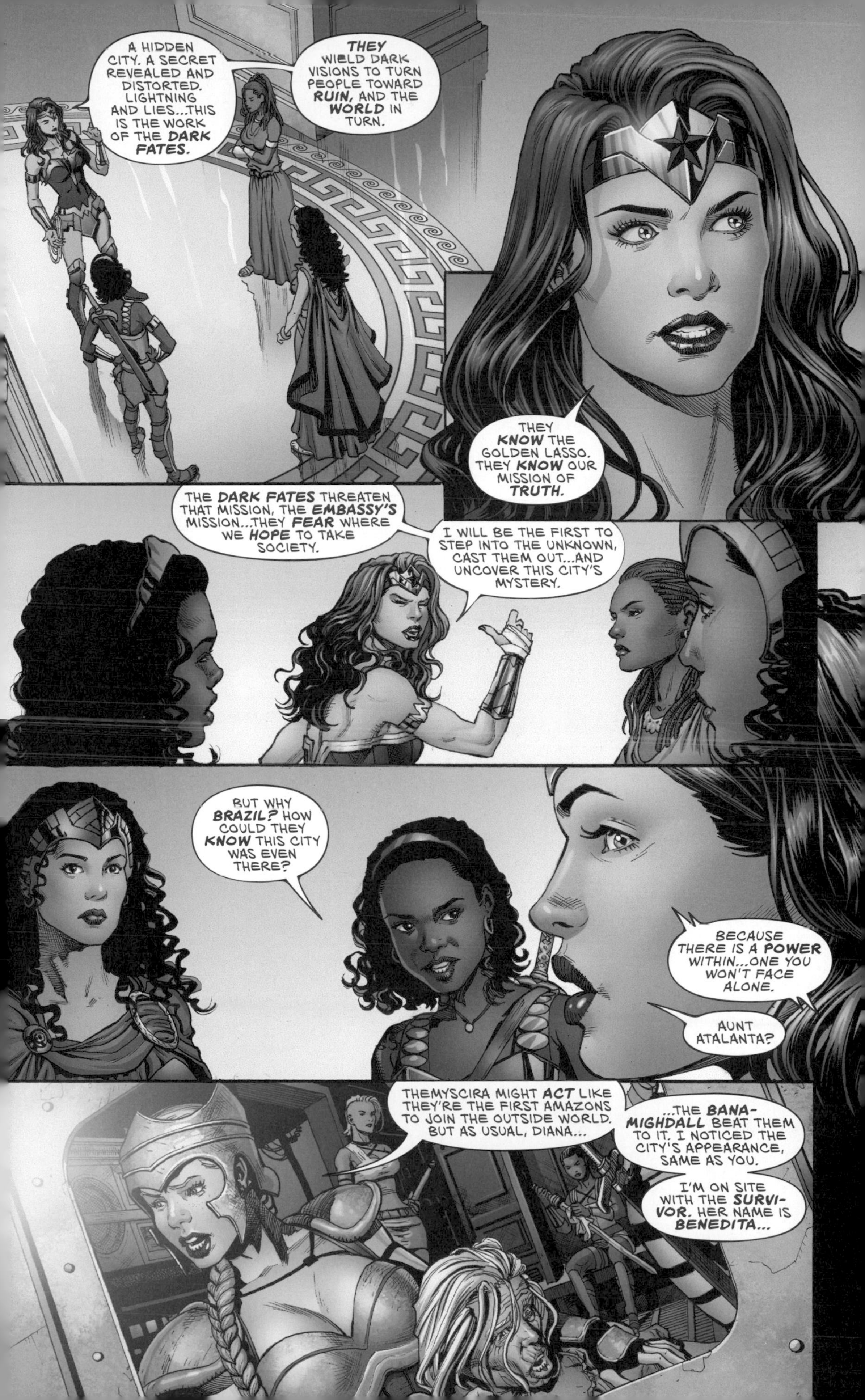
A HIDDEN CITY. A SECRET REVEALED AND DISTORTED. LIGHTNING AND LIES...THIS IS THE WORK OF THE DARK FATES.
THEY WIELD DARK VISIONS TO TURN PEOPLE TOWARD RUIN, AND THE WORLD IN TURN.
THEY KNOW THE GOLDEN LASSO. THEY KNOW OUR MISSION OF TRUTH.
THE DARK FATES THREATEN THAT MISSION, THE EMBASSY'S MISSION...THEY FEAR WHERE WE HOPE TO TAKE SOCIETY.
I WILL BE THE FIRST TO STEP INTO THE UNKNOWN, CAST THEM OUT...AND UNCOVER THIS CITY'S MYSTERY.
BUT WHY BRAZIL? HOW COULD THEY KNOW THIS CITY WAS EVEN THERE?
BECAUSE THERE IS A POWER WITHIN...ONE YOU WON'T FACE ALONE.
AUNT ATALANTA?
THEMYSCIRA MIGHT ACT LIKE THEY'RE THE FIRST AMAZONS TO JOIN THE OUTSIDE WORLD. BUT AS USUAL, DIANA...
...THE BANA-MIGHDALL BEAT THEM TO IT. I NOTICED THE CITY'S APPEARANCE, SAME AS YOU.
I'M ON SITE WITH THE SURVIVOR. HER NAME IS BENEDITA...

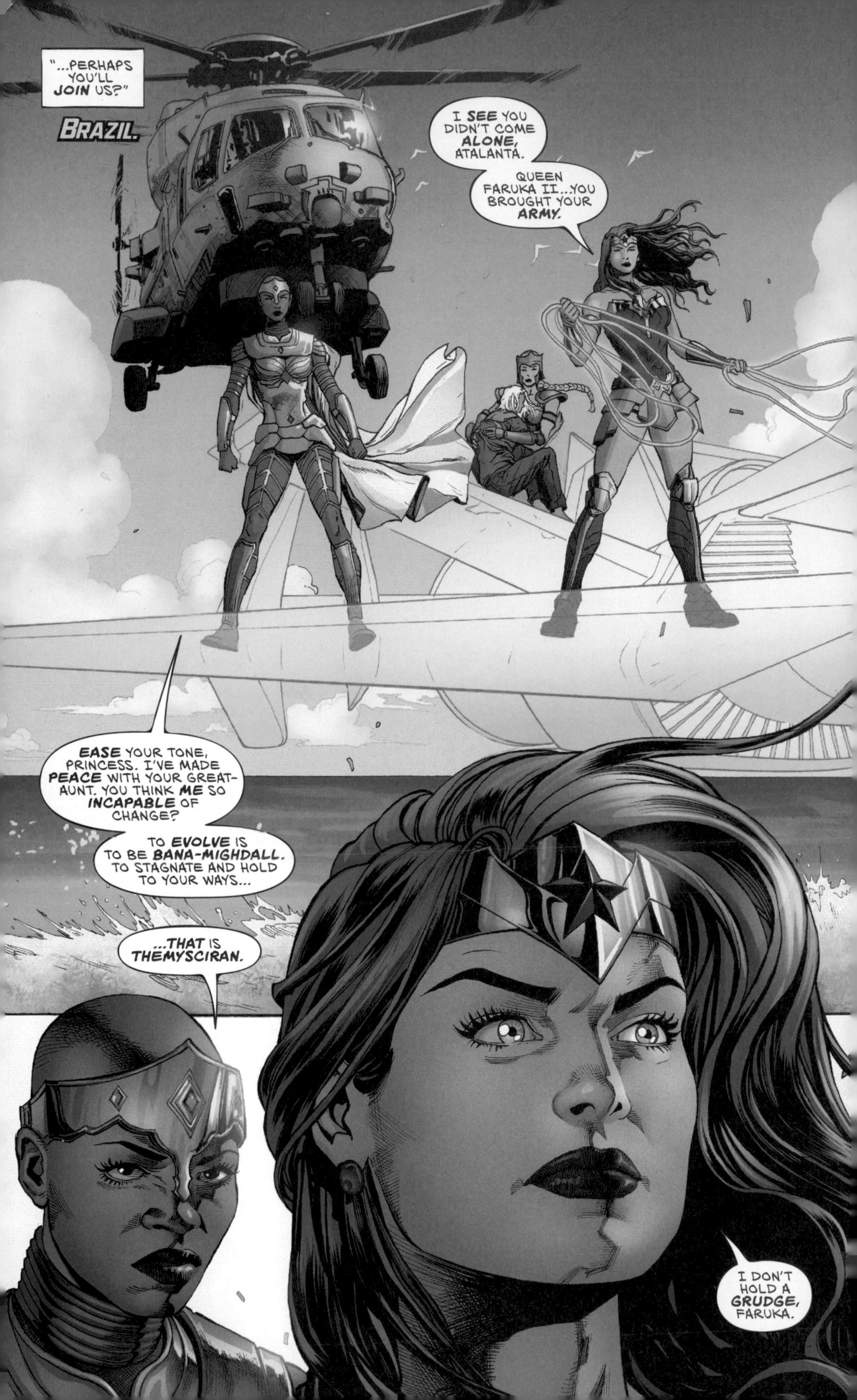
"...PERHAPS YOU'LL JOIN US?"
BRAZIL.
I SEE YOU DIDN'T COME ALONE, ATALANTA.
QUEEN FARUKA II...YOU BROUGHT YOUR ARMY.
EASE YOUR TONE, PRINCESS. I'VE MADE PEACE WITH YOUR GREAT-AUNT. YOU THINK ME SO INCAPABLE OF CHANGE?
TO EVOLVE IS TO BE BANA-MIGHDALL. TO STAGNATE AND HOLD TO YOUR WAYS...
...THAT IS THEMYSCIRAN.
I DON'T HOLD A GRUDGE, FARUKA.

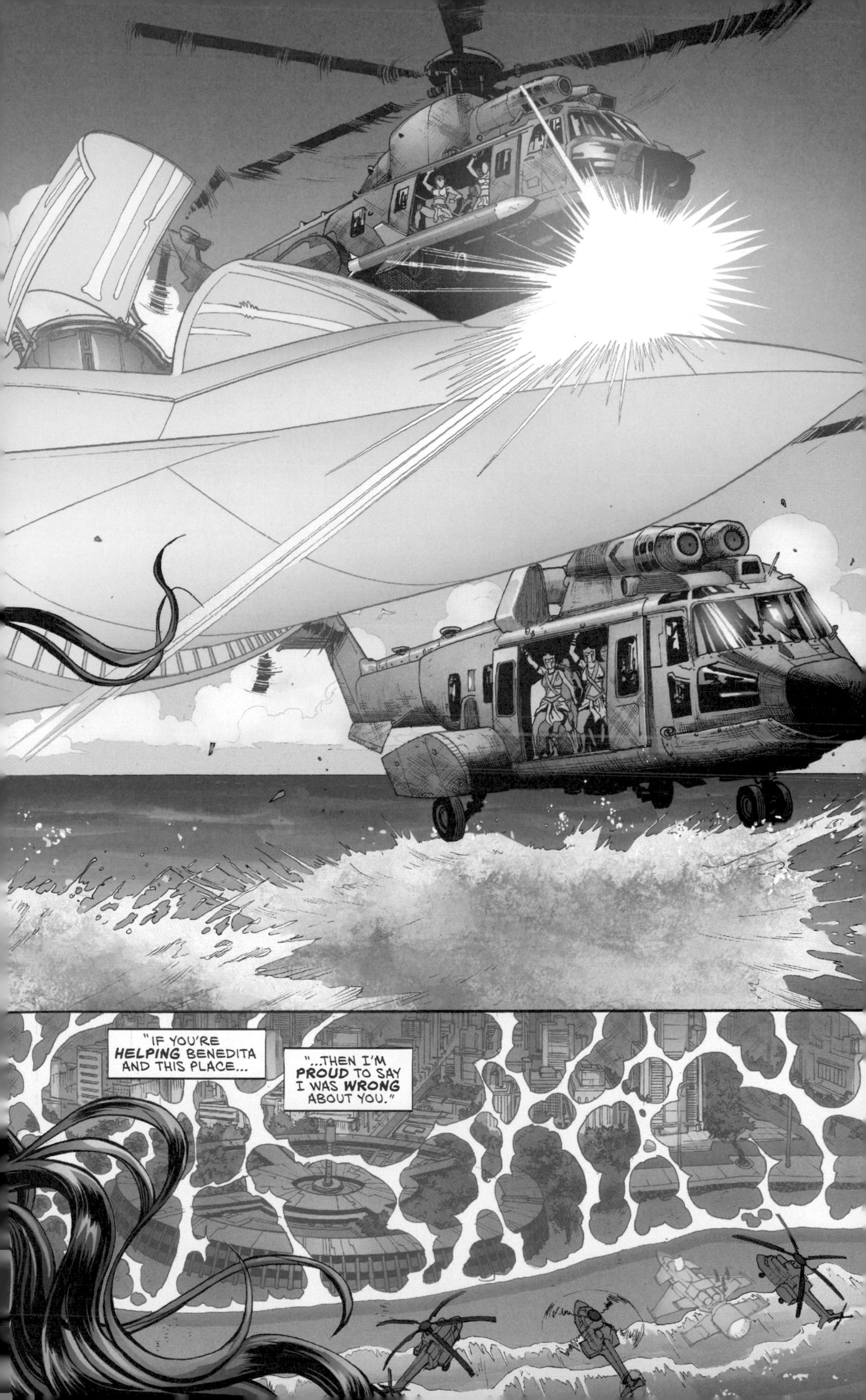
"IF YOU'RE **HELPING** BENEDITA AND THIS PLACE...
"...THEN I'M **PROUD** TO SAY I WAS **WRONG** ABOUT YOU."

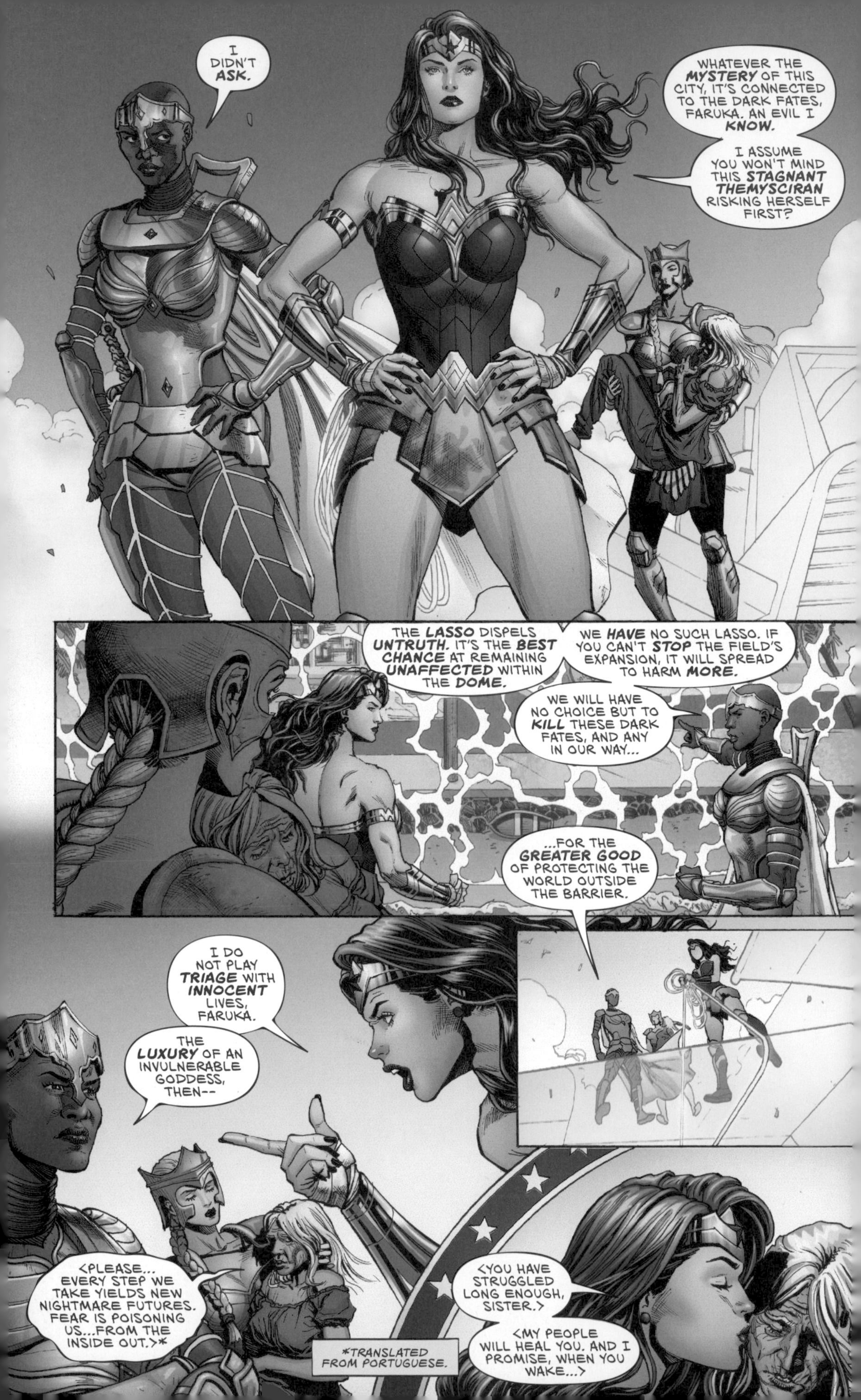

I DIDN'T ASK.
WHATEVER THE MYSTERY OF THIS CITY, IT'S CONNECTED TO THE DARK FATES, FARUKA. AN EVIL I KNOW.
I ASSUME YOU WON'T MIND THIS STAGNANT THEMYSCIRAN RISKING HERSELF FIRST?
THE LASSO DISPELS UNTRUTH. IT'S THE BEST CHANCE AT REMAINING UNAFFECTED WITHIN THE DOME.
WE HAVE NO SUCH LASSO. IF YOU CAN'T STOP THE FIELD'S EXPANSION, IT WILL SPREAD TO HARM MORE.
WE WILL HAVE NO CHOICE BUT TO KILL THESE DARK FATES, AND ANY IN OUR WAY...
...FOR THE GREATER GOOD OF PROTECTING THE WORLD OUTSIDE THE BARRIER.
I DO NOT PLAY TRIAGE WITH INNOCENT LIVES, FARUKA.
THE LUXURY OF AN INVULNERABLE GODDESS, THEN--
<PLEASE... EVERY STEP WE TAKE YIELDS NEW NIGHTMARE FUTURES. FEAR IS POISONING US...FROM THE INSIDE OUT.>*
*TRANSLATED FROM PORTUGUESE.
<YOU HAVE STRUGGLED LONG ENOUGH, SISTER.>
<MY PEOPLE WILL HEAL YOU. AND I PROMISE, WHEN YOU WAKE...>

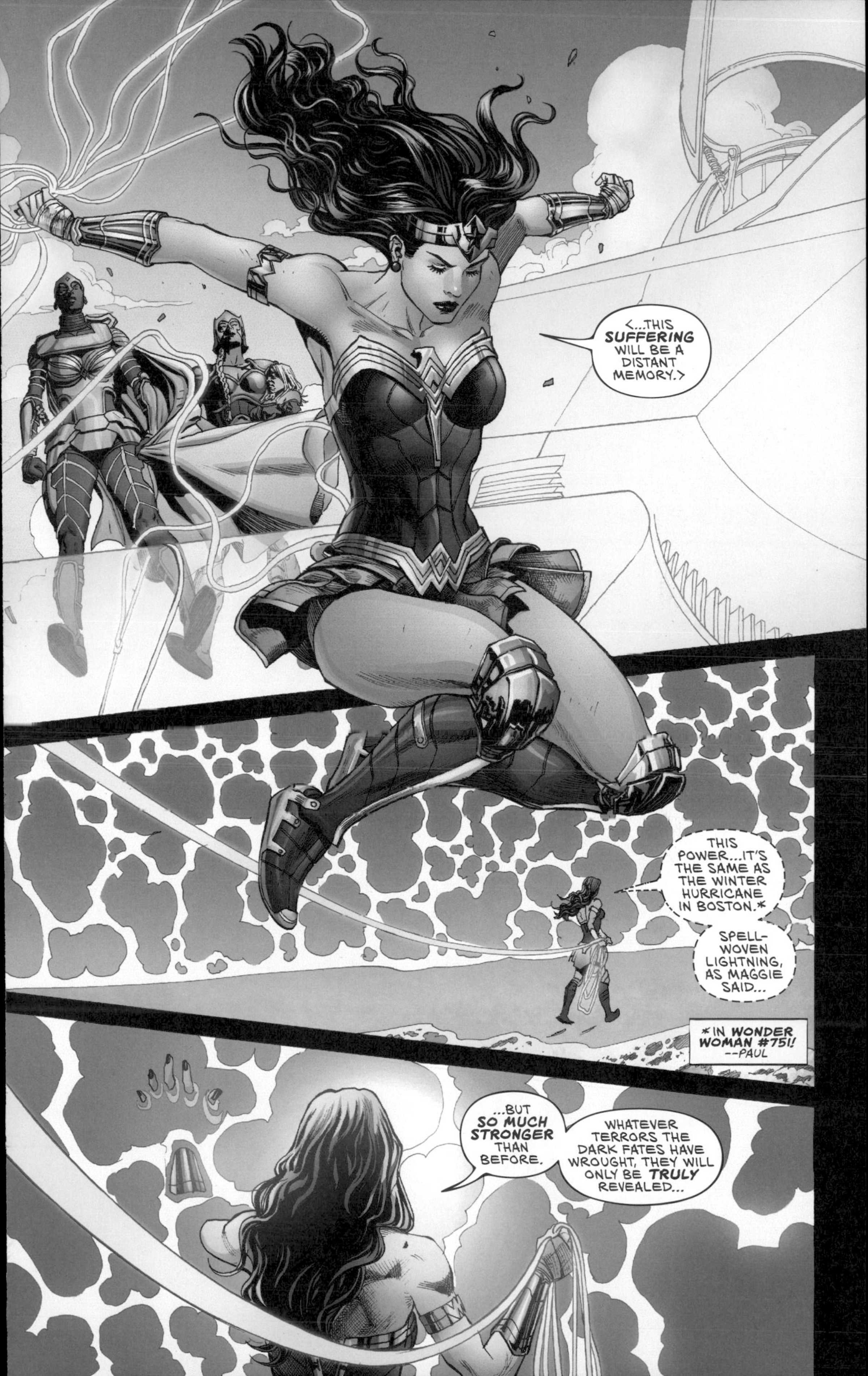

<...THIS SUFFERING WILL BE A DISTANT MEMORY.>
THIS POWER...IT'S THE SAME AS THE WINTER HURRICANE IN BOSTON.*
SPELL-WOVEN LIGHTNING, AS MAGGIE SAID...
*IN WONDER WOMAN #751! --PAUL
...BUT SO MUCH STRONGER THAN BEFORE.
WHATEVER TERRORS THE DARK FATES HAVE WROUGHT, THEY WILL ONLY BE TRULY REVEALED...

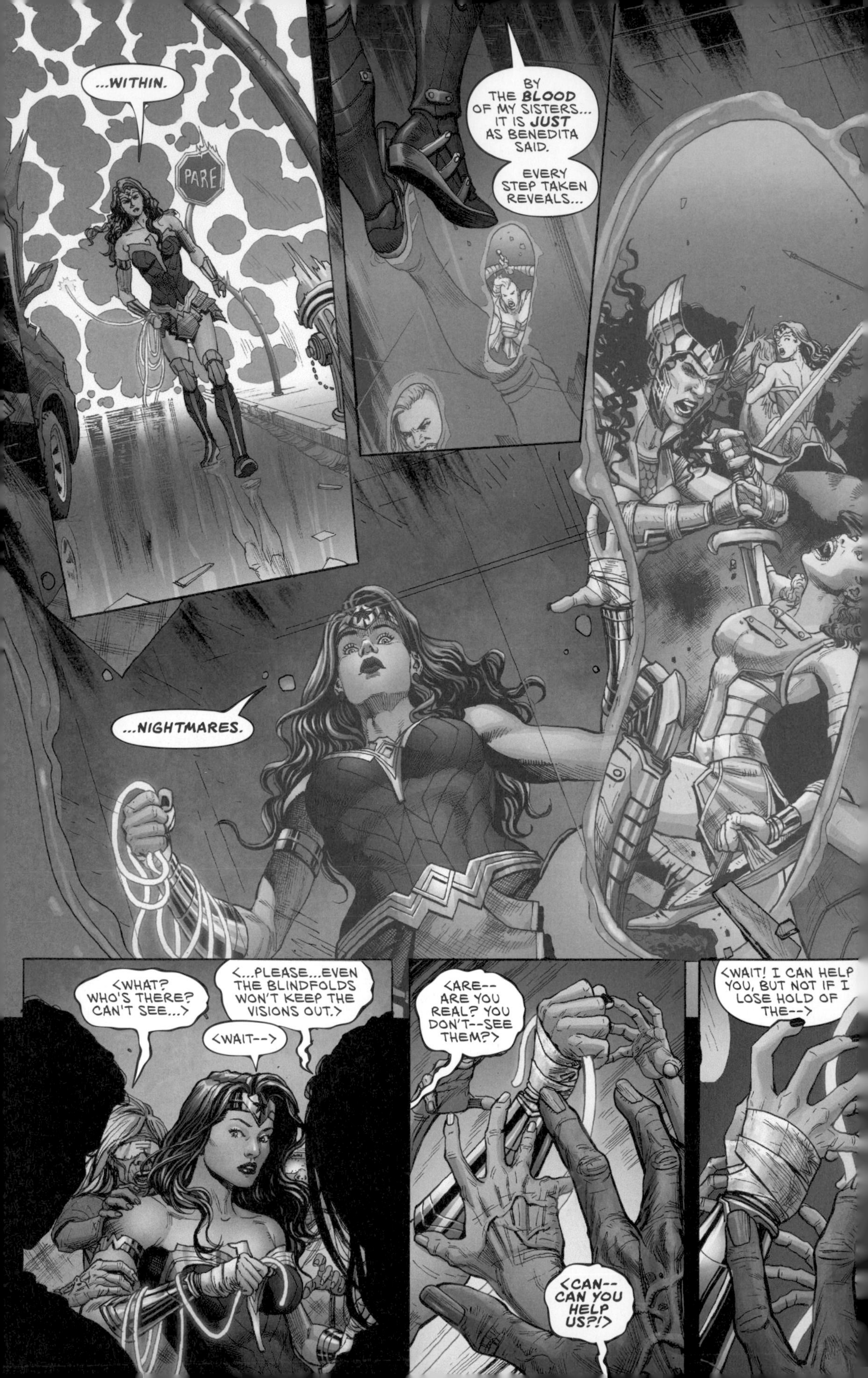
...WITHIN.
PARE
BY THE BLOOD OF MY SISTERS... IT IS JUST AS BENEDITA SAID.
EVERY STEP TAKEN REVEALS...
...NIGHTMARES.
<WHAT? WHO'S THERE? CAN'T SEE...>
<...PLEASE...EVEN THE BLINDFOLDS WON'T KEEP THE VISIONS OUT.>
<WAIT-->
<ARE-- ARE YOU REAL? YOU DON'T--SEE THEM?>
<CAN-- CAN YOU HELP US?!>
<WAIT! I CAN HELP YOU, BUT NOT IF I LOSE HOLD OF THE-->

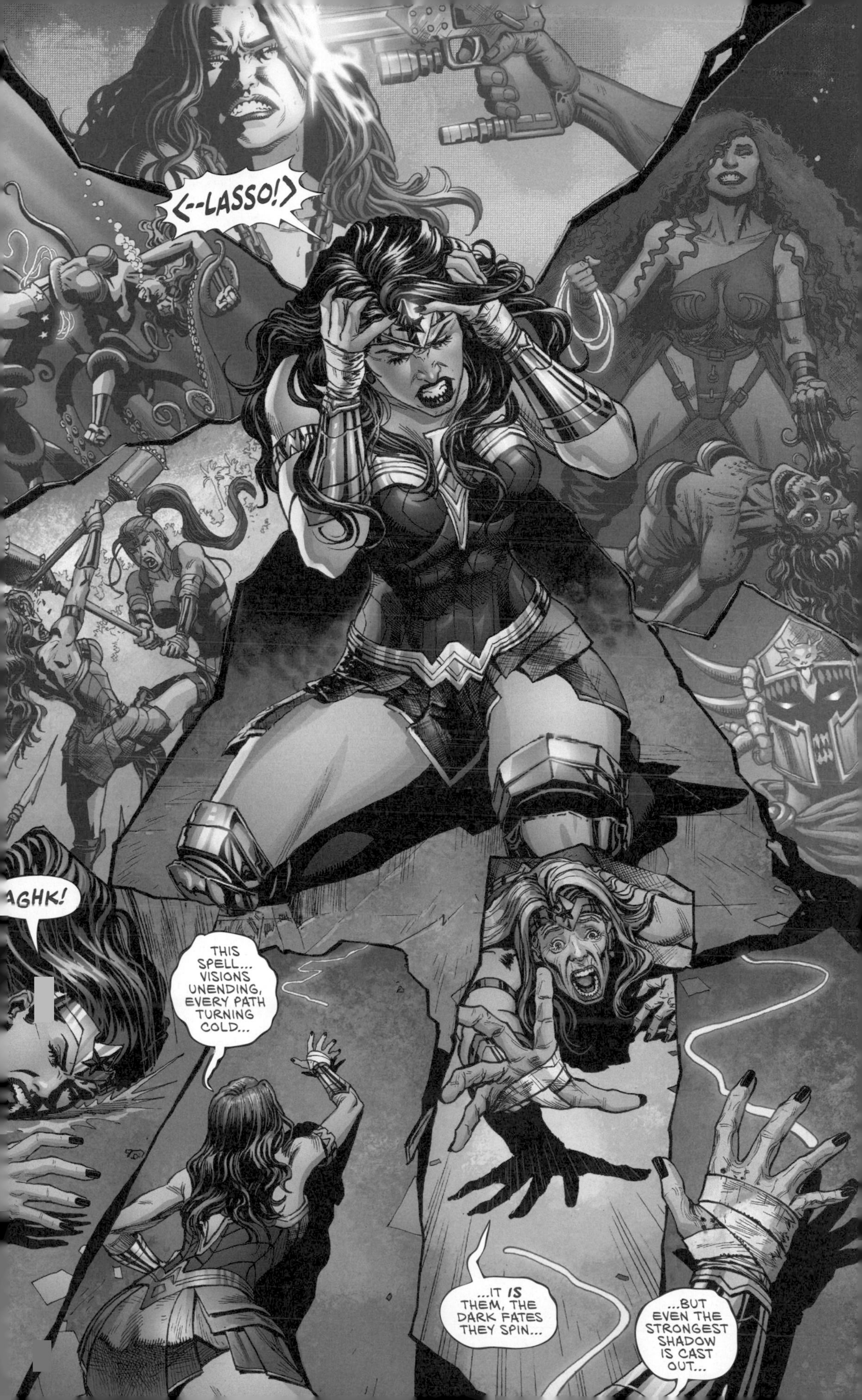
<--LASSO!>
AGHK!
THIS SPELL... VISIONS UNENDING, EVERY PATH TURNING COLD...
...IT IS THEM, THE DARK FATES THEY SPIN...
...BUT EVEN THE STRONGEST SHADOW IS CAST OUT...

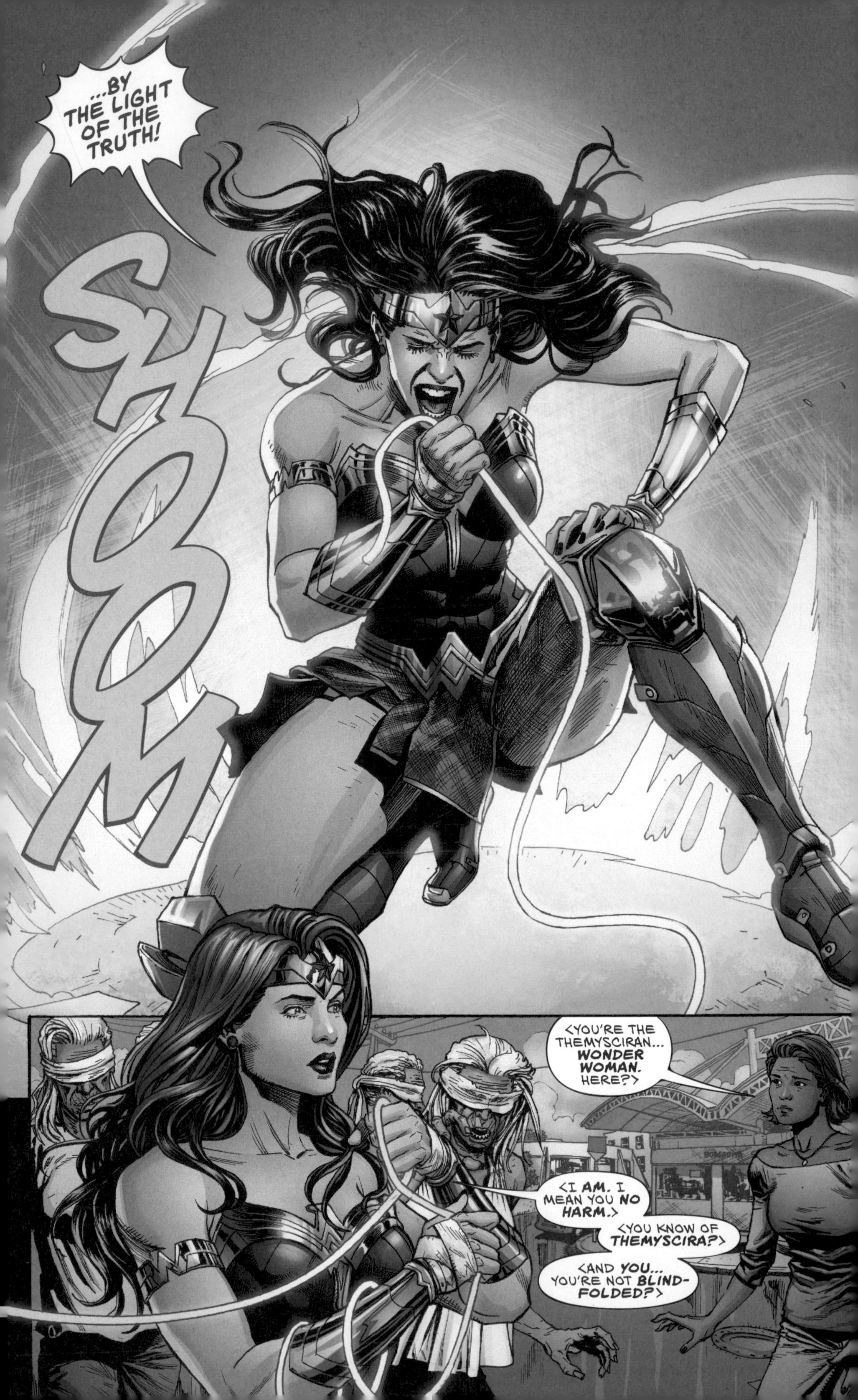
...BY THE LIGHT OF THE TRUTH!
SHOOM
<YOU'RE THE THEMYSCIRAN... WONDER WOMAN. HERE?>
<I AM. I MEAN YOU NO HARM.>
<YOU KNOW OF THEMYSCIRA?>
<AND YOU... YOU'RE NOT BLIND-FOLDED?>

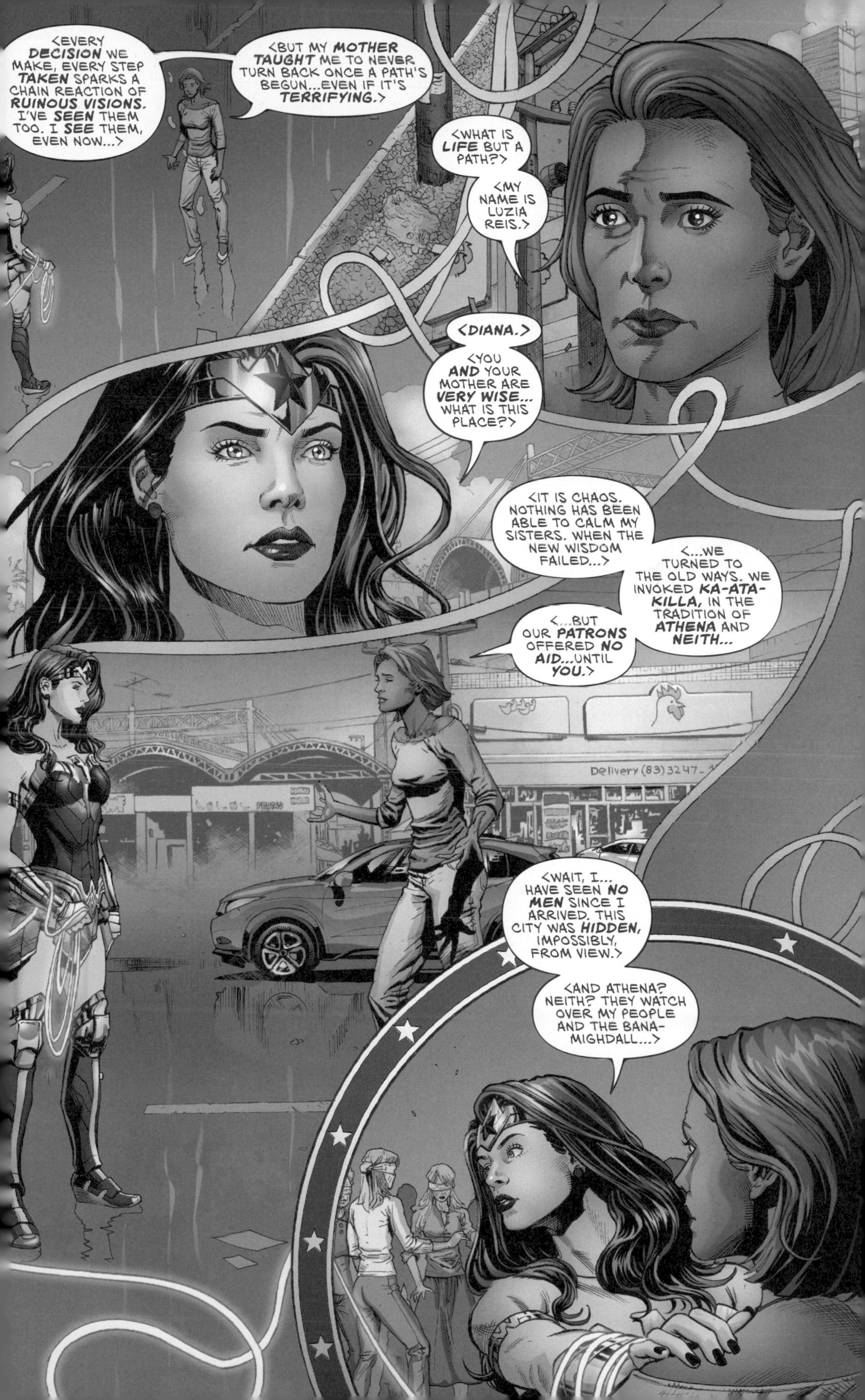

<EVERY DECISION WE MAKE, EVERY STEP TAKEN SPARKS A CHAIN REACTION OF RUINOUS VISIONS. I'VE SEEN THEM TOO. I SEE THEM, EVEN NOW...>
<BUT MY MOTHER TAUGHT ME TO NEVER TURN BACK ONCE A PATH'S BEGUN...EVEN IF IT'S TERRIFYING.>
<WHAT IS LIFE BUT A PATH?>
<MY NAME IS LUZIA REIS.>
<DIANA.>
<YOU AND YOUR MOTHER ARE VERY WISE... WHAT IS THIS PLACE?>
<IT IS CHAOS. NOTHING HAS BEEN ABLE TO CALM MY SISTERS. WHEN THE NEW WISDOM FAILED...>
<...WE TURNED TO THE OLD WAYS. WE INVOKED KA-ATA-KILLA, IN THE TRADITION OF ATHENA AND NEITH...
<...BUT OUR PATRONS OFFERED NO AID...UNTIL YOU.>
Delivery (83) 3247-
<WAIT, I... HAVE SEEN NO MEN SINCE I ARRIVED. THIS CITY WAS HIDDEN, IMPOSSIBLY, FROM VIEW.>
<AND ATHENA? NEITH? THEY WATCH OVER MY PEOPLE AND THE BANA-MIGHDALL...>

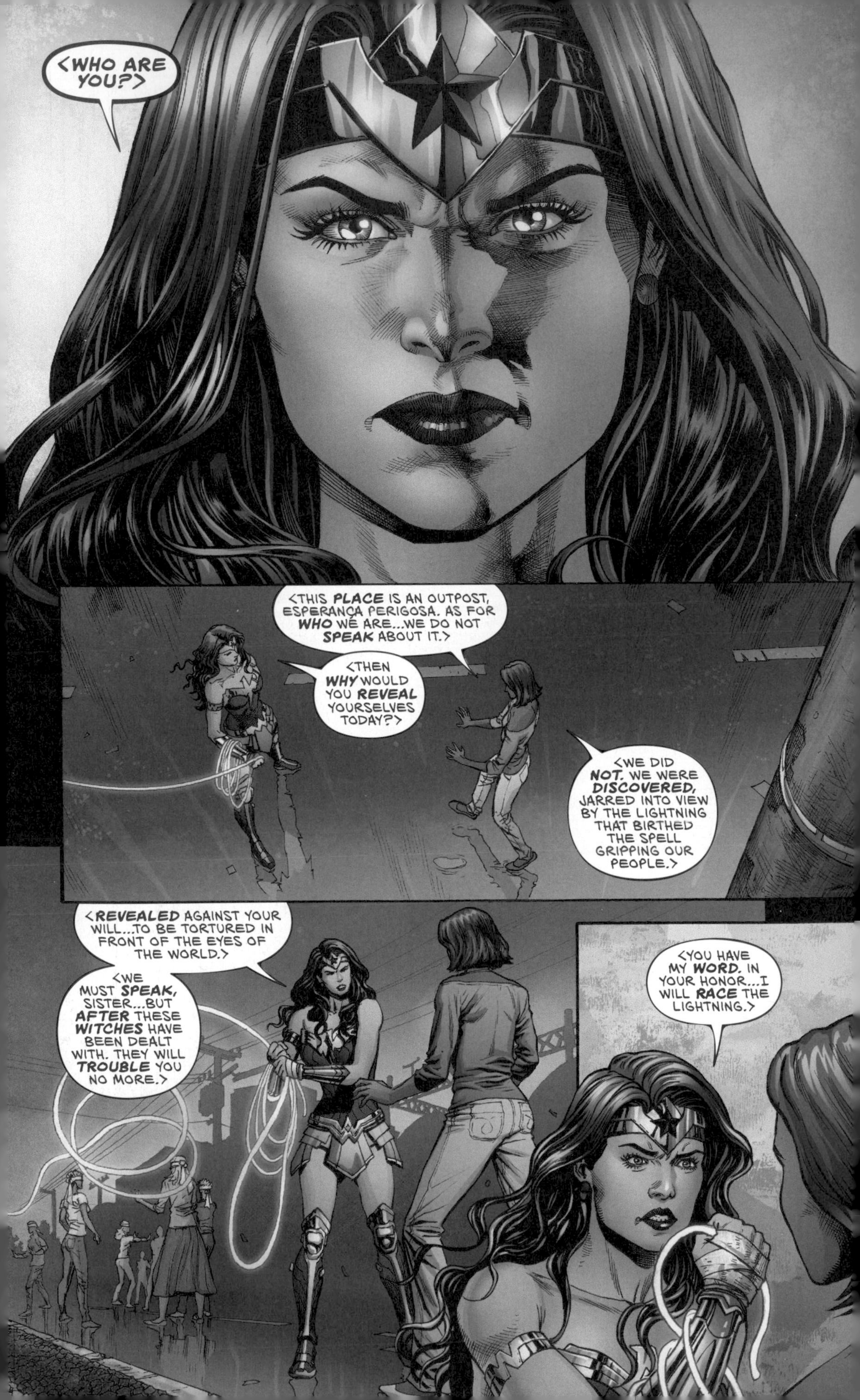
<WHO ARE YOU?>
<THIS PLACE IS AN OUTPOST, ESPERANÇA PERIGOSA. AS FOR WHO WE ARE...WE DO NOT SPEAK ABOUT IT.>
<THEN WHY WOULD YOU REVEAL YOURSELVES TODAY?>
<WE DID NOT. WE WERE DISCOVERED, JARRED INTO VIEW BY THE LIGHTNING THAT BIRTHED THE SPELL GRIPPING OUR PEOPLE.>
<REVEALED AGAINST YOUR WILL...TO BE TORTURED IN FRONT OF THE EYES OF THE WORLD.>
<WE MUST SPEAK, SISTER...BUT AFTER THESE WITCHES HAVE BEEN DEALT WITH. THEY WILL TROUBLE YOU NO MORE.>
<YOU HAVE MY WORD. IN YOUR HONOR...I WILL RACE THE LIGHTNING.>

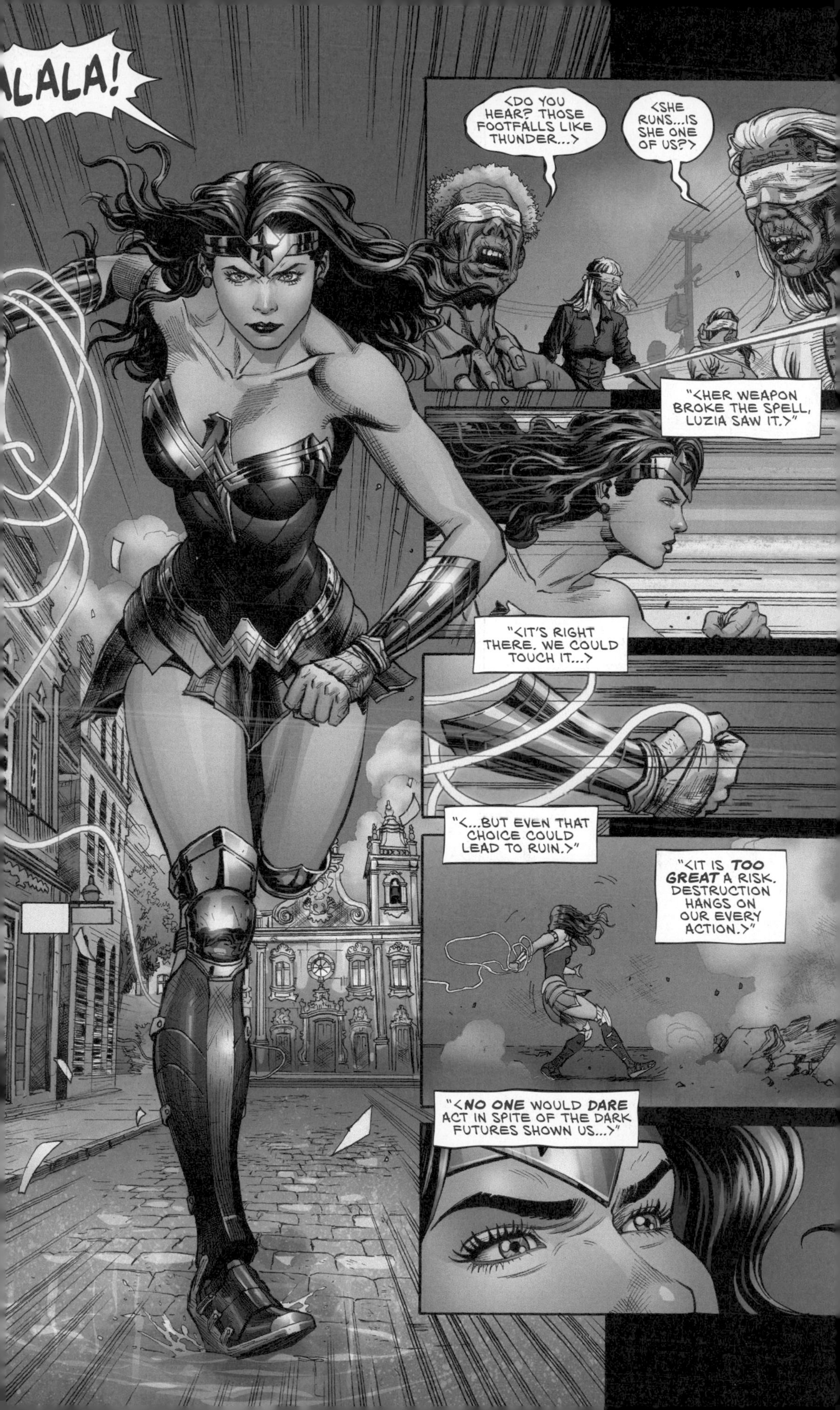

ALALA!
<DO YOU HEAR? THOSE FOOTFALLS LIKE THUNDER...>
<SHE RUNS...IS SHE ONE OF US?>
"<HER WEAPON BROKE THE SPELL, LUZIA SAW IT.>"
"<IT'S RIGHT THERE. WE COULD TOUCH IT...>
"<...BUT EVEN THAT CHOICE COULD LEAD TO RUIN.>"
"<IT IS TOO GREAT A RISK. DESTRUCTION HANGS ON OUR EVERY ACTION.>"
"<NO ONE WOULD DARE ACT IN SPITE OF THE DARK FUTURES SHOWN US...>"

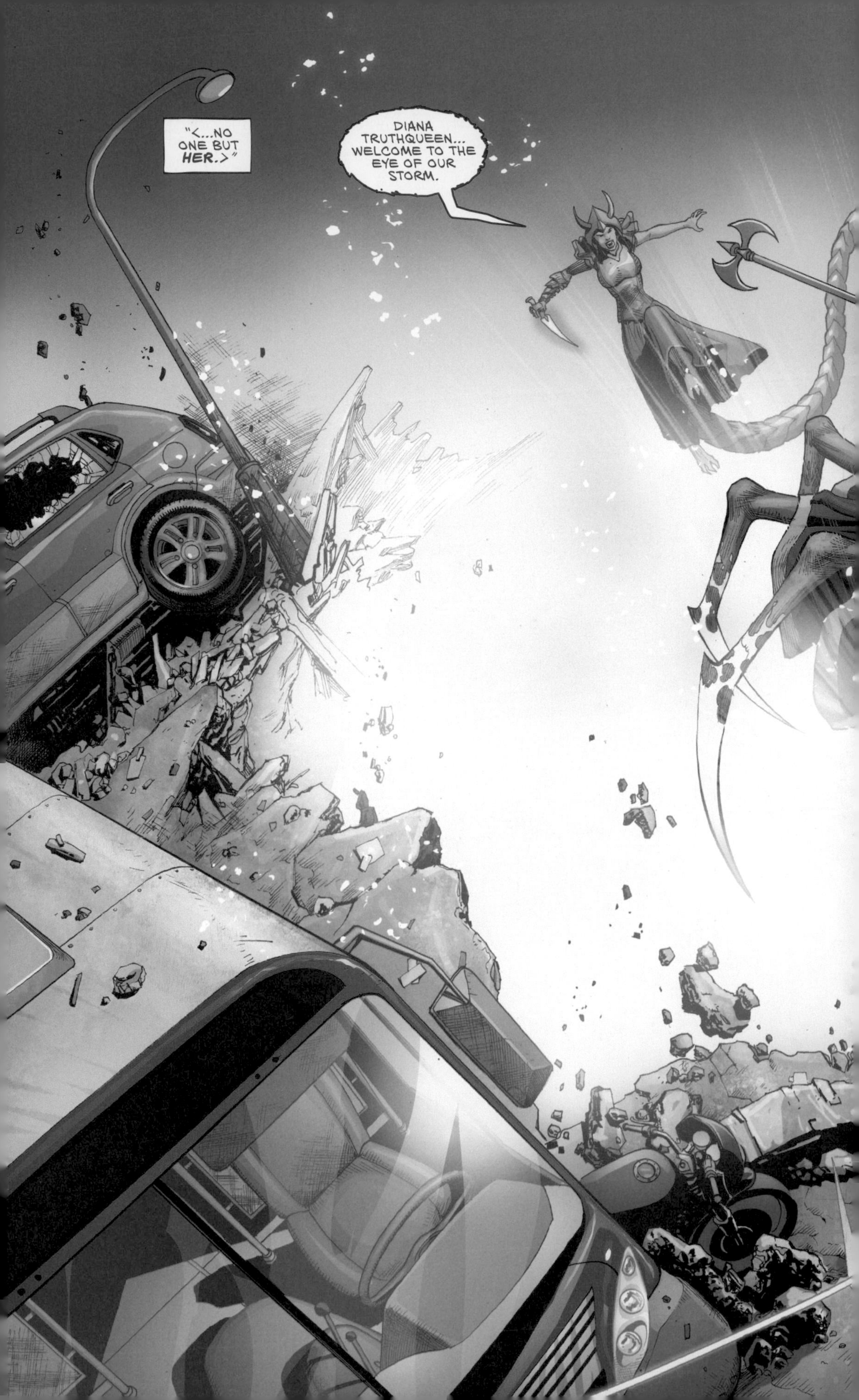
"<...NO ONE BUT HER.>"
DIANA TRUTHQUEEN... WELCOME TO THE EYE OF OUR STORM.

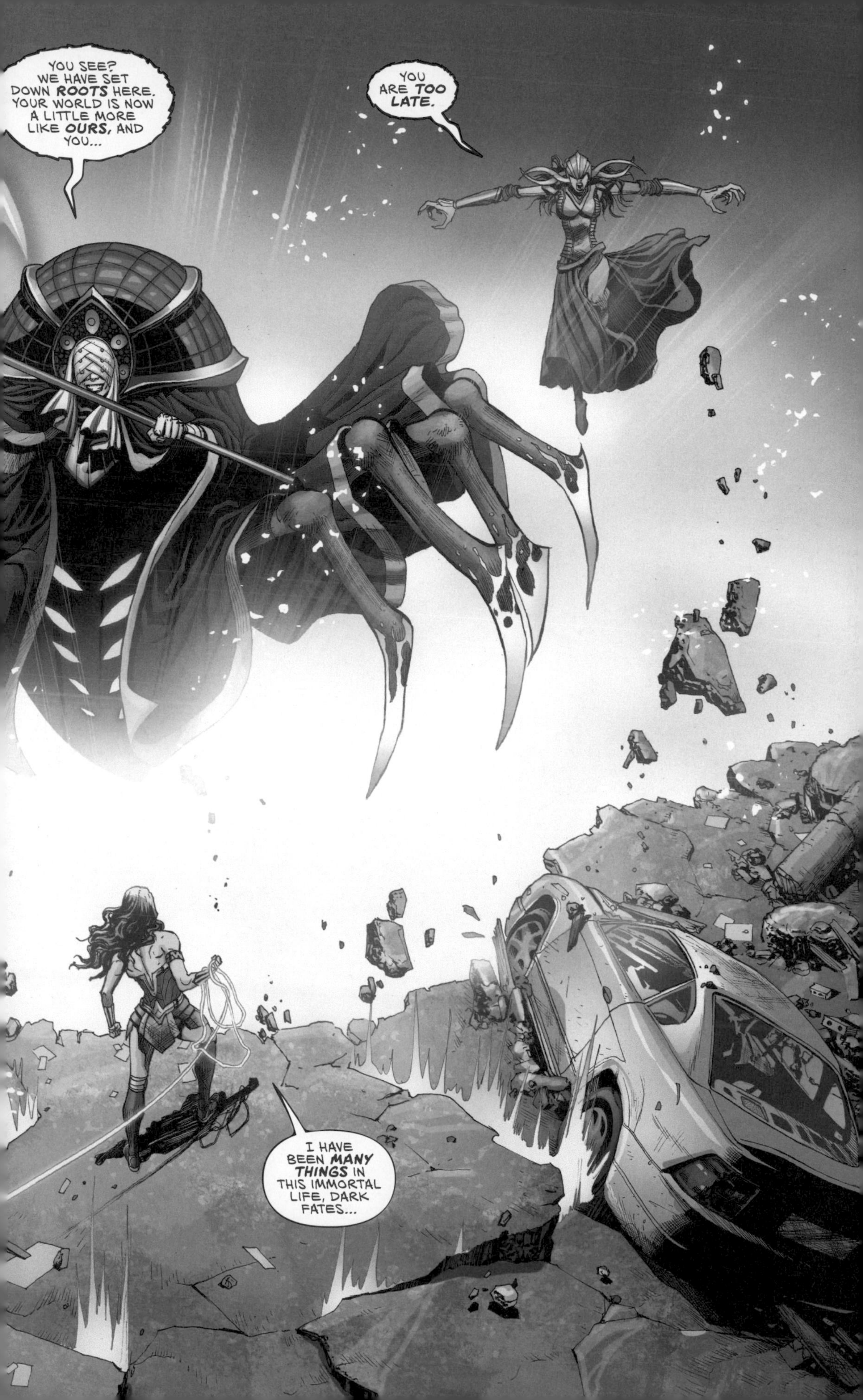
YOU SEE? WE HAVE SET DOWN **ROOTS** HERE. YOUR WORLD IS NOW A LITTLE MORE LIKE **OURS,** AND YOU...
YOU ARE **TOO LATE.**
I HAVE BEEN **MANY THINGS** IN THIS IMMORTAL LIFE, DARK FATES...

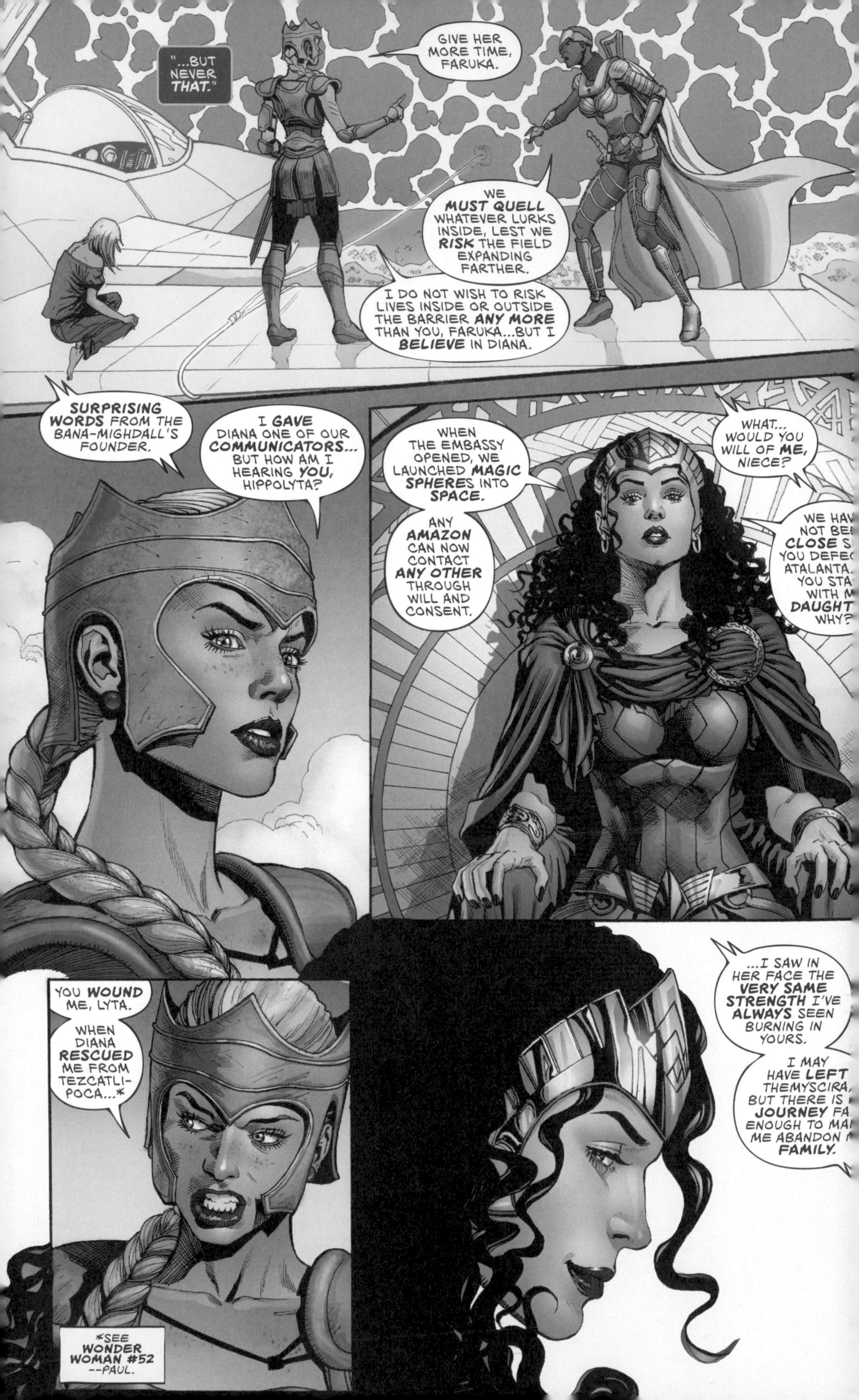
"...BUT NEVER THAT."
GIVE HER MORE TIME, FARUKA.
WE MUST QUELL WHATEVER LURKS INSIDE, LEST WE RISK THE FIELD EXPANDING FARTHER.
I DO NOT WISH TO RISK LIVES INSIDE OR OUTSIDE THE BARRIER ANY MORE THAN YOU, FARUKA...BUT I BELIEVE IN DIANA.
SURPRISING WORDS FROM THE BANA-MIGHDALL'S FOUNDER.
I GAVE DIANA ONE OF OUR COMMUNICATORS... BUT HOW AM I HEARING YOU, HIPPOLYTA?
WHEN THE EMBASSY OPENED, WE LAUNCHED MAGIC SPHERES INTO SPACE.
ANY AMAZON CAN NOW CONTACT ANY OTHER THROUGH WILL AND CONSENT.
WHAT... WOULD YOU WILL OF ME, NIECE?
WE HAV NOT BE CLOSE S YOU DEFE ATALANTA. YOU STA WITH M DAUGHT WHY?
YOU WOUND ME, LYTA.
WHEN DIANA RESCUED ME FROM TEZCATLI-POCA...*
...I SAW IN HER FACE THE VERY SAME STRENGTH I'VE ALWAYS SEEN BURNING IN YOURS.
I MAY HAVE LEFT THEMYSCIRA, BUT THERE IS JOURNEY FA ENOUGH TO MA ME ABANDON FAMILY.
*SEE WONDER WOMAN #52 --PAUL.

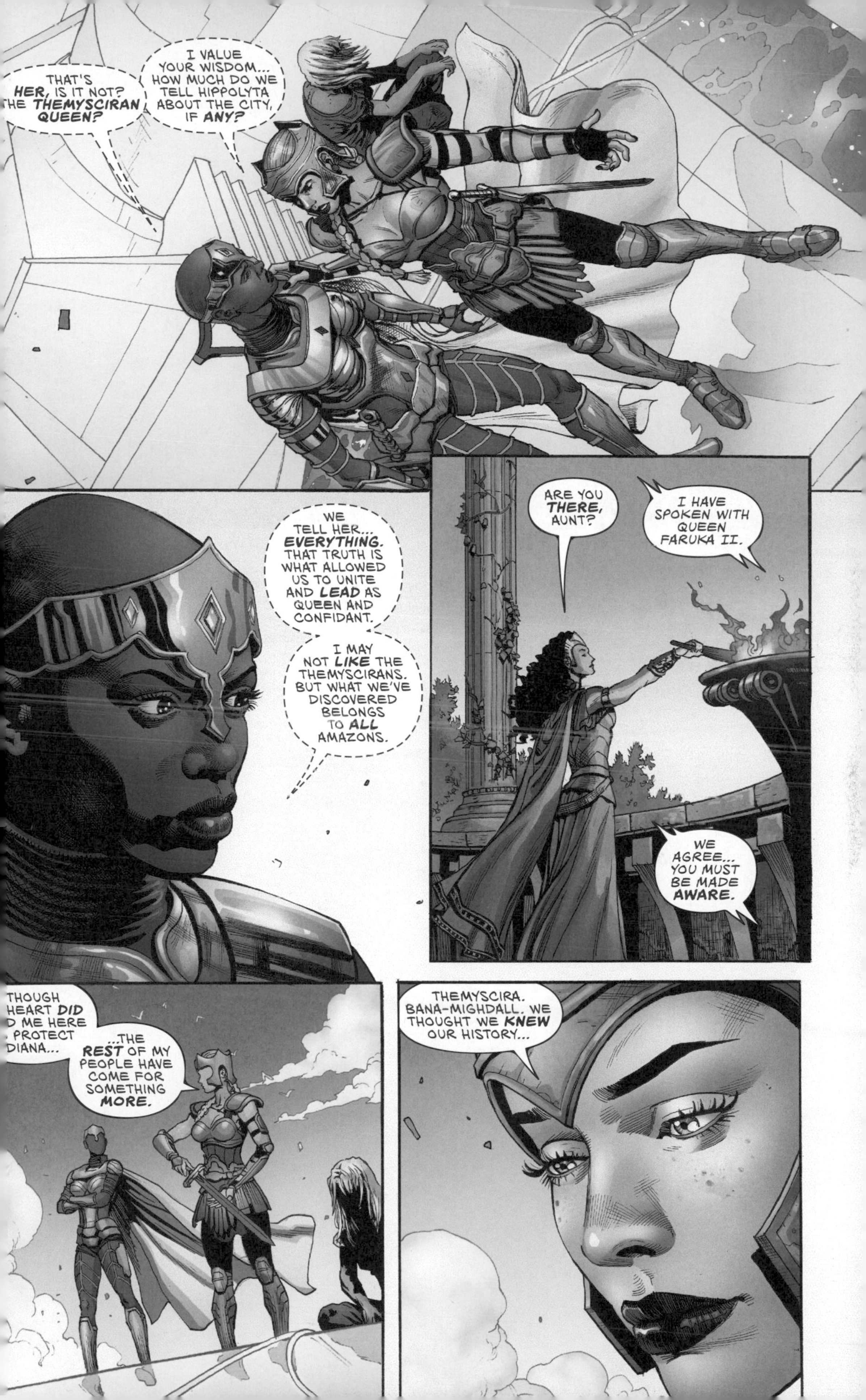
THAT'S HER, IS IT NOT? THE THEMYSCIRAN QUEEN?
I VALUE YOUR WISDOM... HOW MUCH DO WE TELL HIPPOLYTA ABOUT THE CITY, IF ANY?
WE TELL HER... EVERYTHING. THAT TRUTH IS WHAT ALLOWED US TO UNITE AND LEAD AS QUEEN AND CONFIDANT.
I MAY NOT LIKE THE THEMYSCIRANS. BUT WHAT WE'VE DISCOVERED BELONGS TO ALL AMAZONS.
ARE YOU THERE, AUNT?
I HAVE SPOKEN WITH QUEEN FARUKA II.
WE AGREE... YOU MUST BE MADE AWARE.
THOUGH HEART DID D ME HERE PROTECT DIANA...
...THE REST OF MY PEOPLE HAVE COME FOR SOMETHING MORE.
THEMYSCIRA. BANA-MIGHDALL. WE THOUGHT WE KNEW OUR HISTORY...

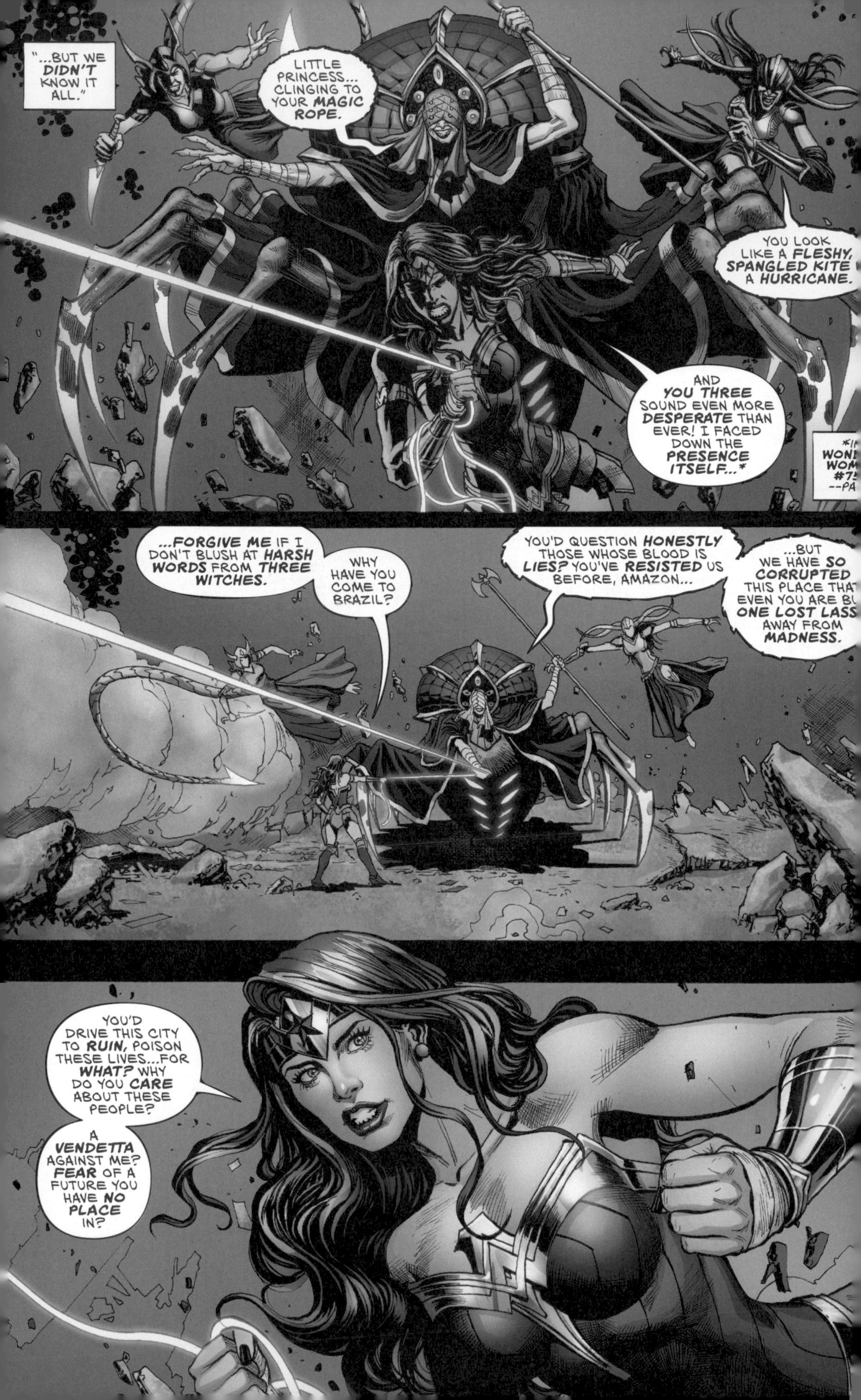
"...BUT WE DIDN'T KNOW IT ALL."
LITTLE PRINCESS... CLINGING TO YOUR MAGIC ROPE.
YOU LOOK LIKE A FLESHY, SPANGLED KITE A HURRICANE.
AND YOU THREE SOUND EVEN MORE DESPERATE THAN EVER! I FACED DOWN THE PRESENCE ITSELF...*
...FORGIVE ME IF I DON'T BLUSH AT HARSH WORDS FROM THREE WITCHES.
WHY HAVE YOU COME TO BRAZIL?
YOU'D QUESTION HONESTLY THOSE WHOSE BLOOD IS LIES? YOU'VE RESISTED US BEFORE, AMAZON...
...BUT WE HAVE SO CORRUPTED THIS PLACE THAT EVEN YOU ARE BU ONE LOST LASS AWAY FROM MADNESS.
YOU'D DRIVE THIS CITY TO RUIN, POISON THESE LIVES...FOR WHAT? WHY DO YOU CARE ABOUT THESE PEOPLE?
A VENDETTA AGAINST ME? FEAR OF A FUTURE YOU HAVE NO PLACE IN?

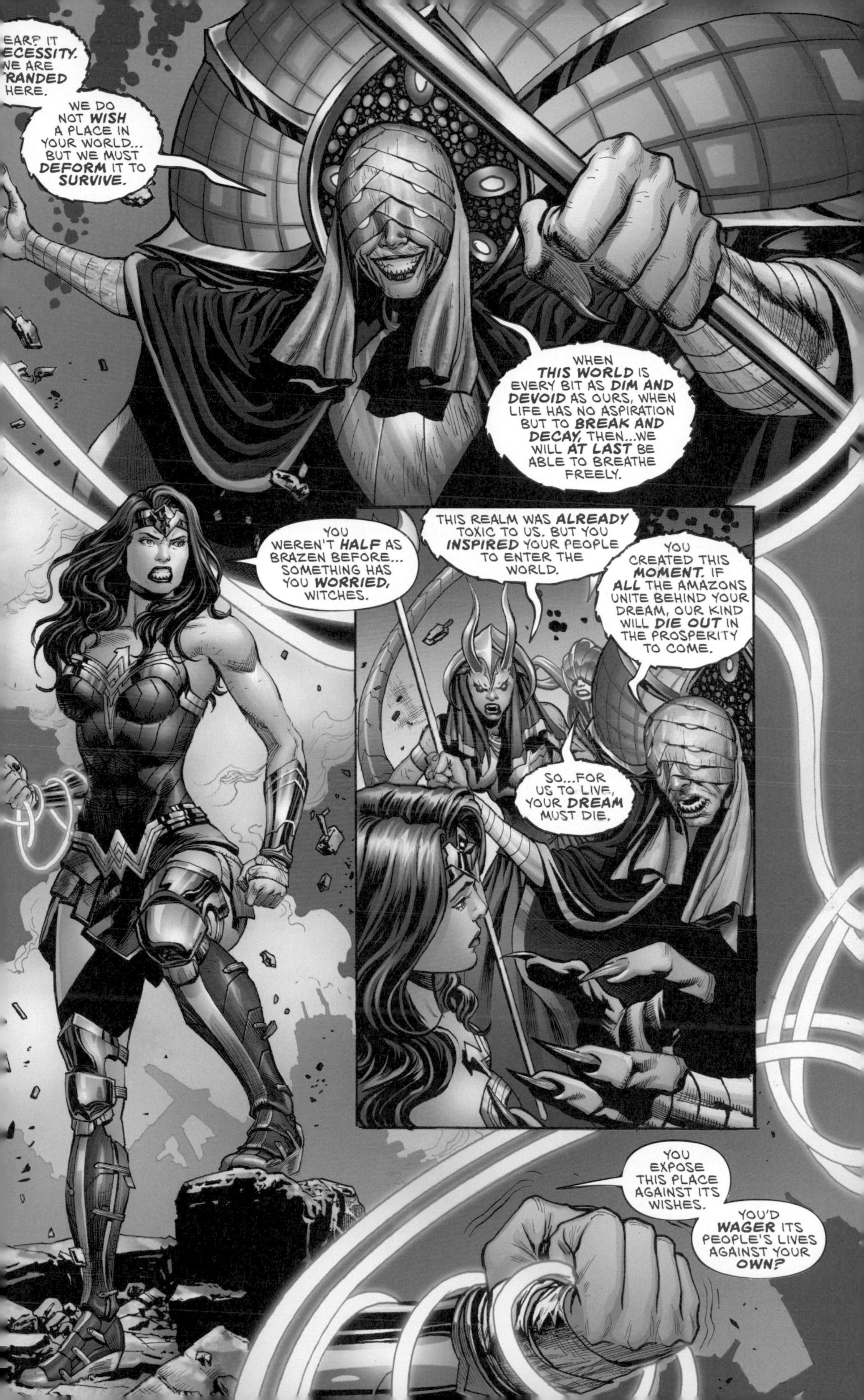
EARF IT ECESSITY. NE ARE RANDED HERE.
WE DO NOT WISH A PLACE IN YOUR WORLD... BUT WE MUST DEFORM IT TO SURVIVE.
WHEN THIS WORLD IS EVERY BIT AS DIM AND DEVOID AS OURS, WHEN LIFE HAS NO ASPIRATION BUT TO BREAK AND DECAY, THEN...WE WILL AT LAST BE ABLE TO BREATHE FREELY.
YOU WEREN'T HALF AS BRAZEN BEFORE... SOMETHING HAS YOU WORRIED, WITCHES.
THIS REALM WAS ALREADY TOXIC TO US. BUT YOU INSPIRED YOUR PEOPLE TO ENTER THE WORLD.
YOU CREATED THIS MOMENT. IF ALL THE AMAZONS UNITE BEHIND YOUR DREAM, OUR KIND WILL DIE OUT IN THE PROSPERITY TO COME.
SO...FOR US TO LIVE, YOUR DREAM MUST DIE.
YOU EXPOSE THIS PLACE AGAINST ITS WISHES.
YOU'D WAGER ITS PEOPLE'S LIVES AGAINST YOUR OWN?

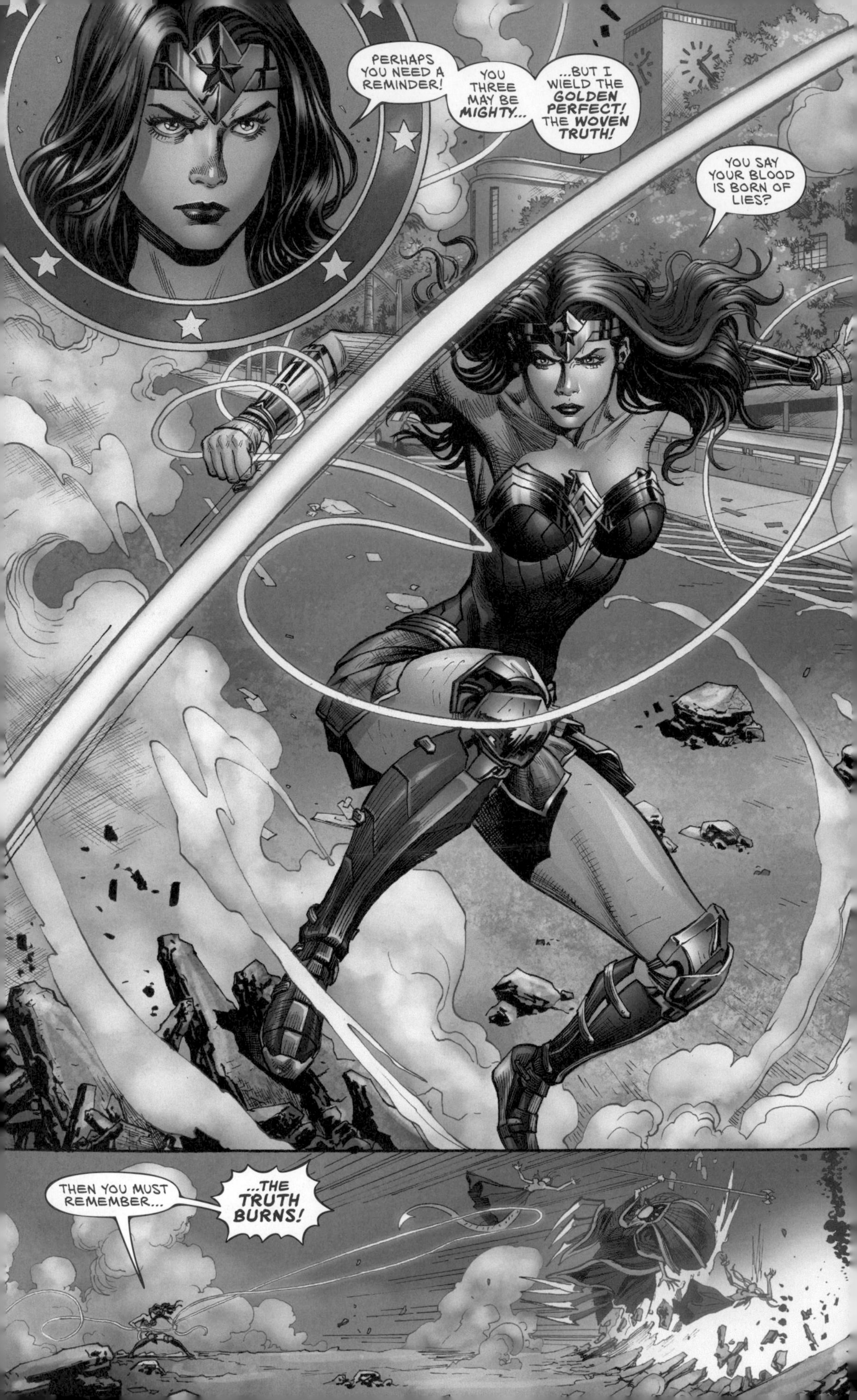
PERHAPS YOU NEED A REMINDER!
YOU THREE MAY BE MIGHTY...
...BUT I WIELD THE GOLDEN PERFECT! THE WOVEN TRUTH!
YOU SAY YOUR BLOOD IS BORN OF LIES?
THEN YOU MUST REMEMBER...
...THE TRUTH BURNS!

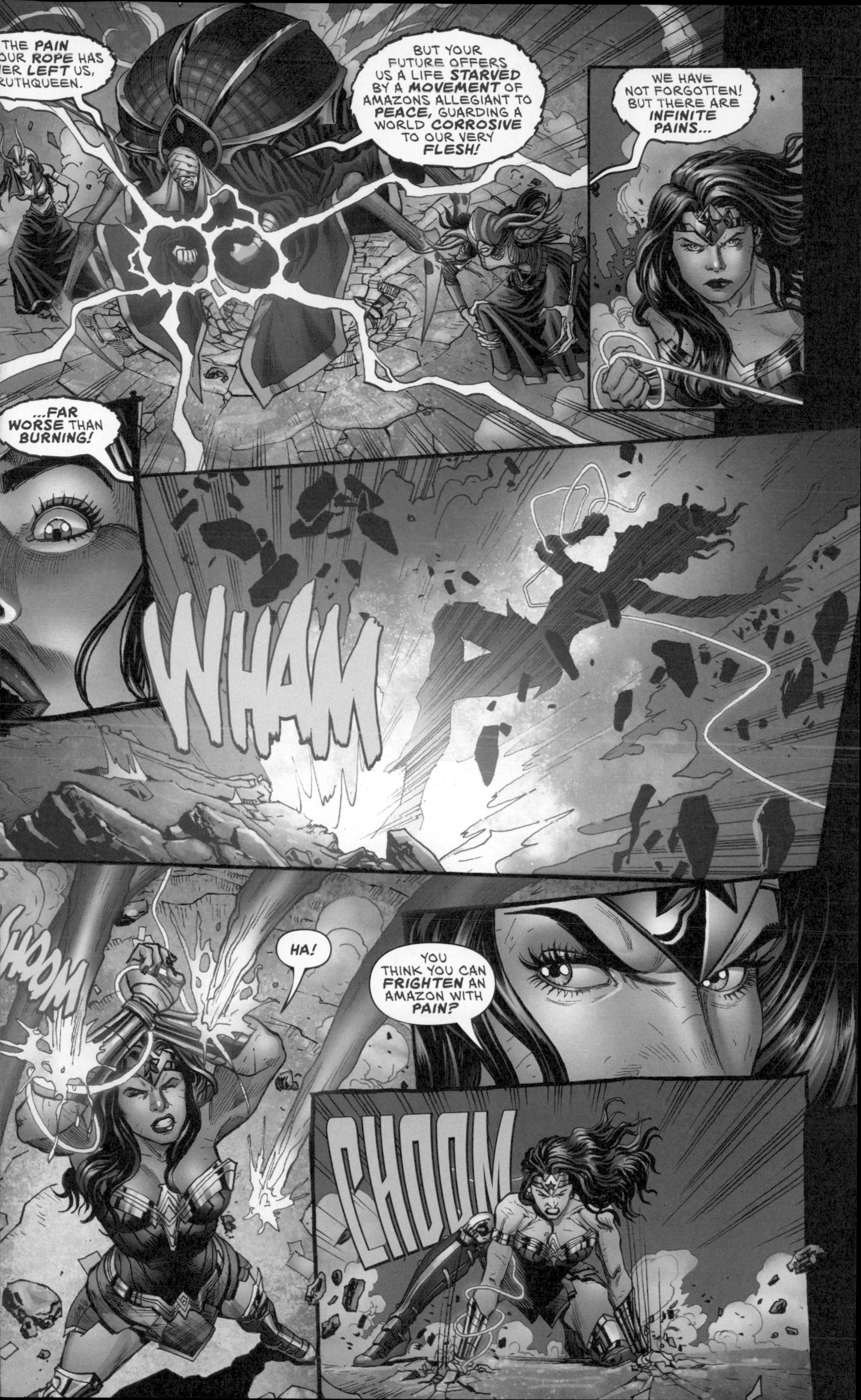
THE PAIN
OUR ROPE HAS
ER LEFT US,
RUTHQUEEN.
BUT YOUR FUTURE OFFERS US A LIFE STARVED BY A MOVEMENT OF AMAZONS ALLEGIANT TO PEACE, GUARDING A WORLD CORROSIVE TO OUR VERY FLESH!
WE HAVE NOT FORGOTTEN! BUT THERE ARE INFINITE PAINS...
...FAR WORSE THAN BURNING!
WHAM
HOOM
HA!
YOU THINK YOU CAN FRIGHTEN AN AMAZON WITH PAIN?
CHOOM

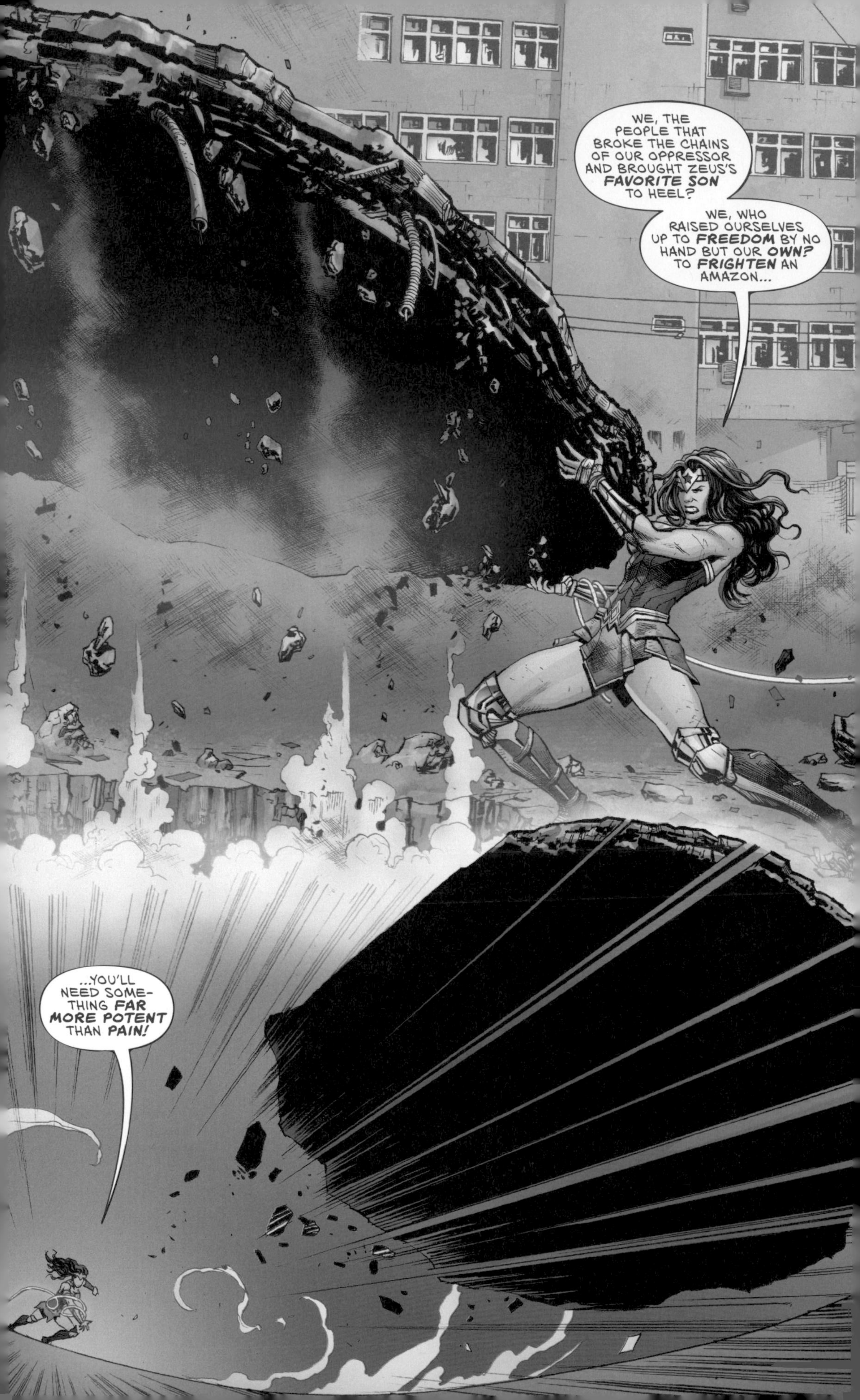
WE, THE PEOPLE THAT BROKE THE CHAINS OF OUR OPPRESSOR AND BROUGHT ZEUS'S **FAVORITE SON** TO HEEL?
WE, WHO RAISED OURSELVES UP TO **FREEDOM** BY NO HAND BUT OUR **OWN?** TO **FRIGHTEN** AN AMAZON...
...YOU'LL NEED SOME-THING **FAR MORE POTENT** THAN **PAIN!**

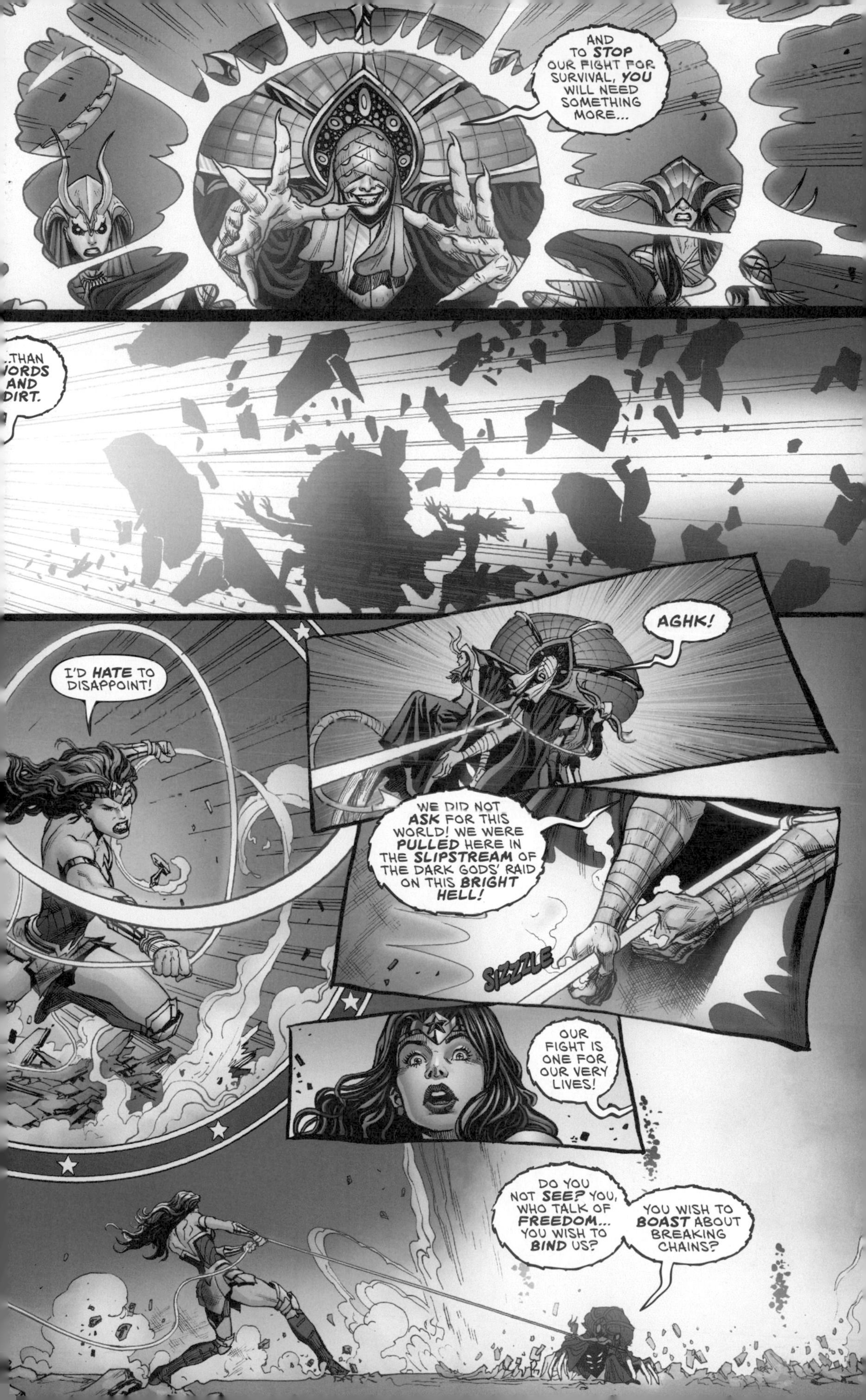
AND TO STOP OUR FIGHT FOR SURVIVAL, YOU WILL NEED SOMETHING MORE...
...THAN WORDS AND DIRT.
I'D HATE TO DISAPPOINT!
AGHK!
WE DID NOT ASK FOR THIS WORLD! WE WERE PULLED HERE IN THE SLIPSTREAM OF THE DARK GODS' RAID ON THIS BRIGHT HELL!
SIZZZLE
OUR FIGHT IS ONE FOR OUR VERY LIVES!
DO YOU NOT SEE? YOU, WHO TALK OF FREEDOM... YOU WISH TO BIND US?
YOU WISH TO BOAST ABOUT BREAKING CHAINS?

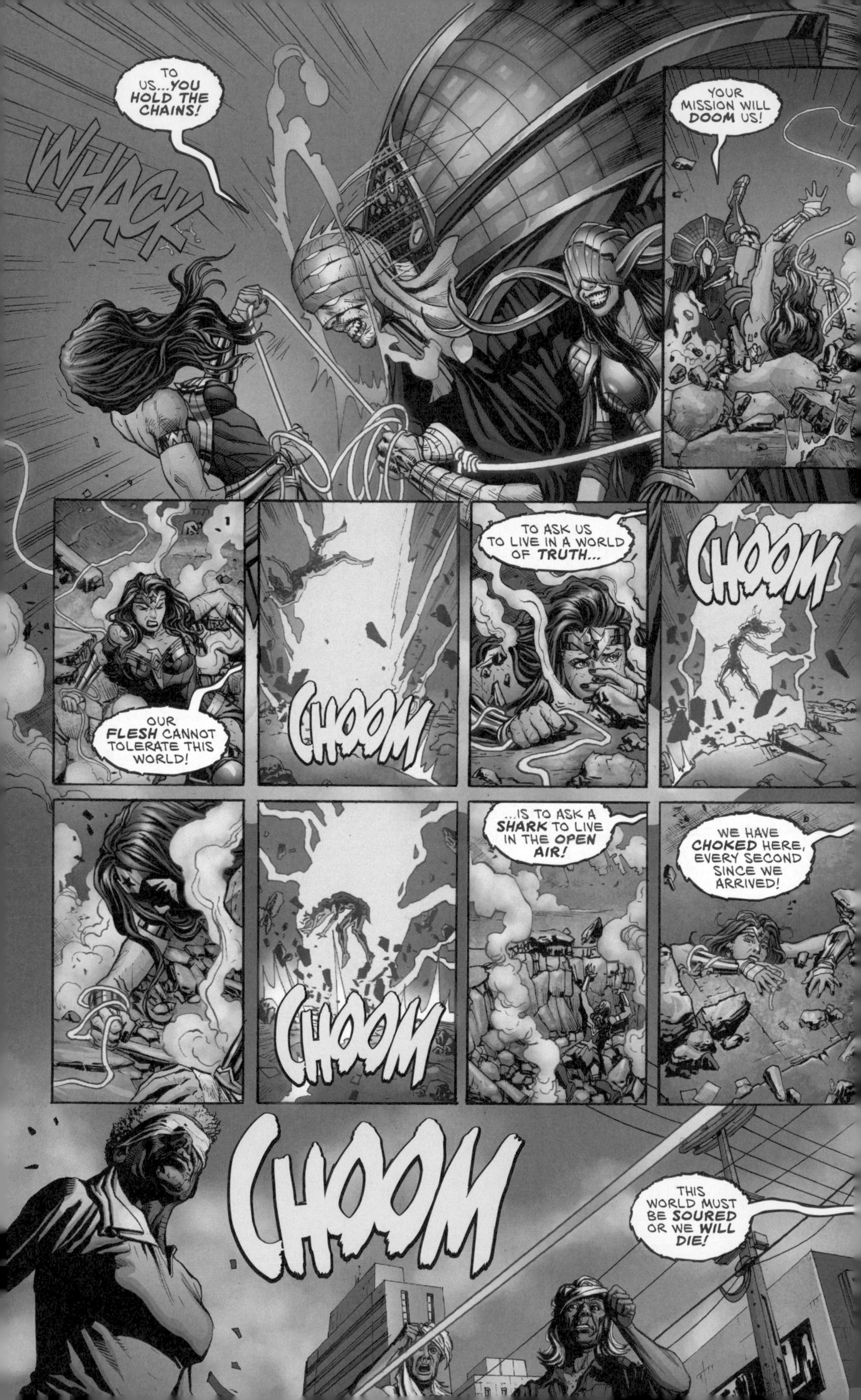
TO US...YOU HOLD THE CHAINS!
WHACK
YOUR MISSION WILL DOOM US!
OUR FLESH CANNOT TOLERATE THIS WORLD!
CHOOM
TO ASK US TO LIVE IN A WORLD OF TRUTH...
CHOOM
CHOOM
...IS TO ASK A SHARK TO LIVE IN THE OPEN AIR!
WE HAVE CHOKED HERE, EVERY SECOND SINCE WE ARRIVED!
CHOOM
THIS WORLD MUST BE SOURED OR WE WILL DIE!

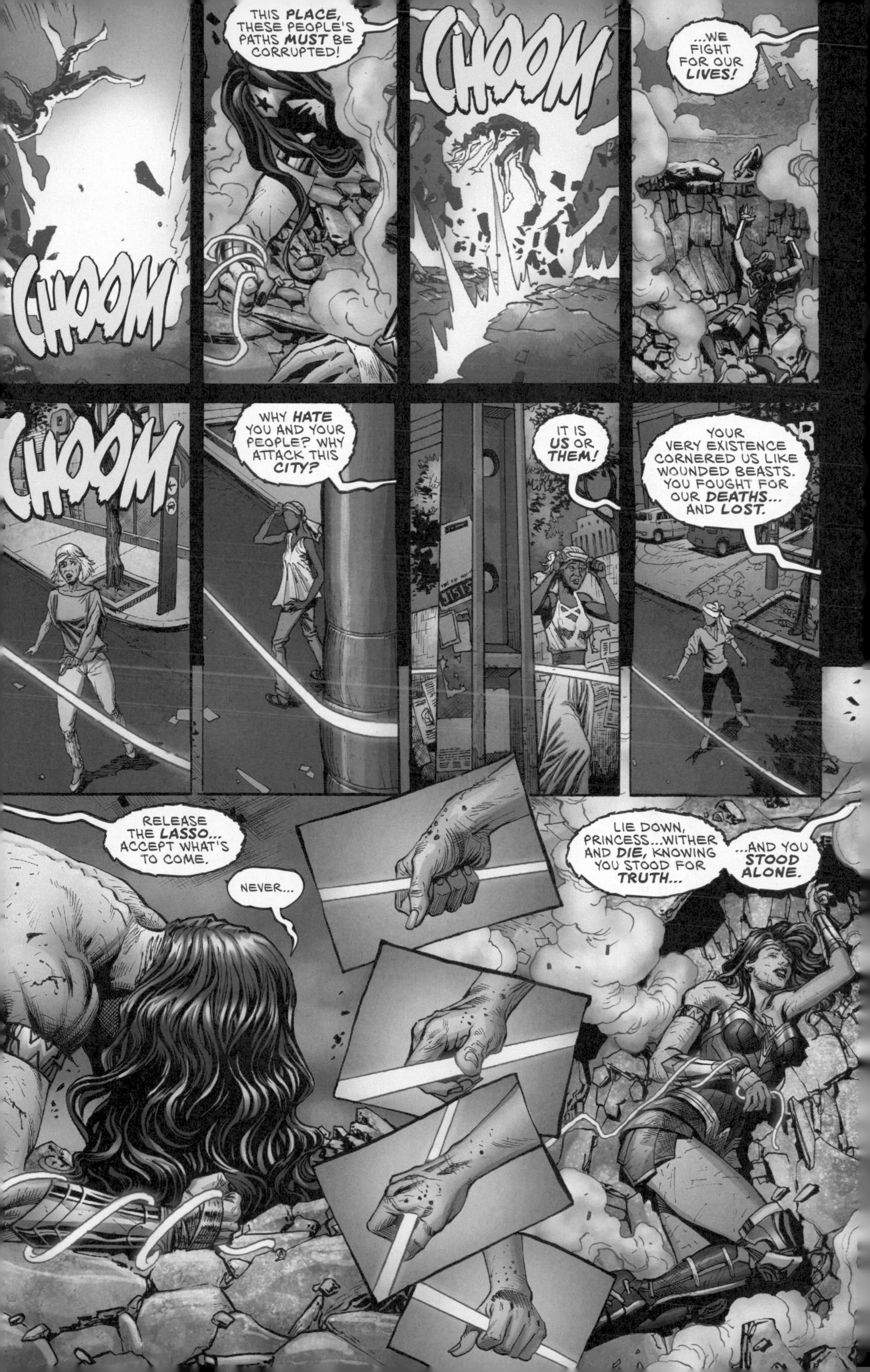
CHOOM
THIS PLACE, THESE PEOPLE'S PATHS MUST BE CORRUPTED!
CHOOM
...WE FIGHT FOR OUR LIVES!
CHOOM
WHY HATE YOU AND YOUR PEOPLE? WHY ATTACK THIS CITY?
IT IS US OR THEM!
YOUR VERY EXISTENCE CORNERED US LIKE WOUNDED BEASTS. YOU FOUGHT FOR OUR DEATHS... AND LOST.
RELEASE THE LASSO... ACCEPT WHAT'S TO COME.
NEVER...
LIE DOWN, PRINCESS...WITHER AND DIE, KNOWING YOU STOOD FOR TRUTH...
...AND YOU STOOD ALONE.

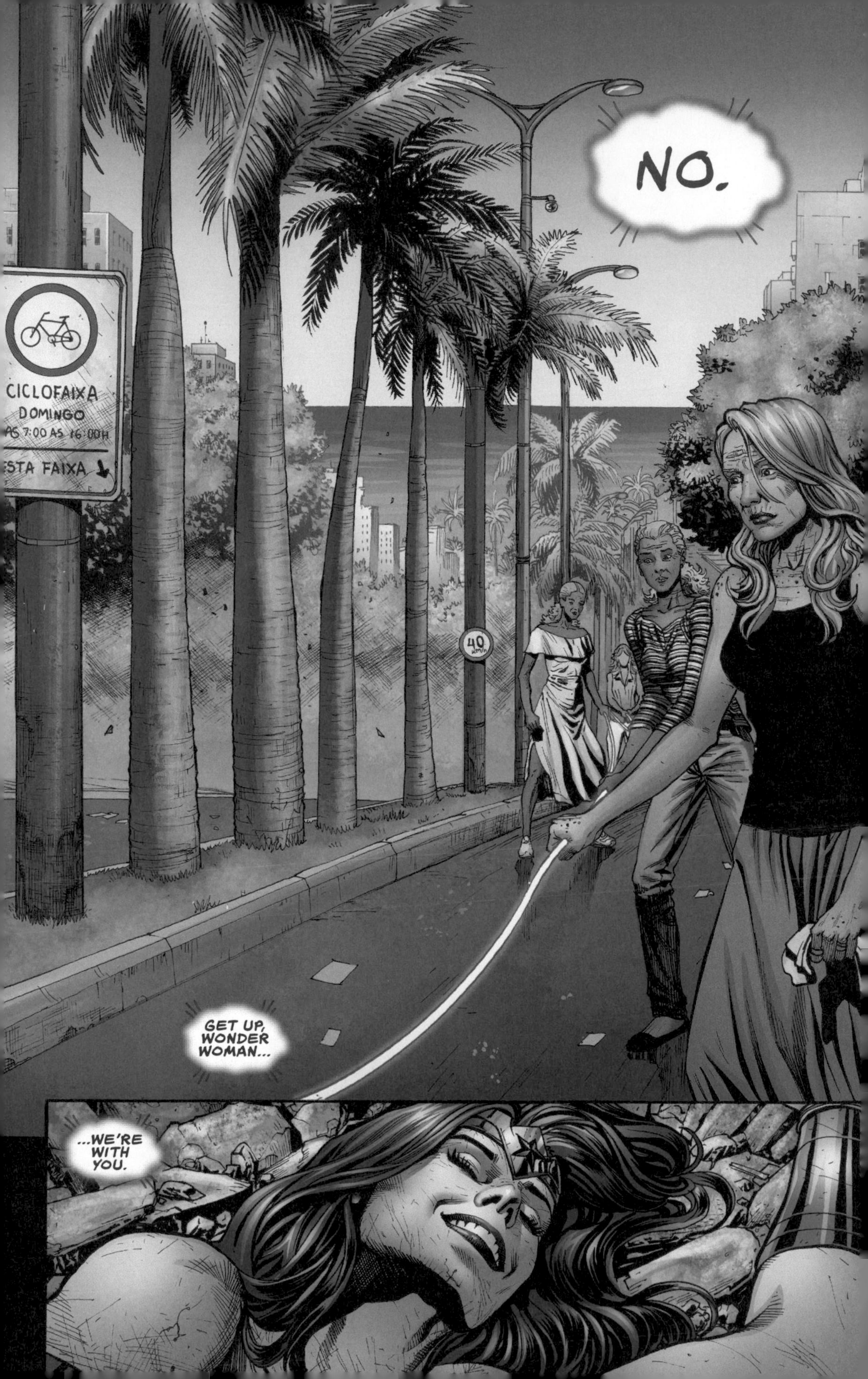
CICLOFAIXA
DOMINGO
7:00 AS 16:00H
ESTA FAIXA
40
NO.
GET UP, WONDER WOMAN...
...WE'RE WITH YOU.

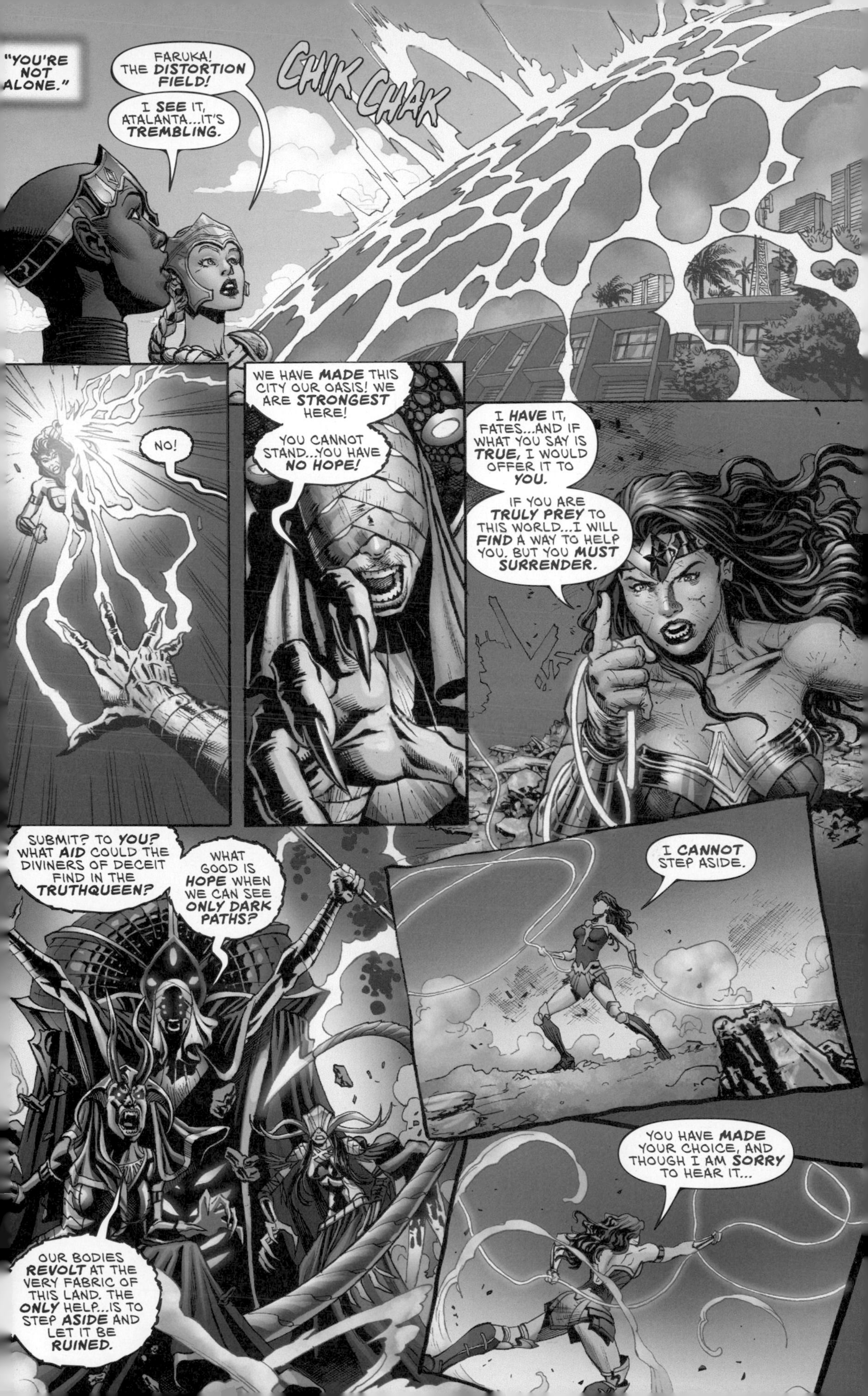
"YOU'RE NOT ALONE."
FARUKA! THE DISTORTION FIELD!
I SEE IT, ATALANTA...IT'S TREMBLING.
CHIK CHAK
NO!
WE HAVE MADE THIS CITY OUR OASIS! WE ARE STRONGEST HERE!
YOU CANNOT STAND...YOU HAVE NO HOPE!
I HAVE IT, FATES...AND IF WHAT YOU SAY IS TRUE, I WOULD OFFER IT TO YOU.
IF YOU ARE TRULY PREY TO THIS WORLD...I WILL FIND A WAY TO HELP YOU. BUT YOU MUST SURRENDER.
SUBMIT? TO YOU? WHAT AID COULD THE DIVINERS OF DECEIT FIND IN THE TRUTHQUEEN?
WHAT GOOD IS HOPE WHEN WE CAN SEE ONLY DARK PATHS?
OUR BODIES REVOLT AT THE VERY FABRIC OF THIS LAND. THE ONLY HELP...IS TO STEP ASIDE AND LET IT BE RUINED.
I CANNOT STEP ASIDE.
YOU HAVE MADE YOUR CHOICE, AND THOUGH I AM SORRY TO HEAR IT...

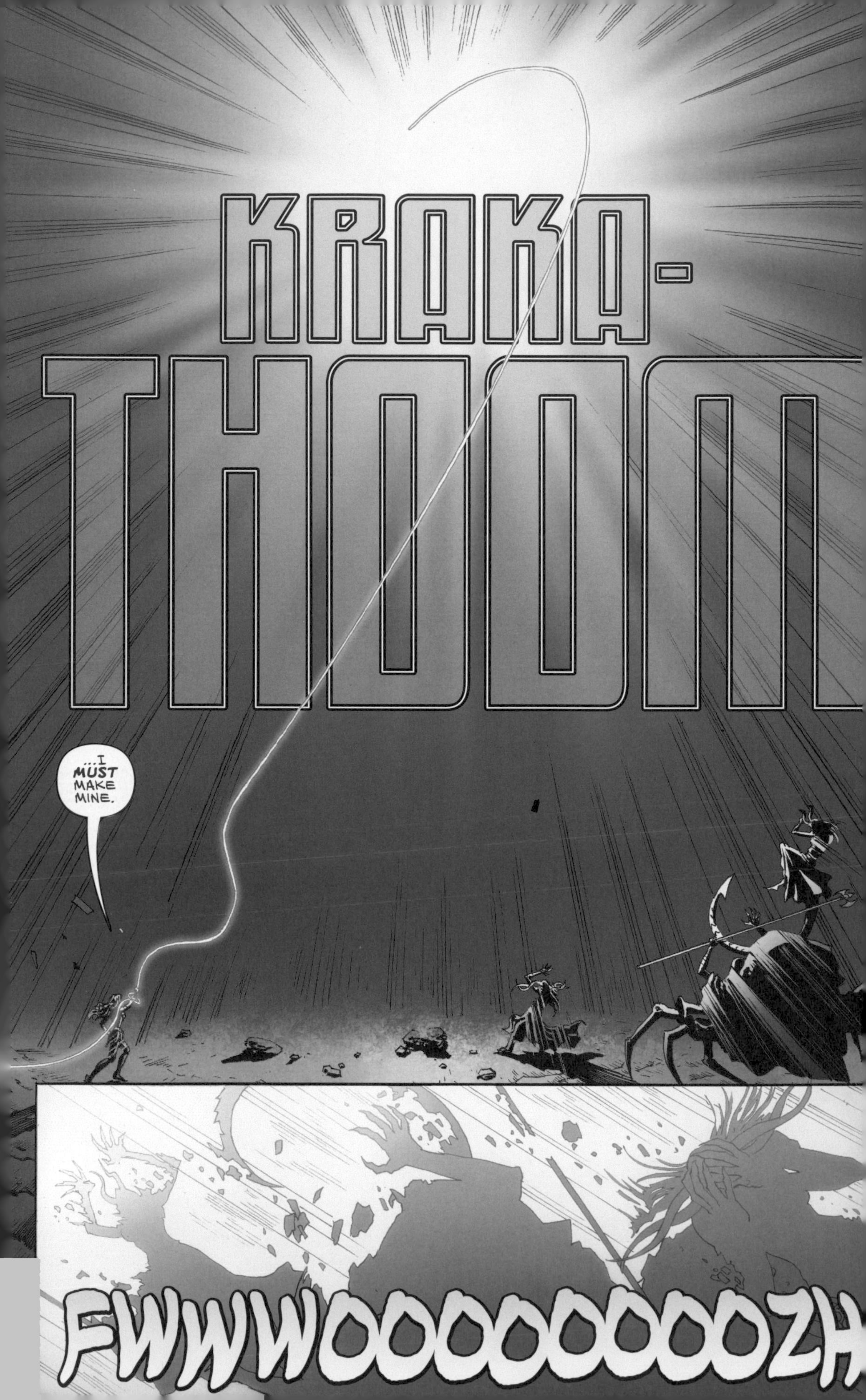
KRAKA-
THOOM
...I MUST MAKE MINE.
FWWOOOOOOOOZH

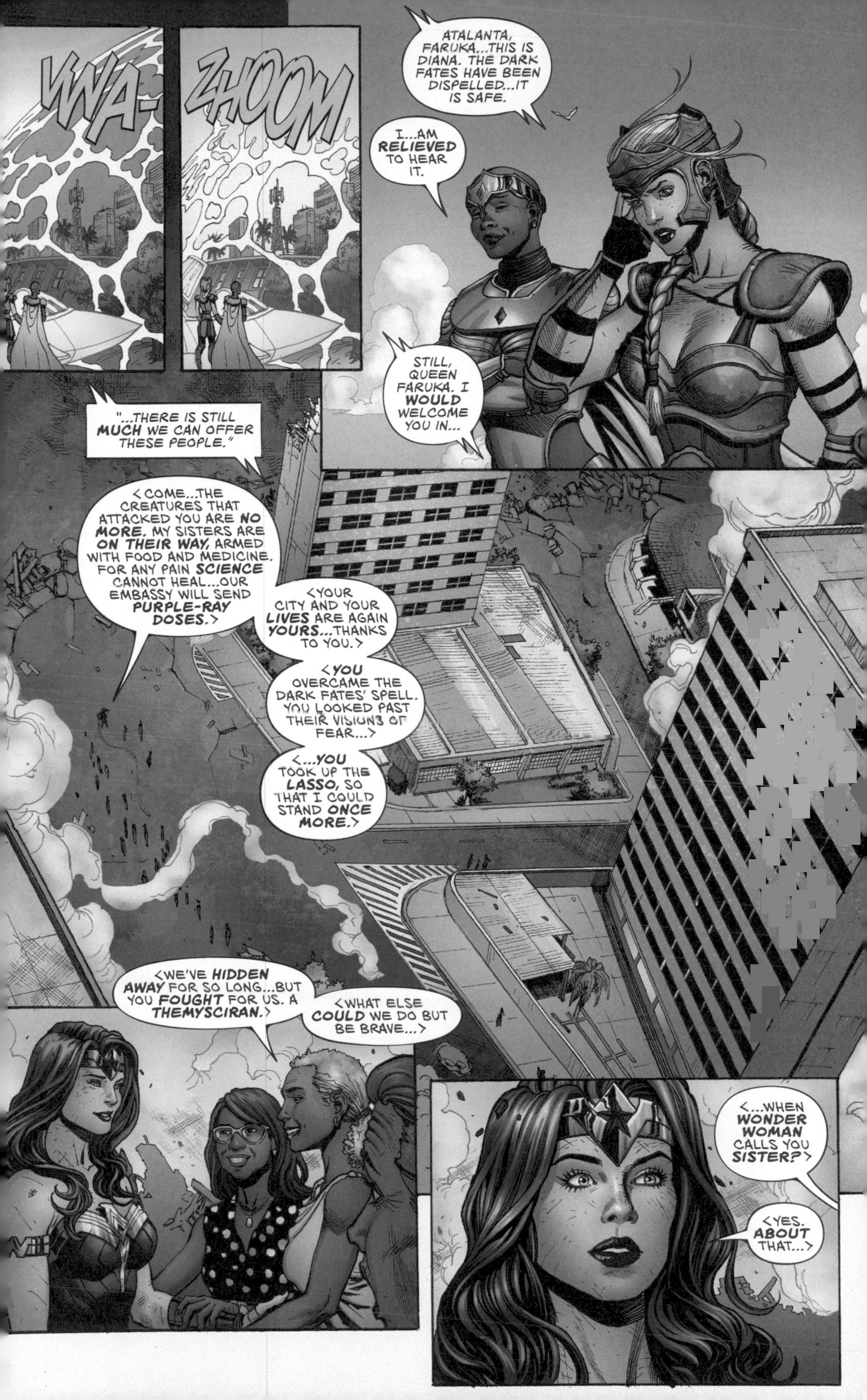
WWA-
ZHOOM
ATALANTA, FARUKA...THIS IS DIANA. THE DARK FATES HAVE BEEN DISPELLED...IT IS SAFE.
I...AM RELIEVED TO HEAR IT.
STILL, QUEEN FARUKA. I WOULD WELCOME YOU IN...
"...THERE IS STILL MUCH WE CAN OFFER THESE PEOPLE."
<COME...THE CREATURES THAT ATTACKED YOU ARE NO MORE. MY SISTERS ARE ON THEIR WAY, ARMED WITH FOOD AND MEDICINE. FOR ANY PAIN SCIENCE CANNOT HEAL...OUR EMBASSY WILL SEND PURPLE-RAY DOSES.>
<YOUR CITY AND YOUR LIVES ARE AGAIN YOURS...THANKS TO YOU.>
<YOU OVERCAME THE DARK FATES' SPELL. YOU LOOKED PAST THEIR VISIONS OF FEAR...>
<...YOU TOOK UP THE LASSO, SO THAT I COULD STAND ONCE MORE.>
<WE'VE HIDDEN AWAY FOR SO LONG...BUT YOU FOUGHT FOR US. A THEMYSCIRAN.>
<WHAT ELSE COULD WE DO BUT BE BRAVE...>
<...WHEN WONDER WOMAN CALLS YOU SISTER?>
<YES. ABOUT THAT...>

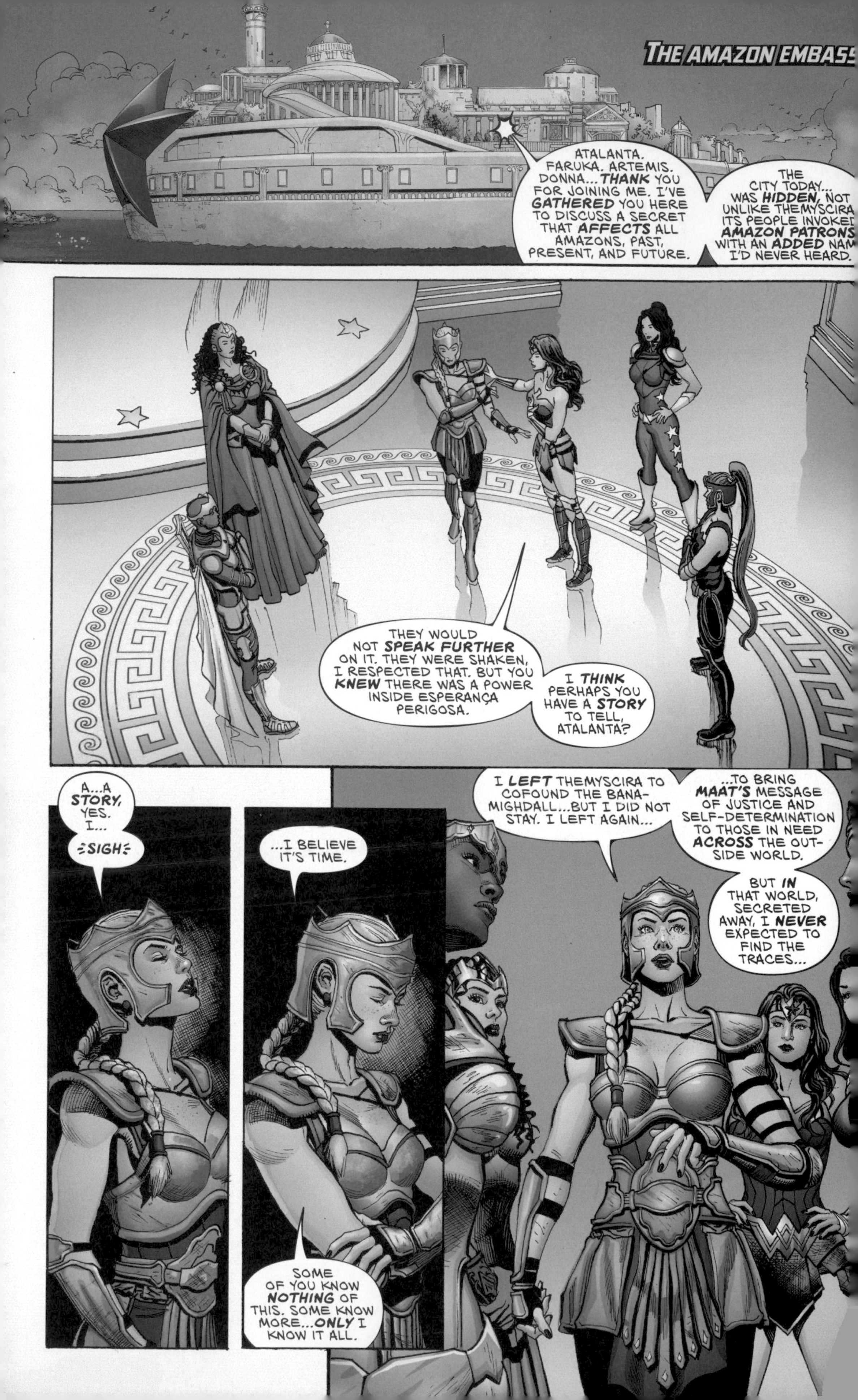

THE AMAZON EMBASS
ATALANTA. FARUKA. ARTEMIS. DONNA... THANK YOU FOR JOINING ME. I'VE GATHERED YOU HERE TO DISCUSS A SECRET THAT AFFECTS ALL AMAZONS, PAST, PRESENT, AND FUTURE.
THE CITY TODAY... WAS HIDDEN, NOT UNLIKE THEMYSCIRA. ITS PEOPLE INVOKED AMAZON PATRONS WITH AN ADDED NAM I'D NEVER HEARD.
THEY WOULD NOT SPEAK FURTHER ON IT. THEY WERE SHAKEN, I RESPECTED THAT. BUT YOU KNEW THERE WAS A POWER INSIDE ESPERANÇA PERIGOSA.
I THINK PERHAPS YOU HAVE A STORY TO TELL, ATALANTA?
A...A STORY, YES. I...
SIGH
...I BELIEVE IT'S TIME.
SOME OF YOU KNOW NOTHING OF THIS. SOME KNOW MORE...ONLY I KNOW IT ALL.
I LEFT THEMYSCIRA TO COFOUND THE BANA-MIGHDALL...BUT I DID NOT STAY. I LEFT AGAIN...
...TO BRING MAAT'S MESSAGE OF JUSTICE AND SELF-DETERMINATION TO THOSE IN NEED ACROSS THE OUT-SIDE WORLD.
BUT IN THAT WORLD, SECRETED AWAY, I NEVER EXPECTED TO FIND THE TRACES...

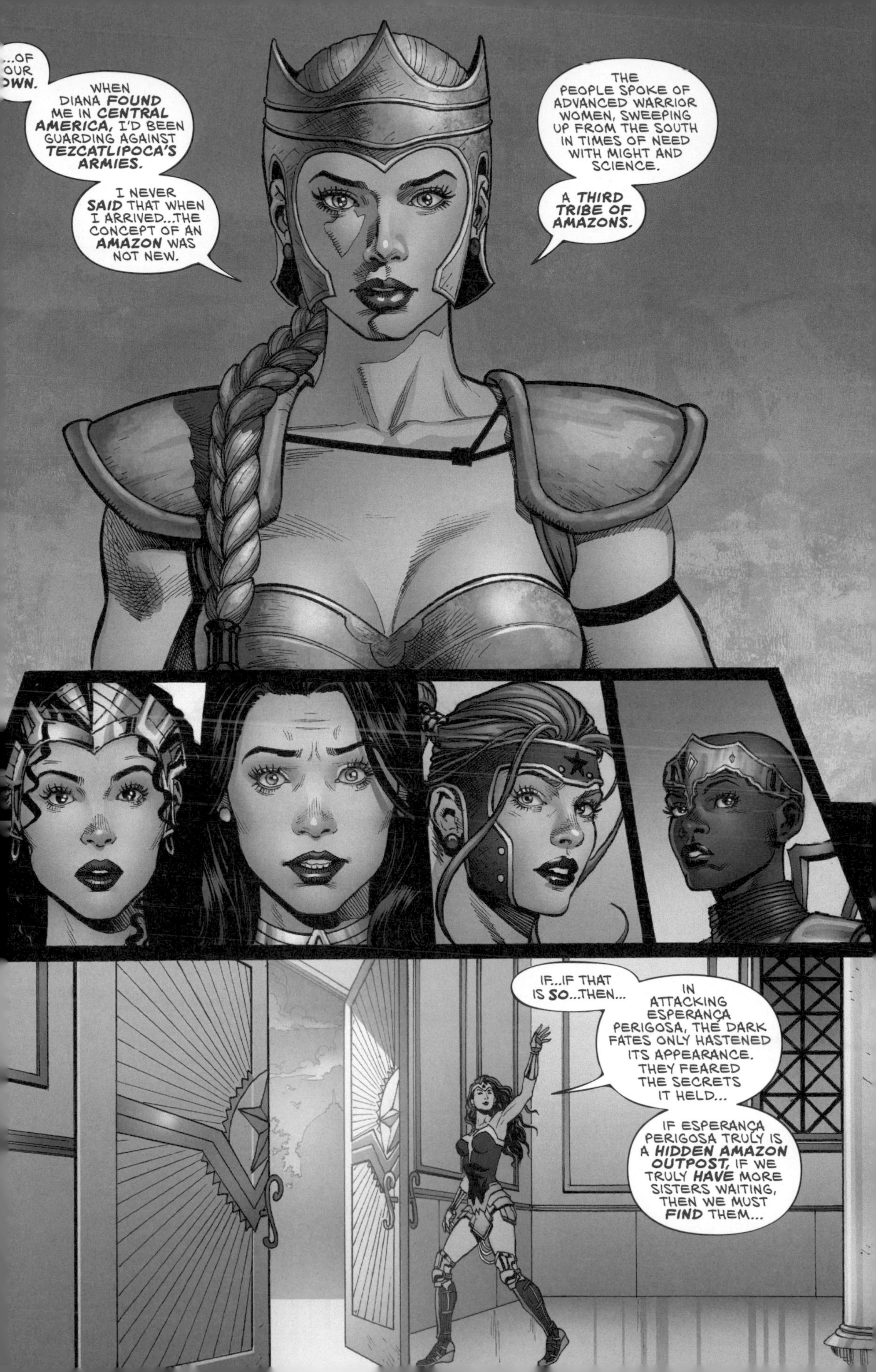
...OF OUR OWN.
WHEN DIANA FOUND ME IN CENTRAL AMERICA, I'D BEEN GUARDING AGAINST TEZCATLIPOCA'S ARMIES.
I NEVER SAID THAT WHEN I ARRIVED...THE CONCEPT OF AN AMAZON WAS NOT NEW.
THE PEOPLE SPOKE OF ADVANCED WARRIOR WOMEN, SWEEPING UP FROM THE SOUTH IN TIMES OF NEED WITH MIGHT AND SCIENCE.
A THIRD TRIBE OF AMAZONS.
IF...IF THAT IS SO...THEN...
IN ATTACKING ESPERANÇA PERIGOSA, THE DARK FATES ONLY HASTENED ITS APPEARANCE. THEY FEARED THE SECRETS IT HELD...
IF ESPERANÇA PERIGOSA TRULY IS A HIDDEN AMAZON OUTPOST, IF WE TRULY HAVE MORE SISTERS WAITING, THEN WE MUST FIND THEM...

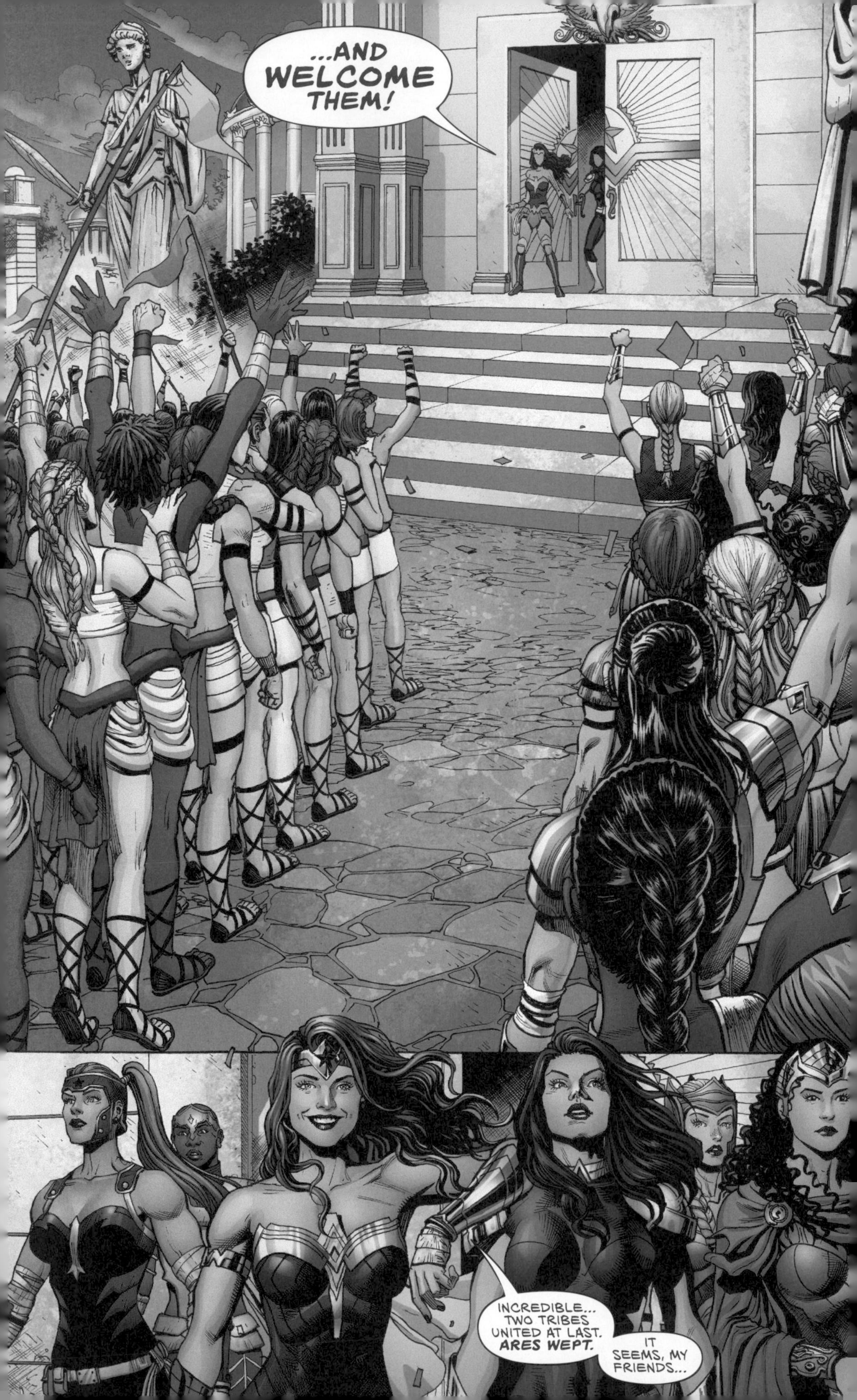
...AND WELCOME THEM!
INCREDIBLE... TWO TRIBES UNITED AT LAST. ARES WEPT.
IT SEEMS, MY FRIENDS...

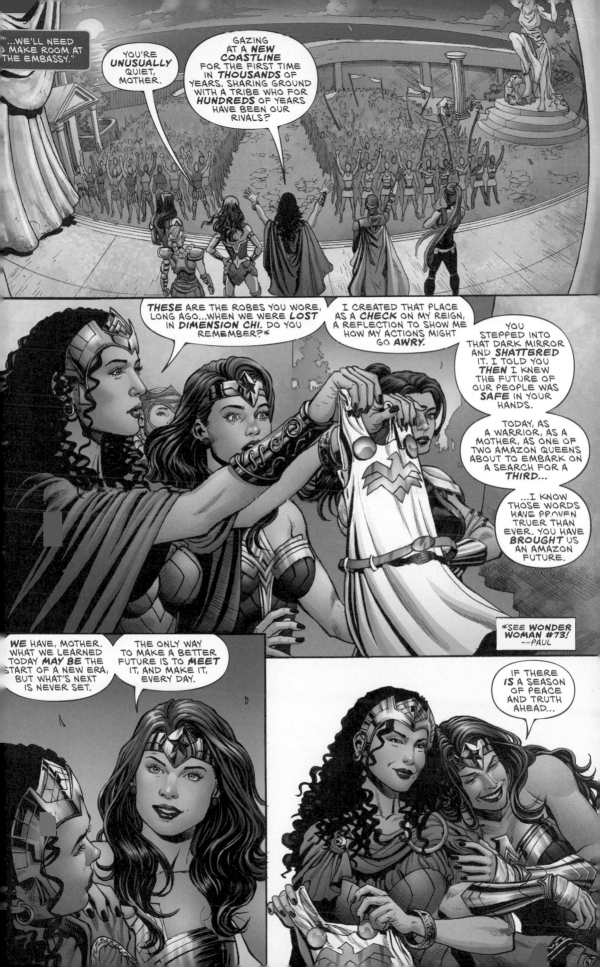

"...WE'LL NEED TO MAKE ROOM AT THE EMBASSY."

YOU'RE *UNUSUALLY* QUIET, MOTHER.

GAZING AT A *NEW COASTLINE* FOR THE FIRST TIME IN *THOUSANDS* OF YEARS, SHARING GROUND WITH A TRIBE WHO FOR *HUNDREDS* OF YEARS HAVE BEEN OUR RIVALS?

THESE ARE THE ROBES YOU WORE, LONG AGO...WHEN WE WERE *LOST* IN *DIMENSION CHI.* DO YOU REMEMBER?*

I CREATED THAT PLACE AS A *CHECK* ON MY REIGN, A REFLECTION TO SHOW ME HOW MY ACTIONS MIGHT GO *AWRY.*

YOU STEPPED INTO THAT DARK MIRROR AND *SHATTERED* IT. I TOLD YOU *THEN* I KNEW THE FUTURE OF OUR PEOPLE WAS *SAFE* IN YOUR HANDS.

TODAY, AS A *WARRIOR,* AS A *MOTHER,* AS ONE OF TWO AMAZON QUEENS ABOUT TO EMBARK ON A SEARCH FOR A *THIRD...*

...I KNOW THOSE WORDS HAVE PROVEN TRUER THAN EVER. YOU HAVE *BROUGHT* US AN AMAZON FUTURE.

*SEE WONDER WOMAN #73! --PAUL

WE HAVE, MOTHER. WHAT WE LEARNED TODAY *MAY BE* THE START OF A NEW ERA, BUT WHAT'S NEXT IS NEVER SET.

THE ONLY WAY TO MAKE A BETTER FUTURE IS TO *MEET* IT, AND MAKE IT, EVERY DAY.

IF THERE *IS* A SEASON OF PEACE AND TRUTH AHEAD...

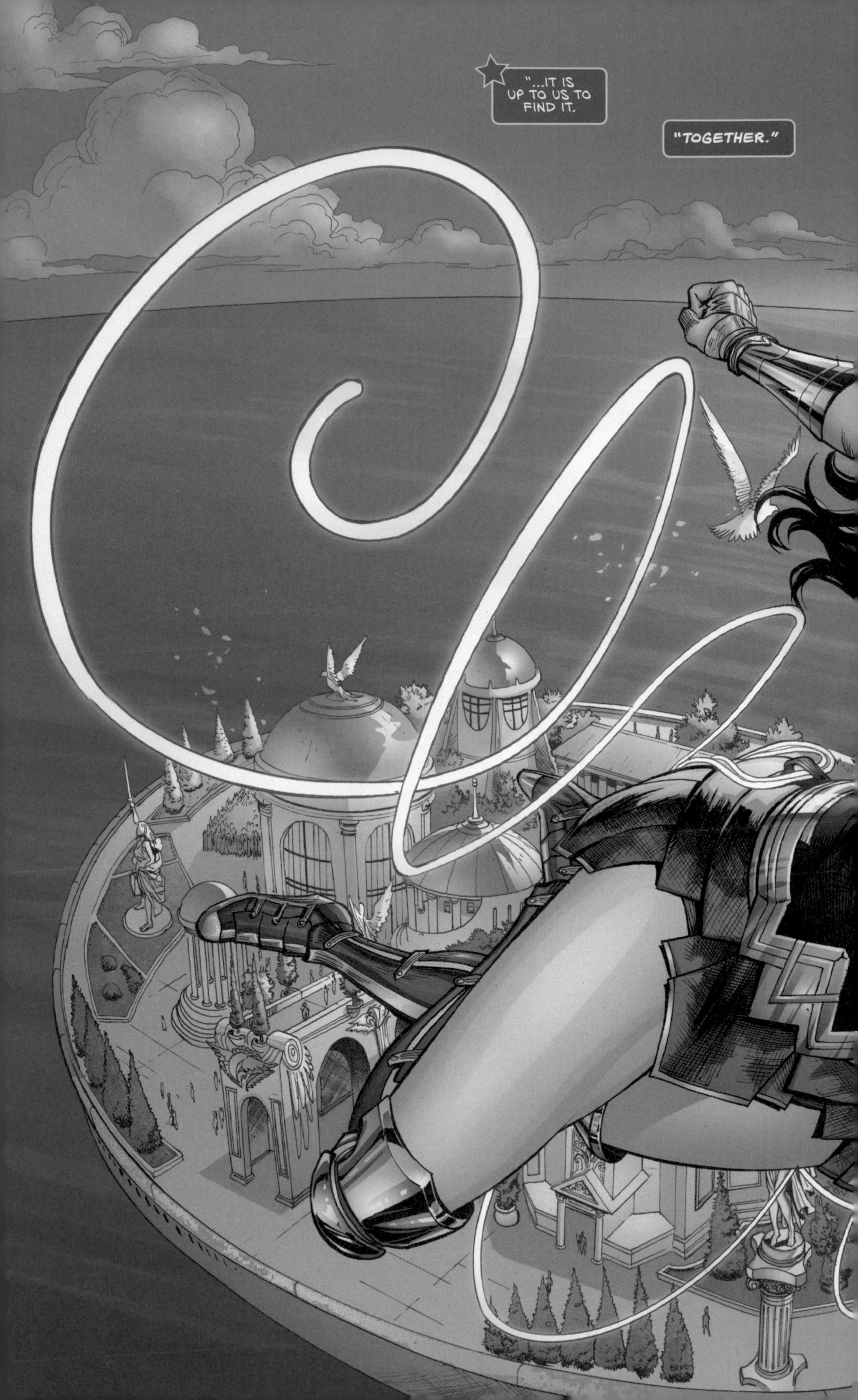
"...IT IS UP TO US TO FIND IT.
"TOGETHER."

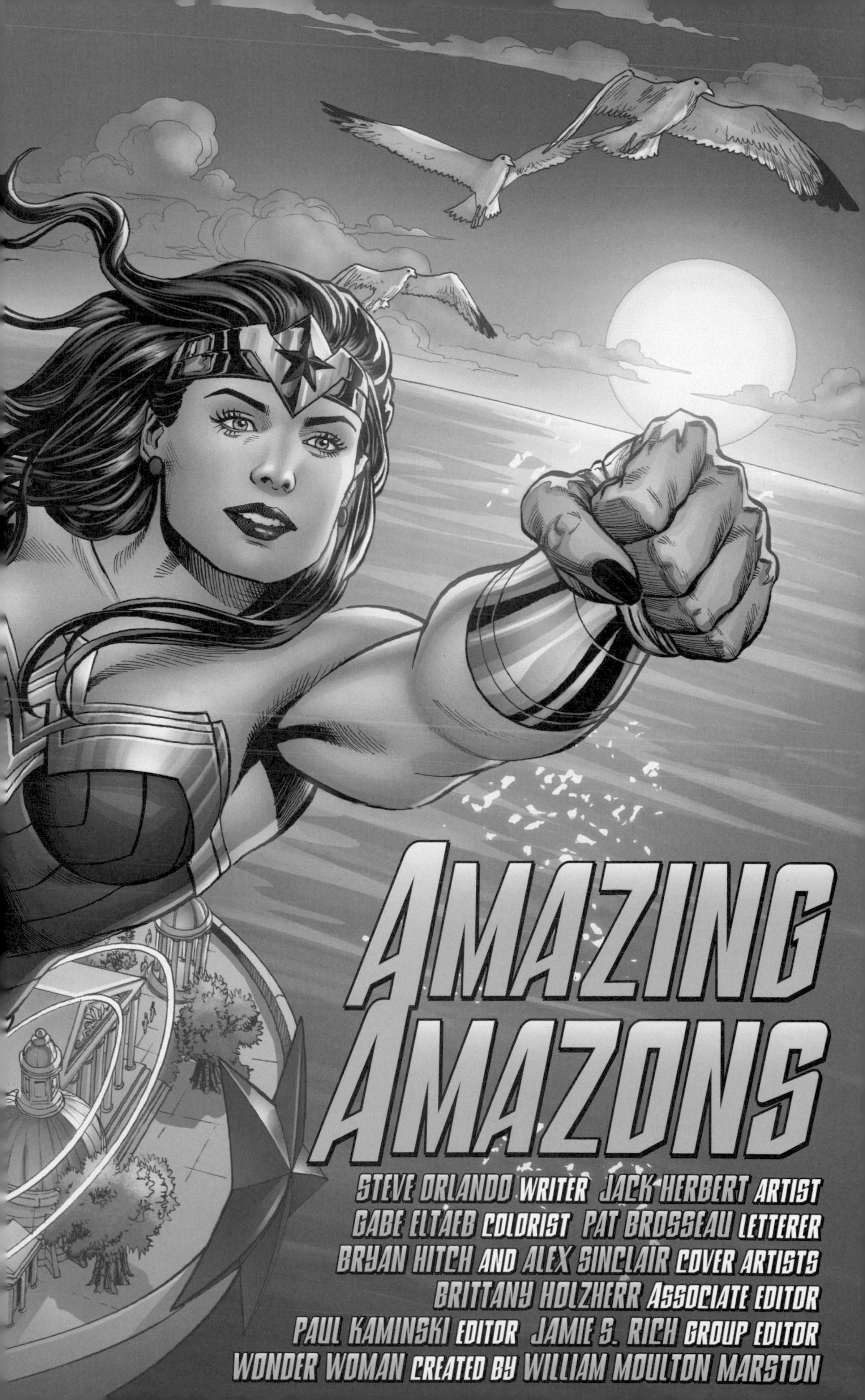
AMAZING AMAZONS
STEVE ORLANDO WRITER JACK HERBERT ARTIST
GABE ELTAEB COLORIST PAT BROSSEAU LETTERER
BRYAN HITCH AND ALEX SINCLAIR COVER ARTISTS
BRITTANY HOLZHERR ASSOCIATE EDITOR
PAUL KAMINSKI EDITOR JAMIE S. RICH GROUP EDITOR
WONDER WOMAN CREATED BY WILLIAM MOULTON MARSTON

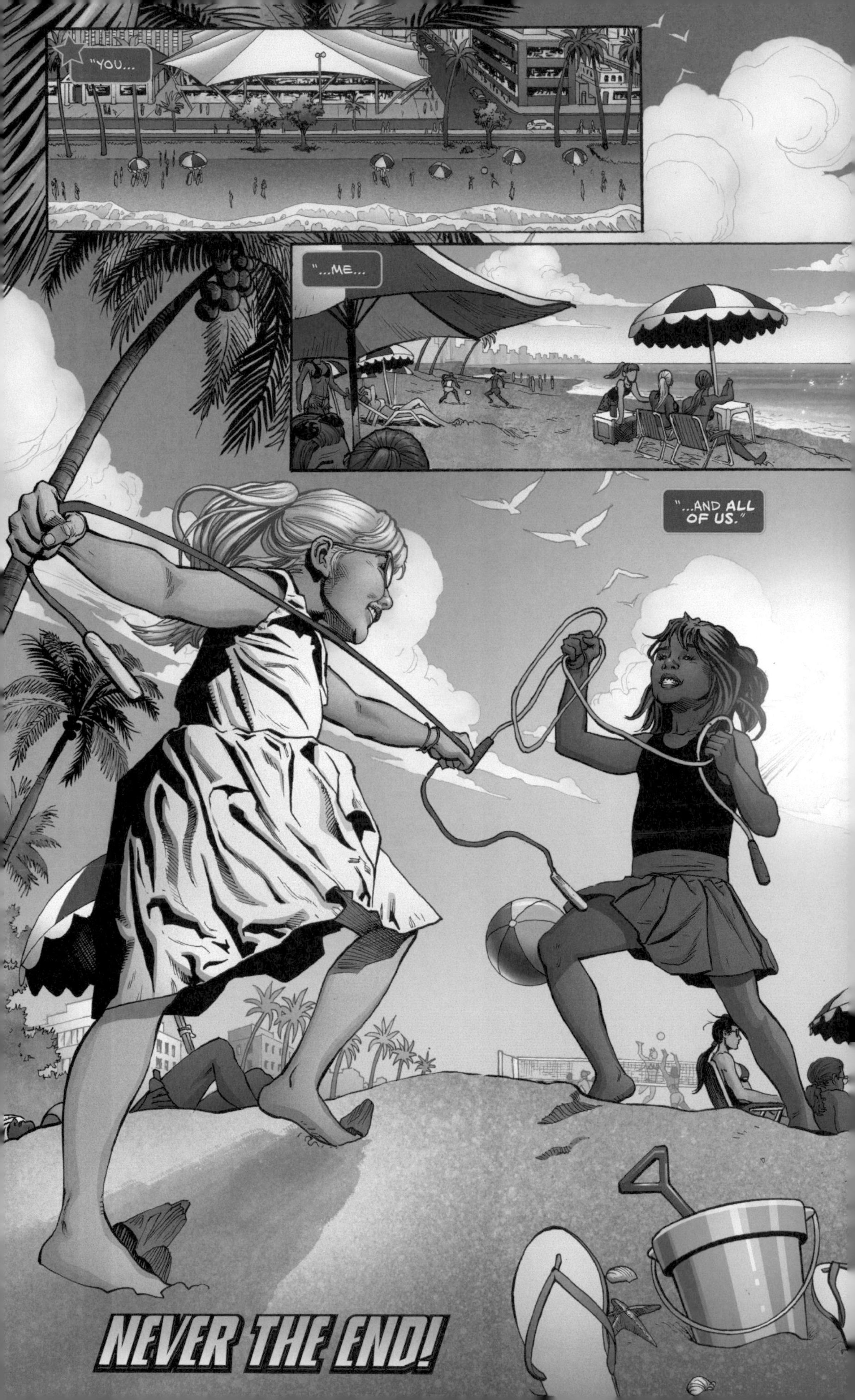
"YOU...
"...ME...
"...AND ALL OF US."
NEVER THE END!

CHARACTER SKETCH GALLERY

WARMASTER & HER HORSEWOMEN

Warmaster
by **V. KEN MARION**

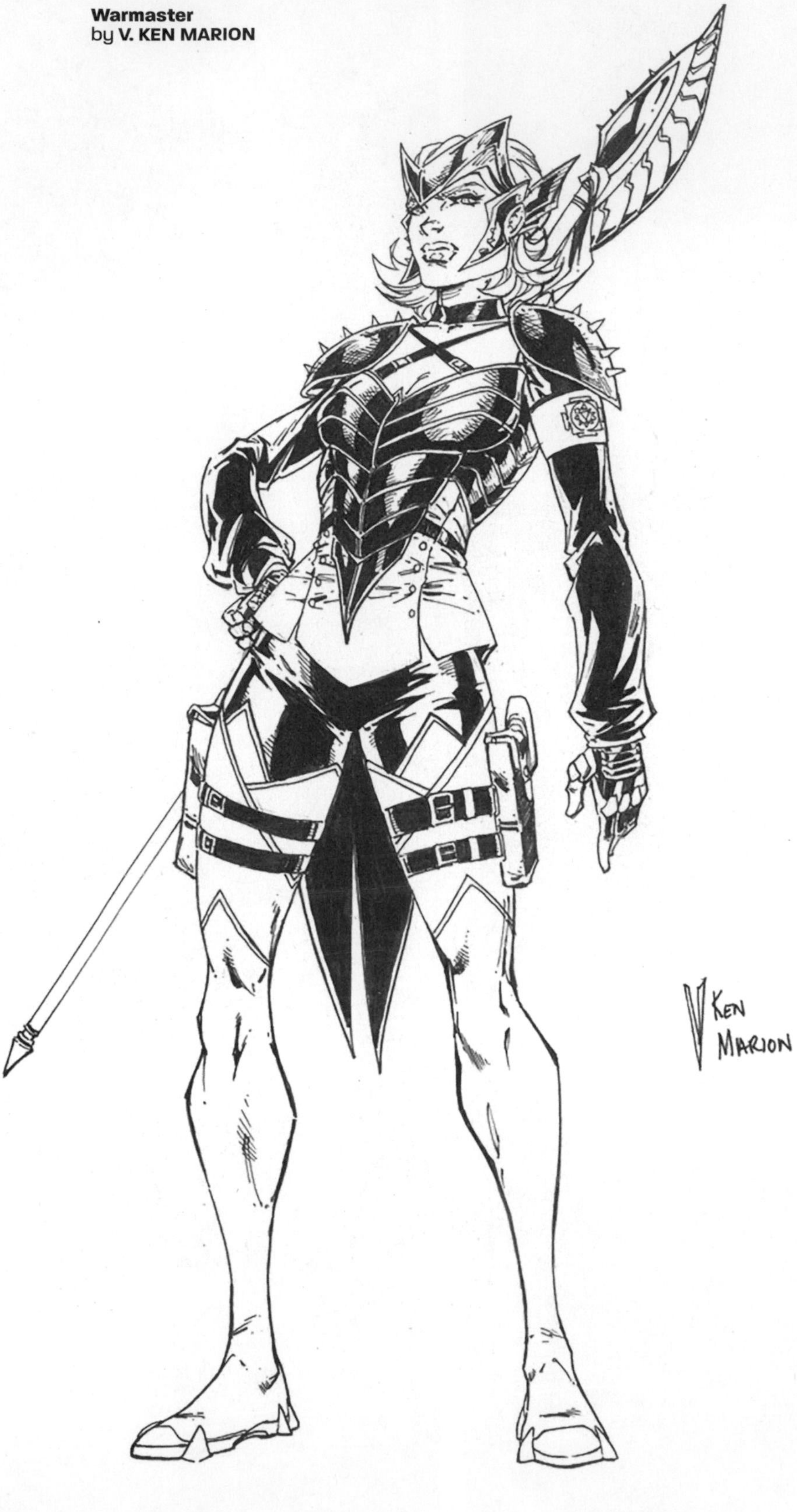
V KEN MARION

Armageddon
by **JESŪS MERINO**

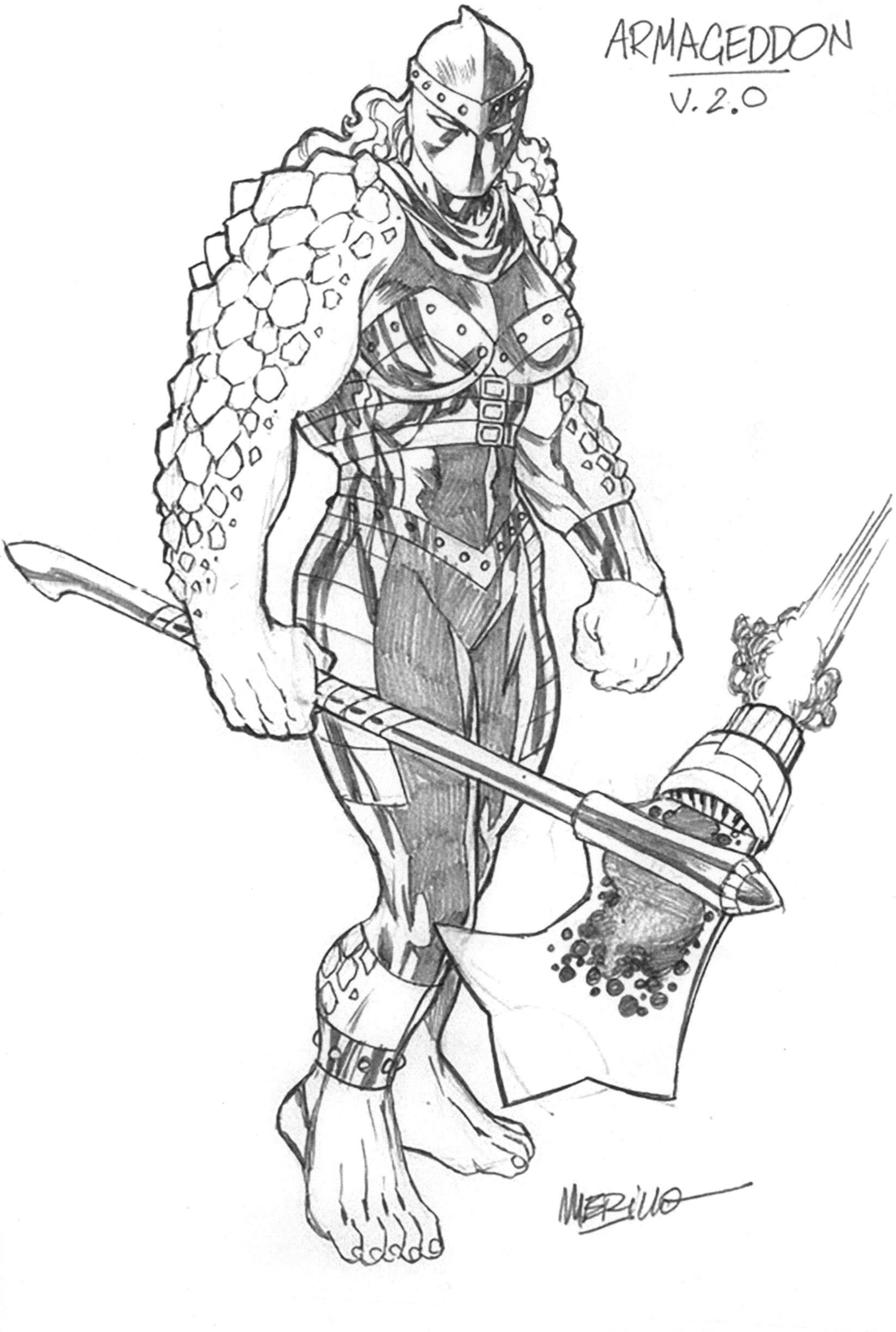
ARMAGEDDON
V.2.0
MERINO

Devastation
by **JESÚS MERINO**

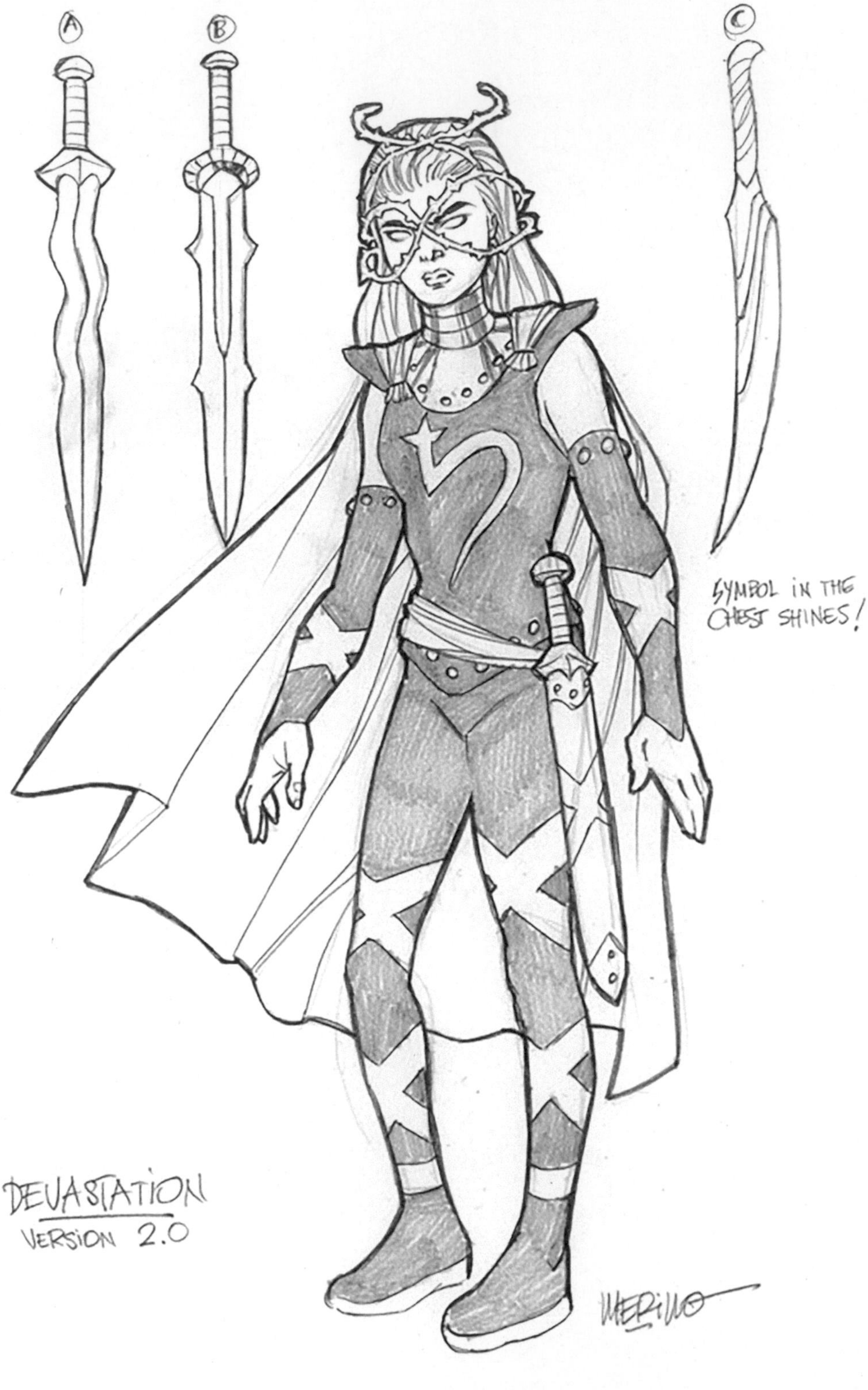
A
B
C
SYMBOL IN THE CHEST SHINES!
DEVASTATION
VERSION 2.0
MERINO

Genocide
by JESÚS MERINO

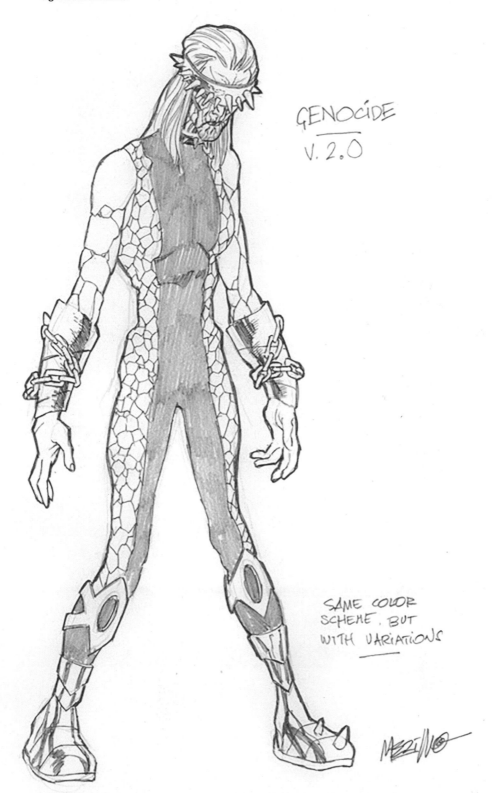

GENOCIDE
V. 2.0

SAME COLOR
SCHEME, BUT
WITH VARIATIONS

WONDER WOMAN AND HER ARSENAL

Invisible Jet
by **KIERAN McKEOWN**

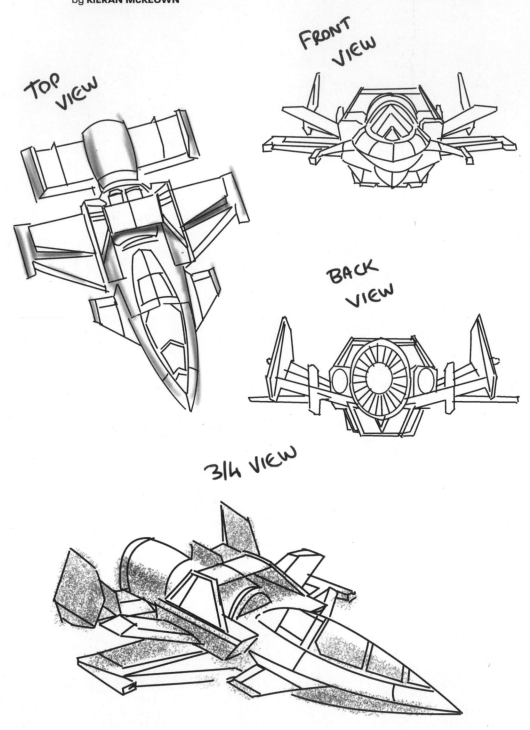

TOP VIEW

FRONT VIEW

BACK VIEW

3/4 VIEW